Judicial Power in a Globalized World

Vincent Anthony de Gaetano

Charles Seale-Hayne Library
University of Plymouth
(01752) 588 588
LibraryandITenquiries@plymouth.ac.uk

Paulo Pinto de Albuquerque • Krzysztof Wojtyczek

Editors

Judicial Power in a Globalized World

Liber Amicorum Vincent De Gaetano

🐎 Springer

Editors
Paulo Pinto de Albuquerque
European Court of Human Rights
Strasbourg, France

Krzysztof Wojtyczek
European Court of Human Rights
Strasbourg, France

UNIVERSITY OF PLYMOUTH

9 0 0 5 7 3 4 5 4 0

ISBN 978-3-030-20743-4   ISBN 978-3-030-20744-1   (eBook)
https://doi.org/10.1007/978-3-030-20744-1

This Springer imprint is published by the registered company Springer Nature Switzerland AG.
The registered company address is: Gewerbestrasse 11, 6330 Cham, Switzerland

Preface

The present volume contains a series of essays in honour of His Excellency Chief Justice Vincent Anthony De Gaetano. Given the professional interests of Chief Justice de Gaetano, it is focused on judicial power in a globalized world. The role and functions of the international and domestic judiciary are currently the object of debate all over the world and particularly in a significant number of European states. This debate is at the heart of the present volume.

The purpose of this book is precisely to address different issues connected with the recent transformations of the judiciary in the context of globalization, at both international and domestic levels. For that purpose we invited a group of Authors coming from the judiciary, the academia and the legal practice, with a great wealth of personal and professional experience that has enriched this volume enormously.

We defined the theoretical framework of the volume by identifying certain general trends and issues to be addressed. The Authors could choose a specific topic falling within this scope and adopt the methodological approach considered as the most appropriate for the proposed topic. In view of the variety of the contributions of the Authors, to whom we are grateful, we are sure that this volume will represent a unique contribution to the scientific debate about the role of courts both internationally and domestically.

Strasbourg, France

Paulo Pinto de Albuquerque
Krzysztof Wojtyczek

Vincent Anthony De Gaetano

Justice Vincent de Gaetano is currently one of the most influential Maltese jurists. Born on 17 August 1952, he studied law at the Universities of Malta, where he got a doctoral degree in 1975, and Cambridge, where he got a degree in criminology in 1977. His doctoral dissertation was entitled "The Genuine Link Theory in Dual Nationality in International Law".

Vincent de Gaetano is first and foremost a judge who made a brilliant career in national and international judiciary. He started to work for the attorney's general office where he was Senior Counsel for the Republic (1979–1988), Assistant Attorney-General (1988–1989) and Deputy Attorney-General (1989–1994). At that time, he was responsible for the general legal advice to the Government in matters of public law, and he played an important role in drafting Maltese criminal law legislation.

In 1994, he was appointed judge of Superior Courts and in 2002 he became the Chief Justice and the President of the Constitutional Court, of the Court of Appeal and of the Court of Criminal Appeal as well as Deputy Chairman of the Commission for the Administration of Justice. During the years spent on the bench in Malta, he endeavoured in particular to implement the standards of the European Convention on Human Rights at national level. In 2010, he was elected judge of European Court of Human Rights in respect of Malta. In June 2018, the Plenary Assembly of the Judges of the European Court of Human Rights elected him President of the Third Section of the Court. His term of office of ECHR judge expired in September 2019.

Justice De Gaetano is a man with diplomatic skills and a long experience in international relations. He was a member of numerous expert bodies of the Council of Europe: the ad hoc Committee of Experts on the Legal Aspects of Territorial Asylum, Refugees and Stateless Persons (CAHAR), the Steering Committee on Legal Co-Operation (CDCJ) as well as the Group of States Against Corruption (GRECO). He also represented Malta in the European Conference of Constitutional Courts, in the Network of Presidents of Supreme Judicial Courts of the European Union and in the Association of the Councils of State and Supreme Administrative Jurisdictions of the European Union.

Justice De Gaetano is also a renowned scholar well beyond the borders of his country. Since 1989, he has taught various legal courses at the University of Malta, including criminal law and criminology. He was also invited to teach as a visiting lecturer at several universities throughout the world. As a prolific academic, Professor De Gaetano wrote numerous publications displaying broad intellectual horizons, a rare linguistic refinement and an in-depth insight of the legal and human issues at stake. These texts address a broad range of topics, especially in the fields of legal theory, international, human rights as well as criminal law.

We had the privilege to sit with Vincent De Gaetano on the bench in Strasbourg for several years. He was a very influential judge of the European Court of Human Rights, especially when he performed the function of President of the Rules Committee. As President of the Third Section of the European Court of Human Rights, he displayed great managerial skills and a genuine availability to build consensus. When dealing with cases, he had the unique capacity of identifying the core of the dispute in synthetic and precise words and of addressing the applicant's complaints and the respondent's reply without avoiding the hard legal questions. His persuasive and rich separate opinions written in remarkably beautiful English were able to reveal a firm *pro homine* approach in human rights cases. Expert in many fields, including criminal law and criminology, he was also recognized by his Strasbourg colleagues as *the* authority in Latin language.

If we had to summarize his personality in a few words, we would say: Vincent De Gaetano is a man of crystal-clear honesty, with a very warm and unpretentious character and an unequalled sense of humour, and a man of unwavering faith and strong legal convictions who always fought for justice whatever the personal price to be paid.

Strasbourg, France   Paulo Pinto de Albuquerque
                                                        Krzysztof Wojtyczek

Contents

The Independence of the Judiciary in Strasbourg Judicial Disciplinary Case Law: Judges as Applicants and National Judicial Councils as Factotums of Respondent States

Kevin Aquilina

Contents

Professor Kevin Aquilina is Dean of the Faculty of Laws, University of Malta.

K. Aquilina (✉)
University of Malta, Faculty of Laws, Department of Media, Communications and Technology Law, Msida, Malta
e-mail: kevin.aquilina@um.edu.mt

© Springer Nature Switzerland AG 2019
P. Pinto de Albuquerque, K. Wojtyczek (eds.), *Judicial Power in a Globalized World*, https://doi.org/10.1007/978-3-030-20744-1_1

1   Introduction

The case law of the European Court of Human Rights (hereinafter 'the ECtHR') contains judgements and decisions where the applicant was a member of the national judiciary who complained that his or her human rights and fundamental freedoms contained in the European Convention for the Protection of Human Rights and Fundamental Freedoms (hereinafter 'the ECHR' or 'the Convention') were breached by the national authorities in disciplinary proceedings through the active participation of a National Judicial Council (hereinafter 'NJC'). Although these councils come by various names in the Member States of the Council of Europe, the generic phrase 'National Judicial Councils' is used in this chapter to refer to them irrespective of their exact textual designation under domestic law.

Invariably municipal laws of Council of Europe Member States establish the legal machinery through which judges are appointed/recruited, promoted, trained, demoted, transferred, disciplined, suspended, removed from sitting on an ongoing case, dismissed from service, have their appointment revoked or promotion withheld, or suffer a reduction of mandatory retirement age from office. What is nonetheless noteworthy about these judicial disciplinary cases that have reached the Strasbourg Court is that national judges are becoming more conscious of their human rights and fundamental freedoms and are finding the courage to challenge their own domestic institutions' decisions breaching their human rights and fundamental freedoms. This developing phenomenon is probably attributable to the shift in interpretation by the ECtHR of the Convention, mainly in its ground breaking *Vilho Eskelinen and Others v. Finland*[1] judgment, whereby it extended the application of the expression 'civil rights and obligations' in Article 6, paragraph 1, of the ECHR to comprise public servants, including judges, as litigants. Further, from a study of the outcome of these cases, it is manifest that judges are more successful before the Strasbourg Court than in their respective national state institutions in so far as human rights and fundamental freedoms violations in disciplinary proceedings are concerned. This is mainly—though not exclusively—attributable to the way national law is drafted without taking full cognizance and due respect for the ECHR when such law is approved by national law making authorities. Nevertheless, the conclusion which can be drawn from those cases that arrived at Strasbourg is an unpleasant one for the national authorities: NJCs pose serious and grave concerns to the Convention both in their composition and operation. Hence, it is imperative for Council of Europe Member States to address this subject in the light of the now emergent and crystallised case law of the Strasbourg Court (and pertinent international and European instruments cited therein) with a view to bring national law and state practice of NJCs (and other competent state authorities replacing and/or supplementing NJCs in judicial disciplinary proceedings) more in line with the ECHR.

2 The Purview of This Chapter

As there is quite a steadily growing amount of Strasbourg case law which factors both a judge as applicant and a NJC as a factotum in the decision making structures of a respondent state, this chapter has had to be selective in its ambit. It therefore deals with only those judgments and decisions of the ECtHR where:

(a) the applicant was a judge performing or having performed duties in the national courts to which s/he had been appointed in terms of domestic law;

---

[1] Appl. No. 63235/00, *Vilho Eskelinen and Others v. Finland* (ECtHR 19 April 2007), hereinafter *Vilho Eskelinen and Others v. Finland*.

(b) the applicant judge sought a remedy before the ECtHR in relation to judicial disciplinary proceedings instituted against him/her[2];

(c) the NJC played a determining role in the disciplinary proceedings against the applicant judge;

(d) the outcome of the ECtHR judgment was decided in favour of the applicant judge, whether in part or in full;

(e) all case law studied in this chapter relates to judgments and decisions mainly delivered by the ECtHR after the *Vilho Eskelinen and Others v. Finland* judgment was delivered;

(f) the term 'judge' is used invariably to refer to all members of the judiciary, howsoever designated in national law, be they judges, magistrates, or Presidents or Vice-Presidents of a Court;

(g) the handful of cases where a national judicial disciplinary authority did not comprise an NJC but another authority are also referred to by way of contrast and comparison; and

(h) the Convention provision in those proceedings which provoked the complaint to the ECtHR by an applicant judge need not necessarily have covered only Article 6 cases but could have included other Convention provisions as well.

3   The *Dramatis Personæ: Applicant Judges*

The *dramatis personæ*—or principal actors in the judicial proceedings to be discussed in this chapter—are mainly twofold: applicant judges and NJCs. This contribution does not consider the role of third party interveners who participated in the proceedings before the Strasbourg Court.[3] Nor does it encapsulate the

---

[2]Not discussed in this chapter are cases where (a) the applicant judge's complaint did not involve discipline namely: (1) Appl. No. 58222/09, *Juračić v. Croatia* (ECtHR 26 October 2011); (2) Appl. No. 33173/05, *G. v. Finland* (ECtHR 27 April 2009); (3) Appl. No. 28396/95, *Wille v. Liechtenstein* (ECtHR [GC] 28 October 1999); (4) Appl. Nos. 6360/04 and 16820/04, *Petrova and Chornobryvets v. Ukraine* (ECtHR 15 August 2008); (5) Appl. No. 12628/09, *Dzhidzheva-Trendafilova v. Bulgaria* (ECtHR 9 October 2012); (6) Appl. No. 43800/12, *Tsanova-Gecheva v Bulgaria* (ECtHR 1 February 2016); and/or (b) where the applicant judge lost the complaint: (1) Appl. No. 47936/99, *Pitkevich v. Russia*, (ECtHR 8 February 2001); (2) Appl. No. 62584/00, *Štefan Harabin v. Slovakia* (ECtHR 9 July 2002); (3) Appli. No. 36593/97, *Muammer Yilmazoğlu*, (ECtHR 12 June 2003); (4) Appl. No. 3964/05, *Serdal Apay v. Turkey* (ECtHR 11 December 2007); (5) Appl. No. 27791/06, *Luigi Tosti v. Italy* (ECtHR 12 May 2009); (6) Appl. No. 51160/06, *Di Giovanni v. Italy* (ECtHR 9 July 2013); (7) Appl. No. 75255/10, *Krstan Simić v. Bosnia and Herzegovina* (ECtHR 15 November 2016); and (8) Appl. No. 2873/17, *Çatal v. Turkey* (ECtHR 7 March 2017).

[3]The Hungarian Helsinki Committee, the Hungarian Civil Liberties Union, the Eötvös Károly Institute, and the Helsinki Foundation for Human Rights of Poland were third party interveners in *Baka v. Hungary* (see paras 5 and 85 of the Second Section judgment and paras 9, 98, 136 and 137 of the Grand Chamber judgment), and the International Commission of Jurists was a third party intervener in *Denisov v. Ukraine* (see paras 7, 42 and 91).

contribution of other state institutions which might not have had a determining effect on the outcome of disciplinary proceedings. As both third party interveners and non-NJCs (such as a Parliament and President of a Council of Europe Member State) do not fall within the category of a NJC, their involvement in judicial disciplinary proceedings will not be considered as such in this chapter.

3.1 A Typology of Disciplinary Proceedings Instituted Against Applicant Judges

The leading case law decided by the ECtHR related to disciplinary proceedings against applicant judges comprises twenty cases.

3.1.1 Where Applicant Judges Won the Complaint

The twenty cases where the applicant judges won the complaint, in part or in full, were: *Albayrak v. Turkey*,[4] *Olujić v. Croatia*,[5] *Kudeshkina v. Russia*,[6] *Özpinar v. Turkey*,[7] *Mishgjoni v. Albania*,[8] *Harabin v. Slovakia*,[9] *Oleksandr Volkov v. Ukraine*,[10] *Saghatelyan v. Armenia*,[11] *Gerovska Popčevska v. The Former Yugoslav Republic of Macedonia*,[12] *Ramos Nunes de Carvalho e Sá v. Portugal*,[13] *Baka v. Hungary*,[14] *Mitrinovski v. The Former Yugoslav Republic of Macedonia*,[15] *Ivanovski v. The Former Yugoslav Republic of Macedonia*,[16] *Jakšovski and Trifunovski v. The Former Yugoslav Republic of Macedonia*,[17] *Poposki and Duma*

---

[4]Appl. No. 38406/97 (ECtHR 7 July 2008), hereinafter *Albayrak v. Turkey*.

[5]Appl. No. 22330/05 (ECtHR 5 May 2009), hereinafter *Olujić v. Croatia*.

[6]Appl. No. 29492/05 (ECtHR 14 September 2009), hereinafter *Kudeshkina v. Russia*.

[7]Appl. No. 20999/04 (ECtHR 19 January 2011), hereinafter *Özpinar v. Turkey*.

[8]Appl. No. 18381/05 (ECtHR 7 March 2011), hereinafter *Mishgjoni v. Albania*.

[9]Appl. No. 58688/11 (ECtHR 20 February 2012), hereinafter *Harabin v. Slovakia*.

[10]Appl. No. 21722/11 (ECtHR 27 May 2013), hereinafter *Oleksandr Volkov v. Ukraine*.

[11]Appl. No. 7984/06 (ECtHR 20 January 2016), hereinafter *Saghatelyan v. Armenia*.

[12]Appl. No. 48783/07 (ECtHR 7 April 2016), hereinafter *Gerovska Popčevska v. The Former Yugoslav Republic of Macedonia*.

[13]Appl. Nos. 55391/13, 57728/13 and 74041/13 (ECtHR [GC] 6 November 2018), hereinafter *Ramos Nunes de Carvalho e Sá v. Portugal*.

[14]Appl. No. 20261/12 (ECtHR [GC] 23 June 2016, hereinafter *Baka v. Hungary*.

[15]Appl. No. 6899/12 (ECtHR 30 July 2015), hereinafter *Mitrinovski v. The Former Yugoslav Republic of Macedonia*.

[16]Appl. No. 29908/11 (ECtHR 21 April 2016), hereinafter *Ivanovski v. The Former Yugoslav Republic of Macedonia*.

[17]Appl. Nos. 56381/09 and 58738/09 (ECtHR 7 April 2016), hereinafter *Jakšovski and Trifunovski v. The Former Yugoslav Republic of Macedonia*.

v. The Former Yugoslav Republic of Macedonia,[18] *Kulykov and Others v. Ukraine*,[19] *Erményi v. Hungary*,[20] *Sturua v. Georgia*,[21] *Kamenos v. Cyprus*,[22] and *Denisov v. Ukraine*.[23]

3.1.1.1   Violated Provisions of the ECHR

There were the below-listed violations of the ECHR in relation to cases instituted by applicant judges before the ECtHR:

(a) thirty-five applicant judges who suffered a violation of Article 6(1)[24];
(b) twenty-two applicant judges who suffered a violation of Article 8[25];
(c) three applicant judges who suffered a violation of Article 10[26];
(d) two applicant judges who suffered a violation of Article 13[27]; and
(e) one applicant judge who suffered a violation of Article 14.[28]

The above statistics are per applicant judge, not per violation or per judgment. Out of the twenty cases studied in this chapter, there were two cases where a judgment was delivered by a Section of the Court which was later confirmed by the Grand Chamber[29]; there were two judgments where four violations of the same

---

[18]Appl. Nos. 69916/10 and 36531/11 (ECtHR 7 April 2016), hereinafter *Poposki and Duma v. The Former Yugoslav Republic of Macedonia*.

[19]Appl. No. 5114/09 and 17 others (ECtHR 19 January 2017), hereinafter *Kulykov and Others v. Ukraine*.

[20]Appl. No. 22254/14 (ECtHR 22 February 2017), hereinafter *Erményi v. Hungary*.

[21]Appl. No. 45729/05 (ECtHR 27 April 2017), hereinafter *Sturua v. Georgia*.

[22]Appl. No. 147/07 (ECtHR 31 January 2018), hereinafter *Kamenos v. Cyprus*.

[23]Appl. No. 76639/11 (ECtHR [GC], 25 September 2018), hereinafter *Denisov v. Ukraine*.

[24]Thirty-five applicant judges in 16 judgments: *Olujić v. Croatia*, *Oleksandr Volkov v. Ukraine*, *Mishgjoni v. Albania*, *Harabin v. Slovakia*, *Saghatelyan v. Armenia*, *Gerovska Popčevska v. The Former Yugoslav Republic of Macedonia*, *Ramos Nunes de Carvalho e Sá v. Portugal*, *Baka v. Hungary*, *Mitrinovski v. The Former Yugoslav Republic of Macedonia*, *Ivanovski v. The Former Yugoslav Republic of Macedonia*, *Jakšovski and Trifunovski v. The Former Yugoslav Republic of Macedonia*, *Poposki and Duma v. The Former Yugoslav Republic of Macedonia*, *Sturua v. Georgia*, *Kamenos v. Cyprus*, and *Denisov v. Ukraine*, and *Kulykov and Others v. Ukraine* (eighteen applicants).

[25]Twenty-two applicant judges in five judgments: one applicant judge in *Özpinar v. Turkey*, *Oleksandr Volkov v. Ukraine*, *Ivanovski v. The Former Yugoslav Republic of Macedonia*, *Erményi v. Hungary*, and eighteen applicant judges in *Kulykov and Others v. Ukraine*.

[26]Three applicant judges in three judgments: one applicant judge in *Albayrak v. Turkey*, *Kudeshkina v. Russia*, and *Baka v. Hungary*.

[27]Two applicant judges in two judgments: one applicant judge in *Özpinar v. Turkey*, and another applicant judge in *Mishgjoni v. Albania*.

[28]One applicant judge in one judgment, *Albayrak v. Turkey*.

[29]*Ramos Nunes de Carvalho e Sá v. Portugal* and *Baka v. Hungary*.

Article (Article 6(1)) was found[30] and one judgment which went direct to the Grand Chamber bypassing the Court's Section.[31] The most violated conventional provision was Article 6(1).

3.1.1.2 Respondent States Responsible for a Violation of the Convention

In all there were 39 judgments delivered by the ECtHR in which a violation of the ECHR was found in respect of twelve Member States cited as respondent states:

(a) One applicant judge in relation to Albania,[32] Armenia,[33] Croatia,[34] Cyprus,[35] Georgia,[36] Portugal,[37] Slovakia[38] and Russia[39];
(b) Four applicant judges in all in relation to Hungary[40] and Turkey[41];
(c) Seven applicant judges in all in relation to the Yugoslav Republic of Macedonia[42]; and
(d) Twenty applicant judges in all in relation to Ukraine.[43]

3.1.1.3 Disciplinary Sanctions Imposed Upon Applicant Judges

A study of the above cases indicates that the applicant judges faced in the vast majority of cases the most severe punishment, that of removal/dismissal from office:

---

[30]*Olujić v. Croatia* and *Oleksandr Volkov v. Ukraine*.

[31]*Denisov v. Ukraine*.

[32]One applicant judge, *Mishgjoni v. Albania*.

[33]One applicant judge, *Saghatelyan v. Armenia*.

[34]One applicant judge, *Olujić v. Croatia*.

[35]One applicant judge, *Kamenos v. Cyprus*.

[36]One applicant judge, *Sturua v. Georgia*.

[37]One applicant judge, *Ramos Nunes de Carvalho e Sá v. Portugal*.

[38]One applicant judge, *Harabin v. Slovakia*.

[39]One applicant judge, *Kudeshkina v. Russia*.

[40]Two applicant judges in *Baka v. Hungary*, and *Erményi v. Hungary* (three judgments were delivered as in the case of *Baka v. Hungary*, there were two judgments—one by the Second Section and another by the Grand Chamber).

[41]Two applicant judges, *Albayrak v. Turkey* and *Özpinar v. Turkey*.

[42]Six applicant judges with four judgments delivered by the ECtHR, one applicant judge in *Gerovska Popčevska v. The Former Yugoslav Republic of Macedonia*, *Mitrinovski v. The Former Yugoslav Republic of Macedonia*, and *Ivanovski v. The Former Yugoslav Republic of Macedonia*; two applicant judges in *Jakšovski and Trifunovski v. The Former Yugoslav Republic of Macedonia*, and *Poposki and Duma v. The Former Yugoslav Republic of Macedonia*.

[43]Twenty applicant judges with three judgments delivered by the ECtHR, one judge applicant, *Oleksandr Volkov v. Ukraine*, eighteen applicant judges in *Kulykov and Others v. Ukraine*, and one applicant judge in *Denisov v. Ukraine*.

(a) one applicant judge was punished by a reduction of the mandatory retirement age[44];
(b) one applicant judge was punished by a transfer[45];
(c) one applicant judge was punished by withholding of a promotion[46];
(d) one applicant judge was punished by a reprimand[47];
(e) thirty-four applicant judges were punished by dismissal from office[48];
(f) one applicant judge was punished by removal from continuing to hear a specific pending case she was seized of[49];
(g) one applicant judge was punished by a suspension from duty[50]; and
(h) one applicant judge was punished by a reduction (of 70%) of salary.[51]

The statistics for the punishment by dismissal from judicial office does not include:

(a) a refusal to be reinstated—there were two cases where more than one punishment was inflicted[52];
(b) a suspension from work (though later the applicant judge was reinstated) but no prompt payment of salary arrears due was made when suspended[53]; and
(c) a dismissal from the position of Vice-President of the Supreme Court and a reduction of mandatory retirement age.[54]

3.1.1.4 National Disciplinary Institutions for Applicant Judges

Not all disciplinary cases involved a NJC. From the twenty cases studied in this chapter, the following observations can be made in relation to NJCs:

(a) there were thirteen cases which involved a NJC as a decision making authority:

---

[44]*Erményi v. Hungary.*

[45]*Albayrak v. Turkey.* But see also Appl. No. 27791/06, *Luigi Tosti v. Italy* (ECtHR 12 May 2009).

[46]*Albayrak v. Turkey.*

[47]*Ibid.*

[48]One applicant judge in *Olujić v. Croatia, Özpinar v. Turkey, Oleksandr Volkov v. Ukraine, Saghatelyan v. Armenia, Gerovska Popčevska v. The Former Yugoslav Republic of Macedonia, Baka v. Hungary, Mitrinovski v. The Former Yugoslav Republic of Macedonia, Ivanovski v. The Former Yugoslav Republic of Macedonia, Erményi v. Hungary, Sturua v. Georgia, Kamenos v. Cyprus,* and *Denisov v. Ukraine,* 2 applicant judges in *Jakšovski and Trifunovski v. The Former Yugoslav Republic of Macedonia,* and *Poposki and Duma v. The Former Yugoslav Republic of Macedonia,* and eighteen applicant judges in *Kulykov and Others v. Ukraine.*

[49]*Kudeshkina v. Russia.*

[50]*Ramos Nunes de Carvalho e Sá v. Portugal.*

[51]*Harabin v. Slovakia.*

[52]*Albayrak v. Turkey,* concerning transfer, withholding of promotion, and reprimand; and *Özpinar v. Turkey,* concerning removal from office and refusal to reinstate applicant judge.

[53]*Mishgjoni v. Albania.*

[54]*Erményi v. Hungary.*

– *Albayrak v. Turkey* and *Özpinar v. Turkey* where the NJC was the Supreme Council of Judges and Prosecutors;

– *Olujić v. Croatia* where the NJC was the National Judicial Council;

– *Kudeshkina v. Russia* where the NJC was the Judiciary Qualification Board;

– *Mishgjoni v. Albania* where the NJC was the High Council of Justice;

– *Ramos Nunes de Carvalho e Sá v. Portugal* where the NJC was the High Court of the Judiciary;

– *Gerovska Popčevska v. The Former Yugoslav Republic of Macedonia*, *Mitrinovski v. The Former Yugoslav Republic of Macedonia*, *Jakšovski and Trifunovski v. The Former Yugoslav Republic of Macedonia*, and *Poposki and Duma v. The Former Yugoslav Republic of Macedonia*, where the NJC was the State Juridical Council;

– *Sturua v. Georgia* where the NJC was the Disciplinary Council of Judges Panel;

– *Kamenos v. Cyprus* where the NJC was the Supreme Council of Judicature; and

– *Denisov v. Ukraine* where the NJC was the High Council of Justice;

(b) there were three cases which involved a NJC but not as a decision making authority:

– *Oleksandr Volkov v. Ukraine* where the NJC was the High Council of Justice which recommended to the Parliamentary Committee on the Judiciary;

– *Kulykov and Others v. Ukraine* where the NJC was the High Council of Justice which recommended to the Parliamentary Committee on the Judiciary in the case of sixteen applicant judges and to the President in the case of two applicant judges; and

– *Saghatelyan v. Armenia* where the NJC was the High Council of Justice which recommended to the President;

(c) there were four cases where an NJC was not involved at all:

– *Harabin v. Slovakia* where discipline was exercised by the Constitutional Court;

– *Baka v. Hungary* and *Erményi v. Hungary* where discipline was administered by Parliament; and

– *Ivanovski v. The Former Yugoslav Republic of Macedonia* where discipline was inflicted by Parliament relying on the conclusion of the (non-NJC) Lustration Commission.

3.1.1.5 National Reviewing Bodies for Applicant Judges

Not all NJCs had their decisions reviewable by higher authority:

(a) there were fifteen cases where NJC decisions were reviewable by a higher authority:

- *Olujić v. Croatia* where the National Judicial Council's decision was review-able by Parliament's Chamber of the Counties and subsequently by the Constitutional Court;
- *Kudeshkina v. Russia* where the Judiciary Qualification Board's decision was reviewable by the Moscow City Court and the Supreme Court;
- *Mishgjoni v. Albania* where the High Council of Justice's decision was reviewable by the Supreme Court and subsequently the Constitutional Court;
- *Ramos Nunes de Carvalho e Sá v. Portugal* where the High Court of the Judiciary's decision was reviewable by the Supreme Court of Justice;
- *Gerovska Popčevska v. The Former Yugoslav Republic of Macedonia, Mitrinovski v. The Former Yugoslav Republic of Macedonia, Jakšovski and Trifunovski v. The Former Yugoslav Republic of Macedonia,* and *Poposki and Duma v. The Former Yugoslav Republic of Macedonia,* where the State Juridical Council's decision was reviewable by the Supreme Court Appeal Panel;
- *Sturua v. Georgia* where the Disciplinary Council of Judges Panel's decision was reviewable by the Disciplinary Council of Judges and, for points of law only, by the Supreme Court;
- *Albayrak v. Turkey* and *Özpinar v. Turkey* where the State Juridical Council's decision was reviewable by the Superior Council's Appeal Panel; and
- *Kulykov and Others v. Ukraine, Denisov v. Ukraine,* and *Oleksandr Volkov v. Ukraine* where the High Council of Justice's decision was reviewable by the Higher Administrative Court;

(b) there were five cases where NJC decisions were not reviewable by a higher authority, namely:

- *Saghatelyan v. Armenia* where discipline was exercised by the President of Armenia on the recommendation of the Council of Justice;
- *Kamenos v. Cyprus* where discipline was exercised by the Supreme Council of Judicature;
- *Harabin v. Slovakia* where discipline was exercised by the Constitutional Court;
- *Baka v. Hungary* where discipline was administered by Parliament; and
- *Erményi v. Hungary* where discipline was administered by Parliament.

(c) there was one reviewable case decided by a non-NJC, that is, *Ivanovski v. The Former Yugoslav Republic of Macedonia,* where discipline was inflicted by Parliament relying on the conclusion of the (non-NJC) Lustration Commission where this decision was initially reviewable by the Administrative Court and subsequently by the Supreme Court.

3.1.1.6 Partial Reparation for Applicant Judges in Terms of Article 41 ECHR

Applicant judges, in certain cases, requested just satisfaction. But the ECtHR did not entertain their requests in quite a number of judgments. Indeed:

(a) *pecuniary damages* were not granted in relation to twenty-nine applicant judges,[55] pecuniary damages were granted only in relation to two applicant judges[56]; pecuniary and non-pecuniary damages were combined in relation to two applicant judges[57]; in relation to one applicant judge, pecuniary damages were reserved,[58] and in relation to three applicant judges no request for just satisfaction was made[59];

(b) *non-pecuniary damages* were not granted in relation to five applicant judges,[60] non-pecuniary damages were granted in relation to 25 applicant judges[61]; pecuniary and non-pecuniary damages were combined in relation to two applicant judges[62]; and

---

[55] *Mishgjoni v. Albania, Harabin v. Slovakia, Saghatelyan v. Armenia, Gerovska Popčevska v. The Former Yugoslav Republic of Macedonia, Ramos Nunes de Carvalho e Sá v. Portugal, Mitrinovski v. The Former Yugoslav Republic of Macedonia, Ivanovski v. The Former Yugoslav Republic of Macedonia, Jakšovski and Trifunovski v. The Former Yugoslav Republic of Macedonia, Poposki and Duma v. The Former Yugoslav Republic of Macedonia, Kulykov and Others v. Ukraine* but only in relation to seventeen (out of eighteen) applicant judges, and *Kamenos v. Cyprus.*

[56] *Albayrak v. Turkey,* and in *Kulykov and Others v. Ukraine* but only to one (out of eighteen) applicants.

[57] *Baka v. Hungary,* and *Erményi v. Hungary.*

[58] *Oleksandr Volkov v. Ukraine.*

[59] *Özpinar v. Turkey, Olujić v. Croatia, Kudeshkina v. Russia.*

[60] *Ramos Nunes de Carvalho e Sá v. Portugal,* and *Kulykov and Others v. Ukraine* but only in relation to four (out of eighteen) applicant judges.

[61] *Mishgjoni v. Albania, Harabin v. Slovakia, Oleksandr Volkov v. Ukraine, Saghatelyan v. Armenia, Gerovska Popčevska v. The Former Yugoslav Republic of Macedonia, Baka v. Hungary, Mitrinovski v. The Former Yugoslav Republic of Macedonia, Ivanovski v. The Former Yugoslav Republic of Macedonia, Jakšovski and Trifunovski v. The Former Yugoslav Republic of Macedonia* but only in relation to second applicant, *Poposki and Duma v. The Former Yugoslav Republic of Macedonia* in relation to second applicant only, *Kulykov and Others v. Ukraine* but only in relation to eleven out of eighteen applicants, *Erményi v. Hungary, Sturua v. Georgia, Kamenos v. Cyprus,* and *Denisov v. Ukraine.*

[62] *Baka v. Hungary,* and *Erményi v. Hungary.*

(c) *costs and expenses* were not granted only in relation to ten applicant judges,[63] cost and expenses were granted in relation to thirty applicant judges[64]; no requests for costs and expenses were made by two applicant judges.[65]

3.1.1.7 Legal Obligation on Respondent States to Put an End to a Breach of the ECHR and Afford *Restitutio in Integrum* in Terms of Article 46 ECHR

In *Volkov v. Ukraine*—the leading case out of the 20 discussed in this chapter—the court reiterated that its judgments are declaratory in nature and that it is up to the respondent state, subject to the Council of Europe Committee of Ministers' supervision, to determine how to put an end to the Convention's breach and afford the applicant a means to reinstate him/her in his/her position before the violation occurred whilst reserving for itself, exceptionally, the type of measure needed to terminate the violation, including identifying which particular means of redress had to be applied. For this purpose, the ECtHR distinguished between general measures and individual measures.

General measures have been applied only once in the judgments surveyed in this chapter—that of *Volkov v. Ukraine*—where the ECtHR requested the taking of a general measure to reform the judicial discipline system: 'These measures should include legislative reform involving the restructuring of the institutional basis of the system. Furthermore, these measures should entail the development of appropriate forms and principles of coherent application of domestic law in this field'.[66] Concluding on this point, the ECtHR emphasised that: 'Therefore, the Court considers it necessary to stress that Ukraine must urgently put in place the general reforms in its legal system outlined above. In so doing, the Ukrainian authorities should have due regard to this judgment, the Court's relevant case-law and the Committee of Ministers' relevant recommendations, resolutions and decisions'.[67] Thus, these general measures are more institutional, structural and systemic rather than individual, and

---

[63]*Kudeshkina v. Russia, Ramos Nunes de Carvalho e Sá v. Portugal, Poposki and Duma v. The Former Yugoslav Republic of Macedonia*, but only in relation to first applicant, and *Kulykov and Others v. Ukraine*, but only in relation to seven out of eighteen applicants.

[64]*Albayrak v. Turkey, Kudeshkina v. Russia, Özpinar v. Turkey, Mishgjoni v. Albania, Harabin v. Slovakia, Oleksandr Volkov v. Ukraine, Saghatelyan v. Armenia, Gerovska Popčevska v. The Former Yugoslav Republic of Macedonia, Mitrinovski v. The Former Yugoslav Republic of Macedonia, Ivanovski v. The Former Yugoslav Republic of Macedonia, Jakšovski and Trifunovski v. The Former Yugoslav Republic of Macedonia, Poposki and Duma v. The Former Yugoslav Republic of Macedonia, Kulykov and Others v. Ukraine* but only in relation to fourteen out of eighteen applicant judges, *Sturua v. Georgia* and *Denisov v. Ukraine*.

[65]*Albayrak v. Turkey* and *Olujić v. Croatia*.

[66]*Volkov v. Ukraine*, para 200.

[67]*Ibid.*, para 202.

addressed only in one case the remedy demanded by the applicant judge. It requested the national authorities to reinstate the applicant judge at the earliest possible time.

As to individual measures, the Court—contrary to the cases listed in the following paragraph—was not of the view that the reopening of domestic proceedings was tantamount to appropriate redress for the violation of Volkov's human rights even though it assumed that the applicant judge's case would be retried by the competent national authorities. Hence, the ECtHR decision was that bearing in mind the very exceptional circumstances of the case, the applicant judge had to be reinstated 'to the post of judge of the Supreme Court at the earliest possible date'.[68]

Individual measures were to be adopted in *Harabin v. Slovakia*,[69] *Gerovska Popčevska v. The Former Yugoslav Republic of Macedonia*,[70] *Ramos Nunes de Carvalho e Sá v. Portugal*,[71] *Mitrinovski v. The Former Yugoslav Republic of Macedonia*,[72] *Jakšovski and Trifunovski v. The Former Yugoslav Republic of Macedonia*,[73] and *Poposki and Duma v. The Former Yugoslav Republic of Macedonia*.[74] As the violation had to be put to an end and reparation for its consequences made through restoring as far as possible the situation existing before the breach occurred, *restitutio in integrum* was advocated. The ECtHR thus was of the view that the appropriate form of redress was the reopening of proceedings by the national authorities and directed respondent states to adopt individual measures in addition to the sums awarded by way of just satisfaction.

In *Özpinar v. Turkey*,[75] the ECtHR noted that Turkish law had been amended to the extent that the decisions of the Superior Council of the Magistracy were subject to review. This, the Court observed, sufficed as just satisfaction to address the conventional violations complained of.

4 The Pre-*Vilho Eskelinen and Others v. Finland* ECtHR Position

4.1 No Access to a Court in Employment Decisions Relating to Civil Servants

One of the previous stumbling blocks for a complainant in the case law of the ECtHR was whether employment decisions concerning civil servants could be challenged

---

[68]*Ibid.*, para 208.

[69]Paras 177 and 178.

[70]Paras 67 and 68.

[71]*Ramos Nunes de Carvalho e Sá v. Portugal*, Grand Chamber, para 222.

[72]Paras 58 and 59.

[73]Paras 57 and 58.

[74]Paras 62 and 63.

[75]Para 92.

before the Court. *Massa v Italy* replied in the negative.[76] The Strasbourg Court ruled that 'employment disputes between the authorities and public servants whose duties typified the specific activities of the public service, in so far as the latter was acting as the depositary of public authority responsible for protecting the general interests of the State, were not "civil" and were excluded from the scope of Article 6 § 1'.[77] This ruling was adopted in subsequent case law in relation to civil servants such as in *Pellegrin v. France*,[78] and also in relation to applicant judges such as in *Pitkevich v Russia*[79] and others which followed it such as *Zubko And Others v Ukraine*.[80] In this respect, pre-*Vilho Eskelinen and Others v. Finland* applicant judges remain remediless.

4.2   *Civil Servants and Judges as Part of the Public Service*

The *Massa v Italy* judgment was applied by *Pitkevich v Russia* to include applicant judges which extended the narrow meaning of a 'civil servant' to include also that of a 'public servant': 'The Court observes that the judiciary, while not being part of ordinary civil service, is nonetheless part of typical public service. A judge has specific responsibilities in the field of administration of justice which is a sphere in which States exercise sovereign powers. Consequently, the judge participates directly in the exercise of powers conferred by public law and perform duties designed to safeguard the general interest of the State'.[81]

---

[76]In *Massa v Italy*, the ECtHR held that: '26. Disputes relating to the recruitment, careers and termination of service of public servants are as a general rule outside the scope of Article 6 para. 1 (art. 6-1) (on recruitment to the civil service, see the *Glasenapp and Kosiek v. Germany* judgments of 28 August 1986, Series A no. 104, p. 26, para. 49, and no. 105, p. 20, para. 35), but State intervention by means of a statute or delegated legislation has not prevented the Court from finding in several cases that the right in issue was a civil one (see, among other authorities, the *Francesco Lombardo and Giancarlo Lombardo v. Italy* judgments of 26 November 1992, Series A no. 249-B, p. 26, para. 17, and no. 249-C, p. 42, para. 16)'.

[77]*Pitkevich v Russia*, note 2, p. 8.

[78]Appl. No. 28541/95, *Pellegrin v France* (ECtHR 8 December 1999).

[79]*Pitkevich v Russia*, note 2.

[80]Appl. Nos. 3955/04, 5622/04, 8538/04 and 11418/04, *Zubko and Others v. Ukraine* (ECtHR 26 July 2006).

[81]*Pitkevich v Russia*, note 2, p. 8.

4.3 Legitimate Limitation of Conventional Rights on Public Servants

In *Vogt v Germany*, the Grand Chamber ruled that civil servants are human beings who enjoy human rights even though a State may expect from them a duty of discretion due to their status.[82] The court was called upon to 'determine whether a fair balance has been struck between the fundamental right of the individual to freedom of expression and the legitimate interest of a democratic State in ensuring that its civil service properly furthers the purposes enumerated in Article 10 para. 2'.[83]

4.4 The Post-Vilho Eskelinen and Others v. Finland ECtHR Position

This interpretation, nevertheless, changed in *Vilho Eskelinen and Others v. Finland*, where the Court reinterpreted in *Pellegrin v France* the functional approach in Article 6, paragraph 1, as follows:

> in order for the respondent State to be able to rely before the Court on the applicant's status as a civil servant in excluding the protection embodied in Article 6, two conditions must be fulfilled. Firstly, the State in its national law must have expressly excluded access to a court for the post or category of staff in question. Secondly, the exclusion must be justified on objective grounds in the State's interest.[84]

5 Confirmed ECtHR Violations of Article 6(1) ECHR in Relation to Applicant Judges

The ECtHR found a number of violations of the ECHR where the applicants were judges sitting on national courts. The rights and freedoms which have been violated by respondent states are identified below:

(a) *Access to a Court*: Saghatelyan v. Armenia and Baka v. Hungary;
(b) *Right to a Public Hearing*: Olujić v. Croatia and Ramos Nunes de Carvalho e Sá v. Portugal;
(c) *Equality of Arms*: Olujić v. Croatia;
(d) *Excessive Length of Proceedings*: Olujić v. Croatia and Mishgjoni v. Albania;
(e) *Tribunal Established by Law*: Oleksandr Volkov v. Ukraine;

---

[82]Appl. No. 17851/91, *Vogt v. Germany* (ECtHR [GC] 26 September 1995), para 53.
[83]*Ibid.*, para 53.
[84]*Vilho Eskelinen and Others v Finland*, para 62.

(f) *Impartiality and Independence of a court or tribunal*: *Olujić v. Croatia*; *Harabin v. Slovakia*; *Oleksandr Volkov v. Ukraine*; *Gerovska Popčevska v. The Former Yugoslav Republic of Macedonia*; *Ramos Nunes de Carvalho e Sá v. Portugal*; *Mitrinovski v. The Former Yugoslav Republic of Macedonia*; *Ivanovski v. The Former Yugoslav Republic of Macedonia*; *Kulykov and Others v. Ukraine*; *Jakšovski and Trifunovski v. The Former Yugoslav Republic of Macedonia*; *Poposki and Duma v. The Former Yugoslav Republic of Macedonia*; *Sturua v. Georgia*; *Kamenos v. Cyprus*; and *Denisov v. Ukraine*;

(g) *Legal Certainty*: as regards (1) the absence of a limitation period for the proceedings against the applicant—*Denisov v. Ukraine and Oleksandr Volkov v. Ukraine*; and (2) the principle of legal certainty and the dismissal of the applicant at the plenary meeting of Parliament – *Oleksandr Volkov v. Ukraine*;

(h) *Adequate time and facilities for defence preparation*: *Ramos Nunes de Carvalho e Sá v. Portugal*.

6 Confirmed Violations of Other ECHR Provisions in Relation to Applicant Judges

Although the bulk of conventional provisions violated in relation to applicant judges have been in respect of Article 6, there were also other conventional provisions which were breached in their respect:

(a) *Violation of Article 8 of the Convention*: *Özpinar v. Turkey*; *Oleksandr Volkov v. Ukraine*; *Ivanovski v. The Former Yugoslav Republic of Macedonia*; *Kulykov and Others v. Ukraine*, and *Erményi v. Hungary*;

(b) *Violation of Article 10 of the Convention*: *Albayrak v. Turkey*; *Kudeshkina v. Russia*; and *Baka v. Hungary*; and

(c) *Violation of Article 13 of the Convention*: *Özpinar v. Turkey*; and *Mishgjoni v. Albania*.

7 Pertinent Principles Enunciated by the Strasbourg Court in Cases Instituted by Applicant Judges

When analysing the Strasbourg cases instituted by applicant judges, a number of principles have been enunciated, some had already been set out in previous case law and have been reaffirmed in relation to applicant judges in the twenty cases studied in this chapter, whilst others are new having been developed specifically in the cases under consideration in this chapter. These principles comprise the following:

7.1 Rule of Law

In *Harabin v. Slovakia*,[85] the Court has held that the judiciary's mission 'in a democratic state is to guarantee the very existence of the rule of law'. In *Erményi v. Hungary*, the Court observed that the expression 'in accordance with the law' required domestic law to be compatible with the rule of law: 'This latter concept, which is expressly mentioned in the Preamble to the Convention and is inherent in all the Articles of the Convention, requires, *inter alia*, that any interference must in principle be based on an instrument of general application'.[86] In *Baka v. Hungary*, the ECtHR quoted the Council of Europe's Venice Commission on Democracy Through Law which had commented on 'the individualised (*ad hominem*) nature of the legislation'[87]: 'laws which are directed against a specific person are contrary to the rule of law'.[88]

7.2 Separation of Powers

The Court noted in two cases studied in this chapter that: 'the notion of the separation of powers between the executive and the judiciary has assumed growing importance in the case-law of the Court.[89] Indeed, the court has been called upon to examine the relationship between Parliament,[90] the President,[91] the Prosecutor General,[92] the Minister of Justice,[93] and NJCs[94] as external agents to the judicial corps, as well as the inter-relationship between the judiciary themselves.[95]

---

[85]*Harabin v. Skovakia*, para 133. See also *Ramos Nunes de Carvalho e Sá v. Portugal*, para 196.

[86]*Erményi v. Hungary*, para 32.

[87]*Baka v. Hungary*, para 154.

[88]*Ibid*, para 117.

[89]*Oleksandr Volkov v Ukraine*, para 103 and *Saghatelyan v. Armenia*, para 43.

[90]*Oleksandr Volkov v Ukraine, Kulykov and Others v. Ukraine, Baka v. Hungary, Erményi v. Hungary, Olujić v. Croatia*, and *Ivanovski v. The Former Yugoslav Republic of Macedonia*.

[91]*Kulykov and Others v. Ukraine*, and *Saghatelyan v. Armenia*.

[92]*Oleksandr Volkov v Ukraine, Denisov v. Ukraine*, and *Saghatelyan v. Armenia*.

[93]*Gerovska Popčevska v. The Former Yugoslav Republic of Macedonia, Oleksandr Volkov v Ukraine*, and *Oleksandr Volkov v Ukraine*.

[94]*Albayrak v. Turkey, Özpinar v. Turkey, Olujić v. Croatia, Kudeshkina v. Russia, Mishgjoni v. Albania, Ramos Nunes de Carvalho e Sá v. Portugal, Gerovska Popčevska v. The Former Yugoslav Republic of Macedonia, Mitrinovski v. The Former Yugoslav Republic of Macedonia, Jakšovski and Trifunovski v. The Former Yugoslav Republic of Macedonia, Poposki and Duma v. The Former Yugoslav Republic of Macedonia, Sturua v. Georgia, Kamenos v. Cyprus*, and *Denisov v. Ukraine*.

[95]*Kamenos v. Cyprus, Sturua v. Georgia, Gerovska Popčevska v. The Former Yugoslav Republic of Macedonia, Mitrinovski v. The Former Yugoslav Republic of Macedonia, Olujić v. Croatia, Oleksandr Volkov v. Ukraine, Gerovska Popčevska v. The Former Yugoslav Republic of*

7.3   Independence of the Judiciary

The doctrine of the independence of the judiciary is a bye-product of the doctrine of the separation of powers: they are indissolubly linked to each other. In *Ramos Nunes de Carvalho e Sá v. Portugal*, the Court linked the rule of law to the independence of the judiciary: 'When a member State initiates such disciplinary proceedings, public confidence in the functioning and independence of the judiciary is at stake; in a democratic State, this confidence guarantees the very existence of the rule of law. Furthermore, the Court has stressed the growing importance attached to the separation of powers and to the necessity of safeguarding the independence of the judiciary'.[96]

7.4   Convention Rights Apply Also to Public Servants

Notwithstanding the fact that judges are public servants, they still are individuals who enjoy conventional rights. In *Albayrak v. Turkey*, the Court found a violation of Article 10 as the domestic state failed to distinguish between the personal views of a judge and information received by a judge by others in the course of his day-to-day activities; unless a nexus can be established between the judge's personal views and what is imparted to him, his opinions have to be considered to be separate.

8   Appearance of Personal Bias

Appearance of personal bias has been a stumbling block upon which ground applicant judges were disciplined. This has taken the form of objective or subjective bias or both.

Macedonia, Mitrinovski v. The Former Yugoslav Republic of Macedonia, Jakšovski and Trifunovski v. The Former Yugoslav Republic of Macedonia, Poposki and Duma v. The Former Yugoslav Republic of Macedonia, Denisov v. Ukraine, Harabin v. Slovakia, Mishgjoni v. Albania, *and Kudeshkina v. Russia.*

[96]*Ramos Nunes de Carvalho e Sá v. Portugal*, para 196.

8.1   Making an Initial Appraisal of Guilt and Subsequently Hearing the Disciplinary Case: Prejudice Through Objective Impartiality

There were cases where the person initiating the disciplinary procedure subsequently participated in the decision making process, finding the applicant judge guilty as charged. Such was the case with *Kamenos v. Cyprus*, *Sturua v. Georgia*, *Gerovska Popčevska v. The Former Yugoslav Republic of Macedonia*, and *Mitrinovski v. The Former Yugoslav Republic of Macedonia*.

8.2   Objective Impartiality Through the Appearance of Personal Bias: National Law Disallowing Judicial Withdrawal

In *Oleksandr Volkov v. Ukraine*, there was a lack of personal impartiality as HCJ's members could not withdraw from hearing the case as no withdrawal procedure was envisaged by law. There were no appropriate guarantees to ensure that the proceedings were objectively impartial.

8.3   Appearance of Personal Bias: Prejudice Through Subjective Impartiality

In *Olujić v. Croatia*, the impartiality of three NJC members was established on the basis of interviews given by the President and two other NJC members during the disciplinary proceedings, expressing bias against the applicant.

In *Oleksandr Volkov v. Ukraine*, two HCJ members, who carried out the preliminary inquiries in the applicant's case and submitted requests for his dismissal, subsequently partook in the applicant's removal from office proceedings. One such member was subsequently appointed HCJ President and presided over the hearing of applicant's case. The role of those members in bringing disciplinary charges against the applicant, based on the results of their own preliminary inquiries, threw objective doubt on their impartiality when deciding on the merits of the applicant's case. Further, personal bias was demonstrated by the Chairman of the Parliamentary Committee on the judiciary who was also an HCJ member. Even though he had not directly criticised the applicant, he had disapproved of applicant's actions.

8.4   Prejudice Through Subjective and Objective Impartiality

In *Gerovska Popčevska v. The Former Yugoslav Republic of Macedonia*, the State Judicial Council was composed of eight judges elected by their peers, the Minister of Justice and the President of the Supreme Court. The latter had expressed an unfavourable view to the applicant and subsequently participated in the impugned professional misconduct proceedings before the SJC. Similar considerations applied to the participation of the then Minister of Justice in the SJC decision to dismiss the applicant notwithstanding that the Minister had requested, as the then President of the State Anti-Corruption Commission, that the SJC review the civil case. The Court considered that the presence on that body of the Minister of Justice, as a member of the executive, impaired the NJC's independence.

In *Mitrinovski v. The Former Yugoslav Republic of Macedonia*, a judge who was a member of the SJC had sought the impugned proceedings. He subsequently took part in the decision to remove the applicant from office. His role in the proceedings failed both the subjective and objective impartiality tests notwithstanding the fact that the said judge was only one of fifteen SJC members. The same situation repeated itself in the case of other judges in *Jakšovski and Trifunovski v. The Former Yugoslav Republic of Macedonia* and in *Poposki and Duma v. The Former Yugoslav Republic of Macedonia*.

In *Denisov v. Ukraine*, the applicant's case was heard and determined by eighteen members, only eight whereof were judges. The non-judicial members constituted a majority capable of determining the proceedings' outcome. Moreover, the majority of the HCJ's members were not employed full-time by the HCJ and the Prosecutor General was an HCJ member. Certain members of the HCJ had shown personal bias. One HCJ judge member, as chairman of the Council of Administrative Court Judges, had proposed Denisov's dismissal to the HCJ. This preliminary involvement had casted objective doubt on this judge's impartiality when he subsequently took part in the HCJ decision on the merits of applicant's case.

9   HCJ Structural Deficiencies Evinced from Strasbourg Case Law

A survey of the case law studied in this chapter indicates that NJCs have contributed to human rights breaches because of their structural deficiencies identified by the Strasbourg Court.

9.1 Difficulties Posed by NJC's Composition

In *Albert and Le Compte v. Belgium*,[97] the ECtHR noted that: 'when disputes to which Article 6 is applicable are determined by organs other than courts, the Convention calls at least for one of the following systems: either the jurisdictional organs themselves comply with the requirements of Article 6 § 1 or they do not so comply but are subject to subsequent control by a judicial body that has full jurisdiction and does provide the guarantees of Article 6 § 1'.[98] Yet, Council of Europe Member States have failed to comply therewith in the cases studied below.

In *Ramos Nunes de Carvalho e Sá v. Portugal*, the proceedings before the CSM, a non-judicial body, were in writing. The applicant was precluded from attending its sittings and making oral submissions both on matters of fact and of law and on the penalties. No evidence from witnesses was heard. On appeal, the Judicial Division of the Supreme Court did not enjoy full powers to review the CSM decision as to the establishments of facts, its review power being limited only to the lawfulness of the decision challenged.

In *Oleksandr Volkov v. Ukraine*, the non-judicial staff appointed directly by the executive and the legislative authorities comprised the vast majority of the HCJ's members such that the applicant's case was determined by sixteen HCJ members attending the hearing, only three whereof being judges. Judges constituted an insignificant decision making minority.

In *Saghatelyan v. Armenia*, the NJC was composed of the President of Armenia, the Minister of Justice and the Prosecutor General. The Council of Justice was presided over by representatives of the executive. The applicant could not contest the NJC's decision before a judicial authority.

In *Kamenos v. Cyprus*, the Supreme Court itself framed the charges against the applicant and then, sitting as the SCJ, conducted disciplinary proceedings. It then decided on and dismissed the applicant's objection concerning the charge sheet which it had framed and also dismissed the applicant from office on the merits.

In *Sturua v. Georgia*, four members of the Disciplinary Council of Judges had first gathered as a Panel to examine the disciplinary charge brought against the applicant. After holding a hearing and examined all the evidence, the Panel found the applicant guilty of a disciplinary offence and dismissed him from office. The same four judges sat as part of the eight-member plenary session of the Disciplinary Council which reviewed on appeal the issues of fact and points of law raised by the applicant before the Panel. On appeal, the same four judges reconsidered their own decision. Half of the bench, including its President, had already expressed their view thereupon.

In *Kulykov and Others v. Ukraine*, as in *Oleksandr Volkov v Ukraine*, the Court concluded that the procedure before the HCJ and Parliament had disclosed a number of structural and general shortcomings, which had compromised the principles of

---

[97] Appl. Nos. 7299/75 and 7496/76 (ECtHR 10 February 1983), para 29.
[98] *Saghatelyan v. Armenia*, para 39.

independence and impartiality, and that the subsequent judicial review had not remedied those shortcomings.

9.2 Reviewing Authority Being Hierarchically Subordinate to the NJC Disciplinary Body of First Instance

In *Denisov v. Ukraine* the HAC judges were also under the disciplinary jurisdiction of the HCJ. This meant that those judges could also be the subject of disciplinary proceedings before the HCJ. The HCJ was not merely a disciplinary authority but an authority with extensive powers with respect to the careers of judges in relation to appointment, discipline and dismissal. The HAC judges were placed in an awkward position being themselves subject to disciplinary proceedings before the HCJ, that same body whose decision they were reviewing. Thus, the HCJ suffered from lack of adequate safeguards as to independence and impartiality.

9.3 Manner of Appointment of the Judiciary on NJCs

The manner of appointment of judges on NJCs has also a bearing in establishing an NJCs independence and impartiality. According to *Oleksandr Volkov v. Ukraine*, the appointed judges on the NJC were not elected by the judicial corps or through election by their peers. Judicial self-governance has to consider the manner of judicial appointment on the NJC. Although ten HCJ members were to be appointed from the judiciary, only three judges were elected by their peers. Seven out of ten judges were appointed from judicially extraneous bodies.

9.4 NJC Members' Dependence on Primary Employer

A shadow of doubt is cast as to the independence and impartiality of NJC part-time members who are dependent—materially, hierarchically and administratively—upon their primary employer. Conflicts of interest may arise between a member's allegiance to the primary employer and to the NJC.

9.5 The Position of Ex Officio NJC Members

The loss of NJC members' primary job, in case of *ex officio* NJC members, means that their NJC membership (as is their salary) is contingent upon an outside source.

Pressure can be put by the outside source on NJC members simply because the primary employer enjoys more clout in terms of salary and allowances, conditions of employment, career prospects, security of tenure, etc. than does the NJC. In *Oleksandr Volkov v. Ukraine*, the Court recalled that had the Minister of Justice and the Prosecutor General to lose their primary job, this would have brought to an end their automatic, *ex officio*, NJC membership.

9.6 Prosecutor General's Involvement as an Ex Officio NJC Member

In *Oleksandr Volkov v. Ukraine*, the Court censored the Prosecutor General's *ex offico* HCJ membership as this could have contributed to a deterrent effect on judges whilst being perceived as a potential threat to the judiciary once he participated actively in court cases. His presence on the NJC which appointed, disciplined and removed judges risked that the latter acted or would act partially in the case of judges with whose decisions he took issue. This same issue also surfaced in *Saghatelyan v. Armenia*.

9.7 Requirement for Substantial Judicial Representation on Judicial Disciplinary Bodies

In *Oleksandr Volkov v. Ukraine,* the ECtHR stressed the need for substantial representation of judges on the relevant disciplinary body. Otherwise there would be an interference in the judicial body from the two other organs of the state, very much in breach of the doctrine of the separation of powers.

9.8 Lack of a Tribunal Established by Law Due to an Illegitimate Set Up of a Judicial Disciplinary Body

In *Oleksandr Volkov v. Ukraine*, the Court determined that as the HAC chamber dealing with the applicant's case was not set up and composed in a legitimate way, there could be no adherence to the principle of a tribunal established by law.

9.9 Lack of Due Consideration for the Proportionality of the Sanction

In *Oleksandr Volkov v. Ukraine,* the proportionality did not figure in the sanctions to be imposed as there were only three possible sanctions which could be applied thereby depriving the opportunity to balance the competing public and individual interests in the light of each case.

9.10 Incompatible Interference with Domestic Law

In *Oleksandr Volkov v. Ukraine,* the Court concluded that the interference with Volkov's human rights was incompatible with domestic law.

9.11 Lack of Forseeability

In *Oleksandr Volkov v. Ukraine,* 'the ECtHR held that the requirements of forseeability were not satisfied. Indeed, there were no guidelines and practice establishing a consistent and restrictive interpretation of the offence of "breach of oath". The absence of appropriate legal safeguards resulted in the relevant provisions of domestic law being unforseeable as to their effects. Due to the vagueness of the offence, any behaviour by a judge could be interpreted to amount to a misbehaviour.

9.12 No Protection Against Arbitrariness

In *Oleksandr Volkov v. Ukraine,* the interference failed to satisfy the requirements of provision of appropriate protection against arbitrariness.

9.13 No Legal Certainty Due to Lack of a Limitation Period

In *Oleksandr Volkov v. Ukraine,* there was no compliance with the principle of legal certainty as no limitation period existed for the proceedings against the applicant. In 2010, the HCJ examined facts dating back to 2003 and 2006. The applicant was therefore placed in a difficult position having to mount a defence concerning events occurring in the distant past. The same point was made in *Denisov v. Ukraine* and in *Ivanovski v. The Former Yugoslav Republic of Macedonia.*

9.14 No Legal Certainty for Applicant's Dismissal at the Plenary Meeting of Parliament

In *Oleksandr Volkov v. Ukraine,* compliance with the legal certainty principle during the plenary meeting of Parliament was missing once the parliamentary decision to dismiss the applicant judge was voted in the absence of a majority of MPs with those present deliberately and unlawfully casting multiple votes on behalf of the absent MPs.

9.15 Inadequate Time and Facilities for Defence Preparation

In *Ramos Nunes Dr Carvalho E Sá v. Portugal* shortcomings in the conduct of the proceedings against the applicant were ascertained in relation to adequate time and facilities for defence preparation.

10 Other Human Rights' Infringements by NJCs

10.1 Insufficiency of Reviewing Powers

The ECtHR has found violations of the principles established in *Albert and Le Compte v Belgium* judgment referred to above in a number of cases related to applicant judges. In *Denisov v. Ukraine* in reviewing the HCJ's decision, which had immediate effect, the HAC's review of applicant's case was insufficient. Accordingly, it was unable to remedy the defects regarding procedural fairness resulting from the proceedings before the HCJ. In *Oleksandr Volkov v. Ukraine,* the Court concluded that the subsequent parliamentary determination of the case did not remove the structural defects of a lack of independence and impartiality. The Court pointed out that the procedure before the HCJ and Parliament had disclosed a number of structural and general shortcomings which had compromised the principles of independence and impartiality, and that the subsequent judicial review had not remedied those shortcomings. To establish whether the reviewing body complied with Article 6, it had to have "full jurisdiction", or provided "sufficiency of review" to remedy a lack of independence at first instance. This was gauged by examining such 'factors as the subject matter of the decision appealed against, the manner in which that decision was arrived at and the content of the dispute, including the desired and actual grounds of appeal'.[99] But the HAC had no power

---

[99] *Oleksandr Volkov v. Ukraine*, para 123.

to quash the decisions and, had it so determined, no identified procedure existed in such eventuality.

In *Olujić v. Croatia*, the NJC's deficiency of not affording a public hearing was not rectified by Parliament's Chamber of Counties and the Constitutional Court once they themselves held no hold public hearings.

10.2   Lack of a Provision of a Public Hearing

In *Olujić v. Croatia*, the NJC failed to hear the disciplinary proceedings in public as requested by applicant even though these proceedings related to a prominent public figure—the President of the Supreme Court. Further, public allegations were earlier made implying that applicant's case was politically motivated. It was both in the applicant's and general public's interest that the NJC proceedings should have been open to public scrutiny.

In *Ramos Nunes de Carvalho e Sá v. Portugal,* no public hearing took place both before the CSM and the Supreme Court's Judicial Division. Public scrutiny was considered by the ECtHR an essential condition for transparency and for the protection of litigants' rights. Yet, he got none notwithstanding the harsh impact on applicant's life and career and the severity of the penalty inflicted. The reviewing body did not enjoy full review jurisdiction though a more thorough review of the disputed facts would have displaced applicant's preoccupations.

10.3   Procedural Unfairness and Unequality of Arms

In *Olujić v. Croatia*, the applicant judge was denied a fair hearing as he was not allowed, in breach of the equality of arms principle, to present his case thereby being put in a disadvantageous position in regard to the Government. When the NJC declined applicant's request to hear witnesses, the proceedings were conducted unfairly as the NJC had permitted only the Government to adduce witnesses.

10.4   Excessive Length of Proceedings

In *Olujić v. Croatia*, the length of proceedings of 6 years before the Constitutional Court (but not before the NJC) exceeded the reasonable time requirement.

In *Mishgjoni v. Albania*, the dismissal proceedings lasted more than 8 years for three levels of jurisdiction. There had been a 4 year delay before the HCJ in the re-examination of the applicant's case in breach of the reasonable time requirement. There was no effective remedy to prevent the continuation of the violation of Article 6, paragraph 1, and for compensation therefor.

10.5   Breach of an Applicant Judge's Privacy: Disproportionality and Arbitrariness

In *Ivanovski v. The Former Yugoslav Republic of Macedonia*, the applicant judge was debarred from working in the public service or academia for 5 years, was not allowed in practice to exercise his law profession and was stigmatised as an informer of the former oppressive secret police. He was deprived of employment opportunities and developing societal relationships. All this affected his reputation having a profound impact on his private life. The applicant judge's argument—that he was acting under compulsion—was not considered by the Supreme Court meaning that the latter's decision was insufficiently thorough to satisfy the 'necessary in a democratic society' test. It therefore could not be considered 'sufficient' in terms of Article 8, paragraph 2. The interference with applicant's privacy was disproportionate to the legitimate aim pursued as it was virtually impossible for him to practice law. The lustration law was adopted 16 years earlier thereby reducing the threat to the newly created democracy because of the passage of time. His relationship with the secret police dated back to 27 years earlier and this made it difficult to maintain that applicant constituted a threat to the State. No assessment was made by the domestic authorities as to whether the applicant constituted such a threat.

In *Erményi v. Hungary*, the interference complained of was not in pursuance of a legitimate aim. The changes in competence of the national courts could have well been achieved without the premature termination of the applicant judge's mandate.

In *Oleksandr Volkov v. Ukraine*, the applicant judge's dismissal from office affected considerably his relationships with others, including those of a professional nature. It also impacted his inner circle procuring tangible consequences for his family's and his material well-being. Moreover, his reputation was at stake in view of the reason brought for his dismissal, namely breach of the judicial oath.

In *Kulykov and Others v. Ukraine*, the Court reached the same conclusion as in *Volkov v. Ukraine* noting that the interference breached the requirements of "quality of law" and this made it unlawful in terms of Article 8 of the Convention.

In *Özpinar v. Turkey*, the removal from office decision related to applicant's conduct, both professionally and privately. The decision harmed her reputation. Although it is possible to encroach upon the private life of judges when their conduct tarnishes the image or reputation of the judiciary, the evidence adduced was inadequate to support the charge and took into consideration various matters unrelated to her professional activity. The applicant was allowed few safeguards in the disciplinary proceedings appearing before the disciplinary body belatedly without having received beforehand the inspection reports. She was not afforded guarantees against arbitrariness, including a guarantee of adversarial proceedings before an independent and impartial supervisory body. This was imperative to the applicant as her removal from office was automatically conducive to loss of the right to practise law. The interference with the applicant's private life had been disproportionate to the legitimate aim pursued.

10.6 Breach of an Applicant Judge's Freedom of Expression: Disproportionality of the Inflicted Sanction: Judge's Right to Express Views in a Professional Capacity on the Administration of Justice and the Judiciary

In *Albayrak v. Turkey*, the interference with freedom of expression was disproportionate to the legitimate aim pursued and the justifications for the interference were
irrelevant and insufficient. No clear and precise evidence was adduced as to what
misbehaviour had been committed by the applicant judge such as in relation to how
the charges levelled against him influenced his judicial duties and impartiality. The
Court reiterated that 'freedom of expression requires that care be taken to dissociate
the personal views of a person from received information that others wish or may be
willing to impart to him or her'.[100]

In *Baka v. Hungary*, the applicant judge's premature termination from office was
the result of the critical views he had expressed in his professional capacity. Issues
related to the separation of powers, the independence of the judiciary, the irremovability of judges and other related points advocated by the applicant judge fell within
the scope of political debate and the public enjoyed a legitimate interest in being
informed about them. The national authorities decision fostered a chilling effect that
the fear of sanction had on freedom of expression against other judges expressing
themselves on matters concerning the administration of justice and the judiciary.

In *Harabin v. Slovakia*, the holding of a public post in the administration of
justice was not considered by the Court tantamount to a conventional right. In
Kudeshkina v. Russia, the Court reiterated that freedom of expression applied to
the workplace and that civil servants also enjoyed it. However, the latter owed a duty
of loyalty, reserve and discretion to their employer and that disclosure of information
obtained in the course of their duties had to be examined in the light of these duties
even if it happens to be a matter of public interest. The judiciary play a special role in
society as they are the guarantors of justice yet when criticised they are subject to a
duty of discretion that precludes them from replying. Judges, because of their *functus
officio*, had to show restraint in exercising their freedom of expression in all cases
where the authority and impartiality of the judiciary was likely to be called into
question. Judges have also to disseminate accurate information with moderation and
propriety. An act motivated by a personal grievance, personal antagonism or the
expectation of personal advantage, including pecuniary gain, did not justify a
particularly strong level of protection. Nevertheless, political speech is of a different
nature. Indeed, a judge is not prevented in making any statements on issues having
political implications. Apart from the fact that important procedural guarantees
where not secured in this case, the Court observed that the sanction of dismissal

---

[100]*Albayrak v. Turkey*, para 47. See also *supra* the previous paragraph in relation to *Özpinar
v. Turkey*.

was disproportionately severe. It could have had a chilling effect on those judges participating in the public debate on the judicial institutions' effectiveness.

10.7 Breach of an Applicant Judge's Right to an Effective Remedy

In *Özpinar v. Turkey*, the applicant judge was unsuccessful in her judicial appeal against the National Legal Service Council's decisions. The Court found that the impartiality of the Council panel that examined challenges to its decisions was highly questionable. During the proceedings, no distinction was drawn between matters related to her private life and those directly connected with her judicial duties. Thus no effective remedy was available to her.

In *Mishgjoni v. Albania*, the Court concluded that the applicant had no remedy to prevent the continuation of the violation of her fair trial right or else to obtain compensation in relation to the excessive length of the dismissal proceedings.

11 Conclusion

11.1 Recommendation for Further Study on the Subject Under Review

This chapter focused on ECtHR cases involving judicial disciplinary judgments with applicant judges and NJCs involved therein. It focused more on the doctrine of the independence of the judiciary and does not consider at great length other doctrines enunciated by the ECtHR which are of direct relevance to the subject under discussion such as the doctrines of the rule of law and the separation of powers.[101] Furthermore, there are other cases instituted by applicant judges relating to non-disciplinary matters (such as appointment, promotion, salary, pension and other conditions of work) not discussed here. Indeed, it is not the purpose of this chapter to consider all these cases which, as time goes by, are—unfortunately—on the increase. Nor does this contribution consider:

(a) preliminary issues of admissibility such as whether disputes relating to the judiciary fall within the ambit of the Convention;
(b) whether the applicant judge had exhausted domestic remedies;
(c) whether the complaint was lodged in a timely manner;

---

[101] Appl. No. 46295/99, *Stafford v. the United Kingdom* (ECtHR [GC] 28 May 2002, para 78; *Oleksandr Volkov v. Ukraine*, para 103; and *Saghatelyan v. Armenia*, para 43.

(d) whether there could have been other breaches of the Convention in relation to an applicant judge which the Court rejected as being manifestly ill-founded;
(e) cases where NJCs were not involved at all in the complaints lodged before the Strasbourg Court; and
(f) where an non-NJC national authority (such as a Parliament[102] or a President)[103] were the disciplinary decision making bodies.

In addition, this chapter does not delve into those complaints lodged by judges decided by the Grand Chamber prior to *Vilho Eskelinen and Others v. Finland*. Nor is reference being made to the rich documentation of international institutions,[104] of Council of Europe institutions[105] (including the Committee of Ministers' Recommendations, Parliamentary Assembly Opinions and Resolutions, Venice Commission opinions/reports, and the Commissioner for Human Rights press releases) and other European institutions[106] cited in the ECtHR case law referred to in this chapter which are relevant to the subject-matter of this chapter, influential and authoritative as they might be. Finally, this chapter does not carry out a comparative study of

---

[102]Other cases not discussed in this chapter where the ECtHR had the opportunity to consider whether Parliament was an independent and impartial tribunal, even if not in relation to an applicant judge, were Appl. No. 13057/87, *Demicoli v Malta* (ECtHR 27 August 1991) and Appl. Nos. 17214/05, 20329/05 and 42113/04, *Savino and Others v. Italy* (ECtHR 28 April 2009).

[103]*Kulykov and Others v. Ukraine* and *Saghatelyan v. Armenia*.

[104]Such as the Seventh United Nations Congress on the Prevention of Crime and the Treatment of Offenders held at Milan (1985) and endorsed by the United Nations General Assembly resolutions 40/32 and 40/146 (1985). Basic Principles on the Independence of the Judiciary. Resource document. United Nations. https://www.un.org/ruleoflaw/blog/document/basic-principles-on-the-independence-of-the-judiciary. Accessed 3 April 2019; the Judicial Group on Strengthening Judicial Integrity (2007). Bangalore Principles of Judicial Conduct and the Commentary thereon. Resource document. United Nations Office on Drugs and Crime. https://www.unodc.org/documents/corruption/publications_unodc_commentary-e.pdf. Accessed 3 April 2019; the International Association of Judges (1999). Universal Charter of the Judge. Resource document. International Association of Judges. https://www.iaj-uim.org/universal-charter-of-the-judges/. Accessed 3 April 2019.

[105]Such as the Consultative Council of European Judges. Magna Carta of Judges (Fundamental Principles). Council of Europe. Resource document. https://rm.coe.int/16807482c6. Accessed 3 April 2019; Consultative Council of European Judges. *Opinion no 10 on the Council for the Judiciary at the service of society* (2007). Council of Europe. Resource document. https://rm.coe.int/168074779b. Accessed 3 April 2019; and the Department of Legal Affairs of the Council of Europe (1998). European Charter on the Statute for Judges. DAJ/DOC (98)23. Council of Europe. Resource document. https://rm.coe.int/16807473ef. Accessed 3 April 2019.

[106]Such as the, the General Assembly of the European Network of Councils for the Judiciary (2007). Judicial Ethics—Principles Values and Qualities. European Network of Councils for the Judiciary. Resource document. https://www.encj.eu/images/stories/pdf/ethics/judicialethicsdeontologiefinal.pdf. Accessed 3 April 2019; and The European Association of Judges Istanbul (2011). Resolution Concerning the Conformity with International Standards of Judicial Independence of the Amendments/Proposed Amendments to the Status of Judges in the Legislation of the Slovak Republic. Resource document. https://www.iaj-uim.org/iuw/wp-content/uploads/2013/06/AEM-resolution-on-Slovakia-2011-eng.pdf. Accessed 3 April 2019.

national laws establishing NJCs or a human rights impact assessment thereupon to determine the extent to which, if at all, do these national laws infringe the ECHR.[107]

11.2   Recommendations for Adoption by Council of Europe Member States

The role of the judiciary—national and international—is a sine qua non for the functioning of a vibrant liberal democracy. Indeed, judges are the guarantors of justice. For this purpose, a number of recommendations can be suggested for implementation by Council of Europe Members States. Essentially, what is being proposed is that first and foremost these States carry out a human rights impact assessment of their national law establishing and regulating NJCs and review mechanisms therefrom in the light of the twenty cases discussed above. Second, after having identified gaps in national law and/or conflicting national provisions with the ECHR, municipal law should be amended to be to brought in line with the Convention as progressively developed by the Strasbourg Court in its case law. Should expert assistance be required, they can always tap on the resources of the Council of Europe's Venice Commission for Democracy through Law. Special regard should be had to the pertinent principles enunciated by the Strasbourg Court in those cases discussed in Sects. 7–10 of this chapter.

By resorting to a teleological interpretation of the ECHR, the Strasbourg Court has—through its judicial activism—contributed to the progressive development of Human Rights Law, a fact for which the Court should be commended for establishing the above-mentioned enunciated principles in its case law where judges were applicants and NJCs factotums of respondent states. However, the Court still needs to rethink the effectiveness of the remedies afforded to ensure that they are effective, sufficient, fair and proportionate to the conventional infringement bearing in mind that out of the applicant judges dismissed from office, only one Member State was requested to reinstate him—in *Oleksandr Volkov v. Ukraine*—and in another case—*Özpinar v. Turkey*—the Court observed that a judicial declaration finding a national law to run counter to the Convention was sufficient just satisfaction.

---

[107] See, for instance, the United Nations Office of the High Commissioner (2019) Submissions for the report on national judicial councils. United Nations Office of the High Commissioner. Resource document.   https://www.ohchr.org/EN/Issues/Judiciary/Pages/ResponsesNJC.aspx.   Accessed 3 April 2019.

References

Consultative Council of European Judges. (2007). *Opinion no 10 on the Council for the Judiciary at the service of society*. Council of Europe. Resource document. Retrieved April 3, 2019, from https://rm.coe.int/168074779b

Consultative Council of European Judges. Magna Carta of Judges (Fundamental Principles). Council of Europe. Resource document. Retrieved April 3, 2019, from https://rm.coe.int/16807482c6

Department of Legal Affairs of the Council of Europe. (1998). *European charter on the statute for judges*. DAJ/DOC (98)23. Council of Europe. Resource document. Retrieved April 3, 2019, from https://rm.coe.int/16807473ef

European Association of Judges Istanbul. (2011). *Resolution concerning the conformity with international standards of judicial independence of the amendments/proposed amendments to the status of judges in the legislation of the Slovak Republic*. Resource document. Retrieved April 3, 2019, from https://www.iaj-uim.org/iuw/wp-content/uploads/2013/06/AEM-resolution-on-Slovakia-2011-eng.pdf

General Assembly of the European Network of Councils for the Judiciary. (2007). *Judicial ethics – Principles values and qualities. European Network of Councils for the Judiciary*. Resource document. Retrieved April 3, 2019, from https://www.encj.eu/images/stories/pdf/ethics/judicialethicsdeontologiefinal.pdf

International Association of Judges. (1999). *Universal charter of the judge*. Resource document. International Association of Judges. Retrieved April 3, 2019, from https://www.iaj-uim.org/universal-charter-of-the-judges/

Judicial Group on Strengthening Judicial Integrity. (2007). *Bangalore principles of judicial conduct and the commentary thereon*. Resource document. United Nations Office on Drugs and Crime. Retrieved April 3, 2019, from https://www.unodc.org/documents/corruption/publications_unodc_commentary-e.pdf

Seventh United Nations Congress on the Prevention of Crime and the Treatment of Offenders held at Milan (1985) and endorsed by the United Nations General Assembly resolutions 40/32 and 40/146 (1985). Basic Principles on the Independence of the Judiciary. Resource document. United Nations. Retrieved April 3, 2019, from https://www.un.org/ruleoflaw/blog/document/basic-principles-on-the-independence-of-the-judiciary

United Nations Office of the High Commissioner. (2019). *Submissions for the report on national judicial councils*. United Nations Office of the High Commissioner. Resource document. Retrieved April 3, 2019, from https://www.ohchr.org/EN/Issues/Judiciary/Pages/ResponsesNJC.aspx

The Selection of Judges and Advocate-General at the Court of Justice of the European Union: The Role of the Panel Established Under Art. 255 TFEU

Francesco Battaglia

Contents

1 Introduction

Since its decision in the case *Les Verts* v. *Parliament* of 1986, the European Court of Justice (ECJ) has repeatedly held that the European Union is an organization based on the rule of law.[1] This principle is now enshrined even in art. 2 TEU, which states that the European Union is founded, among other things, on the values of democracy and rule of law.[2] As regards, then, the content of the rule of law, the ECJ has recently stressed that the very existence of effective judicial review is the essence of the rule

---

Francesco Battaglia is Researcher of European Union Law at the University Sapienza of Rome.

[1]ECJ, Case 294/83, *Parti écologiste "Les Verts"* v *European Parliament*, 23 April 1986, ECLI:EU:C:1986:166.

[2]On the principle of rule of law in the European Union, see Magen and Pech (2018), pp. 235–256.

F. Battaglia (✉)
Sapienza University of Rome, Rome, Italy
e-mail: f.battaglia@uniroma1.it

© Springer Nature Switzerland AG 2019
P. Pinto de Albuquerque, K. Wojtyczek (eds.), *Judicial Power in a Globalized World*, https://doi.org/10.1007/978-3-030-20744-1_2

of law. It follows that in a Union based on the rule of law Courts or Tribunals have to meet the requirements of effective judicial protection, such as to be established by law, to be permanent and to be independent.[3]

The aim of this paper is, indeed, to make some considerations on the requirement of independence and, more specifically, on how judicial appointment mechanisms can influence independence of judges.

In this respect, as early as in 1980s, the European Court of Human Rights underlined that, in order to establish whether a body can be considered "independent", regard must be had, *inter alia*, to the manner of appointment of its members.[4] Thus, a key element to assess the level of independence of a Tribunal is the process through which its judges are selected. In that regard, the European Commission for Democracy Through Law (Venice Commission) has affirmed that where judges are appointed by the governments, there should be guarantees to ensure that the procedures to select them are transparent and independent in practice and that the decisions will be influenced only by objective criteria.[5]

In sum, transparency is essential to recruit the best candidates for judicial posts and minimizing potential political influence in judicial decision-making. Furthermore, a transparent selection process legitimates the judges in the eyes of the public and for gaining public trust.

At the European Union level, before the adoption of the Lisbon Treaty, the selection of judges and Advocate-General at the Court of Justice of the European Union (CJEU) was entirely dominated by governments of the Member State and, thus, the process was not considered transparent enough.[6] It is for this reason that during the Convention on the Future of Europe was suggested to establish a new judicial selection panel responsible for giving an opinion on prospective candidates' suitability to perform the duties concerned. This proposal was finally included in the Lisbon Treaty, under art. 255 TFEU.

Ten years after the establishment of the Panel 255 is, therefore, possible to make a first assessment on how this body improved the transparency of the mechanism to select Judges and Advocate-General of the ECJ and the General Court (GC).

---

[3]ECJ (Grand Chamber), Case C-64/16, *Associação Sindical dos Juízes Portugueses* v *Tribunal de Contas*, 27 February 2018, ECLI:EU:C:2018:117, point 36.

[4]ECtHR, appl. n. 11179/84, *Langborger* v. *Sweden*, 22 June 1989, par. 32; appl. n. 7819/77; 7878/77, *Campbell and Fell* v. *The United Kingdom*, 28 June 1984, par. 78.

[5]European Commission for Democracy Through Law, *Report on the Independence of the Judicial System – Part I: The Independence of Judges*, 16 March 2010, CDL-AD(2010)004.

[6]Kenney (1998), pp. 101–133; Solanke (2009), pp. 89–121.

2 The Establishment of the Advisory Panel

2.1 The Process of Establishment

Article 167 of the Treaty of Rome stated that judges shall have been appointed by common accord of the Governments for a term of 6 years. This provision was reaffirmed by the treaties of Maastricht,[7] Amsterdam[8] and Nice.[9] It means that before the adoption of the Lisbon Treaty the selection of Judges and Advocate General was an act purely internal. Each Member States carried out a domestic selection procedure and then announced the result to the Council. This system lacked transparency and did not give any assurance that the Member States would have followed a merit-based system for the appointment of judges.

As mentioned, such a lack of transparency persuaded the discussion circle on the Court of Justice, established within to the Convention on the Future of Europe, to propose an innovation on the judicial selection process, to be included in Treaty establishing a Constitution for Europe.[10] In particular, it suggested *(a)* that the appointment should have been an act of the Council, even acting by a qualified majority; *(b)* to set up an advisory panel, made up of former members of the Court, representative of national supreme courts and a legal expert chose by the European Parliament, which would have had the task of giving the Member States an opinion on whether a candidates' profile was suited to the performance of their duties, particularly on the basis of objective criteria relating to professional qualifications. In the opinion of the discussion circle, the new advisory panel would have made the judicial selection process more transparent and would have made Member States more demanding in the choice of candidates they would have put forward. The proposed mechanism was similar to the Judicial Appointment Commissions usually established by the Commonwealth States, even if the latter actually play a more powerful role in the election of judges and in some circumstance are even directly responsible for the formal act of appointment.[11]

The Convention accepted only in part the proposal submitted by the discussion circle. On the one hand, the Treaty establishing a Constitution provided for the establishment of the advisory panel, but, on the other, it maintained the appointment as a common accord among member States and not as an act of the Council.[12] The

---

[7]Treaty Establishing the European Community, art. 167, in OJ, C 191, 29 July 1992, 1–112.

[8]Treaty Establishing the European Community, art. 223, in OJ, C 340, 10 November 1997, 1–308.

[9]Treaty Establishing the European Community, art. 223, in OJ, C 325, 24 December 2002, 33–184.

[10]The European Convention, *Final Report of the Discussion Circle on the Court of Justice*, CONV 636/03, 25 March 2003. Available on line at http://www.europarl.europa.eu/meetdocs_all/commit tees/conv/20030403/03c_en.pdf. Last time visited on 18 December 2018.

[11]On the mechanisms established by the Commonwealth states, see van Zyl Smit (2015), pp. 1–56.

[12]Treaty Establishing a Constitution for Europe, Article I-29, in OJ, C 310, 16 December 2004, 1–474.

same mechanism, as already mentioned, is provided by the Lisbon Treaty.[13] Article 255 TFEU, in fact, states that a panel shall be set up in order to give an opinion on candidates' suitability to perform the duties of Judge and Advocate-General of the Court of Justice and the General Court before the governments of the Member States make the appointments of Common accord, as referred to in articles 253 and 254 TFEU.[14]

2.2 A Brief Comparison with the Advisory Panel Established by the Committee of Minister of the Council of Europe

The establishment of the Panel 255 reflects a general trend developed at the International level to open up the process of judicial appointments to scrutiny. Indeed, a similar body was set up in the same period at the level of the Council of Europe. In 2010, the Committee of Ministers of the Council of Europe passed a resolution which established an Advisory Panel of Experts with the mandate to confidentially advise High Contracting Parties whether candidates for election as judges of the European Court of Human Rights (ECtHR) meet the criteria stipulated in the European Convention on Human Rights (ECHR).[15]

However, the Panel established by the Council of Europe has showed to have a lower degree of influence in judicial appointment than the Panel 255. In fact, the Parliamentary Assembly of the Council of Europe (PACE) has often appointed as judges of the ECtHR candidates who had received an unfavorable opinion by the Panel.[16] This has led some scholar to consider this Panel as a weak institutional actor that has understandable difficulties in finding any reasonable space for its already narrow mandate.[17] Indeed, in 2013 a Steering Committee for the Council of Europe suggested some innovation to make the Panel more powerful. In particular, it proposed, *inter alia*, *(a)* that State Parties should not have submitted lists of candidates to the Parliamentary Assembly and the Advisory Panel simultaneously; *(b)* that the Parliamentary Assembly should not have proceeded with the election process without allowing the Advisory Panel a reasonable time within which to inform the State Party concerned of its views on the intended candidates; *(c)* that the State Party concerned not to make public the list of candidates or at least not finally

---

[13]The Treaty on the Functioning of the European Union, art. 255, in OJ, C 83, 30 March 2010, 1–403.

[14]On the establishment of the Panel, see Sauvé (2015), pp. 78–85; Alemanno (2015), pp. 202–221; Dumbrovský (2014), pp. 455–482.

[15]Council of Europe, Committee of Ministers, Resolution (2010)26 on the establishment of an Advisory Panel of Experts on Candidates for Election as Judge to the European Court of Human Rights, 10 November 2010.

[16]See Lemmens (2015), pp. 95–119.

[17]See Bobek (2015), p. 284.

to approve it until the Advisory Panel's views on it have been taken into account.[18] These proposals have been partially accepted by the Committee of Ministers trough a resolution adopted in 2014, which amended the resolution of 2010.[19] Nevertheless, the opinions of the Panel are still frequently disregarded. To give a concrete example, during the period from January 2014 to June 2017, among the 29 lists examined by the Panel, in 9 cases the candidates were maintained on the list despite the Panel's negative opinion.[20]

Furthermore, the Panel is also weakened by the fact that it is not adequately funded and, thus, it has not sufficient means to meet regularly. Budgetary appropriation for the Panel in the Council of Europe's ordinary budget amounts to less 20 thousands euro per year. This amount cover not more than three or four meeting per year.[21]

Unlike the mechanism established by the Council of Europe, the experience of the Panel 255, as will be showed below, seems to be more successful, even if it is not exempt from critical remarks.

3   The Composition and the Activities of the Panel

Art. 255 TFEU states that the Panel shall comprise seven persons chosen from among former members of the ECJ and the GC, members of national supreme courts and lawyers of recognised competence, one of whom shall be proposed by the European Parliament. This provision, thus, does not contain any specific criteria on the recruitment of the members of the Panel except for the fact that it indicates that one member has to be elected by the European Parliament. Neither the Council decision relating to the operating rules of the Panel gives more details on the appointment of its members.[22] It simply clarifies that Members of the Panel may be reappointed only once. In addition, the text of the decisions adopted by the Council to appoint the members of the Panel affirm that, while deciding the members

---

[18]Steering Committee for Human Rights, Report on the review of the functioning of the Advisory Panel of experts on candidates for election as judge to the European Court of Human Rights Strasbourg, 29 November 2013, CDDH(2013)R79 Addendum II.

[19]Council of Europe, Committee of Ministers, Resolution (2014)44, amending Resolution CM/Res (2010)26 on the establishment of an Advisory Panel of Experts on Candidates for Election as Judge to the European Court of Human Rights, 26 November 2014.

[20]Steering Committee for Human Rights, Committee of Experts on the System of the European Convention on Human Rights, Report on the process of selection and election of judges of the European Court of Human Rights, CDDH(2017)R88addI, 11 December 2017.

[21]Advisory Panel of Experts on Candidates for Election as Judge to the European Court of Human Rights, Third activity report for the attention of the Committee of Ministers, Advisory Panel (2017) 2, 30 June 2017.

[22]Council Decision of 25 February 2010 relating to the operating rules of the panel provided for in Article 255 of the Treaty on the Functioning of the European Union, in OJ, L 50, 27 February 2010, 18–19.

of the Panel, account should be taken of a balanced membership of the Panel, both in geographical terms and in terms of representation of the legal systems of the Member States.[23] However, it does not explain who proposes the members to appoint, which criteria the Council has to take into account while appointing and which procedural rules it has to follow. The same considerations apply for the member elected by the Parliament.

Hence, the appointing procedure does not fulfill the principle of transparency, in accordance to which appointments must be made on the basis of clearly defined criteria and by a publicly declared process.

As regards, instead, the activities carried out by the Panel, the decision relating to the operating rules of the Panel states that as soon as the Government of a Member State proposes a candidate, the General Secretariat of the Council shall send that proposal to the President of the Panel. The Panel may ask the government making the proposal to send additional information or other material which the panel considers necessary for its deliberations. Furthermore, except where a proposal relates to the reappointment of a Judge or Advocate-General, the Panel shall hear the candidate; the hearing shall take place in private. Hence, it shows the Panel deliberates only on the basis of confidential information received by Member States proposing the candidate, in particular the *curriculum vitae* in the format defined by the Panel on 25 April 2014, and on the basis of a private hearing with the proposed candidate.[24] This mechanism, of course, is not transparent enough, because interested parties and members of the public are not enabled to scrutinize the way in which the Panel discharge its mandate. Furthermore, even the opinions issued by the Panel are not made publicly available, but they are only forwarded to the Representatives of the Governments of the Member States through the Council, which is consequently in possession of them.[25] On this point, the Panel has expressed the opinion that the full disclosure of its opinions would undermine the aims and quality of the consultation and appointment procedures provided for in Articles 253 to 255 TFEU, notably because it would jeopardise the secrecy of the panel's deliberations and of the intergovernmental conference at which the Member States

---

[23]Council Decision (EU, Euratom) 2017/2262 of 4 December 2017 appointing the members of the panel provided for in Article 255 of the Treaty on the Functioning of the European Union, in OJ L 324, 8 December 2017, 50.

[24]The private hearing takes place only with candidate for a first term of office as Judge or Advocate general. Instead, with regard to the document requested, the Panel calls members States to send *(a)* the essential reasons which led the government to propose the candidate; *(b)* information on the national procedure that led to the candidate being selected, if there was one; *(c)* a letter from the candidate explaining the reasons for the application; *(d)* a CV in the harmonised format defined by the panel at its meeting on 25 April 2014; *(e)* the text of one to three recent publications, of which the candidate is the author, written in or translated into English or French; *(f)* the presentation of one to three delicate legal cases which the candidate has handled in their professional practice, which must not exceed five pages per case. See, Fifth Activity Report of the panel provided for by Article 255 of the Treaty on the Functioning of the European Union, 28 February 2018, 19.

[25]At the request of the Presidency, the President of the Panel shall present that opinion even to the Representatives of the Governments of the Member States' meeting within the Council.

nominate the Judges and Advocates-General.[26] Therefore, the General Secretariat of the Council regularly denies the access to the opinions issued by the Panel on the basis of the exceptions provided by art. 4, parr. 2 and 3, of Regulation1049/2001.[27]

4   The Need for More Transparency

The principle of transparency is not intended only as the right to access documents but, in a broader sense, as the right to be informed on the actions carried out by a specific body so that public can scrutinize the way in which it discharge its mandate.[28]

As argued above, the activities carried out by the Panel are far from being transparent, because its opinions are not made publicly available and are only shared with member States. It follows that the only information available for the public are those released from the Panel and, thus, that people are not aware about how the Panel assesses candidates and which are the reasons of the negative opinions.

On the other hand, the Panel seems to be a powerful body whose opinions are regularly followed by Member States during the selection process of judges and Advocate-General. In this regard, the fifth activity report on the activities carried out from the Panel during the period 2014–2018 affirms that since March 2014 the Panel has assessed 80 candidates for the offices of Judge or Advocate-General, of whom 36 were for the Court of Justice and 44 for the General Court. Of these candidates, 39 were proposed for renewal of their term of office and 41 for a first term office. In total, seven of the 41 opinions on candidates for a first term office have been unfavorable.[29] This means that the Panel has frequently issued unfavorable opinions

---

[26]Fifth Activity Report, 23–24.

[27]Regulation (EC) No 1049/2001 of the European Parliament and of the Council of 30 May 2001 regarding public access to European Parliament, Council and Commission documents, in OJ, L 145, 31 May 2001, 43–48, art. 4 "2. The institutions shall refuse access to a document where disclosure would undermine the protection of commercial interests of a natural or legal person, including intellectual property, court proceedings and legal advice, the purpose of inspections, investigations and audits, unless there is an overriding public interest in disclosure. 3. Access to a document, drawn up by an institution for internal use or received by an institution, which relates to a matter where the decision has not been taken by the institution, shall be refused if disclosure of the document would seriously undermine the institution's decision-making process, unless there is an overriding public interest in disclosure". On the exceptions provided by art. 4 of the regulation 1049/2001, see, *inter alia*, Maes (2014), pp. 475–497; Harden (2009), pp. 239–256; Maes (2008), pp. 577–590; Heliskoski and Leino (2006), pp. 735–781.

[28]On the principle of transparency, see Alemanno (2015), pp. 202–221; Österdahl (2016), pp. 61–79.

[29]Fifth Activity Report of the Panel Provided for by Article 255 of the Treaty on the Functioning of the European Union, 28 February 2018. Available at https://curia.europa.eu/jcms/upload/docs/application/pdf/2018-05/5eme_rapport_dactivite_du_c255_-_en_final_-_public.pdf. Last time visited on 10 February 2018.

on candidates for a first term office which have always been followed by the governments of Member States.

However, it is precisely because of such powerfulness that the Panel should adopt a more transparent policy.

Even the European ombudsman, Emily O'Reilly, through an investigation opened in 2015, highlighted the insufficient transparency of the Panel's practice.[30] The case was submitted to the Ombudsman by the NGO *Access Info Europe*, which considered as a case of maladministration the decision of the Council to deny, on the basis of the exception provided by art. 4 par. 3 of Regulation 1049/2001, access to Panel opinions regarding all judicial candidates nominated for the ECJ and the GC since the Panel's establishment, expressly requested by the complainant.[31]

The main reason for the denial was that, in the view of the Council, Regulation 1049/2001 states that "document" means any content concerning a matter relating to the policies, activities and decisions falling within the institution's sphere of responsibility. Therefore, the opinions issued by the Panel should not be considered as "document", because, while the Council maintains their physical control, they are prepared in the context of an intergovernmental conference, not the Council, and, thus, they do not fall within the Council's sphere of responsibility. It means that, following such an interpretation, Regulation 1049/2001 would apply only to documents authored by an institution and not to documents in possession of the same institution.

Furthermore, the Council has also pointed out that even if the regulation did apply to the Panel opinions, the Council could however deny the access to certain opinions if their disclosure would undermine *(a)* the protection of privacy of the individual or *(b)* the institution's decision making process, unless there is an overriding public interest in disclosure.[32]

In contrast with the argumentation pointed out by the Council, the Ombudsman stated that Regulation 1049/2001 guarantees access to all documents held by an institution and not just those authored by the same institution. Moreover, the Ombudsman explained that the Panel Opinions have to be considered as relating to the activities falling within the Council's sphere of responsibility, because these opinions clearly relate to Council activities.[33]

Nevertheless, the Ombudsman did not find any maladministration in the case concerned, because during the investigation the Council informed her that it had

---

[30]European Ombudsman, Refusal of the Council to publish opinions regarding nominations for the Court of Justice and the General Court, case 1011/2015/TN, opened on 14 July 2015.

[31]For a detailed description of the complaint, see Alemanno A, Lapp C, Delalande A, Khadar L (2015) The EU Public Interest Clinic and Access Info Europe Present: A Complaint to the European Ombudsman Regarding Judicial Transparency. Available at https://papers.ssrn.com/sol3/papers.cfm?abstract_id=2636877. Last time visited on 10 February 2018.

[32]On the exceptions provided by art. 4 of the regulation 1049/2001, *Supra* note 26.

[33]European Ombudsman, Decision in case 1011/2015/TN concerning the refusal of the Council of the European Union to give access to opinions on candidates' suitability to perform the duties of Judge and Advocate-General at the Court of Justice and the General Court of the EU, 4 May 2016.

reassessed its practice as regards the handling of requests for access to documents, held by its General Secretariat, in relation to tasks of support to various intergovernmental bodies or entities, such as the Panel Opinions. Therefore, it decided to process this kind of documents in line with the procedural and substantial legal framework set out in Regulation 1049/2001. On the basis of this policy change, thus, the Ombudsman invited the complainant to submit a new application for access and has encouraged the Council to deal with this application in light of the purpose of Regulation 1049/2001, which ensures the widest possible access to documents.

Indeed, the complainant submitted a new application on 24 May 2016, but the Council rejected it again, stating that the requested opinions were covered by the exception clauses provided by art. 4 of Regulation 1049/2001.[34] In particular, the Council affirmed that the disclosure of the requested documents would have undermined *(a)* the protection of the candidates' commercial interest in the event that they had carried out or had intended to carry out paid work as lawyer or legal adviser; *(b)* the decision-making process leading to the appointment of Judges and Advocate-General. Furthermore, the Council argued that a significant level of transparency is assured by the periodical publication on the activity of the Panel and, thus, it is not necessary to make its opinions publicly available.

Obviously, *Access Info Europe* did not consider the argumentation put forward by the Council satisfactory and, therefore, it referred a new case to the European Ombudsman, together with another complainant, the *HEC-NYU EU Public Interest Clinic*.[35]

Although the case is still pending before the Ombudsman, some remarks can be made on the arguments put forward by the Council in order to refuse access to the opinions of the panel.

Firstly, the decision of the Council seems in contradiction with the advices provided by the Ombudsman on how institutions should handle request of access to documents. In fact, during the first investigation of 2015, the Ombudsman stressed that a key issue which may arise in the context of dealing with such requests is the need to strike an appropriate balance between the protection of the personal data of candidates and the needs of openness and transparency. In this regard, the Ombudsman noted that personal data relating to the professional competence and activities of a public figure, especially a person actually appointed to a high level public post, may not require the same level of protection as might apply in other circumstances. Openness and transparency as regards such personal data will serve to generate trust and confidence in the appointment process, and in the capabilities of the persons actually appointed to high level posts, whilst at the same time striking the right

---

[34]See, Erikson A, Li M, Shalaby O, Transparent Selection of Judges for EU Courts. Complaint to the European Ombudsman, 2017. Available on line at https://papers.ssrn.com/sol3/papers.cfm?abstract_id=3072588. Last time visited on 10 February 2019.

[35]European Ombudsman, The Council of the European Union's handling of requests for access to documents prepared by the Article 255 Panel on Judicial Appointments to the Court of Justice and the General Court of the EU, case 1955/2017/THH, opened on 13 November 2017.

balance with the need to protect personal data.[36] Even the GC, in the case *Dennekamp* v *European Parliament*, held the same position, stating that the distinction between public figures and privates spheres is relevant for the purposes of determining the degree of protection of personal data to which they are entitled. Thus, it would be entirely inappropriate to assess an application for the transfer of personal data in the same way irrespective of the identity of the data subject. Public figures, in fact, have chosen to expose themselves to scrutiny by third parties, particularly the media, even if such a choice in no way implies that their legitimate interests must be regarded as never being prejudiced by a decision to transfer data relating to them. It follows that public figures have generally already accepted that some of their personal data will be disclosed to the public, and may even have encouraged or made such disclosure themselves.[37]

The arguments of the GC are coherent with the well settled case law of the CJEU on the right of access to documents. In fact, GC and ECJ have both repeatedly stated that the right of public access to documents of the institutions is related to the democratic nature of those institutions, as set out in articles 10 and 11 TEU. To that end, Regulation 1049/2001 is intended to give the fullest possible effect to the right of public access to documents of the institution. Thus, any derogations from the principle of the widest possible public access to documents must be interpreted and applied strictly. It means that if the institution concerned decides to refuse access to a document which it has been asked to disclose, it must, in principle, explain how disclosure of that document could specifically and actually undermine the interest protected by the exceptions set out in art. 4 of Regulation 1049/2001.[38] In that context, the fact that information relates to the sphere of professional activities of a public figure is an important element, which should tilt the balance towards greater openness.

In the present case, instead, the Council, in contradiction with the aforementioned approach, has broadly interpreted the exceptions set out in art. 4, par. 3, of Regulation 1049/2001. For example, it failed to explain sufficiently how the judicial

---

[36]In that sense, see also the position expressed the European Court of Human rights in the case *Hannover* v. *Germany* (application n. 59320/00), issued on 24 September 2004, and in particular par. 63, where the Court stated that "a fundamental distinction needs to be made between reporting facts – even controversial ones – capable of contributing to a debate in a democratic society relating to politicians in the exercise of their functions, for example, and reporting details of the private life of an individual who, moreover, as in this case, does not exercise official functions. While in the former case the press exercises its vital role of "watchdog" in a democracy by contributing to impart [ing] information and ideas on matters of public interest, it does not do so in the latter case".

[37]Judgment of the General Court (Fifth Chamber), Case T-115/13, *Gert-Jan Dennekamp* v. - *European Parliament*, 15 July 2015, ECLI:EU:T:2015:497, point 119.

[38]Judgment of the Court (Grand Chamber) of 1 July 2008, Joined cases C-39/05 P and C-52/05 P, *Kingdom of Sweden and Maurizio Turco* v *Council of the European Union*, ECLI:EU:C:2008:374; Judgment of the Court (First Chamber) of 21 July 2011, Case C-506/08 P, *Kingdom of Sweden* v *European Commission and MyTravel Group plc*, ECLI:EU:C:2011:496; Judgment of the General Court (Seventh Chamber, Extended Composition) of 22 March 2018, Case T-540/15, *Emilio De Capitani* v *European Parliament*, ECLI:EU:T:2018:167.

candidates' privacy would have been undermined by disclosure of the Panel Opinions, without taking under consideration that judges are public figures. In addition, it did not even adequately motivated why their disclosure would have undermined the decision-making process leading to the appointment of Judges and Advocate-General.

Furthermore, it seems unsuitable the Council's opinion that a significant level of transparency is assured by the periodical publication on the activity of the Panel and, thus, it is not necessary to make its opinions publicly available. This view is clearly not in line with the principle of the widest access to documents and with the principle of participatory democracy set out in art. 10 TEU, which states that decisions must be taken as openly and as closely as possible to the citizen.

5 Concluding Remarks

The establishment of the advisory Panel responded to the necessity *(a)* to limit the arbitrariness of Member States in judicial appointments and *(b)* to guarantee that proposed candidates met the highest standards. In that regard, the present analysis showed that the Panel has only in part achieved those objectives.

On one side, the judicial appointments is not anymore a monopoly of member States, because an independent advisory body scrutinizes their choices. This contributes to make more objective the selection process. Indeed, statistics show that the Panel has significantly influenced the outcome of judicial selection process. In the period 2014–2018, for example, almost 20% of candidates proposed for a first term office received an unfavourable opinion by the Panel and, consequently, the proposing member States decided to withdraw them.

On the other hand, the Panel showed a serious lack of transparency, which arose problems of democratic legitimacy and accountability in the selection process. In fact, the Panel fulfils its tasks in a completely confidential manner: CVs of candidates are not public, hearings are private and the opinions on candidates are forwarded only to member States. Such a confidential policy risk to undermine public trust in Judges and Advocate-General.

As previously underlined, within a democratic society, such as the European Union, transparency is essential to legitimate decision-making process. Indeed, art. 10 TEU states that decisions must be taken as openly and as closely as possible to the citizen. This principle should drive the Panel to follow a greater transparency policy. In particular, it would be suitable that the candidates hearings were public and that the opinion were made publicly available. Only a greater transparency can strengthen the democratic legitimacy and the accountability of the judicial selection process.

References

Alemanno, A. (2015). How transparent is transparent enough?: Balancing access to information against privacy in European judicial selection. In M. Bobek (Ed.), cit. (pp. 202–221).

Bobek, M. (Ed.). (2015). *Selecting Europe's judges. A critical review of the appointment procedures to the European Courts.* Oxford: Oxford University Press.

Dumbrovský, T. (2014). Judicial appointments: The Article 255 TFEU advisory panel and selection procedures in the member states. *Common Market Law Review, 51,* 455–482.

Harden, I. (2009). The revision of Regulation 1049/2001 on public access to documents. *European Public Law, 15,* 239–256.

Heliskoski, J., & Leino, P. (2006). Darkness at the break of noon: The case law on Regulation No. 1049/2001 on access to documents. *Common Market Law Review, 43,* 735–781.

Kenney, S. J. (1998). The members of the Court of justice of the European Communities. *Columbia Journal of European Law, 5,* 101–133.

Lemmens, K. (2015). Selecting judges for Strasbourg. In M. Bobek (Ed.), *Selecting Europe's judges* (pp. 95–119). Oxford: Oxford University Press.

Maes, M. (2008). La refonte du règlement (CE) nr. 1049/2001 relatif à l'accès du public aux documents du Parlement européen, du Conseil et de la Commission. *Revue du droit de l'Union européenne,* (3), 577–590.

Maes, M. (2014). Le droit d'accès aux documents des institutions européennes: où en est la révision du règlement 1049/2001? *Revue du droit de l'Union européenne,* (3), 475–497.

Magen, A., & Pech, L. (2018). The rule of law and the European Union. In C. May & I. A. Winchester (Eds.), *Handbook on the rule of law* (pp. 235–256). Cheltenham: Edward Elgar Publishing.

Österdahl, I. (2016). Transparency as part of a European rule of law. In W. Schroeder (Ed.), *Strengthening the rule of law in Europe* (pp. 61–79). Oxford: Hart Publishing.

Sauvé, J.-M. (2015). Selecting the European Union's judges: the practice of the Article 255 Panel. In M. Bobek (Ed.), *Selecting Europe's judges* (pp. 78–85). Oxford: Oxford University Press.

Solanke, I. (2009). Independence and diversity in the European Court of Justice. *Columbia Journal of European Law, 15,* 89–121.

Zyl Smit, J. (2015). *The appointment, tenure and removal of judges under commonwealth principles: A compendium and analysis of best practice.* Report of Research Undertaken by Bingham Centre for the Rule of Law, London (pp. 1–56).

Further Reading

Arnull, A. (2006). *The European Union and its court of justice.* Oxford: Oxford University Press.

Bell, J. (2006). *Judiciaries within Europe: A comparative review.* Cambridge: Cambridge University Press.

Benvenisti, E., & Downs, G. W. (2011). Prospects for the increased independence of international tribunals. *German Law Journal, 12,* 1057–1082.

Brinkhorst, L. J. (1998). Transparency in the European Union. *Fordham International Law Journal, 22,* 128–135.

Burbank, S. (2007). Judicial independence, judicial accountability and interbranch relations. *The Georgetown Law Journal, 95,* 909–927.

Crawford, J., & McIntyre, J. (2011). The independence and impartiality of the 'international judiciary'. In S. Shetreet & C. Forsyth (Eds.), *The culture of judicial independence* (pp. 187–214). Leiden: Brill Nijhoff.

Gibson, J., & Caldeira, G. (1998). Changes in the legitimacy of the European Court of Justice: A Post-Maastricht analysis. *British Journal of Political Science, 28,* 63–91.

Kelemen, D. (2012). The political foundations of judicial independence in the European Union. *Journal of European Public Policy, 19*, 43–58.

Krenn, C. (2018). Self-government at the court of justice of the European Union: A bedrock for institutional success. *German Law Journal, 19*, 2008–2030.

Mackenzie, R. (2014). The selection of international judges. In C. Romano, K. Alter, & Y. Shan (Eds.), *The Oxford handbook of international adjudication* (pp. 737–756). Oxford: Oxford University Press.

Mackenzie, R., Malleson, K., Martin, P., & Sands, P. (Eds.). (2010). *Selecting international judges: Principle, process and politics*. Oxford: Oxford University Press.

Malenovský, J. (2011). L'indépendance des juges internationaux. In *Recueil des cours de l'Académie de Droit International de la Haye* (pp. 1–275). Leiden: Brill Nijhoff.

Olsen, J. P. (2017). *Democratic accountability and political order and change. Exploring democratic accountability in an Era of European Transformation*. Oxford: Oxford University Press.

Seibert-Fohr, A. (Ed.). (2012). *Judicial independence in transition*. New York: Springer.

Shetreet, S., & Forsyth, C. (Eds.). (2011). *The culture of judicial independence*. Leiden: Brill Nijhoff.

Szurek, S. (2010). La composition des jurisdictions internationales permanentes: de nouvelles exigences de qualité et de représentativité. *Annuaire Français de Droit International, 56*, 41–78.

The Fair Trial as a Guarantee of the Administrative Procedure

Elena Bindi and Andrea Pisaneschi

Contents

1 Introduction

As a consequence of the ECtHR substantialist approach, the principles established in the European Convention on Human Rights about fair trial do not only apply to judicial proceedings. In some specific cases, these principles can in fact be applied to administrative procedures as well. Nevertheless, the application of art. 6 to administrative procedures is limited to some specific situations and is not aimed at modifying the nature of these procedures.

This paper is based on a joint research by the authors, but paragraphs 1, 2, and 3 are written by Elena Bindi, paragraphs 4 and 5 by Andrea Pisaneschi.

E. Bindi (✉)
University of Siena, Department of Business and Law, Siena, Italy
e-mail: elena.bindi@unisi.it

A. Pisaneschi
University of Siena, Department of Law, Siena, Italy
e-mail: andrea.pisaneschi@unisi.it

© Springer Nature Switzerland AG 2019
P. Pinto de Albuquerque, K. Wojtyczek (eds.), *Judicial Power in a Globalized World*, https://doi.org/10.1007/978-3-030-20744-1_3

This paper investigates the criteria allowing the Court to apply the guarantees of art. 6 to administrative proceedings. In particular, it highlights the difference between French case-law concerning financial markets regulation authorities and the solution adopted in the Italian Grande Stevens v. Italy case. It then dwells on the problematic theory of *ex post* "compensation" for the defaults of the administrative procedure through the process and on the concept of full jurisdiction that has been developed by the Court.

2 Supranational Guarantees for Fair Trial

As is well known, art. 6 of the ECHR only extends the therein established guarantees to criminal and civil proceedings. In particular, its paragraph 1 lays down the fair trial principles referring to civil rights and obligations and to criminal charges only. This article then goes on by developing fair trial guarantees in criminal cases (paras 2 and 3).

Art. 6 develops the right to fair trial in two different meanings: on the one hand, as right to have a trial according to para 1 (right to be heard within a reasonable time by an independent and impartial tribunal), and, on the other hand, as right within the trial, as provided for in para 3. This last covers a range of essential guarantees, both related to the procedure and process, which are aimed at ensuring the real exercise of defence. These guarantees must be assured to anyone charged with a crime. The principle of the presumption of innocence serves thus as *trait d'union* between paragraphs 1 and 3, "the connection between the general clause of the right to process and that concerning specific rights of the defendant in the trial".[1]

Moreover, the catalogue of rights listed in art. 6 is not considered as exhaustive; so these rights have been interpreted by judges in a broad manner. In this way, the adversarial principle, the right to stand on trial, the right to silence and the right against self-incrimination have been added to the rights expressly provided in art. 6 (such as right to be informed promptly; right to have adequate time and facilities for the preparation of the defence; right to defend themselves in person or through legal assistance of his own choosing or, if he has not sufficient means to pay for legal assistance, to be given it free when the interests of justice so require; right to examine or have examined witnesses; right to have an interpreter).[2]

Articles 47 and 48 of Chapter VI of the European Charter of Fundamental Rights essentially reaffirm what is established in art. 6 of the ECHR.[3] The European Charter

---

[1]Chiavario (2012), p. 216.

[2]See Di Stasi (2016), p. 20.

[3]Specifically, art. 47 (entitled "Right to an effective remedy and to a fair trial") establishes that "Everyone whose rights and freedoms guaranteed by the law of the Union are violated has the right to an effective remedy before a tribunal in compliance with the conditions laid down in this Article (paragraph 1). Everyone is entitled to a fair and public hearing within a reasonable time by an independent and impartial tribunal previously established by law. Everyone shall have the

(already entered into force in 2000) has been given legal effects with the reference to it contained in the Lisbon Treaty of 2009. Therefore, the Charter is now part of the primary EU law and can thus assume constitutional level when it codifies the fundamental principles of the European Union or certain general law principles.[4]

Although the fair trial principles are generally applied throughout judicial procedures, it is however worth noting how the ECtHR has acknowledged as the character of the Convention as living instrument: As a consequence, it must be interpreted according to social development.[5] In the light of the above, its scope of application has been interpreted extensively, by attributing an autonomous legal meaning of a substantive nature to the legal concepts contained in the conventional norms (autonomous interpretation).[6] This is in fact the only way to apply rules in an effective manner within diverse State legal systems where legal definitions may have different meanings.[7] Moreover, this is also the only way possible to ensure the compliance with the Convention.

3 Engel Criteria and the Essentially Afflictive Nature of the Sanctions Imposed by the Financial Market Regulation Authorities

The ECtHR has significantly broadened the scope of application of the fair trial principles relying on the autonomous meaning of the legal terms provided for in article 6 ECHR. Despite the fact that this norm only explicitly refers to civil and criminal proceedings, these principles have also been applied to the administrative

---

possibility of being advised, defended and represented (paragraph 2). Legal aid shall be made available to those who lack sufficient resources in so far as such aid is necessary to ensure effective access to justice (paragraph 3)". Art. 48 (entitled "Presumption of innocence and right of defence") stipulates that "Everyone who has been charged shall be presumed innocent until proved guilty according to law (paragraph 1). Respect for the rights of the defence of anyone who has been charged shall be guaranteed (paragraph 2)".

[4]See also Court of Justice EU, 15 October 2009, C-101/08, *Audiolux*, para 63, where it is established that "The general principles of Community law have constitutional status". For some doctrinal views on this matter see, Tizzano (2014), p. 459; Rossi (2016), p. 417.

[5]From ECtHR, 12 July 2001, application n. 44759/98, *Ferrazzini v. Italy*, para 26.

[6]See Sudre (1998), p. 93; Letsas (2004), p. 279; Beumer (2014), pp. 15–17.

[7]While applying art. 6, the Court tends to recognize a limited margin of discretion to the States. The legal remedies topic is indeed a key point of the rule of law, so that the State can't detach too much form the principles provided by art. 6, as interpreted by the Court. Moreover, the Court of Justice of EU shares this interpretation, when repeatedly intervening in order to assure the guarantee of effective legal remedies. See Lambert (1998), pp. 63–89; Arai (2013), pp. 62–105.

proceeding and then to the administrative procedure, when this is aimed at imposing a penalty of criminal nature.[8]

Firstly, the ECtHR has interpreted the term "tribunal" of art. 6 in a substantive way. It is not relevant whether or not the body concerned is part of the judiciary. What counts is, actually, that the body substantially performs judiciary functions. As a consequence, not only the judiciary bodies composing the judiciary system of a country can be placed within the notion of "tribunal". Any public authority in charge of deciding on a criminal charge can be considered as a tribunal, including, therefore, an administrative authority. According to the European Court's case-law the judicial function is defined by the kind of power that a body is exercising in practice.[9]

Secondly, since 1976 the Court has clarified the meaning of the definition of "criminal charge" for the purpose of fair trial. This definition must be interpreted by the Court according to a substantive approach and in an autonomous manner with respect to the diverse classifications provided by the States parties.

The criteria used to define the criminal nature of the sanctions are better known as "Engel criteria", so named because of the case in which they have been laid down for the first time by the ECtHR. These criteria are basically three and they are alternative to each other. The first one is the formal criterion, that is the legal classification given to a sanction by the respondent State. The other two have substantial character, namely the concrete nature of the sanction and the severity of the potential penalty in which the defendant risks incurring.[10]

With reference to the formal criterion, the Court has developed a consolidated case-law according to which the domestic classification of the sanction is not decisive as for the application of art. 6 ECHR, since "the indications so afforded have only a formal and relative value". Moreover, the formal qualification of a

---

[8]See Mirate (2011), p. 550. More generally on the application of art. 6 ECHR in the administrative procedure see Galligan (1997), p. 214; Craig (2003), pp. 753–773; Rabinovici (2012), pp. 149–173; Schindler (2006), pp. 445–466; Vitkauskas and Sîan (2009), pp. 13–81. As for the Italian scholars, see Cassese (2003), pp. 173–239; Mattarella (2012), pp. 113–132; Allena (2012a), pp. 267–300; Pacini (2012), pp. 99–144. Concerning the application of art. 6 ECHR to administrative procedures see ECtHR, 21 January 2014, application n. 4875/11, *Placì v. Italia*, commented by Prudenzano (2014), pp. 1–18.

[9]See ECtHR, 27 September 2011, application n. 43509/08, *Menarini Diagnostics s.r.l. v. Italy*, para 42. The decisions has been commented by many scholars: see, ex plurimis, Letsas (2009); Bombois (2011), pp. 560–571; Basilico (2011), pp. 1–9; Bronkers and Vallery (2012), pp. 44–47; Abenhaïm (2012), pp. 117–134.

[10]See ECtHR, 8 June 1976, application n. 5100/71; 5101/71; 5102/71; 5354/72; 5370/72, *Engel and Others v. Netherlands*. This is the decision in which the Court affirmed that the legal domestic classification is not enough to deny the application of the guarantees coming from the fair trial principle of art. 6 ECHR. With specific reference to the formal criterion, the Court stably considers the domestic classification as "no more than a starting point [because] the indications so afforded have only a formal and relative value". See on that point ECtHR, 21 February 1984, application n. 8544/79, *Oztürk v. Germania*, para 52, in *Riv. it. dir. e proc. pen.*, 1985, 894, commented by Paliero (1985), pp. 894–898. As for scholars, see Goisis (2014), p. 337.

criminal offence is only binding when this qualification is aimed at broadening the scope of art. 6, so as to increase the guarantees of individuals.[11]

As expressly pointed out in the Engel case, the Court does not want to interfere with the free choice of member States of adopting measures of criminal law, that is the *extrema ratio*. On the contrary, the choice of not relying on criminal law is examined by the Court in order to avoid that a different substance is hidden behind the form.[12]

The nature of the sanction refers to its mainly afflictive character rather than to the compensatory or restorative features. Indeed, the aim of the sanction must mainly be that of preventing, suppressing and deterring, in order to prevent similar conducts from being repeated. The purpose of the sanction must therefore be punitive, deterrent and repressive. At the same time, the sanction must be aimed at safeguarding interests that are normally protected by criminal law and has to be applicable to a wide group of recipients.

On the other hand, the severity of the sanction refers to the maximum penalty and depends on both a subjective and an objective assessment.

Moreover, for those sanctions that have an essentially economic content, the principle of severity also concerns the existence of punitive elements of personal affliction. That is to say that the sanction assumes a substantially criminal character when it is socially reprehensible or when it is able to influence the social life and human relations (both professional and personal) of a person.[13]

---

[11]See ECtHR, 8 June 1976, *Engel and Others v. Netherlands*, para 81: "*The Convention without any doubt allows the States, in the performance of their function as guardians of the public interest, to maintain or establish a distinction between criminal law and disciplinary law, and to draw the dividing line, but only subject to certain conditions. The Convention leaves the States free to designate as a criminal offence an act or omission not constituting the normal exercise of one of the rights that it protects. This is made especially clear by Article 7. Such a choice, which has the effect of rendering applicable Articles 6 and 7, in principle escapes supervision by the Court. The converse choice, for its part, is subject to stricter rules. If the Contracting States were able at their discretion to classify an offence as disciplinary instead of criminal, or to prosecute the author of a "mixed" offence on the disciplinary rather than on the criminal plane, the operation of the fundamental clauses of Articles 6 and 7 would be subordinated to their sovereign will. A latitude extending thus far might lead to results incompatible with the purpose and object of the Convention*". See Harris et al. (2009), p. 205.

[12]This is a key point in the ECtHR case-law, since the possibility to apply art. 6 to situations which do not belong to criminal law as for the domestic law is all based on the possibility to examine that choice. Indeed: "*If the Contracting States were able at their discretion to classify an offence as disciplinary instead of criminal, or to prosecute the author of a "mixed" offence on the disciplinary rather than on the criminal plane, the operation of the fundamental clauses of Articles 6 and 7 (art. 6, art. 7) would be subordinated to their sovereign will. A latitude extending thus far might lead to results incompatible with the purpose and object of the Convention. The Court therefore has jurisdiction, under Article 6 (art. 6) and even without reference to Articles 17 and 18 (art. 17, art. 18), to satisfy itself that the disciplinary does not improperly encroach upon the criminal. In short, the "autonomy" of the concept of "criminal" operates, as it were, one way only*". See again ECtHR, 8 June 1976, *Engel and Others v. Netherlands*, paras 81 and 82.

[13]See Bindi and Pisaneschi (2018), pp. 52–78.

The substantialist interpretation of art. 6 of the Convention has had a major impact on the sanctioning procedures of market regulators. In fact, the ECtHR relies on the above mentioned criteria to consider the sanctions issued by the market regulatory authorities as substantially criminal. As a consequence, it applies them the guarantees provided for in art. 6 of the Convention.

When art. 6 of the Convention is applied to essentially administrative sanctions, the consequence is that the procedures by means of which sanctions are imposed do not always comply with the fair trial guarantees. The guarantees of the adversarial principle are ensured in the administrative procedure in a more incomplete manner than with respect to ordinary judicial proceedings.

The application of art. 6 of the Convention to essentially administrative sanctions has the effect that the procedures for imposing sanctions are not always compatible with the guarantees of due process. The guarantees of adversarial proceedings in the administrative procedure are in fact more limited than those of a procedural adversarial nature.[14] In the administrative procedures, the principle of objective impartiality, which should require the separation between the investigation and the decisional phases in order to guarantee the full acknowledgment of documents and equality between prosecution and defence, is often missing. The adversary proceeding has a vertical nature rather than an horizontal one and it is set as an instrument of participation for the private to a public decision, rather than as an instrument of defence. However, when it comes to substantially punitive sanctions, the ECtHR has often reaffirmed that the same authority may not carry out both the investigative and decision-making phases, since this could undermine the principle of impartiality. Specifically, the mere formal and functional division between the two phases would not assure impartiality when there is a hierarchical subordination and an admixture between the decision-making and preparatory bodies. The separation has to be effective and have structural nature. Moreover, the Court has always considered the oral discussion and full knowledge of the proceeding documents as necessary. As to the possibility of presenting evidence, the adversarial principle should be equally guaranteed both with respect to the plaintiff and the defendant. In particular, a public hearing should always be necessary before the authority that decides the sanction.

Ultimately, from a theoretical point of view, a procedure is not a proceeding. Nevertheless, when the procedures are aimed at imposing administrative sanctions which are substantially criminal, the fair trial principles, provided for in art. 6 of the Convention, must be applied according to the Engel criteria.

---

[14]See on that point Cons. Stato, Sez. VI, 12 February 2001 n. 652. In the same sense Cass. Civ., Sez. I, 2 March 2016 n. 4114.

4 *From the French COB and* **Commission Bancaire** *Cases to the Italian* **Grande Stevens**

These principles have been first of all used in France. They contributed to the reform of both the *Commission des opérations de bourse* (COB)—later became *Autorité de marchés financieres*—and the *Commission bancaire*—which has subsequently been reformed with the establishment of the *Autorité de contrôl prudentiel*. The procedural model envisaged for the functioning of the French COB was considered incompatible with art. 6 of the Convention from both the *Cour de cassation*[15] and the *Conseil d'État*.[16]

The regulatory system was amended in 2003, when a new authority was established: the *Autorité de marchés financieres*. This authority is composed of two autonomous and independent bodies: the *Collège* and the *Commission des sanctions*.[17] Later on, two decisions of the ECtHR highlighted two main lacunae in this proceeding, namely the lack of public hearing and the infringement of the right to access to prosecution documents in all its parts.[18]

---

[15]Indeed, the *Court de Cassation* claimed that the presence of the rapporteur at the Commission decision violated the principle of separation between investigation and decision-making phases. Moreover, the Court also considered it in contrast with the impartiality of the body principle, as laid down by art. 6 of the ECHR. The French Cour de Cassation annulled a sanction imposed by the COB following a procedure in which the rapporteur who was in charge for the investigations also had a role in the decision-making phase. See Cour de cassation, Assemblée plénière, 5 February 1999, *Commission des opérations de bourse c. Oury*; decision published in *La semaine juridique (JCP)*, 31 March 1999, n. 13, 636. On this decision see Docouloux-Favard and Pernazza (2003), pp. 1002–1018.

[16]Firstly, the *Conseil d'État* considered that it had to apply the fair trial guarantees only to the judiciary proceedings (see the renowned Avis 31 March 1995, *Ministre du badget c. SARL Auto Méric* (c.d. avis Méric), in *Actualité Juridique Droit Administratif (AJDA)*, 1995, 739. Later on, specifically with the Didier decision of 1999, it extended those guarantees to the administrative procedure (see Conseil d'État, Assemblée, 3 December 1999, in *La semaine juridique (JCP)*, II, 2000, 10267).

[17]On the basis of a report presented by the Secretary-General the *Collège* initiates the procedure by informing the parties and sending the dossier to the *Commission*. The latter nominates a rapporteur who conducts a broad investigative activity and possibly hear the parts asking for it with a request presented with a relation to the *Commission*. The *Commission* then sends the relation to the interested person and convene it in a public hearing. During is hearing an investigation phase can take place and witnesses can be heard. The *Commission* decides then without the *rapporteur*. See Costa (2005), pp. 1174–1182; Linotte and Simonin (2004), pp. 143–147.

[18]See ECtHR, 20 January 2011, application n. 30183/06, *Vernes v. France* and ECtHR, 30 June 2011, application n. 25041/07, *Messier v. France*. As already said, in the first case the Court states that a public hearing before the COB is necessary, since the mere control *a posteriori* made by the Council of State is not enough (see para 32, which states that "compte tenu de l'importance de pouvoir solliciter la tenue de débats publics devant la COB, le seul contrôle ultérieur du Conseil d'Etat n'était pas suffisant en l'espèce. Partant, il y a eu violation de l'article 6 § 1 du fait de l'impossibilité pour le requérant de solliciter la tenue de débats publics devant la COB"). In the second decision the Court highlights that the authority has to inform the defence about all the evidences discharging and against it, since it is not enough that the parties could have full access to

With respect to the *Commission bancaire*, in 2009 the Court considered that the investigating body was subject to the Commission's hierarchical power and that there was not sufficient separation between the person who carried out the investigation and the person who, on the other hand, took the decision.[19] As mentioned above, this decision also led to an organic reform of the *Commission bancaire* through the creation of a new authority called *Autorité de contrôl prudentiel*, which appears to have been drawn up according to the indications of the Court. Here too, the authority is made up of two separate bodies: the *Collège* and the *Commission des sanctions*. The *Collège* decides whether the investigation must be opened and then conducts this phase in an adversarial procedure with the parties. The commission, in turn, decides in accordance with the adversarial principle, following a public hearing. It is important to highlight that in these decisions the defect of objective impartiality of the decision-making body in the administrative procedure could not be balanced by the existence of a subsequent judgment with *full jurisdiction*.

The question of the essentially criminal nature of Consob and Bank of Italy sanctions then came to the attention of Italian judges after the famous Grande Stevens v. Italy decision.[20] In this case, the ECtHR recognized the incompatibility of the sanctioning procedure that, at that time, was governed by the CONSOB, stating that "*It is nevertheless the case that the IT Office, the Directorate and the Commission are merely branches of the same administrative body, acting under the authority and supervision of a single chairman. In the Court's opinion, this amounts to the consecutive exercise of investigative and judicial functions within one body; in criminal matters such a combination of functions is not compatible with the requirements of impartiality set out in Article 6 § 1 of the Convention*".[21]

The organic and formal separation would not guarantee an effective separation between investigative and decision-making functions. This is because, as highlighted by Judges Karakas and Pinto de Albuquerque: "*First, the CONSOB's chairman has the tasks of supervising the preliminary investigation and giving instructions about the functioning of the divisions and directives for their*

---

the case-file. In this way, the counterparty can really affect the decision (see para 52). As it has been noted by Allena (2012b), p. 66, the fact that the ECtHR did not uphold the action in the specific case does not reduce the importance of what has been affirmed by the Court in that decision: as for the highly afflictive sanctions, it is necessary to guarantee the equality of arms since the administrative procedure phase, even when the right to a legal remedy is established. See in detail on that topic Bindi and Pisaneschi (2018), pp. 93–102, and the here mentioned scholars; Salerno (2018), pp. 13–19.

[19]ECtHR, 11 June 2009, application n. 5242/04, *Dubus S.A. v. France*. The Court affirmed that "la société requérante pouvait raisonnablement avoir l'impression que ce sont les mêmes personnes qui l'ont poursuivie et jugée" (para 59). See Zivy and Luc (2010), pp. 85–92; Wils (2011), p. 2022.

[20]ECtHR, 4 March 2014, application n. 18640/10, *Grande Stevens and others v. Italia*. See, *ex multis*, Manetti (2014), pp. 2942–2946; Flick and Napoleoni (2014), pp. 1–13; Abbadessa (2014), pp. 546–552; Allena (2014), pp. 1053–1067; Zagrebelsky (2014), pp. 1196–1198; Barmann (2017), pp. 306–315.

[21]See ECtHR, 4 March 2014, *Grande Stevens and others v. Italia*, para 137.

coordination. Second, the CONSOB's chairman is directly involved in the exercise of the most important inspection powers and other investigative powers attributed to the CONSOB by Articles 115 and 187 octies *of the TUF, upon proposal of the competent directorates. Third, the CONSOB as a Commission may exercise extremely intrusive investigative powers, such as the power to seize property. Fourth, the CONSOB's decision may be motivated* per relationem, *with reference to the preceding procedural acts, and may even be taken by tacit consent of the members of the Commission. All things considered, the CONSOB as a Commission is very far from being an impartial body vis-à-vis the investigatory and prosecutorial bodies of the ITO and ASD. This basic systemic failure of the administrative proceedings is compounded by the grave inequality between the parties".*[22]

However, according to the ECtHR, the defects of impartiality could be compensated by a full jurisdiction judgment by means of which it is possible for the party to challenge the sanctions. In fact, the Court affirms that *"The above findings concerning the CONSOB's lack of objective impartiality and the fact that the proceedings before it did not comply with the principles of a fair hearing are not, however, sufficient to warrant the conclusion that there has been a violation of Article 6 in this case. In this connection, the Court observes that the penalties complained of by the applicants were not imposed by a court at the close of adversarial judicial proceedings, but by an administrative authority, namely the CONSOB. While entrusting the prosecution and punishment of similar minor offences to such authorities is not inconsistent with the Convention, the person concerned must have an opportunity to challenge any decision made against him or her before a tribunal which offers the guarantees of Article 6".*[23]

According to this interpretation, the State could choose where the fair trial guarantees should be ensured, either within the administrative phase or during the judicial one, since this choice is considered to be as the expression of the State's margin of appreciation.

---

[22]See ECtHR, 4 March 2014, *Grande Stevens and others v. Italia*, Partly concurring, partly dissenting opinion of judges Karakas and Pinto de Albuquerque, para 5. On the critical issues of the Consob procedure in respect of these aspects see Torchia (2015), p. 8. See also Allena (2014), p. 1053; Bindi (2014), pp. 3007–3023.

[23]See ECtHR, 4 March 2014, *Grande Stevens and others v. Italia*, para 138. See on the point ECtHR, 2 September 1998, *Kadubec v. Slovakia*, para 57; ECtHR, 16 November 2004, application n. 53371/99, *Čanady v. Slovakia*, para 31 and ECtHR, *Menarini Diagnostics S.r.l.*, para 58.

5 The So-Called Full Jurisdiction and the Problem of the Ex Post Compensation

According to the ECtHR, an administrative procedure concerning essentially criminal sanctions which does not respect the fair trial guarantees can therefore be compensated by a judicial phase with the so-called full jurisdiction.[24] In general, full jurisdiction means the ability of a body to have full jurisdiction over the merit of the case, appraise the facts and assess the evidence. This judicial proceedings have to be without constraints arising from the previous administrative investigations and must entail the possibility of reforming any point of the contested decision, both in fact and law.[25]

The fact that any point must be justiciable may raise some problems in relation to the technical assessments of the administration, according to which markets regulation authorities usually impose sanctions. In this regard, the ECtHR does not allow

---

[24]See, for instance, ECtHR, 21 July 2011, application n. 32181/04 and 35122/05, *Sigma Radio Television Ltd v. Cipro*, para 157, (concerning administrative sanctions—even of pecuniary nature—imposed by the Cyprus control Authority for the communications to the "Sigma TV" and "Radio Porto" companies), where it is stated that *"where the reviewing court is precluded from determining the central issue in dispute, the scope of review will not be considered sufficient for the purposes of Article 6"*.

[25]This is all the more the case where technically complex issues are raised (as pointed out by Allena (2012b), p. 66, as pointed out by the ECtHR in some cases concerning banking supervision procedures. See, for instance, the case *Credit and Industrial Bank v. the Czech Republic*, concerning an insolvency procedure of a bank. In this case, the Court stated that the Czech administrative judge should have examined the substantive reasons at the basis of the administrative procedure, without merely verifying the compliance with the formal conditions (see ECtHR, 21 October 2003, application n. 29010/95, *Credit and Industrial Banck v. the Czech Republic*, parr. 64–65; see also parr. 71–72, in which the Court made it clear that it cannot be considered as compliant with art. 6 ECHR a system in which *"the essential function of the national courts when deciding on matters relating to entries in the Companies Register is to verify that the formal conditions laid down in the relevant legislation for making such entries have been fulfilled"* and in which *"It is not the role of the courts to examine the substantive reasons for which the compulsory administration has been imposed or subsequently extended"*. In other words, as pointed out in the case *Družstevni založna Pria and Others v. the Czech Republic*, the judge should have carried out a point by point analysis of all the relevant factual and legal elements, in order to ascertain whether the bank was indeed in an economic situation justifying compulsory administration, despite the obvious technicality of such a circumstance. See ECtHR, 31 July 2008, application n. 72034/01, *Družstevni založna Pria and Others v. the Czech Republic*, para 111: *"The Court reiterates that, in a given case where full jurisdiction is contested, proceedings might still satisfy requirements of Article 6 § 1 of the Convention if the court deciding on the matter considered all applicant's submissions on their merits, point by point, without ever having to decline jurisdiction in replying to them or ascertaining facts. By way of contrast, the Court found violations of Article 6 § 1 of the Convention in other cases where the domestic courts had considered themselves bound by the prior findings of administrative bodies which were decisive for the outcome of the cases before them, without examining the relevant issues independently"*.

exceptions to the full jurisdiction principle on the assumption that an issue has technical character. Neither, the ECtHR admits that this assessment may be limited or attributed to other organs. When the precondition for the sanction is a technical assessment, even a complex one, the judicial organ cannot reject to re-examine the existence of such precondition; instead, it can call on the assistance of a technical consultant.[26] In short, judicial organs must be able to rule on all the parts of a case.[27]

The full jurisdiction proceedings entails the power of establishing facts according to the exam of their objective features instead of relying on the reconstruction already delineated by the Public Administration. As a consequence, the judge of legality (Court of Cassation) cannot be considered as a full jurisdiction judge.[28] Furthermore, the existence of full jurisdiction has to be assessed in practice, since the ECtHR does not have the competence of ascertaining the compatibility of norms in abstract terms. Conversely, the Court can exercise its jurisdiction with respect to the possible infringement of the fair trial principle in a given legal dispute.[29] At the same

---

[26]ECtHR, 24 November 2005, application n. 49429/99, *Capital Bank Ad. v. Bulgaria*, para 113: "*The Court, for its part, is prepared to accept that the BNB's opinion on this issue carries significant weight because of its special expertise in this area. However, it is not persuaded that the domestic courts, if need be with the assistance of expert opinion, could not themselves ascertain whether the applicant bank was insolvent or not. The difficulties encountered in this respect could also be overcome through the provision of a right of appeal against the BNB's decision to an adjudicatory body other than a traditional court integrated within the standard judicial machinery of the country, but which otherwise fully complies with all the requirements of Article 6 § 1, or whose decision is subject to review by a judicial body with full jurisdiction which itself provides the safeguards required by that provision [. . .]*". See Botta and Svetlicinii (2013), pp. 107–137; Nikolic (2012), pp. 583–588.

[27]See Goisis (2015), p. 558; Allena (2015), p. 71. The authors share the same opinion on that point.

[28]"*It is true that a public hearing was held before the Court of Cassation. However, the latter did not have jurisdiction to examine the merits of the case, to establish the facts and to assess the evidence; indeed, the Government do no contest this. It could not therefore be considered as a court with full jurisdiction within the meaning of the Court's case-law*": cfr. ECtHR, 4 March 2014, *Grande Stevens and others v. Italia*, para 155.

[29]ECtHR, 27 September 1995, application n. 18984/91, *McCann and Others v. United Kingdom*, para 153, where it is established that "The Court recalls that the Convention does not oblige Contracting Parties to incorporate its provisions into national law [. . .] Furthermore, it is not the role of the Convention institutions to examine *in abstracto* the compatibility of national legislative or constitutional provisions with the requirements of the Convention". In the same sense, see ECtHR, 6 September 1978, application n. 5029/71, Klass and Others v. Germany, para 33: "*Article 25 does not institute for individuals a kind of actio popularis for the interpretation of the Convention; it does not permit individuals to complain against a law in abstracto simply because they feel that it contravenes the Convention. In principle, it does not suffice for an individual applicant to claim that the mere existence of a law violates his rights under the Convention; it is necessary that the law should have been applied to his detriment. Nevertheless, as both the Government and the Commission pointed out, a law may by itself violate the rights of an individual if the individual is directly affected by the law in the absence of any specific measure of implementation [. . .]*".

time, the party has the burden of requesting that the judge exercises its functions according to the criterion of full jurisdiction.[30]

However, the view according to which the infringements of art. 6 occurring during the administrative procedure for imposing a sanction can be compensated by the subsequent full jurisdiction trial, raises several interpretative problems.

First of all, administrative sanctions are generally automatically enforceable, while criminal sanctions usually become effective only when the judgment gains force of *res iudicata*. As a consequence, a paradox may arise: an administrative sanction substantially criminal which is imposed in breach of fair trial guarantees might have more noxious consequences than the effects arising from a sanction that is both formally and substantially criminal.

Secondly, even if the opposition proceeding is characterized by full jurisdiction, this judgment will be *a posteriori*. It means that it will concern facts already established in a non-adversarial procedure and presumably according to a previous reconstruction provided for by the public administration.

From the point of view of administrative law, it is difficult to accept the view that the unlawfulness of an act has to be ascertained at the moment of the enactment of the act itself. Likewise, it is difficult to agree that a violation of the guarantees occurred during the administrative procedure may be compensated by means of a subsequent judicial process that may only arise following the enactment of the act.

---

[30]The ECtHR cannot be expected to ascertain an infringement of full jurisdiction if the party relying on the infringement did not have exercised its procedural rights before a national judge. See, for instance, ECtHR, 21 March 2006, application n. 70074/01, *Valico S.r.l. v. Italy*, para 2. For example: "*It is true that the applicants complained about the fact that the court of appeal did not question witnesses [...]. However, they did not indicate any procedural rule which would have prevented such questioning. In addition, the request for questioning of witnesses, made by Mr Grande Stevens in his pleadings of 25 September 2007, did not indicate either the names of the persons whom he wished to have summoned, or the events about which they were to provide evidence. In addition, that request was made on a purely hypothetical basis, for examination only if the court of appeal held that the documents already included in the case file were insufficient or unusable*": ECtHR, 4 March 2014, *Grande Stevens and Others v. Italy*, para 150. Nevertheless, it is important to remember the partly concurring, partly dissenting opinion of judges Karakas and Pinto de Albuquerque, also because of the depth of their reasoning. They think that the Court should have heard the witnesses ex officio, since the adversarial examination is fundamental when severe criminal sanctions are at stake: "*The truly shocking aspect is the total lack of an adversarial examination of the disputed evidence with regard to crucial facts in a hearing before a court of law. The court of appeal unreservedly accepted and endorsed the testimonial evidence collected by the prosecutorial body without giving the applicants an opportunity to conduct an effective cross-examination of the witnesses on the facts of the case*". Because of that, the dissenting opinion does not share the rejection of the application. According to the dissenting judges "*It is obvious that the facts in respect of which the testimony of these witnesses was requested were those referred to in their previous written depositions, collected during the non-judicial stage of the proceedings. It is even more evident that the applicants expected that the witnesses be summoned by the court of appeal, as it could have done using its powers under the law, either at the appellants' request or of its own motion, even without specifying the arguments to be proved*" (ECtHR, 4 March 2014, *Grande Stevens and others v. Italia*. Partly concurring, partly dissenting opinion of judges Karakas and Pinto de Albuquerque, paras 12 and 13).

Moreover, the question of the compensation of an unfair administrative procedure by means of a consequent full jurisdiction judicial process generates a contrast between some fundamental juridical principles (such as the presumption of innocence and immediate enforceability of administrative acts) according to the indications coming from the Grande Stevens decision. Furthermore, this point is neither final in the ECtHR case-law. As affirmed above, the ECtHR based its decisions on the lack of impartiality of the administrative authority with regard to the COB and the *Commission Bancaire*, but it did not take into account the presence of a subsequent full jurisdiction process.

Ultimately, the administrative and judicial proceedings are two different procedures, independent and autonomous one with respect to the other. The administrative procedure is not a process, but it must respect the minimum guarantees related to the adversarial principle when it is aimed at imposing a substantially afflictive sanction, as provided for in art. 6. On the other hand, the judicial process is also autonomous; thus, it cannot allow the revision of all possible defects of the administrative procedure. Both the administrative and jurisdiction functions are different and distinct and governed by diverse principles and rules. Instead, from a dogmatic point of view, the guarantees provided for in art. 6 must be applied to the administrative procedure when it aims at imposing an essentially criminal sanction. This conclusion is the logical consequence of a substantialist approach, but it does not change the nature of the administrative procedure nor it transforms it into a judicial process.

References

Abbadessa, G. (2014). Il caso Fiat-Ifil alla Corte europea dei diritti dell'uomo. Nozione di "pena" e contenuti del principio "ne bis in idem". *Giurisprudenza commerciale, 4*, 546–552.

Abenhaïm, M. (2012). "Quel droit au juge en matière de cartels?", commentaire de l'arrêt CEDH, A. Menarini Diagnostics S.R.L. c. Italie, 27 septembre 2011, req. n° 43509/08. *Revue trimestrielle de droit européen Dalloz, 1*, 117–134.

Allena, M. (2012a). L'art. 6 CEDU come parametro di effettività della tutela procedimentale e giudiziale all'interno degli Stati membri dell'Unione europea. *Rivista italiana di diritto pubblico comunitario*, 267–300.

Allena, M. (2012b) *Art. 6 CEDU. Procedimento e processo amministrativo*. Naples: Editoriale scientifica.

Allena, M. (2014). Il caso Grande Stevens c. Italia: le sanzioni Consob alla prova dei principi Cedu. *Il giornale di diritto amministrativo*, 1053–1067.

Allena, M. (2015). Interessi procedimentali e Convenzione europea dei diritti dell'uomo: verso un'autonomia di tutela? *Il giornale di diritto amministrativo*, 67–76.

Arai, Y. (2013). The margin of appreciation doctrine: A theoretical analysis of Strasbourg's variable geometry. In A. Follesdal, B. Peters, & G. Ulfstein (Eds.), *Constituting Europe - the European Court of Human Rights in a National, European and global context* (pp. 62–105). Cambridge University Press.

Barmann, B. (2017). Dopo il caso Grande Stevens: la via italiana al giusto procedimento. *Giornale di diritto amministrativo, 3*, 306–315.

Basilico, A. E. (2011). Il controllo del giudice amministrativo sulle sanzioni antitrust e l'art. 6 CEDU. *Rivista dell'Associazione italiana dei costituzionalisti, 4*, 1–9. Retrieved March 28, 2019, from https://www.rivistaaic.it/it/rivista/ultimi-contributi-pubblicati/alessandro-e-basilico/il-controllo-del-giudice-amministrativo-sulle-sanzioni-antitrust-e-l-art-6-cedu

Beumer, E. (2014). The interaction between EU competition law procedures and fundamental rights protection: The case of the right to be heard. *Yearbook of Antitrust and Regulatory Studies, 7* (10), 9–34.

Bindi, E. (2014). L'incidenza delle pronunce della Corte EDU sui procedimenti sanzionatori delle autorità amministrative indipendenti. *Giurisprudenza costituzionale, 3*, 3007–3023.

Bindi, E., & Pisaneschi, A. (2018). *Sanzioni Consob e Banca d'Italia. Procedimenti e doppio binario al vaglio della Corte Europea dei diritti dell'Uomo*. Turin: Giappichelli.

Bombois, T. (2011). L'Arrêt Menarini c. Italie de la Cour Européenne des Droits de l'Homme – Droit antitrust, champ pénal et contrôle de pleine jurisdiction. *Cahiers de Droit Européen*, 560–571.

Botta, M., & Svetlicinii, A. (2013). The standard of judicial review in EU competition law enforcement and its compatibility with the right to a fair trial under the EU charter of fundamental rights. In T. Kerikmäe (Ed.), *Protecting human rights in the EU. Controversies and challenges of the charter of fundamental rights* (pp. 107–127). New York: Springer.

Bronkers, M., & Vallery, A. (2012). Business as usual after Menarini? *Mlex Magazine, 3*(1), 44–47.

Cassese, S. (2003). Le basi costituzionali. In S. Cassese (Ed.), *Trattato di diritto amministrativo* (2nd ed., pp. 173–239). Milan: Giuffrè, (I).

Chiavario, M. (2012). Art. 6. In S. Bartole, B. Conforti, & G. Raimondi (Eds.), *Commentario alla Convenzione europea dei diritti dell'uomo e delle libertà fondamentali* (pp. 153–216). Padua: CEDAM.

Costa, D. (2005). L'Autorité des marchés financiers: juridiction? quasi-juridiction? pseudo-juridiction? *Revue Française de Droit Administratif*, 1174–1182.

Craig, P. (2003). The human rights act, article 6 and procedural rights. *Public Law, 4*, 753–773.

Di Stasi, A. (2016). Il sistema convenzionale di tutela dei diritti dell'uomo: profili introduttivi. In A. Di Stasi (Ed.), *CEDU e ordinamento italiano. La giurisprudenza della Corte europea dei diritti dell'uomo e l'impatto nell'ordinamento interno (2010–2015)* (pp. 3–46). Vicenza: Wolters Kluwer-CEDAM.

Docouloux-Favard, C., & Pernazza, F. (2003). Le procedure sanzionatorie della COB e il diritto di difesa. *Rivista del Diritto Commerciale e del diritto generale delle Obbligazioni, 11–12*, 1002–1018.

Flick, G. M., & Napoleoni, V. (2014). Cumulo tra sanzioni penali e amministrative: doppio binario o binario morto? («Materia penale», giusto processo e ne bis in idem nella sentenza della Corte EDU, 4 marzo 2014, sul market abuse). *Rivista dell'Associazione italiana dei costituzionalisti, 3*, 1–13. Retrieved March 28, 2019, from https://www.rivistaaic.it/images/rivista/pdf/3_2014_Flick_Napoleoni.pdf

Galligan, D. J. (1997). *Due process and fair procedures: A study of administrative procedures*. Oxford: Oxford University Press.

Goisis, F. (2014). Verso una nuova sanzione amministrativa in senso stretto: il contributo della Corte europea dei diritti dell'Uomo. *Rivista italiana di diritto pubblico comunitario, 24*(2), 337–358.

Goisis, F. (2015). La full jurisdiction nel contesto della giustizia amministrativa: concetto, funzione e nodi irrisolti. *Diritto processuale amministrativo, 2*, 546–596.

Harris, D., O'Boyle, M., Bates, E., & Buckley, C. (2009). *Law of the European Convention on Human Rights*. Oxford: Oxford University Press.

Lambert, P. (1998). Marge nationale d'appréciation et contrôle de proportionnalité. In F. Sudre (Ed.), *L'interprétation de la Convention européenne des droits de l'homme* (pp. 63–89). Brussels: Bruylant, coll. Droit et Justice.

Letsas, G. (2004). The truth in autonomous concepts: How to interpret the ECHR. *European Journal of International Law, 15*, 279–305.

Letsas, G. (2009). *A theory of interpretation of the European Convention on Human Rights.* Oxford: Oxford University Press.

Linotte, D., & Simonin, G. (2004). L'autorité des marchés financiers, prototype de la réforme de l'État? *Actualité Juridique Droit Administratif (AJDA), 3,* 143–147.

Manetti, M. (2014). Il paradosso della Corte EDU, che promuove la Consob (benché non sia imparziale) e blocca il giudice penale nel perseguimento dei reati di "market-abuse". *Giurisprudenza costituzionale, 6,* 2942–2946.

Mattarella, B. G. (2012). Pubblica amministrazione e interessi. In S. Battini, G. D'Auria, G. Della Cananea, C. Franchini, A. Massera, B. G. Mattarella, et al. (Eds.), *Il diritto amministrativo oltre i confini* (pp. 113–132). Milan: Giuffrè.

Mirate, S. (2011). The right to be heard: equa riparazione e giusto procedimento amministrativo nella giurisprudenza CEDU. *Responsabilità Civile e Previdenza,* 542–558.

Nikolic, I. (2012). Full judicial review of antitrust cases after KME: A new formula of review? *European Competition Law Review, 33*(12), 583–588.

Pacini, M. (2012). *Diritti umani e amministrazioni pubbliche.* Milan: Giuffrè.

Paliero, C. E. (1985). «Materia penale» e illecito amministrativo secondo la Corte europea dei diritti dell'uomo: una questione «classica» a una svolta radicale. *Rivista Italiana di Diritto e Procedura Penale,* 894–898.

Prudenzano, L. (2014). Giusto procedimento amministrativo, discrezionalità tecnica ed effettività della tutela giurisdizionale nella giurisprudenza della Corte europea dei diritti dell'uomo, Corte europea dei diritti dell'uomo, 21 gennaio 2014, ricorso n. 4875/11, Placì v. Italy), Rivista dell'Associazione italiana dei costituzionalisti, Osservatorio costituzionale, pp. 1–18. Retrieved March 28, 2019, from https://www.osservatorioaic.it/images/rivista/pdf/Prudenzano%202014. pdf

Rabinovici, I. (2012). The right to be heard in the charter of fundamental rights of the European Union. *European Public Law, 18*(1), 149–173.

Rossi, L. S. (2016). "Stesso valore giuridico dei Trattati"? Rango, primato ed effetti diretti della Carta dei diritti fondamentali dell'Unione europea. *Il Diritto dell'Unione Europea, 2,* 329–356.

Salerno, F. (2018). Poteri sanzionatori e responsabilità congiunta dei controllori. *Rivista di diritto bancario, 3,* 1–29. Retrieved March 28, 2019, from www.dirittobancario.it/sites/default/files/ allegati/f._salerno

Schindler, B. (2006). Art. 6 (1) ECHR and judicial review of administrative decision making in England and Switzerland: A comparative perspective. *Schweizerische Zeitschrift für internationales und europäisches Recht, 16*(4), 445–466.

Sudre, F. (1998). Le recours aux «notions autonomes». In F. Sudre (Ed.), *L'interprétation de la Convention européenne des droits de l'homme* (pp. 93–98). Brussels: Bruylant, coll. Droit et Justice.

Tizzano, A. (2014). L'application de la Charte des droits fondamentaux dans les États membres à la lumière de son article 51, paragraphe 1. *Diritto dell'Unione Europea,* 429–438.

Torchia, L. (2015). Il potere sanzionatorio della Consob dinanzi alle Corti europee e nazionali, Conference Paper, pp. 1–12. Retrieved March 28, 2019, from https://www.irpa.eu/wp-content/ uploads/2016/03/I-poteri

Vitkauskas, D., & Sîan, L.-A. (2009). *Right to a fair trial under the European Convention on Human Rights (Article 6)* (pp. 1–90). London: Interights. Retrieved March 28, 2019, from https://pt.scribd.com/document/217013881/Manual-for-Lawyers-Right-to-A-Fair-Trial-under- the-ECHR

Wils, W. P. J. (2011). EU antitrust enforcement powers and procedural rights and guarantees: The interplay between EU law, National law, the charter of fundamental rights of the EU and the European Convention on Human Rights. *World Competition: Law and Economics Review, 34* (2), 1–32. Retrieved March 28, 2019, from https://papers.ssrn.com/sol3/papers.cfm?abstract_ id=1759209

Zagrebelsky, V. (2014). Le sanzioni Consob, l'equo processo e il ne bis in idem nella Cedu. *Giurisprudenza italiana, 5*, 1196–1198.

Zivy, F., & Luc, I. (2010). L'équité procédurale devant l'Autorité de la concurrence. *Concurrences, 4*, 85–92.

Judicial Independence: Constitutional Principle or Human Right?

Xavier Bioy

Contents

1   Introduction

The judge Vincent A. De Gaetano (to whom this *Festschrift* is dedicated) was often asked about the expected impartiality of a judge. This was the case as he has held various judicial functions, and he has passed judgement on these requirements in relation to other judges, in countries other than Malta. Better still, he also passed judgement on the conditions and principles of this impartiality in relation to its two-sided aspect: on the one hand, the collective independence of judges due to their status and careers, and on the other hand, the specific assessment of their

Xavier Bioy is Professor of Public Law at Université Toulouse Capitole.

X. Bioy (✉)
Université Toulouse Capitole, Institut Maurice Hauriou, Toulouse, France
e-mail: xavier.bioy@ut-capitole.fr

© Springer Nature Switzerland AG 2019   63
P. Pinto de Albuquerque, K. Wojtyczek (eds.), *Judicial Power in a Globalized World*, https://doi.org/10.1007/978-3-030-20744-1_4

independence in each case. As President of the Constitutional Court, he was also able to see the vital importance of the principle of the separation of powers, which provides the general framework for these institutional guarantees. Therefore, he appreciates the need to associate subjective rights and institutions without confusing them: "Broadly speaking, it can be said that in the espace juridique of the Convention, the Rule of Law requires not only that society is governed on the basis of laws but also that these laws are the result of a democratic process. This requirement of a democratic process, however, goes beyond the mere notion of majority rule and denotes that decision-making should be a participatory process".[1] In this tribute to one of our most distinguished European judges, we have an opportunity to consider and clarify this point.

Indeed, throughout Europe, the role of different national judges (historically seen from the point of view of the legal State and democracy) was significantly affected by the European and international standard of the right to a fair trial, i.e. the rule of law model. Some conceptual frameworks which take their legal form from the Constitution were revised using other concepts from the corpus of human rights. This change could have been the source of confusion in terms of judicial concepts and principles.

The judicial function is the act of "settling a dispute between two parties with regards to the application of law in a specific situation. In a legal system, a court is a body authorised to settle disputes and ensure that the law is applied fairly".[2] We can add an organic dimension to this functional definition, making the judiciary a collection of bodies principally with a judicial function, but not just that.[3] We need to distinguish other functions, which would lead us to settle the long-standing debate that pits trialists (those who believe there are three constitutionally recognised functions) against dualists (those who believe there are only two functions, legislative and executive, with the judiciary relating to one or the other, according to those authors).

Thus, the judiciary, which had already struggled to find its place in the concept of the separation of powers (particularly in France), was also organised by the requirements of independence, impartiality, protection of res judicata, linked to the right to a fair trial. For a large part of the doctrine, and for the judges themselves, these elements have become almost synonymous. Therefore we can sanction involvement by the legislator or government in the administration of justice, either due to violation of the separation of powers, or disregard of judicial independence as part of a fair trial. Sometimes, for the European judge, the separation of powers is just an element of article 6§1 of the Convention, and for constitutional judges, the separation of powers supports the systems to protect the judiciary or justify procedural guarantees during judicial proceedings.

However, this often unfortunately creates confusion, which shows that the culture of human rights can lead, if we are not careful, to a reduction in the complexity of the constitutional culture. The concept of the separation of powers and the judicial notions or "theories" which implement it exceed or go well beyond the sole question

---

[1] De Gaetano (2018).

[2] Magnon (2014).

[3] Troper (1993).

of the judge's independence at the time when they issue a judgement. The constitutional theory firstly aims to determine the centres of political power which are expressed through legal standards, in order to keep them away from each other and therefore moderate power. But it can also attempt to keep a specific function like the judicial function far from the political system.

Another source of confusion comes from the fact that only the "judge" is referenced, without distinguishing between different adaptations or contexts. As noted by Francis Delpérée,[4] we need to firstly distinguish between the independence of the judicial function (as a materially and formally constitutional power to issue rulings to settle legal disputes) and independence of the judiciary (as a body of elected or appointed judges and benefiting from a common status organising their mandate, payment, protections) and finally that of the judge who specifically settles a dispute. The separation of powers (which is inseparable from the first aspect) refers more broadly than the second two elements to the existence of a representative political force, which expresses itself through the formalisation and institutionalisation of a general normative function represented by the identified bodies. On the other hand, judicial independence—even if it depends, amongst others, on the structural and institutional conditions of the organisation and the functioning of legal systems—is assessed specifically in each body and for each judge who issues judgements. Between the two, the organisation of the recruitment and career of judges is an essential administrative and political parameter, but it is strongly tied to national institutional cultures.

France, which has chosen a career judiciary since the First Empire, is an example of this confusion, which undermines the recognition of an authentic judiciary within the conceptual framework of the separation of powers, whilst also reducing the question of the independence of the judge to that of justice in general. Article 16 of the 1789 Declaration of the Rights of Man and of the Citizen (now included in the Constitution) distinguished between guaranteed rights and the separation of powers. The French Constitutional Council and the French State Council now use it indifferently, sometimes with article 64 of the Constitution, which protects the independence of an ordinary judge (the "legal authority").

As much as the independence of a "judicial power" (when legally dedicated by constitutional sources) is based on the independence of the judges required to make a ruling, they are two different legal notions which should not be confused. We can therefore start by underlining the modern requirements in terms of the independence of courts (Sect. 2), before distinguishing them and linking them to the theory of separation of powers (Sect. 3), ending our discussion with the situation in French law (Sect. 4).

---

[4]Delpérée (1996).

2 The Requirement for Judicial Independence and Its Conditions

The human rights discourse, which has an individualistic point of view, focuses on the impartiality of the judge at the point when they issue their ruling. Institutional, organic or functional independence is therefore sidelined in terms of guaranteeing impartiality. The "constitutional" logic, highlighted in the *Loizidou* case, is not the State logic.

2.1 The Human Rights Discourse in Favour of Impartiality

The European Court states that when necessary to maintain the standard of a fair trial, one of the main objectives of the separation of powers is to guarantee the independence of judges. Whilst constitutional law focuses on identifying the powers to be separated, human rights law assumes that the judge is a guarantee for the litigant who, for their impartiality, needs a status establishing their independence. What is an aim for one becomes a condition for the other. As noted by Frédéric Sudre: "statutory independence is the guarantee of functional independence".[5] That is why the question of the status of prosecuting authorities in criminal matters becomes unclear: when an individual's detention depends on these authorities, they must be impartial in each case, and to do this, they must not depend functionally or organically on the executive.[6] However, impartiality has not remained an abstract requirement (which would bring it closer to independence) but it is assessed *in concreto*, with regards to the reality of the situation and its perception by the litigant.[7] It is therefore less and less an institutional principle, and more a subjective right. The same development affected the oversight of retroactive laws: the European Court replaced the idea that the legislative power could never "influence the legal outcome of a case"[8] with the idea of specific and individual assessment of proportionality, which considers restricted access to the court and the public interest supported by the law.[9]

---

[5]Sudre et al. (2019).

[6]ECHR, Gr. Ch., 29 March 2010, *Medvedyev and others vs. France*, n° 3394/03.

[7]ECHR, 24 May 1989, *Hauschildt vs. Denmark, § 47, series A n° 154.*

[8]ECHR, 9 December 1994, *Stran Greek Refineries and Stratis Andreadis vs. Greece*, no 13427/87.

[9]ECHR, 23 October 1997, *National and Provincial Building Society and others* vs. United Kingdom, req. n° 17/1996/736/933-935.

2.2   The Link Between Impartiality and Independence

Within the framework of article 6§1, impartiality requires independence as a guarantee. In turn, when the question of the independence of the courts is considered, the European Court sometimes refers to the principle of the separation of powers, and relies on the rules of national constitutions to assess any potential violation. The constitutionalist tradition, however, aims to initially draw up the outlines of a judicial function which should be organically created, potentially by creating a supreme court responsible for centralising the making of law and/or a high council of justice (or judicial power) which manages the judiciary whilst representing its interests. These constitutional aspects are part of a country's political identity, the choice of political institutions, and only ultimately refer to the matter of the litigant. The independence of the judicial function has its own place to legitimise the courts by the function that they fulfil, and by the links held with the theory of representation.

Unlike other civil servants, judges benefit from specific guarantees, linked to the independence required of judges, which the Court believes to be essential to perform judicial functions. Thus in the case *Baka vs. Hungary*,[10] regarding a measure reducing the length of mandate of supreme court judges, with immediate effect on the current mandate of its president, the European Court condemned the State, referring to the link between the status of judges and the independence of the judiciary as a system (particularly when the seemingly abstract law targets a president considered an opponent by the executive). The measure was at a constitutional level, which would prevent any jurisdictional oversight. The Court subjectivises the effects of constitutional principles relating to judicial independence, either for the benefit of litigants or the judges themselves (§ 108). As a result, the violation of article 6 results from the growing relevance, recognised by international instruments and the European Council, of procedural fairness in cases regarding the dismissal or termination of judges, and notably of the need for an authority independent of the executive and legislative powers to intervene in any decision relating to termination of a judge's mandate.

3   The Constitutional Judicial Function in the Separation of Powers

It is still very difficult to establish a positive theory on the separation of powers which is not just the Montesquieu precept, which states that there should not be just one single body performing all normative functions. The absence of the judicial function leads to confusion between independence and separation.

---

[10]ECHR, GC, 23 June 2016, *Baka vs. Hungary*, n° 20261/12.

3.1 The Difficulty in Determining the Position of the Judicial Function

We will refer here to the "judicial function" and not the "judicial power". We generally understand "power" (in terms of the theory of the separation of powers) as all constitutional bodies which exercise a normative function. For if the function is understood as the constitutional status of a specific normative action (settling disputes and completing related tasks), referring to "jurisdictional power" would imply a form of organic concentration of this function, or at least, a form of institutional representation which is not performed by the legislative power or executive power. It is also not necessary for the constitutional text to use these terms for them to exist legally.

In many political regimes, constitutional texts place the judicial function on the same level as others, giving it a political weight, which is accompanied by suitable forms of institutional autonomy (existence of a higher court of justice,[11] financial autonomy, control of careers, control of judicial disciplinary proceedings, management of resources, etc.). But in others (such as France), several factors can lead to not including the judicial function in the separation of powers: either because the bodies are widely fragmented in "orders" without links between them, or because we do not recognise the judge as having "creator" normative power, or because we do not believe that any form of political power can be implemented. It is precisely this final aspect that impedes any reasoning which attempts to link judicial independence and the separation of powers: the powers which are "separate" (whether this separation is "flexible" or "strict") are required to work together for a common political action and (in a "flexible" manner) to assume a form of "responsibility" which can lead to dismissal of members performing the function. Thus no power is "the subject of the other" and each can be referred to for relevant questions. However the judicial function can relate to the behaviour of the government or assemblies, their action or behaviour; but also, it cannot (except in rare and incorrect exceptions) refer to itself and, also (except when abused), judges can never be held politically liable for having worked incorrectly on a common normative function. The judicial function is not part of the separation of powers in the same way as the others. While we can say that it is a "power" (it makes decisions on political matters), it is "political" (it sometimes makes decisions which affect public life), it is "normative" (the judge is a *de jure* or *de facto* producer of new standards), it is "protected from other powers" (by various independence procedures given to courts or judiciary management bodies), etc., its independence is not another name for its separation from the others.

---

[11]Renoux (2000).

3.2   The Possible Confusion Between Separation and Independence

In France, doctrine is based on a reading which results in a misunderstanding of the judicial function and prevents its institutionalisation: the exaggerated promotion of the role of creator of law when determining what is a power, the lack of an unambiguous theory on representation, and the lack of a theory on the effective responsibilities of judges,[12] leads to disregard for the theory of the separation of powers. The pervasiveness of normative creation to define the notion of power, seems to prevent any consensus on the position of judges, to the extent that this question remains the main bone of contention of the doctrine.

We generally continue to think that the answer to the question of the third power is found in the choice between "willing interpretation" and "knowing interpretation". Yet without doubt, whether we choose one or the other, or whether we combine them, as is often the case, this leads to nothing other than stating that we "need"—for reasons relating to the specific nature of the judicial function—to organically separate it from the others, either to protect it (independence) or to prevent a "government of judges". Neutralising the power of judges starts by preventing them from setting a legal precedent.

However, we do not have an "old" version on one hand where the judge does not exercise a creative function, and a "modern" version on the other hand where we would discover that the judge does. There has always been a consensus on this power, without there being an agreement on the position of the judicial function in the separation of powers, such as enforcement, co-legislation or a third function. Since the organic question of separation of the judicial function is based on a different assessment, that of the guarantee of independence, and the need to protect the other powers from the judge's influence.

Secondly, non-recognition of the judge as a representative, i.e. the dominant choice of an organic theory of representation, limits any vague hope to include judges in the theory of the separation of powers. Conversely, the opposing discourse recognising the quality of the judicial power or counter-power, all the more so when it results in recognising the representative quality of the judge, would require a very legitimate responsibility, a functional legitimacy,[13] which would endorse the transition from a law guaranteed by the State and its judges to a judge creating a social link.[14]

Independence, in general, has other grounds; it is either a requirement of the Constitution as a general guarantee of freedoms by the legislator, or the requirement of a fair trial as a guarantee of impartiality. It is therefore exercised with regards to a larger circle of players, including parties to the trial, public authorities and any pressure group and other judges themselves (which the European Court imposes

---

[12]Bioy (2007).

[13]Krynen (2004).

[14]Raynaud (1993).

itself[15]). It should exist even in a system which does not practice the separation of other powers. This is without doubt the reason why the debate between "trialists and dualists" has always failed. Whether or not there is an independent judicial function, judges must—because they are judges—be protected from pressure. The organic aspect is therefore secondary. The existence of a different European basis undoubt-edly indicates that independence is based on the quality of the right to appeal rather than separation. On the other hand, something that is not the consequence of guaranteed rights is also not caused by separation: judges can be appointed, pro-moted or dismissed (in the event of misconduct) by the executive power.[16]

4   The Specific Case of France

The constitutional law of 3 June 1958 only indicates the separation of the executive and legislative power, so it would seem that few things have changed. The judicial function is growing thanks to the guaranteed rights by the judge and the system of including judges in the created powers. Constitutional Council case law still does not exactly reflect this idea; the Council has continued to call for the separation of powers as a basis for the judge's independence.

4.1   An Informal Judicial Function

The majority of authors in France use the term "authority" for an ordinary judge to deny their status of power. The text's argument here is both false and pointless. Existence as a constitutionally identified and dedicated "power" would not be a *de facto* status but a political choice reflected by the prohibition of "judge-made laws". In France, the judge is not recognised as a power (but they hold it), to avoid competing with the Parliament. Montesquieu described the judge as a "null power"; what the Fifth Republic has reflected in the term "judicial authority", not giving a constitutional status to the administrative judge and specialising the constitutional judge, without a representative body or supreme court in this case. Therefore at best we can only see a disorganised counter-power or a "power to prevent".[17]

In 1958, when the Constitution was being drafted, the State Council confirmed the government's choice to replace the term "justice" with "judicial authority". It also indicates that administrative justice, whilst functionally jurisdictional, is mate-rially and organically related to the executive. From the outset, the dualism of powers positions the courts as a law enforcement function that must remain

---

[15]ECHR, 6 October 2011, *Agrokompleks vs. Ukraine*, 23465/03.

[16]Fabri et al. (2005); Jean (2000).

[17]Hourquebie (2004); Bioy (2016).

independent of the executive: separate from the legislative but only functionally independent from the executive.[18] However this sidelining has not prevented the principle of the separation of powers from being pointed out to prevent violation of judicial independence.

4.2 A Mixture of Legal Principles

In France, we often confuse judicial independence and the separation of powers. It is essentially through guarantees of a fair trial that the judicial function is now recognised by the Constitution, at least through some statutory articles which it dedicates to its bodies. The Constitutional Council is itself protected against a law that attempted to require it to open its archives, which would have allowed pressure to be placed on it. The gathering of prior consent aims to protect the separation of powers.[19] It is up to the Constitutional Council to implement this aspect, firstly by indirect routes, then through the Core Principles. It also underlined that the independence of the High Council of the Judiciary is a guarantee of independence of the judicial authority.[20]

However since the decision dated 21 January 1994, regarding the law on urban planning and construction (93-335 DC), article 16 of the Declaration on Human Rights has become, with its symbolic weight, the centre point of a vast system which organically and functionally makes judges recognised constitutional figures.[21]

In 1980, the Constitutional Council prevented the legislator from condemning court decisions or ordering them in any way, for example by making the court's power to apply sentences subject to a favourable opinion from an administrative commission in order to grant probation. In this case, the legislator misunderstood both the principle of the separation of powers and the principle of judicial independence.[22] The entire "validation laws" system (which involves including in laws the expected effects of an administrative action overturned by a court) must respect both the separation of powers and the rights of the litigant.[23]

Pursuant to art. 16 of the Declaration of the Rights of Man and of the Citizen, which includes various standards, guaranteed rights (the right to a fair trial) seems to be considered more than the separation of powers. Th. Renoux notes that "the separation of powers was never understood by the constitutional court as merely institutional, solely protecting courts, but as a guarantee for the citizen, the

---

[18]Bioy (2013).

[19]Conseil constitutionnel, 9 July 2008, 2008-566 DC, cons. 8.

[20]Conseil constitutionnel, 19 July 2010, 2010-611 DC.

[21]Fraisse (2014).

[22]Conseil constiitutionnel, 2008-562 DC, 21 Feb. 2008, cons. 34.

[23]Decision n° 2013-366 QPC of 14 February 2014: adopting the European terminology.

litigant".[24] The protection of the courts has never been an effect of the separation of powers, but the will to protect the independence required by guaranteed rights.

Nevertheless, the French State Council bases the cancellation of the withdrawal of a judge's appointment on the two-fold argument of independence and the separation of powers[25]: "Considering that the principle of the separation of powers and the principle of judicial independence, as reflected by these constitutional provisions, require that specific judicial guarantees are linked to the role of judge; that they notably mean that the latter cannot be removed from this role, and the specific related guarantees in terms of express provisions of their status and in the conditions set out by the latter".

The functional unification of justice is asserted more than ever, making the protection of res judicata an aspect of the separation of powers, as shown by the decision of the Constitutional Council of 29 December 2005, "2005 amended finance law" which, based only on the separation of powers, regarding a system relating to legislative approval, sets the case law of the court of justice and the State Council against the legislator in the name of the separation of powers and compliance with past res judicata decisions; what Bertrand Mathieu calls "the protection of jurisdictionally acquired situations".[26] In the background, procedural guarantees are creating a more unified judicial function.

However there is more confusion in France: when the French constitutional court bases the constitutional reserve of the administrative judge's power on the "French idea of the separation of powers". How will this dual jurisdiction result in a form of separation of powers? Does this mean that the line between legislative and executive goes through the middle of the judiciary? Does this not rule out any form of unity with the third function?

The reason is actually very old: Blandine Barret-Kriegel[27] has shown how in France, until the sixteenth century, justice appealed to all State functions (notion of "State of justice"), then how, conversely, from the distinction made by Jean Bodin between the *merum* of judges (authority provided by law) and the *mixtum* of the civil judge (judicial activity), the application of the law, the real function of sovereignty became that of administration (notion of "State of finances"). That is why the dualist perception of the separation of powers does not allow for or create an identity for the judiciary. There are many guarantees of independence, but they do not create conditions to include the judiciary in the separation of powers. There is non-interference in the work of the judge, but none of the institution, collaboration, control elements, etc. needed to apply the theory of separation.

The "French style" separation of powers only causes confusion and does not protect the litigant or formalise the judicial function. France is therefore, from this point of view, doubly out of line on the European stage. We need to ensure that the

---

[24]Renoux et al. (2014).

[25]CE, sect., 1 Oct. 2010, n° 311938: JurisData n° 2010-017254.

[26]Mathieu (2006).

[27]Barret-Kriegel (2001).

standard of a fair trial does not impede collective expectations for the creation of a judicial function. Current subjectification through human rights has everything to gain from continuing to be applied with the objectivity of the arrangement of constitutional powers, while remaining separate issues.

References

Barret-Kriegel, B. (2001). *Réflexions sur la justice, Les Chemins de l'État* (Vol. 5). Paris: Plon.

Bioy, X. (2007). La responsabilité du pouvoir juridictionnel. In SEGUR (Ph) (Ed.), *La protection des pouvoirs constitués* (pp. 191–213). Brussels: Bruylant.

Bioy, X. (2013). La transgression de la séparation des pouvoirs. In J.-J. Sueur & P. Richard (Eds.), *La transgression* (p. 220). Paris: Bruylant.

Bioy, X. (2016). L'émergence d'une troisième fonction constitutionnelle: la faculté d'empêcher juridictionnelle. In S. Mouton (Ed.), *Le régime représentatif à l'épreuve de la justice constitutionnelle*, Lextenso, coll. Grands colloques, 2016, p.

Delpérée, F. (1996). La Constitution et les juges. In *Constitution et justice, Recueil des cours de l'Académie internationale de droit constitutionnel, Presses de l'Université des sciences sociales de Toulouse*, p. 55.

Fabri, M., Jean, J.-P., Langbroeck, Ph., & Pauliat, H. (2005). *L'administration de la justice en Europe et l'évaluation de sa qualité*, LGDJ, Montchrestien, coll. Grands colloques.

Fraisse, R. (2014). L'article 16 de la Déclaration, clef de voûte des droits et libertés. *Nouveaux Cahiers du Conseil Constitutionnel, 44*, 23.

Gaetano, V. (2018). *Vincent De Gaetano on the Rule of Law.* https://manueldelia.com/2018/12/vincent-de-gaetano-on-rule-of-law-read-the-speech-here/; site consulted on 3 April 2019.

Hourquebie, F. (2004). *Sur l'émergence du contre-pouvoir juridictionnel sous la Vème République* (678 p). Bruylant.

Jean, J.-P. (2000). Justice: quels modes d'administration et d'évaluation pour un service public complexe qui doit rendre des décisions en toute indépendance? In M. Fabri & P. Langbroeck (Eds.), *The challenge for chance for judicial systems: Developing a public administration perspective.* Amsterdam: IIAS and IOS Press.

Krynen, J. (2004). Introduction. In *La légitimité des juges* (Vol. 1, p. 19). Presses de l'Université des Sciences sociales de Toulouse, Travaux de l'IFR.

Magnon, X. (2014). Retour sur quelques définitions premières en droit constitutionnel: que sont une "juridiction constitutionnelle", une "Cour constitutionnelle" et une "Cour suprême"? Proposition de définitions modales et fonctionnelles, *Mélanges P. Bon*, Dalloz, p. 305.

Mathieu, B. (2006, January 13). Les lois de finances au crible de la sécurité juridique (A propos des décisions 2005-230 et 2005-231 du 29 décembre 2005 du Conseil constitutionnel). *Les petites affiches, 10*, 4–7.

Raynaud, Ph. (1993). Le juge, la politique et la philosophie, *Situations de la démocratie* (p. 110). Gallimard – Le seuil.

Renoux, T.-S. (2000). *Les conseils supérieurs de la magistrature en Europe.* La doc. Frcse.

Renoux, T.-S., de Michel, V., & Magnon, X. (2014). *Code constitutionnel* (p. 257). Litec.

Sudre, F., Milano, L., & Surrel, H. (2019). *Droit européen et international des droits de l'homme* (14th ed.p. 618). PUF.

Troper, M. (1993). La notion de pouvoir judiciaire au début de la révolution française. *Revue du Droit Public*, 842.

The Role of the European Associations and Organisations of Judges in Promoting and Safeguarding the Judicial Independence

Grzegorz Borkowski

Contents

1 Introduction

Supposedly every active member of the European judiciary knows that Vincent Anthony De Gaetano is the judge in respect of Malta on the European Court of Human Rights; quite a lot of them realize that before being elected by the

Grzegorz Borkowski is Judge of the District Court in Radzyń Podlaski, seconded to Regional Court Warszawa-Praga in Warsaw, former Head of Office in National Council of Judiciary.

G. Borkowski (✉)
Civil Division, Regional Court Warszawa-Praga, Warsaw, Poland

© Springer Nature Switzerland AG 2019   75
P. Pinto de Albuquerque, K. Wojtyczek (eds.), *Judicial Power in a Globalized World*, https://doi.org/10.1007/978-3-030-20744-1_5

Parliamentary Assembly of the Council of Europe to the position on the 22 June 2010 he had previously been Chief Justice in Malta and also became President of the Constitutional Court, of the Court of Appeal and of the Court of Criminal Appeal, and Deputy Chairman of the Commission for the Administration of Justice. What might be less commonly known, though, is the fact that Chief Justice Vincent Anthony De Gaetano was also a founding member of the Association of Judges and Magistrates of Malta.[1]

This paper aims to show the importance of the judicial associations in the protection of the judicial independence. Using the Maltese example: the Association of Judges and Magistrates of Malta was formed in January 2001 with the aim of promoting the interests of its members, including:

1. to promote the interests of its members in their professional capacity;
2. to promote the independence of the judiciary;
3. to promote the highest standards of judicial conduct among its members;
4. to promote the general interests of its members, including those interests arising upon retirement from the bench;
5. to promote the exchange of ideas on the administration of justice;
6. to further the cultural, intellectual and legal proficiency of its members;
7. to promote and maintain contacts with judges and magistrates abroad, with national and international associations, and in particular national and international associations of judges and magistrates.[2]

2   The Importance of the Principle of Judicial Independence

2.1   The International Documents Regarding Principle of Judicial Independence

As one can see, promoting the judicial independence is one of the main tasks of the Association of Judges and Magistrates of Malta, which goes perfectly in line with the European standards, reflected in Recommendation CM/Rec(2010)12 of the Committee of Ministers of the Council of Europe to member states on judges: independence, efficiency and responsibilities. According to para. 25 of the Recommendation: "Judges should be free to form and join professional

---

[1]http://www.judiciarymalta.gov.mt/file.aspx?f=650, Accessed 7 Apr 2019.

[2]This goes in line with the Code of Ethics for Members of the Judiciary specifically provides in Rule 27 that "*Members of the Judiciary shall have the right to form their own professional association in order to safeguard their rights and interests, and individual members of the Judiciary shall be entitled to choose freely whether or not to be members of such a professional association. They shall also have the right to affiliate, whether through such professional association or individually, with other associations which may better attain or ensure the aims which their association aspires to.*" See: http://www.judiciarymalta.gov.mt/the-association. Accessed 7 Apr 2019.

organisations whose objectives are to safeguard their independence, protect their interests and promote the rule of law".

The above-quoted paragraph on judicial associations is placed in the chapter of the Recommendation focused on internal independence, therefore one can say that associating among judges is a way for the democratisation of the judiciary. As Gualtiero Michelini, President of MEDEL,[3] puts it: "the gathering of experiences and the participation in delivering the justice service to citizens is contrary to a strictly hierarchical vision of the judiciary, and aims at putting together magistrates in different parts of the territory of the country, with different positions, age, and specialisations, with a view to building common awareness, identifying common problems, needs and requests, addressing as appropriate parliaments, governments, media and civil society".[4]

Leaving Europe for a while, it is worth noticing that the Beijing Principles also recognise this idea when they stipulate that "Judges shall be free subject to any applicable law to form and join an association of judges to represent their interests and promote their professional training and to take such other action to protect their independence as may be appropriate".[5]

Similarly, Principle 9 of the UN Basic Principles on the Independence of the Judiciary states that "Judges shall be free to form and join associations of judges or other organisations to represent their interests, to promote their professional training and to protect their judicial independence". The three objectives, as specified in the UN Basic Principles, namely to: (i) represent the judiciary's interests; (ii) promote their professional training; and (iii) protect their judicial independence, are amongst the most important aims of judges' associations. Therefore, as one can see, the importance of the professional training is in this case directly emphasized and rightly so, as the judicial training, leading to the professionalism of judges is, in the doctrine, perceived as one of the guarantees of the judicial independence (see below). The judiciary, providing important checks and balances on the executive and legislative branches, helps to ensure the rule of law. The judges must therefore have the best possible education available to ensure the democracy remains strong.[6]

There is a great role to be played by the judicial associations, both on the national and supranational level, in defending the judicial independence. It is, therefore, important to understand what the judicial independence really means—as stated in Bangalore Principle of Judicial Conduct of 2002, judicial independence is a pre-requisite to the rule of law and a fundamental guarantee of a fair trial. Without

---

[3]Magistrats Européens pour la Démocratie et les Libertés.

[4]Michelini (2018), p. 184.

[5]Beijing Statement of Principles of the Independence of the Judiciary in the LAWASIA Region, paragraph 9. See also the Principles and Guidelines on the Right to a Fair Trial and Legal Assistance in Africa, Principle A, paragraph 4 (t): "Judicial officers shall be free to form and join professional associations or other organizations to represent their interests, to promote their professional training and to protect their status".

[6]Brunson and Schmucker (2016), p. 196.

the independence of judiciary from other branches of powers and without the inner independence of judges, the right to fair trial would be purely illusory.

The importance of the principle of the judicial independence may be better understood when one realizes that the right to independent tribunal is guaranteed for the European citizens not only in their domestic legal system (either on the constitutional level or in respective procedural provisions), but also in:

– The Universal Declaration of Human Rights—as stated in its article 10: "Everyone is entitled in full equality to a fair and public hearing by an independent and impartial tribunal, in the determination of his rights and obligations and of any criminal charge against him";
– International Covenant on Civil and Political Rights, stating in article 14(1) that: "All persons shall be equal before the courts and tribunals. In the determination of any criminal charge against him, or of his rights and obligations in a suit at law, everyone shall be entitled to a fair and public hearing by a competent, independent and impartial tribunal established by law [. . .],
– European Convention on Human Rights—its article 6 says: "In the determination of his civil rights and obligations or of any criminal charge against him, everyone is entitled to a fair and public hearing within a reasonable time by an independent and impartial tribunal established by law" [. . .];
– Charter of Fundamental Rights of the European Union, which in art. 47 guarantees that: "[. . .] Everyone is entitled to a fair and public hearing within a reasonable time by an independent and impartial tribunal previously established by law [. . .].

There are also numerous international acts dealing specifically with the issue of the judicial independence and, at the European level, these documents include, inter alia:

– the UN Basic Principles on the Independence of the Judiciary,
– the Venice Commission Report on the Independence of the Judicial System—Part I: The Independence of Judges (2010),
– the OSCE/ODIHR Kyiv Recommendations on Judicial Independence in Eastern Europe, South Caucasus and Central Asia,
– the Recommendation of the Council of Europe Committee of Ministers on "Judges: Independence, Efficiency and Responsibilities" adopted in 2010,
– the opinions of the Consultative Council of European Judges,
– the European Charter on the Statute for Judges.

2.2 The Safeguards of Judicial Independence

In the doctrine, the judicial independence is sometimes perceived through its guarantees which may have both procedural and substantive (organizational) aspects. The first ones, i.e. the procedural guarantees, such as: secrecy of debates and voting, court hearings open to public, Judge's discrecy when examining the evidence etc. apply to all kinds of court proceedings (criminal, civil and administrative) and will not be discussed here,[7] whilst within the latter, i.e. organizational aspects, the following guarantees may be found: the sufficient moral and ethical level and professional qualifications, irremovability of a judge, financial independence, *incompatibilitas*, i.e. restriction that a judge may work as a judge only (with the usual exception of an academic career), as well as political neutrality of a judge and disciplinary responsibility.[8]

Nevertheless, the European Court of Human Rights stated that although the notion of the separation of powers between the political organs of government and the judiciary has assumed growing importance in the Court's case-law, neither Article 6 nor any other provision of the Convention requires States to comply with any theoretical constitutional concepts regarding the permissible limits of the powers' interaction. The question is always whether, in a given case, the requirements of the Convention are met and the Court usually examines the three following criteria:

– the manner of appointment of its members and the duration of their term of office,
– the existence of guarantees against outside pressures and.
– whether the body presents an appearance of independence.[9]

Especially the latter two criteria seem to be interesting from the point of view of the judicial associations. In case of the guarantees against outside pressure it must be stressed though, that the Court examines the vulnerability of a judge not only against outside, but also inside pressure. Judicial independence demands that individual judges be free from undue influences outside the judiciary, and from within. Internal judicial independence requires that they be free from directives or pressures from fellow judges or those who have administrative responsibilities in the court, such as the president of the court or the president of a division in the court. The absence of sufficient safeguards securing the independence of judges within the judiciary, in particular vis-à-vis their judicial superiors, may lead the Court to conclude that an applicant's doubts as to the independence and impartiality of a court may be said to have been objectively justified.[10]

There is a broad ECHR case-law related to the issue of appearance of independence. What is at stake is the confidence which the courts in a democratic society must inspire in the public and above all, as far as criminal proceedings are concerned, in the accused.[11] Needless to say, such appearance may be very

---

[7]See more: Borkowski (2014), pp. 5–20, available at: http://journals.pan.pl/Content/93315/mainfile.pdf?handler=pdf. Accessed 7 Apr 2019.

[8]The issue of judges' membership in other than "purely" judicial associations, such as e.g. Masonic lodge, is beyond the scope of this paper. See judgments: Maestri v. Italy [GC §§37-42] and N.F. v. Italy (§ 31) as well as Schabas (2015), p. 511.

[9]See a detailed study by Kuijer (2004), pp. 203–303.

[10]See judgments: Parlov-Tkalcic v. Croatia, § 86; Daktaras v. Lithuania, § 36; Moiseyev v. Russia, § 184.

[11]See judgment Şahiner v. Turkey, § 44.

subjective and the same court may seem independent to someone and not independent to someone else. For this reason the Court is in the position that in deciding whether there is a legitimate reason to fear that a particular court lacks independence or impartiality, the standpoint of the accused is important but not decisive. What is decisive is whether his doubts can be held to be objectively justified, so, in other words no problem arises as regards independence when the Court is of the view that an "objective observer" would have no cause for concern about this matter in the circumstances of the case at hand.[12]

3   The Organisations Providing the Judicial Training

It is often stressed that the initial and continuous training is essential for the judiciary to ensure high ethical standards and competent judges. Without these opportunities, judges cannot reach decisions competently, fairly and efficiently, which can affect the administration of justice more widely. Needless to say, incompetent judges are also more likely to be influenced in their decisions, thereby undermining the principle of independence and impartiality. Judicial associations can, therefore, be involved in developing judges' professional skills, particularly practical skills, although in Europe the professional judicial training is usually performed by the National Training Institutions (NTIs), such as the Judicial Schools, Training Centres etc. Those NTIs may, nevertheless, also create network, promoting standards, good practices, as well as strengthening the judicial independence (see below about EJTN). Judicial associations can also perform important function in raising awareness amongst the public about the judiciary, the law, the legal system and human rights. Taking examples from another side of the Atlantic Ocean, the American Federal Judges Association promotes public education about the judiciary, the Constitution, the role of the courts, judicial independence and the rule of law, as it has a dedicated Civics Education Task Force to evaluate the effectiveness of court websites, and to recommend best practices for public access to information about the courts. Similarly, the Canadian Superior Courts Judges Association's mandate includes promoting public understanding of the role of judges in the justice system.[13]

---

[12]Clarke v. the United Kingdom (dec.).

[13]The Horizon Institute ORG. (2015) https://www.thehorizoninstitute.org/usr/library/documents/main/paper-from-horizon-institute-on-associations-of-judges-in-different-countries-.pdf. Accessed 7 Apr 2019.

3.1 European Judicial Training Network (EJTN)

According to the European Judicial Training Network (EJTN) website, it is the principal platform and promoter for the training and exchange of knowledge of the European judiciary. EJTN represents the interests of over 120,000 European judges, prosecutors and judicial trainers across Europe. Formed in 2000, EJTN's fields of interest include EU, civil, criminal and commercial law and linguistics and societal issues training. The vision of EJTN is to help to foster a common legal and judicial European culture. EJTN develops training standards and curricula, coordinates judicial training exchanges and programmes, disseminates training expertise and promotes cooperation between EU judicial training institutions.

One of the projects in which EJTN is engaged is directly related to the key role of the independent and impartial judiciary in safeguarding the rule of law and making the right to access justice as well as other fundamental rights, as enshrined in the Charter of Fundamental Rights of the European Union and other CoE and international human rights instruments, a reality for every individual.

Following the decision of the European Commission (DG Justice and Consumers Directorate-General) to allocate a grant to organise a series of 6 seminars, one webinar, draft the Manual/Practitioners Guide on aspects of rule of law and the Training Strategy Guide on rule of law EJTN agreed to implement these tasks. The main objective of these seminars is to make the participants reflect on the international and national standards of the Rule of Law and to address aspects of protection of fundamental rights and rule of law as reflected in the ECJ and ECtHR case law, by increasing the understanding of what is the role and daily obligations in private and professional duties of judges and prosecutors, of the EU Member States and six western Balkan nations, namely Albania, Bosnia and Herzegovina, Macedonia, Montenegro, Serbia and Kosovo.

The participating judges and prosecutors learn that the rule of law is a prerequisite for individuals' trust that justice prevails, the prosecution services are autonomous and the courts are impartial. The justice systems firmly anchored in the rule of law are key for the implementation of EU law and for the strengthening of mutual trust. Whatever the model of the national justice system or the legal tradition in which it is based, legality, legal certainty, prevention of abuse of power, independence and impartiality, autonomy, effectiveness and quality are essential rule of law components on which any justice system should be based. These are common qualities which ensure that in all European systems, judiciaries of every branch (civil, criminal and administrative) as well as prosecution services all ensure that the rule of law is guaranteed, especially by the fair, impartial and efficient administration of justice in all cases and at all stages of the proceedings within their competence.

The topics of the seminars cover inter alia such issues as: relationship of judges/ prosecutors in work environment and vis-à-vis other state powers, infringement of the security of tenure of judges and prosecutors, aspects of independence of judges and prosecutors, judicial and prosecutorial integrity: standards of ethical and professional conduct, as well as public discussion and criticism of judges and prosecutors, the role of media and public trust. EJTN activities, such as seminars on human and fundamental rights and, especially, the most popular Exchange Programme allows judges and prosecutors to exchange best practices but also discuss about the problems of the judiciary in their respective countries.[14]

3.2 The European Programme for Human Rights Education for Legal Professionals (HELP)

Another body dealing with the judicial training on the European level is The European Programme for Human Rights Education for Legal Professionals (HELP)[15] which supports the Council of Europe member states in implementing the European Convention on Human Rights (the Convention) at the national level, in accordance with the Committee of Ministers Recommendation (2004) 4, the 2010 Interlaken Declaration, the 2012 Brighton Declaration and the 2015 Brussels declaration. The HELP Network, the only pan-European peer-to-peer Human Rights Training Network, is composed of representatives from National Training Institutions for Judges and Prosecutors (NTIs) and Bar Associations (BAs) of the 47 member states of the Council of Europe.[16] Although it is a body not dealing exclusively with the judiciary and public prosecution, yet its role in the judicial education on the European level, especially outside EU, must be stressed.

As the Secretary General of the Council of Europe noted: "Well-trained judges, with a high level of professional competence, are more likely to withstand improper attempts at influencing their decision making, as well as to ensure more generally that justice is delivered in a fair and independent trial. This is why the Council of Europe also engages in supporting member states in their efforts to strengthen the professional skills and knowledge of judges. Much has been achieved in co-operation with the European Union and its European Judicial Training Network to ensure a coherent approach to human rights training. The Human Rights Education for Legal Professionals (HELP) Programme has developed novel online techniques to cover wider professional audiences in each of our 47 member states".[17]

---

[14]See EJTN web-site: http://www.ejtn.eu/. Accessed 7 Apr 2019.

[15]The author had the honour to be the first Chair of HELP's Consultative Board in 2014–2016: https://www.coe.int/en/web/help/help-consultative-board. Accessed 7 Apr 2019.

[16]https://www.coe.int/en/web/help/home?desktop=true. Accessed 7 Apr 2019.

[17]State of Democracy, Human Rights and the Rule of Law. Role of Institutions, threats to institutions. Report by the Secretary General of the Council of Europe 2018, p. 13, available at: https://rm.coe.int/state-of-democracy-human-rights-and-the-rule-of-law-role-of-institutio/168086c0c5. Accessed 7 Apr 2019.

3.3   The International Organization for Judicial Training (IOJT)

It is worth to mention that there is also an organisation dealing with the judicial training and education on the world level, namely The International Organization for Judicial Training (IOJT) which was established in 2002 in order to promote the rule of law by supporting the work of judicial education institutions around the world. The mission of the IOJT is realized through international and regional conferences and other exchanges that provide opportunities for judges and judicial educators to discuss strategies for establishing and developing training centres, designing effective curricula, developing faculty capacity, and improving teaching methodology. The IOJT is a volunteer, non-profit organization and relies upon the efforts and good will of its members. The organization is governed by a General Assembly of its members which meets every 2–3 years during the international conference. There is an elected Board of Governors which consists of an Executive Committee, Regional Deputy Presidents, additional Deputy Presidents and Governors. As of August 2015, the IOJT has 123 member-institutes from 75 countries.[18]

IOJT's Declaration of Judicial Training Principles in its point 2 state that "To preserve judicial independence, the judiciary and judicial training institutions should be responsible for the design, content, and delivery of judicial training." Also the explanatory commentaries to the declaration show a clear connection between the judicial training and preserving the judicial independence: "By using established best practices, such as conducting needs assessments and evaluations, the judiciary and judicial training institutions can preserve independence and autonomy in providing their training."[19]

On the national level, the educational activities of judicial associations are not always welcomed by the authorities, especially by the administrative branch of power. For example, the Polish Association of Judges "Iustitia" takes active part in the so-called constitutional weeks, organized in both primary and secondary schools all over Poland by Professor Zbigniew Hołda Association,[20] as well in other events aimed at the popularization of the knowledge about the Constitution and the Rule of Law. For this reason, many judges, as well as prosecutors, face the disciplinary charges against them.[21]

---

[18]http://www.iojt.org/About-Us.aspx. Accessed 7 Apr 2019.

[19]http://www.iojt.org/~/media/Microsites/Files/IOJT/Microsite/2017-Principles.ashx.   Accessed 7 Apr 2019.

[20]See: http://stowarzyszenieholda.pl/projekty/tydzien-konstytucyjny/. Accessed 7 Apr 2019.

[21]See the Justice Defend Committee Report: A Country That Punishes (2019) regarding the disciplinary proceedings against judges and prosecutors in Poland at: https://komitetobronysprawiedliwosci.pl/app/uploads/2019/02/Raport-KOS_eng.pdf.   Accessed 7 Apr 2019.

4 The Importance of the Judicial Associations and Organisations on the European Level

4.1 European Association of Judges (EAJ)

Another European judicial association with its world counterpart is the European Association of Judges (EAJ)- member of the International Association of Judges (IAJ). In this case, the relationship is even stronger, as, according to the Art. 1 of the Statutes of the European Association of Judges: The European Association of Judges is a regional organization within the International Association of Judges. EAJ comprises judicial associations from 44 European countries (among them the Maltese Association of Judges and Association of Polish Judges "Iustitia"—see below).[22] According to Art, 2 p. 2 of the Statutes EAJ works to promote closer European cooperation in all areas pertaining to the judiciaries of the member states and international and supranational judiciaries, not exceeding the European level.

The aims of EAJ are perfectly in line with the European standards in this regard. As an association of judges (not a judicial organisation), EAJ is very active in protecting the judicial independence, e.g. by issuing statements, resolutions or open letters.[23] EAJ has also issued in 1993 a commonly referred to document-Judges' Charter in Europe.[24]

4.2 International Association of Judges (IAJ)

The International Association of Judges (IAJ) was founded in Salzburg (Austria) in 1953. It is a professional, non-political, international organisation, bringing together national associations of judges, not individual judges, approved by the Central Council for admission to the Association. The main aim of the Association is to safeguard the independence of the judiciary, which is an essential requirement of the judicial function, guaranteeing human rights and freedom. The organization currently encompasses 90 such national associations or representative groups, from five Continents. The IAJ has four Regional Groups: the European Association of Judges, the Iberoamerican Group, the African Group, the Asian, North American and Oceanian Group.

---

[22]http://www.iaj-uim.org/regional-groups/. Accessed 7 Apr 2019.

[23]See e.g. the common Statement of Platform EAJ, AEAJ, MEDEL and J4J on the unlawful sentence against Murat Arslan, Resolutions on Poland and Serbia (both dated May 2018) or the Open Letter on Poland – available at: https://www.iaj-uim.org/document-author/group-europe-eaj/?orderby=title&order=asc%2F. Accessed 7 Apr 2019.

[24]https://www.iaj-uim.org/iuw/wp-content/uploads/2013/01/Statuto-Giudice-EAJ.pdf. Accessed 7 Apr 2019.

4.3 Magistrats Européens pour la Démocratie et les Libertés (MEDEL)

Another European Judicial Association is, already mentioned above, MEDEL. According to its Statutes, an association denominated "Magistrats Européens pour la Démocratie et les Libertés", abbreviated as MEDEL, has its seat is in Strasbourg. Its goals are as follows:

1. The establishment of a common debate among magistrates from different Countries to support European community integration, in view of the creation of a European political union;
2. the defense of the independence of the judiciary in the face of every other power as well as of specific interests,
3. the democratization of the judiciary, in its recruitment and in the conditions for the exercise of the profession, in particular in face of the hierarchical organization,
4. the respect, in all circumstances, of the legal values specific to the democratic state based on the rule of law,
5. the assertion of the right of magistrates, as of all citizens, to freedom of assembly, association and expression, including the right to form trade unions, to meet and to take collective action;
6. a judicial organization apt to guarantee a public service of justice responding to the principle of transparency, allowing for the citizens' control over its functioning;
7. the promotion of a democratic legal culture through exchanges of information and the study of common topics;
8. the proclamation and the defence of the rights of minorities and of differences, and in particular the rights of immigrants and the most deprived, in a perspective of social emancipation of the weakest.

Following its goals listed above, MEDEL is very active in the field of defending the judicial independence in different European countries, inter alia, by issuing statements, letters and resolutions.[25]

---

[25] See e.g. Statement on the judiciary in Romania (9th March 2019), Letter to Frans Timmermans about the disciplinary proceedings against Judges in Poland (21 February 2019) or Resolution on safeguarding the independence of the Romanian judicial system from secret and unlawful interference of the intelligence agencies (24th May 2018)- all available at: https://medelnet.eu/index.php/activities/an-independent-judiciary/445-resolution-on-safeguarding-the-independence-of-the-romanian-judicial-system-from-secret-and-unlawful-interference-of-the-intelligence-agencies. Accessed 7 Apr 2019.

4.4 Consultative Council of European Judges (CCJE)

MEDEL's statements, as well as those of EAJ or ENCJ and AEAJ (see below) are often referred to by the Consultative Council of European Judges (CCJE),[26] set up by the Committee of Ministers of the Council of Europe in 2000. The CCJE, consultative body concerning independence, impartiality and competence of judges, highlights the essential role of the judicial power in a democratic society. The CCJE is the first body in an international organisation composed exclusively of judges and constitutes therefore a unique body at the European level. All member States may be represented. Members should be chosen in contact, where such authorities exist, with the national authorities responsible for ensuring the independence and impartiality of judges and with the national administration responsible for managing the judiciary, from among serving judges having a thorough knowledge of questions relating to the functioning of the judicial system combined with utmost personal integrity.

To fulfil its mission, the CCJE provides advice and guidance in the form of Opinions. These Opinions are usually prepared by a working group, on the basis of surveys carried out in member States and adopted at its plenary meetings. Until 2018 CCJE has adopted 21 opinions on different topics related to the judicial independence and the rule of law. On the occasion of its 10th anniversary, the CCJE adopted, during its 11th plenary meeting (November 2010), a Magna Carta of Judges (Fundamental Principles) summarising and codifying the main conclusions of the Opinions that it already adopted.[27]

The CCJE may be requested by member States to look into particular problems facing their justice system. It may be asked for assistance by a body of the Council of Europe (Committee of Ministers, Parliamentary Assembly, Secretary General) or by one of its members, in order to provide answers to topical questions and to provide support to the member States, in order to enable them to comply with European standards on some particular situations concerning judges. The CCJE can visit the country concerned to discuss ways of improving the situation, in the legislative and organisational fields. CCJE's Opinions and statements are frequently recalled by the European Court of Human Rights in its judgments relating to the status of judges.[28]

---

[26]See e.g. Report on judicial independence and impartiality in the Council of Europe member States in 2017 (7th February 2018), available at: https://rm.coe.int/2017-report-situation-ofjudges-in-member-states/1680786ae1. Accessed 7 Apr 2019.

[27]See more at: https://www.coe.int/en/web/ccje/home. Accessed 7 Apr 2019 and Borkowski (2016), pp. 203–218, available at: http://www.krs.pl/admin/files/gn%20%20eng%2020160505.pdf. Accessed 7 Apr 2019.

[28]See for example: Morice v. France, Baka v. Hungary, Harabin v. Slovakia.

4.5   European Network of Councils of Judiciary (ENCJ)

There are also judicial associations and organizations at the European level covering a selected parts of the judicial activities. One of the most active in promoting and defending the judicial independence is the European Network of Councils of Judiciary (ENCJ). The ENCJ unites the national institutions in the Member States of the European Union which are independent of the executive and legislature, and which are responsible for the support of the Judiciaries in the independent delivery of justice. The European Network of Councils for the Judiciary (ENCJ) was established in 2004 in Rome. The Network's founders consisted of councils for the judiciary from 13 countries of the European Union, including Poland. The establishment of the ENCJ was intended to fill in the gap in the European integration process to enable the judiciary to keep up with the pace of other authorities in the integration process. According to the ENCJ Statute, the association aims at improving cooperation and mutual understanding between councils of judiciary and members of judiciary profession on the territory of the Member States of the EU and the EU candidate countries. During nearly 12 years of operation the ENCJ has substantially expanded number of its numbers. Starting with the body of 13 founding members in 2015 it reached the number of 22 members and 16 observers.[29]

The mission of the ENCJ concurs to a large extent with the tasks performed by individual judiciary councils, since safeguarding the judiciary independence is seen as one of the most important operational aims for each of them. Over the course of the years the ENCJ has constantly run its analytical and research project called Independence and Accountability.[30]

Like CCJE and MEDEL, ENCJ is also engaged in the defence of the judicial independence in European countries, by issuing statements and opinions of the Executive Board, many of them relating to the current situation in Poland.[31] The 17th September 2018 decision of the ENCJ General Assembly to suspend the National Council of Judiciary (KRS) as ENCJ member was widely commented and recalled in the proceedings before the European Court of Justice in Luxembourg. According to the decision: "It was felt that it was a very sad day, as the KRS was one of the founding fathers of the network and their representatives to the network were very much respected and contributed highly to the work of the network, both in the Board and in the various ENCJ projects over many years".[32]

---

[29]Detailed data available on the Network website: https://www.encj.eu.

[30]See more in: Pałka (2016), pp. 187–202, available at: http://www.krs.pl/admin/files/gn%20%20eng%2020160505.pdf. Accessed 7 Apr 2019.

[31]See: https://www.encj.eu/articles/96. Accessed 7 Apr 2019.

[32]Available at: https://www.encj.eu/node/495. Accessed 7 Apr 2019.

4.6   Association of European Administrative Judges (AEAJ)

The other European judicial association covering some selected judicial activities is the Association of European Administrative Judges (AEAJ) founded in the year 2000. AEAJ Members are: National associations, representing administrative judges from Member States of the European Union and the Council of Europe and individual members, being administrative judges from those countries in which such associations do not exist. Similarly to ENCJ and MEDEL, AEAJ is active in the works of CCJE, but also issues its own statements (e.g. on 23 January 2019 on the situation of judiciary in Poland and in Turkey)[33] as well as presents other important documents and developments regarding the current status of judiciary and the judicial independence in Europe.[34]

The list of the European judicial organisations and associations is, of course, not a full one,[35] but the bodies listed above play a crucial role in supporting the judicial association in European countries and, by doing so, the members of the European judiciary as such, in their everyday work and sometimes struggle, to build and protect the guarantees of the judicial independence. As an example, the recent activities of the Polish Judges Association "Iustitia" may be presented.[36] Iustitia has become extremely active in defending the rule of law in Poland and protecting and supporting the Polish judges who, e.g. face charges in the disciplinary proceedings for openly presenting their criticism toward the changes in the Polish judiciary. In those actions, Iustitia (with more than three and half thousand judges, i.e. more than 30% of the total number of judges in Poland, as members) is constantly supported by the European judicial associations and organisations, such as MEDEL, CCJE, ENCJ, AEAJ, EAJ etc. Such support is extremely important in the difficult times that the members of the Polish judiciary are facing right now. The fact that there are judicial associations and organisations ready to give such a support to their colleagues in Turkey, Poland, Hungary, Romania or whenever the help is needed, is hard to be overestimated and constitutes a solid evidence of the common European values.

---

[33] Available at: https://www.aeaj.org/. Accessed 7 Apr 2019.

[34] See a moving statement of Mr. Diego García-Sayán (UN Special Rapporteur on the independence of judges and lawyers) on the topic of Mr. Murat Arslan's trial available at AEAJ web-site: https://www.aeaj.org/media/files/2019-01-23-51-statement%20conviction.pdf. Accessed 7 Apr 2019.

[35] See for example GEMMI- the European judicial organisation promoting mediation etc.

[36] See the EN web-site: https://www.iustitia.pl/en/. Accessed 7 Apr 2019.

5   Instead of Summary

Instead of summary, it should be noted that, according to already quoted, President of MEDEL -Gualtiero Michelini, there are three main roles of the judicial associations: network and exchange experience, alert other judicial associations, institutions and the public to critical situations, and to identify common problems and trends, and propose ideas and possible solutions.

As for the first aspect, the regular meetings and communications among judicial associations provide a powerful asset in finding a common language, knowledge on what happens outside the court's daily work. "Shaping a common identity of European judges committed to democracy and the rule of law is also an aspect of the specific role of European judges and prosecutors in developing the European case law through interrogating, having a juridical dialogue with, and implementing the judgments of the ECJ and the ECtHR". With regard to alerting to critical situations, G. Michelini stated that "independence of the judiciary is not a privilege for judges and prosecutors, but an essential means of protecting the people's rights. Many difficult situations show that democracy may be fragile, also in Europe now, and that it is essential to preserve it under any contingency, being in a position of professionals tasked with the protection of fundamental rights, and having the expert competence to understand and explain any distortion of the principle of separation of powers". And lastly, it is not sufficient to have principles of external and internal independence of the judiciary or councils for the judiciary just written on paper. It is essential that they are carefully checked and balanced, and that the judiciary perform their functions in a democratic way.[37]

One can only agree with that. After all the judicial independence should be, not only for judges, but for the whole European society, *"as natural as the air we breathe"*.[38] And, using this *licencia poetica*, judicial organisations and associations, help us to keep the air clean.

References

Borkowski, G. (2014). Judicial independence in the light of art. 6 of the European Convention of the Human Rights – Selected aspects. In *Teka Komisji Prawniczej – OL PAN*. Lublin: Polska Akademia Nauk. Retrieved April 7, 2019, from http://journals.pan.pl/Content/93315/mainfile.pdf?handler=pdf

Borkowski, G. (2016). Opinions issued by the Consultative Council of European Judges (CCJE)– Selected aspects. In G. Borkowski (Ed.), *The limits of judicial independence?* Warszawa: Krajowa Rada Sądownictwa. Retrieved April 7, 2019, from http://www.krs.pl/admin/files/gn %20%20eng%2020160505.pdf

---

[37] See note 4, pp. 184–185.

[38] See Laffranque (2014), p. 127.

Brunson, W., & Schmucker, H. C. (2016). Judicial education: A brief history, trends and opportunities. In P. M. Koelling (Ed.), *The improvement of the Administration of Justice*. Chicago: American Bar Association.

Justice Defend Committee Report: A Country That Punishes (2019). Retrieved April 7, 2019, from https://komitetobronysprawiedliwosci.pl/app/uploads/2019/02/Raport-KOS_eng.pdf

Kuijer, M. (2004). The blindfold of lady justice: judicial independence and impartiality in light of the requirements of article 6 ECHR. In *E.M. Meijers Instituut*. Leiden.

Laffranque, J. (2014). Judicial independence in Europe: Principles and reality. In N. A. Engstad, A. L. Froseth, & B. Tonder (Eds.), *The independence of judges*. The Hague: Eleven International Publishing.

Michelini, G. (2018). Standards of professional associations of judges and prosecutors in safeguarding judicial independence. In D. Szumiło-Kulczycka & K. Gajda-Roszczynialska (Eds.), *Judicial management versus independence of the judiciary*. Warszawa: WoltersKluwer.

Pałka, S. (2016). An examination of the independence of the judiciary as an implementation of the objectives and tasks of the European network of councils for the judiciary. In G. Borkowski (Ed.), *The limits of judicial independence?* Warszawa: Krajowa Rada Sądownictwa. Retrieved April 7, 2019, from http://www.krs.pl/admin/files/gn%20%20eng%2020160505.pdf

Report on judicial independence and impartiality in the Council of Europe member States in 2017. Retrieved April 7, 2019, from https://rm.coe.int/2017-report-situation-ofjudges-in-member-states/1680786ae1

Schabas, W. A. (2015). *The European Convention on Human Rights. A commentary*. New York: Oxford University Press.

State of Democracy, Human Rights and the Rule of Law. Role of Institutions, threats to institutions. Report by the Secretary General of the Council of Europe 2018, p. 13. Retrieved April 7, 2019, from https://rm.coe.int/state-of-democracy-human-rights-and-the-rule-of-law-role-of-institutio/168086c0c5

The Horizon Institute. (2015). Retrieved April 7, 2019, from https://www.thehorizoninstitute.org/usr/library/documents/main/paper-from-horizon-institute-on-associations-of-judges-in-different-countries-.pdf

Independence of International Courts

Daniela Cardamone

Contents

1 Introduction: The Proliferation of International Judicial Bodies

Since the end of the Second World War, the number of international courts has increased exponentially all over the world. In a world where national borders are increasingly permeable to people, goods and information, the international community has faced problems that did not allow unilateral solutions. The creation of international jurisdictions has been a necessary instrument for strengthening inter-state cooperation. Their field of action is very broad as these courts decide issues ranging from trade agreements to human rights. They solve commercial disputes of great economic impact in the largest economic superpowers; they can enforce the law of the sea, condemn states for violations of the fundamental rights of their own citizens and punish war criminals all over the world. Given that their decisions are

Daniela Cardamone is Judge in Italy and former member of the Italian Division at the European Court of Human Rights.

D. Cardamone (✉)
Court of Milan, Milan, Italy
e-mail: Daniela.cardamone@giustizia.it

© Springer Nature Switzerland AG 2019
P. Pinto de Albuquerque, K. Wojtyczek (eds.), *Judicial Power in a Globalized World*, https://doi.org/10.1007/978-3-030-20744-1_6

binding, international courts can have a quite significant impact on internal policies of states and on their legal systems. It is estimated that international courts have now issued thousands of legally binding judgments, which result into noticeable changes in the politics and practices of states. Many of these courts have mandatory jurisdiction and are open to non-state actors, such as individuals and societies; this results into a growing influence of their judgments on what have traditionally been considered to be internal aspects of states.[1]

Some have described this phenomenon as "judicialization of the international legal order", which means that international law, which is traditionally the "law of the strongest", is progressively subject to the principles of the rule of law through the will of states themselves".[2]

At the same time, the growing number of Courts and the ever-increasing diversification of issues within their jurisdiction have increased the fragmentation of the international legal order.[3] Such fragmentation arises from the fact that many international tribunals, such as the various courts dealing with fundamental rights, international criminal tribunals, the tribunal of the sea, are sectoral and, therefore, there is a risk that their decisions take into account only the single sector of competence, without worrying about preserving the unity of the international legal system and without taking into account the interpretative divergences that could arise.[4]

2   International Judicial Independence

The phenomenon of the proliferation of international courts has aroused increasing public interest. At the same time, their growing power has raised concerns about their credibility, legitimacy and effectiveness. Concern regarding their legitimacy is closely connected to the problem of their independence. Indeed, legitimacy of international courts, such as that of national jurisdictions, is largely based on their independence.

The issue of the independence of jurisdiction over other powers, which is familiar in domestic law, is relatively unexplored in relation to international courts and tribunals.

In this regard, the first issue to be assessed is whether the independence of international courts should be addressed in different terms. In other words, the questions to be answered are: are international courts impartial dispensers of justice, which adopt decisions based on legal norms? Are they rather a manifestation of state power and influence in international relations whose decisions are inspired by

---

[1]Romano (1999), p. 709 et seq.
[2]The expression "judicialization of the international legal order" is of: Ulfstein (2014), p. 849.
[3]Koskenniemi (2006), p. 3.
[4]Conforti (2007), pp. 2–4.

motives other than strictly legal ones? Are international judges "diplomats in robe"?[5] Do international courts and judges act on the base of the same principles of independence as national legal systems?

In the course of the present analysis, we will see that, while at national level, the legitimacy and authority of the courts are closely linked to their independence, in the context of international tribunals it is less evident what the meaning of independence and impartiality should be. The question therefore arises as the independence of an international judge should be measured according to the national law's standards or based on a different (lower) standard appropriately calibrated for international courts.

At the base of all these questions there is a fundamental issue to analyze: must the independence of the international judiciary be evaluated as that of the national judges, or is there something qualitatively different in the international courts? In other words, is international justice an instrument of international politics such that it should be applied different rules than national jurisdiction and a lower standard of independence?

3 Difference Between National and International Judicial Independence

It is undisputed that judges in each tribunal and international court must be "independent" and "impartial".[6] The notion of judicial independence can be considered an international law *acquis*. For example, Article 10 of the Universal Declaration of Human Rights states that "everyone is entitled in full equality to a fair and public hearing by an independent and impartial tribunal, in the determination of his rights and obligations and of any criminal charge against him".

Article 6 of the European Convention of Human Rights (ECHR) states that "in the determination of his civil rights and obligations or of any criminal charge against him, everyone is entitled to a fair and public hearing within a reasonable time by an independent and impartial tribunal established by law".

Moreover, the international conference, where the international community decided to establish the International Criminal Court (ICC),[7] stated that "there was broad agreement that the Court should be an independent, fair, impartial, effective and broadly representative international criminal judiciary, and that it should be free from political or other influences". It was also stressed that the Court should not

---

[5]This effective definition is from: Voeten (2011), p. 1.

[6]For a general assessment of the principle of judicial independence in international law, see: Meron (2005), p. 359 et seq.

[7]Pursuant to General Assembly resolutions adopted in 1996 and 1997, the Diplomatic Conference of Plenipotentiaries on the Establishment of the International Criminal Court was convened on 15 June 1998 in Rome.

become an instrument of political struggles or a means of interfering in other countries' internal affairs.[8]

The statutes and the rules of the various courts that address the issue set the criteria for holding the function of judge and the requirements to ensure their independence and impartiality.[9]

A few times, these general formulas are supplemented by the rules that establish when judges ought to recuse themselves.[10]

In some cases, the rules governing the functioning of international courts provide for very severe restrictions and prohibit any form of external activity as a necessary instrument to guarantee independence.[11] In other cases, the rules are more flexible but, although the formulations are very varied, the common denominator is always a general commitment aimed at guaranteeing independence and impartiality.

Although, *prima facie*, the concept of judicial independence seems to apply to international judges in the same way as national judges, a series of specific features of the supranational legal system suggest that the direct transposition of the valid principles at national level is not always appropriate.

A crucial difference between the functioning of the two systems is the way in which judgments and decisions are enforced.

At national level, domestic courts play their role within a complex legal system of an original nature (in the sense that it does not derive its validity from any other higher order), in which legislative, executive and judicial power exert sovereignty through binding rules for all citizens. National courts operate within a legal system that has universal scope within the confines of the state and have effective remedies available to execute judgments.[12]

The institutional context in which the international courts operate is substantially different from that in which domestic courts operate. International tribunals do not operate as part of a coherent, unified and sovereign world government. They act within a system without a hierarchical organization and in which the execution of their decisions is left to the will of the same states from which they derive their legitimacy.[13]

---

[8]Press Release, U.N. Diplomatic Conference Concludes in Rome with Decision to Establish Permanent International Criminal Court, U.N. Doc. L/ROM/22 (Jul. 17, 1998).

[9]ICC Statute, Article 40 (2): "Judges shall not engage in any activity which is likely to interfere with their judicial functions or to affect confidence in their independence".

[10]See for example: United Nations Convention on the Law of the Sea: art. 71 (1) "No member of the Tribunal may exercise any political or administrative function, or associate actively with or be financially interested in any of the operations of any enterprise concerned with the exploitation of the resources of the sea or the seabed or other commercial use of the sea or the seabed".

[11]Article 21 paragraph 3 of the European Convention of Human Rights (ECHR) states that: "During their term of office the judges shall not engage in any activity which is incompatible with their independence, impartiality or with the demands of a full-time office; all questions arising from the application of this paragraph shall be decided by the Court".

[12]Dzehtsiarou and Coffey (2014), p. 4.

[13]Dzehtsiarou and Coffey (2014), p. 5.

The execution of international court's judgements depends on much more complex mechanisms that are remitted to the will of states that must agree to execute them. For example, the European Court of Human Rights (ECtHR) does not have the power to enforce its decisions and judgments coercively and Contracting Parties must accept the legitimacy of the Court's judgments, even when it ruled against them.[14] Similarly, without its own enforcement mechanism, the effectiveness of the ICC depends to a large extent on the cooperation it receives from states, the United Nations, regional organizations and other relevant actors, since the investigation phase.[15]

Another aspect that makes the international judiciary particularly fragile is its dependence on states for the financing of its activities. The financial instrument is probably the most important one by which states can affect the proper functioning of international courts. The consultations that precede the adoption of the budget of international courts are not merely financial in nature, but are inspired by political reasons concerning the way states conceive their role in the international legal system.[16]

In light of these considerations, at national level, for example, it would not make sense to question whether and to what extent the level of independence of courts can influence their efficiency.

We refer to the heated debate that took place among scholars regarding the theoretical approach of Posner and Yoo, who have argued that "independence prevents international tribunals from being effective". According to this approach, the more effective international tribunals are "dependent" tribunals, namely staffed by judges controlled by governments through the power of reappointment or threats of retaliation. By contrast, independent tribunals, meaning tribunal that resemble domestic courts, pose a danger to international cooperation.[17]

In this regard, it is interesting to note that even those who have strongly criticized this approach have not affirmed that international judges must enjoy absolute independence but have supported the thesis of "constrained independence". Indeed, the counter-theory of Helfer and Slaughter challenges the conjecture that formally independent courts are correlated with effective judicial outcomes and offer a theory of "constrained independence" in which "states establish independent international tribunals to enhance the credibility of their commitments in specific multilateral settings and then use more fine-graned structural, political and discursive mechanisms to limit the potential for judicial overreaching".[18]

Helfer and Slaughter indeed claim that: "Constrained independence maximizes the benefits of delegation to independent decision makers while minimizing its costs. It allows states to enhance the credibility of their commitments while signalling to

---

[14]Forst (2013).

[15]Sifris (2008), pp. 18–19; Weiner (2013), pp. 545–562.

[16]Blokker (2015), p. 12.

[17]Posner and Yoo (2005), p. 7.

[18]Helfer and Slaughter (2005), p. 44 et seq.

independent courts, tribunals, and quasi-judicial review bodies when they are approaching - or have exceeded - the politically palatable limits of their authority".[19]

4 Ways of Influencing the Actions of International Courts

Although there are profound differences between independence of national and international judges, it is possible to draw up a common definition of judicial independence. It can be affirmed that it is a requirement allowing judges to develop their legal opinion, without being bound by the preferences of other actors. This does not mean that an independent judge "simply applies the law". Independent judges apply the law to specific circumstances and they can be influenced by their cultural approach. Indeed, independence rather allows judges to ignore the preferences and prejudices of outsiders.

Judicial independence is recognized as a significant factor in maintaining the credibility and legitimacy of international courts and tribunals. In this regard, in fact, at least two issues, familiar in national judiciary, have emerged in the international context: first of all, the need to avoid the appearance of bias in international courts and tribunals; secondly, the need to ensure their independence from political bodies.[20]

This problem, however, is more complex at international level, where it is more difficult to identify the entities with respect to which judges should be independent.

Literature is almost exclusively concerned with the degree to which governments influence international tribunals. However, many other actors can concretely influence international judges. For example, non-governmental organizations can lobby governments and inter-governmental organizations for renewed financing, extension of deadlines, and other support[21] or intervene as third party before international courts to challenge national laws, practices and interpretations and to establish precedents,[22] put pressure on governments and intergovernmental organizations, and promote certain interpretations of law.[23]

This results into a potential threat to judicial independence that has received little attention, perhaps because scholars perceive it as more innocuous than the influence of governments or because the study of international law has traditionally been centred on states.

However, what can concretely influence the international tribunals and subject them to what has been called "constrained independence"?

---

[19]Helfer and Slaughter (2005), p. 44.

[20]Mackenzie and Sand (2003), p. 272.

[21]Danner (2006), pp. 35–71.

[22]Van den Eynde (2013), p. 271 et seq; Viljoen and Abebe (2014), pp. 22–44.

[23]Danner and Voeten (2010), pp. 35–71.

States have various ways to influence the actions of international courts. Doctrine highlights a number of potential *ex-ante* and *ex-post* control mechanisms that governments could potentially employ to influence international judges.[24]

The most important determinants of independence in literature are identified in selection and tenure, legal discretion, and control over material and human resources.[25]

Selection and tenure are important components of courts' independence because they help protect judges from governments' reprisals for unfavourable judgments; this means that judicial independence is stronger when governments have fewer opportunities to influence selection and tenure of judges.[26]

An important role in determining overall independence is also played by the level of legal discretion which judges enjoy when they interpret rules.[27]

Another mechanism that can influence the independence of international courts is the participation of states, directly or indirectly, in proceedings; for example, through the intervention as third parties or the appointment of ad hoc (non-permanent) national judges.[28]

According to others, judicial independence increases when governments have less control over the docket of international courts, for example through the granting of mandatory jurisdiction allowing unfiltered access to private actors and/or supranational control agencies.[29]

Even the threat of not executing sentences and decisions can be an implicit form of pressure on international courts. Governments can influence international tribunals by threatening, more or less implicitly, to ignore judgments or even to leave the jurisdiction of a court. Therefore, the more difficult are non-compliance, override and exit, the greater is the independence of an international tribunal.[30]

Moreover, international courts should act only within the limits of the principles of interpretation recognized in international law and ensure that even their "strategic" decisions always move within legal boundaries. Indeed, they are neither legislators nor political bodies. Despite these limitations, international courts and tribunals have a wide margin of discretion with the consequence that it would be difficult for states to claim that they have acted *ultra-vires* and, consequently, to refuse to execute their decisions. It would be wiser for states, as well as for other stakeholders and academic community, to express their criticism about the methods of interpretation applied and/or the results achieved. In any case, international courts, in turn, could be inclined to consider these points of view in order to avoid negative

---

[24] See for an overview Helfer and Slaughter (2005), pp. 44–55.

[25] Keith (2014), p. 3; Keohane et al. (2000), pp. 458–488.

[26] Voeten (2007), p. 4; Torres Pérez (2015), pp. 181–201.

[27] Voeten (2007), p. 4.

[28] Schwebel (1999), pp. 889–900; Kotlik (2008), p. 10.

[29] Alter (2006), pp. 22–49.

[30] Carrubba (2009), pp. 55–69.

consequences in the form of failure to implement judgments or restrictions on funding.[31]

Another form of interaction between international courts and states is based on the principle of subsidiarity. This principle aims to protect national sovereignty by leaving decision-making to states, which are in a better position to protect the fundamental rights of their citizens. International jurisdiction comes into play only when states have proven to fail to protect these rights.[32]

The principle of subsidiarity can provide a guide for international courts in the interpretation of international obligations and, on the other hand, leave room for certain discretion on the part of states. For example, it is known that the ECtHR applies the "margin of appreciation" in its interpretation of the Convention, leaving to states a certain discretion as to the means best suited to achieve the purposes of protection imposed by the Convention itself.

The principle of subsidiarity also leaves room for interaction between international courts and national authorities. National authorities have certain discretion both as regards the interpretation of a judgement issued in a proceeding of which the state was a party, and for the choice of the appropriate means to implement an international court's decision. The binding effects *erga omnes* of the ruling beyond the *res judicata* between the parties pose a question of interpretation and a further possibility of interaction. This means that national authorities, and in particular national courts, play an important role in influencing the interpretation of international courts in future cases. National courts can draw attention to the specificity of domestic law and, through well-motivated opinions, can convince international courts to prefer a different interpretation. An interpretative practice of national courts can amount to the subsequent state practice that international courts must take into consideration.[33]

Finally, national authorities may refuse to implement an international judgment in the national legal order. This position can be supported, for example, in the protection of fundamental human rights in relation to other international obligations, such as international trade agreements. However, it could also have a further effect and encourage other states not to respect international judgments, thereby undermining efforts to promote respect for the international rule of law.[34]

Therefore, in the light of the above considerations, the opinion that the work of international tribunals can never be completely separated from the world of international politics[35] is entirely sharable.

---

[31]Ulfstein (2014), pp. 849–866.

[32]Carozza (2003), pp. 38–79; Kumm (2004), pp. 907–931.

[33]Arnardóttir (2017), pp. 819–843.

[34]Ulfstein (2014), pp. 849–866.

[35]Terris et al. (2007), pp. 1–73.

5 The Concept of Accountability As a Component of Legitimacy: The Relationship Between Independence and Accountability

In light of these considerations, the question arises as to whether national courts should implement international judicial decisions that have been issued by judges who are not independent according to national regulatory standards and who are not accountable.[36]

At the base of this question there is a fundamental concern: does international law grant decision-making authority to international actors who are not accountable?

This issue is at the base of every democratic society where there is a strict correlation between power and responsibility and where responsibility is a fundamental component of democratic legitimacy.

The view that international actors are not sufficiently responsible for their decisions and actions is often exposed as a reason to challenge the legitimacy of international law.[37]

The meaning of accountability is itself extremely complex and depends on the nature of the particular organization concerned. Therefore, when discussing the general concept of accountability in international law, it is difficult to identify a specific definition.[38]

As judicial independence is a fundamental component of democracy, an equally fundamental assumption is that there must be controls over the exercise of judicial power, because uncontrolled power may result in abuse of power.[39]

The concepts of judicial independence and judicial responsibility are not necessarily in conflict. In fact, "mature legal systems are characterized by both judicial independence and judicial responsibility".[40]

As mentioned above regarding the opinion of Helfer and Slaughter on the relationship between independence and effectiveness, the objective of judicial independence is not unconstrained independence. The tendency would be for a level of independence that would ensure a level of independence that allows judges to decide cases "lawfully and impartially, without improper control and influence".[41]

---

[36]Mackenzie and Sand (2003), pp. 272–285.

[37]Von Bogdandy (2013), pp. 361–379.

[38]Grant and Keohane (2005), pp. 36–37.

[39]Sifris (2008), p. 90.

[40]Gewirtz (2005), p. 1.

[41]See for example article 1.1 of the Burgh House Principles on the Independence of the International Judiciary:

> The court and the judges shall exercise their functions free from direct or indirect interference or influence by any person or entity.

Therefore, the challenge would be to balance these two concepts in order to set up an appropriate level of judicial constraint, without compromising the essence of judicial independence.

In other words, according to this approach, international judges should be able to make decisions that do not have inappropriate control by others but, at the same time, there should be a certain level of control by others in the exercise of judicial decision-making.

Nevertheless, an empirical investigation reveals that states are establishing more and more independent courts. Therefore, a question arises: why should states ever agree to bind themselves to the jurisdiction of courts that cannot fully control and which can issue decisions contrary to their national interests?

The answer to this question is that the benefits that states derive from independent international tribunals far outweigh the disadvantages. Independent international tribunals, in fact, strengthen the credibility of international commitments in specific multilateral contexts. They do this by increasing the likelihood that violations of these commitments are detected and accurately labelled as non-compliance.[42]

Such violations create short-term material costs and reputation costs for the state that does not comply with international obligations. Furthermore, the identification of these violations also encourages compliance with obligations in the future, maximizing the binding value of the agreement with respect to all parties involved in the multilateral regime.

For these reasons, states are increasingly ratifying treaties that require the settlement of disputes through international courts. The percentages of ratification are very high; some clear examples of this tendency are the World Trade Organization agreement,[43] the Statute of the ICC[44] and the European Court of Justice (ECJ).[45] Furthermore, states recognize the jurisdiction of independent courts and tribunals even where the decision to do so is optional.[46]

---

[42]Helfer and Slaughter (2005), p. 33.

[43]The WTO exemplifies the first trend. It began its life on January 1, 1995 with 76 members, all of which were automatically subject to the jurisdiction of the WTO's dispute settlement system, including its highly independent appellate body. The number of WTO members quickly surpassed 100, and, as of December 2017, membership had risen to 164.

[44]With 60 ratifications in July 2002, the Rome Statute of ICC enters into force. As of today, 123 countries are States Parties to the Rome Statute of the ICC.

[45]The European Court of Justice (ECJ) has seen its jurisdictional reach expand as more states have joined the Treaty of Rome and the numerous amendments it has spawned. From a six-state trading block, the European Community (now the EU) has now expanded to 28 members. Further enlargements are likely in the next few years.

[46]The ECtHR has perhaps the strongest record in this regard. At the time of the European Convention's founding in 1953, recognition of the ECtHR's jurisdiction was optional. That changed with the adoption of Protocol 11, which made jurisdiction compulsory and granted individuals direct access to the court in all cases. The Protocol, opened for signature in May 1994, could enter into force only if ratified by all European Convention member states. Universal ratification was quickly achieved, however, and the new Court began operating in November 1998.

This is because the disadvantages of setting up independent courts are much lower than those that might seem at first glance. Moreover, judicial independence does not mean that judges do not have to face any limit to their behaviour.

As Helfer and Slaughter claim, "independent" international judges face an even greater host of "structural, political, and discursive constraints, many of which can be manipulated by states themselves. The result is an international legal system in which independent tribunals are unlikely to overstep their bounds and are far more likely to advance states' long-term interests".[47]

6 Conclusion

Our analysis draws the conclusion that, at international level, there is a continuous search for balance between the aspiration to independence, on the one hand, and the responsibility towards the expectations and interests of the main stakeholders, on the other.

In fact, while judicial independence is a fundamental component of democracy, an equally fundamental democratic idea is that there must be controls over the exercise of power.

In this regard, it seems the choice that arises is not between dependent and independent international tribunals but between "complete dependence" and "constrained independence"; this means that states set up independent international courts to improve the credibility of commitments in specific multilateral contexts but then use structural and political mechanisms to control judicial independence.[48]

In conclusion, it seems that the aim of judicial independence of international tribunals, unlike that of national courts, is not "unconstrained independence". Rather, it seems that the tendency is to ensure a level of independence that allows judges to decide cases "lawfully and impartially, without improper control and influence".[49] Therefore, the challenge would be to find a balance so that appropriate restraints are placed without compromising the essence of judicial independence. In other words, states set up independent courts because they are interested in pursuing political goals. Moreover, only through independent tribunals can states actually pursue these interests, where the courts without independence would not be credible.

Therefore, the remaining question is whether it is conceivable a "politically optimal" level of international judicial independence or independence is instead a value to be unconditionally preserved. In this regard, it seems that the independence of international judges is an essential precondition for them to be free from those different forms of pressures, more or less visible and concrete, to which they may be subject. Only in this way, will they be able to continue to guarantee democracy and

---

[47]Helfer and Slaughter (2005), p. 31.

[48]Helfer and Slaughter (2005), pp. 44–55.

[49]See *supra* note n. 44.

fundamental rights and to authoritatively exercise their function of contributing to the affirmation of the rule of law at the international level.

References

Alter, K. J. (2006). Private litigants and the new international courts. *Comparative Political Studies, 39*(1), 22–49. https://doi.org/10.1177/0010414005283216

Arnardóttir, O. M. (2017). Res interpretata, erga omnes effect and the role of the margin of appreciation in giving domestic effect to the judgments of the European Court of Human Rights. *The European Journal of International Law, 28*(3), 819–843. https://doi.org/10.1093/ejil/chx045

Blokker, N. (2015). *The governance of international courts and tribunals: Organizing and guaranteeing independence and accountability - A appeal for research.* European Society of International Law (ESIL) 2015 Annual Conference (Oslo). SSRN: https://ssrn.com/abstract=2709626 or https://doi.org/10.2139/ssrn.2709626

Burgh House Principles on the Independence of the International Judiciary: "The court and the judges shall exercise their functions free from direct or indirect interference or influence by any person or entity". Retrieved April 5, 2019, from https://www.ucl.ac.uk/international-courts/sites/international-courts/files/burgh_final_21204.pdf

Carozza, P. G. (2003). Subsidiarity as a structural principle of international human rights law. *American Journal of International Law, 97*, 38–79. Retrieved April 5, 2019, from https://scholarship.law.nd.edu/cgi/viewcontent.cgi?article=1571&context=law_faculty_scholarship

Carrubba, C. J. (2009). A model of the endogenous development of judicial institutions in federal and international systems. *The Journal of Politics, 71*(1), 55–69. https://doi.org/10.1017/S002238160809004X

Conforti, B. (2007). *Il ruolo del giudice nel diritto internazionale.* Retrieved April 5, 2019, from https://ejls.eui.eu/wp-content/uploads/sites/32/pdfs/Autumn_Winter2007/Il_ruolo_del_giudice_nel_diritto_internazionale_%20Benedetto_Conforti_.pdf

Danner, A., & Voeten, E. (2010). Who is running the international criminal justice system? In D. Avant, M. Finnemore, & S. Sell (Eds.), *Who governs the globe?.* Cambridge studies in international relations (pp. 35–71). Cambridge: Cambridge University Press. https://doi.org/10.1017/CBO9780511845369.003

Danner, A. M. (2006). When courts make law: How the international criminal tribunals recast the laws of War. *Vanderbilt Law Review, 59*, 1. Vanderbilt Public Law Research Paper No. 05-30. Retrieved April 5, 2019, from https://ssrn.com/abstract=822809

Dzehtsiarou, K., & Coffey, D. (2014). Legitimacy and independence of international tribunals: An analysis of the European Court of human rights. *Hastings International and Comparative Law Review, 37*, 271. Retrieved April 5, 2019, from https://ssrn.com/abstract=2584377

Forst, D. (2013). The execution of judgments of the European Court of Human Rights. *Vienna Journal on International Constitutional Law*, (7), 2013. Retrieved April 5, 2019, from https://www.icl-journal.com/media/ICL_Thesis_Vol_7_3_13.pdf

Gewirtz, P. (2005). Independence and accountability of courts. *China Law Review, 1*(1), 11–26. https://doi.org/10.1080/17457230508522943. JSTOR.

Grant, R. W., & Keohane, R. O. (2005). Accountability and abuses of power in world politics. *American Political Science Review, 29*, 36–37.

Helfer, L. R., & Slaughter, A. M. (2005). Why states create international tribunals: A response to Professors Posner and Yoo. *California Law Review, 93*, 899–956.

Keith, K. (2014). Challenges to the Independence of the international judiciary: Reflections on the international court of justice. *Leiden Journal of International Law, 30*(1), 137–154. https://doi.org/10.1017/S0922156516000649

Keohane, R. O., Moravcsik, A., & Slaughter, A. M. (2000). Legalized dispute resolution: Interstate and transnational. *International Organization,* 54(3), 2000, 457–488. Retrieved April 5, 2019, from https://www.princeton.edu/~slaughtr/Articles/IOdispute.pdf

Koskenniemi, M. (2006). *Fragmentation of International law: Difficulties arising from the diversification and expansion of international law.* Report of the Study Group of the International Law Commission, United Nations. Retrieved April 5, 2019, from http://legal.un.org/ilc/documentation/english/a_cn4_l702.pdf

Kotlik, M. D. (2008). *Ad Hoc Judges and Nationality of Judges in the Inter-American Court of Human Rights.* Retrieved April 5, 2019, from http://www.corteidh.or.cr/docs/opiniones/OC_2008/obser_kot_ing.pdf

Kumm, M. (2004). The legitimacy of international law: A constitutionalist framework of analysis. *European Journal of International Law, 15*(5), 907–931. Retrieved April 5, 2019, from http://ejil.org/pdfs/15/5/397.pdf

Mackenzie, R., & Sand, P. (2003). International courts and tribunals and the independence of the international judge. *Harvard International Law Journal, 44*(1), 271–285.

Meron, T. (2005). Judicial independence and impartiality in international criminal tribunals. *American Journal of International Law, 99,* 359–369.

Posner, E. A., & Yoo, J. C. (2005). Judicial independence in international tribunals. *California Law Review, 93,* 1–74.

Romano, C. P. R. (1999). The proliferation of international judicial bodies: The piece of the puzzle. *New York University Journal of International Law and Politics, 31,* 709–751.

Schwebel, S. M. (1999). National judges and judges Ad Hoc of the international court of justice. *The International and Comparative Law Quarterly, 48*(4), 889–900. https://doi.org/10.1017/S0020589300063727. JSTOR.

Sifris, R. (2008). Weighing judicial independence against judicial accountability: Do the scales of the international criminal court balance? *Chicago-Kent Journal of International and Comparative Law, 8,* 88. Retrieved April 5, 2019, from https://ssrn.com/abstract=2292769

Terris, D., Romano, C. P. R., & Swigart, L. (2007). *The international judge: An introduction to the men and women who decide the world's cases* (Loyola-LA Legal Studies Paper No. 2007-18). University Press of New England - Oxford University Press. Retrieved April 5, 2019, from https://ssrn.com/abstract=969035

Torres Pérez, A. (2015). Can judicial selection secure judicial independence? Constraining State Governments in selecting international judges. In M. Bobeck (Ed.), *Selecting Europe's judges. A critical review of the appointment procedures to the European Courts* (pp. 181–201). Oxford: Oxford University Press.

Ulfstein, G. (2014). International courts and judges: Independence, interaction, and legitimacy. *NYU Journal of International Law and Politics.* Pluri Courts Research Paper No. 14-13; University of Oslo Faculty of Law Research Paper No. 2014-14. Retrieved April 5, 2019, from https://ssrn.com/abstract=2433584

Van den Eynde, L. (2013). An empirical look at the Amicus Curiae practice of human rights NGOs before the European Court of Human Rights. *Netherlands Quarterly of Human Rights, 31*(3), 271–313. Retrieved April 5, 2019, from https://ssrn.com/abstract=2350825

Viljoen, F., & Abebe, A. (2014). Amicus Curiae participation before regional human rights bodies in Africa. *Journal of African Law, 58*(1), 22–44. https://doi.org/10.1017/S0021855314000023

Voeten, E. (2007). The politics of international judicial appointments: Evidence from the European Court of Human Rights. *International Organization, 61*(4), 669–701. https://doi.org/10.1017/S0020818307070233

Voeten, E. (2011). *International judicial independence.* Retrieved April 5, 2019, from https://ssrn.com/abstract=1936132 or https://doi.org/10.2139/ssrn.1936132

Von Bogdandy, A. (2013). *The democratic legitimacy of international courts: A conceptual framework*. Retrieved April 5, 2019, from http://www7.tau.ac.il/ojs/index.php/til/article/viewFile/138/115

Weiner, A. S. (2013). *Prudent politics: The International Criminal Court, international relations, and prosecutorial independence*. Retrieved April 5, 2019, from https://openscholarship.wustl.edu/cgi/viewcontent.cgi?article=1452&context=law_globalstudies

Institutional Nature of International Courts and Its Impact on Their Competence

Dmitry Dedov

Contents

1   Conditions of International Cooperation

International justice can be viewed as a stage of social development at the macro level with the participation of states rather than individuals. Those states enjoy their sovereign power. They make their independent decisions to join international organizations, to sign certain international treaties. Their decisions should be based on the recognition that the objectives of an international treaty or organization are in the interests of their members; in other words, by making their decisions the states confirm common interests and common values pursued by the organisation.

The creation of an international court stemmed from the content of an international treaty and the principles of an international organization. The diversity of international courts and international documents does not allow making a detailed analysis of their essence in one small article. It remains possible to emphasize certain objective criteria affecting the competence of those courts. Limiting the scope of the

---

Dmitry Dedov is judge at the European Court of Human Rights elected in respect of the Russian Federation.

D. Dedov (✉)
European Court of Human Rights, Strasbourg, France
e-mail: dmitry.dedov@echr.coe.int

© Springer Nature Switzerland AG 2019   105
P. Pinto de Albuquerque, K. Wojtyczek (eds.), *Judicial Power in a Globalized World*, https://doi.org/10.1007/978-3-030-20744-1_7

intended analysis cannot allow simplifying the task. Nevertheless, it is possible to move from comparatively simple examples to more complex ones.

2 Common Values and Institutional Measures

Indeed, international criminal courts have limited competence related to individual criminal responsibility for the most serious crimes against humanity. These courts operate within the framework of generally accepted norms of criminal procedure and are engaged in establishing relevant factual circumstances. Despite the complexity and enormous scope of their work to establish the facts, as well as discussions about the legitimacy of their decisions, international criminal courts constitute relatively simple example of competence because their competence is narrowly defined in the foundation documents.

There is one serious problem: those states who exercise or who are ready to exercise their power including their military force, they ceased to be under jurisdiction of the International Criminal Court (for example, the Russian Federation and the United States). It is always difficult to share the power of coercion, the power to declare someone guilty. The participation in such courts is based on the presumption that, for various reasons (strong democracy, domestic application of coercion is limited by law) the member state would never become under trial in such court.

At a more advanced stage, there are the courts of economic unions, including the European Union and the Eurasian Economic Union. The foundation treaties of these organizations set out several common goals aimed to achieve the integration in the economic, political and social domains. There are permanent governing bodies of the union, which in general are similar to state bodies of power created on the basis of the principle of separation of powers (executive, legislative and judicial). Also, it is especially important that these supranational entities, which go beyond the concept of an international organization, have extensive and detailed legislation necessary to achieve common goals. It is noteworthy that the Member States of such unions have delegated some of their powers to supranational structures, whose decisions are binding on them.

Under these conditions, international courts of economic unions have a clearly defined competence, apply a developed system of statutes and evaluate specific actions of supranational executive authorities regarding their interference with private interests or consider disputes about their competence on the basis of detailed regulations pursued common goals set out in the foundation treaties. Therefore, the legal framework for judicial decisions is quite detailed, although sometimes it seems to be very complex. In such a situation, the field for criticism of international court decisions is reduced, since supra-state structures cannot arrogate to themselves more powers or broadly interpret their powers than those vested to them by the national authorities by expressing their explicit and unequivocal consent.

3   Rigidity Factor

Also, the member States have taken additional measures to avoid the criticism of the decisions of the international court and its legitimacy: judicial conclusions do not attain the maximum degree of rigidity. The factor of rigidity is important. The high degree of rigidity could be recognized if the decisions of the international court are binding and unpredictable. Enforceability of judgments is a general problem if the competence of the court is wide and if the case-law is not very well established. Therefore, if the decision is non-binding, but predictable and well substantiated, then it is highly likely to be implemented by the State authorities.

It is also important whether the decision is addressed to the person or to the legal document itself. In other words, whether the decision invokes individual or collective responsibility. For example, if the constitutional court comes to the conclusion that the statute contradicts to the national constitution, it does not lead to a personal liability of the members of the parliament for their improper actions or inaction. The constitutional court does not discuss the actions of authorities, it discusses the law. Its legal position is binding for lower courts (law would not be applicable by the courts), and the legislature is recommended to change the regulations. Even if the legislature would refuse to change the statute, and the executive authorities would continue to interfere, the statute would be applied by the courts and all executive decisions would be annulled. This is how the constitutional court could contribute to the process of harmonisation and evolution of law.

The rigidity factor helps to understand the manner of manifestation of power over someone. The supranational institutions need the power to force national institutions to make decisions in the interests of common goals. But their power is different from that one applied to an individual who did not vote for the law enacted by the legislature. In contrary, the national authorities are presented in the supranational bodies and they have accepted the governing rules by consensus. It means that the rigidity factor in international relations is less coercive in nature than at the national level. Therefore, the decision expressed by the international court in an advisory opinion objectively corresponds to the nature of international relations.

Both a long-standing practice of the Court of Justice of the European Union and a newly established practice of the Court of the Eurasian Economic Union show that the advisory opinion has many advantages. It ensures the legitimacy of the decisions of the international court. It strengthens the authority of the international court among the members of the union. And it creates a margin of appreciation for national authorities, that is, conditions for the exercise of power at the national level. This is why the implementation of the advisory opinion becomes more real.

4 Institutional Problems of the European Court of Human Rights

It should be noted that the International Court of Justice of the United Nations also accepts advisory opinions, apparently guided by the same assumptions. Advisory opinions in his case are even more justified, since his task is to interpret abstract norms of public international law, which pays special attention to the independence, independence and sovereignty of its members, as well as the principle of non-interference in the internal affairs of states.

In connection with the latter consideration (the abstract nature of the norms of international law) I approach, in fact, the goal of my research to speak about the international court of human rights, which I understand as an insider, using the example of the European Court of Human Rights ("ECHR", "Court"). Undoubtedly, the legal essence of the ECHR has significant differences compared with other international courts.

It is necessary to begin with the critics of the legitimacy of the ECHR by the member States who ratified the European Convention for the Protection of Fundamental Rights and Freedoms (the "Convention"). The critics reveal the existence of the crisis of legitimacy due to many of the factors mentioned above. The main reason lies, in my opinion, in the distribution of power between international and national institutions. National supreme courts constitute an integral part of the sovereign power. The ECHR is not integrated into such a system of power based on the separation of powers, either at the national or at the supranational level. Even if the delegations of the national parliaments elect the judges of the Court, it does not make it power identical to the sovereign power. It turns out that this is important for legitimacy. For example, this may explain the current crisis in relations between Russia and the Council of Europe. As a result of the sanctions of the Parliamentary Assembly of the Council of Europe, the Russian delegation in general is denied the right to participate in the Assembly, and in particular the right to vote in the election of judges of the ECHR. As a result, over the past 4 years more than half of the judges have been elected without the participation of the Russian delegation of parliamentarians. In this regard, Russia refused to pay contributions to the organization. Moreover, it would be quite reasonable if the Russian Government would refuse to implement the decisions of the ECHR. But this is an example of the direct consequences of a crisis of legitimacy. For other countries, this crisis has happened due to a variety of reasons.

The following are the reasons for criticism. The ECHR actually acts as a legislator, pointing out the mistakes of the legislator, if the quality of the national law is not consistent with the spirit of the Convention. The Court usually attacks excessive or absolute prohibitions, as well as insufficient guarantees of the protection of fundamental rights and freedoms that may lead to the arbitrariness of the authorities. Unfortunately, often the activist position of the Court leads to the fact that the mere insufficiency of guarantees or the formal non-use of these guarantees in relation to a particular applicant may lead to the Court's recognition of a violation of the

Convention, even if it did not cause an arbitrary decision or if it was not associated with the abuse of authority.

The fear of the States Parties is caused by the very unpredictability of the Court's working methods. Although it is possible to speak about the diversity of the Court's methods, the use of each of them in a particular case is often a revelation to the State party. The written procedure increases the risk of unpredictability and enforceability of the Court's decisions. The public hearing do not help a lot, because they are very short and do not allow concentrating on the most important issues. The old position of the Court, namely that he is a master of his own procedure, is also a matter of caution. Russia has always advocated that the Regulations of the Court should be approved by the States Parties, and not by the Court itself. Although the implementation of such a requirement will inevitably cause difficulties with implementation, it should be noted that this does not help to solve the problem of the Court's choice of a particular method of consideration of the complaint. The choice of method can be determined only on the basis of already established practice, but even this is not always the decisive condition.

I ought to note that recently the Court has been working hard to eliminate the uncertainty of working methods. This goal is directly aimed at the activities of the Grand Chamber of the Court, which determines the stages of analysis for certain categories of cases. Recently, this concerns guarantees of protection in criminal proceedings in the absence of witnesses in court or the absence of legal assistance at early stages of the criminal investigation. However, it often happens that the judges of the Grand Chamber are united in defining general principles and methods, although, they disagree on the application of these methods to the circumstances of a particular case.

There are many other reasons for criticism. This also applies to the non-transparent development of the practice of the ECHR (case-law), the actual invention of new rights and freedoms, disrespect for national traditions, as well as the expansion of the control powers of the Court. As a result, States parties lose control over the content of the Convention, they feel themselves to be excluded from the work on the content of the Convention and therefore discredited. This leads to a violation of the principle of subsidiarity, which gives the national authorities the primary role in organizing the protection of fundamental rights and freedoms. They can be said to be offended by the fact that the Court is running ahead of them or trying to outrun them all the time. The court is defended in such cases by the need for an evolutive interpretation of the Convention. However, this interpretation takes place without the participation of national authorities.

As a result, the conclusion of critics is as follows: due to the absence of any control over the judges of the Court, they become irresponsible. In this sense, a negative reaction of supporters of the ECHR to the provision of the Constitutional Court of the Russian Federation with powers to verify the constitutionality of decisions of the ECHR is symbolic, because, in their opinion, the Convention empowers only the ECHR to monitor the compliance by the States parties with their obligations under the Convention. However, these supporters do not take into account that power becomes despotic if there is no control over it.

5   Sources of Legitimacy of the Court and the Scope of Obligations of the Member States

In the absence of such control the international courts of economic unions have to relax their "powerful" pressure on the national authorities. In my view this could be achieved only in the form of advisory opinions. Instead, the ECHR in its judgments always raises a tough question (inevitably, with tough conclusions): whether the Convention has been violated by the state.

In such a situation, the call to respect national traditions can be understood as a call to respect, above all, the sovereignty of the participating States. After long discussions among Russian experts, there was a general opinion that the participation in the Convention does not lead to the restriction of Russia's sovereignty. The Constitution of the Russian Federation contains provisions in general similar to the provisions of the Convention. In this case, the question of the priority of international law does not arise in its usual sense, since the judgments of the Court, although they are a source of international law, in the majority of cases they contain the assessment of the practical actions of national authorities and the manner how they applied the national law.

Indeed, the competence is determined by the institutional conditions in which the Court has to exist and function. The first condition is a basic treaty applied by an international court. In the European Union, this is not only the Treaty of Rome, but also the entire vast array of European Union legislation. In the Eurasian Economic Union there are also general legislative acts, for example, in the field of customs regulation and other areas of the economy. The ECHR has nothing but eighteen articles of the Convention. These norms are very general and abstract, which determines a wide range in the interpretation of the norms of the Convention and their comparison with the norms of national law. This circumstance can be called objective.

There is also a subjective understanding of the nature and nature of the Convention. According to supporters of the active role of the ECHR, the Convention is a law-making international treaty (law-making treaty). It possesses not only the qualities inherent in any multilateral treaty relations, which are based on mutual obligations specified in the contract. The Convention creates positive and negative obligations of the States Parties for the practical implementation of the guaranteed rights and freedoms in the national legal order. This implies the need for an evolutive interpretation of the Convention that meets contemporary needs.

This interpretation lies at the heart of the conflict around the Court and, therefore, at the heart of the crisis of its legitimacy. It gives the Court unlimited creative possibilities, but, unfortunately, does not give the participating States a balancing opportunity to foresee their positive and negative obligations. It can be said that, thanks to the Court's established practice on numerous issues and situations, the national authorities have such an opportunity. However, this does not always remove the problem of uncertainty of state obligations. But it becomes clear why there is a struggle between the ECHR and the national supreme courts in order to determine whether the practice of the Court has finally formed at the time of the decision at the national level.

I do not think that the states, when creating the European system for the protection of fundamental human rights, thought that they would have to undertake many obligations in the future, the nature of which they could not imagine at the time of the creation of the Convention. They pursued more general goals like the prevention of totalitarianism and fascism. These goals were determined by common values (democracy, the rule of law and the protection of fundamental human rights and freedoms) and a common historical heritage. The question is how to achieve these goals? Is every violation of the Convention found by the Court a threat to democracy or the rule of law and a step towards totalitarianism? Of course, not. This means that the Convention contains another idea—to ensure the development of society towards the rule of law and democracy, which are understood as ideals of which achievement should be pursued, and this process is endless. At each stage of such an evolution, an element of uncertainty in the legal and political sense objectively arises. Therefore, a balance between the need to achieve goals and national sovereignty could be achieved by creating mechanisms to reduce such uncertainty and to ensure the predictability of the decisions of the Court. However, the very essence of the Convention is a contradiction: democracy and the rule of law are abstract values, but their characteristics could be determined by the judgments of the Court which are to be adopted on the basis of specific factual circumstances of the case and, most importantly, are binding and mandatory.

The other institutional feature is that the obligations of states are not clearly defined in the Convention as compared with the extensive and detailed legislation of each of the above economic unions, which contain not only detailed norms of a general nature, but also specific regulatory powers that are transferred to the national level. In economic unions, with detailed regulation, the opposite problem arises when national authorities start complaining about the lack of freedom in regulating economic relations. In the case of the ECHR, the results of the interpretation of the Convention by the ECHR may be completely unexpected for national authorities. Within the economic alliances such a surprise is almost excluded.

6   Competence of the ECHR

The third condition is the very broad and uncertain competence of the ECHR in comparison with the national courts. The only limitation specified in the Convention is that the Court cannot act as a court of fourth instance, that is, it does not check the legality and validity of decisions of national authorities, including the judicial institutions. However, the Court evaluates the arguments of the national courts to determine on whether they were sufficient and relevant. The court can also assess whether the restrictions were necessary and how this need was estimated and analyzed by the national courts.

Needless to say about such a detailed and multi-stage analysis as a test for the proportionality of interference with the rights of the applicant by the national authorities. Thus, the Court can very deeply analyze the decisions of national courts, but it can also refrain from this. It can concentrate on certain elements in one case, and not to do that in relation to similar elements in another case. This inevitably leads to the emergence of double standards, even if such contradictory approaches appear sporadically and not intentionally. I will not give specific examples, but most of the dissenting opinions of the judges include the practice of the Court where it takes different approaches, and such opinions are numerous, they speak specifically about the frequent use of double standards.

In general, the ECHR uses any of powers similar to national judicial systems:

- collection and evaluation of evidence,
- establishment and legal assessment of the factual circumstances,
- assessment of the quality of the norms of national law (abstract review of the statutory law),
- evolutive interpretation of the main legal act of the Convention (at the national level, this method corresponds to the evolutive interpretation of the national constitution),
- evaluation of national law through a judicial practice, taking into account its interpretation and explanation by the national supreme courts.
- evaluation of any actions of national authorities, including legal regulation, court decisions and actual actions or inaction of the executive authorities.

It can be said that the ECHR acts as a court of first instance, as an appeal, as a supreme court and as a constitutional court. However, this comparison is not entirely correct since at the same time the ECHR remains to act as an international court which has one main objective—to ensure effective and practical protection of fundamental rights and freedoms. At the same time, the Court has a large degree of independence in decision-making (due to the absence of any institutional influence on it by the national authorities) and a very wide, almost unlimited set of decision-making tools.

7 Conclusion

There is a deep conflict between the very general and abstract nature of the goals and values stated in the Convention, on the one hand, and the generally unlimited powers of the ECHR, which, unlike other international courts, makes tough decisions on violation or non-violation of the Convention. This contradiction does not exist at the national level, where the power to exercise an abstract judicial control (like any other judicial competences) is usually explicitly vested by law.

If the international court is engaged in creating the law (especially a public law), it should be very careful. Normally, at the national level, such a function should be a prerogative of the parliament whose authority is granted through the elections. The judges are experts in the rule of law, their legitimacy and authority arises from their qualities and from the quality of their judgments. Thus, the boundary between the competence of the legislative and judicial authorities is clearly defined.

This contradiction at the international level can be at least partially eliminated with the help of Protocol 16 to the Convention, which provides for the adoption of advisory opinions based on requests made by the national supreme and constitutional courts. The advisory opinions are compatible with the spirit of international organizations and are very much in line with the European human rights machinery. Moreover, the advisory opinions are already utilized by other regional human rights courts. The advisory opinion allows the international court not to make tough decisions and to avoid tensions with the national authorities. Moreover, it leaves the national authorities the opportunity to make final decisions on their own. Unfortunately, this institution is not widely used: so far only nine states have acceded to Protocol 16, and the discussion of this document shows a lack of common understanding even in the Court itself, why advisory opinions are so important for the legitimacy of the Court. Since the Court still continues to find violations of the Convention, it will take time for the Court to change its methods of work and for the States parties to believe in the sincerity of the Court's intentions to limit its power and to achieve the equality in the judicial dialogue. Time will tell.

Human Dignity as a Normative Concept. "Dialogue" Between European Courts (ECtHR and CJEU)?

Angela Di Stasi

Contents

1 Human Dignity: From Semantic Ambiguity Towards a Normative Concept

Although the concept of human dignity is increasingly invoked in the international debate, some commentators consider appeals to human dignity to be little more than rhetoric.[1]

Angela Di Stasi is Full Professor of European Union Law and International Law, Jean Monnet Chair *Judicial protection of fundamental rights in the European Area of Freedom, Security and Justice*, Department of Legal Sciences, University of Salerno.

[1]Any attempt at a historical-philosophical reconstruction of the concept of human dignity clearly *lies* beyond the purpose of this chapter. On the relationship between dignity and freedom we will limit ourselves to mentioning the perspectives outlined by Kant (see in *Fondazione della metafisica dei costumi*, Italian translation by Mathieu, Milano, 1944, pp. 144–145), according to whom human

---

A. Di Stasi (✉)
University of Salerno, Department of Legal Sciences, Salerno, Italy
e-mail: adistasi@unisa.it

© Springer Nature Switzerland AG 2019
P. Pinto de Albuquerque, K. Wojtyczek (eds.), *Judicial Power in a Globalized World*, https://doi.org/10.1007/978-3-030-20744-1_8

From being an ethical and pre-juridical value, a principle informing national catalogues[2] and deontological codes, human dignity aims more and more to assume, in International and European Law,[3] a juridical value as basis and source of the respect of all (or almost all) human rights.

This process has some elements of contradiction. On the one hand, dignity is the informing principle, as we will see below, of old and new catalogues of rights and of international instruments of different kind, which find a common element in the respect of a value, not depriving human dignity of semantic ambiguities that often invalidate its normative contents. On the other hand, the persisting lack, in international instruments, of a juridical definition of human dignity represents the logical consequence of the failed (if not impossible) solution to questions of meta-juridical character.

The well-known criticism of semantic ambiguity—in the sense that dignity is referred to as a vague notion which might be used to support even opposing opinions—is indeed paralleled by the difficulty to provide a full, and above all, shared justification of this idea.[4] Therefore, those who criticize the notion of dignity emphasize its inevitable normative weakness, which would invalidate the concrete possibility of having recourse to it.

In light of these considerations, is it possible to assign to human dignity a normative value that allows for the possibility to make it justiciable? Moving from a short review of some references to dignity in international instruments, we will try to identify some guidelines in the jurisprudence of the European Court of Human Rights (ECtHR) and of the Court of Justice of the European Union (CJEU) and the possible convergence between the respective case-law with regard to the notion of dignity.

---

dignity resides in personal autonomy and in its promotion and respect for the individual's dignity is respect for the individual's autonomy.

[2]See above all, Portinaro (2008), p. 221 when, by drawing on Häberle, he affirms that human dignity is the anthropological-cultural basis for the Constitutional State. The idea of equal dignity *for* all human beings can be found, among others, in the French Constitution dating back to 1789. In the Italian Constitution, the reference to human dignity appears in the first paragraph of art. 3 as "equal social dignity" of citizens and in the second paragraph of art. 41 as a limit to the freedom of private economic enterprise which "cannot be carried out in a way that may cause damage [. . .] to human dignity". But the reference to human dignity as the fundamental value of the whole legal system appears in several other constitutions (see e.g. the Canadian, Danish, Portuguese, Swedish, Swiss, and American Constitutions). Remember the provision of the German Constitution which in art. 1 states: "Human dignity is inviolable. To respect and protect it is a duty of each power of the State".

[3]There is an extensive legal literature on this subject that concerns, of course, several sectors of the legal system. See the publications dating back to the 1980s, by Schachter (1983), pp. 103–110; Feldman (1999), pp. 682–702. See the wide references included, among others, in Beyleveld and Brownsword (2001), Kretzmer and Klein (2002) and Blengio Valdés (2007). We dare refer to Di Stasi (2011). See more recently in the Italian Literature Pirozzoli (2012), Ripepe (2014) and Turco (2018).

[4]Among the critics of such a notion, see above all, Macklin (2003), pp. 1419–1420. In the opposite direction see Andorno (2005), pp. 95–102.

2 Short Review of a Set of International Instruments with Reference to Dignity. Focus on a *Bill of Rights of New Generation*: The Charter of Fundamental Rights of the European Union

The recognition of a normative nature to dignity (or of dignity *tout court*) requires a short review (not meant to be comprehensive) of a set of international instruments, varying both in terms of juridical *vis* (hard law instruments and instruments that, to a large extent, can be considered as soft law) and of more or less recent adoption.

As it is well known, the reference to dignity characterizes the Charter of the United Nations (the Preamble affirms the "faith in fundamental human rights, in the *dignity* and worth of the human person, in the equal rights of men and women and of large and small nations") and represents the basic inspiration of the International Covenant on Civil and Political Rights (ICCPR) as well as of the International Covenant on Economic Social and Cultural Rights (ICESCR).[5] In the Preamble of both of them, it is stated "that [. . .] the recognition of the *inherent dignity* and of the equal and inalienable rights of all members of the human family is the foundation of freedom, justice and peace in the world", and it is recognized "that these rights derive from the *inherent dignity* of the human person".

It is worth noting that reference to dignity is also found in the *Universal Declaration of Human Rights*.[6] Here, there are several mentions of dignity, referred to as *inherent dignity*. In the Preamble, the first *Considerandum* reads as follows: "Whereas recognition of the *inherent dignity* and of the equal and inalienable rights of all members of the human family is the foundation of freedom, justice and peace in the world" while the fifth *Considerandum* used the abovementioned formula: "Whereas the peoples of the United Nations have in the Charter reaffirmed their faith in fundamental human rights, in *the dignity and worth of the human person*. . .". Art. 1 adopts, then, the classical formula according to which "All human beings are born free and equal in *dignity* and rights".[7]

It would be impossible to fully investigate the references to dignity in international conventions of universal application.[8] Many regional instruments also invoke

---

[5]The International Covenant on Civil and Political Rights was adopted and opened for signature, ratification and accession by General Assembly resolution 2200A (XXI) of December 16th 1966 and entered in force on March 23rd 1976, in accordance with article 49. The International Covenant on Economic Social and Cultural Rights was adopted and opened for signature, ratification and accession by General Assembly resolution 2200A (XXI) of December 16th 1966 and entered in force on January 3rd 1976, in accordance with article 27.

[6]The Universal Declaration of Human Rights was adopted by the United Nations General Assembly on December 10th, 1948 with the Resolution 217 A (Doc.A/810), at 71.

[7]The article continues providing that: "They are endowed with reason and conscience and should act towards one another in a spirit of brotherhood".

[8]We only refer, among all of them, to the Convention on the Rights of the Child (adopted and opened for signature, ratification and accession by General Assembly resolution 44/25 issued on November 20th 1989 and in force from September 2nd 1990) and the provisions of its Preamble

dignity.[9] The American Convention on Human Rights Art. 11, para 1 affirms that: "Everyone has the right to have his honor respected and his *dignity* recognized" while Art. 5 of the African Charter on Human and Peoples Rights (1981) states that: "Every individual shall have the right to respect of the *dignity inherent* in a human being".

If, then, the consolidation of human dignity represents the "juridical good" protected by International Human Rights Law,[10] one must give special relevance to the reference to the notion of dignity in the particularly complex field of Bioethics. We must remember that in the *Universal Declaration on Bioethics and Human Rights,* the General Conference of the United Nations Educational, Scientific and Cultural Organization (UNESCO) recognizes that "ethical issues raised by the rapid advances in science and their technological applications should be examined with due respect to the *dignity* of the human person...".[11] Moreover, in Art. 2, para c), among the objectives of the Declaration is "to promote respect for *human dignity* and protect human rights [...]".Art. 3, specifically entitled *Human dignity* and human rights, provides at no. 1 that "Human dignity, human rights and fundamental freedoms are to be fully respected".[12]

In the *Universal Declaration on Bioethics and Human Rights*, even if a specific definition of it still continues to be lacking, human dignity plays, together with the respect for human rights, the role of "the best, if not the only available grounds for the development of international legal standard for biomedicine".[13]

Always in the field of Bioethics, moving from the universal to the regional field (which is here intended in a broad sense)[14] the protection of human dignity represents the basic value of the *Convention for the Protection of Human Rights and*

("Considering that . . . recognition of the *inherent dignity* and of the equal and inalienable rights of all members of the human family is the foundation of freedom, justice and peace in the world, . . . reaffirmed their faith in fundamental human rights and in the *dignity* and worth of the human person...").

[9]See the large number of references to dignity included in the Preamble of the American Declaration of the Rights and Duties of Man (OAS Res. XXX), adopted by the Ninth International Conference of American States (April 1948).

[10]So Arbuet-Vignali (1997), p. 30 et seq., in particular p. 34. See Lauterpacht (1950), p. 69 where he affirms ". . . in relation to both rights and duties the individual is the final subject of all law". We dare refer to Di Stasi (2011).

[11]Adopted by acclamation on 19 October 2005. The Preamble of UNESCO's Constitution refers to "the democratic principles of the *dignity [...]*", and . . . stipulates "that the wide diffusion of culture, and the education of humanity for justice and liberty and peace are indispensable to the *dignity* of men". In the Universal Declaration on the Human Genome and Human Rights (UNESCO), adopted on 11 November 1997, references to human dignity are very many and dignity seems to be linked to the uniqueness and identity of human beings. A similar number of references can be found in the International Declaration on Human Genetic Data adopted on 16 October 2003.

[12]In no. 2 of the same article it is provided that: "The interests and welfare of the individual should have priority over the sole interest of science or society".

[13]So Andorno (2009), p. 224.

[14]Open to be joined by other extra-European States, such as the United States and Canada.

Dignity of the Human Being with regard to the Application of Biology and Medicine.[15] By establishing in Art. 1 that the "Parties [...] shall protect the *dignity* and identity of all human beings and guarantee everyone, without discrimination, respect for their integrity and other rights and fundamental freedoms [...]", the *Convention* carries out the synthesis between bioethical expectations and those of respect of human rights. Here, the respect of dignity is widely specified with reference to the ways to manifest consent.[16]

Within the international instruments in a "bill of rights of new generation" as the *Charter of Fundamental Rights of the European Union* Title I is titled *Dignity* while human dignity becomes the heading of Art. 1, which states "*Human dignity* is inviolable. It must be respected and protected".[17] It is not consecrated as a right to dignity, but it is set up as a general clause, implying the recognition of the character of an inviolable and legally protected good. In the same Title I, dignity is specified as the "Right to the integrity of the person" in Art. 3, which, at no. 2(*a*), provides for "the free and informed consent of the person concerned, according to the procedures laid down by law". It also appears in the Preamble, where human dignity is mentioned as the first value among the "indivisible (and) universal values" on which the EU is founded.[18] It is clear that in devoting the heading of Title 1 to dignity (before Title II "Freedoms" and Title III "Equality"),[19] and adding to it, as an incipit, Art. 1 in its wide conception, the Charter confers on it an almost "holy character": it makes it a sort of "sanctuary", implying that the human being, as unique, unrepeatable, and able of self-determination, is the holder of a value transcending any condition in which he or she may find themselves. But the Charter does not limit itself to assigning to dignity the rank of *character indelebilis*,[20] that is to say recognizing it, as stated in the Explanations to Art. 1 of the Charter, "not only [as] a fundamental right in itself but [as] ... the real basis of fundamental rights".[21] Besides its peculiar systematic choice of assigning to it "the axiological presumption

---

[15]Oviedo, 4 April 1997, hereinafter Convention on Human Rights and Biomedicine. Para 9 of the Explanatory Report (Council of Europe, Directorate of Legal Affairs, DIR/JUR(97) 5) provides that "The concept of human dignity, which is also highlighted, constitutes the essential value to be upheld. It is at the basis of most of the values emphasised in the Convention".

[16]In Chapter II, devoted to Consent, Art. 5 defines as a "General rule" the "free and informed consent" (no. 1) while in no. 3 it provides for the revocability of a given consent.

[17]Such references get, as it is well known, a full normative relevance because (Art. 6, para 1) of the equalization of the legal value of the Charter of Fundamental Rights of the European Union with that of the Treaty on the European Union (TUE) and the Treaty on the Functioning of the European Union (TFUE). See Olivetti (2001), pp. 3–11; Alpa and De Simone (2017), pp. 15–38.

[18]In this regard, we must not forget that the respect for human dignity assumes, in the same treaties, the role of a founding value of the European Union (Art. 2 TUE), and also a principle of the Union's external action (Art. 21, para 1).

[19]On the so called "triangle of Constitutionalism" see Baer (2009), pp. 417–468.

[20]For this definition see Pistorio (2009), p. 39.

[21]See *Official Journal of the European Union*, C-83/02 of 30 March 2010. On the Explanations we dare refer to Di Stasi (2010), pp. 425–454.

of fundamental rights"[22] (thus anticipating its provision, compared with the same "right to life" provided in Art. 2) and using the category of inviolability only for itself, it adds a specification of such value through the subsequent norms and, with regard to the topic at hand, to the already mentioned "right to the integrity of the person". Indeed, in consecrating "the right to respect for his or her physical and mental integrity" (para 1) in the fields of medicine and biology (para 2), Art. 3 of the Charter provides "the free and informed consent of the person concerned, according to the procedures laid down by law" (first alinéa). The innovative character of this norm cannot go unnoticed, since its difficult aim is that of making controversial subjects fall within the range of the fundamental rights of the EU, even if they are the subject of a recommendation or of special conventions binding more or less large groups of States. Although its content does not greatly wander off the provisions of the Convention, the inclusion of such norm in the Title devoted to dignity is very meaningful. The right to respect for physical and mental integrity (Art. 3, para 1) becomes (in para 2) the guarantee of a number of attributes of human dignity, among which there is "the free and informed consent of the person concerned"; however, as regards the ways of its manifestation, we refer "to the procedures laid down by law".

Finally, one cannot forget that in the Charter there are further references to dignity concerning its disciplined applications, with reference to specific categories of individuals: see, *inter alia*, Art. 25 devoted to "the rights of the elderly" which also provides . . . "to lead a life of *dignity*" or "the right to working conditions which respect his or her [. . .] *dignity*" (Art. 31.1).

3   Human Dignity: From Lack of Explicit Reference in the European Convention on Human Rights and Fundamental Freedoms to Increasing Relevance Within the ECtHR Case-Law

Although the European Convention on Human Rights and Fundamental Freedoms is explicitly built on the Universal Declaration of Human Rights, its text does not contain any reference to "dignity".[23] Nevertheless, this concept appears in subsequent Protocol no. 13 to the European Convention,[24] where the abolition of the death penalty is presented as "essential" for the protection of right to life and for "the full recognition of the inherent dignity of all human beings".

---

[22]So Silvestri (2007), p. 2.

[23]Costa (2013), pp. 665–724; McCrudden (2008), pp. 655–724; Kuteynikov and Boyashov (2017), p. 83 et seq. Moreover "dignity" has been included in several later Council of Europe Conventions, notably the Revised European Social Charter (Preamble and Art. 6) and the Convention on Human Rights and Biomedicine (cited above).

[24]Protocol no. 13 to the Convention for the Protection of Human Rights and Fundamental Freedoms, Concerning the Abolition of the Death Penalty in all circumstances, Vilnius, 3.V.2002.

Despite the lack of explicit reference, "respect for human dignity" has assumed paramount importance in the jurisprudence of the ECtHR, as it has been connected to the "very essence of the Convention", alongside human freedoms.[25] This statement, held for example in *Pretty* v. *United Kingdom* and reaffirmed in several other judgments of the Court of Strasbourg,[26] linked "respect for human dignity" to the object and the purpose of the Convention as a whole. Dignity pervades the Convention in a transversal manner, as a principle-value leading the interpretation and application of the provisions of the Convention itself "so as to make its safeguards practical and effective. Any interpretation of the rights and freedoms guaranteed has to be consistent with the general spirit of the Convention, an instrument designed to maintain and promote the ideals and values of a democratic society".[27]

Moreover, the ECtHR refers to dignity with regard to particular rights guaranteed by the Convention, namely the right to life (Art. 2)[28] and the prohibition of torture and inhuman and degrading treatment (Art. 3) that—it is important to underline—must be regarded as the most fundamental provisions of the Convention and as enshrining core values of the democratic societies making up the Council of Europe.[29]

Regarding Art. 3 of the ECHR, in 1973 the European Commission of Human Rights stressed that the expression "degrading treatment" showed that the general purpose of that provision was to prevent particularly serious interferences with human dignity.[30] Later, the Court made explicit reference to this concept in the *Tyrer* judgment, concerning not "degrading treatment" but "degrading punishment".[31] In finding that the punishment in question was degrading within the meaning of Art. 3 of the Convention, the Court had regard to the fact that "although the applicant did not suffer any severe or long-lasting physical effects, his punishment – whereby he was treated as an object in the power of the authorities –

---

[25] Among others, appl. *C.R.* (ECtHR 22 November 1995), para 42 and *S.W.*, para 44.

[26] Appl. No. 2346/02, *Pretty* (ECtHR 29 April 2002) para 65. See also appl. No. 28957/95, *Goodwin* (ECtHR 11 July 2002) para 90; appl. No. 18968/07, *V.C.* (ECtHR 8 November 2011) para 105; appl. Nos. 66069/09, 130/10, 3896/10, *Vinter and others* (ECtHR 9 July 2013) para 113; appl. Nos. 32541/08, 43441/08, *Svinarenko and Slyadnev* (ECtHR 17 July 2014) para 118; appl. No. 61243/08, *Elberte* (ECtHR 13 January 2015) para 142; appl. No. 23380/092, *Bouyid* (ECtHR 8 September 2015) para 89; appl. No. 16483/12, *Khlaifia and others* v. *Italy* (ECtHR 15 December 2016) para 158; appl. No. 23229/11, *Karachentsev* (ECtHR 17 April 2018) para 48.

[27] *Svinarenko and Slyadnev*, cit., para 118.

[28] Appl. No. 78103/14, *Fernandez de Oliveira v Portugal* (ECtHR 28 March 2017).

[29] See appl. No. 14038/88, *Soering* (ECtHR 7 July 1989) para 88. According to Art. 15 ECHR para 2, no derogation from Art. 2, except in respect of deaths resulting from lawful acts of war, or from Art. 3, shall be made under this provision. See among others Webster (2018).

[30] See *East African Asians*, applications nos. 4403/70, 4404/70,4405/70, 4406/70, 4407/70, 4408/70, 4409/70, 4410/70, 4411/70, 4412/70, 4413/70, 4414/70, 4415/70, 4416/70, 4417/70, 4418/70, 4419/70, 4422/70, 4423/70, 4434/70,4443/70, 4476/70, 4477/70, 4478/70, 4486/70, 4501/70, 4526/70, 4527/70, 4528/70, 4529/70, 4530/70, para 192.

[31] Appl. No. 5856/72, *Tyrer* (ECtHR 25 April 1978) para 33.

constituted an assault on precisely that which it is one of the main purposes of Art. 3 to protect, namely a person's dignity and physical integrity" (para 33).

Many subsequent judgments have highlighted the "strong link" between the concepts of "degrading treatment" and respect for "dignity",[32] placing the latter at the centre of Art. 3, even if its relief seems sometimes different from case to case. For example, in the case *Svinarenko and Slyadnev*, the main focus is on the "objectively degrading nature" of the treatment (holding a person in a metal cage during a trial), incompatible with the standards of civilised behaviour that are the hallmark of a democratic society constituting an "affront to human dignity in breach of Art. 3".[33] In *Bouyid* v. *Belgium*, instead, great attention was paid to the "minimum level of severity" demanded for a finding of substantive breach of Art. 3, which was not reached.[34]

There are several references to "dignity" in the cases of persons deprived of their liberty, in which the latter are normally considered in a vulnerable situation[35] and there is an inevitable element of suffering and humiliation involved in custodial measures: this as such will not entail a violation of Art. 3. Nevertheless, as it is clear from the Court's settled case law, under this provision the State must ensure that a person is detained in conditions which are "compatible with respect for his human dignity", that the manner and method of the execution of the measure do not subject him to distress or hardship of an intensity exceeding the unavoidable level of suffering inherent in detention and that, given the practical demands of imprisonment, his health and well-being are adequately secured.[36] Even the absence of an intention to humiliate or debase a detainee by placing him or her in poor conditions, while being a factor to be taken into account, does not conclusively rule out a finding

---

[32]See, for example, appl. No. 30210/96, *Kudła* (ECtHR 26 October 2000) para 94; appl. No. 44558/98 *Valašinas* (ECtHR 24 July 2001) para 102; appl. No. 39084/9711 *Yankov* (ECtHR 11 October 2003) para 114; *Svinarenko and Slyadnev*, cit., para 138.

[33]*Svinarenko and Slyadnev*, cit., para 138.

[34]For some critical findings, see Mavronicola (2016), p. 1, that emphasizes that largely because the ill-treatment was isolated and its concrete effects on the applicants were not significant or in long-term. What the Court failed to appreciate "is that it was the wrong committed against the applicants which reached the minimum level of severity, rather than the harm endured by them". On this topic see also Webster (2016), pp. 371–390. About the minimum level of severity required to fall within the scope of Art. 3 see the well written dissenting opinion of the Judges De Gaetano (with Lemmens and Mahoney).

[35]See, in respect of police custody, appl. No. 21986/93, *Salman* v. *Turkey* (ECtHR 27 June 2000) para 99, and *Bouyid*, cit., para 83.

[36]Among others, see *Kudła*, cit., paras 92–94, and appl. No. 8687/08, *Rahimi* (ECtHR 5 April 2011) para 60; appl. No. 5826/03, *Idalov* (ECtHR of 22 May 2012), para 93; *Svinarenko and Slyadnev*, cit., para 116; appl. No. 11138/10, *Mozer* (ECtHR 23 February 2016) para 178; *Valašinas*, cit., para 102; appl. Nos. 42535/07, 60800/08, *Ananyev and Others* (ECtHR 10 January 2012) para 141; appl. No. 7334/13, *Muršić* (ECtHR 20 October 2016) para 98–99.

of a violation of Art. 3 of the Convention.[37] Indeed, it is incumbent on the respondent Government to organise its penitentiary system in such a way as to ensure respect for the dignity of detainees, "regardless of financial or logistical difficulties".[38]

Moreover, in most cases concerning the detention of ill persons, the Court has examined whether or not the applicant received adequate medical assistance in prison.[39] In this connection, the "adequacy" of medical assistance represents the most difficult element to determine and, adopting a "case-by-case approach" the Court reserves a certain degree of flexibility in defining the required standard of health care.[40] In a recent case concerning a highly dangerous person which had played a prominent role in the Mafia (*Provenzano* v. *Italy*),[41] the Court does not find the applicant's health and well-being not adequately protected. However, reiterating that "the very essence of the Convention is respect for human dignity" (para 152) the ECtHR affirms that in renewing the imposition of the section 41*bis* regime, not only should the statement of reasons militating in favour of renewal have been increasedly detailed and compelling, but the applicant's evolving cognitive deterioration needed to be taken into account: "without providing sufficient and relevant reasons based on an individualised assessment of necessity, would undermine his human dignity and entail an infringement of the right set out in Art. 3" (para 152).

Finally, it is not possible to neglect the undeniable contribution of the ECtHR (and before it of the Commission) in reconstructing, from a jurisprudential point of view, the principle of dignity as well as the right to self-determination of the individual (not without limits) by the interpretation of Art. 8 of the ECHR on the respect for private and family life.[42]

---

[37] See, *inter alia*, appl. No. 28524/95, *Peers* (ECtHR 19 April 2011) para 74; appl. Nos. 5774/10, 5985/10, *Mandić and Jović* (ECtHR 20 October 2011) para 80; appl. No. 35972/05, *Iacov Stanciu* (ECtHR 24 July 2012) para 179.

[38] See, amongst many others, appl. No. 7064/05, *Mamedova* (ECtHR 1 June 2016) para 63; appl. No. 17885/04, *Orchowski* (ECtHR 22 October 2009) para 153; appl. Nos. 36925/10 21487/12 72893/12 73196/12, 77718/12, 9717/13, *Neshkov and Others* (ECtHR 27 January 2015), para 229; appl. Nos. 14097/12,45135/12, 73712/12, 34001/13, 44055/13, 64586/13 *Varga and Others* (ECtHR, 10 March 2015) para 103.

[39] *Mozer*, cit., para 178.

[40] See appl. No. 46468/06, *Aleksanyan* (ECtHR 22 December 2008), para 140.

[41] Appl. No. 55080/13, *Provenzano* (ECtHR 25 October 2018).

[42] Appl. No. 46470/11, *Parrillo* (ECtHR 27 August 2015) para 153; appl. No. 2346/02, *Pretty* . . .cit. para 61.

4   The References to Dignity in the CJEU Case-Law

If dignity is an indeterminate concept, whose meaning cannot be established in absolute *ex ante* but has to be contextualized, it could be useful to define the juridical concept of dignity also within the case-law of the Court of Justice. References to dignity in that matter are heterogeneous: sometimes it is referred to in connection with other rights of the Charter of Fundamental Rights (as Articles 4 and 7), more rarely as an autonomous guarantee and also as "part of EU law" or "general principle of law".

It is significant that, at times, the reference to other articles of the Charter becomes absolute as it happens with reference to Art. 4 referred to for the interpretation and application of a directive because "that value is closely linked to respect for human dignity".[43]

The reference to dignity may be called sometimes "prudent", considering that when it is recalled to by the General Advocate (*Kingdom of the Netherlands v European Parliament and Council of the European Union*),[44] it disappears in the *decisum* and when it is referred to by the Court of First Instance, it often disappears from the grounds of the Court's ruling (*Evonik Degussa GmbH v Commission of the European Communities,* 22 May 2008).[45]

In this context, a first, frequent, jurisprudential mention to dignity is linked to the respect for human dignity, as an essential condition for the exercise of freedom of movement and residence of people and workers, in compliance with Directive 2004/38.[46]

With regard to it, the Court states that: "[. . .] *it is apparent from the settled case-law of the Court that the purpose of Directive 2004/38 is to facilitate the exercise of the primary and individual right to move and reside freely within the territory of the Member States which is conferred directly on citizens of the Union by Article 21 (1) TFEU. Recital 5 of the directive states that that right should, if it is to be exercised under objective conditions of* dignity, *be also granted to the family members of those citizens, irrespective of nationality*[47]".

In this respect, the purpose of the Regulation (EEC) No 1612/68 is also addressed, which requires that, in order for freedom of movement to be guaranteed

---

[43]Case C-353/16, Judgment of the Court of 24 April 2018 para 36.

[44]Case C-377/98, Judgment of the Court of 9 October 2001. It is interesting to note that the Court based its decision nor on Art. 1 of the Charter though it was mentioned in the Advocate General's Conclusions.

[45]Case C-266/06 P, Judgment of the Court of 22 may 2008.

[46]Directive 2004/38/EC of the European Parliament and of the Council of 29 April 2004 *on the right of citizens of the Union and their family members to move and reside freely within the territory of the Member States, amending Regulation (EEC) No 1612/68 and repealing Directives 64/221/ EEC, 68/360/EEC, 72/194/EEC, 73/148/EEC, 75/34/EEC, 75/35/EEC, 90/364/EEC, 90/365/EEC and 93/96/EEC (Text with EEA relevance),* OJ L 158 (2004), pp. 77–123.

[47]Case 246/17, *Ibrahima Diallo* (ECJ 27 June 2018) para 64.

with respect for dignity, optimal conditions must be ensured for the integration of the EU worker family in the hosting Member State.[48]

Dignity plays an undisputed role even regarding third-country citizens, their families and asylum seekers. In particular, with regard to the latter, the Court affirms: *". . .According to that recital, the directive (2003/9) aims in particular to ensure full respect for human dignity and to promote the application of Articles 1 and 18 of the Charter. Thus, those requirements apply not only with regard to asylum seekers present in the territory of the Member State responsible pending that State's decision on their application for asylum but also to asylum seekers awaiting a decision on which Member State will be held responsible for their application*[49]*"*.

Even border guards, performing their duties, are required, *inter alia*, to fully respect human dignity.[50]

In relation to those who are persecuted in their countries because of their sexual orientation, dignity aims to gear the methods of conducting appraisals concerning the alleged sexual orientation of the applicants for international protection. As a matter of fact, the Court of Justice has stated that when the competent authorities request an expert report, procedures must comply, in particular, with the fundamental rights guaranteed by the Charter, such as the right of respect for human dignity enshrined in Art. 1 and the right of respect for private and family life, guaranteed by Art. 7.[51]

With regard to illegal migration, in the notorious case *El Dridi* the Court mentions dignity, clarifying that: *"[. . .] Directive 2008/115 states that it pursues the establishment of an effective removal and repatriation policy, based on common standards, for persons to be returned in a humane manner and with full respect for their fundamental rights and also their dignity*[52]*"*.

Moreover, a significant call to dignity concerns the criminal field, both as a guarantee of suspects and victims of crime (in particular vulnerable subjects) and as a guarantee for conditions of reclusion compatible with human dignity. Regarding the first profile, in accordance with the presumption of innocence, it is necessary to respect the reputation and dignity of the person concerned until a final judgment,[53] as

---

[48] Case 131/85, *Emir Gül* (ECJ 7 May 1986) para 25; Case 413/99, *Baumbast v Secretary of State for the Home Department* (ECJ 17 September 2002) para 50.

[49] Case 179/11, *Cimade, Groupe d'information et de soutien des immigrés (GISTI)* (ECJ 27 September) para 42–43.

[50] Case 23/12, *Mohamad Zakaria* (ECJ 17 January 2013) para 40.

[51] In Joined Cases 148/13, 149/13, 150/13, *A, B, C* (ECJ 2 December 2014) para 65.

[52] Case 61/11, *Hassen El Dridi, alias Karim Soufi* (ECJ 28 April 2011) para 31. See also: case 474/13, *Thi Ly Pham*, (ECJ 17 July 2014) para 20; case 181/16, *Sadikou Gnandi* (ECJ 19 June 2018) para 48; case 82/16, *K.A., M.Z., M.J., N.N.N.,O.I.O., R.I., B.A.* (ECJ 8 May 2018) para 100; case 47/15, *Sélina Affum* (ECJ 7 June 2016) para 4; case 562/13, *Centre public d'action sociale d'Ottignies-Louvain-la-Neuve* (ECJ 18 December 2014) para 42.

[53] Case 474/04, *Pergan Hilfsstoffe für industrielle Prozess GmbH* (ECJ 12 October 2007) para 78. See also, Case 279/02, *Degussa Degussa AG* (ECJ 5 April 2006) para 410: "It must be pointed out that, in inter partes procedures which are liable to result in the imposition of a penalty, the nature and

well as, in order to protect victims of crime, EU law (Council Framework Decision 2001/220/JHA, now Directive 2012/29/EU) obliges each Member State to work to ensure, during the procedure, that all victims receive a duly respectful treatment of personal dignity[54] and that particularly vulnerable victims benefit from specific treatment that meets optimally their situation.[55] As to the second profile, dignity contributes to the promotion of an evolutionary interpretation of the notion of inhuman or degrading treatment, where *the prohibition of inhuman or degrading treatment or punishment, laid down in Article 4 of the Charter, is, in that regard, of fundamental importance, to the extent that it is absolute in that it is closely linked to respect for human dignity [...]*[56]".

Dignity appears also as a parameter of reference with regard to freedom of expression and assembly; in fact, in *Schmidberger* e *Omega* cases the Court highlighted that the exercise of these rights should be in compliance with the rights protected by the Treaty, besides being in conformity with the principle of proportionality (*Schmidberger*, point 77, *Omega*, point 36).

Respect for dignity is also required for the exercise of professions such as, for instance, in the case of the lawyer established in another Member State, where dignity is configured as a parameter of evaluation, together with integrity and probity, for the purpose of access to the profession itself.[57]

Moreover, in the performance of administrative functions, besides gender discrimination in the workplace,[58] behaviours that are harmful to the employees' dignity[59] through intentional or non-intentional harassment[60] are prohibited,

---

amount of the penalty proposed are by their very nature covered by business secrecy until the penalty has been finally approved and announced. That principle follows, in particular, from the need to have due regard for the reputation and standing of the person concerned during a period in which no penalty has been imposed on that person"; Case 62/98, *Volkswagen* (ECJ 4 July 2000) para 281; Case 15/02, *BASF AG* (ECJ 15 March 2006) para 604.

[54]Case 467/05, *Giovanni Dell'Orto* (ECJ 28 June 2007), para 56.

[55]Case 105/03, *Maria Pupino* (ECJ 16 June 2005) para 52; Case 507/10 X (ECJ 21 December 2011) para 25–27.

[56]Case 578/16 PPU, *C. K., H. F., A. S.* (ECJ 16 February 2017) para 59.

[57]Case 292/86, *Claude Gullung* (ECJ 19 January 1988) para 22.

[58]Case 13/94, *P. e S.* (ECJ 30 April 1996), para 22.

[59]In Joined Cases 175/86 and 209/86, *M.* (ECJ 19 April 1988) para 23: "Although it is true that factors appertaining to an official's private life cannot as a general rule justify the imposition of disciplinary measures, it must, however, be admitted that a deliberate failure to comply with several court decisions involving a very substantial sum of money constitutes a fact which may reflect on his position as an official. In this case, such conduct could therefore be regarded as aggravating circumstances".

[60]Case 104/13, *Carlo De Nicola* (ECJ 23 October 2014) para 43–54, particularly para 50: "In accordance with point 2.1 of the Workplace Dignity Policy, it is not relevant that the [harassment] behavior in question is intentional or not. The determining principle is that harassment and intimidation are undesirable and unacceptable behaviors that undermine self-esteem and the self-confidence of those who are victims of it".

especially by those in a hierarchical position.[61] In addition, disciplinary sanctions can be applied to an employee, when the existence of a behaviour that is detrimental to the good functioning of the service or the dignity and reputation of another employee is ascertained.

Furthermore, dignity constitutes a "limit" concerning unfair business-to-consumer commercial practices in the internal market. As the Court affirms: "*Directive 2005/29/EC of the European Parliament and of the Council of 11 May 2005 [. . .] must be interpreted as meaning that [. . .]it does not apply to a national rule [. . .] which prohibits all advertising in relation to the provision of dental care, or to a national rule [. . .] which lays down the requirements of discretion with which the sign of a dental practice must comply*[62]" and "*[. . .] it must be interpreted as not precluding a provision of national law, such as that at issue in the main proceedings, which protects public health and the* dignity *and integrity of the professions of plastic surgeon and plastic doctor by prohibiting any natural or legal person from disseminating advertising for procedures relating to plastic surgery or non-surgical plastic medicine*[63]".

In its judgment of 9 October 2001 (*Kingdom of the Netherlands v European Parliament and Council of the European Union*, points 70–77), the Court of Justice confirmed that the fundamental right to human dignity is part of EU law. Consequently, none of the rights enshrined in the Charter can be used to undermine the dignity of others, since human dignity is part of the very substance of the rights established in the Charter itself and it cannot be prejudiced, even in case of limitation of a right.

Dignity is also a limit to investments in the field of biotechnology and in the use of biological material originating from humans: "*Although Directive 98/44[. . .] states that it seeks to promote investment in the field of biotechnology use of biological material originating from humans must be consistent with regard for fundamental rights and, in particular, the* dignity *of the person. The context and aim of the directive thus show that the European Union legislature intended to exclude any possibility of patentability where respect for* human dignity *could thereby be affected*[64]". As stated in article 5 of the Directive 98/44, the human body, in the

---

[61]Case 585/16, *Carina Skareby* (ECJ 25 July 2018) para 59. See also: Case 132/14, *CH* (ECJ 15 December 2015) para 90 and Case 218/17, *HF* (ECJ 17 September 2017) para 117: "From the entry into force on 1 May 2004, of Art. 12 bis, paragraphs 1 and 3 of the Statute, which provides that "the official shall refrain from any form of psychological or sexual harassment" psychological harassment now means "any inappropriate conduct that manifests itself in a durable, repetitive or systematic manner through behaviors, words, writings, gestures and intentional acts that damage a person's personality, dignity or physical or psychological integrity". On the point, in para 147, it is specified that "negative observations addressed to an agent do not necessarily harm his personality, his *dignity* or his integrity, when they are formulated in measured terms and are not based on illegitimate accusations and without any relationship with objective facts".

[62]Case 339/15, *Openbaar Ministerie* (ECJ 4 May 2017) para 123.

[63]Case 356/16, *Wamo BVBA, Luc Cecile Jozef Van Mol* (ECJ 26 October 2017) para 25.

[64]Case 34/10, *Oliver Brüstle* (ECJ 18 October 2011) para 32.

various stages of its constitution and development, cannot constitute a patentable invention, while, as far as living material of human origin is concerned, the directive defines the patent right in a sufficiently rigorous way so that the human body remains effectively unavailable and inalienable, in order that human dignity can be safeguarded.

In the end, in the highly controversial *Omega* case, dignity emerges as an independent value, where the Court affirms: *"the Community legal order undeniably strives to ensure respect for* human dignity *as a general principle of law*[65]*"*. It is also specified that: *"Community law does not preclude an economic activity consisting of the commercial exploitation of games simulating acts of homicide from being made subject to a national prohibition measure adopted on grounds of protecting public policy by reason of the fact that that activity is an affront to* human dignity".[66]

5 Embryonic Expressions of "Dialogue" Between European Courts (ECtHR and CJEU)

In the present phase of European history within an "integrated"—or basically integrated system of human rights—like the European one, the "circulation" among international judicial systems, both for interpretation or inspiration needs and for parametrical and/or application ends, is by now frequent. An evidence of this is the "selective" reception of (normative and jurisprudential) values existing between the judgments of the ECtHR and CJEU.

Human dignity has become a unifying element in the affirmation of the indivisibility of human rights according to the new needs of human beings. Could it then be considered to have become a normative concept, a central value, as well as the sum and presumption of new values in an international sense of protection of the *homo*— now *homo dignus*, and not only *homo œconomicus* (still the main protagonist of European Union action)?

The brief examination carried out highlighted that both Courts (ECtHR and CJEU) recall dignity interpreting it in light of the fundamental values which inspire both legal systems. Are there elements of convergence in the case-law of the two European Courts?

Some elements in this direction can be found in the reference to norms of the European Convention that perform a supplementary function "in the absence of minimum standards under EU law". Just think, for example, of the reference to the case-law concerning the Art. 3 of the ECHR which is found in some judgments of the CJEU (*ML v Generalstaatsanwalltschaft Bremen* or *Araniosy and Căldăraru*)[67]

---

[65]Case 36/02, *Omega Spielhallen-und Automatenaufstellungs-GmbH* (ECJ 14 October 2004) para 34.

[66]See also, Case 9/74 *Casagrande* (ECJ 3 July 1974) para 773. See: Alpa (1997), pp. 415–426.

[67]C-404/15 e C-659/15 PPU, 5 April 2016 para 90; C-220/18 PPU 25 July 2018, para 90.

regarding detention conditions which guarantee respect for human rights of a prisoner. But these cross-references need further developments, if we are to consider dignity as a unifying element in the growing "dialogue" between the ECtHR and CJEU.

References

Alpa, G. (1997). Dignità. Usi giurisprudenziali e confini concettuali. *Nuova giurisprudenza civile commentata, 13*, 415–426.

Alpa, G., & De Simone, G. (2017). Dignità umana. In AA.VV (Ed.), *Carta dei diritti fondamentali dell'Unione europea* (pp. 15–38). Milano: Giuffrè.

Andorno, R. (2005). La notion de dignité humaine est elle superflue en bioétique? *Revue générale de droit medical, 16*, 95–102.

Andorno, R. (2009). Human dignity and human rights as a common ground for a global bioethics. *Journal of Medicine and Philosophy, 34*, 223–240.

Arbuet-Vignali, H. (1997). Naturaleza y extensión de la protección internacional de los Derechos Humanos y sus vinculaciones con la soberanía. In AA.VV (Ed.), *Héctor Gros Espiell Amicorum Liber* (p. 34). Bruxelles: Brylant.

Baer, S. (2009). Dignity, liberty, equality: A fundamental rights triangle of constitutionalism. *University of Toronto Law Journal, 59*, 417–468.

Beyleveld, D., & Brownsword, R. (2001). *Human dignity in bioethics and biolaw*. Oxford: Oxford University Press.

Blengio Valdés, M. (2007). *El derecho al reconocimiento de la dignidad umana*. Montevideo: A. M.F.

Costa, J. P. (2013). Human dignity in the jurisprudence of the European Court of Human Rights. In C. McCrudden (Ed.), *Understanding human dignity* (pp. 665–724). Oxford: Oxford University Press.

Di Stasi, A. (2010). Brevi osservazioni intorno alle "spiegazioni" alla Carta dei diritti fondamentali dell'Unione europea. In C. Zanghì & L. Panella (Eds.), *Il Trattato di Lisbona tra conferme e novità* (pp. 425–454). Torino: Giappichelli.

Di Stasi, A. (2011). Human dignity: From cornerstone in international human rights to cornerstone in international biolaw? In S. Negri (Ed.), *Self-determination, dignity and end-of-life care*. Leiden: Martinus Nijoff Publishers.

Feldman, D. (1999). Human dignity as a legal value. *Public Law, 1*, 682–702.

Kretzmer, D., & Klein, E. (Eds.). (2002). *The concept of human dignity in human rights discourse*. The Hague: Kluwer Law International.

Kuteynikov, A., & Boyashov, A. (2017). Dignity before the European Court of Human Rights. In E. Sieh & J. McGregor (Eds.), *Human dignity: Establishing worth and seeking solutions* (p. 83 et seq). London: Palgrave Macmillan.

Lauterpacht, H. (1950). *International law and human rights*. London: Stevens & Sons Limited.

Macklin, R. (2003). Dignity is a useless concept. *British Medical Journal, 327*, 1419–1420.

Mavronicola, N. (2016). Bouyid v Belgium: The "minimum level of severity" and human dignity's role in Article 3 ECHR. *Cyprus Human Rights Law Review, 1*, 1–16.

McCrudden, C. (2008). Human dignity and judicial interpretation of human rights. *European Journal of International Law, 4*, 655–724.

Olivetti, M. (2001). Article 1. Human dignity. In W. B. T. Mock & G. Demuro (Eds.), *Human Rights in Europe*. Durham: Carolina Academic Press.

Pirozzoli, A. (2012). *La dignità dell'uomo. geometrie costituzionali*. Napoli: Esi.

Pistorio, G. (2009). Art. 1. Dignità umana. In G. Bisogni, G. Bronzini, & V. Piccone (Eds.), *La Carta dei diritti. Casi e materiali* (p. 39). Taranto: Chimenti.

Portinaro, P. P. (2008). La dignità dell'uomo messa a dura prova. In A. Argiroffi, P. Becchi, & D. Anselmo (Eds.), *Colloqui sulla dignità umana. atti del convegno internazionale* (p. 221). Roma: Aracne.

Ripepe, E. (2014). *Sulla dignità umana e su alcune altre cose*. Torino: Giappichelli.

Schachter, O. (1983). Human dignity as a normative concept. *The American Journal of International Law, 77*, 103–110.

Silvestri, G. (2007). Considerazioni sul valore costituzionale della dignità della persona, Intervention at the trilateral Meeting of the Italian, Portuguese, and Spanish Constitutions (Rome, 1 October 2007). http://www.associazionedeicostituzionalisti.it, 2.

Turco, G. (2018). Dignità e diritti. Un bivio filosofico-giuridico. In V. Marzocco (Ed.), *La dignità in questione. Un percorso nel dibattito giusfilosofico contemporaneo*. Torino: Giappichelli.

Webster, E. (2016). Interpretation of the prohibition of torture: Making sense of 'dignity' talk. *Human Rights Review, 3*, 371–390.

Webster, E. (2018). *Dignity, degrading treatment and torture in human rights law. The ends of Article 3 of the European Convention on Human Rights*. London and New York: Routledge.

The Dialogue Between the European Court of Human Rights and Domestic Authorities: Between Respect for Subsidiarity and Deference

Peggy Ducoulombier

Contents

In the past few years the principle of subsidiarity has become central in the case-law of the European Court of Human Rights (thereafter the Court or the ECtHR).[1] Although this principle supports the European Convention on Human Rights system (thereafter the Convention or the ECHR), the use, or rather misuse, of the subsidiarity principle is often criticised by certain judges or members of the academic world. However, reference to this principle is to be welcomed when used to restore dialogue between domestic authorities, in particular judges, and the Court, so as to improve implementation of its case-law through wider acceptance. The principle of subsidiarity is best understood as an expression of the "shared responsibility" in the protection of Convention Rights, highlighted by recent High Level Conferences.[2]

Peggy Ducoulombier is Professor of Public Law at the University of Strasbourg and Honorary Lecturer at the University of Aberdeen.

[1] See for instance, Spano (2014), pp. 487–502.

[2] See in particular the Brussels Declaration (2015) and Copenhagen Declaration (2018). It must be stressed that the draft Copenhagen Declaration, exploiting the recent developments of European case-law, clearly propounded a conception of subsidiarity which was equivalent to deference

---

P. Ducoulombier (✉)
Research Institute Carré de Malberg (EA 3399), University of Strasbourg, Law Faculty, Strasbourg, France
e-mail: ducoulombier@unistra.fr

© Springer Nature Switzerland AG 2019
P. Pinto de Albuquerque, K. Wojtyczek (eds.), *Judicial Power in a Globalized World*, https://doi.org/10.1007/978-3-030-20744-1_9

131

However, in the difficult times experienced by the Council of Europe and the Court, there is a risk that subsidiarity may lead, under the cover of institutional dialogue, to undue and general deference towards domestic authorities.

In addition, when it comes to the influence of the subsidiarity principle in the Court's reasoning, it may be necessary to distinguish between domestic authorities. If the application of this principle in relation to the Judiciary may be legitimate, as long as the methodology and substance of the European Court's case-law is complied with, in relation to the Legislative power it raises particular issues and involves delicate debates on the relation between democracy and Human Rights.

Judicial deference towards other constitutional powers is well known at the domestic level. For instance, the French Constitutional Council often stresses the fact that it does not enjoy a power of appreciation and decision similar to that of Parliament, thus limiting the constitutional review exercised, in particular with regard certain policy choices.[3] This judicial restraint is based on several ideas such as respect for the democratic principle or respect for institutional competence or expertise. Similar ideas may be found in the Court's case-law, such as the traditional expression of the margin of appreciation doctrine[4] or the more recent occurrences that special weight should be given to the decision of the domestic policy-maker in certain areas.[5] However, the renewed use of the subsidiarity principle carries the risk of transforming the control exercised by the Court and of endangering its position as a counter-majoritarian institution.

---

towards the domestic authorities' decisions. Even if the final declaration is more balanced, traces of the previous draft remain in the emphasis placed on subsidiarity and the margin of appreciation, the need for the Court to focus on serious or systemic violations, etc. However, for an understanding of subsidiarity as leading to a "shared responsibility" in the protection of the ECHR, see §10 of the Copenhagen Declaration: "The Conference therefore: Reiterates that strengthening the principle of subsidiarity is not intended to limit or weaken human rights protection, but to underline the responsibility of national authorities to guarantee the rights and freedoms set out in the Convention". In addition, the Copenhagen Declaration insists on the important of dialogue (see §33 and sq).

[3] See, for instance, for the legislator's decision to open marriage to same-sex couples, Conseil constitutionnel, dec. 2013-669 DC, 17 May 2013, §14.

[4] See ECtHR, *Handyside v. the United Kingdom*, 7 December 1976, app. 5493/72, §48: "[...] By reason of their direct and continuous contact with the vital forces of their countries, State authorities are in principle in a better position than the international judge to give an opinion on the exact content of these requirements as well as on the 'necessity' of a 'restriction' or 'penalty' intended to meet them. [...] Consequently, Article 10 para. 2 (art. 10-2) leaves to the Contracting States a margin of appreciation. This margin is given both to the domestic legislator ('prescribed by law') and to the bodies, judicial amongst others, that are called upon to interpret and apply the laws in force [...]".

[5] See, for instance, ECtHR, GC, *S.A.S. v. France*, 1 July 2014, app. 43835/11, §129: "It is also important to emphasise the fundamentally subsidiary role of the Convention mechanism. The national authorities have direct democratic legitimation and are, as the Court has held on many occasions, in principle better placed than an international court to evaluate local needs and conditions. In matters of general policy, on which opinions within a democratic society may reasonably differ widely, the role of the domestic policy-maker should be given special weight [...]".

If this judicial self-restraint may be understood, and even welcomed for legal or political reasons, the European Court must find the right balance between subsidiarity and control. Minimum standards must be set, below which no one can fall, even the representatives of the Nation. The path of subsidiarity may indeed lead to undue deference to the detriment of the regional protection of Human Rights. This contribution will first distinguish between the different forms of dialogue (1) before examining the impact of the renewed application of the subsidiarity principle on the control exercised by the Court and its authority as a whole (2).

1 Forms of Dialogue Within the European Convention on Human Rights System

The European Court of Human Rights may engage in dialogue with different domestic actors, in particular the Judiciary (Sect. 1.1) and the Legislative power (Sect. 1.2).

1.1 Dialogue with the Judiciary

It is logical that an exchange exists between the European Court of Human Rights and domestic judges who are primary responsible for the correct implementation of the Convention. This is the most evident expression of the subsidiary nature of the ECHR system. However, can this exchange be considered as a dialogue or is it rather a monologue, since it may be expected that domestic judges follow and apply the European Court's case-law without questioning it? Although the Court is reluctant to present the framework of the Convention in a hierarchical manner, according to article 46 ECHR States accept to abide by its case-law. It is therefore logical to conclude that domestic courts will apply the European Court's case-law, at least in cases involving their own States. Some Courts are even ready to follow Strasbourg jurisprudence although involving other countries, as long as this is relevant for the case under their supervision. For instance, the French *Cour de Cassation* stressed the importance of following the relevant European Court's case-law and not only the principles laid down in cases involving France.[6] In cases regarding the non-compliance of the custody regime with the ECHR, the *Cour de cassation* explained that Contracting Parties were expected to follow the European Court's case-law without waiting for their country to be brought before the European Court and condemned at the international stage. A more recent example of the *Cour de*

---

[6]See Cour de Cassation, Plenary Assembly, 15 April 2011, cases 589 to 592. Therefore, even before the case of *Brusco v. France,* 14 October 2010, app. 1466/07, was decided, it was clear from GC, *Salduz v. Turkey,* 27 November 2008, app. 36391/02, that French law was not compliant with article 6 ECHR.

Cassation's willingness to follow the Court's case-law may be found in the evolution of its position following the *Mennesson v. France* and *Labassee v. France* cases, regarding the situation of children born by way of surrogacy.[7]

Does this mean that no genuine dialogue can ever take place between judges? Of course, not. First of all, because not every domestic judge may be as willing as the *Cour de Cassation* to follow Strasbourg case-law. Tentative forms of dialogue have thus occurred with more or less success, depending on the subject or the jurisdiction involved.[8] However, in the past few years, dialogue with the Judiciary, or at least with certain domestic judges, has become tenser and it seems that the preeminent position of the European Court as the legitimate interpreter of the ECHR is questioned.[9] The relations between the Strasbourg Court and the United Kingdom (thereafter UK) Supreme Court may be used as an example of this vigorous dialogue.

According to section 2 of the *Human Rights Act* 1998, which incorporates some of the Convention Rights in the UK legal order, domestic courts must take into consideration the European Court's case-law when it is relevant for the case before them. The way section 2 is drafted is interesting because it does not limit the influence of the European Court's case-law to cases involving the UK. However, section 2 falls short of giving Strasbourg jurisprudence a binding effect on domestic courts as the sole duty of judges is to *take* it *into consideration*. As a result, the UK

---

[7]ECtHR, *Mennesson v. France*, 26 June 2014, app. 65192/11 and *Labassee v. France*, 26 June 2014, app. 65941/11. On July 3rd 2015, in Plenary Assembly case 619 and 620, the *Cour de cassation* reversed its own case-law and accepted that foreign birth certificates should be entered in the French register of births for children born from a surrogate mother, at least regarding their filiation with their biological father.

[8]For instance, after *Kress v. France* (ECtHR, GC, 7 June 2001, app. 39594/98), a dialogue started on the manner in which the former *commissaire du gouvernement* could attend the deliberations without his or her presence being considered as in breach of article 6 ECHR. However, the solution offered by the French Government was not deemed satisfactory by the Court and France was again found in breach of article 6 in *Martinie v. France* (ECtHR, GC, 12 April 2006, app. 58675/00). The proposal, prohibiting the presence of the *commissaire du gouvernement* during deliberations before first instance and appeal administrative courts and allowing it before the *Conseil d'Etat*, unless the parties object, was finally approved by the Court (ECtHR, dec., *Etienne v. France*, 15 September 2009, app. 11396/08). This string of cases may be considered as a form of dialogue between the French administrative judges and Government and the Court, although the result of the dialogue was very much influenced by the European Court. Nevertheless, the good will of both actors in trying to find a compromise on this issue led the Court to be rather tolerant towards other aspects of the internal functioning of French administrative courts. Indeed, in light of ECtHR, GC, *Reinhardt and Slimane-Kaïd v. France*, 31 March 1998, app. 23043/93 and 22921/93, involving the functioning of the *Cour de cassation*, one could have feared that the Court would find France in breach of article 6 again, with regard the communication of the work of the *conseiller rapporteur* to the *rapporteur public* (formerly known as *commissaire du gouvernement*). However, the Court, in the decision *Marc-Antoine v. France*, 4 June 2013, app., 54984/09, decided that there was no breach of the equality of arms principle as the draft judgment was an internal document and parties could understand the main arguments developed by getting access to the general substance of the *rapporteur public*'s conclusions on the case.

[9]Although the Copenhagen Declaration declares the Court to be the authoritative interpreter of the Convention (§26).

Supreme Court considers that there are circumstances allowing domestic judges to depart from the European case-law, including in cases involving the UK. What is striking is that the decision to resist Strasbourg rulings was first presented by Lord Philipps as an opportunity to start a dialogue with the European Court.[10] This development was prompted by the reaction of the Lords to the European Court's judgment in the case of *Al-Khawaja and Tahery*[11] about hearsay evidence. Unhappy with the chamber judgment, the UK supreme judges explained, in *Horncastle*,[12] that in certain circumstances and despite the *Ullah* principle according to which UK courts are expected to follow Strasbourg case-law,[13] domestic judges were entitled to depart from it. As expressed by Lord Philipps

> This is likely to give the Strasbourg Court the opportunity to reconsider the particular aspect of the decision that is in issue, so that there takes place what may prove to be a valuable dialogue between this court and the Strasbourg Court.

At the time, the European Court took the position of the Supreme Court into account and accepted to clarify its case-law,[14] but also defended firmly its position and rejected the criticisms raised against its case-law. However, as the tension grew with the UK, this resolve seemed to fade. Exceptions to the duty to take into consideration have multiplied. Resistance has replaced dialogue as the number of decisions in which UK courts decide to ignore the European Court's case-law has increased,[15] with sometimes strange results at the European level. Two examples

---

[10]This idea is already present in older cases from the House of Lords such as *R v Spear* [2002] UKHL 31 or *R v Lyons (n° 3)* [2002] UKHL 44.

[11]ECtHR, *Al-Khawaja and Tahery v. the United Kingdom*, 20 January 2009, app. 26766/05 and 22228/06.

[12]*R v Horncastle* [2009] UKSC 14, § 11: "The requirement to 'take into account' the Strasbourg jurisprudence will normally result in this Court applying principles that are clearly established by the Strasbourg Court. There will, however, be rare occasions where this court has concerns as to whether a decision of the Strasbourg Court sufficiently appreciates or accommodates particular aspects of our domestic process. In such circumstances it is open to this court to decline to follow the Strasbourg decision, giving reasons for adopting this course". The principles were later elaborated on by Lord Neuberger in the case of *Manchester City Council v Pinnock* [2010] UKSC 45, §48.

[13]*R (Ullah) v Special adjudicator* [2004] UKHL 26. Lord Bingham explained that a court "should in the absence of some special circumstances, follow any clear and constant jurisprudence of the Strasbourg court".

[14]As a result, in the Al-Khawaja case, the Grand Chamber reversed the decision of the chamber and found no violation of article 6 ECHR. ECtHR, GC, *Al-Khawaja and Tahery v. the United Kingdom*, 15 December 2011, app. 26766/05 and 22228/06.

[15]A recent example may be found in *R (on the application of Hallam) v Secretary of State for Justice* [2019] UKSC 2, where the majority of the UKSC departed from the Grand Chamber's ruling in *Allen* (ECtHR, GC, *Allen v. the United Kingdom*, 12 July 2013, app. 25424/09), with Lord Reed and Lord Kerr dissenting. In particular, Lord Reed stressed that none of the arguments used to justify departure from the ECtHR's case-law were present in the case. See §175: "[...] I find it difficult to accept that this court should deliberately adopt a construction of the Convention which it knows to be out of step with the approach of the European Court of Human Rights, established by numerous Chamber judgments over the course of decades, and confirmed at the level of the Grand

may be used in order to illustrate the shift in the "so-called" dialogue between the UK Supreme Court and the European Court of Human Rights.

The first example is drawn from the case of *Vinter*[16] and its follow-up *Hutchinson*.[17] In the first case, the Grand chamber considered that English Law on life imprisonment was not sufficiently clear and, as a result, uncertainty about the possibility of being released led to a breach of article 3 ECHR. However, the Court of Appeal in *Newell and McLoughlin*[18] refused to apply the clear precedent of *Vinter*. In the subsequent similar case of *Hutchinson*, the Grand chamber, instead of maintaining its condemnation of English Law or instead of reversing its *Vinter* position, decided that the case of *Newell* was the clarification that English Law needed to be considered as Convention compliant. When one knows the content of the Court of Appeal case, which is a blatant refusal to comply with *Vinter*, that is, to say the least, a very strange way to put it.

What is even more interesting is the fact that in addition to leading to a direct dialogue with the European Court on UK Law, the position of the UK Supreme Court seems to be given a particular weight in cases involving other countries, even in the absence of a third-party intervention.[19] This can be exemplified by the case of *S., V. and A.*[20] where the Court decided to reverse its long established position on article 5§1c) and preventive detention in light of the judgment of the Supreme Court in *R (on the application of Hicks and others) v Commissioner of Police for the Metropolis*,[21] who favoured the reasoning of the "minority"[22] in the German case of

---

chamber, in the absence of some compelling justification for taking such an exceptional step. For my part, I can see no such justification". Judge De Gaetano's separate opinion in *Allen* was, on the contrary, used by Lord Mance and Lord Wilson to support departing from the Court's judgment. It is now feared that simple disagreement with the decision of the ECtHR suffices to justify departure as Lord Wilson's acerb remarks on Strasbourg case-law seem to indicate (§85-86): "I am, however, persuaded that, in its rulings upon the extent of the operation of article 6(2) of the Convention, the ECtHR has, step by step, allowed its analysis to be swept into hopeless and probably irretrievable confusion. An analogy is to a boat which, once severed from its moorings, floats to sea and is tossed helplessly this way and that [...] the entitlement of the ECtHR [...] to give an autonomous meaning to the articles of the Convention is intended to override any distorted meaning ascribed to them contrary to the Vienna Convention by individual states, not to licence the ECtHR to ascribe a distorted meaning to them [...]". This resistance is also justified by the fact that Lord Wilson does not believe that there is further room for dialogue between the UKSC and the ECtHR (§94). Therefore, it is clear that dialogue can no longer be used as a justification for resistance.

[16]ECtHR, GC, *Vinter and others v. the United Kingdom*, 9 July 2013, app. 66069/09, 130/10 and 3896/10.

[17]ECtHR, GC, *Hutchinson v. the United Kingdom*, 17 January 2017, app. 57592/08.

[18]*R v Newell; R v McLoughlin* [2014] EWCA Crim 188.

[19]For an example of the influence of the UK by way of third-party intervention, see the evolution of the Court's position on the prisoners' right to vote, from ECtHR, GC, *Hirst v the United Kingdom (n°2)*, 6 October 2005, app. 74025/01, to ECtHR, GC, *Scoppola v. Italy*, 22 May 2012, app. 126/05.

[20]ECtHR, GC, *S., V. and A. v Denmark*, 22 October 2018, app. 35553/12, 36678/12 and 36711/12.

[21][2017] UKSC 9.

[22]It must be underlined that the judgment was delivered unanimously. However, judge Lemmens and judge Jaderblöm wrote a separate opinion to highlight their difference in reasoning on the

Ostendorf.[23] Whatever one might think of the correctness of this interpretation, the process and timing leading to this decision is somewhat awkward. Nevertheless, the more the European Court's case-law will enjoy an *erga omnes* rather than an *inter partes* effect, the more important the weight that will be given to domestic courts' interpretation of the Convention.[24]

In that regard, Protocol 16 will institutionalize dialogue with the highest judges,[25] at least for countries which have ratified it. This tool may prove very interesting in order to restore a direct and non-conflictual dialogue between judges as the interpretation of the Convention will be given through a request for an advisory opinion, which will hopefully be followed by the domestic courts, rather than resulting from the review of the domestic authorities' position and condemnation by European Court.[26] However, in case the domestic courts refuse to follow the advisory opinion of the Court, the conflict between the domestic and European Court will be in the open.

1.2 Dialogue with the Legislative Power

Dialogue with the Legislative power is not as direct as with the Judiciary. However, through the analysis of the alleged breach of the Convention such an exchange with Parliaments may occur. Protocol 16 will also increase this form of indirect dialogue as it is likely that most of the questions referred to the Court will be about the compliance with the European Convention on Human Rights of domestic legislation applied by domestic courts. One must stress that Parliaments indirectly dialogue with the European Court when passing legislation. Through various means,[27] they take into consideration European case-law in order to avoid future condemnations by the Court. However, even when consideration is given to European case-law, it may happen that Parliaments pass legislation in contradiction with the European Court of

---

ground that should have been used to conclude that the preventive arrest was not in breach of article 5 ECHR.

[23]ECtHR, *Ostendorf v. Germany*, 7 March 2013, app. 15598/08.

[24]In that regard, it must be highlighted that the Copenhagen Declaration argues for a development of States third-party interventions (see §40 in particular).

[25]One must also mention the development of a dialogue with the highest judges of Contracting Parties through the Superior Courts Network, which value is stressed by the Copenhagen Declaration (§37 b).

[26]See, for instance, the first request for an advisory opinion made by the French *Cour de Cassation* about the sequels of the *Mennesson* and *Labassee* cases, regarding the situation of the intended mother, which is yet to be clarified.

[27]For instance, Parliaments may have specialised Human Rights committee assessing the compatibility of bills with the ECHR, or this question may be an element taken into consideration in the legislative process. The Copenhagen Declaration (§16b), in line with the Brussels Declaration, insists on the role of Parliaments in securing the implementation of the ECHR at the domestic level.

Human Rights' interpretation of the Convention, whether voluntarily or not. For instance, the UK Parliament, due to the principle of Parliamentary supremacy, is free to pass legislation in violation of International Law. According to Section 19 of the *Human Rights Act*, ministers presenting public bills to Parliament must state that they believe the bill to be in compliance with the Convention. However, they may also declare that they are unable to do so but still want the bill to proceed in Parliament. It may be impossible to make such a statement because the case-law of the Court is unclear, unsettled or inexistent or it may be because the government wants the bill to be proceed regardless of the European Court's case-law. Another example of an ambiguous position of a Parliament towards Strasbourg case-law may be found in the debates leading to the French Law banning the concealing of the face in public spaces. Despite reservations being voiced by the *Conseil d'Etat*,[28] mostly based on Strasbourg cases such as *Ahmet Arslan*,[29] the bill was adopted almost unanimously by the two chambers of Parliament and the *Conseil constitutionnel* found it compliant with the Constitution.[30] Worries expressed about the compliance with the Convention appeared unfounded eventually and the ruling of the Court in *S. A.S.* demonstrates that the French Parliament succeeded in passing legislation compatible with the Convention. However, it is interesting to stress that, in this case, the Court was eager to send the message to other Parliaments that the French example should not necessarily be followed. However, when the Belgian Parliament followed suit, the European Court rightly applied the *S.A.S.* precedent to conclude that there was no violation of article 9 ECHR in the case of *Belcacemi and Oussar*.[31] These examples also illustrate the central role played by the principle of subsidiarity in the Court's reasoning, and its impact on the relation between the Court and Parliaments. Some consider that the Court's position has moved from respect to subsidiarity to undue deference towards domestic authorities. However, this criticism may be too strong.

2 Impact of the Renewed Use of Subsidiarity on the European Court of Human Rights

It is true that, in the past few years, subsidiarity has played a key role in the Court's reasoning, often leading to a wide margin of appreciation being given to domestic authorities in an increased number of fields and pushing the control exercised by the

---

[28] *Conseil d'Etat*, Etude relative aux possibilités juridiques d'interdiction du port du voile intégral, 25 March 2010.

[29] ECtHR, *Ahmet Arslan and others v. Turkey*, 23 February 2010, app. 41135/98.

[30] *Conseil constitutionnel*, dec. 2010-613 DC, 7 October 2010, *Act prohibiting the concealing of the face in public*.

[31] ECtHR, *Belcacemi and Oussar v. Belgium*, 11 July 2017, app. 37798/13.

Court away from substance towards procedure. This, in turn, has led to questions being raised about the Court's legitimacy and authority.

2.1 Procedural Control and Increased Level of Abstraction in the Reasoning of the European Court of Human Rights

The renewed place given to subsidiarity has an impact on the Court's method, whether the Court reviews a judicial decision or a legislative interference. In the case of *Von Hannover (n°2)*,[32] the Court explains, in a very pedagogical manner, the consequences for its control of the renewed application of the subsidiarity principle. As long as the Court's case-law is followed by judges and the balancing exercise correctly made, there must be very strong circumstances before the Court is ready to replace the domestic judges' decision with its own view.[33]

As far as legislative interferences are concerned, the reasoning of the Court has been clarified in several cases such as *Evans*,[34] *Animal Defenders International*[35] or *S.A.S.* In all of these cases, the source of the interference had a major bearing on the Court's review, in contradiction with the silence of the ECHR which does not distinguish between the different forms of alleged interferences with Convention rights, whether administrative, judicial or legislative. It is true that the case-law of the European Court had already accepted to give special weight to the decision of the legislative power when certain rights are involved, for which considerations of general or public interest enjoy a particular place such as the first article of the first additional protocol. However, in the aforementioned cases, the Court drew new consequences from the legislative source of the alleged breach, beyond the limits of its traditional jurisprudence. This evolution was based on the necessary respect for the democratic principle or for institutional expertise, although in most cases the main argument remains in fact respect for the democratic principle. The source of the interference has thus become an important element of the scope of the margin of appreciation and of the proportionality test, leading the Court's analysis to focus on general considerations rather than the elements of the case, to the regret of many,

---

[32]ECtHR, GC, *Von Hannover v. Germany (n°2)*, 7 February 2012, app. 40660/08 and 60641/08. This new methodology is supported by the Copenhagen Declaration (§28 c).

[33]See §105 and 107: "[. . .] In exercising its supervisory function, the Court's task is not to take the place of the national courts, but rather to review, in the light of the case as a whole, whether the decisions they have taken pursuant to their power of appreciation are compatible with the provisions of the Convention relied on [. . .] Where the balancing exercise has been undertaken by the national authorities in conformity with the criteria laid down in the Court's case-law, the Court would require strong reasons to substitute its view for that of the domestic courts [. . .]".

[34]ECtHR, GC, *Evans v. the United Kingdom*, 10 April 2007, app. 6339/05.

[35]ECtHR, GC, *Animal Defenders International v. the United Kingdom*, 22 April 2013, app. 48876/08.

including judge De Gaetano.[36] Indeed, this position reflects a classic and problematic conception of democratic legitimacy as being solely based upon electoral legitimacy. However, the Judiciary performs the democratic role of controlling other constitutional powers, including the Legislative power, in compliance with the fundamental principle of the Rule of Law. It is true that judicial deference towards other constitutional powers may also be based upon the constitutional principle of separation of powers, but this deferential position raises concern as to the capacity of courts to act a counter-majoritarian institutions and defend minorities against the undue will of the majority. This risk has been stressed by the European Court in the *S.A.S.* case, without leading to amending the scope of the margin of appreciation. The nature of the subject-matter involved as well as the source of the interference added up to justify the allocation of a wide margin of appreciation and led to the conclusion that there was no breach of the Convention.[37]

Whether the Court defers to the assessment of the domestic Judiciary or Legislative power, the result in terms of reasoning is that the Court's control moves away from substantive towards procedural review. The Court is now more often focusing on whether the Convention, as interpreted by its case-law, has been analysed and applied at the domestic level rather than on the substance of the decision taken by the domestic authorities. It therefore pays specific attention to the process by which legislation was enacted or the procedure according to which the judicial decision was reached. For instance, in the case of *S.A.S.*, the Court insisted on the fact that the position of women wearing the burqa was heard in Parliament, that the vote in Parliament was almost unanimous, that the decision was reviewed by the Constitutional Council etc. By the same token in the case of *Von Hannover (n°2)*, the Court took into account the fact that, following the first *Von Hannover* case, domestic courts amended their position and applied the balancing methodology and criterion developed in the Court's case-law. However, this shift in the methodology of the Court has raised concerns. As far as the Judiciary is concerned, European Court's judges have split over whether or not the domestic courts had sufficiently and correctly followed the Strasbourg court's case-law, demonstrating the subjectivity of this assessment.[38] In addition, as far as the Legislative power is concerned, a unanimous deliberation of Parliament does not protect it from being wrong when it comes to the protection of Human Rights. This is the reason why constitutional

---

[36]See the common dissenting opinion of Judge Ziemele, Sajó, Kalaydjieva, Vučinić and De Gaetano in *Animal Defenders International v the United Kingdom*, spec. pt 9 and 10: "there can be no double standards of human rights protection on grounds of the "origin" of the interference. It is immaterial for a fundamental human right, and for that reason for the Court, whether an interference with that right originates in legislation or in a judicial or administrative act or omission."

[37]We do not disagree with the end result in S.A.S., however we argue that it would have been preferable for the Court to take a strong stance on gender equality rather than building its reasoning on the scope of the margin of appreciation.

[38]See for instance, ECtHR, GC, *Axel Springer AG v. Germany*, 7 February 2012, app. 39954/08 or ECtHR, GC, *Bărbulescu v. Romania*, 5 September 2017, app. 61496/08.

review of Legislation exists. However, whether the renewed place given to subsidiarity and dialogue has led to deference must also be analysed in light of the bigger picture.

2.2 Legitimacy and Authority of the European Court of Human Rights

One can regret the evolution of the Court's reasoning but it would be unfair to portray it as a completely illegitimate move. Indeed, one can also find merit in the decision of the Court to stop the micro-management of Human Rights that an overly sophisticated case-law sometimes reveals. Deferring to the position of the representatives of the Nation or domestic judges in areas linked to the history or cultural aspects of the life of one country may be legitimate and may be considered as the proper way to reconcile 47 different States and legal systems. It is also the result of the better implementation and respect at the domestic level of the Convention. From that point of view, the decision of the Court to restore subsidiarity and dialogue with domestic institutions contributes to its legitimacy and global authority. However, one must not be naïve. The evolution of the Court's interpretation of the Convention is also the result of the general situation of the European Convention system, facing resistance from certain Contracting Parties. In this evolution, it is difficult to assess the part played by a genuine concern for a more balanced interpretation of the Convention and the part played by judicial politics.

The assessment of the correctness of this new position is, of course, a question of balance between subsidiarity and control but also a question of coherence. It is absolutely fundamental that the Court applies these new principles in a coherent manner.[39] But coherence does not require uniformity. It would be impossible and illegitimate to apply the new methodology in a uniform manner as the situation within the Council of Europe is far from being harmonious. Several countries have recently raised concern not only for their overall Human Rights record but more precisely for the protection of the Rule of Law due to attacks on their own Judiciary. In those circumstances, it is not possible for the Court to rely on the subsidiary principle and its consequences. Still, one must be cautious not to create an impression of double standard with countries, such as the UK, for which the Court would be deferential, sometimes to the extreme and not only because its Judiciary may be trusted,[40] and countries for which the Court would apply a strict proportionality test

---

[39]In that regard, certain judges consider that principles of interpretation are not applied consistently by the Court. See the dissenting opinion of Judge De Gaetano and Judge Wojtyczek in the case of *S., V. and A. v. Denmark*.

[40]See, for instance, the double standard criticism raised by the minority in the case of *Animal Defenders International* when compared to the case of *VGT Verein gegen Tierfabriken v. Switzerland*, 28 June 2001, app. 24699/94.

on interferences coming from the Judiciary or Parliament such as Hungary or Poland.[41] However, the position of the Court is necessary to maintain the minimum standard below which Contracting Parties must not fall. As explained by Judge Spano

> the Court may grant deference if national decision-makers are structurally capable of fulfilling [their] task. [. . .] States that do not respect the rule of law, [. . .] and do not ensure the impartiality and independence of their judicial systems, oppress political opponents or mask prejudice and hostilities towards vulnerable groups or minorities, cannot expect to be afforded deference.[42]

3 Conclusion

Are the new forms of dialogue developed in the Court's case-law able to restore faith and trust between domestic authorities and the European Court? It must be stressed that resistance is not necessarily always ill-placed. Indeed, one may agree, for instance, that when it comes to the interpretation of article 6§2 ECHR, the Court has gone too far as Judge De Gaetano himself stressed in its dissenting opinion in the case of *Allen v. the United Kingdom*. It is doubtful, however right the domestic position might be, that departure from the Court's case-law could be perceived as constructive dialogue and not as resistance, pure and simple. The effect that such position may have on the legitimacy of the European system as a whole should lead the Court to pay a particular attention to the coherence of its own reasoning and to err on the side of caution when it comes to the interpretation of the Convention. Otherwise, dialogue will turn into resistance and subsidiarity into undue deference.

References

Spano, R. (2014). Universality or diversity of human rights, Strasbourg in the age of subsidiarity. *Human Rights Law Review, 14*, 487.

Spano, R. (2019). Human rights: Enforcement and effectiveness. In N. Aloupi, D. P. Fernández Arroyo, C. Kleiner, L.-A. Sicilianos, & S. Touzé (Eds.), *Les droits humains comparés, A la recherche de l'universalité des droits humains* (pp. 109–115). Paris: Pedone.

---

[41] In order to mitigate such fears, one may highlight the *Beghal v. the United Kingdom* judgment, 28 February 2019, app. 4755/16 (non-final), in which a chamber of the first section found the 2000 terrorism legislation of the UK in breach of the Convention while, in other cases, the Court seemed more willing to adapt its case-law to the difficult circumstances of fighting terrorism. See, for instance, ECtHR, GC, *Ibrahim and others v. the United Kingdom*, 13 September 2016, app. 50541/08, 50571/08 et sq.

[42] Spano (2019), p. 114.

On Legitimacy for the Exercise of Public Power

Gunilla Edelstam

Contents

Gunilla Edelstam is Associate Professor for Public Law.

G. Edelstam (✉)
Sodertorn University, Huddinge, Sweden

© Springer Nature Switzerland AG 2019
P. Pinto de Albuquerque, K. Wojtyczek (eds.), *Judicial Power in a Globalized World*, https://doi.org/10.1007/978-3-030-20744-1_10

1 Legitimacy in Connection to Unilateral Decision Making

1.1 Unilateral Decisions

Administrative law is a comprehensive part of the legal system. Society is governed to a large extent through administrative law. This paper deals with legitimacy in connection to exercise of public power through unilateral decision-making. A unilateral decision has consequences for the individual concerned. It can for example concern a prohibition, a permit, an allowance, an authorization, an administrative fine, a tax or a duty to perform something (for ex. tearing down a house that was illegally built). Therefore the decision implies power. It implies public power irrespective of whether the individual through the decision receives what he applied for or was denied it.

Unilateral decisions are often made by officials working at administrative author-ities of the state or in local government offices. A law from the Parliament is the basis for the decision-making in both cases.[1] The local governments of Sweden do not have any authority to stipulate regulations as regards to unilateral decisions targeting individuals (natural persons or legal persons). The parliament has through legislation given the local government the duty and power to handle lots of unilateral decision making.

An official is employed by the public authority and it can be his task to make unilateral decisions in individual cases. An administrative case can start with an application from the individual concerned and it is then the task of the official to investigate the case and to make a decision. This applies for issues that have a benign character (for example an investigation on an allowance or a permit of some kind). It is also possible that the official ex officio takes the initiative to investigate a case. This applies for issues that have a burdensome character (for example an investiga-tion on prohibition of some kind or on the loosing of a permit).

Such unilateral decisions are not judicial decisions as they are not made by courts and the judiciary. They are administrative decisions and they imply exercise of public power by officials at the public authorities. However they can to some extent be taken to courts.

1.2 Legitimacy

What is legitimacy in that context? What designates legitimacy in administrative law? In the publication "Legitimacy in European Administrative Law: Reform and Reconstruction"[2] scholars participating in the Dornburg Research Group of New

---

[1]Unilateral decisions can to some extent be made by politicians for ex. by the social board of the local government. The consequences for the politicians might be different as they are not employed.
[2]Ruffert (2011).

Administrative law focused on this question. It was obvious that administrative activities, administrative institutions and also administrative law must be legitimate[3] and that legitimacy has to be designated a legal concept (legitimate refers to situation and legitimacy refers to process or result[4]). This concept however is not self-evident but at any rate legitimacy provides a linkage between basic foundations of the political system and administrative law.[5] Administrative activities, administrative institutions and also administrative law must be legitimate and it is beyond possible acceptance to claim anything contrary to this starting-point. However the broadness of consensus hides all existing uncertainties about the notion of legitimacy. It has to be designated a legal concept but this is not static and it is rather linked to "law in action" than to "law in the books".[6] Persons, procedures and institutional structures in public administration have to seek legitimacy continuously.[7] Legitimacy results as much from events and practices as from legal normativity, i.e. "law in action" and it is[8] important not to conclude that legitimacy is synonymous with legality. We know that on occasion legally irreproachable measures may be considered and experienced as illegitimate.[9] Legitimacy can be given a dual significance.[10] It can refer to the product of social recognition or adequation with a norm or standard. It is to the first definition we refer when considering that an authority has the overall consent of those it concerns. However if a judge states that the court does not have the legitimacy to deliver a judgement he means that it is not in adequation with a norm or standard, there is no support in the law.

Legitimacy can never be taken for granted or conferred once and for all.[11] It is not static but there are some terminological gain that can be drawn from a comparative look at neighbouring notions,[12] such as legality, responsibility and judicial review.

Legitimacy is linked to legality. All that is legal is supposed to be legitimate per se, and illegal actions of government can never be legitimate. Legitimacy is not consumed by legality, and it is crucial to determine where legality ends in administrative law and where the sphere of pure legitimacy begins. This is certainly true for areas of broad administrative discretion.[13]

---

[3]Ruffert (2011), p. 353.
[4]Ruffert (2011), p. 355.
[5]Ruffert (2011), p. 353.
[6]Ruffert (2011), p. 353.
[7]Ruffert (2011), p. 354.
[8]Caillosse (2011), p. 12.
[9]Caillosse (2011), p. 12.
[10]Caillosse (2011), p. 13.
[11]Caillosse (2011), p. 13.
[12]Compare Ruffert (2011), p. 355.
[13]Ruffert (2011), p. 355.

Legitimacy is neighbouring responsibility.[14] Responsibility can be linked to the idea of pecuniary consequences of administrative fault, but it may also be applied as responsibility towards certain principles, structures and values.[15]

There is a relationship between legitimacy and control. Judicial review means that legitimacy can be controlled. Although that does not exist in terminology, there is a common underlying sense of control mechanism being important to legitimatize administrative activity. Above all, judicial control is a special feature of legitimacy of administrative law. If there were not independent courts, administrative activity could not get rid of a power-oriented bias.[16]

In this paper I will deal with legitimacy from these three points of view: legality, responsibility and judicial review. Legal and legality often refers to the law in the book. The source of origin and thus the constitution is important in that context. Legitimacy goes beyond legality and legality is not enough to create legitimacy. Occasionally legally irreproachable measures, i.e. law in action, might be considered and experienced as illegitimate. Legitimacy however is not a precise term or legal term. Some connotations are closely linked to legitimacy. Legality, responsibility and judicial review can be indicated with regard to legitimacy within the administrative law field, when power is exercised by public authorities through unilateral decisions. There is in addition another connotation that needs to be mentioned and that is trust.

1.3 Trust

Trust is the social recognition. It is important that people have confidence in the system i.e. the legislation from the law maker and the application from the decision maker. The power derives from the people in a democracy. A goal should be that people can have trust in the administrative legal system. Administrative law shall promote the common good, the public interest. Trust in the system can diminish if laws are considered not to be in the public interest. Trust is more of a feeling—social recognition—and thus difficult to define but nevertheless of importance to the legitimacy of the legal system. People are dependent on the well-functioning of the administration and the legal administrative system and they will distrust it if it does not function well enough. If for example "the people" (i.e. many of them) discover that immigration in 1 year correspond to a medium sized city of the small country that they live in and they protest against it, this is an expression of distrust. It can be designated in many other ways depending on the person expelling the

---

[14]Accountability is partly congruent with aspects of responsibility but in the true sense of the term it is limited to rather sharply defined mechanisms of the British government system. Compare Ruffert (2011), p. 355.

[15]Ruffert (2011), p. 356.

[16]Ruffert (2011), p. 360.

designation but from a legitimacy point of view it should count as a question of peoples' trust. This distrust is connected not to legality but rather to the wider concept of legitimacy. If people find that the gasoline prices rise too high due to a new tax law, their protests—from legitimacy point of view—can be seen as a question of trust. Democracy and the—from "the people" derived—power has been used, by those in power, in such a way that the people do not have trust in the system and the legislation behind it.

These are examples where "the people" do not have trust in the law maker. Regarding the gasoline tax protests that took place all over France in 2018, it was clear that it was protests against the acting of the legislative power. In the immigration issue the protests were also a question of distrust in the law maker if the legislation made the "middle sized city immigration" possible. If it instead—as the law was in force—would be a question of mistakes or faults by the officials when applying the law in individual cases (giving residence permits) it would be a question of trust or distrust in the public authority and its officials. For example when the Migration authority of Bremen, Germany, during spring 2018 was accused of not following the legislation and thus allowing immigrants residence permits in cases where the law did not allow it, this was an expression of distrust in the public authority regarding how the duties during the investigations were handled.

Trust is another dimension of legitimacy. Some legal matters might be distrusted to such an extent that the power that derived from the people is not accepted by the people. In the gasoline tax protests case in France the politicians obviously found that this was the case. That is why they drew the law back.

2 Legality and Legitimacy

2.1 The Chain of Legitimation

The constitution contains the foundations of law making power. Legitimacy is mediated, and such mediation is maintained by the executive power and thus the official in charge of unilateral decision making. There is a chain of legitimation.[17,18] It is also referred to as the chain of hierarchy. It is a principle of hierarchy with the constitution on top. The legislation that the official applies in a current case shall be in accordance with superior legislation of the "chain". The official must find relevant legislation.

There is a personal legitimation for the official. The personal legitimation implies[19] that every administrative agent has his function conferred upon him by a person who can avail himself of democratic legitimation: a government which is

---

[17]Schmidt Assman (2011), p. 54.

[18]Gonod (2011), p. 4.

[19]Schmidt Assman (2011), p. 54.

legitimatized by parliament names its agents and thus legitimatizes them. This is suitable for administrations which are organized in a hierarchical way.

The chain of hierarchy has as regards to administrative law several levels of national legislation. It can in addition involve international treaties or conventions such as EU legislation and the ECHR (if such stipulations have been made part of the national legal system in accordance with the national constitution). The EU-regulations and directives are on national level mainly part of administrative law. The ECHR puts restrictions on the state, as regards to interference of the state in the rights of individuals, the negative duties of the state. As regards to national administrative law these negative duties are of importance as they lay restrictions as to what legislation the parliament of the state can stipulate as well as what the authorities of the state can be allowed to decide.

Public power derives from the people. In many democracies constitutional and legal concepts of "the people" as the abstract embodiment of ultimate power, provides the root from which the legitimacy of public administration is derived. This is the source of the legislation. At the top of this chain you find the representatives elected by the people. They establish material laws—on what the administration can do as regards to unilateral decision making—but stipulations of legislation can to some degree be delegated to the government or to central administrative bodies. With regard to administrative law there are thus constitutional laws, there are ordinary laws from the parliament (swe. lagar), regulations from the government (swe. förordningar) and regulations from some central authorities (swe. föreskrifter). In this chain with several levels, a rule on a lower level must have support by rules on a higher level. Such issues of legality can be more common within administrative law than in civil or penal law due to the fact that there can be a chain of more levels.

In the chain of hierarchy must be included relevant EU-law and Human Right convention. The constitution stipulates the link to EU-law and EU-legislation take precedence over national law. On national level the EU-legislation in general become part of the administrative legislation and it often deals with material law. The constitution also stipulates the precedence of the ECHR over national legislation.

Conventions and similar agreement with other states must be included in Swedish legislation in order to be binding for courts.[20] We follow a dualistic method and ratifications are not enough if courts are to apply the convention. The convention, ECHR, is ordinary Swedish law but the constitution stipulates that new legislation may not be in contradiction to the ECHR. The ECHR is therefore a restriction as regards to what laws that can be stipulated.

---

[20]Before 1995 when the ECHR became Swedish law the fact that there was an international court, the ECtHR, complicated the situation and it was debated whether the convention was binding for the courts.

2.2   Administrative Law

Administrative unilateral decisions from public authorities have a lack of legality if there is no coherence with higher norms in the chain and the source of origin.

The legislation that is applied when exercising power through unilateral decision making is material legislation with regard to the decision to make and its prerequisites. There is also legislation on formalities such as rules on proceedings and rules on delegation of decision making power.

EU laws are generally part of material administrative law. Procedural legislation as well as the delegation of power to a certain authority is left to the national parliament.[21] ECHR can deal with restriction as regards to national material legislation but it also deals with national court procedure in article 6 which has some influence on the administrative proceeding. The principle of proportionality should be taken into consideration when a unilateral decision is made and can be considered as a matter of legality.

2.3   Interpretation

Issues regarding interpretation of material law and methods used can also be relevant as regards to legality.

Frame-work legislation is sometimes used in administrative law and it deals with material law. In legislation the parliament defines the frame but there is a need for concretization as regards to the prerequisites. That concretization is left to lower instances. Frame-work legislation often gives wide range of possibilities to choose between. Legality of application in such cases can be debated as regards to the support on higher chain-level.

2.4   Concluding Remarks

There can thus be many layers to observe for an official working in a public authority when he shall exercise power through a unilateral decision in a current case. He must apply the relevant material law. He must have delegation of power according to formal law. He must handle the proceeding in accordance with law. Legality is primarily a matter of law in the book and how to interpret it. There is no legitimacy if there is no legality. Most officials dealing with unilateral decision making handle specific cases, on environmental issues, on planning and building, on social allowances, on permits, on prohibitions etc. and therefore, in most cases, it is rather

---

[21]Procedural regulations (for example defence right such as right to information) can be found in the Services Directive, see Edelstam (2012), p. 589.

obvious to a responsible official which law that shall be applied in a current case. However legitimacy goes beyond legality and that is more visible when studying responsibility. The law gives some legitimacy to a unilateral decision but it is not enough. Legitimacy is not consumed by legality.[22]

3 Responsibility and Legitimacy

3.1 Duties and Consequences

Responsibility[23] is neighbouring to legitimacy.[24] Responsibility, dealt with here, regards to the duties that an official has due to his position and the consequences that can occur if he does not fulfil his duties. "Responsibility" goes beyond "legality". It is not just about the "law in the book" but on the law in action". The duties are one side of responsibility. They concern what the official shall fulfil during the handling of a case. The other side of responsibility is the consequences that might be put on the official by courts if he neglects his duties.

The duties involve starting a case and then finding and interpreting applicable legislation as well as finding the facts in the current case and observing objectivity. The official can in addition have some formal duties with regard to defence rights. The duties that will be dealt with belongs to the phase that precedes the decision.

There can be consequences if the official neglects his duties and these consequences can be put on him by the public authority or by courts, for example the penal law court can sentence him for breach of duty to pay a fine or to imprisonment for maximum 2 years.

3.2 Duties

3.2.1 Open the Case

In burdensome cases there is a duty to open a case ex officio according to law and in benign cases there is a duty to start investigation when the individual party applies for a certain decision. The time limit will not be dealt with here but passivity as regards to the starting of an investigation can be of importance when considering whether the official fulfils his duty.

---

[22]Ruffert (2011), p. 355.

[23]Accountability will not be used as term in this context. In the true sense of the term it is limited to rather sharply defined mechanisms of the British government system. Ruffert (2011), p. 355.

[24]Ruffert (2011), p. 355.

3.2.2 The Question of Law

The official must identify the relevant legislation in the mentioned hierarchy which is, in most cases, easy for him as he is employed to handle a certain administrative field, building permits for example. He deals with it more or less every day. It includes material law within the current field, formal procedural law and legislation on delegation of authority. He might have to use methods of interpretation especially as regards to material law. If the legislation as regards to material law contains broadly framed conditions and thus discretionary power the official must make a choice between different possibilities. These issues deal with the "law in the book" i.e. legality.

3.2.3 Fact-Finding[25]

This is law in action and it consists of collecting information, evaluating the information and assessing the burden of proof as well as the use of some principles.

3.2.3.1 Collecting Facts

The duties involve the investigation of the circumstances in the current case. Who shall find out the facts in a current case? In general it is the official in a burdensome case where he himself ex officio opened the case and it can be the individual if he started the case through an application. In benign cases the individual party however might need some help in order to know what facts are needed. This implies a certain duty for the official to help him, at least by informing him on needed facts. If the individual does not have a representative to help him it might be difficult for him to understand that he needs guidance regarding fact finding.

3.2.3.2 Evaluating Proofs

When facts and proofs have been collected it might be necessary—if the case is not evident—for the official to evaluate the proofs/evidences as to relevance and truth. He might have to evaluate information in the current case with regard to its value as proof. There is a free submission of proofs meaning that the party in the case can submit whatever he wants. The official is not bound to accepting only certain proofs. The party is free to try to prove his case in other ways. There is also a free sifting of proofs meaning that the official shall value the weight of the information as proof. A court might value the information differently than the official but still there is a certain freedom.

---

[25]Compare Edelstam (2011), p. 141ff. Compare Edelstam (2016).

3.2.3.3   Standard of Proof and Burden of Proof

The official might also have to decide what the necessary standard of proof is. There is free evaluation of proofs but as regards to the needed standard of proof in an administrative case, it is not "beyond reasonable doubt" that is needed. What is needed instead? In a burdensome case as well as in a benign case this can be essential to the party, which means that it can be essential in order to reach legitimacy. Instead of fact finding, presumptions sometimes are used. If a presumption is used there is no need for evidence. From a legitimacy point of view this might be debated.[26] When may presumptions be used?

When the official shall make a decision on the basis of law and facts and evidences in a current case, he might have to use the burden of proof. This can be used if there is uncertainty regarding how to decide. The relevant standard of proof combined with the placing of the burden will solve the problem when there still is doubt and the investigation cannot reach further.

The basis for traditional designations of burden of proof is that the judge must make a judicial decision even if he is not sure of whether there are sufficient proofs. In administrative law a duty for the public authority and its official to find facts can imply that the burden of proof is on the public authority and not on the individual. If the official in such a case would find that the standard of proof can be placed on a rather low level, that might have an influence on the burden of proof. In a burdensome case (on for example a prohibition of some kind or a withdrawal of a permit) that the authority and its official started ex officio, the burden of proof could maybe be avoided if a lower standard of proof is applied. If instead the duty for the authority to investigate and find facts would be in focus, the burden of proof would be on the public authority. If a duty to investigate and help the individual to find facts exists, the public authority should fulfil this duty before the burden of proof is used in connection to decision making.[27]

3.2.4   Principles[28]

3.2.4.1   Independence

In Sweden there is independence for the decision maker implying that he also is fully responsible for the unilateral decision. This independence has a long tradition and is stipulated in the Swedish constitution. The office of the government is separated from the administrative authorities. The Government takes all important decisions as a collective body. This implies that a minister in the government is not allowed to

---

[26]Compare Edelstam (2011), p. 144f.

[27]Compare Edelstam (1995), p. 190ff.

[28]Independence, impartiality and objectivity have here been designated as principles. As they are stipulated in law this could be debated.

make any statements in an ongoing case. The Swedish constitution stipulates, regarding unilateral decision making, that no authority nor the parliament or a local government may decide on how a public authority shall decide in a case regarding exercise of public power. Independence of the decision maker can be seen as one part of legitimacy. It is a way to avoid a power oriented bias.

3.2.4.2 Impartiality and Objectivity

There is no code of ethics for the officials as in for example the USA and the argument against it has been that the most central and the most demanding in high administrative ethics could not be summarized in some simple points.[29] There are however stipulations regarding impartiality and objectivity that shall be observed during the fact-finding phase.

Impartiality and objectivity concern the relation between the individual party and the official as well as how the case is to be handled. Impartiality can to some extent be defined in legislation. This is however not possible as regards to objectivity. Important is in any case that the public administrative acting should promote the public interest not the personal interest of the official.

The official can be challengeable if for example the individual concerned is his friend or relative or if it concerns himself. He shall not deal with the case if he is challengeable and he should himself renounce the case. Partiality can to some extent be specified in legislation. It is defined in a stipulation in the Swedish Administrative Proceedings Act. Objectivity is harder to define in an administrative procceedings act. However there are some situations that can be described as lacking objectivity. One is about negative influence from an outsider and another is about negative influence from insiders i.e. colleagues.

The first mentioned inappropriate influence from an influencer/outsider on the official/insider involve influence from organised and economic criminality[30] and the relation is profitable for the illegal business activity of the influencer. The official/insider misuses his position by mismanaging his exercise of power, to the benefit of the influencer/outsider. The influencer is in that case helped by the insider. The insider leaks information on the investigation, the way the public authority works and gives advices on how to avoid controls and penalties. The official/insider makes a decision or he avoids making a decision. The insider might gain economically but it is also possible that other things than money is behind his acting or passivity, such as status, need for acknowledgement, need for excitement or dissatisfaction or revenge.

The second mentioned negative influence can be called "negative bureaucratic intellectual fellowship"[31] and it implies that officials at the public authority are

---

[29]Petersson (2007), p. 122.

[30]BRÅ rapport (report from The Swedish National Council for Crime prevention) 2014:4.

[31]Persson (2015), p. 8. Edelstam (2016) p. 139f.

influenced by negative bureaucratic intellectual fellowship and use this fellowship in a negative way, i.e. in a way that do not promote the public good. The negative bureaucratic intellectual fellowship is marked by the feeling of belonging to the chosen and can be used by incompetent officials to exclude citizens that they shall serve. Irrelevant values may have priority to objectivity, for example feministic values in an investigation by the social authorities on the custody of a child.

Corruption is generally thought of as pecuniary corruption and pecuniary corruption is usually criminal in character. The mentioned forms of influences that replace objectivity are not necessarily criminal but nevertheless dangerous to the system. They are part of what can be called institutional corruption and intellectual corruption.[32] The institutional corruption occurs when members of institutions take advantage of their institutional role for personal aggrandizement, in ways not prohibited by law but incompatible with their mission. There is the wrong culture and the wrong tradition. Intellectual corruption can for example imply that authority replaces justification.

Aspects such as objectivity and generally an ethos of office are aspects of importance for the rationality of administrative decisions which shall be secured by the personal legitimacy.[33] The personal legitimacy secures that there is a certain distance between the agent competent to decide and the actual situation of decision.[34] Behind this is the idea of objectivity.[35] Objectivity is thus connected to the chain of legitimation. There is not legitimation for the official if he is not objective in his decision making role.

3.2.5 Defence Rights

There are formal procedural rules with rights for the individual during the handling of the case. They concern for example right for the individual to be informed on new information in his case, to be heard and to see the documents in his case. The official has a duty to guarantee that this happens.[36] The official has for example a duty to notify the individual on new information regarding the facts in his case. He has the right to have a representative. However he must pay the representative himself. In general the individual party will only have written contacts with the official but there can also be some rights for the individual to meet the official in person before the decision is made.

---

[32]Glenn (2010), p. 29f.

[33]See Sect. 2.1.

[34]Schmidt Assman (2011), p. 54.

[35]Schmidt Assman (2011), p. 54.

[36]Compare Edelstam (2007), p. 384ff.

3.3   Consequences

The other side of responsibility is that there might be personal consequences for the official.

An administrative court has the possibility to remit for further investigation of a case that has been taken to administrative court. This is not stipulated in legislation but it can happen when the court finds that the investigation is flawed. However it also happens that the court completes the investigation.

The civil law disciplinary consequences can be either a warning or deduction from salary. This holds true only for public officials of public authorities under the government. Officials that work for an office under the local government cannot have disciplinary consequences. There can be disciplinary consequences for the official if he "deliberately or carelessly disregards duties". This might imply that it must be established that the investigation and the decision was handled wrongly. A notice to quit according to civil law can be the consequence if there are "grounds of fact" (swe. saklig grund). For an official "grounds of fact" can imply neglect or disregard of duty in connection to exercise of power through unilateral decision making. Dismissal according to civil law can take place if the official severely has "neglected his duties". Such consequences can be decided by the public authority that has employed the official. He has possibilities to appeal such a decision to court but it is seldom existing that neglect of duties of this kind are taken to courts. The right for the official to appeal concerns his right to defend himself against the accusations. Cases on damages and breach of duty could give the court better possibilities for a judicial review regarding the responsibilities of the official as the individual has to sue the state or the prosecutor has to prosecute the official.

With regard to paying damages the state or the local government shall pay damages if there is a neglect of duties in a public agency when exercising public power but the official will only have to pay if there is particular reason considering the circumstances.

The stipulation, in the penal code, on breach of duty establishes that an official that deliberately or carelessly in connection to the exercise of public power disregards his duties, can be sentenced for breach of duty. There are other crimes that could be of importance in this context, especially bribery that might be a crime that could be primary to Breach of Duty. Bribery might include a breach of duty in connection to unilateral decision making, for example if the official receives money when he gives a permit. In such case the stipulation on bribery might be applied instead of the stipulation on breach of duty.

3.4   Concluding Remarks

Law in action imply several issues with regard to the duties during the investigation, the duty to start an investigation, the fact finding part, who shall collect of facts and evidence, the standard of proof and the burden of proof. It further more implies a responsibility as regards to the defence rights of the individual concerned and it implies duties of impartiality and objectivity.

The administrative courts are of course the main courts for the judicial review of the exercise of power through unilateral decision making and a mistake or disregards as regards to chain of legitimation or interpretation can be taken to administrative court. They also have the possibility to review how the investigation was handled. In addition neglect of duties can have consequences for the official according to civil law and according to penal law. These responsibilities are vital to legitimacy and they go beyond legality though it is not too easy to define where legality ends and legitimacy takes over. For example is the burden of proof in administrative law a question of legality or legitimacy beyond legality? Irrespective of what the answer is to that question, the instances that could solve questions, on how to deal with fact finding issues such as burden of proof in administrative law cases, are the courts.

4 Judicial Review and Legitimacy

4.1 Unilateral Decisions and Judicial Review

Judicial review means review by courts and there is a relationship between legitimacy and such control. There is a common underlying sense of control mechanisms being important to legitimatize administrative activity and if there were no courts taking on control of activities related to administrative law, administrative activity could not get rid of a power oriented bias.[37]

Unilateral decision making means exercise of public power but it is not judicial power. Judicial power presupposes a court procedure and a judicial decision by the court. Unilateral decision can be reviewed by administrative courts but in addition they can be taken to civil law courts or penal law courts if there has been neglect of duties. If the reason for the review by the penal law court or the civil law court is that an official has neglected his duties, the court must establish that this was the case, in order to be able to decide on the legal consequence (according to penal law or civil law) for the official. Unilateral decisions can this way be reviewed not only by administrative courts but also by penal and civil courts.

4.2 Administrative Law Court

Administrative courts would only have the possibility to review the exercise of power in an unilateral decision if an appeal is made by the individual. If the official at

---

[37]Compare Ruffert (2011), p. 360.

the public authority would approve of an application on for example a permit or an allowance, the issue could not be taken to administrative court. A public authority and its official can, in a burdensome case that was opened ex officio, close down the case.

A unilateral decision can only be appealed if it was negative to the individual concerned, i.e. his application was refused or the public authority that started the burdensome case ex officio made the negative decision (for example a prohibition). However most of the unilateral decisions that can be appealed are not appealed by individual parties.

There are thus a majority of started cases that will not be taken to administrative court. In addition to that there could be cases that were never started due to passivity of the public authority.

Administrative courts can control how questions of law as well as how questions of fact-finding are handled in cases that are appealed. Legality is of course controlled by administrative courts and a decision is changed if needed. But how is the fact finding part of the investigation handled by the administrative courts?

In a study I did[38] on how the Supreme Administrative Court of Sweden treated fact finding issues I found that in cases where there were flaws with regard to the investigation, when the case was dealt with by the Supreme Administrative Court, that issue was in some cases solved by remittal of a case to either the public authority[39] or to the Court of Appeal.[40] In other cases the Supreme Administrative Court completed[41] the investigation itself and in some cases the court used the burden of proof[42] in order to solve the case. It was obvious that the Supreme Administrative Court did not take any responsibility of importance regarding the investigation and the duties of the public authorities in that regard. It was seldom[43] the Court gave leave to appeal for fact finding issues.

4.3   Civil Law Court

Cases on damages could be dealt with by civil law courts. In cases on damages it would be the state that would be summoned in court as the state is responsible for faults and neglects in connection to exercise of power. However such cases regarding the fact finding are extremely rare in courts.

---

[38]Edelstam (1995).
[39]Edelstam (1995), p. 169ff.
[40]Edelstam (1995), p. 181ff.
[41]Edelstam (1995), p. 175ff.
[42]Edelstam (1995), p. 263ff.
[43]Edelstam (1995), p. 367ff.

4.4   Penal Law Court

The official can be prosecuted in penal law court. But it is very seldom that a penal law court is engaged in issues with regard to officials and their dealing with exercise of power through unilateral decision making. There was one case on breach of duty[44,45] were an official in charge had not, despite several reports on child abuse, started an investigation. The child, a German boy with German parents on vacation in Sweden, died. The court found that the official through passivity had committed breach of duty. The court stated that the fact that the activities of the Social welfare service were stipulated in law and involve exercise of public power implies heavy demands on correct and appropriate performances from officials.

There is however in accordance with law a possibility to avoid a penal law trial. An order of summary punishment can be made by a prosecutor. This might diminish court trials with regard to officials and "neglect of duty". It is possible for the prosecutor to issue such an order instead of prosecution in court if the suspect admits to the crime. Another prerequisite is that the penalty can be limited to a fine. The crime "breach of duty" can be limited to a fine. This is a simplified and timesaving procedure for both the official and the prosecutor as the summary punishment does not need to be taken to court and it has the same consequences as a sentence in court. It was used for example on a Director-General (a politician who was appointed by the government) at the National Board of transport. She was in charge of a public purchasing and in connection to that she gave access to confidential information that—if it was revealed to foreign power—could imply dangers to the security of Sweden. She admitted and signed a form and the prosecutor ordered a summary punishment. She was transferred to another post at the government but later she was fired from that post by the government. When the story, concerning the security issue, came out in media two ministers had to leave the government. The Director-General later got the post at the government back, after a trial in the Labour court, to which she had taken the case. She regretted having admitted to a crime, stating that she had done it only to avoid publicity.

The peculiar is that officials can be subject to an order of summary punishment. It happened also in another case where a high profiled politician and former leader of the socialist party had been appointed chief of a public authority. She signed a certificate stating that her body guard was earning a certain sum of money each month but in fact the salary of the bodyguard was much lower. The body guard needed the certificate to by an expensive house (to be granted a loan from the bank) and she, the chief of the authority, got away with an order of summary punishment. Considering the public positions of officials it would be better if the courts would consider, in judicial decisions, how the tasks of the officials should be dealt with. Legitimacy demands that the court can review the acting of the officials and give some guidance as to how officials are to handle their legal responsibility. In the long

---

[44]Hedemora district court B 345/90. 1991-09-26
[45]Edelstam (1995), p. 361.

run this could be of importance to trust. It is after all a question of legitimacy with regard to the activities of the state.

4.5   ECtHR and ECtJ

The ECtHR has possibilities in accordance with article 6 in the ECHR to deal with issues of fact-finding in national courts which might have some influence on the proceeding within public authorities. A precondition for a fair trial, is that the national court can make a judgement not only on legality regarding a unilateral decision from a public authority but also of the facts in the case. If a party in a case asserts that the public authority based its decision on an incorrect value of evidence or an incorrect discretionary evaluation the ECtHR can find that the process of the national court is insufficient and did not fulfil necessary demands according to art. 6:1. In cases against the United Kingdom regarding contacts between parents and their children that were under compulsory care, the parents had taken the cases to court, but the judicial review proceeding was insufficient to allow a true review of the decision by the social authorities.[46]

The EctJ reviews a judicial decision from national courts with regard to legality, the accordance with the EU-legislation, not the fact finding.

4.6   Concluding Remarks

That administrative courts review legality issues is obvious. If it is about material law administrative courts would review and change the decision if needed. If it is a question of delegation and competence of the public authority and its official this would be reviewed and it could be declared invalid. If it is an issue of defence rights that have not been applied it will be reviewed and might be changed if the lack of a defence right caused a lack of investigation. What about fact finding issues? Is law in action controlled i.e. do court review fact-finding? It is of course fine that legality is in focus. However fact-finding contain legitimacy points of view that are important to the system. Who shall control fact-finding if the courts do not and what does it do to legitimacy if the courts do not help with guidance on how to think in such matters? It should be emphasized that administrative law differs a lot from civil and penal law.

---

[46]O,W,B and R against United Kingdom 08.07.1987 ECtHR.

5 Promoting Legitimacy in Administrative Law

Legitimacy results[47] as much from events and practices as from legal normativity, and it is important not to conclude that legitimacy is synonymous with legality but at any rate legitimacy provides a linkage between basic foundations of the political system and administrative law. Society is governed through administrative law and the officials shall exercise the public power in many unilateral decisions. Legitimacy should be a goal for such activities irrespective of whether the issue at stake is more spectacular or just a daily routine matter. Courts have limited possibilities to review unilateral decision making. The matter of legitimacy becomes obvious in more spectacular issues that are published in media and where important public interests are obvious, such as money laundering. Globally money laundering through banks is estimated to comprehend 2 5% of the gross national product of the world. In Sweden, since long known as a country with high trust, i.e. trust in the state and its administration, there are now (2019) two big banks, with branches in other countries, through which money laundering is suspected to have taken place. This is about legitimacy:

- due to the huge amounts of money that have been laundered and due to the fact that the banks have duties to control customers, but obviously do not control all,
- due to the fact that the public authority, the Swedish Financial Supervisory Authority (FSA), has not taken responsibility with regard to supervising the risk of money laundering,
- due to the fact that courts have not had possibilities to make judicial review of money laundering cases,
- due to the fact that citizens can lose trust in the system

Legitimacy diminishes for the important EU directive on money laundering[48] and its implementation, for EU itself and for the nation-states because the law has not been fully applied, because there is not the needed supervision or judicial review and because trust disappears. Legality and responsibility issues have been badly handled, judicial control by courts has not functioned and that can have bad influence with regard to peoples' trust.

The Swedish banks are obliged to report to the National Police Board when they suspect money laundering or financing of terrorism and the supervising of Swedish banks shall be done by the FSA.

The FSA has not acted in its supervisory role as regards to the severe cases of money laundering. For ordinary people though, there has been a comparatively bizarre collection of information on customers in the banks. Ordinary hard working people having contacts with banks know how the personnel of the banks can ask questions that can be quite bizarre, as if you are a suspected criminal. All questions can give a feeling of loss of integrity. In the same time the real dangers regarding

---

[47]Compare 1.2.
[48]2008/60/EC.

money laundering has not been taken into account and the FSA has not made inspections of any importance in such matters.

The FSA can decide a heavy administrative fine for a bank that does not comply with the obligations or withdraw the permit (to be a bank). There are also possibilities to give warnings or remarks. FSA however has not carried through enough supervising activities on the national level. The Director-General of FSA admits to that in an interview.[49]

There might be many reasons for this passivity. One reason could be that there has not been enough money in the budget for the FSA to cover the costs in connection to supervising which means that the state, the parliament and the government has not done enough to support the supervising. It could also imply that the officials of the authority did not know when and how to be active as regards to starting a case. This is connected to fact finding and law in action.

The lack of supervision regarding such money laundering implies shortcomings with regard to taking initiatives to investigate. It puts the state and its authority in peculiar position. The role as supervising authority is not fulfilled. In the same time ordinary hard working people are checked. The banks look where it is easy to look and nobody controls the bank. Distrust with regard to the system can be the result.

The lack of supervision furthermore involves that courts are left out of opportunities to control. No decision from the supervising authority means no appeal to court.

In this paper, on legitimacy in connection to the exercising of public power, the starting point is that legitimacy is a designation that goes beyond legality. The responsibilities of the officials and the judicial reviews are needed to promote legitimacy.

Legality is the basis with regards to applicable legislation but there are parts of the law in action that cannot be found in the book of law. Such issues are the standard of proof and the burden of proof. In addition it can involve the issue of who shall collect facts as well as the issue of when a case shall be started by an official at the authority. Responsibility of officials is not only about legality but also about fact finding. Issues of fact finding are not much checked by the courts. However some of the fact finding issues are questions of law, not in the sense that the answer is to be found in the book of law but in the sense that answers and reflections on how to deal with such issues are important to justice and legitimacy. An issue such as the burden of proof could be assessed by courts with regards to how such an issue should be dealt with. An issue such as the needed standard of proof could be assessed by courts. Such issues have a different meaning in civil and penal law. In penal law "beyond reasonable doubt" is the needed standard of proof. But that is not the case in administrative cases, not even in the burdensome cases. That standard can hardly or rarely be applied when exercising power in administrative law cases. In civil law the parties, the plaintiff and the respondent, must supply the court with facts and proofs and the court must base

---

[49]Sveriges Radio Dagens eko (daily news) 2019-03-08.

its judicial decision on the information from the parties. In administrative law cases the public authority might have to collect some information. How far that is stretched could be assessed by court. It could promote trust in the system.

It is sometimes said that administration differs so much from one public authority to another that it can be difficult to give guidance as to how to deal with fact finding including such things as standard of proof and burden of proof. If we accept that as a reality the consequence will be that fact finding issues are left to the officials. That however can imply loss of legitimacy.

Legitimacy is a value and objectivity is closely connected to this value. The courts have a role in creating this value. If there are "influencers"[50] or if there is a negative bureaucratic intellectual fellowship[51] objectivity disappears and cultures of other kinds are created. This is not easy to change. Many decisions from public authorities cannot be taken to court or are not taken to court. If the individual got what he wanted or if he did not appeal a negative decision, it will not be reviewed by court. The same holds true when the supervising does not function as in the money laundering issues.

However in cases that are taken to court there can be possibilities to pay attention to fact finding issues. Courts can give guidance on how to think with regard to the culture that must exist in order to avoid flaws with regard to objectivity. Even if cases can be very different it should be possible for courts to promote legitimacy by enlightening issues of this kind. Legitimacy is of fundamental importance to the carrying through of the power of the state through unilateral decision making. It is about the law in action and the culture surrounding it and such issues are best handled by courts and the courts can, through their reasoning, give some guidance to officials at the public authorities.

References

BRÅ rapport (report from The Swedish National Council for Crime prevention) 2014:4

Caillosse, J. (2011). Legitimacy in administrative law; Reform and reconstruction. In M. Ruffert (Ed.), *Legitimacy in European administrative law: Reform and reconstruction* (pp. 9–26). Groningen: Europa Law Publishing.

Edelstam, G. (1995). *Förvaltningsmyndigheters utredningsskyldighet – en rättssäkerhetsstudie (Obligation of Administrative Authorities to perform investigations).* Stockholm: Fritzes Norstedts Juridik (with a summary in German).

Edelstam, G. (2007). The right of defence in Fraud investigations. In O. Jansen & P. M. Langbroek (Eds.), *Defence rights during administrative investigations* (pp. 367–413). Antwerpen-Oxford: Intersentia.

Edelstam, G. (2011). Legitimacy issues in administrative law. Historical approach, constitutional approach, fact-finding approach to responsibility from a Swedish perspective. In M. Ruffert

---

[50]See Sect. 3.2.4.2.

[51]See Sect. 3.2.4.2.

(Ed.), *Legitimacy in European administrative law: Reform and reconstruction* (pp. 115–154). Groningen: Europa Law Publishing.

Edelstam, G. (2012). The implementation of the Services directive in Sweden. In U. Stelkens, W. Weiss, & M. Mirschberger (Eds.), *The implementation of the EU Services Directive. Transpositions, problems and strategies* (pp. 589–632). The Hague, The Netherlands: Springer.

Edelstam, G. (2016). Investigation and responsibility – Legal aspects of common interest. In M. Ruffert (Ed.), *The model rules of EU administrative procedures: Adjudication* (pp. 133–140). Groningen: Europa Law Publishing.

Glenn, H. P. (2010). *Legal traditions of the World.* New York: Oxford University Press.

Gonod, P. (2011). Legitimacy in administrative law: Reform and reconstruction. In M. Ruffert (Ed.), *Legitimacy in European administrative law: Reform and reconstruction* (pp. 3–7). Groningen: Europa Law Publishing.

Persson, L. G. W. (2015, May 10). Knoll och Tott spaning. *Expressen* (p. 8).

Petersson, O. (2007). *Den offentliga makten.* Stockholm: SNS.

Ruffert, M. (2011). Comparative perspectives of administrative legitimacy. In M. Ruffert (Ed.), *Legitimacy in European administrative law: Reform and reconstruction* (pp. 351–360). Groningen: Europa Law Publishing.

Schmidt Assman, E. (2011). Legitimacy and accountability as a basis for administrative organisation and activity in Germany. In M. Ruffert (Ed.), *Legitimacy in European administrative law: Reform and reconstruction* (pp. 49–57). Groningen: Europa Law Publishing.

Judicial Integrity and Judicial Independence: Two Sides of the Same Coin

Gianluca Esposito

Contents

1   Introduction

Judicial integrity is a pre-condition to maintaining trust in the judiciary and upholding its independence. Judges are the public face of justice. It is to the courts that citizens and the state turn to make binding legal decisions that can have a great impact on people's lives. As such when judges do not live up to the high standards of integrity and impartiality expected of them, public disquiet is palpable. Hence, preventing corruption within the judiciary is of utmost importance given its instrumental role in combating it. It is society's confidence in the impartiality of individual decisions that forms the core strength of the judiciary as an institution.

One of the worst things that can happen to the judiciary is to be—or to be seen as being—corrupt or corruptible. This shakes trust in the judicial institutions, weakens the independence of the judiciary, and means that the battle against corruption is ultimately lost.

Gianluca Esposito is Executive Secretary of the Group of States against Corruption (GRECO), Council of Europe. The opinions expressed in this article are those of the author and do not necessarily reflect those of the Council of Europe or its bodies.

G. Esposito (✉)
Council of Europe, Strasbourg, France
e-mail: gianluca.esposito@coe.int

© Springer Nature Switzerland AG 2019
P. Pinto de Albuquerque, K. Wojtyczek (eds.), *Judicial Power in a Globalized World*, https://doi.org/10.1007/978-3-030-20744-1_11

The Group of States against Corruption (GRECO)—the Council of Europe anti-corruption body—devoted its 4th Evaluation Round, in part, to the prevention of corruption in the judiciary. The reason is simple: there cannot be an effective fight against corruption without an independent judiciary and there cannot be an independent judiciary without an effective fight against corruption.

The key word is "prevention". Why is that? First, because of the obvious reason that "prevention is better than cure". If corruption is like a virus which, once it enters your body, it spreads all over the place, then taking the right medicines which is tailored to the type of corruption one is facing is surely the right way to go to stop the virus from entering the system or spreading. The second reason is a clear switch in approach to counter corruption. When the more recent international efforts against corruption started a bit more than 20 years ago, there was a widespread belief that, since corruption is a crime, the best and only way to tackle it was to put those responsible behind bars. While repression was and still is very important, when corruption takes place and a conviction is pronounced and served, we have all lost; society has lost. Therefore, the international community realised the importance of preventive tools.

In a number of European (and non-European) countries, the integrity of the judicial institution is under threat, thus undermining the independence of the institutions. Threats to integrity may take many forms, shapes and methods but have in common the aim of ensuring the judiciary is at the service of the "political masters" of the day. This phenomenon, which can be described as "the winner takes it all", is such that, in certain countries, whoever wins a political election changes the rules of the game so fundamentally that it results effectively in a (more or less direct) control of the executive over the judiciary.

This article[1] will discuss the situation of judicial integrity and judicial independence in Europe. It will start by presenting the main elements of judicial independence (Sect. 2) as enshrined in the main Council of Europe's legal instruments in this area,[2] it will continue by stressing the potential threats to judicial integrity and judicial independence, including in light of GRECO's findings and recommendations (Sect. 3), and will conclude by highlighting the trends GRECO identified in the area of judicial independence and judicial integrity, and the means at its disposal to ensure compliance with the Council of Europe's standards in this area (Sect. 4).

---

[1]GRECO (2017) *Trends and Conclusions of Fourth Evaluation Round in the field of Corruption Prevention of MPs, Judges and Prosecutors.*

[2]Council of Europe *European Convention on Human Rights* and the Strasbourg Court case-law, *Committee of Ministers' Recommendation CM/Rec(2010)12 on judges: independence, efficiency and responsibilities,* and the standards developed by the Venice Commission, the Consultative Council of European Judges (CCJE), and GRECO.

2 Key Elements of Judicial Independence: A Pedagogical, Yet Necessary Reminder of the Existing Standards

Judicial independence has been taken for granted for many years. The Council of Europe and its European Court of Human Rights has worked hard to promote it across the Continent, most notably in Central and Eastern Europe after the fall of the Berlin Wall. Yet, there are a number of steps backwards. In some countries, the progress made in the past 15–20 years is being undone. Hence, we need to remind ourselves of the key elements of judicial independence. To this end, the Strasbourg Court's case-law, Committee of Ministers' Recommendation CM/Rec(2010)12 on judges: independence, efficiency and responsibilities and its Explanatory Memorandum, GRECO, the Venice Commission and the Consultative Council of European Judges (CCJE) reports, opinions and recommendations constitute very useful references in this context and are largely used for the reflections that follow in this part.

Judicial independence is a fundamental right of each individual as safeguarded by Article 6 of the European Convention on Human Rights (hereinafter referred to as "the ECHR"). It is not a privilege for judges, but a guarantee for everyone. The independence of each individual judge thus safeguards every person's right to have their case decided only on the law, the evidence and facts and without any improper influence.

It is not possible to summarize here the extensive case-law of the European Court of Human Rights relating to "an independent and impartial tribunal" enshrined in Article 6 of the ECHR. This would also be outside the scope of this article. Nonetheless, as stated in the "Guide on Article 6 of the European Convention on Human Rights – Right to a fair trial", the term "independent" refers to independence vis-à-vis the other powers (the executive and the Parliament) (Beaumartin v. France, § 38) and also vis-à-vis the parties (Sramek v. Austria, § 42). Compliance with this requirement is assessed, in particular, on the basis of statutory criteria, such as the manner of appointment of the members of the tribunal and the duration of their term of office, or the existence of sufficient safeguards against the risk of outside pressures (see, for example, Ramos Nunes de Carvalho e Sá v. Portugal [GC], §§ 153-156). The question whether the body presents an appearance of independence is also of relevance (§ 144; Oleksandr Volkov v. Ukraine, § 103).[3]

A judge cannot have a case withdrawn from him/her without valid reasons for doing so and such decisions should be taken by the competent authorities, such as the President of the court. The notion of "valid reasons" covers all grounds for withdrawal which do not undermine the independence of judges. Efficiency can be a "valid reason". For example, if a judge has a backlog of cases due to illness or other reasons, cases may be withdrawn from that judge and assigned to other judges. Similarly, it may be necessary to withdraw cases from judges who have been assigned a time-consuming case which may prevent them from dealing with other

---

[3]Council of Europe (2018) *Guide on Article 6 of the European Convention on Human Rights – Right to a fair trial.* https://www.echr.coe.int/Documents/Guide_Art_6_ENG.pdf.

cases already assigned to them. In no event should this provision remove the entitlement of parties to withdraw a case, nor the obligation of judges to decline to act in the event of their having an actual or perceived conflict of interest.

Although the notion of the separation of powers between the political organs of government and the judiciary has assumed growing importance in the Court's case-law, neither Article 6 nor any other provision of the Convention requires States to comply with any theoretical constitutional concepts regarding the permissible limits of the powers' interaction. The question is always whether, in a given case, the requirements of the Convention are met (Kleyn and Others v. the Netherlands [GC], § 193). Indeed, the notion of independence of a tribunal entails the existence of procedural safeguards to separate the judiciary from other powers.

That said, the separation of powers is a fundamental guarantee of the independence of the judiciary whatever the legal traditions of member states. In individual cases, judges should be able to decide on their own competence as defined by law without any external influence. Judicial independence would be illusory if executive or legislative bodies were able to interfere in and determine judges' competence in individual cases.

In the notion of independence a clear link is established between independence and impartiality. Both are fundamental rights safeguarded by Article 6 of the ECHR. As the Explanatory Memorandum to Committee of Ministers' Recommendation CM/Rec(2010)12 clearly states, "Independence protects judicial decision making from improper influence from outside the proceedings. Impartiality guarantees that the judge has no conflicts of interest or association with the parties or with the subject of the trial that might be perceived to compromise objectivity".

Decisions of judges can be revised only in appellate (or re-opening procedures in selected circumstances). Revision of decisions outside that legal framework, by the executive and legislative powers or the administration should not be permissible. The administration, executive or legislative powers cannot invalidate, in individual cases, decisions of judges, except in the special cases of amnesty, pardon, and clemency.

Independence, however, does not mean isolation. Judges are part of society and therefore the authorities in charge of the judiciary should enable them to keep in touch with the social and cultural environment in which judges operate.

Judges should be aware that their membership of certain non-professional organisations may infringe their independence or impartiality. GRECO has issued a number of recommendations framing incompatibilities for the judiciary. GRECO stressed that the rules on accessory activities of judges, including arbitration activities in particular, be further developed so as to enhance transparency and to introduce uniform procedures, criteria—and appropriate limits—for granting permission to engage in such activities (Finland §118, recommendation vii), that the rules on incompatibilities and secondary activities be clarified and made more coherent in respect of all persons required to sit as judges or act as prosecutors (Luxembourg §122, recommendation x), that a restriction on the simultaneous holding of the office of judge and that of member of either Chamber of Parliament be laid down in law (Netherlands §96, recommendation v), that a restriction on the simultaneous holding of the office of magistrate and that of a member of local government be laid down in law; and more generally, that the issue of political activity of magistrates be dealt with in all its aspects at legislative level, given its impact on the fundamental principles of independence and impartiality, both real and perceived, of the judiciary (Italy §153, recommendation ix). In Sect. 3, the article will also expand on the tools that GRECO recommended to member states in relation to the management of conflicts of interest.

Judicial independence is not just freedom from improper external influence, but also improper influence from within the judicial system itself. Judges are subject only to the law. Therefore, judicial hierarchical interferences in the exercise of judicial functions cannot be permitted. Instructions from presidents of courts should never interfere in the decision making in individual cases by judges. They should ideally be given in writing and motivated.

There are various systems for the distribution of cases on the basis of objective pre-established criteria. These include, inter alia, the drawing of lots, distribution in accordance with alphabetical order of the names of judges or by assigning cases to divisions of courts in an order specified in advance (so-called "automatic distribution") or the sharing out of cases among judges by decision of court Presidents. What is important is that the actual distribution is not subject to external or internal influence and designed to benefit any of the parties.

In a number of states, variously named independent authorities—known as "councils for the judiciary"—have been established. Their objective is to protect and safeguard the independence of the judiciary. They are involved to a greater or lesser extent in, *inter alia*, the selection, career, professional training of judges, disciplinary matters and court management. The Council of Europe standard regarding these councils is simple: they should be composed by a majority of judges elected by judges.

In a number of countries, this is unfortunately not yet the case. Distribution of seats along political party lines, majority or significant presence of the executive or legislative powers' representatives, direct nomination from the executive power, creation of parallel structure to devoid the councils of the ability to function properly, non-allocation of adequate resources, are all examples of avenues which are practiced in some countries to effectively hamper the ability of these councils to carry out their duties of safeguarding judicial independence.

While councils for the judiciary have proved to be helpful in preserving judicial independence their mere existence does not, in itself, guarantee it. Therefore it is necessary to regulate their composition, appointment of members, respect for pluralism, e.g. to reach a gender balance, transparency and reasoning of their decisions and to ensure that they are free from political or corporate influences.

Independence should not be an obstacle or impediment to efficiency. Both are complementary. However it is necessary to balance independence and efficiency. The search for enhanced efficiency should never compromise independence. Independence protects the judge as a member of a power of the state. Efficiency concerns the judge's role in the justice system from which people expect clarity, speed, cost-effective organisation, courtesy and sensitivity—especially towards victims—and efficiency in the protection of their rights and determination of their obligations.

The independence of judges should be preserved not just when they are appointed but throughout their careers. Career includes promotion and appointment to new positions. Decisions to promote a judge to another position could in practice be a disguised way to sanction an "inconvenient judge". In some countries, the executive or legislative powers maintain a role in judges' careers, and GRECO has highlighted such a shortcoming. GRECO has insisted that decisions concerning judges' careers should be based on objective and transparent criteria, free from considerations outside their professional competence, and be based on merit. Independent authorities, such as councils of the judiciary could be designated to decide on the selection and career of judges.

Irremovability and security of tenures are essential to independence. The latter (security of tenure) means judges cannot, except for disciplinary reasons, be removed from office, until mandatory retirement age unless they have requested early retirement. It also requires, in systems where judges must undergo a probation period before being confirmed in their posts, that the decision on this renewal or confirmation be taken by an independent authority. The former (irremovability) implies that judges cannot receive new appointments or be moved to another post without their consent.

Judges' remuneration is an important element to address when dealing with independence and impartiality. For this reason general principles on judges' remuneration should be established by the law while more specific rules can be set at other levels. An adequate level of remuneration is a key element in the fight against corruption of judges and aims at shielding them from any such attempts.

The assessment of the judge's activity is the appraisal of his/her professional performance following modalities which may vary between judicial systems (hierarchical authority, panels of judges, council for the judiciary, etc.). As the assessment may determine judges' promotion in their careers, it must be implemented having full regard to the guarantees necessary to preserve individual independence. Whatever assessment mechanism exists, appeals should be made possible where the assessment may impact on the career path.

When not exercising judicial functions, judges are liable under civil and criminal law in the same way as any other citizen. Judges should however be protected through "functional immunity", i.e., in the exercise of their judicial functions, judges should only be liable under civil law and disciplinary procedures in cases of malice and gross negligence. GRECO has developed an extensive case-law in the area of immunities. It stressed, among others, that the immunity of ordinary judges be limited to activities relating to their participation in the administration of justice ("functional immunity") (Hungary §154, recommendation xii), and that the power of the Minister of Justice to grant permission for the lifting of functional immunity of judges and prosecutors be transferred to the judiciary (e.g. a panel of high-ranking judges or the High Council of Judges and Prosecutors—HCJP) and that the legislation be made clear to that end (Turkey §194, recommendation xvi).

The above description is not new. As noted earlier, it is the reflection of standards developed by the European Court of Human Rights, multiple Committee of Ministers Recommendations, Venice Commission, CCJE and GRECO reports, opinions and recommendations. Yet, given the ongoing challenges in some quarters to the very basic principles of judicial independence, it is necessary to spell it out for pedagogical purposes as a prelude to Sect. 3 below.

3 Are Judicial Integrity and Judicial Independence Under Threat?

Section 2 above provides a condensed description of the main aspects of judicial independence. Section 3 brings the discussion one step further and analyses if and, if so, to what extent, judicial integrity and judicial independence are under threat. Before attempting to address this question, let me add a few more questions: would a defendant like to be judged by a judge who follows the orders of the government of the day, or by an independent judge? Should a judge also be able to be an MP or a Mayor? Should a judge pay part of his or her salary to the political parties that vote for him or her to be appointed as a judge? Should the vote on the selection of members of the High Council of the Judiciary be based on political party lines? Should prosecutors be hired or fired depending on whether their prosecutions are liked by the political majority of the day?

Answering in the negative to all those questions would be correct, but a number of countries get it wrong as these apparently rhetorical questions simply reflect real-life situations we face in a number of our member states.

For GRECO, judicial independence is an essential pre-condition for an effective fight against corruption. Judges need to be able to make decisions free from real or potential undue influence, including from other branches of the State. If judges are motivated in their decisions by outside influences and considerations (e.g. career progression) other than the laws they are meant to apply, the judicial process is corrupted.

In order to avoid abstractions, this article will briefly describe the situation at the time of writing (March 2019) in four member states: Poland, Romania, Hungary, and Turkey. This description reflects GRECO findings (as of March 2019) concerning the states concerned and it is meant to be neither exhaustive nor stigmatising. The reference to these countries is made for illustrative purposes only.

In Poland, according to GRECO, the amendments to the Laws on the National Council of the Judiciary, the Supreme Court and the Organisation of Ordinary Courts (2016–2018) enabled the legislative and executive powers to influence the functioning of the judiciary in Poland in a critical manner, thereby significantly weakening the independence of the judiciary. GRECO stated that, whereas certain individual amendments of the Laws on the Organisation of Ordinary Courts, Supreme Court and National Council of the Judiciary may in themselves deserve attention, it is precisely the cumulative nature of these amendments against the background of earlier reforms (e.g. the Constitutional Court and the merger of the office of the Prosecutor General with that of the Minister of Justice) that gives rise to particular concern. Most GRECO recommendations to Poland therefore pointed to the need to limit possibilities for the executive (the President of the Republic or the Minister of Justice, as appropriate) to intervene, be it in the internal organisation of the Supreme Court, prolonging the tenure of judges of the Supreme Court and ordinary courts, disciplinary proceedings against judges or the process of appointing and reappointing presidents of ordinary courts and the Supreme Court. Amongst the most pressing concern for GRECO was the lowering of the retirement age for judges. While GRECO did not question the new retirement age as such (nor the possibility of prolonging the service of judges beyond retirement age if necessary safeguards against undue influence are taken into account), it is particularly worrisome that on 3 July 2018 almost 40% of sitting Supreme Court judges saw their tenure terminated, also given the fact that new judges will be appointed by the President on the request of the newly-constituted National Council of the Judiciary, in which 21 out of 25 members have been selected by Parliament, which in itself—as GRECO pointed out– is not in line with the standards of the Council of Europe.[4]

In Romania, in GRECO's views, several proposed changes pertaining to the recruitment and retirement of judges and prosecutors in Law 303/2004 could have, because of their combined effect, a significant impact on the work force and the general capacities of courts and prosecutorial bodies especially since no transitional period has been planned. Magistrates would be able to retire early, after just 20 years of service without any condition of age. This could constitute a powerful incentive for many judges and prosecutors—especially in the higher ranks of the judiciary—to retire very soon. According to certain estimates, regarding the High Court of Cassation and Justice (HCCJ) alone, 94 judges out of 115 are potentially concerned. The intended amendments also contain a proportion of subjectivity in the selection and decision process concerning promotions, which contemplated a two-phased promotion procedure, the latter phase consisting of an assessment of one's past work and conduct. GRECO heard fears that this new system would leave more room for personal or political influences on career decisions, which could impact the neutrality and integrity of the justice system. Against this background, GRECO recommended to Romania that "i) the impact of the changes on the future staff structure of the courts and prosecution services be properly assessed so that the necessary transitional measures be taken and ii) the implementing rules to be adopted by the [Superior Council of Magistracy] for the future decisions on appointments of judges and prosecutors to a higher position provide for adequate, objective and clear criteria taking into account the actual merit and qualifications".[5]

---

[4]GRECO (2018) *Ad hoc Evaluation Poland.* https://rm.coe.int/addendum-to-the-fourth-round-eval uation-report-on-poland-rule-34-adopt/16808b6128.

[5]GRECO (2018) *Ad hoc evaluation of Romania.* https://rm.coe.int/ad-hoc-report-on-romania-rule-34-adopted-by-greco-at-its-79th-plenary-/16807b7717.

In Hungary, a new National Judicial Council was established in 2012, following reform which also added another authority within the judiciary, the National Judicial Office (NJO), headed by a President elected by Parliament as the main authority for the central administration of the judiciary. This system is enshrined in the new Constitution of Hungary (The Fundamental Law) of 2011 which, since then, has been amended a number of times. GRECO recommended that the powers of the President of the National Judicial Office to intervene in the process of appointing and promoting candidates for judicial positions be reviewed in favour of a procedure where the National Judicial Council is given a stronger role.[6] More recently, the creation in Hungary of a parallel administrative court system also raised concerns. The proposed system would give large powers to the Minister of Justice (without effective oversight by a judicial self-administration body) in matters such as selecting and appointing new judges to the Administrative High Court and lower administrative courts; appointing court presidents and judges to senior positions as well as promotions; determining the administrative court's budgets; shaping the new court system during the transitional period of 2019 when new judges, new court presidents and senior judges will be appointed, which will have a long-term impact on the system.[7]

In Turkey, GRECO stressed that an underlying serious concern related to the fundamental structural changes that have taken place since 2016. As a result of these changes, in GRECO's views, the judiciary appears less independent from the executive and political powers than before. The fact that the newly established Council of Judges and Prosecutors (CJP)—replacing the former High Council of Judges and Prosecutors (HCJP)—is made up of members appointed by the President of the Republic and the Parliament and that none are elected by judges and prosecutors themselves, runs counter to the fundamental principle of an independent self-governing judicial body. Furthermore, in GRECO's views, the executive has kept a strong influence on a number of key matters regarding the running of the judiciary: the process of selecting and recruiting candidate judges and prosecutors; reassignments of judicial officeholders against their will; disciplinary procedures; strong organisational links with the Turkish Judicial Academy. GRECO issued several recommendations to Turkey to address and remedy these shortcomings.

These rather diverse situations have one element in common, i.e., the government and/or the Parliament have embarked in legislative initiatives or institutional arrangements which, even when they may seem harmless *prima facie*, are such as to pose—individually or combined—a real, potential or even unintended threat to the independence and integrity of the judiciary.

Against this background, and the concrete examples presented above, it is necessary to recall the key elements that guarantee judicial integrity to preserve

---

[6]GRECO   (2015)   *4th   Round   Evaluation   of   Hungary.*   https://rm.coe.int/
CoERMPublicCommonSearchServices/DisplayDCTMContent?documentId=09000016806c6b9e.
[7]Hungarian Helsinki Committee (2018) *Blurring the boundaries: new laws on administrative courts undermine judicial independence.*

judicial independence—whether in a national or a supranational jurisdiction. These include:

- Judicial independence and the structures separating the three branches of power
- The elaboration and implementation of codes of conduct for the judiciary (which should be "living" documents, regularly updated as needed)
- The management of actual or potential conflicts of interest, including confidential counselling
- Incompatibilities
- Gifts and other benefits
- Supervision of judges' activities: a key issue is to ensure that the supervision and monitoring of judicial conduct does not interfere with judges' independence in decision-making.

These issues are all essential to judicial integrity and to judicial independence—both sides of the same coin: they are too important to our democracies and to the respect of the Rule of Law for threats to them to be left unchecked.

GRECO has devoted the whole 4th Evaluation Round to the prevention of corruption in the judiciary (and in parliaments). Most of GRECO's 49 member states have been evaluated under this round and some, notably Romania and Poland,[8] have also been subject to its new, *ad hoc* evaluation procedure. What have we learned?

First, GRECO identified serious problems with respect to judicial independence and weaknesses in the structures separating the three branches of power. GRECO has been unequivocal in this respect: judicial independence must be recognised and guaranteed by all branches of government. Pressure on judges to refrain from fully exercising their judicial functions or to do so in a biased way not only taints individual judges but also undermines the authority of the judiciary as a fair and impartial arbiter for all citizens.

Second, the vast majority of GRECO member states received recommendations on codes of conduct. A third of these were to adopt such codes and the rest focused on substance and implementation. These texts should stress independence and impartiality as standards of judicial ethics but also refer to clear reasoning of the judgments, institutional responsibility, diligence, active listening, integrity, courtesy to the parties and transparency. In some states, such "codes" include judges' disciplinary regime but ethics standards should not be confounded with the disciplinary regime. Ethics standards aim at achieving in an optimum manner the best professional practices while disciplinary regimes are essentially meant to sanction failures in the accomplishment of duties. GRECO has insisted on the importance of the active involvement of all members of the profession, i.e. judges from all levels, in the development of a set of standards which should ideally be agreed upon following an open debate and discussion on their particular content. These codes need to be detailed and enforceable. Public confidence in the administration of justice is one of

---

[8]GRECO (2018) *Ad hoc evaluations of Poland and Romania.* https://www.coe.int/en/web/greco/ad-hoc-procedure-rule-34-.

the essential components of a democracy. This involves not only respect for independence, impartiality, efficiency and quality but also relies on the quality and integrity of the individual behaviour of judges. Respect by judges of ethical requirements is a duty which comes with their powers.

Third, GRECO has clearly concluded that increased attention to managing conflicts of interest is needed. Rules on when a judge is prohibited from acting and must recuse her or himself from a case are clearly regulated in most jurisdictions. Examples include when the judge is related to one of the parties or has a personal or financial interest in the outcome of a case. GRECO Evaluation reports showed that while judges tended to be well acquainted with these specific rules they were often less aware of conflicts of interest as a global issue. These are conflicts that not only affect their actions in court but extend to choices or decisions made outside court and in their personal life. These can prove particularly important in jurisdictions with few rules governing judges' outside activities or in countries with smaller legal communities where conflicts of interest are difficult to avoid. GRECO has clearly concluded that increased attention to raising judicial awareness of conflicts of interest is needed. This requires training and on-going professional development to ensure judges can identify the range of potential conflicts of interests that may arise as well as knowing how best to address them. Confidential counselling is very important in this context. Thus to avoid confusion and ensure that the rules are properly framed to cover the specificities of the judicial function, GRECO has recommended the rules be streamlined and that where oversight involves external authorities (asset declarations), that there is cooperation with judicial governing bodies.

Fourth, another area where GRECO has noted its concern relates to the political activities of judges in some countries. In most member states, whether in law or in practice, active political activity of judges is prohibited. However, we still have some member states where one can hold simultaneously the functions of judge and member of Parliament or local authority representative. In others, judges pay a part of their salary to the political formation that supports their election in Parliament. These are clearly not in line with the Council of Europe standards and the principle of.

Fifth, as regards gifts and other benefits, judges have a duty to avoid anything that could be construed as an attempt to attract judicial goodwill or favour. If in doubt, judges are expected to err on the side of caution or seek the opinion or permission from a higher judicial authority such as a judicial council, or from dedicated confidential services when these exist. Still, there are some countries where judges may receive presents worth several thousand Euros without declaring them.

Sixth, and finally, as far as the supervision of judges' activities is concerned, it is important to ensure that it does not interfere with judges' independence in decision-making. This requires precision in defining misconduct in a disciplinary sense, and gross misconduct that could lead to dismissal. GRECO identified several factors that are therefore necessary to ensure appropriate monitoring and the enforcement of rules including (i) clear structures; (ii) sufficient capacity of authorities (judicial); (iii) objective criteria; (iv) transparent procedures; (v) review and appeal mechanisms; (vi) sufficiently detailed record keeping of cases and measures taken; and (vii) publicly accessible "case law" (redacted where necessary).

4 Trends and Conclusions

GRECO has identified a number of trends relating to preventing corruption in the judiciary, preserving its integrity and, thus, its independence.

First, the strength and effectiveness of preventive mechanisms are often underestimated. Yet, measures such as an effective systems to manage conflicts of interest, detailed and enforceable codes of conduct, proper regulation of outside activities, transparency about interactions with those seeking to influence judges' activities, help them fulfil the public service mandate with integrity.

Second, one in every five GRECO recommendations points to the need for supervision and enforcement of the legislative framework in place. This is a clear sign that the actual implementation of the existing rules and regulations is a concern. Having a legal framework in place is good, but effectively implementing it is even better. There is therefore a need to place greater emphasis on effectively implementing the existing rules.

Third, and perhaps most worryingly as highlighted above, in certain countries, new legislative initiatives have reversed reforms previously undertaken to comply with GRECO's recommendations. This led GRECO to reassess the new legislation or remind the authorities of the countries concerned of the relevant GRECO recommendations through ad hoc urgent evaluations. There should be no compromise on the principles and values which have preserved Europe's peace and stability for 70 years.

It is against this background that GRECO makes use of all the means at its disposal to ensure countries live up to the commitments they have undertaken when joining it. To achieve this aim, GRECO follows a two-step procedure comprising a mutual evaluation and a compliance program, which is applied to all member states for each evaluation round. The compliance procedure is particularly relevant in this context: it is robust, rules-based, and even-handedly applied process across the membership. In the compliance procedure, GRECO monitors the implementation of the recommendations it has issued to the country in the Evaluation Report. The assessment of whether a recommendation has been implemented satisfactorily, partly or has not been implemented is based on a situation report, accompanied by supporting documents submitted by the member under scrutiny. In cases where not all recommendations have been complied with, GRECO will re-examine outstanding recommendations. Compliance reports adopted by GRECO also contain an overall conclusion on the implementation of all the recommendations, the purpose of which is to decide whether to terminate the compliance procedure in respect of a particular member. Finally, the Rules of Procedure of GRECO foresee a special procedure, based on a graduated approach, for dealing with members whose response to GRECO's recommendations has been found to be globally unsatisfactory. This graduated process starts with more intense scrutiny and reporting and may ultimately end, should a country continuously fail to comply with GRECO's recommendations, with the adoption a public declaration of non-compliance of the country concerned with the Organisation's anti-corruption standards (which include those relating to the independence and integrity of the judiciary, among others).

Ultimately, corruption affects people's lives and erodes Human Rights protection. The potential disruption caused by corruption to Human Rights has been laid bare in a number of areas, including the independence of the judiciary. These links have been brought to light in the work of Council of Europe monitoring or advisory bodies, including GRECO, and also of the European Court of Human Rights. The CCJE adopted an Opinion on preventing corruption among judges which constitute a real road-map to strengthen judicial integrity.[9] The full implementation by each member state of GRECO's country-specific recommendations relating to preventing corruption in the judiciary, coupled with following the Strasbourg Court case-law and the Venice Commission and the CCJE opinions, will go a long way in safeguarding judicial integrity, thereby upholding judicial independence.

---

[9]Council of Europe (2018) *CCJE Opinion No. 21.*

An International Mechanism of Accountability for Adjudicating Corporate Violations of Human Rights? Problems and Perspectives

Marco Fasciglione

Contents

1 Introduction: The Rise of the Business and Human Rights Agenda

Power is becoming less centralized in the international legal system and the fundamental role played by private subjects and entities in exercising power alongside the State has become reality. States are no longer perceived as the only entities involved

---

Marco Fasciglione is Researcher of International Law at the National Research Council – IRISS-CNR, Principal Investigator of the project, *Corporate human rights and environmental due diligence and the Promotion of COrporate REsponsibility (CO.RE)* and Co-Director of the International Summer School on Business and Human Rights. Former legal officer at the European Court of Human Rights.

M. Fasciglione (✉)
National Research Council – IRISS-CNR, Naples, Italy
e-mail: marco.fasciglione@cnr.it

© Springer Nature Switzerland AG 2019
P. Pinto de Albuquerque, K. Wojtyczek (eds.), *Judicial Power in a Globalized World*, https://doi.org/10.1007/978-3-030-20744-1_12

179

in violations of international human rights law and indeed corporations too are increasingly implicated alongside States in breaching international human rights law. This is mainly due to the fact that the process of economic globalization is dismantling the centrality of the State as the subject and the source of the international legal system. Corporate entities, with their capacity to take advantage of the accountability gaps[1] which result from the increasing discrepancy between their power to breach international human rights law and the inability, or the unwillingness, of States to take effective measures in this respect, have become immensely powerful and many of them much more powerful of the majority of States. They generate revenue larger than the GDP of many States, operate on a global basis, exercising in addition considerable influence on policy choices made by States in several domains included in the human rights realm. This shift of power to private sector's entities has not been reflected in a reformulation of the theory on the international legal personality with the corporate entity still remaining "an institution created by states . . . [that] . . . has become a powerful factor in the economic life of nations".[2] The challenges posed by the difficulties in accommodating such new powerful entities in international law had been already anticipated in the '70s by Wilfred Jenks, expressing what he felt to be the real "fundamental issue" at stake: *i.e.* the "relationship between the public interest and the economy when the scale of economy dwarfs the representation of the public interest and the complexity of economic structures escapes the control of any government or legal system". According to his point of view, in particular, this was an issue "on the same order of importance for the future of international law as the control of force, the peaceful settlement of international disputes, the protection of human rights . . .".[3] The release in the 2018 of the Zero Draft of the legally binding instrument and of its draft Optional Protocol, has re-ignited the long-standing debate concerning the creation of international monitoring mechanisms for adjudicating corporate violations of human rights. While monitoring mechanism currently configured under the Zero Draft does not depart from those traditionally operating under international human rights treaties, other options usually advocated by scholars, other experts, and the civil society, also include at the creation of international courts with the specific mandate to deal with human rights violations committed worldwide within corporate activities or, alternatively, and at the regional level, the enlargement of the jurisdiction of already existing courts and tribunals dealing with human rights. Without any claim for exhaustiveness, this paper aspires to provide with some thoughts on the basic

---

[1]Human Rights Council (2008), *Protect, Respect and Remedy: A Framework for Business and Human Rights. Report of the Special Representative of the Secretary-General on the issue of human rights and transnational corporations and other business enterprises, John Ruggie* (7 April 2008) UN Doc A/HRC/8/5, para. 3.

[2]International Court of Justice (1970), *Barcelona Traction, Light and Power Company, Limited (Belgium v. Spain)*, (Judgment 5 February 1970) paras. 38–39.

[3]Jenks (1972), p. 80. For broader reflections on the *modernization* of international law and on the role of human rights agenda in this process, see more recently Pisillo Mazzeschi and De Sena (2018).

elements of the monitoring mechanism configured under the Zero Drafts and some preliminary conjectures as to what an international judicial court on business and human rights could look like.

2 The Enforcement Mechanism of Corporate Violations of Human Rights of the Zero Draft Legally Binding Instrument on Business and Human Rights

After long-standing, and unsuccessful, attempts aimed to regulate the cross-border impact on human rights of corporate entities, on 19 July 2018, the Open-ended intergovernmental working group on transnational corporations and other business enterprises with respect to human rights (OEIGWG), specifically mandated by the UN Human Rights Council to elaborate an international legally-binding instrument to regulate in international human rights law the activities of transnational corporations and other business enterprises,[4] released the Zero Draft legally binding instrument (hereinafter, the Zero Draft) and, soon afterwards, on 4 September 2018, the Zero Draft optional protocol to the zero draft legally binding instrument (hereinafter, Zero Draft OP).[5] The approach of the draft texts conjugates a two-tiered enforcement mechanism grounded upon an international monitoring body, paired with the obligation on member States to enact legal liability for companies on the basis of specific standards or definitions provided in the treaty itself, and to provide access to remedies and other means of enforcement by means of domestic legal systems, including by the setting up of a National Implementation Mechanism (NIM).

Hence, Article 14 of the Zero Draft disciplines the supervision mechanism of the future legally binding instrument. In particular, it envisages the establishment of a Committee of experts in order to monitor and promote the implementation of the Treaty itself, as well as a Conference of State Parties. A careful reading of the draft text reveals that the functions and the tasks attributed to these organisms do not depart from those traditionally performed by existing similar bodies in the current international system of monitoring and supervision of human rights treaties. According to the Zero Draft the Committee of experts, in particular, shall adopt General Comments, interpreting the provisions of the future Treaty, and shall examine periodic reports submitted by States Parties on the implementation of the future instrument in their national legal systems by providing observations and recommendations on their content. Conversely, Zero Draft OP's provisions are

---

[4]Human Rights Council, *Resolution 26/9. Elaboration of an international legally binding instrument on transnational corporations and other business enterprises with respect to human rights* (26 June 2014) UN Doc. A/HRC/RES/26/9, para. 1.

[5]Both Drafts are available at www.ohchr.org. As to the literature on these initial stages of the treaty negotiations, see Deva and Bilchitz (2017); Bilchitz (2016), p. 203 ff.; De Schutter (2016), p. 41 ff.; Fasciglione (2018), p. 629 ff.

quite entirely devoted to regulating the establishment by member States of National Implementation Mechanisms (NIMs) with their main purpose: "to promote compliance with, monitor and implement" the legally binding instrument.[6] The NIM should pursue, accordingly, two broad objectives: (*a*) to establish a mechanism of access to remedy for victims of abuses committed in the context of business activities; and (*b*) to establish procedures for submitting individual and collective complaints.

2.1   The Nature of the National Implementation Mechanisms

At first glance, the establishment under draft Art. 1 of the Zero Draft OP of National Implementation Mechanisms appears to be inspired by the well-known treaty practice concerning national measures for monitoring and implementation, which has met increasing support from States, as a useful means for supervising the correct implementation of the obligations stemming from treaties that States have acceded to in several areas.[7]

Interestingly, National Implementation Mechanism shaped in the current formulation of the Zero Draft OP shall have to fulfil criteria for National human rights institutions, as described in the *Paris Principles*.[8] Draft Art. 2, para. 1, in effect, clarifies that in setting up local NIMs, State Parties must guarantee, among other things, the "functional independence of the National Implementation Mechanisms as well as the independence of its officials and personnel". The implications of this provision are noteworthy. Indeed, it would impede naïve solutions by State Parties, such as attributing the monitoring functions under the future Optional Protocol to the National Contact Points established under the OECD Guidelines for Multinational Enterprises. The OECD National Contact Points, in fact, are governmental bodies and as such they do not comply with the independence requirement enshrined in the Paris Principles. At the end of the day, the best solution for member States in enacting this section of the future Treaty would be to create specific independent

---

[6]Draft Article 1 of the Zero Draft OP.

[7]While this practice is common in the environmental law area, it has only recently been extended to the human rights area. The Optional Protocol of the Convention against Torture and Other Cruel, Inhuman or Degrading Treatment or Punishment (adopted on 18 December 2002 and entered into force in 2006) establishes under Arts. 3 and 17 such a mechanism with the goal of setting up an independent national preventive mechanism for the prevention of torture at domestic level. In a similar vein, Art. 33 of the Convention on the Rights of Persons with Disabilities (CRPD) establishes national implementation and monitoring mechanism in order to supervise the execution of the provisions of this treaty in domestic legal systems (for an analysis on the international mechanisms of follow-up, see Murray (2010), pp. 305–316; and in general Ruiz-Fabri et al. (2000).

[8]United Nations, General Assembly, *Resolution No. 48/134, Principles relating to the Status of National Institutions for the Promotion of Human Rights (Paris Principles)*, (20 December 1993) UN Doc. A/RES/48/134.

institutions charged with the monitoring tasks or, even better, to afford these tasks to National human rights institutions (if already existing).[9]

2.2   Tasks and Functions of National Implementation Mechanisms

According to the Zero Draft OP, National Implementation Mechanisms should perform three main tasks: (*a*) to raise awareness of the business and human rights treaty at the domestic level; (*b*) to conduct review of due diligence obligations under Art. 9 of the Draft Treaty; and (*c*) to run a sort of mediation process.

In the first place, under draft Art. 3, NIMs will be assigned the task of raising awareness of the future instrument at national levels, and this in cooperation with other national institutions, civil society organizations, and other foreign NIMs. Under this function NIMs would be allowed to submit recommendations to the competent authorities of the concerned State. Secondly, draft Arts. 4 and 5 discipline an important, albeit sophisticated, mechanism of supervision of the obligations enshrined in Art. 9 of the Draft Treaty, *i.e.*, to ensure that private sector entities operating within such member States' territory or otherwise under their jurisdiction or control, undertake due diligence obligations throughout such business activities. In particular, Art. 4 fixes a disclosure requirement by establishing that, in order to prevent human rights violations in the context of business activities of a transnational character under Art. 9 of the future Treaty, National implementation institutions shall request "all necessary information from the State Party in whose territory the National Implementation Mechanism operates" concerning implementation of the relevant provisions of the future treaty within the territory or jurisdiction of such State Party. Documents to be disclosed may include reports on non-financial matters (covering both environmental and human rights matters), internal policies outcomes, indicators of environmental and human rights impact assessments, etc. The fulfilment of such information and disclosure objectives implicitly postulates the obligation on corporations to produce and publish reports on such matters. Hence, such an obligation should be explicitly included in the wording of Art. 9 of the Zero Draft. Moreover, under draft Art. 5—to be read in conjunction with Art. 4—member States shall grant to the National Implementation Mechanisms "the competence to conduct reviews on the implementation of due diligence obligations" stemming from Art. 9 of the future Treaty. In doing so, Art. 5 addresses an important gap in the current legal framework on business and human rights. In many domestic legal systems, corporations are required to report on their human rights performance, although there are no consequences to poor reporting, nor is there any systematic process to check the reliability of such reports and of the information contained therein. In these

---

[9]From this perspective, the setting up of NIMs might also operate as a driving force on laggard States to set up their own National human rights institutions.

situations, the requests to NIMs to review corporate performance of their due diligence obligations may be submitted by "victims, natural or legal persons [conducting business activities of a transnational character] or all other persons entitled with a legitimate interest". The procedure may even be initiated *ex-officio* by the same NIM, on the basis of information available to it regarding acts or omissions affecting the implementation of or compliance with such due diligence obligations. This preventive and assessing function affords NIMs extensive powers, including the power to conduct visits and inspections[10] in the facilities of the business entities involved, in order "to monitor the implementation and follow up of due diligence plans or policies". Findings of non-compliance confer on NIMs the power to issue recommendations to the business entities involved. Even if the latter are not under an obligation to implement the recommendations of NIMs, draft Art. 5 clarifies that they are obliged to consider them with a view to ensuring their effective implementation. Should NIMs' recommendations not be considered, the NIM will "inform the competent authorities". In the execution of this mandate, the Mechanism is required to "comply with the minimum requirements of due process of law".

Furthermore, draft Art. 6 configures a non-judicial complaint mechanism based on a mediation mechanism. According to this provision, States Parties may recognize to NIMs the competence to receive and consider complaints "of human rights violations alleged to have been committed by natural or legal persons conducting business activities of a transnational character". The complaint mechanism recognizes the *locus standi* to "victims or a group of victims, their representatives or other interested parties". In these situations, NIMs may initiate a dialogue with member States and other organizations (*e.g.*, NGOs) in order to obtain additional information, and may request States Parties to adopt interim measures.[11] After having examined the complaint, NIMs may assist parties in reaching an amicable settlement of the controversy "consistent with the legal and administrative system of the State party concerned". In this situation, NIMs will be charged with the task of monitoring the fair implementation of the settlement. A possible successive stage to this procedure may be held before the Committee established under Art. 14 of the Zero Draft. Indeed, according to Art. 8 of the Zero Draft OP, the Committee may receive and hear communications from, or on behalf of, individuals or groups of individuals concerning "human rights violations in the context of business activities of transnational character under the jurisdiction of a State Party to the present Protocol". In this respect, draft Art. 9 establishes a partial list of admissibility criteria, clearly inspired

---

[10]Whose definition, however, are not provided by Draft Zero OP. In addition, it also fails in taking into account the likely capacity constraints of such a mechanism to review the implementation of due diligence obligations of the huge amount of companies potentially covered by the instrument in many States.

[11]Draft Art. 6, para. 3(d).

by the practice of international human rights bodies and Courts.[12] Under draft Art. 10, communication is brought to the attention of member States and to the business entities concerned. Interested parties have the obligation to submit observations within 6 months. According to draft Art. 11 and on the basis of the explanations received, the Committee may decide to perform an inquiry and may include the findings of the inquiry in the annual report of its activities.

Even though the aforementioned non-judicial complaint procedure may demonstrate added value, some problems remain. The mechanism is clearly inspired by the practice of the specific instances mechanism of the OECD Guidelines for Multinational Enterprises run, as is well-known, by OECD National Contact Points. The close relationships among these systems create the risk of overlapping between the work of the NIMs in this area and the work of OECD Contact Points. From this perspective, it would make sense to explore ways to merge the two institutions. However, this might prove very difficult, apart from the resistance usually coming from institutions involved in any merging process, due to the fact that it would require an overall reform of OECD National Contact Points mechanisms, since the latter are mainly governmental bodies not complying with the aforementioned functional independence requirement foreseen in Art. 2, para. 1, of the Zero Draft OP with regard to NIMs. As far as NIMs mediation functions are concerned, it may prove to be problematic for NIMs to effectively achieve this part of their mandate. Experience shows, indeed, that States often use mediation instances as delay tactics and that in order to work properly such process would require a realignment of the severe asymmetries existing between involved parties by means of adequate institutional arrangements.

For these and other reasons the enforcement mechanisms currently configured in the Zero Draft has raised increasing skepticism especially within civil society and human rights defenders' organizations.[13] Such criticism has highlighted the fact that both the National Implementation Mechanisms and the international Committee of experts envisaged under the Zero Draft have weak oversight and monitoring powers and that the mediation process, enshrined in the Zero Draft OP, would not provide an effective venue for redressing corporate abuses. This has originated a mounting call for alternative approaches, including the establishment of a completely new international human rights courts on business and human rights, or the enlargement to this specific field area of the scope of the almost positive jurisdictional experience

---

[12]Inadmissibility may be established if the communication is anonymous, manifestly ill-founded or not sufficiently substantiated; if the facts that are the subject of the communication occurred prior to the entry into force of the Protocol for the State Party concerned, unless those facts continued after that date; and if all available domestic remedies have not been exhausted, unless the application of the domestic remedies is unreasonably prolonged or unable to bring effective relief. Surprisingly, the list does not include other common criteria of admissibility, namely: when the same matter has already been examined by the Committee or has been or is being examined under another procedure of international investigation or settlement; and also, the time-limit rule fixing a precise deadline for submitting the communication from the exhaustion of domestic remedy.

[13]See, as for instance, Kletzel et al. (2018).

already existing under regional treaties on human rights. The following pages are devoted to briefly review these *de lege ferenda* alternatives.

3   A Step Further: Is an International Court on Business and Human Rights Desirable?

Three specific questions lie at the core of our subject. First, whether an international court on business and human rights would be desirable and necessary. Second, whether creating such a court is feasible in concrete and third, what kind of form this court, or an alternative judicial mechanism, should take.

As far as the first question is concerned, then, I believe that the answer tends to be an affirmative one. Several reasons, indeed, support the desirability of an international jurisdiction dealing with business and human rights issues.

First, an international court on business and human rights might help in closing abovementioned governance gaps between the scope and impact of economic forces and actors, and the capacity of societies to manage their adverse consequences, that provide the permissive environment for wrongful acts by companies of all kinds without adequate sanctioning or reparation. States, indeed, may be unable to enforce human rights because globalization forces States to aggressively compete with each other to attract investments. The resulting race to the bottom obviously weakens their bargaining power vis-à-vis companies that may have a turnover that is much larger than the national income of the States they are investing in. Also, States may be unwilling to enforce human rights because governments of host States may co-opt companies to collude with them against the local people and the environment. In these two scenarios the classic method of host State responsibility offers no effective remedy because host governments are ether unable to stand up to companies or they can afford to ignore international pressure because of the mineral riches they are able to exploit with the help from foreign business. Corporate self-regulation and soft law instruments are even less likely to provide victims with effective remedies, in these circumstances.

A second point to consider, somewhat connected to the previous one, relies on the circumstance that simply recognizing human rights does not suffice *per se*. Human rights in addition to being binding in substantive terms should also be enforceable. In other terms, such rights must be incorporated into legal systems which secure their effectiveness through appropriate procedures and mechanisms. The very essence of the rule of law is represented in the simple logic expressed in an ancient Latin adage according to which "*ubi jus ibi remedium*" (and vice-versa: where there is a remedy there is a right). Having a right means that somebody has a claim against somebody else, and the other one has a duty to meet this claim. If the duty-bearer does not live up to his or her obligations, the rights-holder has a remedy to hold the duty-bearer accountable. Otherwise, the right would be meaningless. Having a remedy means that the rights-holder can sue the duty-bearer before an independent neutral body, which has the power to decide in a binding manner whether or not the duty-bearer violated his or her obligations. Such an independent neutral body is usually a court. If the court finds that the duty-bearer violated certain obligations, it has the power to order the duty-bearer to provide reparation to the rights-holder.

Well, when corporate violations of human rights are concerned, the contemporary system of international and domestic law remedies is patchy, unpredictable, often ineffective and fragile. Consider the following two legal cases. In July 2017, the Ontario Superior Court dismissed a Rana Plaza class action[14] brought on behalf of Bangladeshis plaintiffs injured in the collapse of the Rana Plaza building in Dhaka in 2013. The plaintiffs were alleging that the enforcement by the defendant, a well-known Canadian garment company, of a corporate social responsibility (CSR) policy created a duty to protect on the defendant itself, on its three affiliates (which had indirectly sourced clothing through factories in Rana Plaza) and on the certification company and its affiliates, which had been engaged to perform two social audits of the factory. The Court in rejecting the claim stated that the defendant (a) had no control over the concerned Rana Plaza factory (a sub-supplier of a defendant's subsidiary), that (b) the alleged duties of care were not existing under Bangladesh law, which the court had established was governing the action under Ontario's choice of law rules and under Ontario law, (c) that the foreseeability element, a necessary element to validly assert a negligence claim, was not met in that case, nor were the victims sufficiently proximate to the defendant to justify whatsoever liability of this latter. Some months later, in its Views of October 2017 on the case *Yassin and others v. Canada*, the UN Human Rights Committee declared non-admissible an individual complaint, against Canada for violations of some ICCPR rights (freedom of movement, minorities' rights) allegedly committed in the West Bank by companies incorporated and domiciled in Québec. The Committee stated that the authors had not provided "(...) with sufficient information about the extent to which Canada could be considered responsible as a result of a failure to exercise reasonable due diligence over the relevant extraterritorial activities of the two corporations".[15] These two cases, one rooted in the realm of the private transnational litigation for the offshore impact of corporate operations, and the other one rooted in the public realm of international human rights law, with its focus on State responsibility, both highlighted the same salient issue of the contemporary discourse on business and human rights: victims of violations of human rights from corporate activities experience various kind of obstacles when seeking to obtaining redress, especially in the home-State of corporations. Aside the legal interactions between private law and public law domains evoked by the running of such gaps, a significant consequence is that in these situations there are not remedies that may be acceded by the victims neither in the State where the damage occurred nor in the State where the corporations has its decision-making organizations: this

---

[14]Ontario Superior Court, *Das v. George Weston Limited*, 2017 ONSC 4129.

[15]See UN Human Rights Committee, *Yassin and others v. Canada* (Communication No 2285/2013), Views October 2017, UN Doc. CCPR/C/120/D/2285/2013, para. 6.7.

leads, ultimately, to one of the greatest failure which may affect legal systems based on the rule of law: . . . . a denial of justice!

Summing up it may be concluded that the need there exists for better judicial protection from corporate human rights abuses, and this at international human rights law or at regional human rights law level. This leads us to turn to a second, and very pragmatic, question: is there a chance for an international jurisdiction on business and human rights to come into existence?

4   Is an International Court on Business and Human Rights Feasible?

The creation of an international court on business and human rights shall have to face several barriers. A first series of barriers concern the impressive economic and political power of corporations. Their lobbying power as well as their political influence might impede at all the establishment of new judicial mechanisms of accountability of corporate breach of human rights or they might try to use this power to pressure judicial forums thereby undermining their independence from corporate interests and conditioning their capacity to perform effectively impartial investigation onto corporate violations of human rights.

With specific regard to the creation of regional mechanisms on business and human rights, another risk to take into consideration is the often-objected argument that the establishment of such jurisdictions, with the connected imposition of binding legal norms on corporations, would encourage forum-shopping by corporations and their escape towards other national jurisdictions with lesser substantive regulations and without fora for judicial accountability. This would have a negative impact on the economies of the host countries by leading, as for example, to an increase of unemployment and in the long run to economic recession.

In the third place, the very same structure of the modern corporation is another barrier to mechanisms for corporate accountability. Multinational corporations, indeed, are simple networks of distinct companies, each one incorporated in a national jurisdiction, more or less tightly connected to one another by investment or contractual links, and which follow a global strategy under a more or less integrated leadership structure. This originates complex problems of allocation of responsibility among the different entities involved, across the several national jurisdictions eventually interested and which might have an impact on the effective exercise of the jurisdiction from an international or regional court on business and human rights. Indeed, the application of the basic principles of corporate law such as the separate corporate personality and limited liability usually operate as a *shield* to deny, avoid or delay legal liability for human rights violations committed by corporate subsidiaries: courts aspiring to affirm their jurisdiction thus are required to *lift the corporate veil* in order to disregard the separate personality of a subsidiary company.

Also, what about supply chains regulation? How a future international court on business and human rights will deal with the fact that nowadays in most industries, large companies rely on a series of contractors and suppliers in a range of countries to produce and transport their products? Today's global supply chains link individual workers with large and small companies across national, political and cultural boundaries. More and more companies do not generally own or operate the end factories in which their goods are produced and they may contract with hundreds, sometimes thousands, of different suppliers annually. As Justine Nolan has masterfully noted the phenomenon involves "broad and sometimes amorphous supply chains begin with the process of sourcing raw materials, and then track the development and distribution of a product that will eventually be brought to the consumer market via a multiplicity of actors".[16] How a future court will accommodate the fact that while each company along a specific supply chain has a responsibility to respect human rights, it is not clear where does that responsibility begin and end? Or, also, in what situation is it reasonable or expected to hold a company accountable for actions that may have occurred because of the actions of other (legally separate) firms?

Finally, on an even more practical level, it should be kept in mind that establishing international courts is a rather expensive affair both in terms of human resources to be recruited and in terms of financial resources that States have to disburse for their functioning. Even by simply extending the scope of the already existing human rights courts, such as the European Court on Human Rights and the other regional courts on human rights, it has to be admitted that these courts do not possess the expertise that would be necessary to deal with corporate violations of human rights. Unfortunately, the subsequent necessity to recruit additional personnel, to organize the Registry, etc. clashes with the endemic lack of resources that historically affects human rights monitoring bodies. Both the European Court of Human Rights, the American Court of Human Rights, the African Court of people Rights and the other United Nations human rights bodies are not exactly a model of prosperity and it may prove to be very difficult to convince States to pay further contributions to these institutions.

Despite the problems outlined above, however, the current gap in international standards applying to corporate human rights violations requires some kind of international mechanism, be it a new forum or an advance within the already-existing human rights supervisory mechanisms. Indeed, countries do not want to deal with these corporate accountability issues alone, so it is hard to imagine that they will regulate corporations without national or international fora to allow that space for them. The following question, then, is which kind of form might the future international court on business and human rights take?

---

[16]See Nolan (2017), p. 42.

5   What Form Might the Mechanism Take?

Several options there exist on the appropriate form and characteristics of a judicial mechanism to address corporate harms.

5.1   The International Court of Justice Model

A first option would involve locating the new mechanism at the International Court of Justice (ICJ) in The Hague. This solution might beneficiate of the particular role of the ICJ as an international forum of longstanding political legitimacy, conjugating the aspiration to universality with the diversity of legal cultures and systems represented in its compositions, as well as "diverse jurisprudential strains, for purposes of producing a new, pluralist, jus gentium-based international law, both substantive and procedural".[17] Attributing to the ICJ jurisdiction on business and human rights cases will beneficiate of the already existing possibility, foreseen in Article 26 of the Statute, to form specialized chambers "for dealing with particular categories of cases [. . .]". All these features would render the ICJ a suitable institution for hosting of a corporate human rights chamber, which would be provided with the highest authority for a human rights court, authority that might be highly needed in such a sensitive domain. The concrete realization of this option, however, would require a radical amendment to the Charter of the United Nations. This might prove being a very tortuous and difficult road due to the qualified majorities that would be required according to Article 108 of the UN Charter.[18]

5.2   The Human Rights Regional Court Model

A second option would involve a reorganization of the existing three regional systems on human rights by attributing to their judicial bodies a specific competence *ratione personae* on corporate entities.

Either the European regional system, the Inter-American system and the African system have already started to deal with business and human rights issues due to the increasing aware of the need to discuss and address corporate responsibility in human rights violations. Two basic perspectives have emerged to date. In the first place, the jurisdictional bodies operating in these systems have looked at the issue

---

[17] See MacWhinney (1991), p. 171.

[18] According to Article 108 amendments to the Charter shall come into force for all Members of the United Nations "when they have been adopted by a vote of two thirds of the members of the General Assembly and ratified in accordance with their respective constitutional processes by two thirds of the Members of the United Nations, including all the permanent members of the Security Council".

through the traditional lenses of the state obligations in the human rights area. Accordingly, they have affirmed two kinds of state duties in relation to corporate negative impact on human rights: a positive obligation to *protect* human rights from corporate violations acting as third parties and a negative obligation to *respect* human rights in relation to corporations acting as state agent.[19] A bulk of case-law has been developed by these judicial bodies with the consequence that nowadays the state duty to protect human rights from third-party, as well as from corporate, violations may be regarded as a well-established principle in the international human rights framework.[20] Secondly, bodies charged with policy-setting functions in these regional systems have started to assess avenues for developing regional policy frameworks dealing with the negative effects on human rights of private sector activities. Exactly in this perspective the Committee of Ministers of the Council of Europe has adopted on 16 April 2014 the declaration on the UN Guiding Principles on business and human rights and on 2 March 2016 the recommendation on the UN Guiding Principles on business and human rights. In the same vein, the General Assembly Organization of American States (OAS), has endorsed the Guiding Principles in June 2014, with the resolution on Promotion and Protection of Human Rights in Business.[21] As far as the African regional system is concerned, it is the African Union that took the lead: on the one side it has started to develop a Policy Framework on Business and Human Rights in 2017[22]; on the other side Article 46C of the recent Amending Protocol to the African Court of Justice and Human Rights adopted in 2014 (the Malabo Protocol), which extends the jurisdiction of the yet-to-be established African Court of Justice and Human Rights (ACJHR), has for the first time admitted a criminal jurisdiction of an international Court over legal persons for purposes of corporate criminal liability.[23] If ratified and entered into force, the Protocol would expand the jurisdiction of the proposed African Court of Justice and Human Rights to adjudicate matters of corporate criminal liability in Africa.

---

[19]It is well-known that such a positive duty is based on the specific formulation of Article 1 common to each regional Convention establishing alternatively that the member States "shall secure to everyone" (ECHR), or "undertake to respect [. . .] and to ensure to all persons subject to their jurisdiction" (ACHR), the rights and freedoms recognized therein, or that the member States "shall recognise [. . .] and shall undertake to adopt legislative or other measures to give effect to them" (ACHPR).

[20]As far as the application of the state duty to protect within the case-law of the ECtHR see Fasciglione (2019), pp. 37–47. As to the American Convention see Orozco-Henríquez (2016), pp. 48–52. As to the African system, see Amao (2008), pp. 761–788.

[21]OAS, General Assembly, *Resolution on Promotion and Protection of Human Rights in Business* AG/RES. 2840 (XLIV-O/14) (4 June 2014) Doc. AG/doc.5452/14 rev. 1.

[22]African Union, Specialized Technical Committee (STC) on Justice and Legal Affairs, *Draft AU Policy Framework on Business and Human Rights* (2017) http://www.africa-eu-partnership.org/sites/default/files/documents/joint_au-eu_press_release_on_stakeholders_validation_workshop_au-hrb_mar.pdf. Accessed 5 April 2019.

[23]African Union, *Protocol on Amendments to the Protocol on the Statute of the African Court of Justice and Human Rights* (27 June 2014) https://au.int/en/treaties/protocol-amendments-protocol-statute-african-court-justice-and-human-rights. Accessed 5 April 2019.

Abovementioned developments, thus, might pave the way for, and facilitate, an extension of the competence of such courts over corporate entities' activities intruding with the rights enshrined in the regional conventions.

A process of reform of the ECtHR, just to focus the regional system closest to us, might involve modifying the modalities according to which cases are allocated. Currently this is made by Section corresponding to the nationality of the judges[24]; the reform might introduce, as for instance, an allocation methodology based on the field of specialization and competencies of the judges.[25] This arguably might require an amendment of the Rules of the Court, e.g. Rule 25 concerning the composition of the Sections, in order to create a permanent corporate chamber formation within the Court. However, the same result might be much more easily obtained on a case-by-case basis by using the possibility that the ECtHR might sit in some special formation dealing with special issues and cases, and therefore by relying on the power of President of the Court to make exceptionally modifications to the composition of the Sections if circumstances so require.[26]

5.3   The International Criminal Court Model

Another option would envisage the creation of an international court dealing with corporate crimes, on the model of the International Criminal Court (ICC). This might be realized by extending the criminal law competence of the ICC to apply to corporate persons, in addition to natural ones. It is well-known that Article 25 (1) ICC Statute makes clear that the Court has jurisdiction over natural persons only. This provision is the result of a hard and very complex negotiation process which saw the French delegation putting forward a proposal providing for the ICC's jurisdiction over legal persons, including corporate entities.[27] Although the proposal received some support from other delegations, it was eventually decided that including legal persons within the new institution's jurisdiction would have shifted the attention from the core goals of the Rome Conference, which were to create an institution that would tackle impunity while securing the maximum number of signatures.[28]

However, a cautious approach should be used when reasoning on attributing to ICC the competence on corporate crimes. Indeed, the main reason of the historical gaps of current international criminal law in prosecuting corporate crimes resides in

---

[24]The Court is composed by five Sections and the Grand Chamber.

[25]This would not be something completely new as a similar approach has been adopted at the Registry's filtering system where a sort of specialist sub-committees put together by skill and competencies there exist.

[26]See Rule 25(4).

[27]See Proposal Submitted by France, UN Doc. A/CONF.183/C.1/L.3, 16 June 1998.

[28]On this issue see Clapham (2000), pp. 139–195.

the circumstance that human rights impact of business activity, however serious, rarely reaches the gravity threshold while meeting the conditions necessary for international crimes to be established. Corporate human rights abuses mainly involve labour issues in the supply chain as well as interferences with economic and social rights. Such violations can be extremely serious but they do not necessarily constitute international crimes. Also, where a conduct from a corporate actor configures an international crime, it is usually regarded as an accessory to the crime and not the principal offender.

In addition, and turning to aiding and abetting criminal responsibility, when business actors engage in criminal behaviour as aiders and abettors of criminal regimes it is only in function of their primary need to do business. Accordingly, while Article 25(3)(c) ICC Statute does provide for the criminal responsibility of aiders and abettors it may happen that, even in presence of an extension of its *ratione personae* competence, the ICC, which has been created to deal with some of the worst imaginable crimes, may be tempted to prioritize the prosecution of perpetrators over the prosecution of corporate aiders and abettors.

On the other side, while these are legitimate concerns, it is true that such an approach may be missing a crucial point. The fact that government officials may consider using the services of the private sector to avoid responsibility. Accordingly, the increase of the deliberate use of private sector services to dilute responsibility or avoid it altogether is a factor that might pave the way for the ICC to pay particular attention to crimes committed by business officials and in the long run to extending its competence over corporate crimes. Even though the institution of an international court dealing with corporate crimes is still far from being established, two important developments have to be pointed out on this path. First, in September 2016, the Office of the Prosecutor of the International Criminal Court issued a Policy Paper on Case Selection and Prioritization in which it indicated that the Office will now "give particular consideration to prosecuting Rome Statute crimes that are committed by means of, or that result in ... the destruction of the environment, the illegal exploitation of natural resources or the illegal dispossession of land".[29] Given that these criminal activities often involve corporate actors, the Policy Paper has raised the expectation for a future increased scrutiny of the human rights impacts of business activity by the ICC. Second, the already mentioned Art 46C of the recent Amending Protocol to the African Court of Justice and Human Rights, has for the first time established a criminal jurisdiction of an international Court over legal persons for purposes of corporate criminal liability. This provision may prove being a fundamental step in defeating the historical lack of equipment of current international criminal law to deal with the human rights impact of business.

---

[29]ICC Office of the Prosecutor (OTP), *Policy Paper on Case Selection and Prioritisation* (15 September 2016) https://www.icc-cpi.int/itemsdocuments/20160915_otp-policy_case-selection_eng.pdf. Accessed 5 April 2019.

6 Conclusions

In this chapter I have sought to illustrate, even if summarily, the reasons according to which, while the setting-up of an international judicial mechanism for adjudicating corporate abuses of human rights norms is needed and desirable, it appears problematic that such an international body might be created in the short run. The subject-matter, indeed, raises more questions rather than providing answers. Furthermore, the very same inception within the OEIGWG of the negotiations on a legally binding instrument on transnational corporations and other business enterprises demonstrate that still there are theoretical and practical barriers and resistances that need to be defeated. Also, what is important that States consider, once they have embarked themselves in a long march on the road for the creation of an enforcement mechanism of a treaty on business and human rights, is that it is worth having an international court, or other similar judicial bodies, on business and human rights only if that court or body is established in a way which its effective operation might be assured. At the end of the day, one may argue that it would be better not to have such a judicial mechanism at all than to have a half-hearted patched-up institution with inadequate competence and feeble authority. On the other side, however, a binding treaty could begin to tackle some fundamental issues at the intersection of business and human rights discourse but also would begin to offer alternative means of remedy for victims. Such move requires of course some form of judicial body providing with enforcement and ensuring the right of victims of human rights violations to an effective remedy and to an adequate reparation for the harms suffered. In order to contribute to a debate that is gaining more and more momentum, some options starting from the current mechanism configured in the Zero Draft have been reviewed. Of course, they will need to be further analyzed and discussed before becoming substantiated proposals.

References

Amao, O. (2008). The African regional human rights system and multinational corporations: Strengthening host state responsibility for the control of multinational corporations. *The International Journal of Human Rights, 12*, 761–788.

Bilchitz, D. (2016). The necessity for a business and human rights treaty. *Business and Human Rights Journal, 1*, 203–227.

Clapham, A. (2000). The question of jurisdiction under international criminal law over legal persons: Lesson from the Rome Conference on an international criminal court. In M. T. Kamminga & S. Zia-Zarifi (Eds.), *Liability of multinational corporations under international law* (pp. 139–195). The Hague: Kluwer Law International.

De Schutter, O. (2016). Towards a new treaty on business and human rights. *Business and Human Rights Law Journal, 1*, 41–67.

Deva, S., & Bilchitz, D. (2017). *Building a treaty on business and human rights. Context and contours.* Cambridge: Cambridge University Press.

Fasciglione, M. (2018). Another step on the road? Remarks on the zero draft treaty on business and human rights. *Diritti umani e diritto internazionale, 12*, 629–661.

Fasciglione, M. (2019). Enforcing the state duty to protect under the UN guiding principles on business and human rights: Strasbourg view's. In A. Bonfanti (Ed.), *Business and human rights in Europe* (pp. 37–47). New York: Routledge.

Jenks, W. (1972). Multinational entities in the law of the Nations. In W. Friedman, L. Henkin, & O. Lissitzyn (Eds.), *Transnational law in a changing society. Essays in honor of Philip C. Jessup* (pp. 70–83). New York: Columbia University Press.

Kletzel, G., López Cabello, A., & Cerqueira, D. (2018). *A toothless tool? First impressions on the Draft optional protocol to the legally binding instrument on business and human rights.* Retrieved April 5, 2019, from http://www.escr-net.org/news/2018/blog-first-impressions-draft-op-protocol-treaty-business-human-rights

MacWhinney, E. W. (1991). *Judicial settlement of international disputes. Jurisdiction, justiciability and judicial law-making on the contemporary international court.* Dordrecht: Martinus Nijhoff.

Murray, R. (2010). The role of national human rights institutions. In M. A. Baderin & M. Ssenyonjo (Eds.), *International human rights law: Six decades after the UDHR and beyond* (pp. 305–316). Farnham: Ashgate.

Nolan, J. (2017). Business and human rights: The challenge of putting principles into practice and regulating global supply chains. *Alternative Law Journal, 42,* 42–46.

Orozco-Henríquez, J. (2016). Corporate accountability and the Inter-American human rights system. *Harvard International Law Journal, 57,* 48–52.

Pisillo Mazzeschi, R., & De Sena, P. (2018). *Global justice, human rights and the modernization of international law.* Cham: Springer.

Ruiz-Fabri, H., Sicilianos, L.-A., & Sorel, J.-M. (2000). *L'effectivité des Organisations Internationales. Mécanismes de suivi et de contrôle.* Paris: Pedone.

Legal Basis for the Establishment
of International Courts

Aleksander Gadkowski

Contents

1   Preliminary Remarks

The past few decades have brought about a major evolution in international law, which affected both its scope *ratione materiae* and *ratione personae*. Over the centuries the substantive scope of its applicability has undergone changes, oftentimes quite dynamically. This resulted naturally from the emergence and development of new areas of international cooperation being regulated by international law. Human rights law is a paradigm example of such an area of international law which has undergone particularly dynamic developments in terms of its substantive scope over the years. On the other hand, the evolution of international law in terms of its

Dr. iur. Aleksander Gadkowski, Lawyer at the Research and Analyses Office of the Supreme Court of the Republic of Poland and Postdoctoral Researcher at the Faculty of Law and Administration at Adam Mickiewicz University in Poznań, Poland. Former Lawyer at the Registry of the European Court of Human Rights (2016–2018). Author of articles on human rights law and European social law.

A. Gadkowski (✉)
Adam Mickiewicz University in Poznań, Faculty of Law and Administration, Poznań, Poland
e-mail: alga@amu.edu.pl

© Springer Nature Switzerland AG 2019
P. Pinto de Albuquerque, K. Wojtyczek (eds.), *Judicial Power in a Globalized World*, https://doi.org/10.1007/978-3-030-20744-1_13

personal scope of application displays a very different trajectory. The scope *ratione personae* initially included states as sovereign entities exclusively and it was only extended in the middle of the twentieth century as a result of a dynamic development of international organisations. The personal scope of international law radically changed to include also IGOs (international governmental organisations) as a result of the advisory opinion of the International Court of Justice of 1949 on Reparation for Injuries Suffered in the Service of the United Nations. Since then international law started to be defined through the lens of a much wider substantive scope than previously. Most importantly, states ceased to be the only entities included in the material scope of international law, and, consequently, also stopped being the only entities creating the regulations of international law.

Over time, the personal scope of international law has undergone even further developments as the legal status of individuals under the framework of international law has started to change as well. Individuals have become increasingly covered by the scope of international law, the best example of which is the international law of human rights. Provisions of this law do not only impose certain obligations on state parties to treaties, but also empower individuals to invoke their rights before international bodies, especially international judicial bodies. Provisions of international human rights law are predominantly self-executing. They bring individuals closer to having international legal personality, because such provisions directly shape the condition of individuals, especially through endowing them with rights and freedoms. Moreover, they are directly applicable in the domestic legal frameworks of state parties. On the other hand, international law also imposes certain obligations on individuals. It provides a framework for holding individuals accountable for serious human rights violations, such as war crimes, crimes against humanity and genocide. In this respect international criminal law is developing quite dynamically. This means that an increasing number of international law provisions are directly applicable and enforceable by individuals, which makes the discussion of individuals' international legal personality particularly topical.

These two above-mentioned characteristics of the evolution of international law in the past few decades are also related to a third one, which is particularly relevant to the topic of this article. The dynamic development of international organisations and the fundamental change in the legal status of individuals have been conducive to the proliferation of international courts and tribunals.[1] Originally, the role of international courts and tribunals was limited to settling international disputes between states as sovereign subjects of international law. These days the jurisdiction of international courts and tribunals has expanded, both in terms of the personal and material scope. The profound development of international organisations has brought about the establishment of judicial control bodies, especially within the framework of regional integration organisations. International human rights conventions have provided the legal basis for the formation of treaty bodies serving control functions and these days we can observe a proliferation thereof. Under some of the

---

[1]Caminos (2013), pp. 55 et seq.

regional systems of international human rights protection these bodies have been granted the status of international courts. With international cooperation flourishing in such areas as economics, trade and investments, an increasing number of arbitral tribunals and quasi-judicial bodies are established, e.g. the International Center for Settlement of Investment Disputes (ICSID), or the special dispute settlement system within the World Trade Organization (WTO). There are also administrative tribunals within the framework of international organisations, such as the United Nations Administrative Tribunal and the Administrative Tribunal of the International Labor Organization. In the area of international criminal law, judicial bodies of various structure and legal status are established. These can be either international tribunals or hybrid tribunals. Finally, "classic" international courts are also established which have a very narrow jurisdiction and settle disputes within a very specialised area of cooperation, an example of which is the International Tribunal for the Law of the Sea (ITLOS). The proliferation of international courts and tribunals is evidenced by the fact there are currently some 40 international bodies exercising judicial functions.[2] Whilst this process demonstrates that those new international institutions are indispensable for settling disputes in numerous areas of international cooperation and that the international community displays trust towards them, it also raises some doubts about the fragmentation of international law.[3] Fragmentation of international law means that the legal system becomes sub-divided into separate sets of legal provisions, diverse from the point of view of their legal nature, and able to function independently or semi-independently within the system of international law, as well as able to shape that system. As certain areas of international law become autonomous, special self-contained systems start to emerge. Still, it is universally agreed that international judicial bodies, despite their profound diversification, belong to the one unified system of international law.[4] Pierre-Marie Dupuy used a metaphor to describe this: "they all speak a language in which the common grammar is international law".[5] Nevertheless, today's international court system undoubtedly is very extensive and diversified and the proliferation of international courts and tribunals, which is caused by transformative changes in contemporary international law, also has an impact on the shape and substance of this area of law.[6]

---

[2]For details see e.g. Cała-Wacinkiewicz (2018), p. 334; Czapliński (2007), p. 130.

[3]Szpak (2014), pp. 31 et seq.

[4]See e.g. Abi-Saab (1999), p. 921.

[5]Dupuy (2007), p. 2.

[6]Sands (1999), p. XXVI.

2 International Courts and Tribunals: International Bodies or Organisations?

Unarguably, international courts belong to a broader conceptual category, namely that of institutions of international cooperation. International cooperation between states can take various organisational forms, some of which are more formalised than others. There is no one universally accepted definition of international institution. Most often these are understood as any institutionalised forms of cooperation between entities (especially states) that strive to achieve a common goal.[7] Therefore, these are mainly international governmental organisations (IGOs) which have international legal personality, distinct from the legal personality of state parties. Having international legal personality implies certain fundamental attributes, namely the ability to act on their own behalf, and within this ability, the right to invoke their rights before international courts and tribunals, known as *ius standi*. Another category of institutions of international cooperation are the so-called "soft organisations". They are similar to international organisations in some respects, however, they do not have international legal personality.[8] Finally, there are also international bodies, often referred to as treaty bodies. They usually serve the functions of control bodies established in international human rights treaties or international environmental law. Although they are established in treaties, they are not international organisations. They exhibit an interesting, separate, atypical hybrid structure, sitting in between "classic" treaty bodies and international organisations. They are largely autonomous and some of them have international legal personality vested on them by the state. Sometimes they also have *ius tractatuum* which they use, for example, to conclude Memoranda of Understanding (MOU). This capacity likens them to that of international organisations.[9] Therefore, it should be emphasized that such international bodies are sometimes treated on a par with the bodies of international organisations, or even with the international organisations *per se*.[10] This is, however, an incorrect assumption. Even though international bodies are established and operate on the basis of treaties or other instruments of international law, or have certain characteristics similar to those of international organisations, they lack one of the most important defining characteristic of international organisations, namely they are not associations of states.

Undoubtedly, international courts and tribunals also constitute institutionalized forms of international cooperation. They are established and operate on the basis of international law instruments, though their legal status is clearly distinct.[11] Most importantly, they have the status of bodies of international organisations, such as the

---

[7]Amerasinghe (2005), pp. 12 et seq.

[8]Klabbers (2002), p. 10.

[9]Gehring (1991), p. 35.

[10]See Schmalenbach (2012), p. 872.

[11]See, e.g., Gadkowski (2018), p. 48.

International Court of Justice (ICJ), which is the principal judicial body of the United Nations (UN). Similarly, the Court of Justice of the European Union (CJEU) is an European Unions (EU) institution. The European Court of Human Rights is a treaty body of the European Convention for the Protection of Human Rights and Fundamental Freedoms, and being a body of an international organisation it operates within the structure of the Council of Europe. Other international regional human rights tribunals are also bodies of regional international organisations, e.g. the Inter-American Court of Human Rights which is an institution of the Organisation of United States, or the African Court of Human and People's Rights which is an institution of the African Union. However, the legal status of the International Criminal Court is different. It is not a body of an international organisation, but, similarly to international organisations, it has its own international legal personality as per art. 4 of the Rome Statute which established the ICC.[12] On the other hand, the ad-hoc international criminal tribunals, namely International Criminal Tribunal for the former Yugoslavia (ICTY) and the International Criminal Tribunal for Rwanda (ICTR) were established as subsidiary bodies of the UN Security Council. Criminal hybrid tribunals, which have some international elements, have yet another legal status. Such tribunals are actually established within the domestic judiciary but operate in conjunction and agreement with international bodies, for example, the Extraordinary Chambers in the Courts of Cambodia (ECCC) and the Special Tribunal for Lebanon (STL). The Panels with Exclusive Jurisdiction over Serious Criminal Offices (East Timor) and The Kosovo War and Ethnic Crimes Court (KWECC) also operate within the domestic judiciaries.[13] On the other hand, there are certain international judicial bodies the status of which was declared in their statutes as that of international organisations. An example of this can be found in the Washington Convention on the Settlement of Investment Disputes between States and Nationals of Other States of 1965.[14] Article 18 of the Convention stipulates that the International Centre for Settlement of Investment Disputes shall have full international legal personality. Thus, the Centre meets the minimum defining criteria for it to be regarded as an international organisation.[15]

International practice in this respect is very diversified and shows that it is not possible to unambiguously categorise all international courts and tribunals within one conceptual category of institutions of international cooperation. Due to the fact that states are not members of international courts and tribunals, it would be difficult to classify them uniformly as instruments of international cooperation, such as international organisations. Thus, international courts and tribunals cannot be universally defined as having international legal personality. Categorising them as international institutions, though, with a diversified and individualised legal status, is fully legitimate. From the point of view of their international legal status,

---

[12]Text of the Rome Statute: UNTS, vol. 2187, p. 90; see: Lee (2002).

[13]Romano et al. (2004).

[14]Text of the Convention: UNTS, vol. 575, p. 159.

[15]Schreuer (2001), pp. 67 et seq.

international courts and tribunals should, therefore, be treated and assessed *a casu ad casum*. Their diversified legal status is undoubtedly the result of the proliferation of international courts and tribunals.[16]

As already mentioned, it would be difficult to classify all international courts and tribunals as institutions of international cooperation. It would be equally difficult to provide an unequivocal definition of an international court/tribunal. Unfortunately defining concepts, even the most fundamental ones, is no mean feat in the domain of international law. Discussing international courts and tribunals in the context of international organisations leads to a conclusion that there is no one universally agreed definition thereof. As an example, definitions proposed by the International Law Commission for the purpose of codification of various areas of international law are very different from one another. International law publications tend to define both "international courts and tribunals" given that both notions, i.e. "courts" and "tribunals" are used interchangeably to signify those international institutions. One of the most popular definitions of the notion was put forward by Christian Tomuschat, according to whom "international courts and tribunals are permanent judicial bodies made up of independent judges which are entrusted with adjudicating international disputes on the basis of international law according to a pre-determined set of rules of procedure and rendering decisions which are binding on the parties".[17] The concept is, therefore, not defined broadly and includes only permanent judicial bodies. Hence, this definition does not cover arbitral tribunals and ad-hoc judicial bodies which are also very important actors in the settlement of international disputes. Excluding arbitral tribunals from the definition might be considered legitimate due to significant differences between international judiciary and international arbitration. However, leaving ad-hoc judicial bodies out of scope of the definition seems questionable.[18] These include, after all, some of the international criminal courts, which, apart from being non-permanent, display all the other "classic" characteristics of international courts. It may of course seem questionable that they are not established in treaties; however, Christian Tomuschat's definition does not feature this element of their legal basis. Nevertheless, such a legal basis (i.e. establishment in an international treaty) seems essential for a court/tribunal to be considered international. As mentioned above, international courts are institutions of international cooperation and as such they operate internationally, in an international environment. To a certain extent they participate in the international community. They are tasked with delivering justice internationally, in accordance with the provisions of international law. In this context it goes without saying that their legal basis is international and it should be emphasized in all definitions or international courts or tribunals. In view of this, Tomuschat's definition should be supplemented with such an international character of the legal basis for the establishment of judicial bodies. It seems that emphasizing the international legal basis is necessary also to

---

[16]Buergenthal (2001), p. 267 et seq.

[17]Tomuschat (2001), p. 1108.

[18]Rosenne (2007), pp. XI et seq.

define other institutions of international cooperation, especially international organisations.

3 The Establishment of International Courts in Treaties and Outside of Treaties

The conclusion that international legal basis is a prerequisite for the establishment of an international judicial body refers not only to courts/tribunals, but all institutions of international cooperation. This is mainly due to the fact that in this way states can demonstrate their will, as the creators and founders of a new institution. Therefore, there is no doubt that it should be an instrument of international law that becomes the legal basis for their establishment. This can be in the form of an international agreement between founders which would have a normative character. The specific forms of such agreements may vary, although as standard these come in the form of treaties. It should be noted that for such agreement to take legal effect it should be governed by international law. This means that parties to such an agreement are states which have international legal personality, though there is a possibility that also international organisations can be parties to such agreements. The notion of agreement should be interpreted broadly, i.e. it can mean various actions undertaken by states to reach an agreement. However, it is vitally important for such actions to be based on measures available in international law, because the newly established judicial institution becomes part of the international legal framework. Therefore, it can be concluded that the agreement as the legal basis for the foundation of an international judicial body definitely reflects the material aspect of its establishment, and this means that it consists in the will of its founders and its normative character related to its substance.

In view of this it can be claimed that the actual legal basis for the establishment and functioning of international courts/tribunals are treaties or other international law instruments. Further, it can be put forward that it is essential for the international law instrument creating an international judicial body to have the element of either explicit or implicit agreement between the founders of the new institution of international cooperation.

According to international law, treaties are not the only possible legal basis for the establishment of international courts/tribunals, nor for the establishment of international governmental organisations. Therefore, even though the establishment of international courts/tribunals in treaties should be given the utmost importance and priority, we should also acknowledge the possibility of the creation thereof by means of resolutions of the bodies of international organisations, both *de facto* and *de iure*. After all, states can express their will in both of these ways, be it directly or indirectly. Law-making resolutions adopted by bodies of international organisations have already gained a strong and well-established position in the system of the sources of contemporary international law.[19]

Undoubtedly the most typical and also desirable situation occurs where the legal basis for the establishment of an international court/tribunal is a legal instrument instituting the body in an international treaty, which clearly and unambiguously expresses the will of its founders. The establishment of a judicial body with such a legal basis gives rise to a self-evident presumption that the body is international in nature. A different situation occurs when a judicial body is not established in an international treaty. In order to prove its international character, it would be necessary to determine whether the founders have entered into any other form of international agreement, which may prove to be challenging.[20] It needs to be emphasized that the law of treaties—in particular the 1969 Vienna Convention on the Law of Treaties—applies to all international treaties which provide the legal basis for instituting international courts or tribunals. However, an international treaty instituting a new international judicial body needs to be something more than just a "conventional" treaty. After all, such an agreement is, in a way, a "constitution" which brings a new international judicial body into existence. Such an international judicial body can also acquire special status, should the treaty grant it with international legal personality. Examples of such regulations can be found in art. 4 of the Rome Statute of the International Criminal Court and art. 18 of the Convention on the Settlement of Investment Disputes between States and National of Other States. The most special of all statutes of international judicial bodies is unarguably the Statute of the International Court of Justice, which is an integral part of the United Nations Charter.[21] The Charter, which can be regarded as a "constitution" of the international community is undeniably the most exceptional international treaty. This stance was confirmed by the ICJ itself in its advisory opinion of 1962 on certain expenses of the United Nations, where the ICJ recognised that "the Charter is a multilateral treaty, albeit a treaty having certain special characteristics".[22] The legal bases of other international judicial bodies can also be found in treaties, e.g. the European Court of Human Rights has its legal basis in the European Convention for the Protection of Human Rights and Fundamental Freedoms of 1949,[23] the International Criminal Court has its legal basis in the Rome Statute of 1998,[24] and the International Tribunal for the Law of the Sea has its legal basis in Annex VI to the United Nations Convention on the Law of the Sea of 1982.[25]

---

[19]D'Aspremont and Besson (2017).

[20]Schermers and Blokker (2011), p. 40.

[21]The text of the Statute: UNTS, vol. 33, p. 993.

[22]See: *Certain Expenses of the United Nations (Article 17, paragraph 2 of the Charter)*, Advisory Opinion, ICJ Reports 1962, p. 157.

[23]Text of the Convention: ETS 005.

[24]Text of the Rome Statute: UNTS, vol. 2187, p. 90.

[25]Text of the Convention: UNTS, vol. 1883, p. 3.

As a result of the proliferation of international courts and tribunals, especially at the turn of the twenty-first century, the generally accepted stance on the possibility of establishing international judicial bodies outside of treaties has also undergone a fundamental change. It was most widely discussed in the context of the foundation of two ad-hoc criminal tribunals, namely the International Criminal Tribunal for the former Yugoslavia (ICTY), and International Criminal Tribunal for Rwanda (ICTR). In a way, the establishment of those two tribunals paved the way for creating the permanent International Criminal Tribunal later on. Both of these ad hoc criminal tribunals came into existence as a reaction of the international community to the violations of international humanitarian law in the armed conflicts in the Balkans and in Rwanda. These tribunals were founded in the UN Security Council resolution based on the powers vested in it in Chapter VII of the UN Charter in a situation classified by the Council as a threat to the peace. On February 22, 1993, the UN Security Council passed Resolution 808 which proclaimed that "an international tribunal shall be established for the prosecution of persons responsible for serious violations of international humanitarian law in the territory of former Yugoslavia since 1991".[26] Subsequently, this precedent was used to establish a similar tribunal for Rwanda. On November 8, 1994, the United Nations' Security Council passed Resolution 955, where it decided to establish "an international tribunal for the sole purpose of prosecuting persons responsible for genocide and other serious violations of international humanitarian law committed in the territory of Rwanda and Rwandan citizens responsible for genocide and other such violations committed in the territory of neighbouring States, between 1 January 1994 and 31 December 1994".[27] The UN Charter does not include any provisions which would give the Security Council the right to establish international judicial bodies. However, in both of the aforementioned cases, the Council used its exclusive power vested in it in Chapter VII of the Charter and took "action with respect to threats to the peace, breaches of the peace, and acts of aggression". The Security Council also acted upon art. 29 of the Charter, which provides that it "may establish such subsidiary organs as it deems necessary for the performance of its functions". The two ad-hoc tribunals became such subsidiary bodies. Even though the status of both of these tribunals has changed these days, they provide good examples of how international courts and tribunals may be established outside of treaties.[28]

---

[26]UN Doc. SC/RES/8087 (1993); for commentary see: Pickard (1995), pp. 435 et seq.

[27]UN Doc. SC/RES/955 (1994); for commentary see: van den Herik (2005), pp. 27 et seq.

[28]On December 22, 2010, the Security Council adopted resolution SC/RES/1966, which created a special Residual Mechanism for Criminal Tribunals which "shall continue the jurisdiction, rights and obligations and essential functions of the ICTY and the ICTR"; for commentary see: Mbengue (2015), p. 201.

4 Concluding Remarks

International courts and tribunals play an increasingly important role in peaceful settlement of international disputes. Their special role in this process has evolved significantly. Traditionally, international courts and tribunals were tasked with settling legal disputes between states in different areas of their international operations. The jurisdiction of the "classic" international court such as the ICJ is still subsidiary and limited to legal disputes between states.[29] However, nowadays there are other courts and tribunals which were established as a result of the evolution of contemporary international law, especially in the areas of international human rights law and humanitarian law. Therefore, their jurisdiction covers different kinds of disputes and in terms of their personal scope it also covers individuals. The fact that individuals can now invoke their rights directly before international courts and tribunals, or can be held accountable for serious violations of international law, has brought about the proliferation of international judicial bodies.[30] As a result, international courts and tribunals can hear cases not only involving different international bodies with legal personality, but also other entities, including individuals, which/who do not have international legal personality. All of these factors resulted in the fact that there are different legal bases for the establishment of international courts and tribunals. The will of the states still plays an essential role in establishing international judicial bodies. However, it does not have to be expressed explicitly and solely in an international treaty. A certain analogy can be drawn to the process of establishing other international institutions, IGOs in particular. Both international courts/tribunals and IGOs can be established in treaties and outside of treaties; a necessary prerequisite, though, is that they are established by means of legal instruments governed by international law.

References

Abi-Saab, G. (1999). Fragmentation or unification: Some concluding remarks. *New York University Journal of International Law and Politics, 31*(4), 919–933.
Amerasinghe, C. F. (2005). *Principles of the institutional law of international organizations.* Cambridge: Cambridge University Press.
Buergenthal, T. (2001). Proliferation of international courts and tribunals: Is it good or bad? *Leiden Journal of International Law, 14*(2), 267–275.
Cała-Wacinkiewicz, E. (2018). *Fragmentacja prawa międzynarodowego.* Warsaw: C.H. Beck.
Caminos, H. (2013). The growth of specialized international tribunals and the fears of fragmentation of international law. In N. Boschiero, T. Scovazzi, C. Pitea, & C. Ragni (Eds.), *International courts and the development of international law. Essays in Honor of Tullio Treves* (pp. 55–65). The Hague: T.M.C. Asser Press.

---

[29]Cançado Trinidade (2014), p. 1 et seq.
[30]Kent et al. (2019).

Cançado Trinidade, A. A. (2014). Reflections on a century of international justice and prospects for the future. In G. Gaja & J. Grote Stoutenburg (Eds.), *Enhancing the rule of law through the international court of justice* (pp. 1–32). Leiden: Brill-Nijhoff.

Czapliński, W. (2007). Multiplikacja sądów międzynarodowych – szanse czy zagrożenia dla jedności prawa międzynarodowego. In J. Kolasa & A. Kozłowski (Eds.), *Rozwój prawa międzynarodowego – jedność czy fragmentacja* (pp. 77–130). Wrocław: Wydawnictwo Uniwersytetu Wrocławskiego.

D'Aspremont, J., & Besson, S. (Eds.). (2017). *The Oxford handbook on the sources of international law.* Oxford: Oxford University Press.

Dupuy, P. M. (2007). A Doctrinal debate in the globalisation Era: On the "Fragmentation" of international law. *European Journal of Legal Studies, 1*(1), 1–19.

Gadkowski, A. (2018). *Treaty-making powers of international organizations.* Poznań: Wydawnictwo Naukowe Uniwersytetu im. Adama Mickiewicza.

Gehring, T. (1991). International environmental regimes: Dynamic sectoral legal systems. *Yearbook of the International Law Commission, 1*(1), 35–56.

Kent, A., Nikos Skoutaris, N., & Trinidad, J. (Eds.). (2019). *The future of international courts. Regional, institutional and procedural challenges.* New York: Routledge.

Klabbers, J. (2002). *An introduction to international institutional law.* Cambridge: Cambridge University Press.

Lee, R. S. (2002). *The international criminal court. The making of the Roma Statute – Issues – Negotiations – Results.* The Hague: Martinus Nijhoff Publishers.

Mbengue, M. M. (2015). Challenges of judges in international criminal courts and tribunals. In C. Giorgetti (Ed.), *Challenges and recusals of judges and arbitrators in international courts and tribunals* (pp. 183–227). Leiden: Brill-Nijhoff.

Pickard, D. B. (1995). Security council resolution 808: A step toward a permanent international court for the prosecution of international crimes and human rights violations. *Golden Gate University Law Review, 25,* 435–462.

Romano, C. P. R., Nollkaemper, A., & Kleffner, J. K. (Eds.). (2004). *Internationalized criminal courts: Sierra Leone, East Timor, Kosovo, and Cambodia.* Oxford: Oxford University Press.

Rosenne, S. (2007). *Interpretation, revision and other recourse from international judgments and awards.* Leiden: Brill-Nijhoff.

Sands, P. (1999). Introduction. In P. Sands, R. Mackenzie, & Y. Shany (Eds.), *Manual of international courts and tribunals* (pp. ix–xxiii). London: Lexis.

Schermers, H. G., & Blokker, N. M. (2011). *International institutional law.* Leiden: Brill-Nijhoff.

Schmalenbach, K. (2012). International organizations or institutions, supervision and sanctions. In R. Wolfrum (Ed.), *Max Planck Encyclopedia of public international law.* Oxford: Oxford University Press.

Schreuer, C. H. (2001). *The ICSID convention. A commentary.* Cambridge: Cambridge University Press.

Szpak, A. (2014). Proliferation of international courts and tribunals and its impact on the fragmentation of international law. *The International Law Annual, 2,* 31–39.

Tomuschat, C. (2001). International courts and tribunals. In R. Bernhard (Ed.), *Max Planck encyclopedia of public international law.* Oxford: Oxford University Press.

van den Herik, L. J. (2005). *The contribution of the Rwanda tribunal to the development of international law.* Leiden: Brill-Nijhoff.

Judicial Review and Life Imprisonment

Davide Galliani

Contents

Davide Galliani is Associate Professor of Public Law and Jean Monnet Professor of Fundamental Rights, University of Milan. This contribution develops some reflections previously exposed in Galliani (2016).

D. Galliani (✉)
University of Milan, Milano, Italy
e-mail: davide.galliani@unimi.it

P. Pinto de Albuquerque, K. Wojtyczek (eds.), *Judicial Power in a Globalized World*, https://doi.org/10.1007/978-3-030-20744-1_14

1 Introduction

The purpose of this article is to demonstrate that the de jure reducibility standard of Life Imprisonment needs to be reconsidered. This is because de jure irreducible Life Imprisonment does not exist. Therefore, instead of the de jure reducible standard, it should be more appropriate to talk about de jure reducible Life Imprisonment by formal and (especially) substantial judicial review. The difference is not purely nominative. The integration of the substantial judicial review makes Life Imprisonment more respectful of human dignity. The new standard is more adequate for the relevant international law and with reference to some principles recognized around the world, as separation of power, judicial review and (of course) human dignity.

This thesis aims to demonstrate the need for making Life Imprisonment reducible through a substantial judicial review and not through a political intervention. In order to illustrate this, the working method inspired by comparative law has been used. Therefore, we will analyze how Life Imprisonment is made reducible in the world and in particular in the European context. The meaning of pardon power and Ministerial power on early release will be considered carefully.

This article will deal with three issues. First, the constitutional provisions related to the power of pardon, with particular attention to the States of the Council of Europe that have Life Imprisonment Without Parole. Second, we will consider the ministerial power on early release. Finally, we will examine the judgments of some Constitutional Courts where the review to Life Imprisonment had to be given to the judge and not to the executive branch. Only a judge is able to evaluate, substantially and not formally, if the detention is still lawful.

The following reflections are addressed to scholars of international law, European law, constitutional law and criminal law, particularly inclined to use the comparative method; furthermore, this contribution could also affect the judges, regardless of their "jurisdiction" (international, European or national).

2 In Which Cases Should De Jure and Therefore De Facto Irreducible Life Imprisonment Be Described?

In order to answer this question, it is essential to focus on Constitutions which do not mention either amnesty or pardon. Only seven Constitutions in the world have no reference to either amnesty or pardon: Andorra, Australia, Bosnia and Herzegovina, Canada, Syria, Saudi Arabia and Yemen. Only two of the forty-seven Member States of the Council of Europe: Andorra and Bosnia and Herzegovina. We can add Canada, which is Observer State of the Council of Europe.

The most comprehensive International Database on amnesty and pardon world-wide,[1] however, reveals that amnesties, in six of these seven Countries mentioned above, have been passed anyway. Andorra is the only State in the world with no constitutional provisions on amnesty and pardon, as well as no practical experience. As a result, out of the 193 Member States of the United Nation, only one, Andorra, could be described as a State with irreducible de jure and de facto Life Imprisonment.

3 Does Life Imprisonment Exist in Andorra?

No. Even though the Constitution does not prohibit Life Imprisonment explicitly (as in the case of the death penalty: article 8), no statute acknowledges it. Therefore, Life Imprisonment in Andorra is not provided by the law, and the maximum penalty is 25 years.

First Consideration From an international and comparative perspective, the de jure and de facto irreducible Life Imprisonment standard seems to be at least problematic. If we consider that among the 193 Member States of the United Nations, there are no States with de jure irreducible Life Imprisonment, what exactly do we mean by de jure reducible Life Imprisonment? If all States around the world allow de jure reducibility of Life Imprisonment, we have to consider only the possibility of de facto irreducible Life Imprisonment.

4 Does Life Imprisonment Exist in the Six of the Seven States with No Constitutional References to Either Amnesty or Pardon But with Practical Experiences of These?

Yes. However, Bosnia and Herzegovina does not have Life Imprisonment-the same situation as in Andorra. Life Imprisonment in Bosnia and Herzegovina is not provided by the law (the maximum penalty is 45 years). If we consider Canada, an Observer State of the Council of Europe, the question of reducibility of Life Imprisonment is simple to solve. Canada has only Life Imprisonment With Parole. Life Imprisonment Without Parole does not exist there and, therefore, Life Imprisonment is always de jure reducible.

Second Consideration If we take a look at the Council of Europe, the de jure and de facto irreducible Life Imprisonment standard is definitely problematic. The only

---

[1]The Amnesty Law Database, created by Professor Louise Mallinder, University of Ulster (http://www.politicalsettlements.org/portfolio/amnesties/: last access: 8 April, 2019).

two States (Andorra, Bosnia and Herzegovina) without constitutional provisions to either amnesty or pardon have no Life Imprisonment. Canada has Life Imprisonment but always with Parole. Considering the Member States and the Observer States of the Council of Europe, the de jure and de facto irreducible Life Imprisonment standard cannot be empirically demonstrated. In Bosnia and Herzegovina the Constitution does not provide either pardon or amnesty. However, we do have here examples of practical experience, even though never with regard to lifers, as Life Imprisonment does not exist. As far as Canada is concerned, this is not a problem, because regardless pardon and amnesty powers, not provided in the Constitution but used de facto, Life Imprisonment is always de jure and therefore hypothetically de facto reducible.

Should such significant relevance be given to criteria with no empirical demonstration? If we cannot talk about de jure irreducible Life Imprisonment for any States in the world, why do we continue to use the criteria of the de jure reducibility?

Why did we previously focus on amnesty and especially pardon powers and not on other early release instruments? When we talk about pardon and amnesty as de jure instruments to reduce sentences, we necessarily adopt a methodology of the comparative law studies. Amnesty and pardon are the most widespread mechanisms provided by Constitutions to reduce sentences. It is quite significant that generally in the judgments involving Life Imprisonment the decisions focus first on pardon and only later, if necessary, on other particular tools, such as amnesty, early release on compassionate or medical grounds etc.[2]

5 How to Deal with States Providing Life Imprisonment Without Parole and, Especially, with Reference to the Pardon Power?

Only 38 of the 193 Member States of the United Nations have Life Imprisonment Without Parole.[3] Of these, ten are Members of the Council of Europe: Bulgaria, Hungary, Lithuania, Malta, the Netherlands, Slovakia, Sweden, Turkey, Ukraine, and the United Kingdom.

---

[2]The most recent book in this subject is Novak (2015).

[3]See Center For Law and Global Justice (2012), p. 25, note 144. These States are: Albania, Argentina, Australia, Brunei Darussalam, Bulgaria, Burundi, China, Comoros, Cuba, Eritrea, Ethiopia, Ghana, Hungary, Israel, Kazakhstan, Kenya, Lao People's Democratic Republic, Liberia, Lithuania, Malta, Marshall Islands, Namibia, Netherlands, New Zealand, Nigeria, Palau, Seychelles, Sierra Leone, Slovakia, Solomon Islands, Sweden, Tajikistan, Tanzania, Turkey, Ukraine, United Kingdom, and Zimbabwe. In note 145, the document underlines that there were twenty-one countries for which researchers could not locate statutory or case law text confirming whether LWOP exists or not. They are: Barbados, Bhutan, Dominica, Equatorial Guinea, Gambia, Grenada, Guyana, Indonesia, Kuwait, Lebanon, Libya, Saint Kitts and Nevis, Saint Vincent and the

It is quite interesting to note that the provisions concerning Life Imprisonment Without Parole in eight of these States have already been judged by the European Court of Human Rights.[4] Therefore, only two States have never been reviewed by the Strasbourg Court, namely Malta and Sweden.[5]

In any case, this aspect is paramount. If it is true that, among these 38 States, all of them have constitutional provisions on amnesty or pardon, it is also theoretically possible that some Constitutions expressly prohibit the use of the pardon power with reference to a particular category of convicts or limit its practice to specific convictions. In this case, and in this case only, de jure irreducible Life Imprisonment actually means de jure irreducible Life Imprisonment. All these potential cases concern States of the United States.[6] No Member States of the Council of Europe that provide for Life Imprisonment Without Parole have express constitutional limitation to the use of the pardon power.

Third Consideration All Member States of the Council of Europe provide for no constitutional limitations to the use of pardon power. All European people, regardless their sentences, could obtain pardon under the law. Once again, it is necessary to repeat the previous question: when we speak about de jure irreducible Life Imprisonment, what exactly do we mean?

Grenadines, Saudi Arabia, South Sudan, Suriname, Syria, Thailand, Trinidad and Tobago, Turkmenistan, and the United Arab Emirates.

[4]In chronological order: (1) United Kingdom: *Vinter and Others v. UK*, Grand Chamber, July 9, 2013 (Article 3, violation) and *Hutchinson v. UK*, Grand Chamber, January 17, 2017 (Article 3, no violation); (2) the Netherlands: *Murray v. Netherlands*, Grand Chamber, April 26, 2016 (Article 3, violation); (3) Turkey: *Öcalan v. Turkey (no. 2)*, Second Section, March 18, 2014 (Article 3, violation) [final] and other cases against Turkey; (4) Hungary: *László Magyar v. Hungary*, Second Section, May 20, 2014 (Article 3, violation) [final]; (5) Bulgaria: *Harakchiev and Tolumov v. Bulgaria*, Fourth Section, July 8, 2014 (Article 3, violation) [final]; (6) Slovakia: *Cacko v. Slovakia*, Third Section, July 22, 2014 (Article 3: violation, no violation) [final]; (7) Lithuania: *Matiošaitis v. Lithuania*, Former Second Section, May 23, 2017 (Article 3, violation) [final]; (8) *Petukhov v. Ukraine no. 2*, Fourth Section, March 12, 2019 (Article 3: violation).

[5]We can not consider *Lynch and Whelan v. Ireland*, Fifth Section, July 8, 2014, app. nos. 70495/10 and 74565/10, a decision of inadmissibility. The reason is that in Ireland Life Imprisonment Without Parole does not appear to exist. The Irish system seems different from the one of the United Kingdom. Also the case of Cyprus is out of our considerations: after *Kafkaris v. Cyprus*, Grand Chamber, February 12, 2008 (Article 3, no violation; article 5, § 4, violation) the State introduced Parole (Release) Board.

[6]Another interesting question here no subject to discussion, is the existence (or not) of a binding international law that prohibits the use of the clemency powers relating to genocide, crime against humanity, and others. In any case, for the Life Imprisonment in the United States, see Flanagan (1995), Berry (2010), Ogletree and Sarat (2012).

6 With Reference to Council of Europe, Who Has the Power of Pardon in the States with Life Imprisonment Without Parole?

In the Republican States, the pardon power is given to the President of the Republic (Bulgaria, Hungary, Lithuania, Malta, Slovakia, Turkey, and Ukraine). In the Monarchies, what is set forth by the law differs from what actually happens nowadays. If in the past the pardon power was a prerogative of the Monarch, now in Sweden, the Netherlands and the United Kingdom the power is substantially a matter held by the Government.

7 Which Are the Possibilities for Judicial Review As Far As Pardon Power Is Concerned?

The power of pardon is by nature a political act. This means, first, that the power of pardon is purpose-free since the goals are not specifically set forth. For this reason, like any other political act, pardon is in principle without judicial review. If the Constitution provides, for example, that 'the Head of State could grant a pardon' or 'pardon shall be granted by the Head of State', how much space could judicial review have? So, basically the power of pardon is judicial review free. Probably the most relevant demonstration of this conclusion is that granting pardon, as well as its refusal, does not need any reason or motivation. If the pardon decree of the Head of State does not contain any motivation, it is easier to understand why there is an absence of judicial review.

However, it is possible to describe some particular forms of judicial review also with reference to the pardon power. For example, if a statute sets forth that pardon can be granted only after conviction, and not before, the Head of State has to comply with this procedural requirement. Otherwise, it is possible (theoretically) to imagine judicial review of the decision. There are also examples that result from language in the statutes. Sometimes, in the statutes (not in the Constitutions) we can find some apparent restrictions to the use of pardon power. The pardon remains a purpose-free power. At most, the statutes can define some constitutional powers more specifically, but they can never change their meaning. If the statutes decide that pardon can be granted taken into account the convict's offences or the victim's opinions or the length of time serving in prison, the nature of the pardon power does not change. The problem in these cases is whether we can imagine judicial review. Maybe yes, but only in this sense-if the Head of State has used its pardon power in a completely arbitrary or grossly unreasonable way.

Even accepting this, we would still have a problem and it might be without solution. To understand if the use of the pardon power is completely arbitrary or grossly unreasonable, we would need to know how the Head of State has taken his decision. Can this be done? No, because the Head of State does not have to explain his decisions.

Fourth Consideration The judicial review of the pardon power is very difficult to imagine, although it cannot be totally excluded. The pardon power remains a purpose-free power without any obligation for motivations. There is definitely very little space for judge intervention.

This also in the case judicial review comes from the Constitutional Courts. The Constitutional Courts can decide which authority has the final decision on pardon. The Constitutional Courts can clarify that, for example in the parliamentary governments, the Head of State has the final decision because he or she (better than the Minister) has a 'neutral' and not a political role. In the end, the conclusion is always the same: the pardon power remain a purpose-free power without any obligations for motivations.

8 Why Are the Possibilities of Judicial Review So Relevant with Reference to the Pardon Power?

We can talk about the de jure reducible standard in the States with Life Imprisonment Without Parole only thanks to the pardon power. In these States, the pardon power is what makes Life Imprisonment de jure reducible. If the pardon power is the only possibility for a lifer without parole in these States, we should at least ask that this lifer

> shall be entitled to take proceedings by which the lawfulness of his detention shall be decided speedily by a court and his release ordered if the detention is not lawful

as provided by Article 5, § 4 of the European Convention of Human Rights.

9 Life Imprisonment and the Minister's Role

Even in case pardon is a governmental power, in the Minister's hands, the previous considerations do not change. The nature of this power is always the same. Pardon is still free of purpose, without any obligation for motivation.

In some States with Life Imprisonment Without Parole (as well as in others too, but we are not going to consider them), the Minister could order inmates' early release. This power usually involves all convicts, and therefore also lifers without parole. In this case too, there could be a statute or another provision (executive and administrative regulations) giving the Minister some indications. However, the power is definitely and with no doubt discretionary. We can discuss the difference between discretionary power and political power, but it would not be relevant for this issue. In both cases, the powers are concessions granted, respectively, by the Head of State and the Minister.

The Minister uses his power to satisfy the statute or other provisions, but (1) as in the case of pardon power, also in the case of early release there is no duty for specific motivations[7] and (2) only the purposes of the power of early release are binding, but not how these purposes are reached.

Could the possibility of early release in the Minister's hands be described as a right? No, absolutely not. No duties, no rights. If the Minister had the obligation to grant early release for those cases provided by statutes or other regulations, the conclusion could be different. It is important to repeat: in none of the States in the world, the Minister has the obligation to grant early release. It is a concession of the Minister who uses his/her 'clemency' power to grant early release. His power is discretionary. From an inmate's point of view, we can discuss, as far as early release is concerned, about a privilege, not a right.[8] The Minister may decide for early release, but he is not law obliged. As a consequence, the space for judicial review is too limited.

We could consider some judicial review space also in the case of early release by the Minister, but it is anyway very limited. The judge, for example, can take a decision regarding law violation, irrationality and procedural lack. Some examples may explain better. If the statute sets forth that early release should be granted in case life expectancy is less than three months, and the Minister ignores this rule, we can imagine a (limited) space for judicial review with reference to the unlawful grant of early release. The case of irrationality is more difficult, but we can try to explain it-a statute sets forth early release in case of inability to ambulate and the Minister does not grant it to a lifer with medically verified inability to walk (for example) more than five metres. In this case, we might see a (limited) space to judicial review. The last example is the simplest. If the Minister takes his decision with procedural lack, the judicial review could have spaces (for example, the Minister deny to grant early release without requesting the compulsory but not-binding opinion of the Parole Board or Prison Director).

In these cases, we probably can discuss the existence of formal judicial review. Regarding the substantial judicial review, the conclusion is that the spaces are very limited. If the Minister does not grant early release with specific and detailed motivations, the spaces for judicial review, also in the extreme cases of the arbitrary and capricious use of the power, appear extremely limited. It is difficult to gain real, actual, complete and substantial judicial review.

Is this formal and very limited judicial review enough? No. The judge can never decide if continuing detention is lawful compared to the original sentence. However,

---

[7]This point is crucial. In some cases, it can happen that the Minister explains the motivations of his or her decision. For example, the Minister could send a 'personal' letter to lifer. Does the Minister have to do this? No. These particular cases are not usual and especially are not provided by law. In most cases, the Minister uses only one words: 'no'. This is what law allows. See for more (interesting) reflections, Griffin and O'Donnel (2012), and Griffin (2015).

[8]See the excellent book of Appleton (2010).

only the judge has the duty to disclose the reasoning and the documents used for the decision. The procedure will be made transparent only with the judge, as only the judge is formally independent and impartial from the parties. Finally, only the judge is substantially bound to respect the jurisdictional procedures and guarantees-one of the most important of them is the adversarial way to reach the final decision.

Fifth Consideration In case the possibility to allow an early release is a Minister's power, due to the nature of this power, it is very difficult to show a concrete, actual and especially substantial possibility of judicial review. Early release power is by nature discretionary, with no duty for motivations. Therefore, a convict does not have a right but a privilege. This is the reason why in front of a privilege (and not a right) the judicial review should be described as very limited.

10   Life Imprisonment, the Purposes of the Penalties and the Minister's Role

The last, but not least important, observation is that we can examine the States in which Life Imprisonment (often mandatory) has only one purpose-punishing the convict. Without considering the merit of this choice, this is what happens in some States.[9] It can also occur that lifers, in some of these States, are not allowed to ask for early release to a judge or (at least) a parole board. The only possibility is early release by the Minister.

This (apparently) entangled system, however, shows an evident contradiction, with relevant consequences even to the basis of the Rule of Law. On one hand, the sole punitive purpose of Life Imprisonment makes early release a privilege (not a right), but, on the other hand, the judicial review on early release should guarantee something that is not possible to guarantee. The contradiction is clear and undeniable-if early release is a privilege, and not a right, the space for a substantial judicial review is fictional, unreal, and nonexistent.[10]

The Rule of Law, realised by a real separation of powers, an actual judicial review, and a material guarantee of the human dignity, is a conquest that does not deserve formal deference. The Rule of Law deserves substantial, valid and reasonable observance.[11]

---

[9]Apart from the importance of rehabilitation, highlighted by the Resolutions of the Council of Europe (see Appendix), in some of these States, where Life Imprisonment has only retributive scope, the deterrent goal of penalties is deny because it is against human dignity!

[10]Without considering that, in the case of mandatory Life Imprisonment, the problem doubles. The space of the judicial review is limited at the beginning and at the end.

[11]This is the common thread of the most important book on Life Imprisonment ever published: van Zyl Smit (2002). See also Lécuyer (2012). More recently: van Zyl Smit and Appleton (2016, 2019).

11 Relevant Constitutional Court's Judgements

In Italy, the Constitutional Court, in sentence no. 204 of July 4, 1974, declared the constitutional illegitimacy of the Minister's power to grant conditional release ('liberazione condizionale') that has been allowed also for Lifers (only) since 1962, using these words (our translation):

§2. Conditional release represents a particular aspect of the executive moment of the penalty and it is part of the ultimate and decisive goal of the penalty itself that is to tend to the social rehabilitation of the convicted (. . .).

'Thanks' to article 27, § 3 of the Constitution,[12] conditional release has acquired a more incisive weight and value than in the past. It represents, by nature, a peculiar aspect of the penal treatment and its application took a peremptory duty to legislator to consider not only the rehabilitation goal of the penalty, but also to arrange all adequate instruments to achieve this goal and the forms trough which this goal can be guarantee.

As a result, by virtue of constitutional article (no. 27, §3), arise the right of the convicted in order that, occurring the conditions provided by law (the 'secure rehabilitation', 'sicuro ravvedimento', ndr), the continuing punitive pretence be reviewed to verify if the quantity of the expiate penalty has positively carry out its rehabilitation goal. This right shall obtain a valid and reasonable jurisdictional guarantee.

There is no doubt that the law in force is completely deficient of this guarantee. The law determines an abnormal sequence of interventions and responsibilities, which move from the judge of the executive moment ('giudice di sorveglianza', ndr) to the Minister of Justice.

In such a significant phase of the executive moment of the penalty, this connection between an authority of the judiciary and an authority of the executive power contrasts with the guarantee of the personal liberty which the article 24 of the Constitution,18 within Article 13,19 ensures the judicial safeguard for.

It should be noted that the Minister of Justice has such a wide discretionary power that he or she can disregard the opinion of the judicial authority as far the request for the application of the conditional release. The judicial authority, thanks' to its functions on the executive moment of the penalty provided by law, is the only adequate authority who can evaluate the real and concrete existence of the objective and subjective conditions (especially the second one) that are essential to grant conditional release.

The disharmony of the system is even more unacceptable after law no. 1643, November 25, 1962, that has modified the original text of Article 167 of the Penal Code extending the application of the conditional release to the Life Imprisonment convicted.

Due to law no. 1634 of the 1962, conditional release had taken, with no doubt, a different appearance and dimension compared to what provided for by the legislator in 1930. Albeit subject to predetermined conditions, we are facing an actual surrender by the State to further realization of the punitive pretence with reference to certain convicts, surrender that surely cannot depend on an authority of the executive power, but on the judicial power, with all guarantees both for the State and for the convicted'.

---

[12] Article 27, § 3 of the Italian Constitution: 'Punishment cannot be inhuman treatment and must aim at the rehabilitation of the convict' ('Le pene non possono consistere in trattamenti contrari al senso di umanità e devono tendere alla rieducazione del condannato').

The Italian Constitutional Court did not care about the subsequently legal vacuum. A hypothetical renunciation by the State to the further realization of the punitive pretence cannot depend on an authority of the executive power. After the historical sentence no. 204 of 1974, all Italian Constitutional Court judgments on Life Imprisonment have declared constitutional because of the possibility to obtain conditional release under real and concrete judicial review.

Considering the first decision of the Italian Constitutional Court directly concerning Life Imprisonment, sentence no. 264 of November 22, 1974, decided five months after the sentence no. 204, the words used are unequivocal:

> Sentence no. 204 of 1974 is a remarkable judgment by which the Constitutional Court declared unconstitutional the law which attributed to the Minister of Justice the power to grant conditional release. This will therefore be granted no more in relation to discretionary decisions of political power, but on the basis of a court decision, which the person is entitled to apply to, and with the guarantees proper of the judicial proceedings ensuring the offender has taken such a behaviour so as to feel his rehabilitation secure.

Sixth Consideration Substantial judicial review, in case of Life Imprisonment Without Parole, is fundamental not only for the convicted but also for the State. The judicial review allows to protect society, not only inmates.

12 Conclusion

It is noteworthy that in sentence no. 204 of 1974 of the Italian Constitutional Court, the judges did not take into account the issue of the pardon power, provided by the Constitution. They could have referred to it, but they did not.

Another Constitutional Court, whose importance is recognized worldwide, had used clear words:

> Implementing a prison sentence in accordance with human dignity requires that the person sentenced to life imprisonment retains the opportunity to regain his freedom. The possibility of pardon alone is not sufficient.[13]

What will the destiny of the Minister's power be? We can conclude with an unequivocal statement:

> However, with the wider recognition of the need to develop and apply, in relation to mandatory life prisoners, judicial procedures reflecting standards of independence, fairness and openness, the continuing role of the Secretary of State in fixing the tariff and in deciding on a prisoner's release following its expiry has become increasingly difficult to reconcile

---

[13]"Zu den Voraussetzungen eines menschenwürdigen Strafvollzugs gehört, daß dem zu lebenslanger Freiheitsstrafe Verurteilten grundsätzlich eine Chance verbleibt, je wieder der Freiheit teilhaftig zu werden. Die Möglichkeit der Begnadigung allein ist nicht ausreichend" (45 BVerfGE 187, June 21, 1977). Thanks' to Professor Dirk Van Zyl Smit for the translation.

with the notion of separation of powers between the executive and the judiciary, a notion which has assumed growing importance in the case-law of the Court.[14]

From a more general point of view, it is paramount that States allow judges to use their powers. If the decision on lifers' early release continues to be a political issue, some of the most important principles of the Constitutional States may be only theoretical and not practical. These principles are the separation of powers and the respect for human dignity.

If politicians have the 'last word' on lifers, they might use the detainee as a means to obtain votes during an election campaign (or not to lose them during their term). This would mean a violation of the human dignity, a right any person, whether in prison or not, must have.

References

Appleton, C. (2010). *Life after life imprisonment*. Oxford: Oxford University Press.

Berry III, W. (2010). More different than life, less different than death. The argument for according life without parole its own category of heightened review under the eighth amendment after Grahamv. Florida. *Ohio State Law Journal, 71*(6), 1109–1147.

Center For Law and Global Justice (School of Law, University of San Francisco). (2012). *Cruel and Unusual. U.S. Sentencing Practices in a Global Context*. https://www.usfca.edu/law/academics/centers/human-rights-in-criminal-sentencing-project

Flanagan, J. (Ed.). (1995). *Long-term imprisonment. Policy, science, and correctional practice*. Thousand Oaks, CA: Sage.

Galliani, D. (2016). The reducible life imprisonment standard from a worldwide and European perspective. *Global Jurist*, (1), 81–99.

Griffin, D. (2015). The release and recall of life sentence prisoners: Policy, practice and politics. *Irish Jurist, 53*, 1–35.

Griffin, D., & O'Donnel, I. (2012). The life sentence and parole. *British Journal of Criminology, 52*, 611–629.

Lécuyer, Y. (Ed.). (2012). *La perpétuité perpétuelle. Réflexion sur la réclusion criminelle à perpétuité*. Rennes: Universitaires de Rennes.

Novak, A. (2015). *Comparative executive clemency: The constitutional pardon power and the prerogative of mercy in global perspective*. New York: Routdlege.

Ogletree Jr., C., & Sarat, A. (Eds.). (2012). *Life without parole. America's new death penalty*. New York: New York Universities Press.

Van Zyl Smit, D. (2002). *Taking life imprisonment seriously in national and international law*. The Hague: Kluwer Law International.

van Zyl Smit, D., & Appleton, C. (Eds.). (2016). *Life imprisonment and human rights*. Oxford: Hart.

van Zyl Smit, D., & Appleton, C. (2019). *Life imprisonment. A global human rights analysis*. Cambridge: Harvard University Press.

---

[14]European Court of Human Rights, *Stafford v. UK, Grand Chamber*, May 28, 2002, § 78 (unanimously finding violation of Article 5, § 1 and Article 5, § 4).

Anti-Constitutional Constitutionalism: Minority Against Minority (Its Impact on International Law)

Armen Harutyunyan

Contents

The modern democratic state, which no longer knows the personal usurpation of power, becomes a link in the process of self-organization of modern society, in which conflicts arise and are resolved and exhausted in the process of adding together political unity and government.

Therefore, only if the task of organizing and preserving political unity is solved, the state becomes a reality and a uniform acting force. The concept of state can be understood only if it is considered from two aspects: as a source, constantly organizing, protecting and developing further unity, and as a "constituted" power acting on this basis.

Both of these aspects of activity are connected to each other by numerous invisible threads. Thus, the content and successful outcome of the state authority's activity depend on the success of the organization of political unity, and this, in turn, depends on whether the "state" finds approval and support. Therefore, modern development does not allow avoiding the problems of organizing political unity and isolating the "state" from its sociological substrate.

"The organization of political unity" does not mean the achievement of a harmonious condition of universal consent. It does not result in the abolition of social, political or institutional differences through overall unification. It should not be thought of without the existence and meaning of conflicts in the human society. Conflicts are able to prevent the 'ossification', the strengthening of already frozen forms. They are almost the only driving force that could not come to exist without historical turns. The absence of conflicts or their solution by force can lead to a stable immobility of the existing, which means—the inability to use the changed conditions and to bring forward new forms: then the moment of the collapse of the existing will

A. Harutyunyan (✉)
European Court of Human Rights, Strasbourg, France
e-mail: armen.harutyunyan@echr.coe.int

© Springer Nature Switzerland AG 2019
P. Pinto de Albuquerque, K. Wojtyczek (eds.), *Judicial Power in a Globalized World*, https://doi.org/10.1007/978-3-030-20744-1_15

become inevitable, and the disturbances will be even greater. A good example of this are the velvet revolutions in Armenia and Ukraine.

It depends not only on the existence of conflicts, but also on how they are overcame and regulated. Therefore, we should talk about ensuring the formation and preservation of political unity, by resolving conflicts; not to ignore or suppress conflicts for the sake of political unity and not to reject political unity for the sake of resolving the conflict.

Constitution is the fundamental law within the society. It defines the guidelines according to which a political unity is formed and the tasks that the state is facing should be properly understood. It regulates the whole process of overcoming conflicts within the society, the organization and the process of forming political unity and the activities of the state. It creates and normalizes the basis of the general legal regime. In general, it is a fundamental, structural plan based on elaborated principles for the legal regulation of the life of the society.[1]

Constitutionalism as a system that establishes the legal framework for the relationship of society and an individual with the government can be real and putative.

Currently, in most countries of the world there is a very unfavorable social situation that constantly reproduces and stimulates people's anti-legal attitudes. Legal nihilism has acquired a new quality, its nature, causes, spheres of influence have changed, it became spontaneous and it often turns into legal chaos. Relations between the state and society are developing on the basis of not real, but formal constitutionalism, which, on the one hand, is a consequence of amorphous stable groups and interests of citizens, on the other hand, is a consequence of the inability or unwillingness of the ruling elite to accept the new rules of the game as mandatory for all groups, including themselves. Today's geopolitical realities do not allow these elites to challenge democracy, that's why go along the path of formalizing democratic institutions and deprive of their essence—they formally exist, but do not function.

The constitution is designed in order to the state and its citizens limit themselves for mutual benefit. Constitutionalism as opposed to arbitrariness needs institutional guarantees, i.e. in such an organization of authority, in which all its branches restrict each other, relying on a system of checks and balances.

Today, many states only declare humane values, democratic freedoms and equal civil rights. As a result, human values deform and personality degrades.

If we want to avoid dictatorship, then one power must be balanced by another through a system of checks and balances, i.e. the separation powers is required. In this sense, the constitution is more than a list of competencies of certain state bodies.[2]

Political freedom acquires guarantees if the power is not in the same hands. In order for the power to stop the power, it is necessary, therefore, to divide it.[3]

---

[1]Hesse (1981), pp. 22–28 (in Russian).

[2]Shayo (2001), pp. 77, 78 (in Russian).

[3]Jacquet (2002), p. 90 (in Russian).

In the post-Soviet space, for example, the ruling elites more often rely on a democratic method of government—the rule of the majority.[4] Liberalism accepts the majority rule as a method, but not as an indicator of what the solution should be. To the doctrinal democrat, the fact that the majority wants something is sufficient reason to consider it as a good, for him, the will of the majority determines not only the content of the law, but also the fact that it is a good law. The liberal thinks that the opinion of the minority should be heard and discussed. History many times proved that the position of the minority was more correct. For the liberal, democracy means a system of guarantees for the minority, not a dictatorship of the majority. The liberal is concerned primarily with the limiting of an aggression of the majority, while the doctrinal democrat knows only one criterion—the existing opinion of the majority. The danger lies within the possibility of being in a situation of dictatorship of the majority.

When the desire of the majority of the people will be accomplished, there will be always a danger that it will overwhelm the minority.

Democratic and liberal traditions agree that a decision must be made by the majority. At the same time, if the doctrinal democrat considers it desirable that as many questions as possible should be decided by a majority vote, then the liberal is convinced that it is necessary to limit the number of questions that must be resolved in this way. The doctrinal democrat believes that the majority should have the right to decide what kind of power is needed and how to use it, while for the liberal democrat it is important that the power of the majority is limited by the long-term principles.

The fundamental concept of a doctrinal democrat is the concept of sovereignty. For him, it means that the rules of the majority cannot be limited. The ideal of democracy, which was originally aimed at preventing authoritarian power, thus becomes a justification for a new authoritarian government through the formalization of the system of checks and balances. We are seeing this trend in many modern countries. The authority of a democratic decision should be based on the fact that it is accepted by the majority of the society, which is united by common convictions, principles; it is necessary that the majority obey these principles, even if their immediate interest is to violate them. The passing majority should not try to formalize the system of checks and balances, the principle of rotation of power and other "general principles" in order to make the majority permanent and designs it for themselves. Dialectics will inevitably lead to a situation in which the majority, de facto becoming a minority, will rule the "majority rule", thereby suppressing individual freedom. This is the danger that threatens to many modern societies. The idea of individual freedom is central to the liberalism.[5]

The majority's authority, which represents the majority of the population, is acceptable only if the minority has a chance during the election process to become a majority, and also if the existence of the minority is not suppressed. If the minority

---

[4]In our opinion, this method of government is common in most modern states.

[5]Hayek (1960), pp. 90–102.

has no prospects, the system is unacceptable. If the position of the minority is unbearable, then, despite the public peace, an uprising will follow, because the minority has nothing to lose. The constitution, as the guarantor of the order, meaning the prerequisite of its own existence, implies that the position of the minority is satisfactory and temporary.

The principle that provides with an approval of government actions by the majority does not mean that the majority is morally entitled to do what it prefers. Democracy is not an unlimited government. A democratic government needs guarantees of individual freedom, like any other government. If democracy is a means rather than a purpose, its boundaries should be defined in accordance with the purpose that we want to achieve. This purpose is to guarantee and protect human rights. The effectiveness of the organization of the power in modern societies can be assessed by the degree of protection of human rights. In this regard, the perspective of freedom depends on whether the majority makes it an object of conscious choice or not. The constitution should take care of the protection of minority. To some extent, this protection is ensured by the guarantees of fundamental human rights and freedoms, to which specific group rights and privileges of the protection of the minority are added. But the abuse of power by the majority can hardly be completely excluded. Therefore, the constitution contains institutional and procedural rules that protect the minority. Such an institutional protection might be ensured by a Constitutional court.[6]

The nicety of the modern global constitutional situation lies within the fact that, very often, the political majority, having lost its position in the society, tries to retain power by using an administrative resource. It leads to the fact that the political majority sitting on the administrative resource becomes a minority within the society. There is a suppression of the opposition and total disregard of the individual's dignity—the basis of fundamental rights and freedoms. And the political majority loses its position because it tries to govern not on the basis of liberal values. It gradually evolves into the dictatorship of the majority. Therefore, having lost public support, the dictatorship of the majority is transformed into the dictatorship of a minority. In countries where the political opposition acts on the basis of liberal values, not formally, but actually proceeds from the constitutional concept of the rule of fundamental human rights and freedoms that are based on the dignity of the individual, retains the support of the overwhelming majority of the people and sooner or later displaces the dictatorship.

In this situation, we have the classical formula of the majority and minority. Constitutionalism replaces unconstitutionality. Such a liberal-oriented majority respects the interests of the minority and is ready to give a place to the minority after the results of the election.

Thus, constitutionalism as a system that establishes the legal framework for the relationship between society and the individual with the government becomes real

---

[6]Shayo (2001), pp. 66–69. (in Russian).

and is based on constitutional principles only. Here we are dealing with constitutional constitutionalism.

If the opposition uses the rhetoric of a liberal democracy only in order to gain the power, from the value perspective it does not differ from the authority. In that case two scenarios are possible:

A. The opposition, that makes deals with the authorities, "incriminates itself" by such a behaviour, etc., it is recognized as non-democratic and loses the majority within the society and becomes a minority. Politically, there is a "struggle" between the power of the minority and the opposition of the minority. A major part of the society becomes apathetic and the whole political system loses its legitimacy. Constitutionalism, as a system that establishes the legal framework for the relationship of society and the individual with the government, becomes putative and relies on the principles that contradict constitutional principles. In that case we are dealing with unconstitutional constitutionalism.

B. The opposition came to power "honestly", but did not stand the test of power and slipped into the dictatorship of the majority and became a political minority relying on administrative resources. And again the same cycle, which we indicated above, begins. In that case there is a danger of an agreement with the opposition, and through various imitation and manipulative technologies, for quite a long time, to distract the people and close the way to politics to the new political forces. Such a conspiracy is an imitation of the minority's struggle with the minority. There is again the functioning of unconstitutional constitutionalism. It lasts exactly as long as civil society consolidates and prepares for the revolution. That is exactly what was going on in the Republic of Armenia during 25 years, until the revolution took place, thanks to the new generation that did not know the Soviet government and were more determined. Now everything depends on whether the new government will stand the test of power.

These formulas are somewhat simplified representation of the situation. Authority and opposition are not two powers. They are more multifaceted and multi-levelled. But if you look at the essence, discarding the display technology of the distraction from the primary to the secondary, we note that this is the case in the most countries of the world. There are not so many real dictatorships that do not hide their priorities. There are not so many states with the deep democratic traditions, where political and legal cultures, developed civil society and independent judiciary do not allow the political system (no matter what disturbances are) to leave the paradigm of constitutional constitutionalism.

Thus, there is a crisis of the constitutional state. This crisis, by the way, also affected developed democracies: the USA, France, Italy, and others. Although, in these countries constitutionalism is still based on constitutional principles, future is unclear. There is a blurring of the value system on which constitutional constitutionalism is based. Within the EU, this is seen in some countries of the Central and Eastern Europe: Poland, Hungary, etc. But what is happening in France is also a demonstration of the crisis of constitutionalism. The constitution as a social contract between the society and the state no longer suits the majority of society. The

President of the Republic, Mr. E. Macron, proposed to formalize the approach through the municipalities on the three issues: France, taxes, immigrants. From the constitutional point of view it is a legal step made towards the revision of the social contract. The step aimed at the civilized resolution of contradictions between society (the majority) and the state (government). So far, everything is within the paradigm of constitutional constitutionalism.

From the perspectives of International Law, it is unquestionable; crisis of constitutionalism is causing problems for International Law. Stable constitutional states are resources for stability of International Law. Crisis within them automatically impacts International Law as well and creates also crisis of it.

Legal science and jurisprudence should develop a theory, which would allow to a certain extent to rely on existing social values as social facts. For instance, due to changes in public opinion in many countries, including European ones, there is a reconsideration of the family and its values.

It is necessary to have a transparent legal methodology applicable in cases when it comes to the inclusion of the new values in constitutional law or when it is necessary to give life to the values laid down in the constitution. Undoubtedly, there are values that have, rather, a formal legal character, and values that are accessible to public perception. For instance, the principle of the rule of law is a legal value, and judges possess more competence in its interpretation. But, of course, constitutions contain the concepts of social values, which are considered to be legal, and at the same time are open to everybody. Thus, it can be written down in the constitution that the past injustice must be revised or that the dignity of the person is the highest value, etc.[7]

To some commentators, any references to values in constitutional law seem highly questionable. A good example is Carl Schmitt, who regretted that in German courts the post-war consideration of human rights was guided by the values. At a more general level, beyond the legal sphere, Heidegger interpreted values as part of the metaphysical decadence of the West and oblivion of the true essence of being. It is true that under the cover of the sometimes rather exalted conversation about values, and social interests, political forces pursue their own goals, which often are completely devoid of ethical content. Thus, there is a reasonable ground to be sceptical of statements about values and to ask sensitive questions about the origin and the content of such values. Undoubtedly, in this area naivety cannot be tolerated.

But we can't actually get away from the value theories during judicial control over human rights and that's all the complexity.

Any ethical theory of human rights is obviously universalistic. It is connected not only to the interpretation of the given catalogues of human rights, but it also points the way to a much larger and more complex topic—the general theory of the legitimacy of human rights that fits into the cultural, political, and social context and may possibly reinforce with the help of theoretical approaches the fragile culture of human rights that has developed since 1945.

---

[7]Constitutional values in the theory and judicial practice, a collection of reports, M., 2009, A. Shayo, Introduction, pp. 8–9 (in Russian).

We should not forget that human rights in our time are under the protection of many institutions, that includes courts with broad competencies. However, they are based on nothing else but on the constant conviction of the citizens of our planet that only life in the light of such rights is fair for the realization of the best possibilities of human nature. In that sense, the ethical theory of the type that was described above can apparently do a favour to the cosmopolitan tradition of human rights.[8]

If we will not rely on these values, as indicators of the essence of the political system and political groups (personal dignity as the basis of the fundamental rights and freedoms; the fundamental rights and freedoms as the supreme values), then we risk being not just under the dictatorship of the majority or minority. Here everything is more or less clear. But we risk being under the dictatorship of unclear. When society will be atomized, there will be no longer a political unity. This will be the situation of the irreconcilable struggle of minorities with minorities for the "great" ideas of democracy and freedoms. But the only freedom that we will receive will be the freedom from humanity.

References

Hayek, F. A. (1960). *The constitution of liberty* (pp. 90–102). New York: University of Chicago.

Hesse, K. (1981). *Basics of constitutional law of Germany* (pp. 22–28). Moscow: Juridicheskaya literatura.

Jacquet, J.-P. (2002). *Constitutional law and political institutions* (p. 90). Moscow: Jurist.

Shayo, A. (2001). *Self-restraint of power: (Short course of constitutionalism)* (p. 77, 78). Moscow: Jurist.

---

[8]Ibid., Matthias Malmann: The Theory of Values and the Practice of Constitutional Justice., pp. 15–16.

Human Rights Due Diligence in International Law: Where Do We Go from Here?

Beatriz Mateus de Albuquerque

Contents

Beatriz Mateus de Albuquerque holds a LLM on Transnational Law from King's College London, a LLM on Law in a European and Global Context from Católica Global School of Law and a law degree from the Portuguese Catholic University Lisbon.

B. Mateus de Albuquerque (✉)
King's College London, London, UK

© Springer Nature Switzerland AG 2019   229
P. Pinto de Albuquerque, K. Wojtyczek (eds.), *Judicial Power in a Globalized World*, https://doi.org/10.1007/978-3-030-20744-1_16

1   Introduction

Since the Rana Plaza disaster in 2013, garment supply chains and their problematic working conditions have caught world-wide attention. The United Nations Guiding Principles on Business and Human Rights (UNGPs)[1] have been a landmark development, but more is to be done if we want to see real changes in companies. The European Union (EU) has the potential to be this change vector.

My research questions are whether the time is ripe to set a European-wide binding standard on human rights due diligence (HRDD)for the garment sector and, if yes, what format and content should this standard have. To reply to these questions, this paper will analyse the most important domestic initiatives to establish mandatory HRDD legislation. We are experiencing in Europe an accelerated shift from voluntary to legally binding HRDD requirements, particularly in global supply chains. Due to this growing trend in domestic legislations, there is an urgent need for European-level harmonization.

The Conflict Minerals Regulation[2] will also be studied and analysed as a case study, since it is the sole example of internationally binding HRDD legislation. It establishes supply chain due diligence requirements that could be, to a certain extent, transferred to garment supply chains. Lastly, the current panorama in the garment sector will be discussed and recommendations for a future EU proposal will be made, based on the comparative analysis of the national and international instruments mentioned in this research.

2   Human Rights Due Diligence: In Search of a Concept

The concept of HRDD arose from the second pillar of the UNGPs—business responsibility to respect. It seeks to 'identify, prevent, mitigate and account'[3] for how companies address human rights impacts. This responsibility is 'the biggest single responsibility placed on businesses'[4] by the Special Representative on Business and Human Rights John Ruggie. The use of due diligence concept was a 'clever and deliberate tactic'[5] used by Ruggie, because it is a familiar term both in the business and human rights field. Nonetheless, the same concept is used with different meanings in these areas. Corporate due diligence focuses on the investment risks for

---

[1]Un Doc A/HRC/17/31.

[2]Regulation (EU) 2017/821 of the European Parliament and of the Council of 17 May 2017 laying down supply chain due diligence obligations for Union importers of tin, tantalum and tungsten, their ores, and gold originating from conflict-affected and high-risk areas (OJ L 130, 19.5.2017, p. 1–20). (Conflict Minerals Regulation).

[3]Guiding Principle ('UNGP') 15.

[4]Harrison (2013), p. 107.

[5]Bonnitcha and McCorquodale (2017a), p. 900.

the company, whereas HRDD is characterized for covering a wide number of stakeholders, including individuals and communities harmed by the company's activities.[6] In a nutshell, the former includes a 'thorough investigation of the assets and liabilities of the firm', while the latter 'requires a shift from considering the risk to the company to risk to potential victims of corporate action'.[7]

The UNGPs concretize in detail the due diligence process in Principles 17 to 21, establishing four main phases, which are the identification and assessment of adverse human rights impacts; action upon and integration of the findings; tracking responses and communicating results. Yet, there is no definition of the concept.[8] In order to provide some clarity on the issue, the Office of the High Commissioner for Human Rights (OHCHR) proposed a definition. HRDD 'comprises an ongoing management process that a reasonable and prudent enterprise needs to undertake, in light of its circumstances [. . .] to meet its responsibility to respect human rights'.[9] One important remark is that putting in place a HRDD process does not necessarily imply no responsibility for the company.[10] HRDD can help prevent or mitigate potential human rights violations and, in case there has already been a violation, remediate them.[11] It should be context specific, considering the effort the company put in identifying the impacts it could have on human rights, putting in place systems to deal with them. The crucial element is whether the company was or ought to have been aware of the risks.[12] One further element of HRDD highlighted by the OHCHR is its ongoing character, which contrasts with the corporate due diligence, because this is usually a once-off process performed before a specific transaction.[13]

Both the OECD Guidelines for Multinational Enterprises[14] (OECD Guidelines) and the OECD Due Diligence Guidance for Responsible Business Conduct[15] followed the concept of HRDD in a similar way. Additionally, the OECD has been working on sectorial guidance developing its Guidelines according to the particularities of each sector that I will further address below.[16]

HRDD in supply chains is particularly difficult due to the complexity and dynamism of modern global chains, the increasingly high number of actors involved

---

[6]Nolan (2017), p. 246.

[7]Lundan and Muchlinski (2012), p. 189.

[8]Since this is not the topic of this article, I am not addressing the scholarly debate on this issue. I will only briefly refer to the official position of the UNHCHR. See Bonnitcha and McCorquodale (2017b), and Ruggie and Sherman (2017), pp. 921–928.

[9]UN Human Rights Office of the High Commissioner for Human Rights, 'The Corporate Responsibility to Respect Human Rights: An Interpretive Guide' (OHCHR, 2012). (p. 4).

[10]UNGP 17.

[11]Commentary to UNGP 17.

[12]McCorquodale et al. (2017), p. 200.

[13]McCorquodale and Smit (2017), p. 224.

[14]OECD, Guidelines on Multinational Enterprises, 2011.

[15]The OECD Due Diligence Guidance for Responsible Business Conduct was adopted in May 2018.

[16]See Sect. 4.

and the lack of specific guidance in many sectors. It is important to start by identifying all the suppliers, because the HRDD must cover the entire supply chain, otherwise the root causes of human rights violations will persist. This exercise tends to be difficult, since there is no end-to-end visibility in the supply chains and companies do not know all their suppliers or under which conditions they are working. The existing HRDD practices nowadays are still in their infancy, in the beginning of their 'human rights journey'.[17] Beyond the first tier of the supply chain, it is more difficult to trace back the suppliers and the existing HRDD processes diminish dramatically. The further it is in the chain away from the company, the less leverage it has to influence its suppliers.

As above-mentioned, the majority of the companies that already conduct HRDD have difficulties in fulfilling all of its components. For instance, in 2017 the first 'Corporate Human Right Benchmark' produced concluded that the phase of observing and identifying which human rights risks might exist is achieved by roughly one third of all the observed companies. Worse still, corporate action based on the received information is even more difficult and the results drop off dramatically, with 97% of the companies scoring 0's.[18]

Additionally, the phase of remediation is being marginalized by companies. The communication and explanation of the efforts and results achieved must also be publicly available in a transparent way, including publication of the supplier list, production sites, audit reports and action plans with specific targets.

Furthermore, HRDD should be performed by every corporation, independently of its size. 'Meaningful HRDD is much more a question of the individual set-up of the supply chains than of the size of the company'.[19] Nonetheless, the bigger the corporation, the more responsibility it has, because the probability of having a long and complex supply chain that ends in high-risk areas is bigger as well.

3 Domestic HRDD Legislation: The Trend to Harden Due Diligence Obligations

This chapter focuses on the most developed HRDD legislative initiatives that are currently emerging at a domestic level, namely in France, Germany, the Netherlands and Switzerland.[20] In all the analysed countries, the debate on business and human

---

[17]McCorquodale et al. (2018), p. 67.

[18]Corporate Human Rights Benchmark – Key Findings 2017. https://www.corporatebenchmark. org/sites/default/files/2017-03/CHRB_Findings_web_pages.pdf [16/07/18] See the explanation for the score system on p. 6.

[19]Clean Clothes Campaign – Position Paper on HRDD, March 2016, p. 4.

[20]Therefore, I will not address the UK Modern Slavery Act, although it includes a 'transparency in supply chains' provision that requires annual reporting by certain companies on the steps they took to avoid modern slavery in their supply chains. A report of the Parliament's Joint Committee on Human Rights recommends the creation of legislation on a duty to prevent human rights abuses and

rights, and particularly on HRDD, has been shifting gradually, from a conception where all the initiatives should be voluntary to a defence of mandatory legislation. We are currently observing a European development at different speeds, with clear frontrunners and some countries completely staying behind.

3.1   France

Currently, the French Law on Duty of Care[21] is at the forefront in terms of human rights due diligence. Its legislative process was not without difficulties. The initial proposal intended to create a new liability regime and provided for 'a reversal of the burden of proof from victims to companies'.[22] The law was referred to the highest French court, the Constitutional Council, which considered that most of the text was according to the Constitution, apart from the civil fine for non-compliance with the duty of care, whose vague terms breached the principle of legality.[23]

The law covers the same spectrum of human rights as the UNGPs and it is not limited to a specific sector or risk of human rights violation. It establishes an obligation of vigilance, meaning an obligation for large parent companies[24] to perform HRDD for all activities carried out by the company itself, its subsidiaries, subcontractors and suppliers 'with which the company maintains an established commercial relationship',[25] under penalty of paying a fine. So, it also includes entities not directly under the control of the enterprise. In practice, it affects around 200 companies.[26] Companies are obliged to design a HRDD plan, report on its implementation and disclose it. Article 1 establishes very concrete requirements that the plan must fulfil. It follows the same HRDD structure as in the UNGPs. Interested parties can file a complaint to judicial authorities if the company still fails to design it,[27] 3 months after an unsuccessful formal notice. There can also be compensation when the obligations, such as the publication of an appropriate vigilance plan, have not been met and that lack of action has caused damage.[28]

---

an offence for the failure to prevent those, along the entire supply chain. This would include conducting HRDD. See 6th report of the session 2016/17, 'Human Rights and Business 2017: Promoting responsibility and ensuring accountability', §193.

[21]Loi no. 2017-399 du 27 mars 2017 relative au devoir de vigilance des sociétés mères et des entreprises donneuses d'ordre (JORF n°0074 du 28 mars 2017).

[22]Cossart et al. (2017), p. 317.

[23]Decision 2017-750 DC of 23 March 2017.

[24]Companies must be incorporated or registered in France for 2 consecutive fiscal years that employ either at least 5000 people themselves and through their French subsidiaries or employ at least 10,000 themselves and through subsidiaries located in France and abroad.

[25]Loi no. 2017-399, art. 1: *avec lesquels est entretenue une relation commerciale établie.*

[26]Huyse and Verbrugge (2018), p. 37.

[27]*Ibid*, p. 37.

[28]Loi no. 2017-399, art. 2.

The new law has been criticized, because the burden of proof still lies with the injured party, which means victims will have to prove that the company was faulty and that there is a causal link with the harm they suffered.[29] This signifies an unsurmountable barrier for many victims to access justice. Another criticism relates to the scope of the law, since it only covers 'businesses with whom the company has a stable, regular and ongoing relationship', which disregards areas that can be particularly risky, such as small suppliers that do not have a stable relationship with the company.[30] Another point of concern is that France will put itself in a competitive disadvantage if it is the sole one to establish such restrictive rules for its companies.[31] The argument made is that it would be preferable to wait for an instrument at the European or international level to avoid incoherence and competitive drawbacks between countries. But, as Dominique Potier stated, 'France cannot wait for the EU to take a stand',[32] the laws must change at a domestic level first in order to incentivize the EU to harmonize them. The hope of the French is that it will happen just as it happened with the EU Directive on Non-Financial Reporting[33] that was modelled after the French law on the same matter.

3.2 Germany

There is still no HRDD law in Germany, but the German National Action Plan (NAP) addresses this topic extensively. Companies are expected to perform HRDD and, if by 2020 half of the companies with more than 500 employees have not integrated HRDD into their corporate processes, the 'Federal Government will consider further action, which may culminate in legislative measures'.[34] This falls short of mandatory obligations, but at least puts some pressure on German companies by admitting that possibility in the near future.

There already exists a proposal for a binding HRDD law presented by several German NGOs. The proposal would cover large companies whose corporate seat, headquarters or principal place of business is in Germany and small and medium enterprises (SMEs) only when they are from high-risk sectors or areas,[35] just like its French counterpart. It would include documentation and reporting obligations and

---

[29]ECCJ, 'French Corporate Duty of Vigilance Law – Frequently Asked Questions', 24 March 2017, p. 5.

[30]Triponel and Sherman (2017), p. 3.

[31]Eckert (2016), p. 55.

[32]Assemblée Nationale, Rapport n°3582 (2016), p. 6.

[33]Directive 2014/95/EU of the European Parliament and of the Council of 22 October 2014 amending Directive 2013/34/EU as regards disclosure of non-financial and diversity information by certain large undertakings and groups (OJ L 330, 15.11.2014, p. 1–9).

[34]German NAP on Business and Human Rights (2016–2020), p. 12.

[35]Amnesty International, Brot für die Welt, Germanwatch and Oxfam, 'Legislative Proposal: Corporate Responsibility and Human Rights', 15 June 2017, p. 3.

supervision by regulatory authorities (which are not defined yet but could possibly be trade registry offices or customs offices[36]) that could require companies to consult with affected parties or create grievance mechanisms.[37] Non-fulfilment of due diligence obligations triggers civil law liability. Other consequences can be 'exclusion from foreign trade incentive programs, subsidy allocations or public procurement contracts'.[38]

In relation to the garment sector, Germany developed a multi-stakeholder initiative called 'Partnership for Sustainable Textiles', which englobes 98 companies representing 50% of the entire German textile market.[39] This is however a strictly non-binding initiative. It is a step forward for the German garment sector, but it lacks, amongst others, deadlines for companies to implement the requirements, the obligation to share information to suppliers and a sanctioning mechanism.

3.3   The Netherlands

In February 2017, a Child Labour Due Diligence Bill[40] was adopted by the lower house of the Parliament, but its approval is now dependent upon the Senate.

The law was supposed to enter into force in January 2020. It has a broad scope, covering not only all Dutch companies, but also foreign ones that deliver to the Dutch market twice or more a year. The justification for this scope is that the legislative purpose is to protect consumers. Consequently, they should be able to trust that the companies from which they purchase do not work with child labour.[41] They would have to state to a regulatory authority (not yet defined which) that they performed adequate HRDD in the entire supply chain to prevent the occurrence of child labour and create an action plan to prevent it. Even though the consequence for the failure to submit a statement is a fine, there will only be enforcement if third parties complain.[42] The consequences can even be the imprisonment of the responsible director or fines up to 750,000 or 10% of the company's annual turnover.[43] This law prioritizes the HRDD process itself to the detriment of reporting obligations, since the statement is to be submitted only once, in contrast to the French law, which requires an annual statement.

---

[36]*Ibid*, p. 6.

[37]*Ibid*, p. 4.

[38]*Ibid*, p. 5.

[39]Huyse, 'Belgium', p. 32.

[40]*Wet Zorgplicht Kinderarbeid.*

[41]MVO Platform, 'Frequently Asked Questions about the Dutch Child Labour Due Diligence law', 14 April 2017 https://www.mvoplatform.nl/en/frequently-asked-questions-about-the-new-dutch-child-labour-due-diligence-law/ [27/07/18].

[42]*Ibid.*

[43]*Ibid.*

The Netherlands has developed in 2016 a sectoral partnership agreement for textile and garment as the first of several projected sector covenants. By December 2017, 65 enterprises were already included and 58 shared their lists of suppliers, consequently identifying 2800 suppliers in 49 countries.[44] Although this partnership agreement has a voluntary character, as soon as companies enter it they must comply with the provisions in the agreement. The consequence of failing to comply is expulsion. The obligations are carrying out supply chain due diligence, establishing an action plan, reporting on the progress and participating in collective activities.[45]

In comparison to the German partnership agreement, the Dutch has several unique elements, such as the existence of a dispute and complaints mechanism for victims, the obligation to provide full transparency of the entire supply chain, only accessible by the *Sociaal-Economische Raad*, which then publicly shares an overview of the information. Furthermore, companies can only withdraw from the agreement after 2 years of signing in. These characteristics show that the Dutch partnership agreement is at a more advanced level than the German one. Both initiatives started cooperating in January 2018 to incentivize companies to conduct HRDD and harmonize their practices. They will benefit from shared knowledge and establish common projects. As mentioned above,[46] the main concern is that both countries will be in competitive disadvantage because the EU will not level the playing field any time soon.

3.4 Switzerland

In 2015, a coalition of NGOs started the 'Responsible Business Initiative' (RBI),[47] which was submitted to the federal authorities in October 2016. The initiative intended to amend the Swiss Constitution with a view to include a provision demanding that Swiss companies and the ones under their control would have to respect all internationally recognized human rights both in Swiss territory and in their activities abroad.[48] Additionally, it would establish mandatory HRDD following the UNGPs logic—identify impacts, act upon them, report and account for actions taken. It does not focus on one specific sector.[49] It applies to all companies,

---

[44]Huyse, 'Belgium', p. 30.

[45]*Ibid.*

[46]See Sect. 3.2.

[47]Consult the RBI with an Explanatory Report in www.corporatejustice.ch. [27/07/18].

[48]Peter Burckhardt and Anya George, 'Business and Human Rights – What Swiss companies need to know', *Schellenberg Wittmer newsletter*, November 2017 https://www.lexology.com/library/detail.aspx?g=483d670c-93cb-4480-b518-a604b7aa9489 [17/07/18], p. 3.

[49]I will not address the Federal Act on Private Security Services Provided Abroad, which includes a disclosure requirement, but only for security purposes.

except SMEs. It is only applicable to the latter in case they work in a high-risk sector or area, as the French law.

This proposal was not approved by the Federal National Council. In May 2018 the Legal Affairs Committee of the National Council issued a counter-proposal, which was approved in June 2018. The Council of States will still have to vote on the new proposal.[50]

Although the counter-proposal maintains key elements of the RBI, such as mandatory HRDD and parent company liability, it has been watered down to allow consensus. The civil liability regime has been severely restricted and victims can only file complaints for 'three violations: damage to life, damage to personal integrity, or violation of property rights'.[51] The personal scope of the counter-proposal was also restricted to large companies fulfilling several requirements and high-risk SMEs. Moreover, there is no longer provision to use all internationally recognized human rights and environmental standards, but only international standards in instruments ratified by Switzerland.

3.5   Preliminary Conclusion

There are different degrees of HRDD legislation, going from a merely reporting obligation[52] to an explicit link between HRDD obligations and civil liability.[53] Having mandatory and clear rules on HRDD coupled with an accountability mechanism increases legal certainty and businesses' compliance. It is useful to have regulations with a hybrid character, combining mandatory features with some flexibility for the businesses to decide how they want to achieve the established objectives. The French law, which is the best example of hard law in HRDD currently, leaves some leeway for businesses to decide which is the best implementation process to follow.[54]

There are as well different ways of implementing mandatory HRDD, be it through a sectorial approach like the Dutch bill on child labour or through a cross-sectorial law like the French one. There is a clear shift towards mandatory HRDD at state-level. The Council of Europe's recommendation recognizes it and incentivizes

---

[50]Swiss Coalition for Corporate Justice, 'Another step towards the adoption of a mandatory HRDD in Switzerland', 16 July 2018. http://corporatejustice.org/news/7046-another-step-towards-the-adoption-of-a-mandatory-hrdd-bill-in-switzerland [20/07/18].

[51]Simon Bradley, 'Swiss firms lack 'unified approach' on business and human rights', *Swissinfo*, 14 June 2018.

[52]Such as the Non-Financial Reporting Directive, which was not addressed in detail here, precisely because it only establishes a reporting obligation and does not contain a substantive HRDD requirement.

[53]Such as the French law or the Swiss Initiative.

[54]Eckert, 'The French Attempt', p. 52.

States to continue down this path.[55] The enactment of these different laws increases the pressure on the EU. In 2016, several Member States launched a green card initiative to push the Commission towards mandatory HRDD legislation.[56] The European Coalition for Corporate Justice also demands to see this shift at a European level.[57] Since the French law is the most detailed, ambitious and human rights focused one, a future garment legislative initiative should at least replicate its main achievements at the EU level.

4 International HRDD Legislation: The Conflict Minerals Regulation as a Case Study

This chapter analyses the Conflict Minerals Regulation from a comparative perspective, since it is the only binding international legislation on HRDD. By studying its context, legislative procedure and content, it will be easier to conceive what future legislation on the garment sector will look like and what challenges it might face.

4.1 Context

Many of the world richest countries in minerals have a great problem of violence, conflict and corruption that extends to the extraction, transport and trade of minerals. The commerce of minerals is deeply linked with human rights abuses and has been known to finance armed militias that increase the violent environment in these countries. In consequence, companies that deal with minerals benefit from and fuel these human rights violations. This panorama, unfortunately, tends to be 'rather rule than exception'.[58]

The value of the mineral trading industry world-wide is estimated at €200 billion.[59] The Great Lakes region in Africa is the epicentre of the problems regarding conflict minerals. The Democratic Republic of Congo (DRC) is the best studied case on this matter. Although its civil war ended in 2002, it was estimated that in 2008 there were 'still 45.000 people dying every month and that finances of conflict

---

[55]Recommendation CM/Rec(2016)3 of the Committee of Ministers to Member States on human rights and business.

[56]ECCJ, 'Members of 8 European Parliaments support duty of care legislation for EU corporations', 31 May 2016 http://corporatejustice.org/news/132-members-of-8-european-parliaments-support-duty-of-care-legislation-for-eu-corporations [20/07/18].

[57]Huyse, 'Belgium', p. 38.

[58]Hofmann et al. (2018), p. 115.

[59]EC, FAQ Responsible Sourcing of Minerals Originating Conflict-Affected and High-Risk Areas: Towards an Integrated EU Approach, memo/14/157 of 5 Mar. 2014, p. 7.

minerals and the fight for these resources were a central driver for this' and that armed groups 'receive 90% of the profits'.[60]

Many social problems occur in the extraction phase, where small and artisanal mining happens in a grey legal area, due to the absence of governmental control and exploitation by armed militias.[61] In the transport phase there is no verification of documents, which facilitates the traders' job of erasing the signs of conflict associated with these minerals by mixing them with legally exported ones.

The EU is the world's largest single market[62] and a valuable player in the global trade of minerals. Therefore, it has the bargaining power and capacity to change the reality, by stopping being complicit in abuses and blocking access to conflict minerals at least in European companies and their supply chains.

4.2 Legislative Procedure

The Conflict Minerals Regulation entered into force in June 2017 and will take full effect on 1 January 2021. This way, importers are allowed some time to adapt to the new rules, although the Commission incentivizes Member States to start implementing the Regulation as soon as possible to educate importers and allow competent authorities to gain monitoring experience before 2021.

Prior EU legislation dealt with sourcing of natural resources, such as the Regulation on the international trade in rough diamonds[63] or the Directive which seeks transparency in the extractive and logging industries,[64] but the Conflict Minerals Regulation is rooted on the already existing international standards endorsed by the OECD on responsible mineral supply chains,[65] which are followed by 43 States[66] and consequently represent a widely harmonised standard.

The European Commission (EC) had already expressed some criticism regarding the impact of the OECD Guidance, because its voluntary character did not motivate companies to comply with it.[67] This is one of the reasons to push for binding rules in

---

[60]Prendergast and Lezhnev, cited in Hofmann, 'Conflict minerals', p. 119.

[61]BSR, Conflict minerals and the democratic Republic of Congo (2010) https://www.bsr.org/reports/BSR_Conflict_Minerals_and_the_DRC.pdf [15/06/18].

[62]'Advice Note to Companies, Member States and The European Commission', p. 2.

[63]Council Regulation (EC) No. 2368/2002 of 20 December 2002 implementing the UN certification of the Kimberley process for the international trade in rough diamonds (OJ L 358, 31.12.2002, pp. 28–48).

[64]Directive 2013/34/EU of the European Parliament and of the Council of 26 June 2013 on the annual financial statements, consolidated financial statements and related reports of certain types of undertakings (OJ L 182, 29.6.2013, p. 19–76).

[65]OECD, Due Diligence Guidance for Responsible Supply Chains of Minerals from Conflict-Affected and High-Risk Areas, version 3 (2016) ('OECD Guidance').

[66]*Ibid*, p. 2.

[67]Voland and Daly (2018), p. 48.

this area, according to the Commission. The fact is that several African countries have adopted legislation implementing the OECD Guidance, such as the DRC, Rwanda, Uganda and Burundi, but there are significant problems with the efficacy of these rules.[68]

The Regulation is the European counterpart to the article 1502 of the American Dodd-Frank Act introduced in 2010 that requires companies listed on US stock exchanges that use conflict minerals in their supply chains to disclose annually the origins of those minerals and perform due diligence. The EU tried to learn from Dodd-Frank Act's mistakes by extending the Regulation's scope to all high-risk areas in the world in order to avoid opportunistic moves away from the countries englobed in the Regulation.[69]

Initially, the Commission proposed a voluntary self-certification scheme for importers that raised much criticism and was overturned by the European Parliament (EP) that considered it as insufficient. According to the EP Committee on Development, the Commission's proposal was 'based on "do no harm" approach, [but] risks doing no good either'.[70]

The lack of attention paid to downstream[71] producers who would not be under the scope of the Regulation allows them to prefer non-responsible importers that supply conflict minerals at a lower cost.[72]

In the end of the negotiations, agreement was reached for mandatory obligations for importers, except small volume ones. The EP tried to include mandatory obligations for smelters and refiners[73] (both upstream actors), but the final version of the Regulation merely encourages them to follow the OECD Guidance.

As for downstream actors, the final version of the Regulation was not as ambitious as the Parliament's proposal, which would apply the Regulation to them as well, although on a voluntary basis. The EP clearly wanted to emphasize the importance of having a due diligence mechanism in the entire supply chain.[74]

However, there is some room left for future binding rules, but currently it is only assumed that 'if downstream companies source from upstream companies based in the EU, the minerals they source should already be compliant with the Regulation'.[75] The Commission stated that it might consider additional legislation if it understands that the current rules are insufficient to incentivize responsible behaviour down the

---

[68]Commission Staff Working Document, Impact Assessment, 5 March 2014, SWD(2014) 53 final, p. 14 (Impact Assessment).

[69]Voland and Daly (2018), p. 48.

[70]EP, Opinion of the Committee on Development for the Committee on International Trade on the proposal for a regulation on conflict minerals (COM(2014)0111 – C7-0092/2014 – 2014/0059 (COD)), p. 3.

[71]See definitions for 'upstream' and 'downstream' actors in OECD Guidance, p. 32.

[72]EP, *At a glance, plenary - 13 May 2015*, p. 2.

[73]EP, texts adopted, P8_TA(2015)0204, amend.43.

[74]*Ibid*, amends.71 and 91.

[75]Voland and Daly (2018), p. 61.

supply chain.[76] The reason for this different treatment is that upstream actors are in a unique position to control the origins of the minerals they use, because after them it will be technically impossible to track back their origins further down in the supply chain. Downstream companies often argue they do not have leverage over the smelters to obtain due diligence information, even if they identify them.[77]

4.3   Content

The Regulation's main objective is to 'facilitate and promote the responsible and transparent sourcing of minerals from conflict-affected and high-risk areas'.[78] This will be done through a process of due diligence,[79] which aims at tracking the minerals flow 'from mine to export at country level',[80] through databases and independent audits to all supply chain actors. In contrast with the OECD Guidance which covers all minerals and the entire supply chain, the Regulation focuses on firms located upstream in the supply chain, which raised criticism because it allows for 'strategic relocation'.[81] This means that companies using tin, tantalum and tungesten minerals ('3TG') that are based in the EU and would fall under the scope of the Regulation can move outside and still import into the EU without facing the onerous costs of the due diligence obligations under the Regulation. It also has a more limited material scope, only covering 3TG, their ores, and gold originating from conflict-affected and high-risk areas, independently of whether they are imported as raw materials or metals. However, in comparison with the Dodd-Frank Act which only applies to the DRC and 9 adjoining countries,[82] the geographical scope of the Regulation is much broader, potentially applying to the entire world.[83]

One important point of the Regulation is that it does not oblige companies to stop sourcing from conflict-affected countries if they comply with their due diligence requirements appropriately. Even in areas not considered risky there might be conflict minerals, so what counts is how the minerals are sourced and not necessarily where they are sourced from. In brief terms, importers will need to adopt a supply chain policy following the OECD Guidance and incorporate it into contracts with

---

[76] *Ibid,* p. 54.

[77] 'Impact assessment', p. 25.

[78] 'Advice note', p. 1.

[79] Although the Regulation does not specify that it is HRDD, it will be assumed to be so since most of the risks are related to possible human rights violations.

[80] Hofmann et al. (2018), p. 117.

[81] Bergkamp (2017).

[82] Art.1502(e)(4) Dodd-Frank Act.

[83] The EU Regulation covers 3TG sourced from mines that can be spread all over the world in case the countries where they are located export to the EU.

suppliers,[84] assess possible risks and implement strategies to mitigate those adverse impacts,[85] have their activities audited by independent third parties[86] and publicly disclose the audit reports and their due diligence policies.[87] Additionally, the Commission must establish an up-to-date list of global responsible smelters and refiners to increase transparency for downstream actors.[88]

Although the Regulation is applicable to EU importers of 3TG, it also has implications outside the EU, since these actors must ensure that the imported minerals are sourced by responsible smelters and refiners.

4.4 Preliminary Conclusion

The EU bodies realized it was crucial to have an EU-level intervention, not only to provide more leverage in comparison with possible action by individual Member States, but also because there was the necessity of addressing 'the demand-side of minerals originating from conflict zones'.[89] Instead of waiting for Member States to create their own rules that would treat differently companies in the EU internal market, the EU opted to harmonise and consolidate due diligence processes. These arguments could also be used regarding garment supply chains, since there is currently a very fragmented situation throughout Europe.[90]

One of the main arguments against a mandatory due diligence process in an EU regulation is the so-called 'market distortion' argument. Such a Regulation would create a de facto 'embargo' on the countries that have a risk of having conflict minerals, because companies would search for the least burdensome way of complying with the requirements by avoiding importing from those areas. Consequently, local conflict-free traders will be worse off, since they make the effort to source responsibly, but do not have the same levels of demand as before.

Before and during the negotiations of the Regulation, many scholars and entities insisted on turning the OECD Guidance standards for the downstream part of the supply chain[91] into mandatory legislation, which in the end did not happen. One argument is that companies need either to see a short-term benefit to act or to be

---

[84]Regulation Art.4.

[85]Regulation Art.5.

[86]Regulation Art.6.

[87]Regulation Art.7.

[88]Regulation Art.9.

[89]'Impact Assessment', p. 4.

[90]See Sect. 5.2.

[91]CIDSE, *Securing a strong and effective EU regulation for supply chain due diligence to stop complicity in funding conflicts* (2015) https://www.cidse.org/publications/business-and-human-rights/securing-a-strong-and-effective-eu-regulation-for-supply-chain-due-diligence.html [08/06/2018].

forced by law,[92] especially if they do not face the public directly. It is essential that these rules 'have teeth and they need to be tailored to closely reflect how the relevant supply chains work'.[93] That is why it makes sense to have specific rules for each sector that is particularly prone to incur in human rights abuses.

The task this Regulation dictates is not an easy one. Implementing due diligence mechanisms throughout the entire supply chain is increasingly complex and requires the collaboration of geographically dispersed actors. It is necessary to create a relation of both trust and power between the different tiers of the supply chain to ensure compliance and commitment at every level.[94] A similar task will be needed in the garment sector and that is why a parallel Regulation should be created. Although the 5-step framework for due diligence in the OECD Guidance[95] could easily be transferred to the garment sector, there is a critical difference that must be considered. The 'choke point' for traceability and due diligence in the mineral supply chain happens in the refiners and smelters phase,[96] because after that it is physically impossible to separate and identify the different mineral components and their origins. In the garment supply chains, although there are several stages of product modification, it never gets to a point where they are no longer separately identifiable. In that regard, the garment supply chain traceability is facilitated.

The case of conflict minerals is a paradigmatic example of an area of law that has been gradually 'hardened'. It is still early to analyse the impacts that mandatory human rights due diligence has on this field, but 'it has structural features that give cause for optimism'.[97] Its effects will spread throughout the entire supply chain and beyond the EU. As Cullen recognizes, having mandatory rules on HRDD for this sector is 'only the beginning of the impact of HRDD on supply chain management'.[98] Other fields, such as the garment sector, are next in line.

---

[92]Constantin Blome, 'Policy Brief', *University of Sussex*, May 2016, p. 4.

[93]Schwartz (2016), p. 182.

[94]Hofmann et al. (2018), p. 129.

[95]See Annex I of the OECD Guidance.

[96]OECD, 'OECD Forum on Due Diligence in the garment and footwear sector – session notes', January 2018, p. 16.

[97]Cullen (2016), p. 776.

[98]*Ibid*, p. 778.

5   The Case for International HRDD Legislation in the Garment Sector

This chapter is dedicated to the garment sector. After presenting the sector's characteristics, I will analyse the EU Flagship Initiative on the Garment Sector[99] ('the Initiative'), the procedure and spirit behind it and the current position of EU actors. Finally, I will draw some lessons from the comparison between this Initiative, the Conflict Minerals Regulation and the several above-mentioned domestic initiatives.

5.1   Characteristics

The garment industry globally plays an increasingly important role in the economy employing more than 75 million people and being 2.86€ trillions worth.[100] Therefore, it is worryingly problematic that it is one of the sectors where the risk of human rights abuse is higher. The global garment supply chains are increasingly complex, with numerous tiers and actors involved in them. Consequently, the levels of transparency in these supply chains are very low, which leads to higher risk of human rights violations. It becomes very difficult to trace back a garment to its origins through subsidiaries and subcontractors spread all over the world and to check if their clothes have been ethically produced.

According to the Business and Human Rights Resource Centre, 'over 80% of the allegations of abuse by EU textile companies concerns extra-territorial human rights impacts'.[101] It is thus crucial for European brands to be able to trace their products and the components from which they are made to their origins, since it is usually before entering the EU market that human rights violations occur.

The garment industry usually consists of low-skill production and is well-known for its labour-intensive character that materialises itself in excessively long working days and overtime hours. It can happen due to pressure put by retailers that frequently change, cancel or rush orders to meet the deadlines for the numerous production cycles per year that brands have. This market is increasingly competitive and characterized by low prices and high volumes. Such an environment is prone to the occurrence of forced labour. Other common problematic issues in the garment sector include the lack of a living wage and regular contracts, lack of freedom of

---

[99]European Parliament resolution of 27 April 2017 on the EU flagship initiative on the garment sector (2016/2140(INI)).

[100]EP Committee on Development, 'Report on the EU Flagship Initiative on the garment sector', A8-0080/2017, 28 March 2017, p. 18.

[101]Business & Human Rights Resource Centre, Briefing 'European textile industry and human rights due diligence: key developments, human rights allegations & best practices', April 2018, p. 2.

association, child labour and poor occupational safety and health protection. Violence towards workers is also registered, as well as human trafficking.[102]

There are several structural issues identified in the garment sector irrespectively of their geographical location. One of them is the high percentage of women working in this field, which rounds 75% globally and, in some countries, such as Bangladesh or Cambodia, it reaches 80% and 90%, respectively.[103] Due to this factor, many of the existing violations are gender-related such as sexual harassment, pregnancy discrimination and gender-discrimination regarding wages. Many of these women are low-skilled and work in precarious situations, which increases their vulnerability to abuses in the workplace. According to a study,[104] all the analysed hotspot countries had gender equality as a core gap in the garment sector.

Another element that raises human rights concerns is the persistence of illegal subcontractors in the garment sector. The working conditions in small informal factories or house workshops are worrying, because they are 'neither visible, nor audited by international agencies'.[105] It is, thus, a privileged scenario for human rights abuses. This generally happens without the knowledge of the retailers that give orders to suppliers that then subcontract, even when it is prohibited by their contracts, to other unregistered actors that constitute further tiers down the chain. Consequently, brands do not feel responsible for these people's working conditions. However, these workers are in special need of protection, because they often lack any work contracts and are not aware of their legal rights or where they stand in the supply chain.[106] This outsourcing of work happens in order to meet production demands, when the nominated supplier does not have the capacity to finish the order in time or does not have the ability to perform certain specialized tasks. It tends to be of a short-term duration.

---

[102]Steve Banker, 'The Risk of Human Trafficking in the Supply chain', *Forbes,* 27 July 2015. https://www.forbes.com/sites/stevebanker/2015/07/27/the-risk-of-human-trafficking-in-the-supply-chain/#17a479db17ed [06/08/18].

[103]The World Bank (2017): In Bangladesh, Empowering and Employing Women in the Garments Sector, http://www.worldbank.org/en/news/feature/2017/02/07/in-bangladesh-empowering-and-employing-women-in-the-garments-sector and Human Rights Watch (2015): "Work Faster or Get Out", https://www.hrw.org/report/2015/03/11/work-faster-or-get-out/labor-rights-abuses-cambodias-garment-industry [06/08/18].

[104]AETS, 'Study on the responsible management of the supply chain in the garment sector', December 2016, p. 117.

[105]*Ibid*, p. 16.

[106]Nina Ascoly, 'The Global Garment Industry and the Informal Economy: Critical Issues for Labor Rights Advocates', IRENE/CCC Discussion Paper, September 2004, p. 6.

5.2   The EU Flagship Initiative on the Garment Sector: Its Origins and Developments

Since the collapse of the Rana Plaza, many public and private initiatives to sustainably improve the garment supply chains have been launched all over the world. In fact, the garment sector is the one with more ongoing sustainability initiatives.[107] There is a trend towards establishing codes of conduct, self-assessments, multi-stakeholders initiatives or partnerships between organisations, such as H&M and the ILO or Inditex and IndustriALL. Although the intention of these initiatives is laudable, the fact that they are not harmonised and sometimes overlap is problematic. This proliferation of standards demonstrates growing awareness in the sector, but it mainly leads to a confusing and unpredictable environment for actors that want to comply. These initiatives do not necessarily cover the same spectrum of issues, since many of them have a targeted and sectorial nature and are therefore likely to leave large governance gaps.

Businesses are concerned about this panorama. H&M in 2016 has sent a policy statement to the Commission complaining about the 'multiple and parallel initiatives that are counterproductive and sometimes duplicative' and that slow down progress.[108] That is why there is an urgent necessity to have an overarching instrument coordinating the efforts and harmonising the standards and best practices in this sector. A 'demand-side' European common framework that obliges companies to comply if they want their products in the EU market would be more effective.[109] Furthermore, it would encourage a race to the top and reward the most diligent companies with the 'first-mover advantage'.[110]

The EU is the second largest economy in the world and a key player in the garment industry and trade, since it imports almost half of the world's total clothing production[111] and is the second largest exporter of textile and apparel products after China.[112] It has the power to act and introduce real changes in the garment supply chains.

The informal consultations for an EU garment initiative started back in 2014, when the Commission promised to act upon it.[113] In 2015, it released a trade strategy called 'Trade for All' that intended to promote human rights and ethical trade and committed itself to promote responsible supply chains. In 2017, it published a 'Staff

---

[107]EP Committee on Development, 'Report', p. 7.

[108]Halldin, 'H&M's comments on EU-Garment Initiative and National Initiatives', June 2016.

[109]Business and Human Rights Resource Centre, 'Briefing', p. 11.

[110]*Ibid*, p. 7.

[111]EP Committee on International Trade, 'Opinion of the Committee on International Trade for the Committee on Development on the EU Flagship initiative on the garment sector', 28 February 2017.

[112]The Initiative, p. 5.

[113]EP, Briefing 'Improving global value chains key for EU trade', June 2016, p. 5.

Working Document on Sustainable Garment Value Chains' (CSWD).[114] With this document, the Commission intended to demonstrate its commitment towards sustainability in garment supply chains and how it has been concretized in its participation in numerous cooperation projects. The entire document is focused on EU development cooperation activities that the Commission is aiding financially. It seems that the Commission is just excusing itself for the lack of regulation in this area, as if throwing money into the problem would solve it. These cooperation measures, although valuable, have not been effective enough in addressing human rights and labour-related issues.[115]

The EP has been the most active actor at the EU level. In April 2017, the EP approved a resolution demanding, *inter alia,* mandatory HRDD legislation for garment supply chains at the EU level based on the OECD Due Diligence Guidance for Responsible Supply Chains in the Garment Sector and Footwear Sector[116] and bearing in mind the ILO standards.[117] The resolution was adopted by 505 votes to 49,[118] which sends a clear message to the Commission. The EP calls on the Commission 'to go beyond it' the CSWD.[119]

The Council of the European Union has also commented on this topic. It welcomes the CSWD as an 'important first step that should lead to further ambitious efforts in the garment sector that extend beyond development cooperation'.[120] Furthermore, the Council 'takes good note of the EP Resolution'.[121] All in all, it seems that the Council is discretely backing up the Parliament's effort to have comprehensive binding regulations for the garment sector.

There is agreement between the Commission and the Parliament that the main priorities addressed by the EU should focus on women's economic empowerment; decent work and living wages; and transparency and traceability in the value chain.[122] Regarding the first category, the Commission refers the implementation of the EU gender action plan 2016–2020[123] as a priority to increase female entrepreneurship. To make progress in the other categories, the involvement of many

---

[114]SWD(2017) 147 final.

[115]The Initiative, §5.

[116]OECD, 'OECD due diligence guidance for responsible supply chains in the garment sector and footwear sector', 2017. (OECD Garment Guidance).

[117]See ILO Resolution of 10 June 2016 on decent work in supply chains and the ILO Tripartite Declaration of Principles concerning Multinational Enterprises and Social Policy (2017, 5ed.).

[118]Cécile Barbière, 'MEPs demand tough rules for textiles', *Euractiv,* 28 April 2017 https://www.euractiv.com/section/global-europe/news/meps-demand-tough-rules-for-textiles-importers/ [25/07/18].

[119]EP Committee on Development, 'Report', §5.

[120]Council of the European Union, 'Sustainable Garment Value Chains – Council conclusions', 9381/17, 19 May 2017, §2.

[121]*Ibid,* §12.

[122]See CSWD and the explanatory text of the report on the Initiative by the Committee on Development.

[123]12249/15 - SWD(2015) 182 final.

actors is needed, such as public authorities, trade unions, businesses and the international community.[124]

5.3 Preliminary Conclusion: Recommendations and Lessons Learned

For a future legislation on garment supply chains, several points should mandatorily be addressed. The proposal should have human rights protection as its main focus and not only a general sustainability goal. It should also closely follow the sector-specific recommendations provided in the OECD Garment Guidance and turn them into binding rules, as happened in the conflict minerals sector. This was wise because these provisions are already tested and implemented by many companies that would then be subjected to the Regulation. The proposal should also be aligned with the above-mentioned ILO core standards.

Regarding the choice of instrument, the panorama in Europe, as argued above, lacks coordination and needs urgent European-wide coordination. Consequently, like in the conflict minerals sector, a regulation would be the most appropriate instrument, precisely because it 'ensures the highest level of harmonisation across Member States and guarantees sufficient authority over participating operators'.[125]

There must be an obligation to perform HRDD according to the OECD Garment Guidance and to justify how it is conducted. Each enterprise should have a plan where there would be detailed information on how to prevent and mitigate harm in its own operations and in its supply chain. All above-mentioned domestic initiatives require the same. According to the OECD Garment Guidance, clear timelines for each action should be provided.[126] The criteria for the action plans should be clearly detailed in the proposal. These binding obligations should preferentially be set out for both upstream and downstream segments of the supply chain, since responsibility for unethical practices lies with every actor through the supply chain equally. Following the recent example of the Conflict Minerals Regulation, the proposal should at least bind European importers to perform appropriate HRDD.

To identify risks and to monitor their progress regarding HRDD, more than auditing is needed, since sometimes these audits only reveal a snapshot in time and not the real conditions behind it.[127] Nonetheless, these site-level assessments are a crucial element to ensure conduction of HRDD. There is currently an 'auditing fatigue', since it is the most commonly used mechanism by brands to monitor their suppliers, although it risks becoming just a bureaucratic exercise. Auditors must have adequate technical competences to evaluate the situations and must be

---

[124]CSWD, p. 20.

[125]EC, 'Proposal for a Regulation', p. 6.

[126]OECD Garment Guidance, p. 72.

[127]AETS, 'Study', p. 36.

independent third parties. Suppliers must be especially controlled when there are increased risks, changes or information gaps. Other monitoring systems such as surveys and data analysis techniques that measure key performance indicators are further possibilities.[128]

An incentives' system should be created to award companies that have effective HRDD practices. Measures such as procurement advantages, support through export credits or beneficial tax and customs regulations have been proposed.[129] Another possibility that could be included is the establishment of sustainable production criteria. If companies could prove their goods fulfilled these criteria, these goods could be considered certified as being produced sustainably. Consequently, tariff preferences could be applied for these enterprises.[130] For instance, in Article 9 of the Regulation, the Commission committed to establish an up-to-date public list of global responsible suppliers and refiners, which benefited them by limiting their scrutiny by Member States. This is also an incentivising measure for companies that could be applied for clothing enterprises. Labelling techniques can also be developed for companies with 'fair clothing'.

Traceability and transparency in the supply chains are indeed two of the main concerns in the garment sector that should be carefully regulated. The same standards must be applied through the entire supply chains so that the human rights impact can be adequately measured and compared in relation to other supply chains. These rules on transparency should be binding to oblige companies that want to enter the EU market to disclose the necessary details about their entire supply chains. These could be the names and addresses of all their unit productions[131] or at least the names of specific high-risk sub-suppliers and their countries of origin.[132] The EP Committee on Employment and Social Affairs suggested that a reporting system that would link every actor, from producers to retailers, participating in the supply chain would be appropriate.[133] A public online database with all relevant information on each actor of the supply chain could be set up by the Commission.[134]

There is a current trend towards voluntary disclosure set by many garment industry giants,[135] even without a legal obligation to do so. This proves that the main excuse for companies not to become more transparent, which is that it harms their competitive position in relation to other companies that do not disclose

---

[128]The Initiative, §17.

[129]Business and Human Rights Resource Centre, 'Briefing', p. 16.

[130]EP Committee on International Trade, 'Opinion', §8.

[131]Open letter to the EC, 'High time for the European Commission to impose transparency in the garment supply chain', 24 April 2017.

[132]OECD, 'OECD Forum', p. 9.

[133]EP Committee on Employment and Social Affairs, 'Opinion of the Committee on Employment and Social Affairs for the Committee on Development on the EU Flagship initiative on the garment sector', 10 February 2017, §22.

[134]The Initiative, §14.

[135]Clean Clothes Campaign, Human Rights Watch, Global Union et al., 'Follow the thread – the need for a supply chain transparency in the garment and footwear industry', 2017, p. 13.

anything, does not stand, at least for big brands. In fact, it improves their reputation by guaranteeing that they are not afraid of being held accountable for abuses that might occur in their supply chains. Additionally, it creates a healthy competition between companies to implement the best HRDD strategy possible, since the market will prefer products from companies with good HRDD practices.[136] The public is currently more concerned with these issues and brands want to protect their reputation as much as possible. By disclosing such sensitive information, awareness is raised, and consumers can now make informed decisions and change their purchasing practices accordingly. Although transparency is an important step towards accountability, by itself it does not improve working conditions in the supply chains. It should be established as supplementary to other HRDD requirements. Additionally, companies should also be obliged to regularly report on their HRDD practices and policies in a statement, including 'due diligence management systems, most significant risks of harm in the organization's own operations and its supply chain, and the plan to mitigate and prevent such harm'.[137] Such a complete disclosure obligation was also established by the Conflict Minerals Regulation in article 7, where each importer must send yearly to the Member State competent authority a list of established documents. The French law also obliges companies to report on their HRDD plans' implementation regularly.

Since gender inequality in the garment sector is such a common characteristic, rules to eliminate it should be at the core of the proposal. Particular attention should be paid to women's social and labour rights, wage equality, maternity protection and women's participation in collective bargaining.[138] Some suggestions to empower women could be to have focussed market access or to use alternative channels for women entrepreneurs, such as digital platforms only for them.[139] Just like women, children are also especially vulnerable to exploitation and child labour is another major concern in the garment sector. The proposal should require countries to ratify and implement the ILO conventions, namely the ILO convention 182 on the worst forms of child labour. However, this is not enough. Children's rights should be a central focus of the proposal. The provisions on this topic could be modelled after the Dutch bill.

SMEs compose more than 90% of the EU garment market[140] and they can be found at all stages of the supply chain. Since they might lack the leverage or resources that multinational enterprises have to improve transparency or carry out due diligence, special attention should be paid to avoid disproportionately burdening them. Nonetheless, they are still obliged to conduct HRDD. There are strengths

---

[136] Angelica Dziedzic, Celine Lelievre and Jonathan Povilonis, 'Towards EU legislation on human rights due diligence – case study of the garment and textile sector', *HEC-NYU EU Clinic*, 2017, p. 28.

[137] OECD Garment Guidance, p. 90.

[138] EP Committee on International Trade, 'Opinion', §20.

[139] AETS, 'Study', p. 118.

[140] OECD, 'OECD Forum', p. 6.

associated to SMEs—due to their usually less formal operating structure, they can more easily implement procedural chances and embed due diligence into their decision-making processes.[141] The Committee on International Trade suggests the creation by the EC of a specific helpdesk for them, as well as tailored capacity-building programmes.[142]

The Conflict Minerals Regulation exempted importers that did not surpass a certain threshold.[143] The same logic could possibly be applied for the garment proposal, although it would be preferable to include every enterprise and modify adequately the obligations for SMEs. Otherwise many risky supply chains would be left unregulated. Another possibility could be exempting SMEs, except if they are considered to be of high risk, following the French, Swiss and German examples. Skills and management training should be promoted by the Initiative for all companies, regardless of their size, to raise awareness of their labour rights and to help sharing best practices.

Additionally, one of the main problems of voluntary initiatives is the lack of an appropriate access to remedy for victims and their families and to hold the perpetrators accountable. Currently, all the existing mandatory HRDD laws focus more on the prevention than on remediation. The EC should pay special attention to this issue which is problematic across all business and human rights sectors. Operational-level grievance mechanisms must be established according to ILO conventions and following the recommendations of the OECD Garment Guidance.[144] They must be effective and transparent to facilitate access by victims.

Without penalties, EU instruments have more difficulties in being effectively implemented. Therefore, there should be a minimum requirement clause that would then be developed by each Member State. That is the easiest way to achieve consensus between the signatory parties. Civil or criminal liability linked to failure to conduct appropriate HRDD and consequent human rights violations must be established at state level following the example of the French law and the German and Swiss initiatives.

6 Conclusion

There is still a long way to go in the garment sector for many companies to adequately perform HRDD and have transparent supply chains. But as the Clean Clothes Campaign bluntly states, 'a system of corporate accountability that requires people to scramble on the ground for brand labels is the antithesis of

---

[141]*Ibid*, p. 6.

[142]EP Committee on International Trade, 'Opinion', §4.

[143]See the Regulation, art.1(3).

[144]OECD Garment Guidance, chapter 6.

transparency'.[145] And this is what companies, countries and the civil society are gradually understanding.

'Conflict minerals are providing the fertile ground to develop international standards that may become hard law in the future'.[146] It is still an initial step, but it establishes useful precedent for other sectors. The study of domestic examples demonstrates the will of several States to effectively implement change by hardening the UNGPs' standards.

I conclude that it is high time for the European Commission to 'stop dragging its feet' and act according to the Parliament's proposal, it can even be considered a moral duty to act.[147] For the domestic initiatives to be truly effective, the EU must act, and act rapidly. The EU has the power to level the playing field for its garment companies and their supply chains, reaching way beyond the European borders.

References

Book Chapters

Lundan, S., & Muchlinski, P. (2012). Human rights due diligence in global value chains. In R. Van Tulder, A. Verbeke, & L. Voinea (Eds.), *New policy challenges for European multinationals* (pp. 181–201). Bingley: Emerald Group Publishing Limited.

McCorquodale, R., & Smit, L. (2017). Human rights, responsibilities and due diligence – Key issues for a treaty. In S. Deva & D. Bilchitz (Eds.), *Building a treaty on business and human rights* (pp. 216–237). Cambridge: Cambridge University Press.

Nolan, J. (2017). Human rights and global corporate supply chains. In S. Deva & D. Bilchitz (Eds.), *Building a treaty on business and human rights* (pp. 238–265). Cambridge: Cambridge University Press.

Journal Articles

Bonnitcha, J., & McCorquodale, R. (2017a). The concept of 'due diligence' in the UN guiding principles on business and human rights. *European Journal of International Law, 28*(3), 899–919.

Bonnitcha, J., & McCorquodale, R. (2017b). The concept of 'due diligence' in the UN guiding principles on business and human rights: A Rejoinder to John Gerard Ruggie and John F. Sherman, III. *European Journal of International Law, 28*(3), 929–933.

Cossart, S., Chaplier, J., & Beau de Lomenie, T. (2017). The French law on duty of care: A historic step towards making globalization work for all. *Business and Human Rights Journal, 2*, 317–323.

---

[145]Clean Clothes Campaign, 'Follow', p. 1. regarding the Rana Plaza disaster.

[146]Martin-Ortega (2013), p. 45.

[147]Open letter to the EC, 'High time', cited above.

Cullen, H. (2016). The irresistible rise of human rights due diligence: Conflict minerals and beyond. *The George Washington International Law Review, 48*, 743–780.

Harrison, J. (2013). Establishing a meaningful human rights due diligence process for corporations: Learning from experience of human rights impact assessment. *Impact Assessment and Project Appraisal, 31*(2), 107–111.

Hofmann, H., Schleper, M., & Blome, C. (2018). Conflict minerals and supply chain due diligence: An exploratory study of multi-tier supply chains. *Journal of Business Ethics, 147*, 115–141.

Martin-Ortega, O. (2013). Human rights due diligence for corporations: From voluntary standards to hard law at last? *Netherlands Quarterly of Human Rights, 31*(4), 44–74.

McCorquodale, R., Smit, L., Neely, S., & Brooks, R. (2017). Human rights due diligence in law and practice: Good practices and challenges for business enterprises. *Business and Human Rights Journal, 2*, 195–224.

Ruggie, J., & Sherman, J. (2017). The concept of 'due diligence' in the UN guiding principles on business and human rights: A reply to Jonathan Bonnitcha and Robert McCorquodale. *European Journal of International Law, 28*(3), 921–928.

Schwartz, J. (2016). The conflict minerals experiment. *Harvard Business Law Review, 6*, 129–183.

Voland, T., & Daly, S. (2018). The EU regulation on conflict minerals: The way out of a vicious cycle? *Journal of World Trade, 52*, 37–63.

Policy Documents

AETS. (2016, December). Study on the responsible management of the supply chain in the garment sector.

Amnesty International. (2017, June 15). Brot für die Welt, Germanwatch and Oxfam. Legislative Proposal: Corporate Responsibility and Human Rights.

Business & Human Rights Resource Centre. (2018, April). Briefing 'European textile industry and human rights due diligence: key developments, human rights allegations & best practices'.

Clean Clothes Campaign. (2016, March). Position on Human Rights Due Diligence.

Clean Clothes Campaign, Human Rights Watch, Global Union et al. (2017). Follow the thread – the need for a supply chain transparency in the garment and footwear industry. https://cleanclothes.org/resources/publications/follow-the-thread-the-need-for-supply-chain-transparency-in-the-garment-and-footwear-industry/view

Commission Staff Working Document, Impact Assessment, 5 March 2014, SWD(2014) 53 final.

Committee on Development. (2017, March 28). Report on the EU flagship initiative on the garment sector. A8-0080/2017.

Committee on Employment and Social Affairs. (2017, February 10). Opinion of the Committee on Employment and Social Affairs for the Committee on Development on the EU Flagship initiative on the garment sector.

Committee on International Trade. (2017, February 28). Opinion of the Committee on International Trade for the Committee on Development on the EU Flagship initiative on the garment sector.

Constantin Blome. (2016, May). *Policy Brief*. University of Sussex.

Council of the European Union. (2017, May 19). Sustainable Garment Value Chains – Council conclusions. 9381/17.

Directorate-General for International Cooperation and Development of the European Commission. (2017, March). The responsible management of global value chains in the garment sector.

Dziedzic, A., Lelievre, C., & Povilonis, J. (2017). *Towards EU legislation on human rights due diligence – case study of the garment and textile sector*. HEC-NYU EU Clinic.

European Commission. FAQ Responsible Sourcing of Minerals Originating Conflict-Affected and High-Risk Areas: Towards an Integrated EU Approach, memo/14/157 of 5 March 2014.

European Commission. (2017a, September 7). Follow up to the European Parliament resolution of 27 April 2017 on the EU Flagship initiative on the garment sector.

European Commission. (2017b, April 24). Commission Staff Working Document – Sustainable garment value chains through EU development action. SWD(2017) 147 final.

European Parliament. (2014, August). Briefing 'Workers' conditions in the textile and clothing sector: just an Asian affair? Issues at stake after the Rana Plaza tragedy'.

European Parliament, Opinion of the Committee on Development for the Committee on International Trade on the proposal for a regulation on conflict minerals (COM(2014)0111 – C7-0092/2014 – 2014/0059(COD).

European Parliament. (2015, May 13). At a glance, Plenary.

European Parliament. (2016, June). Briefing 'Improving global value chains key for EU trade.

European Parliament. (2017, April). EU flagship initiative on the garment sector – at a glance.

Huyse, H., & Verbrugge, B. (2018). *Belgium and the sustainable supply chain agenda: Leader or laggard?* KU Leuven.

ILO. (2016, June 10). Resolution concerning decent work in global supply chains.

ILO. (2017). Tripartite declaration of principles concerning multinational enterprises and social policy (5th ed.).

OECD. (2016). Due Diligence Guidance for Responsible Supply Chains of Minerals from Conflict-Affected and High-Risk Areas, version 3.

OECD. (2017). OECD Due Diligence Guidance for Responsible Supply Chains in the Garment and Footwear Sector.

OECD. (2018, January). OECD Forum on Due Diligence in the garment and footwear sector – session notes.

Open Letter to the European Commission. (2017, April 24). High time for the European Commission to impose transparency in the garment supply chain.

Swiss Coalition for Corporate Justice. (2018, July 16). Another step towards the adoption of a mandatory HRDD in Switzerland. Retrieved July 20, 2018, from http://corporatejustice.org/news/7046-another-step-towards-the-adoption-of-a-mandatory-hrdd-bill-in-switzerland

Swiss Coalition for Corporate Justice, 'The Initiative Text with Explanations – Factsheet V'. Retrieved July 17, 2018, from https://corporatejustice.ch/wp-content/uploads//2018/06/KVI_Factsheet_5_E.pdf

Online Sources

Barbière, C. (2017, April 28). MEPs demand tough rules for textiles. *Euractiv*. Retrieved July 25, 2018, from https://www.euractiv.com/section/global-europe/news/meps-demand-tough-rules-for-textiles-importers/

Bergkamp, P. (2017). *The EU conflict minerals regulation: The uncertain effects of supply chain due diligence*. Corporate Financial Lab. Retrieved June 10, 2018, from https://corporatefinancelab.org/2017/07/10/the-eu-conflict-minerals-regulation-the-uncertain-effects-of-supply-chain-due-diligence/

BSR, Conflict Minerals and the Democratic Republic of Congo. (2010). Retrieved June 15, 2018, from https://www.bsr.org/reports/BSR_Conflict_Minerals_and_the_DRC.pdf

Burckhardt, P., & George, A (2017, November). Business and Human Rights – What Swiss companies need to know. *Schellenberg Wittmer Newsletter*. Retrieved July 20, 2018, from https://www.lexology.com/library/detail.aspx?g=483d670c-93cb-4480-b518-a604b7aa9489

Business and Human Rights Resource Centre. *Switzerland: Debate intensifies around initiative for responsible business conduct launched by NGO coalition*. Retrieved July 17, 2018, from https://www.business-humanrights.org/en/switzerland-ngo-coalition-launches-responsible-business-initiative

CIDSE. (2015). *Securing a strong and effective EU regulation for supply chain due diligence to stop complicity in funding conflicts.* Retrieved June 8, 2018, from https://www.cidse.org/publications/business-and-human-rights/securing-a-strong-and-effective-eu-regulation-for-supply-chain-due-diligence.html

ECCJ. (2016, May 31). *Members of 8 European Parliaments support duty of care legislation for EU corporations.* Retrieved July 20, 2018, from http://corporatejustice.org/news/132-members-of-8-european-parliaments-support-duty-of-care-legislation-for-eu-corporations

McCorquodale, R., Holly, G., & Smit, L. (2018, June 6). Making sense of managing human rights issues in supply chains. *British Institute of International and Comparative Law.* https://www.biicl.org/documents/1939_making_sense_of_managing_human_rights_issues_in_supply_chains_-_2018_report_and_analysis_-_full_text.pdf?showdocument=1

MVO Platform. (2017, April 14). *Frequently Asked Questions about the Dutch Child Labour Due Diligence law.* Retrieved July 27, 2018, from https://www.mvoplatform.nl/en/frequently-asked-questions-about-the-new-dutch-child-labour-due-diligence-law/

Others

Ascoly, N. (2004, September). The Global Garment Industry and the Informal Economy: Critical Issues for Labor Rights Advocates. *IRENE/CCC Discussion Paper.*

Bradley, S. (2018, June 14). Swiss firms lack 'unified approach' on business and human rights. *Swissinfo.*

Corporate Human Rights Benchmark, Key Findings 2017 Retrieved July 16, 2018, from https://www.corporatebenchmark.org/sites/default/files/2017-03/CHRB_Findings_web_pages.pdf

ECCJ. (2017, March 24). French Corporate Duty of Vigilance Law – Frequently Asked Questions.

Eckert, V. (2016). *The French attempt to legalize human rights due diligence: Is France leading the European Union in Business and Human Rights?* (Master Thesis, Lund University).

Triponel, A. & Sherman, J. (2017, May). Legislating human rights due diligence: Opportunities and potential pitfalls to the French duty of vigilance law. *Corporate and M&A Law Committee Newsletter.*

International Courts and Tribunals as Determiners of the Law on State Responsibility

Is an UN Convention on State Responsibility Still Necessary?

Cezary Mik

Contents

1   Introduction

The roots of the international law (IL) of State Responsibility (SR) are without doubt customary. The customary legal status of some fundamental principles concerning the international responsibility of States has been confirmed by international courts and tribunals since being established. The PCIJ acquis occupies a special place in

C. Mik (✉)
International and European Law, Cardinal Stefan Wyszynski University, Faculty of Law and Administration, Warszawa, Poland
e-mail: c.mik@uksw.edu.pl

© Springer Nature Switzerland AG 2019
P. Pinto de Albuquerque, K. Wojtyczek (eds.), *Judicial Power in a Globalized World*, https://doi.org/10.1007/978-3-030-20744-1_17

this field.[1] However, the scope of the customary rules on SR has never been unequivocally determined. Some of the rules were developed in the legal practice after judicial decisions were made. Nevertheless, relatively many remain controversial as to their status and content.

Several official and private attempts to elaborate and adopt a convention on SR before World War II were unsuccessful. Finally, in 1954 the UN International Law Commission (ILC) was given the task to "undertake the codification the principles of international law governing State responsibility".[2] After several significant reversals, its work was completed by the adoption of the Articles on Responsibility of States for Internationally Wrongful Acts (ARSIWA; Articles) in 2001. However, until now the Articles have not been transformed into a convention. What is more, thanks to international courts and tribunals and despite the unclear legal status at least of some of the ARSIWA provisions, the Articles came to have to a live of their own. Thus, two questions need to be answered: (i) how judicial decisions may determine the legal position of the rules contained in the ARSIWA; and (ii) is a convention which is based on SR necessary?

To this aim we should: (i) undertake a short legal analysis of the ARSIWA; (ii) determine the function that judicial decisions play in relation to SR, especially in confirming the ARSIWA provisions as having legal status; (iii) consider the necessity of adopting of a UN convention on SR.

2 ARSIWA as a Soft Regulation of the State Responsibility

The ARSIWA is a set of 59 articles in four parts.[3] Part One concerns the internationally wrongful act (Article 1–27). It consists of five chapters pertaining to general principles, attribution of conduct to a State, breach of an international obligation, responsibility of a State in connection with the act of another State, and the circumstances precluding wrongfulness. Part Two is devoted to the content of SR (Article 28–41). It is composed of three chapters on general principles, reparation for injury, and serious breaches of obligations under *juris cogentis* norms. Part Three is about the implementation of SR (Article 42–54) and includes two chapters on the invocation of responsibility by an injured State and countermeasures. The last part comprises general provisions (Article 55–59). The ARSIWA are not a ready convention. It contains neither a preamble nor final clauses, there are no provisions on the terms used in it, or a dispute settlement.

---

[1]Tams (2015), pp. 292–296.

[2]UN GA resolution 799 (VIII), 7 December 1953, 24 abstentions.

[3]Commentaries to the ARSIWA: Yearbook of the ILC 2001, vol. II, Part II, United Nations 2008, pp. 31 and seq.; http://legal.un.org/docs/?path=../ilc/texts/instruments/english/commentaries/9_6_2001.pdf&lang=EF. Accessed: 6 March 2019.

The ILC recommended draft articles on SR to the UN General Assembly (GA). According to the ILC Statute (Articles 1, 15, 20),[4] it could do only that with a view to the conclusion of a convention or to convoke a conference to conclude a convention (Article 23(1) c) or d)).[5] Nevertheless, during the work of the ILC, significant discrepancies appeared as to the final result of the work (code—G. Fitzmaurice; convention—H. Waldock) and as to the course of action recommended to the GA. A compromise was finally reached and the ILC recommended that the GA take note of the draft and "decided further to recommend that the GA consider, at a later stage, and in light of the importance of the topic, the possibility of convening an international conference of plenipotentiaries to examine the draft articles on responsibility of States for internationally wrongful acts with a view to adopting a convention on the topic". It added that "the question of the settlement of disputes could be dealt with by the above-mentioned international conference, if it considered that a legal mechanism on the settlement of disputes should be provided in connection with the draft articles".[6] Thus, the ILC, first, proposed the convocation of the conference with a view to adopt a convention "at the later stage", not at once. This may suggest that not all matters were unresolved and uncontroversial. Also, it was aware that not all issues were regulated in the draft.[7]

The reaction of the GA was rather cautious.[8] In its resolution of 12 December 2001 it took note of the Articles and "commends them to the attention of Governments without prejudice to the question of their future adoption or other appropriate action".[9] There was no mention about future codification conference. However, since 2001 and every three years, the UN GA adopts a resolution on SR (without vote).[10] On its request, since 2007, the Secretary General publishes reports containing State comments on further action regarding the Articles[11] and the

---

[4] A/RES/174(II).

[5] The ILC may use other options. It adopts draft principles (allocation of loss in the case of transboundary harm, 2006), guiding principles (unilateral declarations, 2006), guide to practice (reservations, 2011), conclusions (fragmentation, 2006, identification of customary law, 2018). On the shift from legislative to non-legislative codifications: Bordin (2014), pp. 538–546.

[6] ILC Yearbook 2001, vol. I, pp. 304–305.

[7] To unresolved issues belonged: (1) the definition of damage and injury; (2) Part Two, Chapter Three (Consequences of serious breaches of certain obligations); (3) separate Chapter on countermeasures (necessity, sufficiency), three controversial Articles 51, 53, 54; *LaGrand*: necessity of review of principle of cessation and related Articles; (4) dispute settlement (Part Three, first reading), future form of the Articles (is a convention the only option). J. Crawford, Fourth report on State responsibility, A/CN.4/517 and Add.1.

[8] On debate in the ILC and GA: Caron (2002), pp. 861–866.

[9] A/RES/56/83, without vote.

[10] A/RES/59/35 (2 December 2004), A/RES/62/61 (6 December 2007), A/RES/65/19 (6 December 2010), A/RES/68/104 (16 December 2013), A/RES/71/133 (13 December 2016).

[11] Responsibility of States for internationally wrongful acts. Comments and information received from Governments. Report of the Secretary-General: A/62/63 (9 March 2007) and A/62/63/Add. 1 (12 June 2007), A/65/96 (14 May 2010) and A/65/96/Add.1 (30 September 2010), A/68/69 (27 March 2013) and A/68/69/Add.1 (28.6.2013).

compilation of international courts and tribunals referring to the ARSIWA.[12] In addition, in its last resolution the UN GA requested the Secretary General to prepare a technical report listing the judicial references to the ARSIWA as well as references to the Articles made in submissions presented by States before international courts and tribunals.[13] The Articles as a general law were basically meant for regulating responsibility in traditional inter-State relations (Article 33).[14] It is interesting that specialized tribunals resolving disputes between States and individuals (mostly ICSID tribunals[15]) invoke them more often than traditional arbitration or the ICJ.

Formally, the ILC draft articles have preparatory value. However, the ARSIWA case (and some newer drafts) are different. International courts and tribunals have started to refer in their judicial decisions to its provisions as an expression of codification of customary law (but not only). As a result, they become a part of international legal practice.[16] In 2013 the UN GA acknowledged that a growing number of judicial decisions refer to the ARSIWA. Since 2004 it has also recognized the importance and usefulness of the Articles and commends them to the attention of Governments, "without prejudice to the question of their future adoption or other appropriate action". The ARSIWA have acquired a kind of normative autonomy.

# 3	Determination of Rules on SR by International Courts and Tribunals: The Role of ARSIWA

## 3.1	Determination of Rules of Law as a Function of International Courts and Tribunals

According to Article 38 of the ICJ Statute,

1. The Court, whose function is to decide in accordance with international law [...], shall apply:
    d. subject to the provisions of Article 59, judicial decisions [...] as subsidiary means for the determination of rules of law.

---

[12]Responsibility of States for internationally wrongful acts. Compilation of decisions of international courts, tribunals and other bodies. Report of the Secretary-General: A/62/62 (1 February 2007; it contains decisions pertaining draft articles from before they had been finally adopted), A/65/76 (30 April 2010), A/68/72 (30 April 2013), A/71/80 (21 April 2016) and A/71/80/Add.1 (20 June 2017). Not all decisions compiled in reports expressly refer to the ARSIWA.

[13]Report of 20 June 2017, A/71/80/Add.1.

[14]Crawford (2002b), pp. 886–888.

[15]Critical analysis: Kurtz (2010), pp. 200 and seq.

[16]Tams (2018), p. 77: "it is important to note the very unusual features of the process of legal development of the law of State responsibility: its length (lasting, even on a conservative estimate that only begins with Ago, from 1963 to 2011); its openness (with changes of direction and major doctrinal debate) and its almost discursive character (with constant feedback loops be-tween the ILC, governments and other actors of international law)."

Although Article 38 determines the applicable law before the ICJ, it is commonly perceived as a rule listing the main sources of IL.[17] However, the function of judicial decisions (not only those of the ICJ) is different. They are subsidiary means for the determination of the (international) rules of law.[18]

Three questions require some comments. First, judicial decisions are mentioned without any further qualification so decisions of international and national courts and tribunals can be taken into account. Strictly speaking, the judiciality of decisions should refer to decisions binding for the parties of the dispute. They can originate from all courts and tribunals, including arbitration and organs which have the authority to decide. But broadly speaking, all products of international courts and tribunals (esp. advisory opinions, in extreme cases even separate or dissenting opinions of judges) and all decisions of *quasi*-judicial bodies (i.e. WTO panels and Appellate Body, or Human Rights Committee) may be included in this category. ICJ decisions take the most prominent place among all international judicial decisions. Secondly, judicial decisions are not primary sources of IL, they are only subsidiary. Subsidiarity is the central notion describing the role of decisions within IL. They should not replace main sources, but be applied as a supplementary, interpretative instrument.[19] They can be used mostly *infra* or *intra legem,* and in principle neither *praetor legem* nor *contra legem* (they cannot constitute an autonomous source of law). Third, judicial decisions serve as means for determining of the rules of law. Here, the key concept is determination. It is unclear notion,[20] but it should not be detached from the subsidiary function of judicial decisions. Formally, determination does not refer to creation. Judicial decisions may be used for the determination of all international rules of law, irrespectively of their primary source. However, their role in relation to customary law and general principles of law may be more determinative. At times, the determination is interpreted as establishing law and judicial decisions as precedents.

In practice, the role of judicial decisions is more important for international rules of law than it might result from a formal reading of Article 38 ICJ Statute. Their role may be analysed as to all the main sources, but bearing in mind that there is no treaty on SR and that dominant arguments favour the customary status of the majority, if not all, provisions of the ARSIWA, it is sufficient to restrict our scrutiny to judicial decisions as a means of determining the customary status of ARSIWA provisions.

---

[17]See Pellet (2006), pp. 735 and seq.

[18]Thirlway (2014), pp. 5–8.

[19]Thirlway (2014), p. 8, explains: "they do not normally purport to be ultimate sources, but rather intermediaries". According to the author, judicial decisions are "material rather than formal sources, but material sources having a special degree of authority" (p. 117).

[20]Pellet (2018), pp. 33–34.

3.2 International Courts and Tribunals as Determiners of Customary Law on SR

3.2.1 Traditional Approach to Customary International Law (CIL)

The idea of CIL is old. We are used to thinking that custom is an extremely early source of IL. At the same time, conditions of identifying of a customary rule were not clear. At present, we consider that the traditional vision of customary law is based on two elements: (i) practice of States (*usus*) and (ii) their acceptance of a rule as a legal rule (*opinio juris sive necessitatis*). This concept is generally accepted in legal theory and practice, and from judicial perspective. It was also the assumption for the ILC Draft conclusions on the identification of CIL adopted in 2018 (conclusion 2).[21] Both elements of a custom should be ascertained separately, but have to be shown together (conclusion 3). It is clear that the judicial decisions of international (but not national[22]) courts and tribunals cannot constitute a proof of State practice or their acceptance. As conclusion 13 (1) states,

> Decisions of international courts and tribunals, in particular of the International Court of Justice, concerning the existence and content of rules of customary international law are a subsidiary means for the determination of such rules.

The rule follows closely the language of Article 38 (1) (d) ICJ Statute. As the ILC explains in the commentary to conclusion 13, decisions of international courts and tribunals are an aid in the identification of customary rules.[23] They cannot supersede State practice. They are only subsidiary means for the determination of the existence and content of customary rules. They have no binding force except between parties. Their role is ancillary "in elucidating the law, rather than being themselves a source of international law". Thus, the ILC rejected the opinion that judicial decisions can be formal precedents. Simultaneously, it pointed out it did not mean that such decisions are not important for the identification of customary rules.

The Commission observed also that "Decisions of courts and tribunals [. . .] may offer valuable guidance for determining the existence or otherwise of rules of customary international law". However, "[t]he value of such decisions varies greatly, however, depending both on the quality of the reasoning (including primarily the extent to which it results from a thorough examination of evidence of an alleged

---

[21]The UN GA welcomed the draft conclusions (without vote). Resolution of 20.12.2018, A/73/10, annex. The Assembly "brings them to the attention of States and all who may be called upon to identify rules of customary international law". The Conclusions with commentaries (ILC Report 2018, pp. 149–150): http://legal.un.org/docs/?path=../ilc/texts/instruments/english/commentaries/1_13_2018.pdf&lang=EF. Accessed: 6 March 2019.

[22]On the role on national courts: Olesson (2013), pp. 615 and seq.; Nollkaemper (2007), pp. 760 and seq.

[23]For the ILC, decisions of the WTO bodies and procedural or interlocutory orders are judicial decisions. It attributes also some weight to separate and dissenting opinions of judges. At the same time the ILC is silent as far as i.e. Human Rights Committee views are concerned.

general practice accepted as law) and on the reception of the decision, in particular by States and in subsequent case law. Other considerations might, depending on the circumstances, include the nature of the court or tribunal; the size of the majority by which the decision was adopted; and the rules and the procedures applied by the court or tribunal. It needs to be borne in mind, moreover, that judicial pronouncements on customary international law do not freeze the law; rules of customary international law may have evolved since the date of a particular decision." It added: "The skills and the breadth of evidence usually at the disposal of international courts and tribunals may lend significant weight to their decisions".

According to the classical theory of CIL, the first component of custom is primarily State practice (conclusion 4). Judicial decisions cannot substitute State practice. This practice comprises both physical and verbal acts (conclusion 6).[24] Under certain circumstances, it may include inaction.[25] Practice has to be general, which means it must be sufficiently widespread and representative, as well as consistent. Provided that the practice is general, no particular duration is required (conclusion 8). However, if it is to be sufficiently widespread and representative, its developmentmust take some time. Thus, the time aspect is not completely irrelevant,[26] as a customary rule can not be instantly created.

The second element of CIL is the acceptance of the general practice as law. It must be undertaken with a sense of legal right or obligation (conclusion 9). The requirement of acceptance is a guarantee the conscious participation of States in practice, the proof of their consent. States which oppose the emerging customary rule may express their objection. Here also some time to react is needed. If the practice is general and accepted, it is then binding for all States, except persistent objectors (conclusion 15).[27] Judicial decisions are a means for determination of both elements of a custom.

---

[24]See, however, *Continental Shelf* Case (Libya v. Malta), Judgment of 3 March 1985, ICJ Rep. 1985, p. 13 (at 29), para. 27; *Legality of the threat or use of nuclear weapons*, Advisory Opinion of 8 July 1996, ICJ 1996, p. 226 (at 253), para. 64.

[25]A state's failure to act may be considered practice if three conditions are fulfilled: (1) if the conduct of the other state calls for a response (*Pedra Branca* Case, Malaysia/Singapore), which in his opinion "implies that the relevant practice ought to be one that affects the interests or rights of the State failing or refusing to act"; (2) "a State whose inaction is sought to be relied upon in identifying whether a rule of customary international law has emerged must have had actual knowledge of the practice in question or the circumstances must have been such that the State concerned is deemed to have had such knowledge" (*Fisheries* Case); (3) the inaction should be maintained "over a sufficient period of time". Therefore, acquiescence understood as qualified silence is relevant. M. Wood, Third report on identification of customary international law, A/CN.4/682, 27 March 2015, points 23–25.

[26]See the ICJ, *Navigational and Related Rights Case* (Costa Rica v. Nicaragua), 13 July 2009. The Court held that it is particularly significant that Nicaragua did not contest a "practice which had continued undisturbed and unquestioned over a very long period". It refused to acknowledge that "the customary right extends to fishing from vessels on the river." It stated that "There is only limited and recent evidence of such a practice". ICJ Rep. 2009, p. 213 (at 265–266), paras. 141, 143.

[27]In assessing a general practice and its acceptance as law, regard must be had to the overall context, the nature of the rule, and the particular circumstances in which the evidence in question is to be

3.2.2 The ARSIWA as Traditionally Perceived CIL

3.2.2.1 Before the Adoption of ARSIWA

If we wish to apply the traditional approach to the ARSIWA, it would be useful to distinguish two periods: before and after the adoption of the Articles. Without doubt, some basic rules relating to SR existed before the LN or UN were established and were practised and accepted by States.[28] The most crucial of them were confirmed by the PCIJ, and later accepted by the ICJ[29] and other courts and tribunals[30] and they have been incorporated in the ARSIWA. As a consequence, some Articles existed as customary rules before the adoption of the ARSIWA and retain that status at present. The last Special Rapporteur on SR, J. Crawford, listed among them "The principles that (i) the breach of an international obligation invokes the responsibility of the state; (ii) the state cannot rely on its municipal law as grounds for failure to comply with its international obligations; and (iii) for every international wrong there was an injured state (entailing the idea that responsibility was essentially bilateral)".[31] Undoubtedly, these principles fulfil the criteria of two-elementary concept of the CIL and belong to it.

Such customary principles, however, represent a limited set of rules and as with all customary rules are not very detailed. As the ICJ held in the *Gulf of Maine Case*,[32]

> A body of detailed rules is not to be looked for in customary international law which in fact comprises a limited set of norms for ensuring the co-existence and vital co-operation of the members of the international community [. . .].

Customary rules can regulate powers and procedures to a limited extent. For them, it is more difficult to regulate exceptions than principles.

In addition, in the field of SR at least some concepts remained unclear and not fully acceptable for States until the end of the work of the ILC, and some had been

---

found (conclusion 3.1). The ILC is silent as to the moment of determination of a customary rule. Meanwhile, in most cases the existence and the content a customary rule is determined *a posteriori*. As a result, States may have no idea that the practice will be the base for custom and that they can react as persistent objectors.

[28]Crawford (2013b), p. 8, noted that the formation of "general part" of the law of SR, "occurred only late, at the beginning of the 20th century, and that formerly the law of State responsibility was at best in its infancy".

[29]Tams, pp. 297–301.

[30]See *Materials on the Responsibility of States for Internationally Wrongful Acts*, United Nations Legislative Series, ST/LEG/SER.B/25, New York: United Nations 2012. The structure of the Materials is based on the ARSIWA, even if only some judicial decisions refer to Articles or their earlier versions.

[31]Crawford (2013a), p. 72.

[32]*Delimitation of the Maritime Boundary in the Gulf of Maine Area* (Canada v. United States of America), Judgment of 10 October 1984, ICJ Rep. 1984, p. 246 (at 299), para. 111.

maturing during its work.[33] Until 1963 the attention of the ILC had been focused on SR for injury to aliens, then the shift took place and the Commission took a broader perspective. Moreover, under the influence of the judicial decisions or publicists, certain new ideas were introduced, such as internationally wrongful act or obligations *erga omnes*. During the work responsibility had been separated from liability. Damage ceased to be a necessary condition of responsibility. In the final reading of the ARSIWA stakeholders introduced new formulas of the discussed concepts (countermeasures), assimilated relatively new ideas (peremptory norms) or rejected concepts which had been accepted (international crimes and delicts of States).[34] However, both practice and acceptance of these concepts were precarious. Thus, the Articles corresponding with such ideas cannot be considered customary at least at the moment of their adoption by the ILC.

One may argue that the Articles, like many other draft articles, are the result of dialogue between States commenting on the Articles, judicial practice which accompanies the work of the ILC and doctrinal opinions. There had been two sources of State influence in the drafting of the Articles. First, the Special Rapporteur while compiling authorities and drafting the Articles, was expected to base his reasoning and commentaries on various State practices and jurisprudence in national and international courts. The scope and extent of the ILC draft is already constrained by State practices and *opinio juris*. Secondly, States may exert a subtler influence on the ILC through their comments on the ILC drafts.[35] The Commission made efforts to take into account State practice, but only 21 governments had submitted comments on the draft Articles and only a few have done so regularly.[36] In a general debate on the ARSIWA in 2001 only 68 governments were involved.[37]

In its commentaries, the ILC pointed out (introduction, Article 56) that the ARSIWA constitute at the same time a codification and a progressive development of IL.[38] But, it cautiously determined the individual provisions as customary, citing judicial decisions (Articles 4—conduct of organs of a State, 25—state of necessity, 38—interest, 44—exhaustion of local remedies in the context of admissibility of claims). The ILC also held that a provision is well-established, sometimes invoking case law in support. This expression can be understood as well as an endorsement of its customary status, ex. Articles 13 (international obligation in force for a State), 36 and 37 (compensation, satisfaction), 50 (2) and 51 (dispute settlement between

---

[33]See Analytical Guide to the Work of the ILC: State responsibility, http://legal.un.org/ilc/guide/9_6.shtml. Accessed: 6 March 2019.

[34]Crawford (2002a), pp. 1 and seq.

[35]Wong (2018), p. 5.

[36]Wong (2018), p. 6.

[37]Crawford and Olesson (2005), p. 960.

[38]As Article 15 ILC Statute states, "progressive development of international law" means the preparation of draft conventions on subjects which have not yet been regulated by IL or in regard to which the law has not yet been sufficiently developed in the practice of States, while "codification of international law" denotes the more precise formulation and systematization of rules of IL in fields where there already has been extensive State practice, precedent and doctrine.

injured and responsible States and countermeasures; proportionality in countermeasures). Simultaneously, the ILC indicated that only Articles 41 (1) (consequences of a serious breach of an obligation; duty to cooperate) and 48 (2) (invocation of responsibility by a State other than an injured State; scope of claims) may reflect the progressive development of IL. This means, however, the ILC was fully aware that the ARSIWA as a whole did not constitute CIL.

Last but not least, the ILC stated in the commentary to Article 56 (Questions of SR not regulated by these Articles) that one of its functions is to preserve the application of the rules of CIL concerning SR on matters not covered by the Articles. The Articles do not purport to state all the consequences of an internationally wrongful act even under existing IL and there is no intention of precluding further development of the law on SR. For example, the principle *ex injuria jus non oritur* may generate new legal consequences in the field of responsibility.

The corollaries of reading Article 56 in the context of its commentary are the following : (i) Articles do not constitute a full set of principles (there is a place for rules not included, including CIL; some of them may belong to general law, others to special law); (ii) the ARSIWA do not preclude further development of the regime of SR, including CIL; (iii) it is not excluded that further development of CIL on SR can undermine or correct principles accepted in the Articles, but not recognized as customary; (iv) taking into account that provisions in the written text are more precise than customary rules, one can assume that even if we accept that an article has customary nature, it is only in principle, to some extent. In these circumstances, it would be difficult to say that the ARSIWA belonged to the CIL at the moment of their adoption.

3.2.2.2   After the Adoption of the ARSIWA

Almost 20 years have passed since the adoption of the Articles. What has changed over this period of time concerning their customary status? Traditionalist will say we should verify general State practice and its acceptance as law as a basic source and analyse international case-law and teachings as subsidiary. However, the situation remains unclear. The practice is not easy to scrutinize. The attitude of States towards GA resolutions on the ARSIWA is not uniform.[39] There is limited access to the diplomatic acts and correspondence of some States, and no legislation based on the Articles. Only a part of domestic courts invoke them, but solely on several provisions. States are also divided as to the nature of certain principles contained in Articles. Legal opinions expressed by States are not always convergent. Few treaties possess explicit clauses on SR. Some concepts are still not sufficiently explored or remain controversial (state of necessity,[40] countermeasures, consequences of violations of obligations resulting from peremptory norms, due diligence, *erga omnes*

---

[39]See also point 3.
[40]Wong (2018), p. 8.

obligations and generally various types of obligations). International judicial decisions refer to the ARSIWA as a whole or their individual provisions as CIL. But
many references are not based on examination of State practice and its acceptance as
law. Thus, even nowadays, while using the traditional model of CIL, it is problematic to validate the customary nature of the ARSIWA.

3.2.3 ARSIWA as an Expression of Modern Concepts of CIL or Judicial Precedents

3.2.3.1 Modern Concept of CIL

Identifying rules of CIL in a traditional way is an incredibly challenging exercise,
especially if one attempts to make sense of the multiple claims, counterclaims,
actions and omissions of the 193 States that compose the international community.[41]
Moreover, contemporary international life is under strong pressure from many
agents—political, economic, cultural, moral (ethical), scientific and technological
and others. Hence, new interpretations of CIL appear. They relate mostly to technical
methods of evidencing customary law, but have important substantive effects.[42]
Thus, modern approaches to the CIL are based on the restriction of the relevance of
State practice and on paying special attention to presumed or general consent (lack of
contestation) of States or nature of the rule as an obvious element of every legal
order. Instead of practice, resolutions of international organizations or ILC draft
articles and judicial decisions are willingly exploited. This new look at CIL is
noticeable in the case law of the ICJ, but not only.

As S. Talmon argues the ICJ uses three methods of reconstruction of customary
rules: induction, deduction, and assertion. However, only induction corresponds
with two-elements theory. Yet, there are four situations where this method cannot
be used: (i) "state practice is non-existent because a question is too new" (*Gulf of
Maine* Case, 1984); (ii) "state practice is conflicting or too disparate and thus
inconclusive" (*Libya/Malta Continental Shelf* Case, 1985); (iii) "*opinio juris* of
states cannot be established" (*North Sea Continental Shelf*, and *Qatar/Bahrain*
Cases, 1969 and 2001); (iv) "there is a discrepancy between state practice and *opinio
juris*" (*Nicaragua* Case, 1986). In such situations, the Court should declare *non
liquet*, but it does not. It reaches for the deductive method. The rules are inferred
from existing rules and principles of CIL, general considerations concerning the
function of a person or an organization or from principal legal systems of the world
(but not from postulated values). The ICJ sometimes also uses assertion as its
method of reasoning. This occurs when the Court considers a specific custom
notorious, and also when it rules as a legislator, without going into the analysis of

---

[41]Rightly, Bordin (2014), p. 547.
[42]See i.a. Lepard (2010), *passim*.

traditional elements of a custom or even contrary to these elements. The Court refers to ILC works[43] or its own decisions.[44]

In turn, N. Petersen wrote that "'modern' customary international law is often primarily characterized not by methodological rigour but, rather, by an attempt to reconcile legal interpretation with considerations of efficiency or moral intuitions about human rights and the international community that most international lawyers share. In the absence of methodological constraints, customary law seems to be an entry gate for the 'progressive' development of international law and a tool for judicial law-making".[45] However, the strategies of identification of the CIL depend on the circumstances of each individual case and the preferences of the affected parties.

Petersen examined 48 decisions issued by the ICJ between 1949 and 2015 (95 instances in which the Court identified customary rules). In most cases the evidence of customary rules was based on the paper practice i.e. treaties (mostly law-making treaties), GA resolutions and draft articles of the ILC (more than 63%).[46] He concluded that, by contrast, "even though state practice is seen as a constitutive element of customary international law in most international law textbooks and treatises, it only plays a marginal role in the case law of the ICJ". "State practice is often difficult to observe and rarely homogenous". Instead, the ICJ referred more often to the general consent of the parties as to the existence of customary rule (not its application), own decisions or State practice in general (if the Court examines state practice thoroughly, it usually comes to the conclusion that a principle of CIL does not exist; *Jurisdictional Immunities*, 2012). In judgments in which the ICJ confirmed the positive existence of a customary rule, practice was a mere auxiliary instrument. It usually confirmed a result that had already been found through other means (*Pulp Mills*, 2010). The only judgments where the Court analysed state practice in detail are cases that concern the bilateral practice of the parties (*Navigational Rights*, 2009, *Right of Passage*, 1960).[47]

Nevertheless, issuing decisions promoting modern customary law is dangerous. Claims concerning their arbitrariness and the pre-emption of legislative function by courts may be formulated. This may provoke negative reactions of States, not only in a cases decided, but also towards international judicial activity in general.

---

[43] Since 1997. See Bordin (2014), p. 544.

[44] Talmon (2015), pp. 421 and seq. Alschner and Charlotin (2018), pp. 89 and seq., mention that the ICJ made 1865 self-references between 1948 and 2013 (against 126 judgments being examined self-citation appeared in 101).

[45] Petersen (2017), p. 363.

[46] First, they were used as a legitimation device. The ICJ has been relying on treaties or UNGA resolutions in order to show that the specific principle was accepted by the vast majority of the international community. Second, the Court has been using written texts to add specificity to the often vague, unwritten principles. Petersen (2017), pp. 368, 372–375.

[47] Petersen (2017), pp. 366 and seq.

3.2.3.2 Judicial Decisions as Precedents

As a rule, at least globally, judgments or other formally binding decisions of international courts and tribunals are binding exclusively for the parties.[48] Decisions made at the regional level sometimes have extended effects.[49] Nevertheless, decisions can formally neither add or diminish the rights and obligations of the parties of a dispute,[50] nor *a minori ad maius* confer rights or impose obligations on third parties. The dominant opinion is there is no place for precedents in IL. Judicial decisions cannot be an autonomous source of that law.

Formally, this is true. However, we have to bear in mind that: (i) many international rules are extremely general, they require interpretation which is close to filling gaps (especially many customary rule or general principles of law need determination not only as to their content, but also their existence); (ii) the main function of judicial bodies is to settle a dispute between parties, however, there is no place for *non liquet*[51]; so, the court has to issue a decision even if there is an impression that there is no rule of law at all[52]; (iii) an additional function of international courts is to pronounce in the form of advisory opinions; although they are formally non-binding[53] their regulatory impact is not restricted to asking subjects; (iv) today, there are many international courts and tribunals (we talk of their multiplication/proliferation). There is no hierarchy between them (decisions made by any court are not binding for each other). They are not bound by their own decisions. However, at the same time there is a dialogue between courts and tribunals, a kind of 'free movement' of judicial decisions. The form of decisions which are mutually cited is not important.[54] They are reciprocally respected. ICJ decisions have special authority,[55] albeit not all are uncontroversial.[56] Courts and tribunals are

---

[48]See Article 59 of the ICJ Statute, Article 296 together with Article 287 of the UNCLOS (it concerns the ICJ, ITLOS, arbitration); Article 31 (3), 33 of the ITLOS Statute; Article 46 (1) of the ECHRs; Article 68 (2) of the AMCHRs; Article 30 of the Protocol to the AfCharterHPsRs. See also Article 84 of the 1907 Convention for the pacific settlement of international disputes.

[49]See, however, the Article 105 of the ICC Rome Statute (the sentence of imprisonment shall be binding on all States Parties).

[50]*Explicite* Article 19 of the WTO DSU.

[51]See, however, Thirlway (2016), pp. 122–125.

[52]This principle is sometimes explicitly pronounced in legal bases of courts and tribunals.

[53]Explicite Article 5 of the Protocol No. 16 to the ECHRs. It is interesting that in most cases there is no regulation of effects of advisory opinions.

[54]There is no difference between judgments and advisory opinions.

[55]Shahabuddeen (1997), esp. pp. 67 and seq. His position is cautious. Also Alschner and Charlotin (2018), p. 90, who consider 111 ICJ judgments and 45 PCIJ decisions as precedents.

[56]See i.e. GA vote on resolutions on compliance with the ICJ judgments in *Military and Paramilitary Activities in and against Nicaragua* (1986; A/RES/41/31, until 1989), or *Avena and Other Mexican Nationals* (2004; A/RES/73/257) and on follow-up to the Advisory Opinion on *Legality of Force* (1996; until now).

willing not to depart from their own determinations (what is called 'line of jurisprudence'), except where there is good reasons to do so.[57]

The cautious conclusion can be that in the judicial practice of IL we do not know the legal precedents, but we should acknowledge the existence of *de facto* precedents.[58] Of course, not all judicial decisions are precedents, and not all international courts and tribunals have the same precedential capacity.[59] In tackling international problems on a precedential basis, international courts and tribunals should act in a self-restrained way, taking into account State attitudes to the maximum possible extent.

3.2.3.3 Non-traditional Approach to the ARSIWA: Between Modern Custom and Precedent

In the case of modern CIL, a customary rule is not based on State practice, but rather on the resolutions of international organizations, ILC draft articles and other documents and judicial decisions. The essential role to play in the determination of customary rules are international courts and tribunals. At least the silent approval for the results of such a determination is required.

In the field of SR the role of resolutions of international organizations is almost non-existent. As UN Secretary General reports show, the ARSIWA are referred in judicial decisions quite extensively. Their authoritative position is in principle accepted by States, courts and scholars. This results from the methods of draft-making, conceptual quality and consistency as well as the position of the ILC itself. The Articles, as other non-legislative codifications, are sometimes even compared to *Corpus Iuris Civilis, American Restatements* or the soft codification of the UNIDROIT.[60] However, the provisions of the Articles are invoked in judicial decisions rather as confirmation of a customary nature of a rule than its basis. Courts and tribunals cite each other. Even if decisions can be an evidence of the existence of a modern customary rule, courts and tribunals do not rule on each provision of the ARSIWA.

Finally, at least silent States approval for the ARSIWA is necessary. Meanwhile, they diverge in many respects. Some States are afraid the negotiation of a convention on SR, because it may reopen discussions about consensually accepted concepts and provisions. In fact, however, this means there is no stable support for all the

---

[57]Pellet (2018), p. 38.

[58]See also Hernández (2014), pp. 166–193.

[59]Boyle and Chinkin (2007), pp. 293–300. On specific features of court's precedents and arbitration precedents: Forteau (2016), and Fernández Arroyo (2016), respectively pp. 87 and seq. and pp. 113 and seq.

[60]Bordin (2014), p. 547.

articles.[61] Other States declare that several provisions should be modified.[62] For them, these provisions are certainly not binding. Only a small group of States clearly highlight the fact that the ARSIWA reflect CIL.[63]

As concerns judicial precedents, P. Dailler emphasized that the ARSIWA were based principally on them, to a far greater extent than on State practice and doctrine, references to which are far less systematic. It's much easier to find cases than to compile State practice.[64] Precedents are more politically neutral than State practice. They are also more precise than customary rules. In this context, Dailler noticed that the Commission referred mostly to 9 judicial decisions in the Commentary to the ARSIWA (2 of PCIJ, 6 of the ICJ, 1 arbitral tribunal). It used them in order to confirm different (yet not all) the articles.[65] J. Crawford expressed more moderate opinion. He wrote: "The ILC in codifying the law of state responsibility had to lay down general rules, which to some extent involved inventing them. The rules of state responsibility have been derived from cases, from practice, and from often unarticulated instantiations of general legal ideas (ex. Article 48)".[66] Ch. Chinkin and A. Boyle, on the other hand, recognized that "The law relating to state responsibility is a classic example of 'lawyer's law' ripe for codification by an expert body of international lawyers. There were remarkably few precedents for the ILC to drawn up".[67] In any case, most of the Articles cannot be classified as based on precedents at the moment of their adoption.

Currently, the number of judicial decisions referring to the Articles is increasing. The UN Secretary General statistical report (2017) discloses that, from 1 January 2001 to 1 January 2016, international courts and tribunals referred to the ARSIWA[68] in 163 cases with 392 references.[69] However, as resulting from the UN Secretary General reports, only in some cases rules contained in Articles were described as customary or well-established. In others they were superficially asserted as axiomatic, without any reflection as to their legal nature. When they are applied, sometimes the reasoning of the court and that of the ILC is not fully convergent.[70] Thus, it is difficult to assert that in such situations precedents can be established.

---

[61] Australia, Canada, New Zealand, 2016; UK, UN SG report, 2010; US, UN SG report, 2007; Nordic countries, UN SG report, 2007.

[62] Kuwait, UN SG report 2007; Articles 10 (conduct of an insurrectional or other movement), 12 (existence of a breach of an international obligation), 23 (force majeure), 24 (distress), 26 (compliance with peremptory norms) are mentioned in this context.

[63] Germany, UN SG report, 2010; UK, UN SG report, 2016.

[64] Dailler (2010), p. 41.

[65] Dailler (2010), pp. 43–44.

[66] Crawford (2013a), p. 74.

[67] Boyle and Chinkin (2007), p. 182.

[68] The ICJ has referred to earlier versions of the drafts on SR since 1997 (*Gabčikovo*).

[69] The report covers also 50 cases with 202 references in opinions of judges appended to a decision, 157 cases with 792 references in submissions by parties to a dispute.

[70] See more Crawford (2013a), pp. 81–85.

In addition, in most cases different international courts refer to the same articles relating to attribution and breach. Except Articles 25 (state of necessity) and 31, 34–36 (reparation), courts refer to other articles incidentally (from 1 to 6 times). As to the range of Articles [Articles 18 (coercion), 19, 46 (plurality of injured States), 53 (countermeasures), 54 (measures taken by States other than an injured State)] there is no judicial practice, albeit the issue of SR is at stake.[71] It is not easy to explain such an approach. At times, the parties do not refer to them, and the courts are silent. However, sometimes they do and are also silent.[72]

Leaving these dilemmas aside for a while, we can say that there general consensus between States concerning the basic rules on SR enshrined in the ARSIWA. We can assume that the rules inserted in the first three parts of the Articles relating to the fundamental principles on SR, rules on attribution and breach as well as the part on reparation in principle belong to them. They impose with such force that no States can ignore them. These Articles should be treated as belonging to positive IL, especially as they are inextricably linked to the law itself and present in every legal order. There are no legal obligations without accepting the principle of responsibility. In other cases, however, the Articles may be contested and then it would be necessary to confirm their existence and content by proving their non-modern customary status.

4 Case for Convention on State Responsibility for Internationally Wrongful Acts

4.1 General Remark

When the legal status of the ARSIWA is uncertain and only some of their rules are generally recognized as customary or based on *de facto* precedents, it is reasonable to consider whether any new steps should be taken, for example: (i) no further action taken (no convention or other action); (ii) a convention may be adopted, but not now; (iii) negotiate a convention on the basis of the ARSIWA; (iv) adopt Articles by the GA in the form of a declaration or resolution. The most challenging idea is to elaborate a convention. More than 100 States presented their positions on this topic.[73] They can be divided in three groups: (i) in favour of a convention (over

---

[71] See i.a. *Jurisdictional Immunities of the State* (Germany v. Italy), Judgment of 3 February 2012, I.C.J. Reports 2012, p. 99; *Questions relating to the Obligation to Prosecute or Extradite* (Belgium v. Senegal), Judgment of 20 July 2012, I.C.J. Reports 2012, p. 422; *Whaling in the Antarcic* Case (Australia v. Japan), Judgment of 31 March 2014, I.C.J. Reports 2014, p. 226; *Obligation to negotiate access to the Pacific Ocean* (Bolivia v. Chile), Judgment of 1 October 2018, nyr.

[72] *Ex. Application of the Interim Accord of 13 September 1995* (the former Yugoslav Republic of Macedonia v. Greece), Judgment of 5 December 2011, I.C.J. Reports 2011, p. 644.

[73] See Crawford and Olesson (2005), pp. 960–965, on early controversies which appeared during debate on ARSIWA in the UN.

half); (ii) those against it (8 States, including US, UK, Canada, Australia, NZ, Israel; their number is static); (iii) those with an intermediate position (almost half; with a possible positive decision in the future).[74]

4.2 No Further Action on SR

According to some States, the most important, albeit political, argument against the adoption of a convention, is a lack of wide support among States.[75] In particular the UK argue that States generally accepted the ARSIWA in their current form. The Articles reflect an authoritative statement of IL and have been referred to by international courts and tribunals, writers and, more recently, domestic courts. It is difficult to see what would be gained by the adoption of a convention. The ARSIWA are already proving their worth and are entering the fabric of IL through State practice, decisions of courts and tribunals and the literature. They are referred to consistently in the work of foreign ministries and other government departments. The impact of the Articles on IL will only increase with time, as is demonstrated by the growing number of references to the Articles in recent years. This achievement should not be put at risk negotiation on a convention would be complex and uncertain as to their results (old issues may be reopened, debates may be fruitless, new compromises would be necessary).[76] It may weaken current consensus. Even were a text to be agreed, it is unlikely that it would enjoy as wide support as the Articles have had. If few States were to ratify a convention, that instrument would have less legal force than the ARSIWA. There is a significant risk that a convention with a small number of participants may have a de-codifying effect, may serve to undermine the current status of the Articles and may be a "limping" convention, with little or no practical effect.[77] It is interesting that for the UK, the very breadth of the Articles, both in terms of their scope and formulation, means that it is still premature to say that they reflect in their entirety CIL or a settled consensus of views among

---

[74]Pacht (2014), pp. 445–447.

[75]See broadly Pacht (2014), pp. 447–462.

[76]Negotiations could cause the unwarranted change to long-accepted rules, through an ill-advised vote, adoption by consensus of a "watered-down" text, or by means of dismemberment of those components which are more controversial or whose inclusion in the text might be considered to be more in the nature of *de lege ferenda* than *lex lata*. There is a risk of politicisation of law-making process. It is in the interest of weaker states not to have a convention, some states want to scuttle the idea of conventional regulation by the conference. Pacht (2014), pp. 448–449.

[77]The convention could attract few ratifications, or many reservations, leaving the instrument languishing with a prolonged entry into force, or anaemic ratification rate, and accordingly casting doubts as to the legal authority of the rules on State responsibility contained therein (risk of marginalization). Pacht (2014), pp. 447–450. See also the position of Australia, Canada and New Zealand, the UN SG report, 2016.

States. There remain elements of uncertainty and disagreement (UN SG reports, 2007, 2010, 2016).[78]

4.3   Convention Yes, But Not Yet

Slightly less categorical is the standpoint of the Nordic countries. They share the opinion that the ARSIWA express to a large extent customary law. In principle, they support the idea of a future convention on SR. However, they believe that the Articles, should not be eroded by compromises and package-deals at a diplomatic conference. The moment to start negotiations has not yet come (UN SG reports, 2007, 2010). A similar approach is adopted by the Netherlands. It additionally stresses that negotiations at this moment may unravel the fragile balance in the Articles or result in the adoption of a convention that may never enter into force or one that will not acquire universal or at least quasi-universal participation. With respect to controversial articles, the practice of States as well as the decisions of international courts, arbitral tribunals and other bodies can make a significant contribution to the development of CIL and that the crystallization of these Articles into CIL will benefit from more time (UN SG report, 2010).

4.4   Convention: Yes

There are a fair number of States who are adherents of a convention on SR.[79] However, they constitute two groups. First one, represented by Austria is in principle in favour of a convention. However, it maintains that the project should only be pursued if there are sufficient assurances that the current structure and balance of the ARSIWA will be maintained[80] and a renewed discussion of their substantial provisions avoided and if there are realistic prospects for a wide ratification and acceptance of such a convention (UN SG report, 2016).

The majority of States belongs to second group. They support the idea of incorporation of the ARSIWA provisions into a convention. This would certainly contribute to the respect of IL and for peace and stability in international relations as a third pillar of the international legal order.[81] States must not be over-cautious about

---

[78]See also the US opinion; the UN SG report, 2007. According to Germany, the elaboration of a convention depends on confirmation customary status of ARSIWA by all States and courts. The UN SG report, 2010.

[79]See also broadly Pacht (2014), pp. 462–471.

[80]As to Lithuania, negotiations should not prejudice the importance of the ARSIWA as a reflection of CIL and practice (UN SG report, 2010).

[81]El Salvador, UN SG reports, 2010, 2013, 2016.

it. State responsibility is only interested in secondary rules and not primary rules that define the obligations of States. It would not make sense to proceed in the development and codification of this matter and continue to proceed in others like diplomatic protection, liability and the responsibility of international organizations when the main principles that guide the development of the latter are those that apply to State responsibility. The ARSIWA have undergone a period of maturation. Judicial decisions proves that the Articles are ready for codification (UN SG reports, 2007, 2013).[82]

Mexico considers that "[o]nly a binding instrument could offer the guarantees and certainty necessary to enable injured States to obtain reparation. States tended to disparage so-called 'soft law'. It was doubtful that a declaration would make the significant contribution to the codification of international law warranted by five decades of effort". They deserve a place, "together with the Vienna Convention on the Law of Treaties, as one of the fundamental pillars of public international law". Avoiding the adoption of a convention could cause an imbalance that would be created where primary rules were more comprehensively codified than secondary rules. This imbalance could in the long term be detrimental to the coherence and effectiveness of IL. State practice and judicial decisions also show that the Articles contain the formulation of certain customary rules widely accepted by States. The existence of customary rules and principles related to SR is independent of their potential formulation in a convention. The adoption of a treaty would be without prejudice to the process of forming CIL in the matter. On the contrary, a convention could have a continuous and positive impact on the development of customary law, as in the law of treaties (UN SG report, 2010; Mexico, CELAC, UN SG report, 2016).

4.5 Declaration as an Alternative or First Step to Convention

A small group of States favour a declaration on SR as an alternative for a convention. In such a case it would be an autonomous instrument or a first step in adopting a convention. Thus, Qatar leans towards the adoption by the GA of a consensus declaration that could contribute, by being cited in judicial decisions, to the consolidation of Articles and lay the foundations for the next phase in the process of the adoption of a treaty on SR (UN SG reports, 2010, 2013). Also Chile promotes the fact that the ARSIWA have not been enshrined in a binding legal framework, let alone the absence of a decision regarding their future adoption more than ten years after their submission, and does not support the interpretation that their importance is recognized. It is unacceptable that such an issue would figure in the deliberations of the UN Sixth Committee every three years without any progress being made on the resulting resolution adopted. For Chile the adoption of a

---

[82]See also France, the UN SG report, 2010.

declaration would constitute a transitional measure on the road towards a convention (UN SG report, 2013).

4.6   Assessing Options. Conclusions

A no-change option expresses opportunistic pragmatism. It aims at leaving the problem to international courts and tribunals and, to some extent, to State practice and the doctrine. Its main justification is a fear that by initiating negotiations and adopting a convention States may destroy the existing acquis in the form of the ARSIWA and related case-law without replacing it with anything.[83] Such a risk exists. However, is the present state of affairs really unproblematic? The Articles constitute a non-binding instrument made by a small number of experts with the modest participation of States. Non-binding texts are poor vehicles for the development of positive law. Only some articles are accepted generally and without reservation. Others remain uncertain and controversial. Judicial decisions refer to them in many cases superficially, without determining their legal status. Besides, there is no guarantee that the courts and state practice will follow the ARSIWAs and that doctrine will not find better solutions.[84] Judicial decisions can also solidify Articles which are controversial as binding and have little support from States.[85] They can be only progressive developer of IL, not their codificator, or even recessive developer of law.[86]

Pacht rightly observed that "the Articles were formulated as a legal instrument in the sense that they were intended to establish a unitary system of rules on SR". They are "structured in a composite manner, and are meant to be read cumulatively". "It is precisely the equilibrium of the text, which is used by those opposing a treaty to maintain that a treaty negotiation would be a threat. However, it is equally (if not more) plausible to argue that such balance is also threatened by the piecemeal application of the Articles by states and the courts and tribunals, especially through the auto-interpretation and application of the rules. To put it bluntly, it is much easier for a court or a tribunal to pick and choose from the provisions of a text which is strictly-speaking non-binding, than to choose to selectively apply the provisions of a treaty". The legal position of those provisions "would have enjoyed the greater legal security of being encapsulated in a treaty than they enjoy at present in a formally nonbinding text where they are subject to the vicissitudes of opinions as to their *de lege ferenda* nature".[87]

---

[83]Crawford et al. (2001), pp. 969–970.

[84]On difficulties in interpreting judicial decisions: Dailler (2010), p. 40.

[85]Crawford and Olesson (2005), p. 968, mention about case-law concerning Articles 40, 46, and 51.

[86]Pellet (2018), pp. 41–55.

[87]Pacht (2014), pp. 466–467.

By adopting the GA declaration instead of a convention is an option, but it does not add anything new, except if some provisions were to be changed or added to the Articles. But then, all allegations connected with convoking a conference should be recalled. Additionally, the view that the codification is outdated, and there are new forms of international law-making, is overestimated. Treaties are negotiated and concluded, even if and sometimes because their subject-matter is controversial. The level of their ratification depends on a host of reasons.[88]

The arguments put forward against drawing up a convention are unconvincing. A diplomatic conference to negotiate a treaty would allow for the participation of all States and would provide a forum for a political understanding/consensus on some of the most controversial provisions. As a rule, judicial decisions cannot replace them in international law-making, without the risk of proclaiming rules inappropriate and unacceptable for States. The ARSIWA should be an important basis for a future convention and default position (any deletion or modification would require at least a 2/3 majority during the preliminary rounds of a conference).[89] Judicial decisions should play a key role in determining the content.[90] Pacht aptly wrote that if something is be difficult, this is not in itself a convincing reason not to try. There is no compelling reason to assume that States would wish to renegotiate the ARSIWA *de novo*. The conference could be limited to more controversial or unresolved issues. To suggest that the law contained in those provisions will "harden" over time despite the opposition of States is misguided.[91] A convention could prevent the increasing deformalization of IL, and contribute to its stabilization and legal certainty. It can influence as States-parties as non-State-parties, contributing to develop clear rules of CIL. Leaving the matter to CIL only, determined by international courts and tribunals or doctrine, could be considered as tantamount to accepting the uncertainty inherent in these subsidiary means.

A Convention could clarify, complete or correct the ARSIWA provisions. There remain aspects of the law of state responsibility which were not covered, such as the responsibility of states for wrongful acts committed against other international actors, including international organisations.[92] Some issues were excluded consciously from the Articles, such as due diligence or the need for *mens rea* requirements. There are also inconsistencies or ambiguities in the ARSIWA. For example, it seems that Article 48(3) might subject the possibility of the invocation of responsibility by a state other than an injured state to the operation of the nationality of claims rule in Article 44(a), thereby significantly limiting the potential scope of such an invocation. This has been acknowledged by the Commission itself which, in the

---

[88]Pacht (2014), pp. 454–455.

[89]Pacht (2014), p. 452.

[90]Tams (2015), pp. 301–305.

[91]Pacht (2014), p. 451.

[92]There are limited differences between the ARSIWA and Articles drafted by the ILC on responsibility of international organizations (2011). Perhaps, it would be useful to join them in one convention.

commentary to the corresponding provision in the 2011 Articles on the Responsibility of International Organizations, sought to retroactively clarify the meaning of Article 48. Then there is a class of issues in the Articles for which there exist differences of opinion. These are not limited to larger issues of countermeasures and serious breaches of peremptory norms. Questions have also been raised about some of the more technical provisions. For example, the United Kingdom has placed on record its concern about "interpretative uncertainties in a number of aspects relating to attribution", and has noted that "[e]xperience had also indicated the need for greater clarity about the principle of aid or assistance set out in article 16. Given its potential for covering virtually all forms of state interaction, the text presented some fairly significant gaps".

When considering a conference on convention on SR some preparatory efforts could be made. For instance, it would be useful to draw a questionnaire for States where all provisions of the ARSIWA would be split into individual sentences. States would have some time for a decision whether they are ready to accept a particular sentence or not. If not, what would their suggestion to delete, change (how) or complement (how) the sentence/provision.

References

Alschner, W., & Charlotin, D. (2018). The growing complexity of the International Court of Justice's self-citation network. *European Journal of International Law, 29*(1), 83–112. https://doi.org/10.1093/ejil/chy002

Bordin, F. A. (2014). Reflections of customary international law: the authority of codification conventions and ILC draft articles in international law. *International and Comparative Law Quarterly, 63*(3), 535–567. https://doi.org/10.1017/S0020589314000220

Boyle, A., & Chinkin, C. (2007). *The making of international law*. Oxford: Oxford University Press. https://doi.org/10.1093/law/9780199213795.001.0001

Caron, D. (2002). The ILC articles on state responsibility: The paradoxical relationship between form and authority. *American Journal of International Law, 96*(4), 857–873. https://doi.org/10.2307/3070682

Crawford, J. (2002a). Introduction. In *The International Law Commission's articles on state responsibility. Introduction, text and commentaries* (pp. 1–60). Cambridge: Cambridge University Press.

Crawford, J. (2002b). The ILC's articles on responsibility of states for internationally wrongful acts: A retrospect. *American Journal of International Law, 96*(4), 874–890. https://doi.org/10.2307/3070683

Crawford, J. (2013a). The International Court of Justice and the law of state responsibility. In C. J. Tams & J. Sloan (Eds.), *The development of international law by the International Court of Justice* (pp. 71–86). Oxford: Oxford University Press. https://doi.org/10.1093/acprof:oso/9780199653218.003.0005

Crawford, J. (2013b). *State responsibility. The general part*. Cambridge: Cambridge University Press. https://doi.org/10.1017/CBO9781139033060

Crawford, J., & Olesson, S. (2005). The continuing debate on a UN Convention on state responsibility. *International and Comparative Law Quarterly, 54*(4), 959–972. https://doi.org/10.1093/iclq/lei045

Crawford, J., Peel, J., & Olesson, S. (2001). The ILC's articles on responsibility of states for internationally wrongful acts: Completion of the second reading. *European Journal of International Law, 12*(5), 963–991.

Dailler, P. (2010). The development of the law of responsibility through the case law. In J. Crawford, A. Pellet, & S. Olleson (Eds.), *The law of international responsibility* (pp. 37–44). Oxford: Oxford University Press. https://doi.org/10.1093/law/9780199296972.001.0001

Fernández Arroyo, D. P. (2016). Les décisions arbitrales comme précédent. In *Le précédent en droit international* (pp. 113–134). Paris: Éditions A. Pédone.

Forteau, M. (2016). Les décisions juridictionnelles comme precedent. In *Le précédent en droit international* (pp. 87–112). Paris: Éditions A. Pédone.

Hernández, G. I. (2014). *The International Court of Justice and the judicial function.* Oxford: Oxford University Press. https://doi.org/10.1093/acprof:oso/9780199646630.001.0001

Kurtz, J. (2010). The paradoxical treatment of the ILC articles on state responsibility in investor-state arbitration. *ICSID Review – Foreign Investment Law Journal, 25*(1), 200–217. https://doi.org/10.1093/icsidreview/25.1.200

Lepard, B. D. (2010). *Customary international law. A new theory with practical applications.* Cambridge: Cambridge University Press. https://doi.org/10.1017/CBO9780511804717

Nollkaemper, A. (2007). Internationally wrongful acts in domestic courts. *American Journal of International Law, 101*(4), 760–799. https://doi.org/10.1017/S0002930000037714

Olesson, S. (2013). Internationally wrongful acts in the domestic courts: The contribution of domestic courts to the development of customary international law relating to the engagement of international responsibility. *Leiden Journal of International Law, 26*(3), 615–642. https://doi.org/10.1017/S0922156513000277

Pacht, L. T. (2014). The case for a convention on state responsibility. *Nordic Journal of International Law, 83*(4), 439–475. https://doi.org/10.1163/15718107-08304003

Pellet, A. (2006). Commentary on article 38 of the statute. In A. Zimmermann, C. Tomuschat, & K. Oellers-Frahm (Eds.), *Statute of the international court of justice. A commentary* (pp. 677–792). Oxford: Oxford University Press. https://doi.org/10.1093/law/9780199692996.001.0001

Pellet, A. (2018). Decisions of the ICJ as sources of international law? In *Decisions of the ICJ as sources of international law. Gaetano Morelli Lectures Series, Vol. 2 – 2018* (pp. 7–61). Rome: International and European Papers Publishing. https://doi.org/10.15166/978-88-943616-0-5

Petersen, N. (2017). The International Court of Justice and the judicial politics of identifying customary international law. *European Journal of International Law, 28*(2), 357–385. https://doi.org/10.1093/ejil/chx024

Shahabuddeen, M. (1997). *Precedent in the World Court.* Cambridge: Cambridge University Press.

Talmon, S. (2015). Determining customary international law: The ICJ's methodology between induction, deduction and assertion. *European Journal of International Law, 26*(2), 417–443. https://doi.org/10.1093/ejil/chv020

Tams, C. (2015). Law-making in complex processes. The World Court and the modern law of State responsibility. In *Sovereignty, statehood and state responsibility. Essays in Honour of James Crawford* (pp. 287–306). Cambridge: Cambridge University Press. https://doi.org/10.1017/CBO9781107360075.022

Tams, C. (2018). *Decisions of the ICJ as sources of international law. Gaetano Morelli Lectures Series, Vol. 2 – 2018* (pp. 63–106). Rome: International and European Papers Publishing. https://doi.org/10.15166/978-88-943616-0-5

Thirlway, H. (2014). *The sources of international law.* Oxford: Oxford University Press. https://doi.org/10.1093/law/9780199685394.001.0001

Thirlway, H. (2016). *The International Court of Justice.* Oxford: Oxford University Press. https://doi.org/10.1093/law/9780198779070.001.0001

Wong, E. (2018). *The missing "custom" in the customary international law – Understanding the undue restriction of states' influence in the creation and crystallisation of law of state responsibility.* Retrieved February 6, 2018, from https://www.docdroid.net/wZ1iACp/state-responsibility-enoch.pdf

In Search of the Optimal Court Administration Model for New Democracies

Piotr Mikuli

Contents

There is no uniform definition of court administration in the literature. In particular, the delimitation between court administration and court governance in model terms is extremely difficult to delineate.[1] In the strict sense, court administration covers the technical, organizational and material conditions under which courts operate, such as the establishment of judicial agendas, the supervision of budgets and the supervision of extrajudicial staff. It also covers the internal functioning of courts, which may—to a greater or lesser extent—relate to the sphere of the dispensation of justice. In a wider sense, court administration also concerns many activities related to the functioning of the entire court system. Thus, the second category also applies to the decisions concerning the structure of courts, the process of creating courts, certain types of supervision of judges, disciplinary proceedings, etc.

In this paper, I disregard the solutions adopted for the appointment of judges, the legitimacy of the judiciary and its responsibility, including disciplinary proceedings. I emphasize, above all, the issue of court administration in the strict sense of the term. After a brief presentation of possible court administration models, arguments in favour of the judicial autonomous model will be presented.[2] This model can function independently of the differences in the aforementioned solutions. I also disregard the problem of correlating this autonomous model with the problem of

Piotr Mikuli is Professor and the Head of the Chair in Comparative Constitutional Law, Jagiellonian University. This paper builds upon a research project financed by the National Science Centre, Poland, according to the decision DEC-2016/21/B/HS5/00445.

[1]Mikuli (2017a), p. 1.
[2]See Mikuli et al. (2019), p. 73 ff; Smith (2017), p. 144 ff; Gee et al. (2015), p. 64 ff.

P. Mikuli (✉)
Chair of Comparative Constitutional Law, Jagiellonian University, Kraków, Poland
e-mail: p.mikuli@uj.edu.pl

© Springer Nature Switzerland AG 2019
P. Pinto de Albuquerque, K. Wojtyczek (eds.), *Judicial Power in a Globalized World*, https://doi.org/10.1007/978-3-030-20744-1_18

credibility of the third power in the historical context of a new democracy—that is, the verification of the judicial environment at the beginning of a political transformation in a situation where at least some of its members were connected to the overthrown authoritarian, or totalitarian, system.

Regardless of the system of government adopted in a democratic state, the separation of the judiciary from the legislature and the executive is necessary for implementing the principle of the rule of law. Today's democracies have developed a number of safeguards to ensure both the independence and autonomy of the judiciary and the high competencies of people responsible for the dispensation of justice. Such guarantees are offered not only by provisions of the Constitution but also by provisions of judicial procedures.

In many countries, councils of the judiciary are institutions tasked with safeguarding the principle of judicial independence. I believe that the activities of councils should be included in court administration in a broader sense. The judicial council model created mainly in Southern European countries has become popular in many others, including post-authoritarian countries in Latin America and Central and Eastern European countries. Councils can serve as a forum for discussion on the functioning of courts and planned reforms and contribute to the development and implementation of the necessary mechanisms to ensure the transparency of the activities of the third power.[3] According to the European Network for the Councils for the Judiciary (ENCJ), established in Rome in 2014, which associates several judicial councils operating in Europe, the councils are supposed to play an important role in ensuring the proper functioning of the justice system. According to ENCJ, the council should consist of judges or, in the case of its mixed-up composition, judges should constitute no fewer than half of the council members.[4] Regardless of their institutional composition or structure, councils are intended to ensure that a number of competencies related to the judiciary are exercised independently of the executive and legislative bodies. I am of the opinion that a mixed composition may be an

---

[3]Generally speaking, in constitutional systems where judicial councils function, one may distinguish two models. The first one occurs in some Nordic states and is characterized by the fact that there is a specific organizational merger of the council as a collegial organ and a unit dealing with administrative matters of courts. In the second model, which occurs in some Southern European states (Spain, Italy, and also France), the judicial council does not possess any competencies in the scope of court administration, but it plays a crucial role in the process of judicial appointments and disciplinary proceedings of judges. However, in many countries, hybrid measures exist which are hard to qualify to one of these two models.

[4]B.C. Smith rightly argues that '[e]ven the establishment of a judicial council, designated to distance the appointment of judges and the management of the judiciary from the political process, will not guarantee judicial independence if the executive controls its membership'. In this context, he uses the examples of Malaysia and Kazakhstan. See Smith (2017), p. 56. However, it seems that these arguments may be more relevant at the beginning of the process of democratic transition. In Poland, for example, similar views were presented to justify the capture of the judicial council by the ruling party as well as to explain other measures taken towards the judiciary, while the facts are completely different. The overwhelming majority of Polish justices were appointed after 1989 and they are in their forties.

important advantage of this type of body; then the council becomes a platform for discussion and working out a position with representatives of the legislative and executive powers[5] as well as representatives of different legal jobs and lay persons. In this model, the council goes beyond the entity which is only a kind of self-government of the judges.[6]

Although in many democratic countries, such as Austria, Germany, Finland, Luxembourg, the Czech Republic and Latvia, there are no judiciary councils,[7] these institutions seem to have many advantages. They can provide a kind of buffer for limiting the influence of political factors on judicial bodies. The literature explains that judiciary councils aim to strengthen the autonomy of judges while preserving the external accountability of this power so as to strike a balance between these two values.[8] Arguments that are critical of councils are sometimes raised from academia.[9] These include the allegation that judiciary councils limit the accountability and checking of judiciary bodies and petrify the status quo in the interests of the most prominent representatives of the judiciary.[10] The alternative in this case should certainly not be to increase the competencies of the government administration in relation to the judiciary, especially in relatively less stable political systems, where the legal and political culture leaves much to be desired. This can lead to a deliberate undermining of the independence of courts and the autonomy of judges for current political gain. M. Bobek believes that the relatively strong position of the Department of Justice towards courts does not necessarily mean that the judicial system is less independent or effective, since 'the transformation of the judicial branch is primarily about building ethical consensus and accountability and not

---

[5]However, it does not mean that the most desirable model for the council is one in which representatives of the legislative or the executive would have the same number of members as judges. This might create a wrong impression that greater involvement by such members strengthens the legitimacy of the judiciary. See Bałaban (2015), p. 45.

[6]On one hand, this allows for articulating a position on behalf of the whole community of judges; on the other hand, it is also important for other functions, including quasi-auditing functions, such as agreeing on positions on proposed reforms or the inclusion of political—by definition—powers (i.e. the executive and the legislature), in activities aimed at strengthening and safeguarding the independence of the third power.

[7]In these countries, the processes for recruiting judges and court administration are primarily the responsibility of the Ministry of Justice.

[8]Garoupa and Ginsburg (2008), p. 4 ff.

[9]Bobek and Kosař (2014), pp. 1257–1292; See also Kosař (2016). Confront also Selejan Gutan (2018), pp. 1709–1740.

[10]M. Bobek, D. Kosař refers to the case of Slovakia, where the council was dominated by prominent judges with a communist background. They juxtapose this with the situation in the Czech Republic, where the lack of a judicial council and a most powerful Minister of Justice contributed to the necessary reforms of the judicial system. In the same context, B.C. Smith mentions the cases of Romania and Indonesia, where, as he emphasizes, judicial councils have represented rather corporate interests of certain judges, so that their reform and control function may have been questioned. See Smith (2017), pp. 149–150.

about institutions'.[11] However, everything has to be considered in a certain context. The risks of a possible pathological emancipation of the judiciary and the danger of its direct politicization should be balanced.[12] The question is, 'Which dangers are greater, especially now that populism is growing even in stable democracies'? In this sense, the answer is obvious. The 'assault' on the operation of courts (which we are unfortunate to witness in Poland[13] and Hungary), aimed at subordinating them to politicians, may be an irresistible temptation, and references to the idea of democracy (understood in its simplified sense) serve, then, only as an effective propaganda trick and a smokescreen.[14] Political practice may obviously undermine the significance of all reasonable, normative solutions. However, it should be remembered that normative regulations can either contribute to the crystallization of a higher political and legal culture or lead to the consolidation of certain pathologies. Therefore, greater safeguarding of the independence of the judiciary is of great importance in this context.

Of course, in many democratic countries, court administration—both in narrow and broad senses—is sometimes also entrusted to entities associated with the executive. This may raise doubts as to whether such a solution is compatible with the principle of the separation of powers and independence of courts and judges. In particular, new democracies have not had the opportunity to develop traditions that guard them against abuses. Therefore, explicit constitutional and legislative provisions seem all the more necessary in these countries to ensure more consistent separation between the judicial bodies and the other two powers in order to limit political abuse. In countries of stable democracy, a high legal and political culture limits the scope for possible abuse.[15] However, this differentiation between old and young democracies is only partly justified. The point is that even in countries with a stable democracy, the legal and constitutional culture can turn out to be an insufficient safeguard against undesirable practices. This is even more evident at a time of growing populism and smear campaigns against judges and courts. Moreover, populist forces in new democracies can—and often do—allow certain formal regulations which provide for the executive to exert a significant influence on the

---

[11]Bobek (2010), p. 251 ff.

[12]Mikuli (2017b), p. 183.

[13]I am referring, in the context of this paper, to the unconstitutional capture of the Polish National Council of the Judiciary by the politicians of the ruling party. See Mikuli (2017c), see also Sadurski (2018).

[14]See Mikuli (2017b), pp. 182–183 and Mikuli et al. (2019), p. 172.

[15]As the former Polish Chief Justice, the late S. Dąbrowski, emphasizes, 'The system works fairly well under conditions of a stable democracy and an absence of threats to the autonomy of judges. The defect of this system is that if there is a crisis of democracy, guarantees of the independence of the courts and the autonomy of judges may prove inadequate [. . .]. It is pointed out in the literature that it is easy to imagine a situation in which the Justice Minister's supervision over the courts comes dangerously close to indirect influence on the merits of the dispensation of justice. These rights vested in the Justice Minister do not arise out of the Constitution, and as competencies of the executive branch affecting the judicial branch, they represent a major departure from the constitutional principles'. Dąbrowski (2009), p. 411.

judiciary to function in 'old' democracies to legitimize the activities aimed at politicizing the judiciary. To do so, they tend to refer to Western models viewed, of course, only formally, without looking at the current standards of the legal and political cultures in this respect. That is why I am of the opinion that a more formal approach should be implemented in both old and new democracies.

On the matter of court administration in its strict sense, one can distinguish three main models, which have their own subtypes.[16]

From the general theoretical point of view, the so-called executive model includes a wide amalgamate of systemic and internally heterogeneous solutions. This model was developed is the oldest one and, as such, it is still widely used worldwide, with some modifications. At the entity level, the court administration competencies may be delegated to a minister, responsible employees of a ministry's department or a government agency subordinate to, and supervised by, the government or the minister. Sometimes, the structure of a special agency and its relationship with the ministry may be of such a character that one may have some doubts as to whether it still adheres to an executive model.[17]

At the same time, the so-called partner model of court administration assumes that administrative activities are performed by entities that are independent of the government, but may constitute either a part of the state administration or have a hybrid nature—which is generally difficult to classify from the point of view of the principle of separation of powers. In this approach, there can also be an agency that is separated from the Department of Justice, but is formally subordinated to a respective minister; its competencies can include widely understood administrative matters, such as the establishment of a budget for the judiciary. In the partnership model, the detailed scope of delegated tasks, as well as organizational issues, may be the subject of bilateral arrangements between the executive and representatives of the judiciary in the form of frameworks documents.[18] Thus, the systemic status of a unit responsible for court administration may vary and fluctuate from a very close

---

[16]This is only a proposal. One can find other systematizations in the literature. In this paper, I accept the scheme included in Fox et al. (2017), p. 187 ff.

[17]Confront, for instance, the systemic position of the Swedish National Court Administration (*Domstolsverket*). See 'The Swedish Judicial System', Regeringskansliet, June 2015, pp. 5, 21 (http://www.government.se/49ec0b/contentassets/9ebb0750780245aeb6d5c13c1ff5cf64/the-swedish-judicial-system.pdf).

[18]An example of this is Her Majesty's Courts and Tribunal Service in England and Wales. It is financed by a part of the budget allocated to the Department of Justice. According to the framework document, the Lord Chancellor is obliged to make every effort to reach an agreement with the Lord Chief Justice on the financing of the Service. The framework agreement clearly states that neither the Lord Chancellor nor the Lord Chief Justice may interfere directly or indirectly with the day-to-day work of the Service. The Scottish Courts Service, however, is an office that is not included within the structure of the department, nor is it an agency subordinated to the Scottish executive. It is currently (since 2010) independent, although it remains within the structure of the state administration; therefore, it forms a part of the Scottish executive. In the latter case, the partnership model is subject to particular modification, moving towards independent, but extra-judicial, court administration.

relationship with the Department of Justice to a quasi-independent agency, but not, at least directly, subordinated to the judicial power.[19]

In turn, the third model can assign the competency to manage and administer courts (court business), in a general theoretical sense, directly to the judiciary, given the following:

1) Administrative activities may be carried out by individual courts on their own behalf or by offices attached to them; this solution is used at the level of the highest judicial bodies.
2) Administrative activities may be carried out and supervised by a separate office connected only to the judiciary.[20]

In this second type, it should be emphasized that a characteristic feature is that members of this office (entity) are, in principle, exclusively judges selected with a normatively specified parity.[21] An important role in the model of autonomous court administration by the judiciary is played by the legal status of administrative employees, including officials of the court staff, such as clerks. The method of their selection (recruitment) and the material content of the employment relationship are determined without taking into account the requirements typical of the civil service.[22] Judicial officials are deemed to be officers and employees of the judicial branch.[23] A normative expression of this trend may be the adoption of a separate act

---

[19]As an example of the latter, one may point to the Irish Court Service, which is a separate institution whose board is composed mainly of judicial members; however, it remains responsible before the Minister of Justice.

[20]In this case, this unit should depend on the judiciary's power, subject to specific mechanisms. For instance, the head and members of the board of such institution might be appointed by bodies of judicial self-government or by a judicial council. The creation of a separate unit is preferable from an efficiency perspective in the case of lower courts, due to their dispersion.

[21]Fox et al. (2017), p. 195 ff. The United States offers an example of a country with an autonomous model. The administrative activity of courts is carried out and supervised by a separate office connected only to the judiciary. In federal courts, the Administrative Office of the U.S. Courts is such an entity. The office is headed by a director, who is responsible for the supervision of all administrative matters relating to the clerical staff of the federal courts. The director is appointed and dismissed by the Chief Justice after obtaining the opinion of the Judicial Conference of the United States. This is an annual meeting convened by the Chief Justice and attended by, among others, chief judges of all judicial circuits. The Conference is the body that oversees the activities of the Office and determines the policy relating to the administration of the federal courts. The task of the Conference in this respect is primarily to review and analyse the work of courts and prepare recommendations for them, aimed at harmonizing the procedures and effectiveness of proceedings. The Conference is also obliged to carry out studies on currently binding court procedures. The Administrative Office is responsible for the integrated court management and financial planning system.

[22]Fox et al. (2017), p. 199.

[23]See e.g. § 332 Section (f.4) of 28 U.S. Code circuit executive; § 332 Section (h.4) of 28 U.S. Code circuit executive and court staff within the United States Court of Appeal for The Federal Circuit; § 601 of 28 U.S. Code Director and Deputy Director of Administrative Office.

on the staff of the agency subordinated to, and supervised by, the central judicial authority.[24]

Obviously, an organ responsible for court administration is subordinated to the judicial power, but it must cooperate with other state authorities belonging to different branches of government.[25] These relationships can take various forms, such as the provision of current information[26] and cooperation in preparing and implementing the budget. The budget and funds allocated for the judiciary are also subject to approval in the legislative process of the parliament.

Each of the analysed models has various advantages and disadvantages.[27] As far as the executive model is concerned, it can be argued that the executive—being the one responsible for the administrative functioning of the state and for the implementation of financial policy—should also be able to have a real impact on courts as organizational units. However, the principle of separation of powers and the independence of the judiciary seem to be most important and should prevail in this case. This is what leads me to question this model. First and foremost, there are no clear guidelines for the separation of the jurisdictional and administrative spheres of the activities of courts. The partnership model seems to offer an interesting solution, but the participation of judges, or even their representatives, in the process of bargaining and making mutual concessions with the executive may hamper the authority of courts and may prove inefficient. Even the establishment of an independent agency is not always an optimal solution due to the unauthorized interference of a partner with its composition and directions of action. It seems that the judicial autonomous model raises the fewest doubts.

The advantage of the judicial autonomous model over the others can be justified as follows. First, this model is most in line with the principle of the independence of the judiciary in the organizational sense; it protects young democracies, in particular, from attempts to undermine the independence of the judiciary by taking measures which may, at least indirectly, affect the sphere of jurisdiction. Second, the judicial autonomous model is universal in nature, as it is independent of the solutions adopted for the appointment of judges, promotions, etc.[28] Even if we were to consider it desirable for the judiciary and the other two powers to have close relations in this respect (by referring to the need to ensure 'democratic legitimacy' or 'accountability of judges'), there is no excuse for depriving the judiciary of its autonomy in the field of administrative matters. After all, it would be just as absurd, even under the conditions of the parliamentary system, for parliament to interfere

---

[24]Fox et al. (2017), p. 200.

[25]Fox et al. (2017), p. 198.

[26]This includes annual reports addressed to Congress by a Chief Justice on the proceedings of Judicial Council of United States (§ 331 of U.S. 28 Code); copies of annual report of the activities of the Administrative Office and state of business of court are submitted to Congress and Attorney General (§ 604 Section (4) of U.S. 28 Code).

[27]Fox et al. (2017), p. 98.

[28]Confront Kosař (2018).

with the current administrative activities of the government by, for example, laying down its rules of procedure or making decisions on current expenses, orders and other activities of the office providing services to ministers. Third, the judicial autonomous model does not preclude the introduction of appropriate auditing elements for courts' administrative activity, such as for the necessary maintenance of the discipline of public finances or compliance with other criteria, like reliability and economic efficiency. Relevant institutions, such as audit chambers and auditor courts, may fulfil the competencies in this respect.

References

Bałaban, A. (2015). Konstytucyjne przesłanki niedopuszczalności nadzoru administracyjnego Ministra Sprawiedliwości nad sądownictwem (Tezy). In P. Ziętarski (Ed.), *Model nadzoru nad działalnością sądów i pracą orzeczniczą sędziów* (pp. 47–59). Warszawa: Kancelaria Senatu.

Bobek, M. (2010). The administration of courts in the Czech Republic – In search of a constitutional balance. *European Public Law, 16*(2), 251–270.

Bobek, M., & Kosař, D. (2014). Global solutions, local damages: A critical study in judiciary councils in Central and Eastern Europe. *German Law Journal, 15*(7), 1257–1292.

Dąbrowski, S. (2009). The boundaries of permissible interference in the judicial branch by the executive and legislative branches. In T. Wardyński & M. Niziołek (Eds.), *Independence of the judiciary and legal profession as foundations of the rule of law. Contemporary challenges.* Warsaw: LexisNexis.

Fox, N., Firlus, J., & Mikuli, P. (2017). Models of court administration: An attempt at comparative review. In P. Mikuli (Ed.), *Current challenges in court administration* (pp. 187–200). The Hague: Eleven International Publishing.

Garoupa, N., & Ginsburg, T. (2008). Guarding the guardians: Judicial councils and judicial independence. *John M. Olin Program in Law and Economics Working Paper* No. 444. Retrieved April 8, 2019, from https://chicagounbound.uchicago.edu/cgi/viewcontent.cgi?referer=https://www.google.pl/&httpsredir=1&article=1221&context=law_and_economics

Gee, G., Hazell, R., Malleson, K., & O'Brien, P. (2015). *The politics of judicial independence in the UK's changing constitution.* Cambridge: Cambridge University Press.

Kosař, D. (2016). *Perils of judicial self-government in transitional societies.* Cambridge: Cambridge University Press.

Kosař, D. (2018). Beyond judicial councils - Forms, rationales and impact of judicial self-governance in Europe. *German Law Journal, 19*(7), 1567–1612.

Mikuli, P. (2017a). Developments in courts administrations – Prologue. In P. Mikuli (Ed.), *Current challenges in court administration* (pp. 1–7). The Hague: Eleven International Publishing.

Mikuli, P. (2017b). Tug of war between the judiciary and the minister of justice: On court administration in Poland. In P. Mikuli (Ed.), *Current challenges in court administration* (pp. 167–186). The Hague: Eleven International Publishing.

Mikuli, P. (2017c). An explicit constitutional change by means of an ordinary statute? On a bill concerning the reform of the national council of the judiciary in Poland, *International Journal of Constitutional Law* Blog. Retrieved April 8, 2019, from http://www.iconnectblog.com/2017/02/an-explicit-constitutional-change-by-means-of-an-ordinary-statute-on-a-bill-concerning-the-reform-of-the-national-council-of-the-judiciary-in-poland/

Mikuli, P., Fox, N., & Puchta, R. (2019). *Ministers of justice in comparative perspective.* The Hague: Eleven International Publishing.

Sadurski, W. (2018). *Bad response to a tragic choice: The case of Polish Council of the Judiciary, VerfBlog*. Retrieved April 8, 2019, from https://verfassungsblog.de/bad-response-to-a-tragic-choice-the-case-of-polish-council-of-the-judiciary/

Selejan Gutan, B. (2018). Romania: Perils of a "Perfect Euro-Model" of judicial council. *German Law Journal, 19*(7), 1709–1740.

Smith, B. C. (2017). *Judges and democratization. Judicial independence in new democracies*. London: Routledge.

How 'Liberal' Democracies Attack(ed) Judicial Independence: An Anecdote from De Gaulle's France

Mathias Möschel

Contents

1 Introduction

It is no secret that former President Charles De Gaulle's sympathy for judges—and arguably for law and lawyers more broadly—was rather limited. Statements such as "[i]n France the only Supreme Court is the people"[1] or "[r]emember the following: there is first France, then the State and then, as long as these two other major interests are guaranteed, the law"[2] have been attributed to him. While similar proclamations in any national context might raise some eyebrows, they are more problematic in a country that has been historically rather diffident towards judges and where the

---

Mathias Möschel is Associate Professor at Central European University. The author wishes to thank Elsa Bourdier for helping locate precise references to newspapers of the time of the events. Any errors and omissions are the author's alone.

[1] *"En France, la cour suprême, c'est le peuple"*. De Gaulle made this statement supposedly in conjunction with the ratification of the European Convention on Human Rights, which he opposed and it is referred to in various places. See e.g.: Favoreu (1992), p. 500.

[2] *"Souvenez-vous de ceci: il y a d'abord la France, ensuite l'Etat, enfin, autant que les intérêts majeurs des deux sont sauvegardés, le droit."* This citation is mentioned in: Foyer (2006), p. 7.

M. Möschel (✉)
Central European University, Legal Studies Department, Budapest, Hungary
e-mail: moschelm@ceu.edu

P. Pinto de Albuquerque, K. Wojtyczek (eds.), *Judicial Power in a Globalized World*, https://doi.org/10.1007/978-3-030-20744-1_19

"government by judges" (*le gouvernement des juges*)[3] functions as a sort of scare-crow seen as either bringing France back to the arbitrariness of courts under *Ancien Régime* or as importing American judicial problems.[4] Given such an unfavourable context to an independent and strong judiciary, it comes as little surprise that "De Gaulle's" Constitution of the Vth Republic—which is still France's constitution today (hereinafter the 1958 Constitution)—had extremely limited constitutionality control of legislation[5] and did not intend to fully consider the judiciary amongst the actual powers of the State, only referring to it as "judicial authority".[6] Another reason for this choice seems to be that judges are not elected and therefore cannot be considered a state power but only an authority.[7]

Beyond these rather well-known aspects of De Gaulle's attitudes towards law and courts, what is possibly less known, today, is that these statements did not remain simply verbal or at constitutional design level but translated into concrete attempts and instances of bridling judicial independence. This contribution intends to focus on one such instance which uncannily resembles some of the techniques used in contemporary Europe, but I will come back on this point *infra*.

2 Judicial Independence in the 1960s

The broader context within which this anecdote took place is related to the independence of Algeria and the creation of a secret organization in February 1961, called *Organisation de l'Armée Secrète* (OAS). This organization was composed of a number of army members: generals (e.g. Raoul Salan, Maurice Challe, André Zeller, Edmond Jouhaud), officers and normal soldiers (e.g. André Canal), but also civilians (e.g.: Yves Godard, Pierre Lagaillarde, Jean-Jacques Susini) who opposed the independence of Algeria and the end of the French presence there. The OAS was formed when it became clear that De Gaulle had changed his opinion concerning the future of Algeria by calling for a referendum on Algeria's independence which

---

[3]See on this expression: Lambert (2005).

[4]On this observation see: Chapsal (1984), p. 133. At the time, the critique was about the American Supreme Court's *laissez-faire* liberalism which served to strike down a whole set of labour law protective statutes.

[5]In its initial version, Article 61 of the Constitution only allowed the President, the Prime Minister and the presidents of the two parliamentary houses to raise the issue of constitutionality of legislation and such a control could only take place before legislation entered into force. These criteria were later broadened by amending the French Constitution. Moreover, starting from its famous Freedom of association decision (Decision no. 71-44 DC of 16 July 1971) the Constitutional Council, France's constitutional court, extended its review to assess legislation also against fundamental rights and principles.

[6]See Title VIII of the 1958 Constitution, entitled "*De l'autorité judiciaire*". On this understanding of the judiciary not as a power but as an authority, see: Costa (1960), p. 261.

[7]See on this point, Foyer (2006), p. 66.

eventually took place on 5 July 1962. The OAS organized a series of terroristic attacks and murders, including an attempted *coup d'état* in April 1961, and two assassination attempts on President De Gaulle in September 1961 and August 1962.

As a reaction to some of these events, De Gaulle used his emergency powers under Article 16 of the Constitution to create a series of exceptional tribunals that had to try some of the members of the OAS who had been caught.[8] One of these tribunals was the High Military Tribunal (*haut tribunal militaire*) charged to deal with the high level officials. A Special Military Tribunal (*tribunal militaire spécial*) was in charge of dealing with the lower ranking ones. The High Military Tribunal was then abolished by De Gaulle in May 1962 after it had essentially not convicted General Salan to death. The details relating to this trial will be discussed more in detail here below. The High Military Tribunal was then substituted by the Military Court of Justice (*Cour militaire de justice*). Its creation was instead annulled by the French Supreme Administrative Court (the *Conseil d'Etat*, hereinafter CdE) in the famous *Canal* judgment of October 1962[9] for having been adopted *ultra vires* by De Gaulle. The General had disliked this decision so much that he immediately set out to create a commission to reform and to reign in the CdE.[10] The reform failed or simply petered out and still today serves as an example to show the independence of the CdE from the Executive but also of how the anecdote told here below was not the only attempt for De Gaulle to influence the independence of the judiciary.[11]

An important aspect for the purpose of this short narrative is that the hearings of the High Military Tribunal were taking place on the premises of the Paris Palace of Justice, where the Court of Appeals and also the French Supreme Court (*Cour de cassation*) are located. This had also been the practice for earlier exceptional tribunals, such as the High Court of Justice (*Haute-Cour de Justice*) which had been created to deal with crimes committed by certain personalities during the Vichy Regime from 1940 to 1944. Some of its most important hearings, such as those concerning the Admiral Esteva and the Maréchal Pétain, had taken place in the Palace of Justice.[12] Locating the hearings of the High Court of Justice within the

---

[8]For a critical assessment of this French "tradition" of exceptional tribunals, see: Jaffré (1962), pp. 229–337.

[9]CdE, *Canal, Robin et Godot*, 19 October 1962, *Rec. Lebon*, p. 552.

[10]In approving ways on this judgment and on the failed reform, see: Mitterrand (2010), pp. 139–143. Very critically instead: Foyer (2006), pp. 238–241.

[11]Arguably, for the French understanding and history of the judiciary, the administrative court system is not conceived of being part of that state power. This can be seen from the 1958 Constitution itself, where the administrative court system is not mentioned under Title VIII on judicial authority, leaving the CdE almost unmentioned in the 1958 Constitution. But from the human rights logic and the perspective of the European Court of Human Rights the CdE certainly is deemed to be part of the judiciary, despite the finding of some minor procedural issues tainting its functioning under Article 6 (right to a fair trial). See the famous judgment: *Kress v. France*, no. 39594/98, 7 June 2001.

[12]*Id.*, pp. 101 and 105.

courts instead of in the political space of *Palais Bourbon*[13] had been a conscious choice by De Gaulle. In his own words he "was particularly careful not to influence the prosecution, the investigation and the judgments" and in order to ensure that "the discussions [would be] undisturbed by manifestations or movements to those present [he] refused to let the High Court sit in the hall of the Palais Bourbon – as many had insisted – installing it instead in the Palais de Justice and assuring it the security of a considerable police guard".[14]

2.1 The Anecdote

Unsurprisingly, the High Military Court followed this practice and it was precisely around this issue of security police relating to another high profile trial before this exceptional tribunal that the events at the basis of this contribution unfolded.[15] In fact, end of April 1962 General Raoul Salan had been "caught" in Alger and had been brought before the High Military Court where his trial started on 15 May 1962.

For that highly publicized event, the Justice Minister feared demonstrations in favour of the accused and therefore ordered the police forces to heavily control or even block access to the Palace of Justice. This led to long queues and some (physical) altercations between the police forces and the court employees (judges, lawyers etc.) trying to enter the building. Some of them went to a nearby café from where they called Marcel Rousselet, the First President (*Premier Président*) of the Paris Court of Appeals, to inform them of this situation. Thereupon, Rousselet immediately left a solemn audience over which he was presiding to protest in public against this interference of the (executive) forces of order with the judges. The image of a judge fully dressed in his official red robe with an ermine collar and the brooch of the Legion of Honor on his chest, loudly protesting on the stairs of the Palace of Justice left its mark (see the picture here below).

---

[13]Palais Bourbon is the name attributed to the building of the National Assembly. It should be mentioned that something that had been called *Haute-Cour* already existed under France's Third Republic and it dealt with acts of treason by Ministers and the Senators were the judges of this political court. However, given that the Senate had disappeared and that under the Vichy Regime many Senators had voted in favour of Maréchal Pétain, it was difficult to use this institution to judge collaborators of the Vichy Regime. *Id.*, pp. 91–92.

[14]De Gaulle (1967), p. 793.

[15]The main elements of the story are taken from descriptions published in Jaffré (1962), p. 290 and Monnerville (2003), pp. 211–212.

Marcel Rousselet on the stairs of the Palais de Justice. *Photo Credit: Agence Diffusion Presse (A.D. P.—20 September 1962)*

After the incident, Rousselet received a letter from the prefect (*préfet*)[16] whose tone he deemed unacceptable. He asked the Justice Minister, Jean Foyer, to discuss the issue with the Interior Minister who in turn should have talked to the prefect about this; to no avail. As a consequence, Rousselet refused to appear at any audience until the end of the judicial year.

One may wonder: why such a fuss over something that seems to be a detail? The reason for Rousselet's protest is that normally security of the Palace of Justice is ensured by special *judicial* forces under the orders of the First President of the Paris Court of Appeals and not by *executive* forces of order. The sending of police to the Palace of Justice was seen both as an infringement of the specific powers of the First President and also as an infringement of the broader principle of separation of powers.

However—and now comes the truly problematic point—De Gaulle had not appreciated Rousselet's public and dramatic "intervention". Less than two months after the event, the government issued a regulation (*ordonnance*) which dealt with judges in Algeria and the provisional retirement age of judges.[17] While predominantly dealing with the situation of judges in Algeria and what would happen with

---

[16]This is essentially representative of the central government and the chief administrator at the local level.

[17]Ordonnance no. 62-780 du 12 juillet 1962 relative à la situation des magistrats en service en Algérie et à la limite d'âge provisoire des magistrats.

them after Algeria's independence, the regulation also specified that "in order to take into account the return to the French mainland of judges who had previously been working in Algeria [. . .], the retirement age of ordinary judges is fixed at 67 years of age".[18]

That this otherwise anodyne provision applied almost exclusively to Rousselet becomes clear when considering the other provisions of this regulation. On the one hand, it explicitly excluded judges from the French Supreme Court, of which he was not a judge.[19] On the other hand, the retirement age was to be introduced progressively, meaning that from 15 September 1962 only those judges who were 18 months older than 67 had to retire and from 15 September 1963 everyone above 67.[20] Being born on 6 December 1893, 'coincidentally' Rousselet fell into the first group, meaning that he had to retire only two months later. Hence, behind the issuance of seemingly neutral rules (retirement age of judges) with an objective justification (the return of judges from Algeria for whom places needed to be created), an uncomfortable judge could be set aside by the Executive. Ironically, another provision of the regulation then provided that a decree would determine the conditions at which the retirement age would return progressively to its initial levels, i.e. once it had obtained its stated (and not-so-stated) goals.

2.2 The Reactions to the 'Forced Retirement'

There are a number of interesting observations that can be made from this story. The newspapers of the time did not really go into any detailed analysis around this forced retirement and what it meant for judicial independence. A first article in *Le Monde* simply refers to the instrument at the time it was adopted.[21] A second article in that same journal later mentions that Rousselet was allowed to claim his retirement (*faire valoir sa retraite*) on 15 September 1962,[22] thus seemingly giving the impression of a voluntary departure. *Le Figaro* instead was a little more open about what really happened by describing the story as follows:

> [W]ith great sadness, we have seen Mr. Marcel Rousselet departing. He was at the same time a great judge, a man of letters and a scrupulous historian. His smiling friendliness combined with an extreme sensitivity had always opened all hearts to him, which is why the opening ceremony of the new judicial year yesterday in which he did not take part anymore – because he had been incited to retire - left a melancholy mark on this first event of the judicial year 1962-1963.[23]

---

[18]*Id.* art. 16.

[19]*Id.* art. 16.

[20]*Id.* art. 17. Quite generously the regulation specified that for these judges the pension would be calculated as if they had reached 70 years of age (*Id.* art. 18).

[21]La limite d'âge des magistrats est ramenée à 67 ans, *Le Monde*, 14 July 1962, p. 8.

[22]See: M. Marcel Rousselet devient le premier Président honoraire de la Cour de Paris, *Le Monde*, 9–10 September 1962, p. 12.

[23]Bochin (1962), p. 14; also cited in Jaffré (1962), p. 290, note 1.

The event was (also) little commented upon or noted in academic literature. For instance, in a large book on the history of justice in France which runs over 1244 pages, this remarkable event is mentioned only twice *en passant*.[24] Another passing reference to this story in an academic journal was published at the occasion of Marc Rousselet's death.[25]

Most publications where this story is mentioned in more detail are rather non-academic essays that describe or critique how France's Presidents have, *inter alia*, perceived and treated justice and courts. Here we could subdivide the publications into two groups.

The first one directly critiques—or defends—De Gaulle's actions and conception of the State and of justice more broadly.[26] Amongst the critics, the story is mentioned as one of the examples showing how De Gaulle undermined France's rule of law in various ways. What is fascinating is that amongst the most fervent critics one finds two very prominent political figures: François Mitterrand, France's later President, and Gaston Monnerville, France's Senate President, the second-highest institution in France, from 1946 to 1968. The former mentions the event in quite some detail in his (in)famous work *"Le coup d'état permanent"* which constituted a sort of opening of his political campaign against De Gaulle in 1964.[27] The latter, instead tells the story in his autobiography, in which he (also) offers a scathing critique of how De Gaulle (regularly) undermined the Constitution and constitutional safeguards during the time period of his Presidency.[28]

At the same time, De Gaulle's former Justice Minister during that time, Jean Foyer, tells a rather different story in defense of the President and, accessorily, of himself.[29] In his version, Rousselet was indeed in charge of the security forces for the Palace of Justice, but had delegated those powers to a colleague who had coordinated the security measures around this specific trial with the prefect. Around 1 PM a lawyer, Maurice Garçon, who was also member of the famous *Académie française*, tried to enter the premises but was asked to identify himself. Outraged that as a famous *académicien* he would have to follow such instructions he called Rousselet from a nearby café. Rousselet then showed up on the stairs of the Palace of Justice as already described, allegedly less out of institutional motivations as for personal reasons: having written an important book on the history of the judiciary in

---

[24]Royer et al. (2016), pp. 1118 and 1124.

[25]Nécrologie: le Premier Président Marcel Rousselet (1984) *Revue internationale de droit comparé*, *36*, 161–162.

[26]See in this group the already mentioned work by Jaffré (1962), p. 290 but also the book by Besson (1973), p. 354, fn. 1. The interesting thing about this author was that Besson had been named General Prosecutor of the Paris Court of Appeals (1949), of the French Supreme Court (1951) and later of the High Military Tribunal (1961), one of those exceptional jurisdictions mentioned above. In 1962, he was "relegated" to a post as governmental counsellor of judicial affairs which he held for a few weeks only. See on this: Royer et al. (2016), p. 1124.

[27]Mitterrand (2010), pp. 216–218.

[28]Monnerville (n. 15).

[29]The details of this version can be found in: Foyer (2006), pp. 222–224.

France,[30] he was hoping to also become a member of the *Académie française* and Garçon was supposed to support this endeavour. Moreover, Foyer explains the continuation of Rousselet's indignation and the request of excuses from the prefect to his being associated to the political camp of François Mitterrand via his son, who was working closely in the former's cabinet. As to the accusation that after this event the retirement age of judges was lowered in order to get rid of Rousselet, Foyer also finds this caused by political instrumentalization and laconically states that "[o]ne attributes to others those bad actions that could have been taken by oneself" and that "the accusation was grotesque".[31]

A second group amongst the critical accounts in non-academic essays is of a later stage and actually relays the story with regard to the change of heart and attitude of François Mitterrand when he became France's President himself in 1981. Indeed, these critiques are mostly based on the fact that in 1964 he had still highlighted the permanent *coup d'état* by De Gaulle. However, once Mitterrand came to power almost twenty years later, he did not follow what he had preached in the past[32] and actually did not take judicial independence seriously either, as demonstrated by the infamous *Broglie* trial during which he had tried to force the resignation of the judge presiding the trial.[33]

3 Lessons for Today?

Apart from a brief analysis of the publications that commented or described the anecdote at the time, what is also interesting to see how it uncannily resembles contemporary events and developments, especially in Hungary and Poland. Generally we have come to refer to such developments as the rise of "illiberal democracy",[34] "abusive constitutionalism",[35] "populist constitutions"[36] or some combination of these or similar expressions. One of the key instruments in such regimes—whatever name is given to them—is the use of unconstitutional constitutional amendments.[37] De Gaulle's controversial use of Article 11 instead of Article 89 to amend the French Constitution in 1962 so as to introduce a President directly elected by the people is a textbook example for such an amendment.

Another easy and beloved target for illiberal or populist regimes are judges and judicial independence. And here we have seen in more recent years subtler

---

[30]Rousselet (1957).

[31]*Id.*, p. 224.

[32]See e.g.: Jamet (1984), pp. 124–125 and Coignard and Lacan (1989), p. 95.

[33]Coignard and Lacan (n. 32), *ibid.*

[34]Arguably the term has been coined in 1997 (Zakaria 1997, p. 22) but has since then been popularized by Hungary's Prime Minister, Viktor Orbán.

[35]Landau (2013), p. 189.

[36]Landau (2018), p. 521.

[37]See most recently on such amendments: Roznai (2017).

techniques emerge in order to control 'unruly' judges, namely via the reduction of the retirement age of judges. Hungary and Poland have been most famous for doing so.[38] However, as the described events and reaction demonstrate, De Gaulle had already 'invented' it more than half a century ago. In other words, one could say that Hungary and Poland have 'simply plagiarized' some of De Gaulle's arsenal of 'illiberal' tools in France.

This contribution intends to shed a little more light on this somewhat forgotten story by linking it to similar attacks on judicial independence today. I am aware that there are some contextual differences between then and now, i.e. France at that time was struggling with a war-like situation which is not the case in contemporary Hungary and Poland. Nevertheless, this anecdote highlights that attacks on judicial independence also took place—and do take place—in more established liberal democracies in ways that uncannily resemble what happens nowadays in other geographical realities. Indeed, threats to rule of law and constitutionalism are not limited to illiberal democracies but are probably part and parcel of liberal ones. On the one hand, this may mean that we need to unearth similar stories from the books of history or archives so as not to forget them. On the other hand, it also demonstrates that we need to remain vigilant not only in illiberal/young democracies but also in more established ones.

References

Besson, A. (1973). *Le mythe de la justice*. Paris: PLON.
Bochin, R. (1962, September 18). Séance solennelle de rentrée à la cour d'Appel de Paris, *Le Figaro*, p. 14.
Chapsal, J. (1984). *La vie politique sous la Ve République* (2nd ed.). Paris: PUF.
Coignard, S., & Lacan, J.-F. (1989). *La République bananière*. Paris: Belfond.
Costa, J. L. (1960). Nécessité, conditions et limites d'un pouvoir judiciaire en France. *Revue française de science politique, 10*, 261.
De Gaulle, C. (1967, translation). *The complete war memoirs of Charles De Gaulle*. New York: Simon and Schuster.
Favoreu, L. (1992). De Gaulle et le Conseil constitutionnel. In *De Gaulle en son siècle, Tome 2 : La République*. Paris: Plon.
Foyer, J. (2006). *Sur les chemins du droit avec le Général : mémoires de ma vie politique, 1944–1988*. Paris: Fayard.
Halmai, G. (2017). The early retirement age of the Hungarian judges. In F. Nicola & B. Davies (Eds.), *EU law stories. Contextual and critical histories of European jurisprudence* (pp. 471–488). Cambridge: Cambridge University Press.
Jaffré, Y.-F. (1962). *Les Tribunaux d'exception. 1940–1962*. Paris: Nouvelles Editions Latines.
Jamet, D. (1984). *A chacun son coup d'état*. Paris: Editions du Quotidien.

---

[38]The literature on this and the various constitutional law and European Union Law implications is quite vast. For the sake of brevity on the situation in Hungary, see: Halmai (2017), pp. 471–488; on the situation in Poland, see: Sadurski (2018); on the broader situation also with regard to the (non-) reaction by European institutions, see: Kovács and Scheppele (2018), p. 189.

Kovács, K., & Scheppele, K. L. (2018). The fragility of an independent judiciary: Lessons from Hungary and Poland - and the European Union. *Communist and Post-Communist Studies, 51,* 189.

Lambert, E. (2005 [1921]). *Le gouvernement des juges*. Paris: Dalloz.

Landau, D. (2013). Abusive constitutionalism. *UC Davis Law Review, 47,* 189.

Landau, D. (2018). Populist constitutions. *The University of Chicago Law Review, 85,* 521.

Mitterrand, F. (2010 [1964]). *Le coup d'état permanent*. Paris: Les Belles Lettres.

Monnerville, G. (2003 [1980]). *Vingt-deux ans de présidence*. Paris: le cherche midi.

Rousselet, M. (1957). *Histoire de la magistrature francaise: de origines a nos jours*. Paris: PLON.

Royer, J.-P. , Jean, J.-P., Durand, B., Derasse N., & Dubois, B. (2016). *Histoire de la justice en France du XVIIIe siècle à nos jours* (5th ed.). Paris: PUF.

Roznai, Y. (2017). *Unconstitutional constitutional amendments: The limits of amendment powers*. Oxford: OUP.

Sadurski, W. (2018). Polish Chief Justice of the Supreme Court Under Pressure: What Now?, *Verfassungsblog*. https://doi.org/10.17176/20180705-161545-0

Zakaria, F. (1997). The rise of illiberal democracy. *Foreign Affairs, 76,* 22.

Powers Conferred Upon the EU and the Powers of the Court of Justice: The Protection Afforded to Same-Sex Couples in a Stable Relationship

Barbara de Mozzi

Contents

1   The Case Law of the European Court of Human Rights on the Protection of Same-Sex Couples' Rights

It is proposed to analyse how the powers conferred upon the EU condition the powers of the Court of Justice in applying the EU Charter of Fundamental Rights, especially in comparison with the ECHR's jurisdictionary remit. The occasion for this appraisal is the analysis of the case law on the protection of the rights of same-sex couples of, respectively, the Court of Justice and the European Court for Human Rights.

The European Court of Human Rights' position on the need for a juridical recognition and protection of same-sex couples is well known, especially in the light of articles 8 and 14 of the ECHR. The question of how to reconcile the non-recognition of same-sex marriages—namely the absence of any legal protection

Barbara de Mozzi is Associate Professor at University of Padova.

B. de Mozzi (✉)
Faculty of Law, Padua University, Padova, Italy
e-mail: barbara.demozzi@unipd.it

© Springer Nature Switzerland AG 2019   301
P. Pinto de Albuquerque, K. Wojtyczek (eds.), *Judicial Power in a Globalized World*, https://doi.org/10.1007/978-3-030-20744-1_20

(in some states) for them—with the European Convention on Human Rights has on many occasions been referred to the European Court for Human Rights, with particular reference to articles 12 ("Right to Marry"), 14 ("Prohibition of Discrimination") and 8 ("Right to Respect for Private and Family Life"). The Court has, on the one hand, ruled that same-sex couples are in need of legal recognition and their relationship protected, although leaving to the national laws of the contracting states the choice of whether or not to extent the institution of marriage to same-sex couples (article 12 of the European Convention on Human Rights and article 9 of the EU Charter of Fundamental Rights) (Schalk and Kopf, v. Austria).[1]

While article 12 of the European Convention on Human Rights expressly refers to a marriage between man and woman, the Court observed that major social changes have taken place in the institution of marriage since the adoption of the Convention, especially since article 9 of the EU Charter of Fundamental Rights that guarantees the right to marry and establish a family, without any reference to the partners' sex (but "in accordance with the national laws governing the exercise of these rights").[2]

On the other hand, the Court recognised that a state failing to fulfil its obligation to guarantee a legal framework able to provide same-sex unions adequate protection infringes article 8 of the European Convention on Human Rights (Oliari and others v. Italy), but without prejudice to the state's discretion on how such civil partnerships should be regulated.[3]

The European Court of Human Rights recently acknowledged that the Italian State's non-recognition that the homosexual partner of an Italian citizen was entitled to a residence permit on family grounds (Taddeucci and McCall v. Italy)[4] violated articles 8 and 14 of the European Convention on Human Rights.[5]

These principles were recently reaffirmed in the Orlandi and others v. Italy judgement,[6] regarding the non-recognition of the legal effects of same-sex marriages contracted abroad.

The legal effects of same-sex marriages contracted abroad by Italian citizens are governed by legislative decree 7/2017, which amended legislative decree No. 218/95, by introducing the provision that such marriages have the legal effects of a registered civil union. The Orlandi judgement, as well as others against Italy,

---

[1]ECtHR, 24th June 2010, Schalk and Kopf v. Austria. See also Scherpe (2013), p. 83.

[2]See also ECtHR, 15th March 2012, Gas and Dubois v. France; ECtHR, 16th July 2014, Hamalainen v. Finland; ECtHR 9th June 2016, Chapin and Charpentier v. France.

[3]ECtHR, 21th July 2015, Oliari and others v. Italy. See also ECtHR 7th November 2013, Vallianatos and others v. Greece; Ragone and Volpe (2016), p. 451.

[4]EChHR. 30th june 2016, Taddeucci and McCall v. Italy.

[5]EChHR 23rd February 2016, Pajic v. Croatia. "Although Article 8 does not include a right to settle in a particular country or a right to obtain a residence permit, the State must nevertheless exercise its immigration policies in a manner which is compatible with a foreign national's human rights, in particular the right to respect for his or her private or family life and the right not to be subject to discrimination". See also Alpa (2016), p. 108; Persano (2016), p. 11; Sperti (2016), p. 2336.

[6]ECtHR, 14th December 2017, Orlandi and others v. Italy.

ruled that the Italian State violated article 8 of the European Convention on Human Rights on the Right to Respect for Private and Family Life. The Italian State, in this case, failed to afford any form of protection—prior to legislative decrees 76/2016 and 7/2017—to the plaintiffs' union, a same-sex marriage contracted abroad, because it neglected to register the union either as a marriage or a civil union. The Italian State was, consequently, ordered to make "just satisfaction" in respect of non-pecuniary damage to the injured party.[7]

These judgements accept the idea—which transpires from numerous other rulings by the European Court of Human Rights—that article 8 of the Convention is not limited to just imposing negative obligations upon Member States. In fact, article 8 imposes positive obligations upon the competent authorities which—respecting the margins of appreciation reserved to the States—are required, by striking a balance between individual and societal interests, to put in place the measures necessary to protect the development of affective relationships.

Naturally, failure to respect human rights by a Member State can be challenged before the ECtHR regardless of the sphere of action where the violation purported took place.

Various European institutions and the Council of Europe have also suggested that Member States take due account of the variety of family models and guarantee that same-sex unions should be able to enjoy the same rights and advantages of a marriage by allowing same-sex couples to register such unions.

2 The Court of Justice's Position

The Court of Justice appears to have adopted a more cautious approach.

It is recognised that the Court of Justice has hitherto only dealt with the protection of same-sex couples in anti-discriminatory terms. Thus there are situations in which member states—while having regulated same-sex unions so as to make the condition of a partner in a same-sex civil union "comparable" to that of a spouse—had, unreasonably, excluded the former from specific benefits reserved to a spouse.

In the judgements passed on the cases Maruko,[8] Römer[9] and Hay,[10] the Court of Justice declared that by excluding a worker in a civil solidarity pact with a person of the same sex (if regulated in the Member State) from certain benefits (such as, for example, days of special leave and a salary bonus) which, instead, were conceded to a married worker, a State was culpable of direct sexually orientated discrimination (prohibited by directive No. 78/2000/EU) whenever its national law prohibits same-sex marriages and when "in the light of the objective of and the conditions relating to

---

[7]See also Morozzo Della Rocca (2017), p. 584.
[8]CJEU, Maruko, 1st April 2008, C-267/06. See Biagioni (2014), p. 376; Moschel (2009), p. 37.
[9]CJEU 20th May 2011, C-147/08.
[10]CJEU, Hay, 12th December 2013, C-267/12. Rizzi (2015), p. 47.

the grant of those benefits, that employee is in a comparable situation to an employee who marries".[11]

Those principles apply, regardless of whether the discrimination derives from national law or from a collective labour agreement, as the latter is subject to constraints deriving from European anti-discrimination legislation.[12]

In practice, discrimination occurs, in the view of the Court of Justice, when a nation regulates civil partnerships or unions in such a way that a couple joined in a civil union can be deemed "comparable" to a married couple, and, at the same time, unreasonably refuses to afford that protection (such as, for example, pension benefits) to the worker in a civil union although affording it to a married worker under national law or collective labour agreements.

Instead, no protection, in an anti-discriminatory sense (in the light of directive No. 78/2000/EU), exists (because the situations are not comparable) in a nation where a couple in a same-sex union is not afforded protection "similar" to that of a married couple, as, for example, in Italy before law No. 76/2016.

On the other hand, the Court has never—to the best of our knowledge—thoroughly considered the potentiality of reading articles 7 and 21 of the EU Charter of Fundamental Rights together (corresponding to articles 8 and 14 of the foregoing European Convention on Human Rights), in order to ascertain if—without prejudice, as stated, to the Member States' discretion as to whether same-sex couples can be legally married (article 12 of the European Convention on Human Rights, article 9 of the Nice Charter)—the non-recognition of any legal protection for such homoaffective relationships is in conflict with stable same-sex couples' right to be afforded appropriate protection for their private and family life.

The reasons for such a different approach[13] are to be found in the European Union's lack of legislative competence on matters of civil status, the limited "scope of application" of the Charter of Fundamental Rights as also the difficulty of identifying an "facilitating law"—other than the anti-discriminatory law—that would allow the model fact situation of same-sex couples in a stable relationship to fall within the remit of European Union law.

In this regard, a recent ruling passed by the Italian Constitutional Court on the system of sanctions introduced by legislative decree No. 23/2015 in the case of unlawful dismissal[14] restated—in line with the case law of the Court of Justice[15]— that in order for a provision of the EU Charter of Fundamental Rights to be directly invoked between private subjects so as to disapply a national provision in contrast with the principle it enshrines, the former must assert a principle that is "sufficient in itself to confer on individuals an individual right which they may invoke as such"[16];

---

[11]CJEU, Hay, 12th December 2013, C-267/12.

[12]See also art. 16 dir. no. 78/2000. CJEU 13th September 2011, C-447/09; CJEU 7th June 2012, C-132/11.

[13]See di Bari (2012), p. 221.

[14]Constitutional Court, 8th November 2018, no. 194, in www.dejure.it.

[15]CJEU, Küçükdeveci, 19th January 2010, C-555/07.

[16]CJEU, Association de médiation sociale, 15th January 2014, C- 176/12.

and benefit from an act of community law that has given expression to that principle. "The national court, faced with a national provision falling within the scope of European Union law which it considers to be incompatible with that principle, and which cannot be interpreted in conformity with that principle, must decline to apply that provision, without being either compelled to make or prevented from making a reference to the Court for a preliminary ruling before doing so".[17]

Therefore, it is necessary to move from the premise that the powers conferred upon the EU condition the powers of the Court of Justice in applying the EU Charter of Fundamental Rights, especially in comparison with the ECHR's jurisdictionary remit. The Nice Charter does not constitute a means for protecting fundamental rights in sectors other than those in which the European Union can exercise its specific competence. Thus, in practice, the CFRUE's provisions apply to Member States when they act in the area where Union legislation applies.[18] However, the simple fact that a law falls in a sector in which the Union has legislative competence will not entail that the Charter can be applied if—in practice—the Union has never exercised this legislative power. Nor will the issue of simple "recommendations" by European institutions suffice.

Nevertheless, even given this premise, it should be asked if space actually exists to enable the Court of Justice—in the future—to go beyond reading questions in merely anti-discriminatory key (directive no. 78/2000)—and assess compliance with the principles under articles 7 (respect for private and family life) and 21 (principle of non-discrimination) of the EU Charter of Fundamental Rights of a Member State's legislation that—by not making provision to regularise single-sex unions—precludes the same-sex partner of a citizen of the same State (or a Union citizen) from being able to benefit from a residence permit on family grounds (unlike a heterosexual partner who has the legal means of marriage to have his or her family status recognised). This would have the consequence of disapplying discordant national legislation on the grounds that it contrasts with the foregoing principles, and when its content is sufficiently precise, of conferring upon the individuals "an individual right which they may invoke as such".

In the light of the competence of the European Union on the matter of free movement, the answer to this question would seem to be positive.

3 Italian Case Law

As is known, the Court of Justice handed down a very important ruling, C-673/16, which goes beyond the rules of mere anti-discrimination, regarding the right of sojourn of a non-EU "spouse" who married an EU national of the same sex in a member state other than that in which the couple resides.

---

[17]CJEU, *Kücükdeveci*, 19th January 2010, C-555/07.
[18]Constitutional Court no. 194/2018. See also article 52 of the Nice Charter.

Before dwelling on this rule, it is necessary to analyse the argumentative avenues that national case law had to follow in a country such as Italy—lacking up until 2016, a legislation to protect same-sex civil unions—in order to afford protection to same-sex couples.

Prior to legislative decree No. 76/2016, the relevant case law on civil unions had recognised that a same-sex couple married abroad had the right to prosecute their emotional relationship when one of the spouses took up residence in Italy.

Some national courts based this solution (before law No. 76/2016 was passed) not upon articles 7 and 21 of the Charter but instead upon a community-law interpretation of the word "spouse" (pursuant to article 9 of the EU Charter of Fundamental Rights), contained in article 2, subsection 1, letter b), No. 1 of legislative decree No. 30/2007 that implemented article 2 of directive 38/2004, and which was intended (according to the court) to refer not only to married heterosexual couples but also, in an inclusive sense, to same-sex couples married abroad.

This solution (a community interpretation of the word "spouse" pursuant to domestic law) did not, however, appear very convincing given that in Italian domestic law the word "spouse" unquestionably refers to persons of different sexes.

In any case, this interpretative option would still have left the partners of same-sex couples, who had not married abroad and were only "in a civil union", without protection.

The Constitutional Court and the Supreme Court of Cassation made cautious but important appeals to the legislator so that it would, at least, make provision to regulate specific situations in which a homoaffective relationship required specific protection.

In particular, the Constitutional Court, although frequently excluding that the non recognition of same-sex couples' right to marry stood in contrast to articles 2, 3, 29, and 117 subsection 1 of the Constitution, nevertheless, brought stable same-sex couples under the aegis of article 2 of the Constitution, deeming them to be social groups furthering the development of human personality.[19]

Subsequently, it took the next step by recognising a need for legislative action in order to regulate a particular situation whereby, notwithstanding a sex change in one of the spouses of a married couple, the two spouses still wished to remain in a union (no longer heterosexual) which—considering the spouses' previous life as a married couple—still called for protection as a "form of community".[20]

This implicitly indicated the path that the legislator could follow for a—much wider—measure to regulate stable same-sex unions.[21]

In the wake of these rulings, the Supreme Court recognised that—in certain circumstances—the absence of a legislative framework designed to protect the affective and relational nucleus that characterises a same-sex union (protected

---

[19]Constitutional Court, 15th April 2010, n. 138, in www.dejure.it.

[20]Constitutional Court no. 170/2014, in www.dejure.it; Cassation, 21th April 2015, no. 8097, in www.dejure.it.

[21]See also Cassation, 14th May 2018, no. 11696.

under article 2 of the Constitution) could determine a violation of fundamental rights arising from the relationship in question.[22]

4 The Coman Case

At the European level, the Court of Justice's ruling, C- 673/16, constitutes an important step forward in the protection, albeit still partial, of same-sex couples.[23] The issue referred to the regulation of the right of residence of a "family member" (same-sex spouse) of a Union citizen who had established a family life with said family member, and then returned to his or her country of origin. The conditions regarding the concession of the right should not, in principle, be more strict than those provided for by Directive 2004/38 on free movement, as otherwise every useful legal effect of article 21, subsection 1, of the TFEU would be forfeited.[24]

The ruling—in recognising the right of residence—dwelt upon the meaning given to the word "spouse" in the context of directive 2004/38 (art. 2, subsection 2, letter a); which it held to be "neutral" with respect to sex.[25]

In a situation such as the one in question Member States have no powers of discretion in choosing whether or not to concede the right of residence to a same-sex spouse regularly married in a different State. On the contrary, the right of residence of a partner in a civil union on the basis of the legislation of a Member State, depends on the circumstance of whether or not the state treats same-sex unions as equivalent to heterosexual marriages (directive 2003/38, art. 2, subsection 2, letter b).

The limit of public policy remains unaffected (in this regard the respect for national identity) although it is to be interpreted restrictively: the recognition of a same-sex marriage contracted abroad for purposes of granting a derived right of residence to a citizen of a third State, does not prejudice the institution of marriage in the first Member State (in the circumstance of its being reserved to persons of different sexes).

The Coman case does not resolve the question of the right to enter the territory of a State of a partner in situations where same-sex couples albeit not "married" abroad had (only) entered into a "de facto" same-sex, "family" relationship there, or who had contracted a registered civil union abroad and the host Member State does not treat registered civil union as equivalent to marriage (see article 2, subsection 2, letter b, directive 38/2004). In other words, the judgement does not resolve situations that such couples had to face in countries such as Italy and Croatia, before (due to the

---

[22]Cassation 9th February 2015, no. 2400, in www.dejure.it. Also see Cassation 15th March 2012, no. 4148, in www.dejure.it.

[23]CJEU, Coman, 5th June 2018, C-673/16. See Gyeney (2018), p. 149; Battaglia (2018), p. 21; Lang (2018), p. 13; Penasa (2018), p. 18; Dunne (2018), p. 383; Titshaw (2016), p. 45.

[24]See also CJEU 12th March 2014, C-456/12.

[25]See also Bell and Selanec (2016), p. 221.

ECtHR "Oliari" and "Pajic" judgements) registered civil unions were regulated in these countries.

Second, nor does the Coman judgement address the question of the nature of the protection afforded to a same-sex spouse, married abroad, in a country whose constitution expressly proscribes the right to have same-sex marriages recognised.

As we shall see this question is also raised with respect to same-sex couples who -although not married abroad- had established a "family" life in that country, when the Constitution of the host Member State prohibits the recognition of such relationships.

In the Coman case—centred upon article 21 of the TFEU—the Court of Justice in interpreting the word "spouse" as per article 2, subsection 2, letter a) of directive 2004/38 drew upon article 7 of the EU Charter of Fundamental Rights, which was then read, by the Court, in conjunction with article 8 of the European Convention on Human Rights and especially with the Convention's case law: ECtHR statued, indeed, that "the relationship of a homosexual couple may fall within the notion of 'private life' and that of 'family life' in the same way as the relationship of a heterosexual couple in the same situation."[26]

The Court clarifies "that a national measure that is liable to obstruct the exercise of freedom of movement for persons may be justified only where such a measure is consistent with the fundamental rights guaranteed by the Charter".[27]

Likewise, in the Staatssecretaris case,[28] European Court of Justice reads directive no. 2003/86 in the light of article 7 of the EU Charter of Fundamental Rights, in conjunction with article 8 of the European Convention on Human Rights. The measures concerning family reunification, such as measures for the withdrawal of a residence permit issued to family members, "must be adopted in conformity with fundamental rights, in particular the right to respect for private and family life guaranteed by Article 7 of the Charter, which contains rights corresponding to those protected by Article 8 (1), of the ECHR".[29]

It does, nevertheless, seem that the EU Charter of Fundamental Rights could be used in a more incisive manner in the foregoing situations: for example, when the same-sex partner in a civil union registered abroad asserts a right to freely reside in a territory of a Member State by virtue of his/her being a "family member" of a Union citizen who exercises his/her right of free movement (or—as stated, returns to his/her country of origin), in the event that the host State does not afford protection to same-sex civil unions.

In such a case, the partner in a civil union certainly could not demand the disapplication of national law, either on the basis of article 2, subsection 2, letter a) or on the basis of article 2, subsection 2 letter b) of the directive.

---

[26]ECtHR, Vallianatos, 7th November 2013; ECtHR, Orlandi, 14th December 2017.

[27]CJEU, Coman, 5th June 2018, C-673/16.

[28]CJEU, 14th March 2019, C-557/17.

[29]CJEU, 14th March 2019, C-557/17.

However, he or she could arguably request the disapplication of a discordant national law (also in its horizontal relations) insofar as contrary to articles 7 and 21 of the EU Charter of Fundamental Rights.

Directive no. 2004/38, indeed, can be deemed the "facilitating law"—other than the anti-discriminatory law (directive no. 2000/78)—that would allow the model fact situation of same-sex couples in a stable relationship to fall within the remit of European Union law.

5 Conclusions

The Court of Justice, in the light of community jurisdiction on the matter of the free movement of citizens, will very probably be called upon to determine whether a member state's legislation complies with the principles of articles 7 (respect for private and family life) and 21 (non-discrimination) of the EU Charter of Fundamental Rights when the member state in question not only fails to make any provision to regularise same-sex unions but also excludes a same-sex partner of the citizen of that state (or a community citizen) from being able to benefit from a residence permit for family reasons. This would consequently render the national legislation of this state inapplicable on the grounds of its being at variance with the foregoing principles, whose content is sufficiently precise as to confer a "right" upon individuals, and one that may be invoked as such.

Essentially, it is possible to envisage—in the future rulings of the Court of Justice—an extension to partners in registered civil unions contracted in a State other than that of the destination Member State, of forms of protection currently recognised by the Court of Justice (the Coman case) as applicable to the single same-sex "spouse", married abroad.

It is well known that European Union is required, under Article 4(2) TEU, to respect the national identity of the Member States, inherent in their fundamental structures, both political and constitutional.[30] In the Coman case the Court limited itself to stating that, on the one hand, the "obligation to recognise such marriages for the sole purpose of granting a derived right of residence to a third-country national does not undermine the national identity or pose a threat to the public policy of the Member State concerned"; on the other hand, that the "concept of public policy as justification for a derogation from a fundamental freedom must be interpreted strictly, with the result that its scope cannot be determined unilaterally by each Member State without any control by the EU institutions".[31]

It must, however, be asked if it were possible or not to arrive at different solutions in a legal framework where the Constitution explicitly prohibited the recognition of such same-sex civil unions.

---

[30]See also, to that effect, *Bogendorff von Wolffersdorff*, CJEU, 2 June 2016, C-438/14.

[31]ECtHR, Coman, 5th June 2018, C-673/16.

The circumstance that the EU Charter of Fundamental Rights—which has the same legal value as a treaty—, construed in conformity to the ECHR, claims a form of protection for the "private and family life" of same-sex couples (in the ambit of subjects falling under the shadow cone of the Union law) appears to constitute a bulwark for the protection of such subjects' rights.

And the force of this claim is such that not even a surmised constitutional prohibition of a Member State on the recognition of same-sex unions could prevent the recognition of the unions for the limited purpose of free movement.

Instead, the solution will be quite different in the case, for example, of the request for the issue of a residence permit for family reasons in favour of the second or third wife of a European citizen of the Muslim faith who had contracted marriage abroad, the polygamous marriage. In the event of a polygamous marriage, where the sponsor already has a spouse living with him in the territory of a Member State, Directive no. 2003/86 statues that the Member State concerned "shall not authorise the family reunification of a further spous". Neither the principle of the protection of family life in conjunction with principle of non-discrimination (Article 7 of the Nice Charter of Fundamental Human Rights) could be invoked, since, in this case, in the balance between individual and societal interests, the latter would prevail.[32]

In any case, a very fecund dialogue is found to be taking place on this subject matter between the courts, especially the European Court of Human Rights and the European Court of Justice.[33]

Similarly it emerges that, albeit commencing in a soft-footed manner, the Court of Justice (in the ambit of the shadow cone cast by Union law) may today afford an effective protection of fundamental human rights, precisely in the light of the principle of the primacy of EU law.

Furthermore, such protection is probably more "immediate" than that afforded—at present—by the ECtHR. Whereas, according to Italian constitutional case law, the ordinary judges can't disapply internal rules, contrary to the ECHR.

References

Alpa, G. (2016). La tutela giurisdizionale dei diritti umani Relazione al convegno "Il diritto privato nella giurisprudenza della Corte europea dei diritti dell'uomo", Padova, 15-16 maggio 2015. *La Nuova giurisprudenza civile commentata, 1,* 108.

Battaglia, F. (2018). La definizione di "coniuge" ai sensi della direttiva 38/2004: Il caso "Coman" e "Hamilton". *OIDU - Ordine Internazionale e Diritti Umani, 3,* 21.

---

[32] See also Sandulli (2018), p. 335.

[33] See also CJEU 26th March 2019, C-129/18, SM, "It is apparent from the case-law of the European Court of Human Rights that the actual relationship which a child placed under the *kafala* system maintains with its guardian may fall under the definition of family life, having regard to the time spent living together, the quality of the relationship, and the role which the adult assumes in respect of the child".

Bell, C., & Selanec, N. B. (2016). Who is a "spouse" under the citizens' rights Directive? The prospect of mutual recognition of same-sex marriages in the EU. *European Law Review, 5,* 661.

Biagioni, G. (2014). On recognition of foreign same-sex marriages and partnerships. In D. Gallo, L. Paladini, & P. Pustorino (Eds.), *Same-sex couples before national, supranational and international jurisdictions* (p. 376). Springer.

di Bari, M. (2012). *Same-sex unions in the EU system of protection of fundamental rights: The role of courts at national supranational and international level "after Lisbon"* (p. 221). Lap Lambert Academic Publishing.

Dunne, P. (2018). Coman: Vindicating the residence rights of same-sex "spouses" in the EU. - *European Human Rights Law Review, 4,* 383.

Gyeney, L. (2018). Same sex couples' right to free movement in light of member states' national identities: The legal analysis of the Coman case. *Iustum Aequum Salutare, XIV,* 149.

Lang, A. (2018). Il mancato riconoscimento del matrimonio tra persone dello stesso sesso come ostacolo alla libera circolazione delle persone nell'Unione: il caso "Coman". *GenIUS, 2,* 13.

Morozzo Della Rocca, P. (2017). Il diritto alla coesione familiare prima e dopo la legge n. 76 del 2016. *Giurisprudenza italiana, 3,* 584.

Moschel, M. (2009). Germany's life partnerships: Separate and unequal. *Columbia Journal of European Law, 16,* 37.

Penasa, S. (2018). Matrimonio tra persone dello stesso sesso e libertà di circolazione dei cittadini europei e dei loro familiari: osservazioni a "cerchi concentrici" sul caso "Coman c. Romania" della Corte di giustizia. *Diritto, immigrazione e cittadinanza, 3,* 18.

Persano, F. (2016). Il caso "Pajic": è in contrasto con la CEDU la legge di uno Stato contraente che disponga il diritto al ricongiungimento familiare esclusivamente a favore di "partners" eterosessuali. *Osservatorio costituzionale, 3,* 11.

Ragone, S., & Volpe, V. (2016). An emerging right to a 'gay' family life? The case of Oliari v. Italy in a comparative perspective. *German Law Journal, 17,* 451.

Rizzi, F. (2015). Il caso "Hay" e la Corte di giustizia: una nuova dottrina contro la discriminazione delle coppie omosessuali. *Rivista giuridica del lavoro e della previdenza sociale, 1*(2), 47.

Sandulli, S. (2018). La legalizzazione della poligamia è davvero così lontana? *Familia, 3,* 335.

Scherpe, M. (2013). The legal recognition of same-sex couples in Europe and the role of the European Court of Human Rights. *The Equal Rights Review, 10,* 83.

Sperti, S. (2016). Clausola risolutiva espressa. Rilascio del permesso di soggiorno per motivi familiari anche a partner dello stesso sesso. *Giurisprudenza italiana, 11,* 2336.

Titshaw, S. (2016). Same sex spouses lost in translation? How to interpret 'spouse' in the EU Family Migration Directives. *Boston University International Law Journal, 34,* 45.

Internal Organisation of Regional Human Rights Courts: The European Court of Human Rights and the Inter-American Court of Human Rights

Roberta Muscat and Guillem Cano Palomares

Contents

1 Introduction

The end of World War II was followed by the much awaited birth of two main regional human rights systems—one in Europe under the organisation known as the Council of Europe (CoE) and the other in the Americas within the Organisation of

The authors wish to thank Marta Cabrera Martín, legal adviser to the President and the Secretary of the Inter-American Court of Human Rights and former lawyer at the Registry of the European Court of Human Rights, for the useful comments and suggestions she has made to this contribution.

R. Muscat (✉) · G. Cano Palomares
European Court of Human Rights, Strasbourg, France
e-mail: roberta.muscat@echr.coe.int

© Springer Nature Switzerland AG 2019
P. Pinto de Albuquerque, K. Wojtyczek (eds.), *Judicial Power in a Globalized World*, https://doi.org/10.1007/978-3-030-20744-1_21

American States (OAS). Both these organisations have their own mechanisms for protecting their people (as well as any individual on their respective territories) from their Governments—courtesy of the Governments themselves. The founding Member States of these two intergovernmental organisations cradled their first born, respectively, the European Convention on Human Rights (the European Convention) which opened for signature in Rome on 4 November 1950 and entered into force in 1953, and the American Convention on Human Rights (the American Convention) which opened for signature on 22 November 1969 and entered into force in 1978. These relatively short—yet so important—texts represent, together with other instruments, the foundations of today's international human rights law. Already at the time, there was no doubt that the two conventions would eventually need to be interpreted and that a system of enforcement would be required to ensure that the Governments are brought to task when they fail to fulfil their commitment to the cause as expressed by their ratification of these two conventions. To that end, the European Commission on Human Rights and the European Court of Human Rights on the one hand and the Inter-American Court of Human Rights on the other hand, were established. In respect of the European system, in 1998, the two-tier system, of the Commission who had jurisdiction to decide on the admissibility of applications or issue reports in respect of admissible applications that could eventually be decided by the Court, was abolished in favour of the single Court we know today.

2 The Jurisdiction of the Courts

2.1 The European Court of Human Rights

The European Court of Human Rights (ECtHR) deals with contentious cases brought by any person, non-governmental organisation, or group of individuals, against States (represented by their Governments), whereby a right arising from the European Convention or its Protocols is alleged to have been breached. The ECtHR also has jurisdiction to hear inter-state cases in so far as Article 33 of the European Convention provides that any High Contracting Party may refer to the Court any alleged breach of the provisions of the Convention and the Protocols thereto by another High Contracting Party. All the 47 Member States have accepted the jurisdiction of the ECtHR. Indeed, today this is a compulsory requirement for membership to the CoE.

The ECtHR may also, at the request of the Committee of Ministers, or if asked by the highest courts and tribunals of the High Contracting Parties,[1] give advisory

---

[1]This is a novelty resulting from the coming into force of Protocol No. 16, on 1 August 2018. It applies only to those States that have ratified the Protocol (currently 11 State Parties to the Convention).

opinions on legal questions concerning the interpretation of the European Convention and the Protocols thereto.

The supervision of the execution of the judgments of the ECtHR is in the hands of the Committee of Ministers of the CoE, a statutory decision-making body made up of the Ministers for foreign affairs of the Member States.[2] However, since the entry into force of Protocol No. 14, the Court has also jurisdiction to examine the question whether a State Party has complied with a final judgment of the Court, in accordance with the procedure described in Article 46 § 4 of the European Convention.

2.2 The Inter-American Court of Human Rights

The Inter-American Court of Human Rights (IACtHR) deals with contentious cases submitted by the Inter-American Commission of Human Rights or by State Parties to the American Convention. Of the 35 State Members of the OAS 20 are currently under the compulsory jurisdiction of the Court.[3] The main difference with the European system is that there is no right of individual petition to the Court. Individuals can only lodge petitions with the Inter-American Commission on Human Rights (a non-judicial body), which is competent to examine their admissibility, adopt reports on the merits of admissible petitions and eventually submit a case to the IACtHR.[4] The system is more similar to the two-tier system that existed in Europe before the entry into force of Protocol No. 11 to the European Convention (1998), with the European Commission on Human Rights and a non-permanent European Court of Human Rights.

The IACtHR also deals with requests for advisory opinions submitted by Member States (not their highest courts like in the European system) and organs of the OAS.[5] Unlike the European system, the IACtHR's advisory jurisdiction is not confined to the interpretation of the founding treaty (the Convention) but covers also the interpretation of other treaties concerning the protection of human rights in the American states. Finally, the IACtHR, unlike the ECtHR, is responsible for supervising the execution of its own judgments.[6]

---

[2]The role and functions of the Committee of Ministers are set out in Chapter V of the Statute of the Council of Europe ETS No. 001.

[3]Trinidad and Tobago and Venezuela, which had accepted the compulsory jurisdiction of the Court, have denounced the Convention.

[4]According to Articles 51 and 61 of the American Convention.

[5]Article 64 of the American Convention.

[6]The legal grounds for this competence can be found in Article 65 of the American Convention and Article 30 of the Statute of the IACtHR. See *Baena Ricardo et al. (270 workers) v. Panama*, 28 November 2003, where the IACtHR came to the conclusion that the intention of the States was to grant the Court the authority to monitor compliance with its decisions.

3 The Composition of the Courts

3.1 The ECtHR

The ECtHR is made up of forty-seven judges, one with respect to each Member State, who are elected by the Parliamentary Assembly of the CoE after a special committee scrutinises the candidates' qualifications and the national procedure (as a result of which the Member States would have presented a list of three judges). According to Article 23 of the European Convention the judges shall be elected for a period of 9 years and may not be re-elected; they however hold office until they are replaced. The ECtHR can consider cases in various formations, namely in Single-judge formation, Committees of three judges, Chambers of seven judges and a Grand Chamber of seventeen judges.[7] Under the European Convention system, when sitting as a single judge, a judge shall not examine any application against the High Contracting Party in respect of which that judge has been elected. Conversely, the judge elected in respect of the High Contracting Party concerned shall sit as an *ex officio* member of the Chamber and the Grand Chamber,[8] deciding on the admissibility or/and merits of a case which has not been declared inadmissible *de plano*.[9]

The ECtHR is directed by its President and two Vice-Presidents who are elected by the plenary court for a period of 3 years.[10] According to Rule 25 of the Rules of Court[11] each judge shall be a member of a Section. The composition of the Sections shall be geographically and gender balanced and shall reflect the different legal systems among the High Contracting Parties. There are currently five Sections and each Section is composed of between nine to ten judges. Each Section has a President and a Vice-President, the former's role is, *inter alia*, to preside at the sittings of the Section and Chambers of which he or she is a member and to direct the Sections' work. The Section President's duties may be carried out by the Vice-President of the Section when required.[12] Section Presidents and Section Vice-Presidents are elected for a period of 2 years, and may be re-elected only once.[13]

Vincent De Gaetano, in whose honour this *liber amicorum* is being put together, was elected as ECtHR judge in June 2010 and took office on 20 September 2010. During his office he was elected as Vice-President of Section and from 3 November 2015 to 31 August 2018 served as Vice-President of Section IV. He was then elected President of Section and has been President of Section III since 1 September 2018. We take this opportunity to congratulate him on his ascending career within the

---

[7]Article 26 § 1 of the European Convention.
[8]Article 26 §§ 3 and 4 of the European Convention.
[9]Rule 29 (3) of the Rules of Court.
[10]Article 25 of the European Convention.
[11]The last edition of the Rules of Court entered into force on 1 August 2018.
[12]Rule 12 of the Rules of Court.
[13]Rule 8 of the Rules of Court.

ECtHR (as well as that before), which is undoubtedly the result of his hard work, commitment, legal acumen, sense of justice, and last but not least his personality.

3.2 The IACtHR

The IACtHR is composed of seven judges, who are elected by an absolute majority vote of all the States Parties to the Convention, in the General Assembly of the OAS, from a list of candidates proposed by any of those States which wish to put forward a candidate.[14] They are elected for a term of 6 years and may be re-elected only once.[15] The President and Vice-President of the Court are elected by the plenary court for a period of 2 years and may be re-elected. Unlike the ECtHR, the IACtHR does not sit permanently and therefore the judges do not have to reside in the city or country where the Court has its seat, namely in San José, Costa Rica. They shall however remain at the disposal of the Court and shall travel to the seat of the Court or to the place where the Court is holding its sessions as often and for as long a time as may be necessary.[16]

One of the main differences with the European system is that the IACtHR is not composed of as many judges as State Parties to the Convention. As a result, the necessity of having the judge, national of the State Party against which a case was lodged, to sit on the examination of such case was raised. Before 2009, the IACtHR sitting judges had the right to hear cases against their own countries. If the respondent State did not have a national sitting among the seven judges of the court, or if such national withdrew from hearing the case, the respondent State was allowed to appoint an *ad hoc* judge to decide on the case against that country. However, in a remarkable advisory opinion delivered in September 2009, the IACtHR reversed its position.[17] It found that the *ad hoc* judge system established by the American Convention (Article 55) was only applicable to inter-state cases, but not to cases originating in individual petitions. It also considered that sitting judges who were nationals of the State Party concerned had an obligation to withdraw from the individual case submitted against that State, contrary to the letter of Article 55 § 1 of the American Convention which stipulated that the judge, being a national of any of the States Parties to a case, shall have a right to hear that case. The IACtHR considered that the *ad hoc* judge system was justified only in the context of inter-state cases, since it had been intended to preserve procedural equity between the parties. In reply to the argument that this figure guaranteed a better understanding of

---

[14] Articles 52 and 53 of the American Convention. Each of the States Parties may propose up to three candidates.

[15] Article 54 § 1 of the American Convention.

[16] Article 16 of the Statute of the IACtHR.

[17] See Advisory Opinion OC-20/09 on Article 55 of the American Convention, 29 September 2009. This position was reflected in Article 19 of the Rules of Procedure of the IACtHR.

the domestic law of the respondent State, the IACtHR considered that this role could be fulfilled by expert evidence submitted by the parties to the case, as well as by the presentation of *amicus curiae*.[18] The IACtHR also pointed out that the possibility for the judge to provide information on the domestic law or the facts without the presence of all parties to the proceedings was inappropriate, having regard to the principle of due process. Most importantly, the IACtHR, seeking to strengthen the perception of the judge's impartiality, considered that the nationality of a judge sitting on a case was related to the perception of the justice applied by the Court, especially in the context of individual petitions, and thus his or her presence in the composition deciding cases against his or her own country must be avoided.

4   The Registry/Secretariat

4.1   The ECtHR

In 1994 with the adoption of Protocol No. 11 to the European Convention, which set up the permanent court (referred to as the ECtHR in this article), the then Article 25 of the Convention was introduced. It provided that the ECtHR shall have a Registry and that its functions and organisation shall be laid down in the Rules of Court.[19] The responsibility for the organisation and activities of the Registry falls on the Registrar who is elected by the plenary court for 5 years and may be re-elected.[20] The plenary may also elect one or more Deputy Registrars for the Court on the same lines.[21] According to Rule 18 of the Rules of Court the Registry shall be divided into Section Registries which shall offer the legal and administrative services required by the Court. Each Section shall be assisted by a Section Registrar, its deputy and, in practice, the officials of the Registry assigned to that Section. The former Article 25 of the Convention also provided that "the Court shall be assisted by legal secretaries". The latter notion was dropped in subsequent amendments via Protocol No. 14[22] which dealt with the introduction of non-judicial rapporteurs assisting Single-judge formations. However, the latter function does not replace the former. Albeit oddly formulated in the former Article 25, the concept of legal secretaries was understood as covering all the lawyers in the Registry employed to assist the ECtHR in various ways by undertaking diverse legal tasks, but which did not fall under any of the other identified categories of Registry staff mentioned in the Rules of Court, such as the Registrars. Today the Rules of Court refer to persons having that same role as officials of the Registry who shall be appointed by the Registrar under the

---

[18]Article 44 of the Rules of Procedure of the IACtHR.

[19]See current Article 24 § 1 of the European Convention.

[20]Rule 15 and 17 of the Rules of Court.

[21]Rule 16 of the Rules of Court.

[22]See the explanations set out in § 58 of the Explanatory Report to Protocol No. 14.

authority of the President of the Court.[23] Since 2010, non-judicial rapporteurs, who shall assist the Court sitting in its single judge formation, function under the authority of the President of the Court (by whom they are appointed) and are also part of the Registry.[24]

More recently, on 23 June 2014, the Rules of Court were also amended to officialise the long standing assistance provided to the ECtHR by the Jurisconsult, whose role is to ensure the quality and consistency of its case-law by providing opinions and information to the different formations and members of the ECtHR.[25] In practice, the Jurisconsult is assisted by a Deputy Jurisconsult and a team of experienced lawyers who may assist in formulating opinions and who follow Chamber deliberations enabling the Jurisconsult to have a comprehensive awareness of all the cases delivered in Chamber formation. The Jurisconsult, as well as his team, are also members of the Registry. The Jurisconsult acts as the manager of an entire department which covers some support services, mainly the Research and Library Division and the Case-law Information and Publications Division. The current Jurisconsult, Lawrence T. Early, was and remains a greatly respected and appreciated mentor to both the authors of this piece and is held in high esteem by judges and lawyers in and outside the ECtHR.

Quite apart from the organisation and roles derived from the official texts as mentioned above, the Registry has evolved to cater for the needs of the ever increasing workload of the ECtHR and to maximise its effectiveness.

The lawyers (officials of the Registry, previously known as legal secretaries) are usually attached to the Section where the judge elected in respect of their State (commonly known as national judge) sits. The case-processing lawyers are grouped in divisions which may be country specific (which is normally the case with high case-count countries) or which group a number of low case-count countries. Generally lawyers work on cases lodged against the State of which they are nationals which usually corresponds to the State from which they have obtained their law degree. The reason is self-evident. Since lawyers process cases concerning human rights issues arising from domestic procedures and laws, proficiency in the language and in the domestic legal framework at issue in the case are an asset. All members of the Registry are recruited on the basis of open competitions, and are required to adhere to strict conditions as to their independence and impartiality.[26] According to vacancy calls regularly published online,[27] they are required to have thorough knowledge of their national legal system and a very good knowledge of one of the two official languages of the CoE (English and French) and knowledge of the other, apart from an excellent knowledge of their own language. Case-processing lawyers

---

[23]Rule 18 and 22 of the Rules of Court.

[24]Rule 18A of the Rules of Court.

[25]Rule 18B of the Rules of Court.

[26]https://www.echr.coe.int/Documents/Registry_ENG.pdf. Accessed 3 April 2019.

[27]Lawyers at the Registry are staff members of the CoE, the organisation within which the ECtHR functions.

examine and deal with applications lodged with the ECtHR by taking care of the legal analysis as well as maintaining correspondence with the applicants and, where appropriate, with Governments and third parties. They prepare case-files for the examination by the non-judicial rapporteur or judge-rapporteur as the case may be, and then for submission to the Court in its different formations. They also attend the Court's deliberations, draft judgments, decisions, minutes, reports, notes and other documents. Where necessary they undertake studies and research relating to the case-law of the Convention and national law for use by the Chamber or the Grand Chamber.

The entry into force of Protocol No. 14 and the establishment of the Single-judge formation (by which a judge sitting alone, assisted by a non-judicial rapporteur, can declare applications inadmissible) brought about further changes within the Registry. With a view to making the most of this new procedure the ECtHR set up a new Filtering Section which has been operational since 2011. Its principal function is to carry out a thorough, accurate and immediate sifting of cases to ensure that all applications are placed on the appropriate procedural track. By centralising resources and streamlining working methods, it was intended to minimise the time taken to respond to applicants' complaints and to reduce the backlog of unexamined cases.[28] Statistics today show that it has indeed been successful, and the Filtering Section continues to develop new working methods to ensure it remains relevant and effective in the light of the challenges and constraints faced by the ECtHR.

Last but not least, the Registry has other departments such as Administration (mainly dealing with human resources and budget), Communications (Press, Visitors and Public Relations), Information Technology and Language. These sectors are indispensable to the functioning of the ECtHR in each of their supportive functions. For example, while the Information Technology Department continuously seeks to ameliorate and assist in implementing innovative working methods, the Communications Department ensures that knowledge of the ECtHR and its case-law is widespread and that the ECtHR remains accessible to the public.

There are currently some 640 staff members in the Registry, including lawyers, administrative and technical staff and translators.

4.2 The IACtHR

The IACtHR has a Secretariat, which functions under the immediate authority of the Secretary,[29] and has currently 16 case-processing lawyers. The Secretary is elected

---

[28]https://www.echr.coe.int/Documents/Filtering_Section_ENG.pdf. Accessed 3 April 2019.

[29]Article 59 of the American Convention and Article 14 of the Statute of the IACtHR. According to Article 14.4 of the Statute, the staff of the Secretariat shall be appointed by the Secretary General of the OAS, in consultation with the Secretary of the Court.

by the Court for a term of 5 years and may be re-elected.[30] He or she is assisted by a Deputy Secretary.[31] The cases are assigned to the lawyer independently from their nationality. Since January 2014, one legal division is in charge of the supervision of the execution of judgments. In November 2013 a new legal officer was appointed as Legal Director. He supervises the legal work of the lawyers (quality check of draft judgments, resolutions, case management). The Secretariat has other staff: legal assistants, secretaries and trainees attached to the case-processing lawyers. It has a financial and administrative director and other support staff (librarians, information technologists, etc.). The total number of staff (excluding trainees and support divisions) is approximately 60.

The role of the case-processing lawyers and the Secretariat in general is vital for the functioning and the everyday work of the IACtHR, given that its judges do not sit full time. Each case-processing lawyer prepares drafts and notes for the adjudication of the cases submitted to the Court. He/she is aided by legal assistants and trainees, who usually contribute to the drafting of the facts or the summary of the arguments of the parties. The Legal Director quality-checks the draft judgments prepared by the case-processing lawyers but there is also a lawyers' meeting in which the Secretary, the Deputy Secretary and all the lawyers give their comments on the draft judgment presented by the case-processing lawyer. In this meeting issues of case-law consistency are raised. Only after this meeting has taken place is the final draft judgment sent to the judge-rapporteur and later to all the judges. However, the judge-rapporteur usually gives instructions to the lawyer during the drafting process. The case-processing lawyers attend the private deliberations of the IACtHR in cases for which they have prepared drafts and notes. They also process the correspondence of the Court with the parties and sit in the public hearings held before the IACtHR together with the Secretary and the Deputy Secretary.

5 The Courts' Workload

On 1 January 2019, there were 56,350 cases pending before the ECtHR which had been allocated to a judicial formation. In 2018 the ECtHR delivered 2738 judgments and 40,023 decisions (inadmissible or struck out). In the same period 19,550 applications were disposed of administratively (via the Rule 47, explained below) and 7644 applications were communicated to the respondent Governments.[32]

As regards the IACtHR, at the end of 2018, there were 32 contentious cases pending, 25 cases in which provisional measures were applied (active provisional measures), and 194 cases at the stage of supervision of execution. The productivity of the IACtHR in terms of judgments could be compared to that of the Grand

---

[30]Article 7 of the Rules of Procedure of the IACtHR. His/her functions are described in Article 10.

[31]Article 8.1 of the Rules of Procedure of the IACtHR.

[32]https://www.echr.coe.int/Documents/Stats_analysis_2018_ENG.pdf. Accessed 3 April 2019.

Chamber of the ECtHR. For instance, in 2018 the IACtHR delivered 28 judgments (21 judgments on admissibility, merits and reparations and 7 interpretation judgments).[33] During the same year the Commission submitted 18 new contentious cases to the IACtHR. It is however difficult to compare the workload of both Courts, since the IACtHR does not have to deal with the filtering of inadmissible cases, which is the sole responsibility of the Inter-American Commission.[34]

6 Procedure and Working Methods

6.1 The ECtHR

The ECtHR has adopted various procedures and working methods which have helped it better serve the interests of human rights in Europe, be it by maximizing its efficiency and output or intervening in a timely manner.

When an application reaches the ECtHR it has to be compliant with Rule 47 of the Rules of Court, which means it has to contain all of the information requested in the relevant parts of the application form provided by the Court. If the application is not properly filled in, an applicant (or his representative if such exists) is informed about the failures in its completion enabling him or her to re-lodge an application complying with the relevant requirements. The six-month period referred to in Article 35 § 1 of the European Convention is interrupted only when a complete application is sent to the Court. It is therefore wise for applicants to send in their application in a timely manner, for them to have enough time to comply with the relevant requirements if they have failed on their first try. A rigorous approach in the application of Rule 47, as of 2014, has penalised applicants who left it to the last days before the expiry of the time-limit to lodge their applications which were incomplete. However, such a system has saved time in the Registry's registration process and the allocation of a case to a judicial formation given that a complete and clear application allows court (Registry) officials to determine speedily the judicial pathway the application will take.

An application may be assigned to a Single-judge formation if it is evidently inadmissible (such as for example, where an application is out of 6 months, or an applicant failed to exhaust domestic remedies, but also in the case that the complaints are manifestly ill-founded on the basis of the ECtHR's case-law). As of recent the ECtHR has adopted a one-in one-out policy concerning such cases, which means that evidently inadmissible cases will be processed a few days or weeks after they

---

[33]The Grand Chamber of the ECtHR, in 2018, delivered 14 judgments and one strike-out decision.

[34]For instance, in 2017 the Inter-American Commission received 2494 new petitions. At the end of the year, there were 4002 petitions pending initial evaluation and 2622 petitions pending in the admissibility and merits phases. See the Annual Report of the Inter-American Commission, 2017, chapter II: http://www.oas.org/en/iachr/docs/annual/2017/TOC.asp. Accessed 3 April 2019.

have reached the Court. This has enabled applicants to have a decision in a much shorter time span than used to be the case in the past when cases were dealt with, mainly, in a chronological order.[35] This is not to say that cases which are not declared inadmissible in the immediate months following their lodging will not be declared inadmissible at a later stage by any one of the judicial formations.

When a case is not evidently inadmissible it will be decided by a Committee or Chamber. With the introduction of Protocol No. 14, Article 28 of the European Convention provides that a Committee may, by a unanimous vote, declare an application inadmissible or strike it out of its list of cases, where such decision can be taken without further examination; or declare an application admissible and render at the same time a judgment on the merits, if the underlying question in the case, concerning the interpretation or the application of the Convention or the Protocols thereto, is already the subject of well-established case-law of the ECtHR. Their decision or judgments will be final. In line with this extended competence of the Committee a number of practices have been adopted enabling cases to be determined speedily.

Of particular interest is the well-established case-law (WECL) procedure, which applies to cases of a repetitive nature, such as length of proceedings or conditions of detention. In such cases no observations are asked for from the parties, unless they wish to do so. The original procedure, developed a little less than a decade ago, allowed for an increase in the handling of repetitive cases and a multitude of strike-outs[36] which till then were less common. However, this approach reached its apex after 2015, by means of the WECL fast-track procedure implemented via highly effective IT tools—known as WECL modules. This system requires less drafting and is based on automatic processing via specific IT systems. The internal deadlines are shorter and the life time of an application is consequently also reduced. The WECL fast-track procedure is to be commended for its time-saving but also because it is able to prevent the emergence of a backlog of WECL cases. In the period 2015–2017 the WECL fast-track procedure accounted for a substantial proportion of the total number of communications, judgments and decisions by the Court: 48% in 2015; 61% in 2016; 47% in 2017.[37] Some of such cases end up being settled between the parties, either on the basis of a proposal already made by the Registry or on agreement between the parties themselves. If a settlement is reached the application is normally struck out in accordance with Article 39 of the Convention. If the parties do not agree to settle the case, the respondent Government may make a declaration acknowledging the violation of the Convention and undertaking to provide the applicant with redress. This is known as a unilateral declaration, which, if accepted by the judges deciding on the case, can lead to the striking out of the application under Article 37 § 1 (c) of the European Convention, even if the applicants wish the

---

[35]Without prejudice to the application of the ECtHR's Priority Policy.

[36]Under Article 37 § 1 (c) or Article 39 of the European Convention.

[37]Period 1 January to 31 October 2017. Statistics prepared for the Court's meeting with Government Agents on 4 December 2017.

examination of the case to be continued. This system enables an economy of time and resources as it avoids having to proceed to judgment when the Court is satisfied with the terms of the unilateral declaration and considers that respect for human rights as defined in the Convention and the Protocols thereto do not require it to continue the examination of the application (Article 37 § 1 *in fine*).

Another tool which has allowed the ECtHR to act on the situation concerning repetitive cases is the pilot judgment procedure. Indeed, when a domestic problem becomes the subject of a number of identical applications before the Court, the latter will aim to select some applications and process them in accordance with the pilot-judgment procedure.[38] Such a procedure allows for the adoption of a judgment, in a leading case, which will indicate to the respondent State the measures which need to be taken to correct the systemic problem. On the expiry of the time-limit set in that judgment, the Court will review the position in the light of any general or individual remedial measures taken at national level in response to the pilot judgment. A further tool within this procedure is the possibility for the ECtHR to adjourn or freeze the examination of all the other cases related to the same systemic issue. Such an approach is subject to the State acting promptly upon the delivery of the final judgment. In this way a balance is reached between the interests of the persons suffering from this same problem clogging the system, and that of other persons whose cases require a timely, yet individual, examination by the ECtHR.

As to the procedure before the Chamber, in order to maximise its resources (by diminishing the number of cases to be dealt with in a Chamber and thus lightening the Section agendas), at the present time, their competence has in practice been "limited" mainly to complex cases which have not been subject to the ECtHR's assessment previously. In particular, cases that may potentially bring about a development, a change or a clarification of the case-law remain to be examined by Chambers as well as cases presenting a novel factual context in which existing case-law principles are to be applied.[39] Thus, while until 2017 all non-repetitive cases were, as a rule, examined by Chambers, today, non-repetitive cases which are nonetheless based on already established general principles and do not create jurisprudential novelty, or are not of particular importance to the State concerned, are considered as falling into a category of "Broader WECL" and are dealt with by Committees.

Another exercise undertaken by the ECtHR to relieve it from certain tasks is shifting some of its ground work onto Governments who have accepted to take it on instead. In particular, this refers to the Immediate simplified (IMSI) communication procedure. This novel approach means that it is no longer for the court (Registry) officials to sift through all the documents in detail and prepare a statement of facts, which is then quality checked by Registrars and examined judicially. Through the

---

[38]See Rule 61 of the Rules of Court. See, for instance, the case *Torreggiani and Others v. Italy*, nos. 43517/09 and 6 others, 8 January 2013.

[39]See for more details the Follow-up to the CDDH Report on the Longer-Term Future of the system of the European Convention on Human Rights—GR-H (20 February 2018).

IMSI procedure the respondent Government is informed of the subject matter of an application and the Convention issue raised in the case is indicated to them. It is then for the Government to prepare a statement of facts which will eventually be used by the Registry for the preparation of the case. This procedure reaps its fruits and avoids an excessive burden on the Governments, particularly when applications appear likely to be struck out, *inter alia*, on the basis of a unilateral declaration or a friendly settlement i.e. situations where a statement of facts becomes less relevant or even unnecessary. The IMSI procedure may apply to any case, irrespective of whether it is assigned to a Committee or a Chamber.

The most recent development in the ECtHR procedure, introduced throughout the Court in 2019 and applicable to both the Chamber and Committee procedures, is the compulsory non-contentious procedure. In practice this means that once a case is communicated to the Government, a period of 12 weeks will be dedicated to the parties to allow them the possibility of reaching a settlement, or of the Government to submit a unilateral declaration. Only once it is clear that none of these avenues will be pursued, will the contentious phase take off and the parties proceed to submit observations on the case. This does not mean that a settlement cannot be reached at a later stage if the parties so wish. This system is in principle applicable to any type of case although it seems logical to have some exceptions, such as, for example, in cases suitable for the pilot procedure.

When it comes to procedures, one of the few which has remained unchanged is the Grand Chamber procedure. A case may reach the Grand Chamber either via relinquishment by a Chamber[40] or via a referral request.[41] Relinquishment is possible when a case pending before a Chamber raises a serious question affecting the interpretation of the Convention or the Protocols thereto, or where the resolution of a question before the Chamber might have a result inconsistent with a judgment previously delivered by the Court. Referral is possible only after a judgment has been delivered by the Chamber and if one of the parties so requests within 3 months from the delivery of that judgment. According to Article 43 § 2 of the Convention, a panel of five judges of the Grand Chamber shall accept the request if the case raises a serious question affecting the interpretation or application of the Convention or the Protocols thereto, or a serious issue of general importance. Thus, the panel acts as a filter which allows for the Grand Chamber not to be overburdened.[42] This step is extremely relevant bearing in mind that the Grand Chamber procedure is both complex and lengthy compared to the procedures before the other formations.

Finally, this section would not be complete if a few words were not spent on the ECtHR's power to indicate interim measures in proceedings before it.[43] According

---

[40]Article 30 of the European Convention.

[41]Article 43 of the European Convention.

[42]For instance in 2018, the panel of the Grand Chamber considered 120 referral requests but only accepted them in 5 cases. See Annual Report ECtHR 2018, p. 162: https://www.echr.coe.int/Documents/Annual_report_2018_ENG.pdf. Accessed 3 April 2019.

[43]Rule 39 of the Rules of Court.

to Rule 39 of the Rules of Court, the Chamber or, where appropriate, the President of the Section or a duty judge may, at the request of a party or of any other person concerned, or of their own motion, indicate to the parties any interim measure which they consider should be adopted in the interests of the parties or of the proper conduct of the proceedings. Generally the ECtHR applies Rule 39 where an applicant faces imminent risk of serious and irreparable damage. Indeed the vast majority of cases in which Rule 39 has been applied concern deportation and extradition proceedings and involve complaints that the applicant will be at real risk of a violation of Article 2 (the right to life) or Article 3 (the right not to be subjected to torture or inhuman treatment) of the Convention, if returned to the receiving State.

6.2 The IACtHR

The comparison between the ECtHR and the IACtHR in terms of procedure and working methods is not self-evident, given the differences in size, competence and workload between both jurisdictions. However, there are some interesting aspects of the IACtHR's procedure and practices which are worth mentioning.

The Victim's Legal Assistance Fund of the IACtHR was established by the General Assembly of the OAS, by way of Resolution AG/RES. 2426 of 3 June 2008. The purpose of this Fund is to cover the cost of litigation before the IACtHR for those alleged victims who lack the necessary economic resources. These costs may cover the presentation of evidence by the victims as well as the travel expenses for the attendance at the public hearing of the alleged victims, witnesses, experts and representatives. It is the President of the Court who decides which costs may be funded through the Fund.[44] The financing of the Fund depends on voluntary contributions from the Member States of the OAS, the permanent observer States, other States and donors that may wish to collaborate with the Fund.[45] The IACtHR in its final judgment may order the respondent State to reimburse expenditures made from the Fund.[46] Similarly, before the ECtHR, once a case is communicated to the respondent Government, applicants may, upon a decision by the President, receive legal aid if they cannot afford to instruct a lawyer and if the Court considers it is necessary to grant such assistance for the proper conduct of the case.[47] However, the amount allocated by way of legal aid is low and represents only a contribution to the legal costs. The sum awarded in legal aid is paid by the CoE.

Until 2009, the alleged victims who could not bear the costs of a legal representative were represented by the Inter-American Commission on Human Rights. After

---

[44]See, for instance, Order of the President of the IACtHR, 18 December 2013, case of the Garifuna Community and its members v. Honduras.

[45]Norway's contributions to the Fund represented 80% of the contributions in 2017.

[46]Article 5 of the Rules for the Operation of the Victim's Legal Assistance Fund of the IACtHR.

[47]Rules 100 to 105 of the Rules of Court set out the details of such legal aid.

the 2009 reform of the Rules of the Court, in cases where alleged victims are acting without duly accredited legal representation, the Court may, of its own motion, appoint an Inter-American Defender to represent them during the processing of the case.[48] For this purpose, the IACtHR signed a memorandum of understanding with the Inter-American Association of Public Defenders (IADEF). The latter appoints one of their public defenders to assume the legal representation of the alleged victim during the entire proceedings. The legal representation before the IACtHR by the person appointed by the AIDEF is provided free of charge. The Inter-American defender will charge only the expenses arising from the defence. The IACtHR will contribute by paying the reasonable and necessary expenses that he or she incurs to the extent possible via the Victims' Legal Assistance Fund. Conversely, before the ECtHR, while legal representation is not obligatory until communication of a case to the respondent Government—and even then it is subject to some exceptions—the ECtHR does not appoint a legal representative to act for the applicant. It is the applicant's responsibility to seek such representation, if necessary via the bar associations of the respective States.

The IACtHR holds one and up to three special sessions per year outside San José. Contracting States invite the Court to hold these sessions in their territory. During these sessions the IACtHR holds public hearings, deliberates on cases and organises public seminars on specific topics, normally at the premises of the highest courts of the host country. This practice is very positive for the visibility of the IACtHR in many Contracting States and contributes to the strengthening of the dialogue between the Court and national authorities, including domestic courts and tribunals. This practice is not shared by the ECtHR which has its permanent seat in Strasbourg.

The IACtHR may order provisional measures (under Article 63 § 2 of the American Convention) that are precautionary in nature, like the ECtHR's interim measures. The IACtHR's provisional measures also serve a protective purpose, as they are "*not only precautionary in the sense that they maintain a legal situation, but fundamentally protective because they protect human rights*".[49] Provisional measures of protection are ordered by the IACtHR to guarantee the rights of specific individuals or groups of individuals who are in a situation of: (a) extreme gravity and (b) urgency, and (c) risk of suffering irreparable harm. The Inter-American Commission can request the IACtHR to order provisional measures at any time, even if the case has not yet been submitted to the jurisdiction of the Court, while the representatives of the alleged victims can do so only if the measures relate to a case that the Court is already examining. The IACtHR may also order such measures *ex officio* at any stage of the proceedings. Provisional measures may be extended after the IACtHR has already judged on the merits, for instance if the victims

---

[48] Article 37 of the Rules of Procedure of the IACtHR. Although the cases are submitted to the Inter-American Court by the Inter-American Commission and not by the alleged victims, the alleged victims can participate in the written and oral proceedings before the Court (Articles 40, 46 and 51 of the Rules of Procedure of the IACtHR).

[49] See the order of 8 September 2004 in the matter of *Luisiana Ríos et al. regarding Venezuela*, para. 5.

continue to receive threats at the stage of supervision of the execution of the judgment.[50] The Court or its President may decide to call for a public or private hearing to verify the implementation of the provisional measures and even order any procedures that are required, such as on-site visits to verify the actions that the State is taking.[51] The ambit of application of provisional measures is generally wider than that in the practice of the European system. For instance, the IACtHR has frequently ordered the State to provide security measures, by permanent escort or guard, to persons whose life and integrity were threatened.[52] It has also ordered a State to protect the offices of a newspaper which had been the object of attacks and threats, as well as to protect the life, personal integrity and freedom of expression of the people working for that newspaper.[53]

Under Article 63 § 1 of the American Convention, the IACtHR is empowered to rule that the consequences of the violation be remedied and that fair compensation be paid to the injured party. In most of its judgments the IACtHR awards measures of reparation which cover restitution (for instance, the release of a person unlawfully deprived of liberty), satisfaction (public acts to acknowledge the international responsibility of the State, publication of the judgment in the official language of the country), rehabilitation (medical and psychological care), guarantees of non-repetition (legislative measures, training of public officials), the obligation to investigate, prosecute and punish the human rights violations found, and pecuniary compensation. This goes far beyond what the ECtHR normally does in its judgments, which are in principle declaratory and only exceptionally contain indication of general and/or individual measures (other than financial compensation) that the respondent State should take to execute the judgment, either on the basis of Article 46 of the European Convention or in the context of a pilot-judgment procedure. Unlike the European system, where this responsibility lies with the Committee of Ministers of the CoE, the IACtHR supervises itself the execution of each of the measures ordered in its judgments, through a fully jurisdictional procedure involving all the parties which includes public hearings and the issuance of orders, by which the IACtHR assesses the degree of compliance by the State and gives further instructions for compliance.[54]

---

[50]For instance, in the case of *García Prieto et al. v. El Salvador*, judgment of 20 November 2007 and order of 3 February 2010.

[51]In 2017, the IACtHR visited a prison in Brazil in order to verify the compliance with provisional measures applied with respect to persons deprived of their liberty in that prison, in the case of *the Plácido de Sá Carvalho Prison Complex with regard to Brazil*.

[52]Case of *Barrios Family v. Venezuela*, order of 30 May 2013.

[53]Case of *"El Nacional" and "Así es la Noticia" Newspapers v. Venezuela*, order of 6 July 2004.

[54]For a comparison between the American and the European human rights protection systems in terms of reparation, execution of judgments and monitoring of the execution of judgments, see Saavedra Alessandri et al. (2017), pp. 211–267.

7 Conclusion

In recent years the ECtHR and the IACtHR have intensified their cooperation in the form of institutional visits by their respective Presidents and judges, staff exchanges and joint seminars as well as publications. The importance of this cooperation cannot be overstated given the similarity of the rights and freedoms protected by the respective treaties governing the work of the two courts, the existence of equivalent principles of interpretation and the increasing similarity of the issues brought before them. This strengthening of institutional cooperation has improved judicial dialogue and increased the cross-references to each other's jurisprudence. However, this article has shown that both courts have kept their differences in terms of composition, internal organisation, workload, procedure and working methods. This is not unexpected given that the Inter-American system of human rights protection has not evolved in the same direction as the European one. Their structural difference makes the comparison between both courts inevitably difficult. Nevertheless, it is possible to draw certain parallelisms and identify good practices with regard to their internal organisation and functioning. For example, on the one hand, the practice of the IACtHR on reparation, as well as its experience in the supervision of the execution of its judgments, may become an interesting source of inspiration for the ECtHR, especially now that the ECtHR is increasing its involvement in matters of execution, as a result of the use of the pilot-judgment procedure and the possibilities offered by Article 46 of the European Convention (notably under Article 46 § 4). On the other hand, the new procedural tools used by the ECtHR in handling repetitive cases (WECL, friendly settlements, unilateral declarations, pilot-judgments) and the working methods of its Registry could prove useful in its turn to the IACtHR, which may, in the future, also be confronted with cases of a repetitive nature.

Reference

Saavedra Alessandri, P., Cano Palomares, G., & Hernández Ramos, M. (2017). Reparación y supervisión de sentencias. In J. García Roca & E. Carmona Cuenca (Eds.), ¿Hacia una globalización de los derechos? El impacto de las sentencias del Tribunal Europeo y de la Corte Interamericana (pp. 211–267). Pamplona: Thomson Reuters Aranzadi.

The Notion of Judicial Independence: Impartiality and Effectiveness of Judges

Péter Paczolay

Dilexi iustitiam et odivi iniquitatem.

Contents

1 The Role of Judicial Independence

The independence of the judiciary serves as a shield for the judicial process in a well-working democratic society: it provides for the protection of the judicial system both against external influences and also to the individuals who have recourse to courts in order to settle their disputes. When speaking of judicial independence and the quality of judicial decisions, we are analysing two sides of the same coin: guaranteeing the independence of judges is as important as improving the quality of judicial decisions

Péter Paczolay is Professor of Law and Political Science, University of Szeged, former President of the Constitutional Court of Hungary (2008–2015) and Judge at the European Court of Human Rights, Strasbourg, France.

P. Paczolay (✉)
European Court of Human Rights, Strasbourg, France
e-mail: Peter.Paczolay@echr.coe.int

© Springer Nature Switzerland AG 2019
P. Pinto de Albuquerque, K. Wojtyczek (eds.), *Judicial Power in a Globalized World*, https://doi.org/10.1007/978-3-030-20744-1_22

as the two notions are strongly inter-dependent. Therefore I approach the topic of judicial independence focusing on impartiality and effectiveness.

Serving as the strongest guarantee of the rule of law and the protection of human rights, judicial independence is regarded as one of the most eminent general principles of law. This is evident from the extensive international literature and a large number of international documents acknowledging the need to ensure the independence of the judiciary and the functioning of the judicial system in the interest of the society.[1] The principle of the independence of judges means that judges can administer justice only while being independent of the parties to the case and of institutions of State power, political and public associations, natural and legal persons.[2] This concept is one of the most archaic principles paving the development of today's functioning judicial systems, as already Montesquieu warned his readers that there is no liberty if the power of judging is not separate from legislative power and from executive power. If it were joined to legislative power, the power over the life of the citizens would be arbitrary, for the judge would be the legislator. If it were joined to executive power, the judge could have the force of an oppressor.[3]

The term "independent" refers to independence *vis-à-vis* the other branches of power[4] and also *vis-à-vis* the parties to a particular case.[5] With regard to the question of independence from other branches, parliamentary systems tend to give priority to the functional cooperation of the legislative and executive branches. The same tendency is strengthened by the political interpenetration of the two branches resulting from the rule of the parties of the parliamentary majority in both of them. The closely interwoven relationship of the legislative and executive branches is based on party politics,[6] as politics in parliamentary systems mean to a large extent party politics. Party politics in practice transcend the constitutional distinction between the legislature and the executive.[7] As a consequence, the legislative and executive branches are in effect no longer separated but rather form a solid political block. Therefore, in parliamentary systems it is necessary to vest the judiciary with substantive independence in order to limit the possibility of abuse of power by the other branches, and to effectively protect the liberties of citizens.[8] This underlines

---

[1]Bangalore Principles of Judicial Conduct; Kyiv Recommendations on Judicial Independence in Eastern Europe, South Caucasus and Central Asia from 2010; Burgh House Principles on the Independence of the International Judiciary.

[2]*Campbell and Fell v United Kingdom*, no. 7819/77, 7878/77, ECtHR 1984, § 78.

[3]Montesquieu (1992), p. 157.

[4]*Beaumartin v France*, no. 15287/89, ECtHR 1994, § 38.

[5]*Sramek v. Austria*, no. 8790/79, ECtHR 1984, § 42.

[6]Sajó and Uitz (2017), p. 144.

[7]*"When a government party makes a policy decision, therefore, it can be effectively impossible to determine whether this is a decision of the party in government, the party in parliament, or indeed the wider party organization in the country as a whole. In practice it is likely to be a complex interaction between all three."* Laver (2008).

[8]For the importance of the separation of powers between political organs and the judiciary see: *Stafford v. the United Kingdom* [GC], no. 46295/99, ECHR 2002-IV, § 78.

the importance of judicial independence from the point of view of political science, too.

Obviously, there is a vast amount of necessary interferences between the judiciary and other branches of power. The legislator regulates the organization, the competences, the procedures of the courts under constitutional guarantees, it may define the tenure, the conditions of the appointment of judges, and it can also play a role in their dismissal.[9] For instance, the executive power may appoint judges or intervene in the nomination process and administer courts and tribunals, or heads of State may grant pardons thus overruling or eliminating the effects of lawful judicial decisions. However, these functions do not necessarily mean an influence on the work of judges. As pointed out by the European Court of Human Rights ('ECtHR' or 'the Court') in *Flux v. Moldova*, the appointment of judges is permissible unless the appointed judges are influenced or pressured by the executive power in the performance of their judicial duties.[10] Similarly with regards to the separation from the legislative branch, in *Sacilor Lormines v. France* the Court stated that even if the judges are appointed by the Parliament, it does not *per se* result in them being subordinate to or instructed by the authorities when carrying out their adjudicatory role.[11] The legitimacy of these necessary interferences was pointed out in a more general sense in *Kleyn v. the Netherlands*, where the Court stated that "*neither Article 6, nor any other provision of the Convention requires States to comply with any theoretical constitutional concepts regarding the permissible limits of the powers' interaction. The question is always whether, in a given case, the requirements of the Convention are met.*"[12]

As we know, the American vision of separation of powers, enshrined also in the US Constitution, elevated the judiciary to the rank of the third branch of power. However, the judicial branch has less powers than the political branches (the legislative and the executive), the "least dangerous branch" in the wording of the Federalist Papers.[13] Its main role is to check the other two branches, mainly through constitutional review.

The crux of judicial independence is therefore not solely the strict separation of the judiciary but rather focusing on safeguards of judicial impartiality.[14] It can be achieved by guaranteeing judges freedom from the influence of external forces, and by setting strict incompatibility rules (e.g. in new democracies prohibiting party membership, thus severely limiting the judges' right of association).[15]

---

[9]Wittes (2009).

[10]*Flux v. Moldova* (no. 2), no. 31001/03, ECtHR 2007, § 27.

[11]*Sacilor-Lormines v. France*, no. 65411/01, ECtHR 2006, § 67.

[12]*Kleyn and Others v. the Netherlands* [GC], nos. 39,343/98 and 3 others, ECtHR 2004, § 193.

[13]Hamilton et al. (1961), p. 465.

[14]CCJE Opinion No. 1(2001), paras. 11, 12; Council of Europe, Challenges for judicial independence and impartiality in the member states of the Council of Europe, SG/Inf(2016)3rev, para. 34.

[15]*Morris v. the United Kingdom*, no. 38784/97, ECtHR 2002-I, § 58.

The independence of the judiciary has both an institutional and an individual aspect.[16] The institutional aspect comprises of the independence and autonomy of the judicial branch from the political actors and other influences (e.g. media pressures). It includes also the arrangements for functional operation and its adequate financing. The individual aspect refers to the independence and impartiality of the judge and not of the judiciary as such. The judge is independent and subject only to the law. This refers to its independence from political and any other interference, independence from the parties, from politicians, and any other person or institution. It means the personal liberty of the judge in judicial decision-making. Impartiality is the other side of the same requirement: the judge should decide the case without external pressures and interference.[17] Judicial independence is not to be considered as the personal privilege or the innate right of the judge but as a guarantee of the functioning of the third branch of power. This leads us to the responsibility of judges in exercising their power in an appropriate and effective manner.[18]

2 European Regulations and Documents

At the European level the right to an independent and impartial tribunal is guaranteed by Article 6 of the European Convention on Human Rights ('the Convention'):

> 1. In the determination of his civil rights and obligations or of any criminal charge against him, everyone is entitled to a fair and public hearing within a reasonable time by an independent and impartial tribunal established by law. (...).[19]

As the Convention's interpretative body, the ECtHR elaborates on certain aspects of judicial independence and helps crystallizing applicable thresholds through its jurisprudence. However, as the Venice Commission's systemic overview of the European standards of judiciary independence rightly noted, the case-law of the Court, by its very nature, does not approach the issue in a systematic way.[20]

The most authoritative text, besides the Convention, on the independence of the judiciary at the European level—although being solely a soft law measure—is Recommendation (94)12 of the Committee of Ministers on the Independence, Efficiency and Role of Judges. It provides that *"the independence of judges should be guaranteed pursuant to the provisions of the Convention and constitutional principles, for example by inserting specific provisions in the constitutions or other legislation or incorporating the provisions of this recommendation in internal*

---

[16]Sajó and Uitz (2017), p. 319.

[17]Sajó and Uitz (2017), p. 319. See also: *Campbell and Fell v. UK, Henryk Urban* and *Ryszard Urban v. Poland.*

[18]I do not address here the closely connected question of *'Qui custodiet ipsos custodes'.*

[19]European Convention on Human Rights, Article 6(1).

[20]Venice Commission, European Standards on the Independence of the Judiciary, A Systematic Overview. Study No. 494/2008, para. 1.

law."[21] By this statement, the Recommendation links the Convention and national constitutions, indicating that States should incorporate the European standards into their own national constitutions thereby creating a more solid and general standard similarly in all Member States.

Also an important and comprehensive text is *Opinion No. 1 of the Consultative Council of European Judges (CCJE) on standards concerning the independence of the judiciary and the irremovability of judges.*[22] The CCJE analysed the standards set in Recommendation (94)12, the relevance of these standards and any other international standards to problems in these fields. Other Opinions of the CCJE are also relevant in this context, e.g. CCJE Opinions no. 6 on Fair Trial within a Reasonable Time, no. 10 on the Council for the Judiciary in the Service of Society and no. 11 on the Quality of Judicial Decisions. Also, the Magna Carta of Judges (Fundamental Principles) was adopted by the CCJE in November 2010.[23]

The European Commission for Democracy through Law of the Council of Europe (better known as the Venice Commission) adopted a *Report on Judicial Appointments* (CDL-AD(2007)028) in 2007 which covers issues of particular importance for judicial independence.[24] Later on in 2010 the Venice Commission adopted two general reports on the most important European standards applicable to the judiciary that constitute a key reference for the Commission in the assessment of country-specific legislation regulating the judiciary and the guarantees of its independent functioning.[25]

The reports underline that the independence of the judiciary has both an objective component, as an indispensable quality of the judiciary as such, and a subjective component as the right of an individual to have his/her rights and freedoms adjudicated by an independent judge. Without independent judges there can be no correct and lawful implementation of rights and freedoms. Flipping to the other side of the coin, the report emphasizes that the independence of the judges in a given society depends on several factors. In addition to the institutional rules guaranteeing

---

[21] Council of Europe, Recommendation (94)12 of the Committee of Ministers on the Independence, Efficiency and Role of Judges, Principle I, 2(a).

[22] Consultative Council of European Judges (CCJE), Opinion n. 1 on standards concerning the independence of the judiciary and the irremovability of judges, CCJE (2001) OP N°1.

[23] Judicial Independence

2. Judicial independence and impartiality are essential prerequisites for the operation of justice.

3. Judicial independence shall be statutory, functional and financial. It shall be guaranteed with regard to the other powers of the State, to those seeking justice, other judges and society in general, by means of national rules at the highest level. The State and each judge are responsible for promoting and protecting judicial independence.

[24] European Standards on the Independence of the Judiciary: A Systemic Overview, Venice Commission, Strasbourg, 3 October, 2008.

[25] Report on the independence of the judicial system part I: The independence of judges. Adopted by the Venice Commission at its 82nd Plenary Session (Venice, 12-13 March 2010), CDL-AD(2010) 004.

independence, the personal character and the professional quality of the individual judge deciding a case, and the legal culture as a whole in a particular society are also of major importance. However, even the best institutional rules cannot work without the good will of those responsible for their application and implementation. The implementation of existing standards is therefore at least as important as the identification of new standards needed.[26]

Not only did the Venice Commission provide general reports addressing the sphere of judicial independency, it also analysed particular legal situations and draft laws of certain States with regard to their compatibility with the Council of Europe's standards on the rule of law, e.g. in the case of Ukraine and Albania in 2015 and Poland in 2017.

In the case of Ukraine in 2015, where the regime change left a corrupt judiciary appointed under dubious circumstances,[27] the independency of the judiciary was in such a crisis that the government proposed to dismiss all judges and to appoint the new judiciary under new criteria. This proposal was submitted to the Venice Commission for opinion, and although the Commission recognized the risk of such political influence, as well as the need for extraordinary measures to remedy these shortcomings,[28] they objected to the idea from a rule of law perspective. As the Commission stated:

> 73. ... [E]xtraordinary measures should indeed be aimed at identifying the individual judges who are not fit to occupy a judicial position. In this respect, dismissal of every member of the judiciary appointed during a particular period would not be an appropriate solution to the problems indicated by the authorities. That is particularly so in the case of judges who were appointed in a lawful manner in a country which had a democratic system, although imperfect in many respects and allowing too great a political influence in the appointment of judges.

As a conclusion, the Commission stated that the transformation of the Ukrainian judiciary into a competent and transparent system is to be achieved in a fair and proportionate manner, not compromising judicial independence.[29] Furthermore, they pointed out that in order to meet the European standards with regard to the independency of the judiciary, the problems to be eliminated do not lie in the law itself, rather in Ukrainian constitutional provisions.[30] With this, the Venice Commission implied that in order to reform the judiciary to conform to European standards, a State must remedy deficiencies originating from the constitution itself.[31]

---

[26]Report on the independence of the judicial system part I: The independence of judges. Adopted by the Venice Commission at its 82nd Plenary Session (Venice, 12–13 March 2010), CDL-AD(2010) 004, paras. 6–7, 10.

[27]Sajó and Uitz (2017), p. 156.

[28]Venice Commission Opinion, Ukraine, 2015, para. 73.

[29]Venice Commission Opinion, Ukraine, 2015, para. 91.

[30]Venice Commission Opinion, Ukraine, 2015, para. 92.

[31]Venice Commission Opinion, Ukraine, 2015, para. 13.

With regard to the Albanian situation, where the constitutionalisation of independency standards in the post-communist era resulted in constitutional guarantees being conferred upon judges who were not yet independent and impartial in practice, the need for revising constitutional provisions was similarly on the table.[32] The Albanian Parliament's Ad Hoc Committee requested the opinion of the Commission with regard to the overall reform of the Albanian judiciary submitted in the form of Draft Amendments to the Constitution.[33] The amendments focused on the independency of the system in several regards, addressing both the permanent institutional arrangements of the judiciary and the prosecution service, as well as the cleansing of the ranks of the judiciary—similarly to the Ukranian example.[34]

With special regard to the notion of independency, the Venice Commission analysed firstly the institutional arrangements surrounding prosecution, pointing out the importance of specifying whether the amendments refer to internal or external independence by their wording.[35] This clarification was noted to be of utter importance as to the required level of transparency within the different prosecutorial institutions and between the prosecution and the executive.[36] Likewise, the Commission scrutinized the planned vetting of the sitting judges and prosecutors due to the alleged high level of corruption. Hereby the Commission made reference to the Ukrainian situation presented above, noting, that such measures may have been appropriate in an exceptionally critical political context such as the one in Albania.[37] However, the Commission also noted that in any case due regard must be paid to the independency standards rooting from Article 6 of the ECHR.[38] They stated that in case the process is *"a general measure, applied equally to all judges, decided at the constitutional level, and accompanied by certain procedural safeguards and not related to any specific case a judge might have before him/her"*, it is compatible with the standards of Article 6.[39] However, due regard must be paid to exclude possibilities where the vetting procedure is abused in order to influence the judge's position in a particular case.[40]

A third key opinion by the Venice Commission regarding the independence of the judiciary was delivered in the case of Poland in 2017. The reasons for preparing the government's amendments were to increase the efficiency of the judiciary, enhance judges' accountability, reduce procedural delays and strengthen professionalism.[41] Although the Commission recognised the need for reforming the Polish judicial

---

[32]Venice Commission Opinion, Albania, 2015, para. 8.

[33]Venice Commission Opinion, Albania, 2015, para. 1.

[34]Venice Commission Opinion, Albania, 2015, para. 9.

[35]Venice Commission Opinion, Albania, 2015, para. 84.

[36]Venice Commission Opinion, Albania, 2015, para. 84–85.

[37]Venice Commission Opinion, Albania, 2015, para. 100.

[38]Venice Commission Opinion, Albania, 2015, para. 107.

[39]Venice Commission Opinion, Albania, 2015, para. 107.

[40]Venice Commission Opinion, Albania, 2015, para. 107.

[41]Venice Commission Opinion, Poland, 2017, para. 6.

system, as well as the possibility of the renewal of the judiciary,[42] it still concluded that the measures presented in the amendments by the Polish government, together with past acts passed on the Public Prosecutor's Office *"enable the legislative and executive powers to interfere in a severe and extensive manner in the administration of justice, and thereby pose a grave threat to the judicial independence."*[43] This conclusion was the result of several key aspects combined.[44] First, the Commission stated that the planned immediate replacement of the sitting members of the National Council of the Judiciary would lead to the politicisation of the body.[45] Second, it concluded that the lowering of the retirement age would have a drastic immediate effect on the independency of the judiciary, combined with the planned discretionary power of the President and the Minister of Justice to extend the Supreme Court judges' and judges' mandates beyond that age if they consider it advantageous.[46]

The opinions of the Venice Commission have an important impact even on the jurisprudence of the ECtHR, as the opinions are often quoted among the relevant international forums and in Council of Europe materials related to the subject of the case.[47]

3 Standards to Determine Judicial Independence at the European Court of Human Rights

The basic principles relevant to the independence of the judiciary should be set out in constitutions or equivalent texts.[48] These principles include the judiciary's independence from other state powers resulting in judges being subject only to the law, being distinguished solely based on their different functions, and their irremovability.[49]

---

[42]Venice Commission Opinion, Poland, 2017, para. 11.

[43]Venice Commission Opinion, Poland, 2017, para. 129.

[44]Venice Commission Opinion, Poland, 2017, para. 95.

[45]Venice Commission Opinion, Poland, 2017, para. 31.

[46]Venice Commission Opinion, Poland, 2017, paras. 51 and 109.

[47]In the case *Baka v. Hungary* [GC], no. 20261/12, ECtHR 2016, for example, the Court referred to Opinion on the draft law on introducing amendments and addenda to the Judicial Code of Armenia (term of office of court presidents), adopted at its 99th Plenary Session (Venice, 13–14 June 2014, CDL-AD(2014)021), and to the Joint Opinion of the Venice Commission and the Directorate of Human Rights (DHR) of the Directorate General of Human Rights and the Rule of Law (DGI) of the Council of Europe, on the draft law on amendments to the Organic Law on General Courts of Georgia, adopted by the Venice Commission at its 100th Plenary Session (Rome, 10–11 October 2014, CDL-AD(2014)031. On how the impact of Venice Commission opinions are reflected in the case-law of the Court, see Bode-Kirchhoff (2014), pp. 55–72.

[48]Venice Commission, The Division for Independence and Efficiency of Justice of the Council of Europe, The various aspects of external and internal independence of the judiciary, Guido Neppi-Modona, 2012, CDL(2012)035.

[49]"It is true that the irremovability of judges by the executive during their term of office must in general be considered as a corollary of their independence and thus included in the guarantees of

The jurisprudence of the ECtHR serves as a yardstick for the determination of independency. In this regard the Court noted that the manner of appointment of its members and the duration of their term of office, the existence of guarantees against outside pressures and the question whether the body presents an appearance of independence are the criteria to be taken into account.[50] The Court has also underlined the judiciary's necessary independence from the legislative. The principle of the rule of law and the notion of fair trial enshrined in Article 6 preclude any interference by the legislature with the administration of justice designed to influence the judicial determination of the dispute.[51]

Another aspect raised by the Court concerns judicial independence within the system of the administration of justice itself. Judicial independence demands individual judges to be free not only from undue influences outside the judiciary, but also from within. This internal judicial independence requires them to be free from directives or pressures from the fellow judges or those who have administrative responsibilities in the Court such as the president of the Court or the president of a division in the Court.[52] The absence of sufficient safeguards securing the independence of judges within the judiciary and, in particular, *vis-à-vis* their judicial superiors, may lead the Court to conclude that an applicant's doubts as to the impartiality of a court may be said to have been objectively justified.[53]

Thus, the Court's case-law has addressed several aspects of the principle of judicial independence: independence from the parties, independence from the executive and legislative powers, and internal judicial independence as well.

The rules of incompatibility are also an essential element of judicial independence. As even the appearance of independency is a factor examined by the Court, judges should not put themselves into a position where their independence or impartiality may be questioned—even if only at the outset. This justifies national rules on the incompatibility of judicial office with other functions and is also a reason why many states restrict political activities of judges.[54]

The Court set up a system of tests for the determination of impartiality and independence, composed of a subjective and an objective test for analysis. The existence of impartiality must be determined firstly by the subjective test, meaning

---

Article 6 para. 1 (art. 6-1). However, the absence of a formal recognition of this irremovability in the law does not in itself imply lack of independence provided that it is recognised in fact and that the other necessary guarantees are present." *Campbell and Fell v United Kingdom*, no. 7819/77, 7878/77, ECtHR 1984, § 80.

[50]*Campbell and Fell v United Kingdom*, no. 7819/77, 7878/77, ECtHR 1984, § 78; *Kleyn and Others v. the Netherlands* [GC], nos. 39343/98 and 3 others, ECtHR 2004, § 190.

[51]*Stran Greek Refineries and Stratis Andreadis v. Greece*, Series A no. 301 B, ECtHR 1994, §. 49.

[52]*Moiseyev v. Russia*, no. 62936/00, ECtHR 2008, § 182.

[53]*Parlov-Tkalčić v. Croatia*, no. 24810/06, ECtHR 2009, § 86.

[54]*Piersack v Belgium*, no. 8692/79, ECtHR 1982, § 30; *Bajaldziev v Former Yugoslav Republic of Macedonia*, no.4650/06, ECtHR 2011, §§ 30–32.

that on the basis of the personal conviction of a particular judge in a given case.[55] The Court stated in *Padovani v. Italy* that this personal impartiality of a judge must be presumed until there is proof to the contrary.[56]

As to the objective test, the Court in the *Bajaldziev* case stated that "*when applied to a body sitting as a bench it means determining whether, quite apart from the personal conduct of any of the members of that body, there are ascertainable facts which may raise doubts as to its impartiality.*"[57] In this respect even appearances may be of some importance, as the Court referred to the famous saying "*justice must not only be done, it must also be seen to be done*" of the High Court of Justice of England.[58]

The Court further reflected on the appearance of independency and impartiality as a factor of determination in the *Procolo v. Luxembourg* and the *Piersack v. Belgium* cases. In the *Procolo v. Luxembourg* case it stated that for finding a violation of Article 6 of the Convention with regards to independency and impartiality, it is enough to cast doubt on the institution's structural impartiality as that doubt in itself is sufficient to vitiate impartiality, and this makes it unnecessary for the Court to look into the other aspects of the complaint.[59] *In Piersack v. Belgium* the Court pointed out that what is at stake is the confidence which the courts in a democratic society must inspire in the public.[60] Thus, any judge in respect of whom there is a legitimate reason to fear a lack of impartiality must withdraw.[61] The concepts of independence and objective impartiality are closely linked and may require joint examination. This was the approach applied in *Oleksandr Volkov v. Ukraine*.[62] As regards to the requirement of impartiality, the Court held that the tribunal must be subjectively free of personal prejudice or bias and must also be impartial from an objective viewpoint; it must offer sufficient guarantees to exclude any legitimate doubt in this respect.[63]

An important institutional and structural element to be taken into consideration whether a tribunal could be considered "independent" is the manner of appointments of judges: according to the notion of the separation of powers[64] between political

---

[55] *Bajaldziev v Former Yugoslav Republic of Macedonia*, no.4650/06, ECtHR 2011, § 30; *Nikolov v. the former Yugoslav Republic of Macedonia*, no. 41195/02, ECtHR 2007, § 19.

[56] *Padovani v. Italy*, Series A no. 257-B, ECtHR 1993, § 26; *Morel v. France*, no. 34130/96, ECtHR 2000-VI, § 41; *Bajaldziev v Former Yugoslav Republic of Macedonia*, no. 4650/06, ECtHR 2011, § 31.

[57] *Bajaldziev v Former Yugoslav Republic of Macedonia*, no. 4650/06, ECtHR 2011, § 32.

[58] *Bajaldziev v Former Yugoslav Republic of Macedonia*, no. 4650/06, ECtHR 2011, § 32.

[59] *Procola v Luxembourg*, no. 14570/89, ECtHR 1995, § 45.

[60] *Piersack v Belgium*, no. 8692/79, ECtHR 1982, § 30.

[61] *Piersack v Belgium*, no. 8692/79, ECtHR 1982, § 30.

[62] *Oleksandr Volkov v. Ukraine*, no. 21722/11, ECtHR 2013, § 107.

[63] *Haarde v. Iceland*, no. 66847/2, ECtHR 2017, § 103.

[64] "The notion of separation of powers between the executive and the judiciary ... has assumed growing importance in the case-law of the Court." *Stafford v. the United Kingdom* [GC], no 46295/ 99, ECtHR 2002-IV, § 78.

organs of the government and the judiciary developed by the Court's case-law, the appointment of judges both by the legislature and the executive is permissible, provided that appointees are free from influence or pressure when carrying out their adjudicatory role.[65]

As a final element, judicial decisions should not be subject to any revision outside the appeals process. The Court held that the mere existence of a power of the Government to block the implementation of a judicial decision gave rise to the violation of Article 6(1) in that the applicant's civil rights and obligations were not "determined" by a "tribunal" within the meaning of that provision.[66] The Court also added that "for an individual litigant it is the consequences of litigation - the operative provisions of a judgment - which are of importance."[67]

4 Quality of Justice: Predictability and Stability of Judicial Decisions

Providing judges with the guarantees of independence is not autotelic; judges are expected to exercise their function impartially and effectively. Turning now to the requirement of effectiveness, it is a recent trend in the examination and study of the judiciary that special attention is to be paid to the criteria of the quality of justice. Different, sometimes overlapping projects have been launched worldwide in order to define such criteria. Judges themselves, as well as the public always had clear views on the quality of justice drawn from their personal experiences or based on reactions to shortcomings in the judicial system. Similarly, courts everywhere and always are criticized for being slow and expensive.[68]

The Council of Europe therefore launched an important initiative by creating the European Commission for the Efficiency of Justice ('CEPEJ'). The CEPEJ reports on the evaluation of judicial systems give a good overview about how the various judicial systems work and what the main trends are. Moreover, the CEPEJ created a working group on the quality of justice in 2007. One of the tasks of this working group is to collect information concerning initiatives taken by member states to promote and increase the quality of adjudication and further legal work in the courts. Another task is to develop concrete instruments for the member states in the area of court quality.

---

[65] *Maktouf and Damjanović v. Bosnia and Herzegovina* [GC], nos. 2312/08 and 34179/08, ECtHR 2013, § 49; *Thiam v. France*, no. 80018/12, ECtHR 2018, § 59.

[66] *Van der Hurk v Netherlands*, no. 16034/90, ECtHR 1994, §§ 44–55.

[67] *Van der Hurk v Netherlands*, no. 16034/90, ECtHR 1994, §§ 44–55.

[68] European Commission for Efficiency of Justice (CEPEJ), Checklist for promoting the quality of justice and the courts adopted by the CEPEJ at its 11th plenary meeting (Strasbourg, 2–3 July 2008).

CEPEJ made it clear that it does not aim to produce neither a theory of quality of justice, nor a definition of quality of justice. Rather, it aims to promote the quality of work within justice systems and to give policy makers and judicial practitioners concrete tools for improving the quality of their own system, taking into account their specificities.

Why are the stability, consistency and predictability of judicial decisions important? The first answer has to do with political philosophy. The role and legitimacy of the judiciary in modern political communities that are democracies are different from the other branches of power. The judiciary, being a counter-majoritarian institution, is independent from the will of the majority that is from democratic processes in a more general way. Consequently, the counter-majoritarian logic of judicial bodies is legitimate as far as their decisions are not arbitrary, inconsistent, contradicting or groundless. The unlimited power of having the final say in disputes has to be counter-balanced by a strict scrutiny of the consistency and constancy of the procedures and decisions. As a legitimate inference, it may be concluded that the quality of justice is the ground for the legitimacy of a court.

But is it possible to define the quality of justice at all? The main element in the judicial process is the decision itself. The decision with all its consequences is the function that a court is expected to fulfil. Even if we say that it is hard to define the quality of justice, judges have to reflect consciously on the values of consistency and predictability. Legal certainty is a basic value that judges try to ensure in the legal system. However, sometimes judges forget that legal certainty is not only a requirement for the law-maker, the law-enforcement or for the individuals but legal certainty has to prevail in the judicial process itself.

What are the possible tools to achieve at least a relative stability in the jurisprudence? When adjudicating a case and interpreting the law, courts develop and apply a number of tests, like balancing, proportionality etc. The coherent use of these tests endorses that all interested parties calculate the likelihood of the favourable decision of the respective court. In more difficult cases, involving very distinctive factual backgrounds and new legal challenges, it is difficult to follow even the well-established jurisprudence of courts. Nonetheless, such cases offer opportunity for the restatement of the respective jurisprudence.

Undoubtedly, there will always be decisions causing surprises and the predictability of jurisprudence does not instantly mean that the decisions of courts are evident. Indeed this is the central and most essential function of the notion jurisprudence: to keep looking for an efficient balance between predictability and flexibility.[69]

---

[69]Dworkin (1986), pp. 147–150.

5 Conclusion

We observe nowadays continuous attacks on the courts by amending the respective constitutional provisions and laws, by cutting back the budget, by curtailing the term of judges, by not executing judicial decisions. However, without underestimating the dangers of these attacks, one may say that the judiciary has always been under threats. Such outstanding American presidents as Thomas Jefferson or Abraham Lincoln openly attacked the judiciary, and Kelsen had to leave not only the Constitutional Court created by him but also Austria. Consequently, there is no reason for panicking, we should rather keep in mind that—as the Hungarian Constitutional Court put it—the realization of the State under the rule of law is an ongoing process.[70] We have to fight day by day for an appropriate political and legal culture.

References

Bode-Kirchhoff, L. (2014). Why the road from Luxembourg to Strasbourg leads through Venice. In K. Dzehtsiarou, T. Konstadinides, T. Lock, & N. O'Meara (Eds.), *Human rights law in Europe: The influence, overlaps and contradictions of the EU and the ECHR*. New York: Routledge.

Consultative Council of European Judges (CCJE), Opinion n. 1 on standards concerning the independence of the judiciary and the irremovability of judges, CCJE (2001) OP N° 1.

Council of Europe, Challenges for judicial independence and impartiality in the member states of the Council of Europe, SG/Inf(2016)3rev.

Council of Europe, Recommendation (94)12 of the Committee of Ministers on the Independence, Efficiency and Role of Judges.

Dworkin, R. (1986). *Law's empire*. Cambridge, MA: Harvard University Press.

European Commission for Efficiency of Justice (CEPEJ), Checklist for promoting the quality of justice and the courts adopted by the CEPEJ at its 11th plenary meeting (Strasbourg, 2–3 July 2008).

Hamilton, A., Madison, J., & Jay, J. (1961). The Federalist Papers [1787-8] Mentor.

Kritz, N. J. (Ed.). (1995). *Transitional Justice* (Vol. III). Washington, DC: United States Institute of Peace Press.

Laver, M. (2008). Legislatures and parliaments in comparative context. In B. Weingast & D. Wittman (Eds.), *Oxford handbook of political economy*. Oxford: Oxford University Press.

Montesquieu, Ch.-L. (1992 [1758]). *The spirit of the laws* (A. M. Cohler, B. C. Miller, & H. S. Stone, Trans. Eds.), Cambridge University Press

Report on the independence of the judicial system part I: The independence of judges. Adopted by the Venice Commission at its 82nd Plenary Session (Venice, 12-13 March 2010), CDL-AD (2010)004.

Sajó, A., & Uitz, R. (2017). *The constitution of freedom: An introduction to legal constitutionalism*. Oxford University Press.

Venice Commission, European Standards on the Independence of the Judiciary, A Systematic Overview. Study No. 494/2008.

Venice Commission, The Division for Independence and Efficiency of Justice of the Council of Europe, The various aspects of external and internal independence of the judiciary, Guido Neppi-Modona, 2012, CDL(2012)035.

Wittes, B. (2009). *Confirmation wars: Preserving independent courts in angry times*. Rowman & Littlefield.

---

[70] 11/1992. (III.5.) Constitutional Court decision on the statute of limitation, in Kritz (1995), p. 631.

Disciplinary Liability of a Judge for a Legal Error: A Threat to Judicial Independence?

Taras Pashuk

Contents

1 Introduction

It is accepted that disciplinary liability of judges may target judicial conduct in the office (for example, lack of respect towards parties) and outside the office (such as membership in a political party). It is also acknowledged that disciplinary liability may be a tool for checking the managerial effectiveness of a judge (for example, ensuring promptness of court proceedings). The problematic issue falls within the area of disciplinary control over the decisional competence of a judge because such control involves legal assessment of the judge's decision outside the judicial process in the case. This, in turn, may pose a threat to judicial independence.

There is no uniform approach as regards the possibility of examining the content of judicial decisions in disciplinary proceedings for possible legal errors. On the one hand, the risks of interfering with judicial independence may prompt a suggestion that no such substantial review of judicial activity should be allowed. On the other

T. Pashuk (✉)
European Court of Human Rights, Strasbourg, France

© Springer Nature Switzerland AG 2019
P. Pinto de Albuquerque, K. Wojtyczek (eds.), *Judicial Power in a Globalized World*, https://doi.org/10.1007/978-3-030-20744-1_23

hand, the considerations of judicial ethics and public confidence in the competent judiciary may point to the need for providing certain disciplinary control over the substance of decisional activity of a judge. So what approach should be chosen as regards the possibility of disciplinary liability of judges for their legal mistakes? This problem could be addressed on the basis of comparative-law analysis, with reference to the international law standards in the area.

2   Immunity from Disciplinary Liability for the Substance of Judicial Decisions

In many established democracies where judiciaries have their long-standing traditions, it is a well-accepted idea that the interpretation and application of law is not subject to disciplinary control, except for appeal and judicial review. Subject to certain reservations, this approach is taken, for example, in France, Belgium, the USA, and Canada.

The review of the content of judicial decisions by a disciplinary authority may result in the following negative consequences. Firstly, it may limit judicial independence in the decision-making process and encroach upon the principle of separation of powers. Secondly, it may turn the disciplinary proceedings into "*quasi* appeal" proceedings where the issues which have to be examined in the ordinary procedural way according to the judicial hierarchy will be examined by a disciplinary authority. Thirdly, it may bring about the situations where the disciplinary body may take over the precedent-making authority since the judges being under the jurisdiction of the disciplinary body will be induced to take into account the findings of that body in previous cases. Fourthly, this affects the *res judicata* principle as regards court decisions that are final but are later subjected to disciplinary review as to their substance.

In June 2010 the OSCE Office for Democratic Institutions and Human Rights together with the Max Planck Institute for Comparative Public Law and International Law organized a regional expert meeting which concluded with the adoption of a set of recommendations aimed to further strengthen judicial independence in the countries of Eastern Europe, South Caucasus and Central Asia. Within the domain of judicial accountability the meeting made the following recommendation:

> ... Disciplinary responsibility of judges shall not extend to the content of their rulings or verdicts, including differences in legal interpretation among courts; or to examples of judicial mistakes; or to criticism of the courts.[1]

In line with the same rationale, the Venice Commission has considered, in one of its opinions, that control over disciplinary issues, requiring compliance with personal and professional obligations of judges, does not encompass the possibility of reviewing the content of judicial decisions, or evaluation of how the judges apply

---

[1]OSCE Office for Democratic Institutions and Max Planck Minerva Research Group and Human Rights, *Kyiv Recommendations on Judicial Independence in Eastern Europe, South Caucasus And Central Asia* (2010), § 25.

the law. The correction of mistakes as to the application of the law when rendering a resolution is to be made by way of appeal, but not through disciplinary proceedings.[2]

3 Searching for the Limits of Immunity from Disciplinary Liability for a Legal Error

However, leaving the matter to be resolved exclusively by way of appeal proceedings is not always sufficient to address judicial misconduct. The grounds for appeal are strictly defined and may not cover particular procedural decisions of a judge or his actions in the court proceedings. Certain rulings and judgments are simply not open to appeal. Moreover, appeal and disciplinary systems pursue different objectives, and accomplishing of both objectives in some cases requires both appeal review and disciplinary proceedings. Appeal review seeks to correct prejudice to a particular party in the past while judicial discipline seeks to prevent potential prejudice to future litigants and the judiciary in general. Vindication of personal rights of an individual defendant does not necessarily protect the public from a judge who repeatedly and grossly abuses his/her judicial power. Moreover, the disciplinary system's goal of preventing potential prejudice to the judicial system itself cannot depend on a party's decision in litigation to expend the time and money associated with pursuing the issue of judicial conduct that may be examined on review. The possibility of an appellate remedy for a particular judicial act, therefore, does not automatically and necessarily divest the judicial disciplining authority of the jurisdiction to review the same conduct.[3]

Therefore, in view of the lack of sufficient control over the judiciary and the need to react to obvious judicial arbitrariness, the principle of functional immunity from disciplinary action was not interpreted in absolute terms and there emerged a trend in the domestic legal systems providing for a certain scope of disciplinary control over the substance of judicial activity. Accordingly, analysis of conditions under which a legal error can be elevated to a judicial misconduct deserving disciplining has become one of the sensitive parts of the discussions in this field.

4 The Limits of Immunity for a Legal Error: French Experience

In France the history of development of this issue is interesting. As early as 8 February 1981, the Superior Council of the Judiciary was cautious enough to admit that immunity for a legal error was not indefinite by saying that such a

---

[2]Venice Commission & the CoE Directorate General of Human Rights and Legal Affairs, *Joint opinion on the law amending certain legislative acts of Ukraine in relation to the prevention of abuse of the right to appeal* (2010), § 39.

[3]Gray (2004), p. 1248.

principle finds its limit when a judge has, in a gross and systematic way, gone beyond his/her competence or ignored the framework of his/her jurisdiction, so that (s)he has, despite appearances, produced only the act which has nothing in common with jurisdictional activity. Later in its decision of 5 May 1982 the Council of State adopted the same position by rejecting the complaint brought before it against the decision of the Superior Council of the Judiciary which had sanctioned the judge concerned.[4]

In 2007 the French legislator attempted to expand the grounds for disciplinary liability of judges by adding the following phrase in the organic law on the status of the judiciary: "one of the breaches of the duties of his status shall be a serious and deliberate violation by a magistrate of a rule of procedure constituting an essential guarantee of the rights of the parties, committed within the framework of judicial proceedings closed by a court decision which has become final". That issue was immediately brought before the Constitutional Council which declared that amendment unconstitutional. The Constitutional Council noted that whereas "the independence of the judicial authority, guaranteed by Article 64 of the Constitution, and the principle of the separation of powers, proclaimed by Article 16 of the Declaration of 1789, do not prohibit the organic legislator to expand disciplinary liability of magistrates on to their judicial activity by providing that a serious and deliberate violation of a procedural rule constituting an essential guarantee of the rights of the parties may incur such liability, the same principles preclude initiation of disciplinary proceedings where the violation has not been previously established by a court decision which has become final."[5]

In 2010 that principle was incorporated in section 43 of the organic law on the status of the judiciary providing as follows: "[O]ne of the breaches of the duties of judicial status is a serious and deliberate violation by a magistrate of a rule of procedure constituting an essential guarantee of the rights of the parties, *established by a court decision that has become final* [emphasis added]."[6]

Accordingly, following the position of the Constitutional Council, the French legislation makes the balance between the disciplinary liability of a judge and his/her independence by admitting the disciplinary liability of judges to their judicial activity on the substantive grounds of "serious and deliberate violation by a magistrate of a rule of procedure constituting an essential guarantee of the rights of the parties". However, it provides a procedural safeguard as the disciplinary liability is possible only in cases where this particular violation of the official duty has been previously established by a decision of court which has become final. This additional procedural condition, however, raised criticism as to the availability of realistic opportunities of ensuring disciplinary control in this regard and as to the existence of a fair balance between the two principles (judicial independence and liability).

---

[4]Conseil constitutionnel, *Commentaire de la décision n° 2007-551 DC du 1er mars 2007.*

[5]Conseil Constitutionnel, Décision n° 2007-551 DC du 1 mars 2007.

[6]Loi organique relative à l'application de l'article 65 de la Constitution (2010), article 21.

5 The Limits of Immunity for a Legal Error: The US Experience

In the USA the federal statute provides that a federal judge is subject to disciplining if (s)he "has engaged in conduct prejudicial to the effective and expeditious administration of the business of the courts".[7] The litigants try to use the complaints procedure to appeal judicial decisions, but the statute directs, on the federal level, the dismissal of any complaint that is "directly related to the merits of a decision or procedural ruling".[8] Nevertheless, a measure of judicial liability for the substance of judicial decision remains to be a possibility on the federal level.

As regards state jurisdictions, many State codes of judicial conduct address this issue. The codes establish that a judge should perform the duties of judicial office impartially, competently, and diligently, specifying in comments that a "good-faith error" of fact or law does not violate this rule. In particular, such comment is included in judicial conduct codes in Arizona, Colorado, Connecticut, Georgia, Idaho, Indiana, Iowa, Kentucky, Maryland, Massachusetts, Montana, Ohio, Pennsylvania, Washington, West Virginia and Wyoming.

An explanation of what may constitute a "bad-faith error" has been made in the comments to the Massachussetts Code of Judicial Conduct, which claims that "in the absence of fraud, corrupt motive, or clear indication that the judge's conduct was in bad faith or otherwise violates this Code, it is not a violation for a judge to make findings of fact, reach legal conclusions, or apply the law as the judge understands it".[9]

According to the comments to the Arizona Code of Judicial Conduct, "a pattern of legal error" or "an intentional disregard of the law" may constitute misconduct.[10] The Maine Code of Judicial Conduct states that an error of law in a judicial decision, "whether recognized on appeal or not", shall not constitute a violation of the Code unless the judge's action demonstrates "wilful or repeated disregard of explicit requirements of the law".[11] According to the advisory note to that rule, the terms of Rule 2.2 emphasise that to give rise to an ethical concern, the error of law or failure to be "faithful to the law" at issue must be much more serious and apparent than an error of law that may lead to a trial court action being vacated or criticized for an error of law on appeal.[12]

In upholding the distinction between honest legal errors and the mistakes which require disciplinary sanctions the judicial conduct organisations underline that

---

[7]28 U.S. Code, section 351 (a).

[8]28 U.S. Code, section 352 (b) (A) (ii).

[9]Massachusetts Supreme Judicial Court Rules, Rule 3:09: Code of Judicial Conduct (2016), Comment to Rule 2.2.

[10]Arizona Code of Judicial Conduct (2009), Comment to Rule 2.2.

[11]Maine Code of Judicial Conduct (2017), Rule 2.2.

[12]Maine Code of Judicial Conduct (2017), Advisory Notes for Rule 2.2, p. 33.

merely legal errors are to be remedied in the ordinary way of judicial review of the court decisions. For example, the Massachusetts Commission on Judicial Conduct pointed out in its annual report that "the Commission does not have the power to determine whether a judge made the correct decision; that is for appellate courts."[13] Similar reservations have been made by the Kansas Commission on Judicial Qualifications[14] and the Maine Committee on Judicial Responsibility and Disability.[15]

6 The US Case Law on Elements of a Legal Error Amounting to a Disciplinary Offence

In practical terms, however, the question arose how those general ideas about separation of judicial decision-making from disciplinary control should be applied. The question was addressed back in 1985 in the State of Maine in the case of Judge Benoit. The Supreme Judicial Court of Maine, while reviewing those findings, concluded that the appropriate way to evaluate the alleged violations of the Code of Judicial Conduct is to apply an objective standard. The objective inquiry that one must make is whether *"a reasonably prudent and competent judge would in all the circumstances of a given case have concluded that the conduct was both obviously and seriously wrong"*.[16] Subsequently, that standard was maintained by other states in the USA.

In parallel, other US jurisdictions advanced other elements. For example, in Oklahoma jurisdiction a number of qualifying factors have been distinguished to characterise a legal error as disciplinary offence. In a case concerning removal of a judge from office the court reasoned in the following manner:

> 19. ... We recognize that the fear of jeopardy of punishment has the potential of chilling judicial independence. ... A balance must be struck between independence and accountability and a line must be drawn between mere legal error correctable by appeal and acts which are obviously and seriously wrong and amount to excessive use of judicial authority.
>
> 20. While the line may not always be clear, ... factors which may be considered in determining whether certain actions rise to the level of judicial misconduct. ... include **the availability of appeal, the nature of the judge's conduct, the extent of the court's jurisdiction, the motive of the judge, the egregiousness of the error, and the frequency of the offending conduct. A pattern of misconduct is certainly more serious than an isolated incident**[emphasis added]. These factors mediate the sensitive line between judicial misconduct and mere error."[17]

---

[13]Massachusetts Commission on Judicial Conduct, 2017 Annual Report, p. 1.

[14]Kansas Commission on Judicial Qualifications, 2015 Annual report, p. 13.

[15]Maine Committee on Judicial Responsibility and Disability, 2015 Annual Report, p. 3.

[16]Supreme Judicial Court of Maine, *In the Matter of Benoit* (1985).

[17]Court on the Judiciary of Oklahoma, Appellate Division, *State Edmondson v. Colclazier* (2002).

In California, the relevant elements were set out in the following way (case references omitted):

> ... [A] judge must be free not only to make the correct ruling for the proper reasons, but also to make an incorrect ruling, believing it to be correct. The determination whether a legal error provides the basis for discipline thus requires an inquiry into additional factors that demonstrate more than legal error, alone.

> In summary, a judge who commits legal error which, in addition, clearly and convincingly reflects **bad faith, bias, abuse of authority, disregard for fundamental rights, intentional disregard of the law, or any purpose other than the faithful discharge of judicial duty**, is subject to investigation [emphasis added]. Mere legal error, without more, however, is insufficient to support a finding that a judge has violated the Code of Judicial Ethics and thus should be disciplined.[18]

In Louisiana, a judge may be disciplined for "a legal ruling or action made contrary to clear and determined law about which there is no confusion or question as to its interpretation and where this legal error was egregious, made in bad faith, or made as part of a pattern or practice of legal error."[19]

The Supreme Court of Kentucky made the following opinion on this topic (footnotes and internal quotation marks omitted):

> [A] judge's conduct must be more than an erroneous legal decision made in good faith. Accordingly, a judge may be properly sanctioned for a legal error when the judge acted in bad faith, engaged in a pattern of misconduct, or when the judge's legal ruling or action [was] made contrary to clear and determined law about which there is no confusion or question as to its interpretation.[20]

In 2014 the New Jersey Supreme Court ruled that in order to be subject to judicial disciplining, there must be a "clear and convincing proof" of an objective legal error under the *Benoit* test and that the error must be *"made contrary to clear and determined law about which there is no confusion or question as to its interpretation"*.[21]

Despite this plurality of approaches in the US jurisdictions, there appear to be common features as regards the elements of such judicial misconduct. Notably, the *actus reus* of a legal error amounting to a disciplinary offence should consist of: (a) a continuing pattern of legal error, or (b) a single egregious error. As regards the *mens rea*, those violations may be committed (a) in bad faith, with a specific malicious intent, or (b) in bad faith, even though the intent was not based on a specific malicious motive, or (c) in negligent disregard of duties (even though the negligent offences constitute relatively rare case law).

---

[18]Supreme Court of California, *Oberholzer v. Commission on Judicial Performance* (1999).

[19]Supreme Court of Louisiana, *In re Boothe* (2013).

[20]Supreme Court of Kentucky, *Alred v. Commonwealth judicial conduct commission* (2012).

[21]Supreme Court of New Jersey, *In the Matter of Louis M.J. Dileo, a Former Judge of the Municipal Court* (2014).

Continuing Pattern of Legal Errors   The repeated and uncorrected legal error is obviously more serious than an isolated instance. Commission of multiple errors, or unacceptable judging that continues over a period of years, may indicate that the judge has not maintained professional competence in the law.[22] The New Mexico Judicial Ethics Book therefore admits that it is more likely to impose a measure of disciplinary liability when there is a pattern of legal error, indicating that the judge lacks competence in the law. Continuous conduct of this sort demonstrates that a judge has not maintained professional competence in the law and is not fit to hold the office.[23]

Egregious Legal Error   When a single error (or two) leads to a complaint of misconduct, the disciplinary body has to be careful in determining whether the error constitutes misconduct. It has been considered appropriate for the Commission to act only if the legal principle that has been ignored or overlooked by the judge is so fundamental that it raises a serious question about the judge's competence.[24] Therefore, an extremely serious legal error can subject a judge to disciplinary action, even if there is no continuous pattern of violations. Those cases do not necessarily involve a malicious motive of the judge. Evaluation that measures the egregiousness of a legal error is, admittedly, somewhat subjective, but the courts seem to agree that a legal error is serious enough to amount to misconduct when judges deny individuals their basic or fundamental rights.[25]

"Mens Rea" Elements of a Legal Error Amounting to Disciplinary Offence   The US case law takes account of the specific state of mind of a judge accused of judicial misconduct. It matters whether the judge acted with a specific bad motive (corruption, fraud, revenge, racial considerations, intent to benefit or bring harm to a party), or whether (s)he made a disciplinary offence without malice but still acting intentionally, or he basically neglected his official duties which resulted in misconduct. It is appropriate to emphasise that in the US case law negligent misconduct may result in disciplinary liability of a judge. Notably, in 1996 the New York Court of Appeals upheld the removal of a non-lawyer, town court justice, who had been censured twice for improperly jailing two defendants for their failure to pay restitution and fines when, in fact, they had paid—a problem caused by the judge's faulty and sloppy record-keeping.[26] Another New York judge was removed from office for, among other things, repeated neglecting notification of litigants of their rights, including the right to counsel (*In re Esworthy*, 568 N.E.2d 1195, 1196 (N.Y. 1991)).[27]

---

[22]Lubet (1998), p. 72.

[23]New Mexico Judicial Education Center (2011), pp. 4–6.

[24]Stern (2004), pp. 1558–1559.

[25]Shaman (1988), p. 9.

[26]Stern (2004), p. 1556.

[27]New Mexico Judicial Education Center (2011), pp. 4–6.

7 The Limits of Immunity for a Legal Error: Raising the Discussion on to the International Level

On the universal level the issue of judicial independence has been regularly addressed in the system of the United Nations. Within the framework of those discussions the issue of disciplinary liability has arisen. We would only point out that in 2007 the UN Human Rights Committee in one of its comments admitted that judges could be dismissed "on serious grounds of misconduct or incompetence".[28]

Outside the UN system, similar approach was expressed by the International Bar Association (IBA) in 1982. In the Minimum Standards of Judicial Independence the grounds for removal for judicial misconduct were formulated in the following way:

> 30. A judge shall not be subject to removal unless by reason of a criminal act or through gross or repeated neglect or physical or mental incapacity he/she has shown himself/herself manifestly unfit to hold the position of judge.[29]

In the European system of human rights protection, the Council of Europe has developed a number of instruments regarding enforcement of judicial independence and efficiency of the judiciary, including disciplinary oversight. In 2002 the Consultative Council of European Judges (CCJE)—a body of the Council of Europe— issued its Opinion No. 3 (2002) where it emphasised that misconduct must be "serious and flagrant" to give rise to a disciplinary action.[30] Later, in its Opinion No.10 (2007), the CCJE, while expressing concerns as to the practice of expanding judicial liability to the issues of "purely jurisdictional matters" in certain states, still underlined the need to impose disciplinary sanctions on judges who "neglect" their cases through "indolence" or who are "blatantly incompetent".[31]

The scope of disciplinary liability of judges was further clarified in the Recommendation Rec(2010)12 of the Committee of Ministers of the Council of Europe adopted on 17 November 2010. That instrument set out the following principle:

> 66. The interpretation of the law, assessment of facts or weighing of evidence carried out by judges to determine cases should not give rise to civil or disciplinary liability, except in cases of malice and gross negligence.[32]

---

[28]UN Human Rights Committee (HRC), *General comment no. 32, Article 14, Right to equality before courts and tribunals and to fair trial*, 2007, § 20.

[29]IBA, Minimum Standards of Judicial Independence, 1982.

[30]Consultative Council of European Judges of the Council of Europe, *Opinion no. 3 (2002) on the principles and rules governing judges' professional conduct, in particular ethics, incompatible behaviour and impartiality*, § 60.

[31]Consultative Council of European Judges of the Council of Europe, *Opinion no.10 (2007) to the attention of the Committee of Ministers of the Council of Europe on the Council for the Judiciary at the service of society*, §§ 62–63.

[32]Committee of Ministers of the Council of Europe, *RecommendationCM/Rec(2010)12 to Member States on judges: independence, efficiency and responsibilities*.

This was an important provision. Firstly, it addressed specifically the issue of possible imposed disciplinary liability for legal errors. The answer was positive: judges may be disciplined for their errors in the interpretation of law, assessment of facts and evaluation of evidence. Secondly, the Recommendation specifies the requirement for the *mens rea* of the actor: liability may arise only if "malice" or "gross negligence" has been established in the course of disciplinary proceedings. Nevertheless, the Recommendation does not make an attempt to describe the *actus reus* elements of the offence.

The Venice Commission in its opinions has also pointed out certain factors which should be taken into account when drafting legislation on exceptional expansion of judicial accountability on to the field of judicial adjudication. Notably, when it comes to the requirements for mental elements of the disciplinary offence arising from a legal error made by a judge, the Venice Commission expressed the following considerations:

> 22. The legal interpretation provided by a judge in contrast with the established case law, by itself, should not become a ground for disciplinary sanction unless it is done in bad faith, with intent to benefit or harm a party at the proceeding or as a result of gross negligence. While judges of lower courts should generally follow established case-law, they should not be barred from challenging it, if in their judgment they consider right to do so.[33]

The above overview of the current state of international soft law suggests that it delicately addresses the possibility of judicial liability for a legal error. The interpretation and application of law is a core function of the judiciary but disciplinary liability should not be excluded from legal decision-making by a judge. A disciplinary offence is characterised by such terms as "serious misconduct or incompetence", "indolence", or "blatant incompetence". Assessment of mental elements is necessary in the disciplinary proceedings, and it is referred to as "malice" or "gross negligence" as well as "bad faith, with the intent to benefit or bring harm to a party at the proceedings or as a result of gross negligence".

8 Concluding Observations

Comparative analysis of domestic approaches in France and in the USA as well as the overview of the international standards on this matter suggests that disciplinary liability of a judge for a legal error lies within the sensitive area of interaction between two fundamental principles of the modern society: the principle of independent adjudication and the need for public confidence in the competent justice. Judicial independence cannot be a shield for an incompetent judge and the law

---

[33]Venice Commission & the CoE Directorate of Human Rights & the OSCE Office for democratic institutions and human rights, *Joint Opinion on the draft law on disciplinary liability of judges of the Republic of Moldova* (2014), §§ 20–22.

should permit, rather on exceptional grounds, disciplinary interference with the adjudicating function which may entail content-based analysis of judicial decisions.

The criteria for such interference are necessarily developed in broad terms, however the use of normative technique is sometimes inappropriate as it often does not make due distinction between the *actus reus* and *mens rea* elements of the disciplinary offence.

In order to prevent the over-inclusive approach taken by the disciplinary authorities, the *actus reus* of the legal error subject to a disciplinary action should be understood as referring to an egregious legal mistake. In practical dimension it is important to take into account the standard which should be applied in such cases. In order to classify a legal error as deserving a disciplinary action, the US objective reasonableness test appears to be appropriate. On the basis of that standard a legal error would amount to a disciplinary offence if *a reasonably prudent and competent judge would in all the circumstances have concluded that the conduct was both obviously and seriously wrong*.

Disciplinary proceedings against a judge should necessarily include investigation into the mental element of conduct. Such analysis should permit to distinguish (a) a good-faith legal error which cannot be subject to a disciplinary action, and (b) a bad-faith legal error which deserves disciplinary measures. The bad-faith criterion may consist of (i) any specific intent which is different from faithful compliance with the judicial duty (including corruption, fraud, revenge, racial considerations, intent to benefit or bring harm to a party); (ii) wilful misconduct (where specific malicious motive has not been established but there is no doubt about clear intent to make a legal error) (iii) gross negligence with regard to the judicial duty (not involving any intent to make an error).

Furthermore, there are *external factors* relevant for the determination whether or not the legal mistake should be treated as a disciplinary offence. Firstly, *the ambiguity/clarity of law and availability of divergent/uniform case law*: this factor importantly predetermines whether there is merely a disputable interpretation and application of law or a legal error. Apparently, where the law is vague and there is no settled case law or where the case law is divergent, the legitimate judicial discretion is wider, this resulting in the scope of disciplinary interference being narrower. Secondly, *frequency of legal errors*: while the sole instance of legal error may not constitute a disciplinary offence for *de minimis* considerations or because there is no material to put in the question of the good-faith conduct of the judge, repetition of minor errors or a continuing pattern of error may disclose a disciplinary issue. Thirdly, *reversibility of legal error*: where a legal error cannot be corrected by means of ordinary review procedures (either because such a measure is not open to appeal or because the scope of review does not extend on to that matter), such error is more likely to be treated as disciplinary misconduct in view of the irreparability of the wrong caused by such error. Therefore, it may not be excluded, for example, that similar legal errors will be differently viewed in the light of disciplinary law, depending on whether or not the error may be reversed on appeal.

References

28 U.S. Code, Judiciary and Judicial Procedure. Retrieved April 9, 2019, from https://www.law.cornell.edu/uscode/text/28/352

Arizona Code of Judicial Conduct. (2009). Retrieved April 7, 2019, from http://www.azcourts.gov/portals/137/rules/Arizona%20Code%20of%20Judicial%20Conduct.pdf

Committee of Ministers of the Council of Europe, RecommendationCM/Rec(2010)12 to Member States on judges: Independence, efficiency and responsibilities, 17 November 2010. Retrieved April 7, 2019, from https://rm.coe.int/16807096c1

Conseil constitutionnel, Commentaire de la décision n° 2007-551 DC du 1er mars 2007, *Les Cahiers du Conseil constitutionnel, Cahier n° 22*. Retrieved April 7, 2019, from https://www.conseil-constitutionnel.fr/sites/default/files/as/root/bank_mm/commentaires/cahier22/ccc_551dc.pdf

Conseil Constitutionnel, Décision n° 2007-551 DC du 1 mars 2007. Retrieved April 7, 2019, from http://www.conseil-constitutionnel.fr/conseil-constitutionnel/francais/les-decisions/acces-par-date/decisions-depuis-1959/2007/2007-551-dc/decision-n-2007-551-dc-du-1-mars-2007.1170.html

Consultative Council of European Judges of the Council of Europe, Opinion no. 3 (2002) on the principles and rules governing judges' professional conduct, in particular ethics, incompatible behaviour and impartiality, Strasbourg, 19 November 2002. Retrieved April 7, 2019, from https://rm.coe.int/16807475bb%20-%20P228_38580

Consultative Council of European Judges of the Council of Europe, Opinion no.10 (2007) to the attention of the Committee of Ministers of the Council of Europe on the Council for the Judiciary at the service of society, Strasbourg, 23 November 2007. Retrieved April 7, 2019, from https://rm.coe.int/168074779b

Court on the Judiciary of Oklahoma, Appellate Division, *State Edmondson v. Colclazier,* No. CJAD-01-2, 14 June 2002.

Gray, C. (2004). The line between legal error and judicial misconduct: Balancing judicial independence and accountability. *Hofstra Law Review, 32*(4), 1245–1280.

IBA, Minimum Standards of Judicial Independence, 1982.

Kansas Commission on Judicial Qualifications, 2015 Annual report. Retrieved April 7, 2019, from http://www.kscourts.org/appellate-clerk/general/commission-on-judicial-qualifications/2015-Annual-Report.pdf

Loi organique n° 2010-830 du 22 juillet 2010 relative à l'application de l'article 65 de la Constitution. Retrieved April 7, 2019, from https://www.legifrance.gouv.fr

Lubet, S. (1998). Judicial discipline and judicial independence. *Law and Contemporary Problems, 61*, 59–74.

Maine Code of Judicial Conduct. (2017). Retrieved April 7, 2019, from http://www.courts.maine.gov/rules_adminorders/rules/text/mc_jud_conduct_plus_2017-9-5.pdf

Maine Committee on Judicial Responsibility and Disability, *2015 Annual Report*. Retrieved April 7, 2019, from http://www.jrd.maine.gov/pdfs/jrd_ar15.pdf

Massachusetts Commission on Judicial Conduct, *2017 Annual Report*. Retrieved April 7, 2019, from https://www.mass.gov/files/documents/2018/05/15/CJC%202017%20Annual%20Report_1.pdf

Massachusetts Supreme Judicial Court Rules, Rule 3:09: Code of Judicial Conduct. (2016). Retrieved April 7, 2019, from https://www.mass.gov/supreme-judicial-court-rules/supreme-judicial-court-rule-309-code-of-judicial-conduct

New Mexico Judicial Education Center. (2011). *New Mexico judicial ethics handbook*. University of New Mexico School of Law.

OSCE Office for Democratic Institutions and Max Planck Minerva Research Group and Human Rights, Kyiv Recommendations on Judicial Independence in Eastern Europe, South Caucasus And Central Asia. (2010, June 23–25). Retrieved April 7, 2019, from https://www.osce.org/odihr/kyivrec

Shaman, J. M. (1988). Judicial ethics. *Georgetown Journal of Legal Ethics, 2*(1), 1–20.

Stern, G. (2004). Judicial error that is subject to discipline in New York. *Hofstra Law Review, 32*(4), 1547–1563.

Supreme Court of California. (1999). *Oberholzer v. Commission on Judicial Performance. 20 Cal 4th 371, 84 Cal.Rptr.2d 466; 975 P.2d 663.*

Supreme Court of Kentucky. (2012). *Alred v. Commonwealth judicial conduct commission.* No. 2011–SC–000558–RR.

Supreme Court of Louisiana, *In re Boothe* (2013), 12–1821 (La.1/29/13), 110 So.3d 1002.

Supreme Court of New Jersey, *In the Matter of Louis M.J. Dileo, a Former Judge of the Municipal Court* (072095), D-66-12 (N.J. 2014).

Supreme Judicial Court of Maine, *In the Matter of Benoit*, 487 A.2d 1158 (Me. 1985).

UN Human Rights Committee (HRC), General comment no. 32, Article 14, Right to equality before courts and tribunals and to fair trial, 23 August 2007, CCPR/C/GC/32. Retrieved April 7, 2019, from http://www.refworld.org/docid/478b2b2f2.html

Venice Commission & the CoE Directorate General of Human Rights and Legal Affairs, Joint opinion on the law amending certain legislative acts of Ukraine in relation to the prevention of abuse of the right to appeal, No. 588/2010, CDL-AD(2010)029), Strasbourg, 18 October 2010. Retrieved April 7, 2019, from http://www.venice.coe.int/webforms/documents/default.aspx?pdffile=CDL-AD(2010)029-e

Venice Commission & the CoE Directorate of Human Rights & the OSCE Office for democratic institutions and human rights, Joint Opinion on the draft law on disciplinary liability of judges of the Republic of Moldova, no. 755 / 2014 (CDL-AD(2014)006), Strasbourg / Warsaw. (2014, March 24). Retrieved April 7, 2019, from http://www.venice.coe.int/webforms/documents/default.aspx?pdffile=CDL-AD(2014)006-e

Institutional Communication as a Means to Strengthen the Legitimacy of Constitutional Courts

Paolo Passaglia

Contents

1 Introduction

The legitimacy of constitutional and supreme courts is certainly one of the most challenging subjects that scholars of constitutional and comparative constitutional law must address.[1] Indeed, the subject cannot be overlooked: the legitimacy of the judiciary, and especially of the highest judicial bodies, is related, on the one hand, to the implementation of democracy and, on the other, to the historical evolution of constitutionalism.

Paolo Passaglia is Full Professor of Comparative Law at the University of Pisa; *pro-tempore* Scientific Coordinator of the Comparative Law Area of the Research Department, Constitutional Court of the Italian Republic.

---

[1]With regard to the legitimacy of constitutional courts, for a comparative perspective, see *inter alia*, Favoreu (1994), p. 557 ff.; Sunstein (1997), p. 61 ff.; Sadurski (2005), Garlicki (2009), p. 227 ff.; Mezzetti (2010), p. 307 ff.; Calamo Specchia (2011) and Butturini and Nicolini (2017).

P. Passaglia (✉)
University of Pisa, Law Department, Pisa, Italy
e-mail: paolo.passaglia@unipi.it

© Springer Nature Switzerland AG 2019
P. Pinto de Albuquerque, K. Wojtyczek (eds.), *Judicial Power in a Globalized World*, https://doi.org/10.1007/978-3-030-20744-1_24

Achieving (or searching for) a balance between these principles is a milestone for any constitutional or supreme court. Thus, it is no coincidence that this is one of the most debated topics in scholarship, nor that the debate dates back at least to the eighteenth century. In this regard, a starting point may be the relationship between the judiciary and politics suggested by Article 10 of the law of 16–24 August 1790 on the judicial organization of France after the Revolution of 1789, according to which "*les tribunaux ne pourront prendre directement ou indirectement aucune part à l'exercice du pouvoir législatif, ni empêcher ou suspendre l'exécution des décrets du Corps législatif sanctionnés par le Roi, à peine de forfaiture*".[2]

Based on these premises, for courts, the balance between democracy and constitutionalism generally consisted in the establishment of limits within which judicial review could develop, so as to draw a line beyond which political power could be exercised "freely". In other words, only when political decisions affected the cornerstones of the legal order would courts have the power (and the required legitimacy) to create the conditions for limiting democracy with constitutionalism.

If courts are 'anti-majoritarian' institutions,[3] their legitimacy depends on the anti-majoritarian function that they capable of exercising. Courts can never replace the legislature, but neither can they tolerate major infringements upon the core of the legal order simply because democratic consensus may support these violations. In this regard, the US Supreme Court, during World War II—a time when individual rights were understandably not among the main concerns of political decision-makers and when public needs were probably more urgent than private concerns—dared to write incredibly effective words: "[*t*]*he very purpose of a Bill of Rights was to withdraw certain subjects from the vicissitudes of political controversy, to place them beyond the reach of majorities and officials and to establish them as legal principles to be applied by the courts. One's right to life, liberty, and property, to free speech, a free press, freedom of worship and assembly, and other fundamental rights may not be submitted to vote; they depend on the outcome of no elections*".[4]

When dealing with these issues, the very foundation of the legitimacy of courts is at stake, so that it is only by focusing on how courts protect fundamental rights that it is possible to (try to) ascertain the significance of judicial review within a given legal order. However, this is not the only perspective from which the legitimacy of courts may be analysed; or, rather, in addition to the "traditional" approach to studying the legitimacy of courts, another approach can be proposed, one that is certainly less

---

[2]The principle was strengthened when it was enshrined in the Constitution: see the Constitution of 1791, Title III, Chapter V, Article 3 of which reads as follows: "*les tribunaux ne peuvent s'immiscer dans l'exercice du pouvoir législatif ou suspendre l'exécution des lois*". Borrowing from Montesquieu's words, this downgraded "*la puissance de juger, si terrible parmi les hommes*" to a function "*pour ainsi dire, invisible et nulle*" (de Secondat de Montesquieu (1748), Livre XI, Chapitre VI).

[3]Reference is made to the "*Counter-Majoritarian Difficulty*" evoked by Bickel (1962), p. 16 ff.

[4]See Justice Robert Jackson's majority opinion: *West Virginia State Board of Education v. Barnette*, 319 U.S. 624, at 638 (1943).

fundamental, but that should not be disregarded nonetheless. In recent years, this approach has attracted growing interest, not only because of its interdisciplinary nature, but also because of the impact that the outcome of these studies can have in terms of explaining certain strengths or shortcomings, or suggesting practices that courts could adopt.

The reference is to the approach that courts adopt to communicate their activities. This subject, which is only apparently ancillary, is actually becoming increasingly significant, because it shows how the legitimacy of courts is not simply an absolutely necessary feature of the system, but is also an aspect that must be put into practice, to create consensus and support, among the public, for the constitutional or supreme court in question.

In the last few decades, communication as a means to create consensus has attracted a great deal of attention, including in the field of legal studies. In this regard, the development of the law on institutional communication is highly significant, although it was at first essentially focused on the relationship between politics and society, on the assumption that the former needed a way to effectively send messages to the latter, so as to ensure its own visibility and ultimately create or strengthen consensus. At least during this initial phase, the judicial branch was excluded from the dynamics, precisely because courts—strictly speaking—do not need consensus to enjoy legitimacy, as their legitimacy derives from the function they perform: therefore, a sort of presumption was implicitly followed, according to which institutional communication was not a function that courts needed to carry out.

This presumption progressively faded, however, as it emerged that legitimacy is not only a *corollary* of the courts' role in the legal order. In other words, legitimacy is a twofold concept: on the one hand, it results from the simple fact that supreme and constitutional courts are the protectors of their constitutions; on the other, it derives from the activity that these courts specifically carry out. This form of legitimacy requires the possibility of expressing some kind of consensus, mainly on the judgments delivered by the courts; however, this consensus in turn requires courts to make their judgments truly accessible to the public. Accessibility is not an issue of concern to lawyers and scholars alone; on the contrary, it must be taken to regard public opinion in general, at least when it comes to the courts' essential rulings and seminal decisions. Courts need to speak directly to people who do not possess specific legal knowledge, even if highly technical and complex matters frequently characterize the courts' judgments.

Communication has therefore become necessary for courts too. Awareness of the importance of communication for legitimacy grew progressively, to the point that it is undisputable today, such that if anything, the time has come to question the traditional adage that "courts speak with judgments". The adage is still used today, but increasingly wearily and rarely: clearly, this growing difficulty cannot be a coincidence.

The changes occurring in the courts' attitudes towards shaping views on judicial activity are too evident to be overlooked. After all, if institutional communication has reached constitutional and supreme courts, and, to some extent, has become a component of their activity, it certainly cannot be ignored when it comes to determining the position of courts in the legal order.

The brief remarks that follow in this text result from this finding. The aim pursued is, simply, to describe some of the salient features of the ongoing process of the establishment of communication between constitutional and supreme courts on one hand, and public opinion on the other.

2 Legitimacy as a "Position-Based Reward" and the Emergence of Communicative Needs

As noted above, the legitimacy of constitutional and supreme courts traditionally derives from their role in the legal order, so that it could be described as a "position-based reward". On a historical view, this was particularly true for the systems and historical and political contexts in which the entrenchment of ways to protect the Constitution was conceived as a barrier against the 'drifts' that the law, once defined as "the expression of the general will" could not avoid. This type of legitimacy, however, can certainly be assumed as a fact that is invariably connected to the existence of a system of constitutional adjudication.

If legitimacy derives from the function of protecting the Constitution, it is clear that the basis for constitutional courts' legitimacy flows not from democracy, but rather from rationality. In this regard, the 'consecration' of the courts' role could be identified in the definition proposed by Charles Evans Hughes well before becoming Chief Justice of the United States: "[w]e are under a Constitution, but the Constitution is what the judges say it is".[5] That is, the legitimacy of supreme and/or constitutional courts is the result of their giving a voice to the legal order's 'fundamental law', through a logical and argumentative process in which they express the authority conferred upon them. Courts performed this historical role wherever liberal democracies were established, with very few exceptions. Even in the French legal system—in which the influence of the Jacobin tradition considerably delayed the entrenchment of a judicial form of protection of the Constitution—the legitimacy of the *Conseil constitutionnel* was finally achieved, as demonstrated by the increasingly clear superseding of the opinion that André Laignel, a Socialist member of the *Assemblée nationale*, sought to express as late as 1981: "*Vous avez juridiquement tort parce que vous êtes politiquement minoritaire*".[6] This was one of the last few expressions of a traditional conception of the relationship between politics and the

---

[5]Speech delivered at the Chamber of Commerce, Elmira, New York, 3 May 1907 (published in *Addresses and Papers of Charles Evans Hughes, Governor of New York, 1906–1908*, New York, 1908, 139), when Evans was State Governor. Shortly after (in 1910), he was appointed Associate Justice of the Supreme Court, a position he maintained until 1916. He then returned to the Supreme Court in 1930, as Chief Justice.

[6]This argument was made during the session of 13 October 1981, in reply to the centre-right opposition's protests against the law on nationalization that was to be passed.

judicial branch, one that would soon be swept away by the assessment (truly definable as 'revolutionary') that, in the words of Louis Favoreu, "*la politique a [vait] été saisie par le droit*".[7]

On the whole, the above commentary can still be applied to describe the roots of the legitimacy enjoyed by courts, as it is indisputable that these arguments are as valid today as they were decades ago. Nevertheless, the relevant theoretical consid- erations must be examined in light of the actual practice—and indeed, in practice, there have been changes, albeit ones that fall beyond the scope of standard textbooks on constitutional or comparative constitutional law.

If the roots of legitimacy have not changed, the forms through which legitimacy is strengthened did transform. Theoretical legitimacy as a "position-based reward" can no longer be conceived of as independent from the legitimacy deriving from the specific activity performed by the courts. The changes did not concern the way in which courts exercise their role: with regard to their activity, today as in the past, legitimacy is based essentially on their legal reasoning and on their ability to develop a rational argumentative process that readers can understand and follow. What has profoundly changed is how the messages relating to the courts' activity are con- veyed. This change only partially affected the courts, because it was (and is) mainly the outcome of transformations that involved (and continue to involve) society generally.

Therefore, the changes did not directly affect constitutional and supreme courts and their place in the system, but rather the societies in which they operate. Moreover, these changes are far from insignificant, as the rationality founding the courts' legitimacy must contend with the idea that "*dans un monde où les médias jouent le rôle d'une caisse de résonance et d'une loupe grossissante, les émotions comptent plus que jamais*".[8]

If emotions guide the perception of the messages, then the image of "wise men" (as constitutional judges in France continue to be called) who, from the height of an ivory tower, declare what the Constitution is, risks being replaced by the shocking image that Bob Dylan suggests in Jokerman: "judges dying in the webs that they spin".

Given the above considerations, courts may choose either to continue to operate as they always have, risking loss of the legitimacy 'capital' with which they are structurally endowed, or to adapt to the needs of society, without denaturing their own essence, of course, but accepting the challenges posed by modernity.

Clearly, this is a purely fictitious alternative, because if constitutional courts wish to continue to exercise their role, they cannot close themselves off from the world: to re-propose the idea of "speaking through judgments" would lead to precisely such a closure, for the simple reason that this way of conveying messages is no longer capable of allowing the courts to be heard. Scholars of communication studies note that "the medium is the message",[9] as societies have always been shaped more by the

---

[7]Favoreu (1988).

[8]Moïsi (2008), p. 5.

[9]McLuhan (1994).

type of media with which men communicate than by the content of communication. And because this is the age of social media, it is simply unthinkable that communication should rely solely upon a formal, complex and often complicated text, as a judgment is (and must be).

The idea that the recipient must adapt to the forms of expression chosen by the party sending the message is unsustainable in general, and even more so when the recipient has several options to choose from when receiving the message. A court that engages in only traditional (and anachronistically limited) forms of communication would be deluding itself of being able to stimulate recipients to make an effort to comprehend more complete information. In practice, such a court, being unable to force its recipients to read, would be entrusting the dissemination of the contents of its judgments to other parties entirely.

In fact, the risk of adopting such a closed attitude is of letting the mass media, instead of its judgments, speak for the court, with a very real risk that the contents of the judgments, often difficult to understand, would be excessively simplified.

In other words, it is now a basic fact that, if courts wish to be masters of their fate, they must become communicators themselves. Then, the real problem is to elaborate schemes that are capable of guiding institutional communication. This seems far from easy, also because the prevailing practices were developed with and for political and representative bodies, such that they only partly apply to judicial bodies.

Whatever the pattern followed, it is indisputable that communication policies can no longer be considered as purely contingent to judicial activity. Many examples could be mentioned in this respect. However, in the comparative sense, the most emblematic is probably that of the Supreme Court of the United Kingdom.

As is well known, the Constitutional Reform Act 2005 provided for the replacement of the Appellate Committee of the House of Lords with the Supreme Court of the United Kingdom. Therefore, a wholly new court was created, with regard to form. However, the body was much less novel in other respects, as the same Law Lords on the Appellate Committee became the first members of the Supreme Court; in addition, the case law of the House of Lords was 'incorporated' into the new institution, also as a set of horizontal precedents. These elements of continuity demonstrate that the purpose of the Constitutional Reform Act 2005 was not to address criticisms of the existing system. At the same time, it was not a merely 'cosmetic' operation. The point is precisely that, in practice, the system worked as if there was a firm separation between the second chamber of Parliament and the highest judicial body; however, the interpenetration between the legislative and judicial branches was perceived to be no longer sustainable at the dawn of the twenty-first century, from the symbolic and communicative points of view. It is no coincidence that the Constitutional Reform Act made drastic changes to the functions of the Lord Chancellor, retaining only those as Secretary of State for Justice, and removing therefrom the roles of member of the highest court and speaker of the upper chamber. It was also considered that formal respect for the principle of separation of powers could no longer be avoided, essentially because the appearance, if not the substance, was too far removed from principles that had been considered fundamental for centuries. The principles were fundamental especially for British constitutional law, if it is true that the principle of separation of powers was elaborated by Montesquieu in the chapter of his *Esprit des Lois* dedicated to "*La constitution d'Angleterre*".[10]

To establish a clear separation between the legislator and the judicial body, the seat of the Supreme Court was moved to a different building (located on the other side of Parliament Square, exactly across the Parliament): the independence of the Supreme Court was to be shown in also geographic terms, so as to be more readily perceivable by the public.

The British case appears to be emblematic. However, it is fair to state that all supreme and constitutional courts pay increasing amounts of attention to being open to the public and making their role easier to understand, also thanks to a specific communications policy. While it is now undisputed that such an approach has been adopted, the effectiveness of the actions undertaken and the choices made in implementing institutional communications remain to be clarified. Despite the good intentions, the choices made have not always led to the selection of effective means. After all, given that courts must deal with matters that are inevitably highly technical, Karl Popper's warning sounds particularly appropriate: "[i]t is impossible to speak in such a way that you cannot be misunderstood."[11]

Therefore, an analysis of constitutional and supreme courts' institutional communications requires an understanding of how these bodies 'speak', to evaluate whether they do so in a way that allows for comprehension and, ultimately, if through their 'speech', they are able to enhance their legitimacy.

This will be the subject of the following sections. As space constraints prevent conducting an extensive analysis here, some of the most significant communication policies affecting the relationship between constitutional and supreme courts and public opinion will be outlined. A limited set of cases will be examined, with the hope that they can offer, some interesting elements that indicate general trends. The judicial bodies that will be considered are the supreme courts of the United States and of the United Kingdom, the constitutional courts of Germany, Italy and Spain, and the French Constitutional Council.

3   The Quest for Simplification in Drafting Judgments

In all countries, legal discourse is, in itself, anything but easy to understand for the general public. Of all legal texts, judgments are probably the most complex, especially because they are inevitably weighed down by various technicalities. To this inconvenience, which is to a large extent unavoidable, in recent years, courts have attempted to provide some remedies.

---

[10]de Secondat de Montesquieu (1748), Livre XI, Chapitre VI.
[11]Popper (2002), p. 29.

In the case of the Italian Constitutional Court, for example, the changes were minimal: in recent years, the only innovation noted is that, where the judge-rapporteur is not the same judge who drafted the decision, this fact is now expressly declared at the beginning of the judgment. In the past, this was not specified, leaving readers with the task of verifying whether the name of the judge indicated at the beginning of the judgment (the judge-rapporteur) corresponded to that at the end (the author). The change is minimal and is directed essentially to the most attentive readers, certainly not to the general public. Its limited impact certainly does not disprove the observation that the Italian Court tends to preserve the traditional style of drafting decisions.

In this regard, the Italian example is by no means isolated, as the general trend is to maintain tradition. However, two exceptions deserve attention.

The Supreme Court of the United Kingdom, again, provides useful material for a case study. Although formally maintaining the traditional style of decision-making, the Supreme Court produced a change of great importance: ever since it began rendering judgments, in October 2009, the Court has progressively reduced the frequency of *seriatim* opinions, which characterized the judicial activity of the House of Lords (as well as that of many other British courts). This to the point that, today, it is rare to find a Supreme Court judgment setting out the individual opinions of the members of the panel. Instead of a series of individual opinions, the ordinary form of drafting judgements now consists in entrusting to a single judge the task of drafting the legal reasoning underlying the judgment, with which the majority of the Court agrees. Dissenters are left to explain their reasons in separate opinions. This has led to a clear *rapprochement* to the American "Opinion of the Court" model, which has the indisputable benefit of making the sense of judgments and their legal basis much easier to grasp, compared to traditional *seriatim* opinions.

The second exception concerns the French Constitutional Council, which, in 2016, openly engaged in strengthening the intelligibility of judgments, even reversing deeply rooted traditions.

Starting with Judgments No. 2016-539 QPC and 2016-540 QPC, of 10 May 2016, in fact, *"le Conseil constitutionnel a décidé de moderniser le mode de rédaction de ses décisions"*,[12] to simplify them and to (be able to) draft a more articulated legal reasoning section.

It is worth recalling that, by virtue of a longstanding custom, contrary to most other constitutional courts, the judgments of the Constitutional Council were articulated on the *"Vis-Con-Dis"* scheme typical of French jurisdictions. According to this scheme, judgments were divided into three parts: the *visas*, which listed the acts and provisions that formed the standard for the Council's decision; the *considérants*, the paragraphs in which the legal reasoning was set out; and the *dispositif*, consisting in the declaration of unconstitutionality or conformity to the Constitution of the challenged provisions. The framework of the judgment was structured on a main

---

[12]*Communiqué du Président du 10 mai 2016*, http://www.conseil-constitutionnel.fr/conseil-constitutionnel/francais/actualites/2016/communique-du-president-du-10-mai-2016.147341.html.

clause, which was always identical and which, divided into two parts, would begin the judgment and then would close the part providing the legal reasoning ("*Le Conseil constitutionnel* [. . .] *décide*"). Between the two fragments of the proposition, the paragraphs of the *visas* and of the *considérants* were inserted. In grammatical terms, therefore, the *visas* and the *considérants* were subordinate clauses of the main sentence.[13]

In concrete terms, the 'modernization' operated in May 2016 resulted in the removal of the "*Vis-Con-Dis*" scheme. The references previously contained in the *visas* remain, of course, at the beginning of the judgment, even if they are no longer introduced by the term "*vu*". The most significant changes were made to the legal reasoning section, which, because the *considérants* were removed, is now composed of paragraphs (which are numbered, as were the *considérants*) that contain separate periods. The *dispositif* was left essentially unchanged.[14]

With these changes, the judgments of the Constitutional Council have undoubtedly approached—at least in terms of their formal framework—those of the other constitutional courts. The judgments have become more readable. In fact, overcoming the constraints of the "*Vis-Con-Dis*" scheme opened the way to the possibility of providing a legal reasoning that can span several paragraphs, without necessarily being inserted into subordinate clauses. Thus, the new drafting system allowed the Council to write less synthetic accounts of its legal reasoning, and paved the way to developing the form of writing to make it more easily accessible. Obviously, it would be improper to infer, from the removal of the *considérants per se*, that a pivotal change in the style of decision-making has occurred: the framework of the judgments of the Council has been simplified, but the argumentative style was not revolutionized for this very reason. Indeed, in this regard, it may be noted that, at least to date, there has been significant continuity between the judgments rendered before and after May 2016. The fact that the structural constraints have loosened is, therefore, to be considered nothing more than a first step towards a more open way of drafting the court's legal reasoning. In the next few years, it will be possible to establish whether, after this first step, others will follow, and whether these other steps will actually be oriented towards drafting more readable and intelligible judgments.

Although still incomplete, this evolution in the Constitutional Council's style of decision-making gives an idea of the degree to which constitutional and supreme courts can shift towards a more communications-oriented approach. It is clear that much has been done. However, it is also clear that, when intervening on elements that are, to a large extent, mere details (as they concern only the form of drafting), it is impossible to overcome communication difficulties with only this type of change.

---

[13] For an analysis of the drafting of the judgments of the French Constitutional Council and the legal reasoning provided therein, see, recently, Baranger (2012), Guillaume (2012), p. 49 ff.; Canivet (2013), p. 236 ff.

[14] The reform of the style of drafting the judgments of the Constitutional Council was also analysed by one of its members: see Belloubet (2017), p. 7 ff.

The key issue, however, is whether constitutional and supreme courts can really do more. It is certainly possible to propose and elaborate further simplifications to the style of drafting judgments, but probably, these simplifications cannot touch upon anything except marginal aspects. This is because any simplifying intervention absolutely cannot risk resulting in trivialization: the message contained in a judgment is inevitably complex, such that it is impossible to do more than make some adjustments of style and structure, to avert the risk of distorting the court's product.

In light of the above, it must be acknowledged that the bulk of courts' institutional communication must be conducted on different grounds: in any event, judgments must remain the 'moment' when the courts fully express their legal reasoning, in all of its complexity and with all applicable technicalities.

4   Official Comments to Judgments

An interesting—and equally atypical—effort to reconcile observance of the traditional decision-making style with the need to develop the intelligibility of judgments comes, again, from France.

One of the tasks that is usually conferred upon legal scholars is to write comments on judgments. In this regard, the case law of the Constitutional Council is no exception. Nevertheless, the Council itself has experimented with a way to present judgments that can foster understanding, by scholars, of their most significant implications and their unexpressed argumentative foundations.

In fact, almost every judgment is accompanied with an official comment, which is drafted by the General Secretariat and is published on the institution's website.[15] These comments have assumed prominence in the institutional communications activity carried out by the Council.

To the extent that the official comments are drafted by the General Secretariat and not by the judges, they cannot be attributed with authoritative value. Therefore, the analysis they carry out cannot be considered to indicate the Council's real intent. Nevertheless, the fact that they are prepared within the institution is, in itself, a basis for according to these comments an extremely high degree of reliability, to the point that they can be considered irreplaceable instruments for scholars seeking to comprehend the actual decision-making process, which choices led to adopting certain solutions instead of others, etc. Of course, these are still relatively technical texts, so that their recipients are essentially lawyers: in essence, institutional communications are conveyed only minimally from these comments. Their function is mainly that of fostering comprehension of what was not expressed in the judgment: despite the reform of May 2016, the judgments of the Constitutional Council remain rather cryptic, sufficiently so that even skilled lawyers may find them difficult to

---

[15]See https://www.conseil-constitutionnel.fr/decisions: for each judgment, its text and the official comment is provided and freely downloadable.

understand. In any event, it is noteworthy that, due to their structure, style and availability online, the Constitutional Council's official comments can be easily consulted by the public, and shed light on many of the elements and arguments that guide the Council in rendering its judgments.

5 Judgment Summaries

As noted above, the real institutional communications activity, that which targets public opinion and other institutions, uses the means analysed thus far only to a limited extent. Actually, it is hard to dispute that the communication activity engaged in by courts mainly consists in the dissemination of summaries that briefly describe the key contents of judgments.

In this regard, constitutional and supreme courts follow basically two models: (*a*) the syllabus and (*b*) the press release.

(*a*) A syllabus, which is also called a "headnote", is the text that typically accompanies the judgments of the Supreme Court of the United States. It is a synthesis of the judgment and is placed at the beginning of the judgment itself, with the warning that "*the syllabus constitutes no part of the opinion of the Court but has been prepared by the Reporter of Decisions for the convenience of the reader.*"[16]

The merely informational nature of the syllabus, together with the fact that it is considerably shorter than the judgment, makes the task of the person drafting the syllabus extremely sensitive, as his or her interpretation of the judgment risks creating a level of trust in the reader that might, perhaps, be misplaced. Despite this drawback,[17] the syllabus is clearly a precious means of disseminating an accurate account of the main approaches taken by the Supreme Court when addressing the issues raised in the writ of *certiorari*. On the communications level, the level of detail and the technical nature of the syllabus imply that the reader, to be able to truly and concretely comprehend the judgment summarized, must have a certain degree of legal knowledge. Therefore, it would be improper to identify the syllabus' target as being the general public. It is unquestionable, however, that the provision of

---

[16]This warning is included in all judgments of the Supreme Court, together with a reference to the judgment in the case *U.S. v. Detroit Timber & Lumber Co.*, 200 US 321, 337 (1906), in which the Court addressed the issue of differences between the syllabus and the judgment. The Court clarified that the text drafted by the Reporter of Decisions is not official: the syllabus "gives his understanding of the decision", and nothing more.

[17]This drawback could not be eliminated by conferring official and authoritative character upon the syllabus. This occurs, for instance, with the summaries of the judgments of the Canadian Supreme Court, which are not separated from judgments, and must therefore be considered as a part of it (in fact, the syntheses are also sent for official translation). The authoritative nature of the synthesis could avoid interpretations and expectations arising from non-official texts, devoid of any legal bases; nevertheless, precisely this authoritative nature would exacerbate the problems deriving from any conflict there may be between the synthesis and the actual judgment, because, in this case it would be very difficult to identify objective criteria to solve the conflict.

a syllabus considerably increases the number of subjects who can obtain autonomous information on the contents of the judgment without having to rely on mass media. The greatest value of the syllabus, however, lies not so much in its potential (for the Supreme Court's messages to reach further recipients), but rather in its effectiveness: a synthetic text that precedes an often long judgment appears to be an invitation to read. An invitation that—it is fair to imagine—is accepted in a statistically non-negligible number of cases: the syllabus, in other words, significantly increases the actual number of readers of the Court's judgments.

(b) A typical tool in any public communication policy is the press release. The adoption of the practice of drafting press releases expresses a much clearer choice than that of providing syllabuses, as the name and—above all—the gap between the press release and the judgment make the different targets and functions of the two texts clear. This diversity is reflected in the clearest of differentiations regarding the source, thus excluding any doubt as to which text must prevail in case of conflict. Indeed, it is undisputed that press releases cannot have official and/or authoritative nature.

Actually, press releases do not form a unitary category, because there is a wide variety of press releases, which respond to needs that may be highly diverse. Among others, an important distinction can be made between "necessary" press releases and "non-necessary" press releases.

Necessary press releases are the indefectible complement to any judgment, or at least to the vast majority of them. The Supreme Court of the United Kingdom and the French Constitutional Council opted for this type of press release, seeking to engage in direct dialogue with the public to give an account of the judicial body's overall activity, as if to strengthen its own role and legitimacy, presenting all that the body does in a concise but sufficiently explanatory manner.

Non-necessary press releases, on the contrary, are adopted by those courts that deliver many judgments, so that a selection is needed for those that truly deserve dissemination. A press release is published only for the judgments that actually have general value: given the high number of direct individual appeals and the consequent litigation brought before them, both the German Federal Constitutional Court and the Spanish Constitutional Court have opted for this solution. Although such a solution is probably obligatory in light of the number of judgments that the courts must deal with, it proves to be not devoid of significance, in terms of the idea that it implies: indeed, non-necessary press releases could also be defined as "selective", because when it must be decided whether to associate a press release to a judgment, the choice that is made is, actually, to stress the importance that the Constitutional Court recognizes to the judgment. In other words, the press release is a further element of evaluation offered to the public.

Selective press releases are also used by the Italian Constitutional Court, which produces an extremely limited number of press releases compared to its foreign counterparts. However, for a long time, it was not the number that made the Italian experience peculiar.

Before drafting press releases based on the German model, the press releases that were issued by the *Palazzo della Consulta* until 2017 provided not a concise and usable presentation of the contents of the judgment, but rather mere information on the solution adopted by the Court in a certain case: it was not possible to infer the Court's legal reasoning from those releases, because the final decision was communicated only in very broad terms. Indeed, press releases were issues only for particularly important judgments, and the dissemination of the outcome of the case mainly served to defuse rumors in the mass media on how the Court might be deciding the cases.[18]

Evidently, the Italian experience simply does not include the press releases (or syllabuses) prepared by other courts. This is proved by the attempt, in 2016, to introduce a further tool, first called a "synopsis", and later a "synthesis", which was a text prepared by one of the judicial assistants of the judge who drafted the decision, and presented to the Court's Press Office for publication on the Court's website. This document was soon abandoned in favour of a new type of 'real' press releases, which are prepared for the most important judgments and are published on the Court's website.

6   The Use of Social Media

Browsing the Internet, it is easy to see how supreme and constitutional courts have all created well-designed websites, that are very rich in terms of content and that have expanded over the years, in parallel with the growing attention to accessibility and usability.

In this regard, there is such a wealth of data that it would be interesting to compare the courts' websites. This comparison could provide interesting indications on how the different courts perceive their role and identify the main recipients of their messages.[19] The point is that a study of this type, which would nevertheless be valid today, could be at least partially regarded as a 'rearguard' investigation, as the real issue increasingly appears to be not websites, but rather the courts' use of social media.

The practice followed by the various courts differs remarkably, even if a common trend may be identified in that openness to social media characterizes, to a greater or lesser extent, all of the institutions taken into consideration here. The social network that appears to be the most 'successful' in this respect is Twitter: there are official accounts for the supreme courts of the United States and the United Kingdom, as well as for the Canadian Supreme Court, but also for the German and the Spanish Constitutional Courts and the French Constitutional Council. Even Facebook is used, especially by the French Council and the Canadian Supreme Court. The latter is particularly active, as it also has an official account on LinkedIn.

---

[18]The peculiarities of the press releases issued by the Italian Constitutional Court are analysed by Gragnani (2013), p. 531 ff.

[19]A comparative analysis of the websites of several constitutional courts was carried out by Costanzo (2016), p. 667 ff. As far as the website of the Italian Constitutional Court is concerned, see Passaglia (2017), p. 113 ff.

This increasingly widespread attention shows how a social media presence can be a vital channel for reaching out to the public, and thus ultimately strengthen legitimacy in relation to the activities actually carried out.

Although the tool must necessarily be handled with caution, in that the risk of trivializing messages must necessarily be considered, it must be admitted that social media allow for direct interaction between the institution and the public. For the first time, constitutional and supreme courts are truly able to bypass the mass media, to make their presence clear to the public. In this regard, provided that it is correctly set up, and the potential of the relevant tools is adequately exploited, a communicative activity is a fundamental asset in the effort to take an active part in communication society today.

In light of the above, the policy of the Italian Constitutional Court appears to be at least debatable. This is not a reference to the enduring importance of the annual press conference held by the President of the Court, which affirms the role of the mass media as a pivotal tool for disseminating the Court's work[20]: this traditional event is still useful, provided, however, that it does not catalyse the shift of communication efforts towards indirect channels. What continues to make the Italian Court peculiar is its general refusal to use social media, presumably because the Court believes that it is able to disseminate information on its activity through its website and traditional communications tools. However, the most recent trends in the communication society appear to suggest that the social communications policy of the Italian Court should be deeply rethought.

7   The Use of Foreign Languages

Communication increasingly projects beyond national borders, with the purpose of implementing a form of 'cultural' legitimacy, which courts seek by participating in transnational judicial dialogue.

In this regard, there is obviously a language divide, which inevitably favours Anglophone courts and compels the other courts to use forms of communication that allow for making their activity known abroad. This is why non-Anglophone courts show increasing levels of attention to the translation of their judgments into other languages, of course mainly English.

The ways in which the objective of "making themselves known" is pursued changes considerably depending on the court. Indeed, some courts are more active than others, to the point that they translate into English all of their most important judgments and, sometimes, even the related press releases: this is the case, for example, of the German Federal Constitutional Court. Other courts have a less

---

[20]It should be noted that the press conference, in addition to being open to journalists, is also broadcasted live on television. The audience that the event manages to attract, however, is rather limited, also because the conference is held in the morning.

stringent policy, but still tend to translate "as much as possible", not only into English, but also into other languages: in this regard, the example of the French Constitutional Council is revealing, as its judgments are sometimes translated into English, but also German, Spanish and Italian depending on the language skills of the collaborators and interns in the Council's Legal Department. Even the Italian Constitutional Court, since 2007, has been relatively active with reference to the translation of its judgments to English, with an average of more than a dozen translations per year.

The translation of judgments, as part of the courts' communications policies, is of the utmost importance; nevertheless, it cannot in itself suffice to enable the full inclusion of the case law of non-Anglophone courts into transnational judicial dialogue. A foreign scholar or lawyer, who is not expected to possess deep knowledge of the national legal order in which a judgment was rendered, may encounter great difficulties in grasping the real meaning of the court's legal reasoning and ruling, even if it is translated in a language that he or she understands perfectly. Therefore, a complementary activity—namely, a brief presentation of the salient points addressed by the judgment—is essential. This is purportedly the fundamental objective of the Codices database and of the thrice-yearly *Bulletin on Constitutional Case-law* edited by the Commission for Democracy through Law (the so-called Venice Commission).[21] Nevertheless, the selection of judgments, as well as the absence of rigid standards in terms of presentation are shortcomings that are not easy to overcome. Indeed, there is longstanding experience with countries creating repertories in scarcely homogeneous forms, and of selecting the judgments to be reported according to criteria that are not always indisputable, in terms of the real impact of the judgments from a comparative point of view.

If even the Venice Commission does not appear—at least for the moment—to have found suitable forms with which to effectively convey the essential contents of the courts' judgments, it may be appropriate, and indeed necessary, to entrust the task to legal scholarship. In other words, it does not seem improper to enrich the role of legal scholars with further implications: not only that of 'watchdogs' for the courts, but also of 'facilitators' of dialogue at all levels, by shedding light on the core of the most important judgments, for the benefit of public opinion but also—by choosing to write in English—of the transnational legal community.

8 Final Remarks

The previous pages provide a brief review of the issues considered to be some of the most significant with regard to the institutional communications policies of constitutional and supreme courts. This paper should be considered as a step towards a

---

[21]The *Bulletin* is freely available at https://www.venice.coe.int/WebForms/pages/?p=02_02_Bulletins.

broader research effort, and as no more than an inventory of problems that the comparative method seems to be able to address with good results.

The interlocutory nature of these pages, moreover, is combined with the provisional nature of research conducted in a field that is undergoing major changes. The development of new forms of communication will require courts to move in new directions to bolster their legitimacy, both within the institutional framework and in public opinion, not to mention in transnational judicial dialogue. Thus, the opportunity to identify past trends must be associated with a prospective view, that can help to account for the full complexity of the challenges posed by the communication society to constitutional and supreme courts. These challenges are common to all institutions, but present peculiarities for constitutional and supreme courts. Indeed, the jurisdictional nature and the sensitivity of the functions these bodies perform place them at the crossroads between the implementation of representative democracy and the impossibility to do without a means to protect the basic rules of the system which, as such, must be considered as a non-removable part of the system, and the importance of which must be constantly expressed and disseminated—certainly through judgments, but also through institutional communications.

References

Baranger, D. (2012). Sur la manière française de rendre la justice constitutionnelle. Motivation et raisons politiques dans la jurisprudence du Conseil constitutionnel. *Jus Politicum*, 7, 2012, Retrieved April 3, 2019, from http://juspoliticum.com/article/Sur-la-maniere-francaise-de-rendre-la-justice-constitutionnelle-478.html

Bellloubet, N. (2017). La motivation des décisions du Conseil constitutionnel: justifier et réformer. *Les Nouveaux Cahiers du Conseil constitutionnel, 55/56*, 7.

Bickel, A. M. (1962). *The least dangerous branch. The supreme court at the bar of politics.* Indianapolis, IN: Bobbs-Merrill Co.

Butturini, D., & Nicolini, M. (Eds.). (2017). *Giurisdizione costituzionale e potere democraticamente legittimato.* Bologna: Bononia University Press.

Calamo Specchia, M. (Ed.). (2011). *Le Corti Costituzionali. Composizione, Indipendenza, Legittimazione.* Turin: Giappichelli.

Canivet, G. (2013). La motivation des décisions du Conseil constitutionnel. In S. Caudal (Ed.), *La motivation en droit public* (p. 236). Paris: Dalloz.

Costanzo, P. (2016). La Corte costituzionale come 'nodo' della Rete. In *Scritti in onore di Gaetano Silvestri* (Vol. I, p. 667). Turin: Giappichelli.

de Secondat de Montesquieu, C. (1748). *De l'esprit des lois.* Geneva.

Favoreu, L. (1988). *La politique saisie par le droit. Alternances, cohabitation et Conseil constitutionnel.* Paris: Economica.

Favoreu, L. (1994). La légitimité du juge constitutionnel. *Revue internationale de droit comparé*, 557.

Garlicki, L. (2009). La légitimité du contrôle de constitutionnalité: problèmes anciens c/ développements récents. *Revue française de droit constitutionnel*, 227.

Gragnani, A. (2013). Comunicati-stampa del Palazzo della Consulta anziché provvedimenti cautelari della Corte costituzionale?. *Giurisprudenza costituzionale*, 531.

Guillaume, M. (2012). La motivation des décisions du Conseil constitutionnel. *Annuaire international de Justice constitutionnelle*, 49.

McLuhan, M. (1994). *Understanding media: The extensions of man (1964)*. Cambridge, MA: MIT Press.

Mezzetti, L. (2010). Teorie della giustizia costituzionale e legittimazione degli organi di giustizia costituzionale. *Estudios Constitucionales*, 307.

Moïsi, D. (2008). *La géopolitique de l'émotion: Comment les cultures de peur, d'humiliation et d'espoir façonnent le monde*. Paris: Flammarion.

Passaglia, P. (2017). Qualche osservazione sulla comunicazione pubblica della Corte costituzionale. In G. L. Conti & P. Milazzo (Eds.), *Studi pisani sul Parlamento, VII. La crisi del Parlamento nelle regole sulla sua percezione* (p. 113). Pisa: Pisa University Press.

Popper, K. (2002). *Unended Quest: An Intellectual Autobiography (1976)*. New York: Routledge.

Sadurski, W. (2005). *Rights before courts*. Dordrecht: Springer.

Sunstein, C. R. (1997). Introduction – The legitimacy of constitutional courts: Notes on theory and practice feature: Questioning constitutional justice: Introduction. *East European Constitutional Review, 6*, 61.

Third Parties Involved in International Litigation Proceedings. What Are the Challenges for the ECHR?

Pere Pastor Vilanova

Contents

1   Foreword

Since this book is a tribute to Judge De Gaetano, I consider that justice has been done to him on account of the exceptional nature of his professional career as both a national and an international judge. More personally, I have had the honour of spending time with him in his capacity as President of the Third Section of the European Court of Human Rights, where he has demonstrated great wisdom and humanity. I have learned much from him, and thank him most sincerely. It is now my turn to express my gratitude to him through this written contribution, which concerns the application of Article 36 of the European Convention on Human Rights. I am

Pere Pastor Vilanova is Judge at the European Court of Human Rights. The views expressed herein are personal. I would like to warmly thank Ms Camila Dupret Torres for her valuable collaboration in both the research and the writing of this article.

P. Pastor Vilanova (✉)
European Court of Human Rights, Strasbourg, France
e-mail: pere.pastorvilanova@echr.coe.int

© Springer Nature Switzerland AG 2019
P. Pinto de Albuquerque, K. Wojtyczek (eds.), *Judicial Power in a Globalized World*, https://doi.org/10.1007/978-3-030-20744-1_25

aware that he is not indifferent to this question, as illustrated by the recent Committee judgment in the case of *Buttigieg and Others v. Malta*, where the third-party intervention was accepted (see Sect. 3 below). This was a very generous application of Article 36 (see Sect. 3.1.1), and would appear to support the thesis developed in the following lines. . .

2 Introduction

Cases before the European Court of Human Rights ("the Court") involve not only the applicant(s) on the one hand and the respondent member State(s) on the other.[1] A significant number of cases in fact involve third parties, through the intervention mechanism laid down in Article 36[2] of the European Convention on Human Rights ("ECHR") and Rule 44 of the Rules of Court. Article 36, headed "Third party intervention" states:

1. In all cases before a Chamber or the Grand Chamber, a High Contracting Party one of whose nationals is an applicant shall have the right to submit written comments and to take part in hearings.
2. The President of the Court may, in the interest of the proper administration of justice, invite any High Contracting Party which is not a party to the proceedings or any person concerned who is not the applicant to submit written comments or take part in hearings.
3. In all cases before a Chamber or the Grand Chamber, the Council of Europe Commissioner for Human Rights may submit written comments and take part in hearings.

Accordingly, four categories of interveners are envisaged. The first paragraph consecrates the right of State Parties of the applicant's nationality to intervene. Article 36 § 2 addresses two other types of third party, namely third States and "any person concerned".[3] The first group are States which are neither a party to the proceedings nor concerned by the first paragraph of Article 36, and the second group encompasses two subcategories, *amici curiae* and other persons who are also "concerned" by the proceedings.[4] Finally, the third paragraph sets out the right of the Council of Europe Commissioner for Human Rights to take part in the proceedings.

It would appear that since the first intervention in 1979[5] about two hundred cases have involved third-party interventions. Cases in which the applicant's State of nationality has intervened are quite rare (13 cases), whereas interventions by third

---

[1]While most cases oppose persons or groups of individuals to Member State(s) in the sense of Article 34 of the Convention, others are inter-State cases within the meaning of Article 33 of the Convention, and oppose exclusively Member States.

[2]Article 36 ECHR was initially introduced by Protocol No. 11, 11 May 1995.

[3]The text of Article 36 § 2 is taken from the former version of Rule 37 § 2 of the Rules of Court.

[4]The French version of Article 36 § 2 refers to "*toute personne intéressée*".

[5]I refer to the United Kingdom, in the case of *Winterwerp v. the Netherlands*, no. 6301/71, 24 October 1979.

States are significantly more frequent. The category of persons "concerned" by the proceedings amounts for 141 cases, including 37 before the Grand Chamber. A total of 23 interventions have been made by the Commissioner for Human Rights.[6] Although not all interventions are equally valuable to the Court, it is fair to assert that most include scientific information, international and comparative-law studies and an assessment of the current practice of other courts that is useful for the Court as it interprets and applies the rights set out in the Convention.[7]

The diversity of interveners and the differences between them suggest that the purpose of their intervention also varies. All of these interventions are of importance. However, due to length constraints, this article prioritizes the issue of persons "concerned" by the proceedings, and more specifically the "original parties" to the domestic proceedings—as opposed to *amici curiae*. The position adopted in this article is that the original parties' rights and interests should be guaranteed through the availability of a genuine and effective possibility to participate in the proceedings pending in Strasbourg. For that purpose, intervening should be a right rather than a mere possibility that is left to the discretion of the President of the Court or of the Chamber. To be effective, such a right should entail notification by the Court to the original parties of the existence of the proceedings in question.

3 Intervening Before the Court, a Right or a Possibility?

The Convention sets out a possibility to intervene, but one that varies depending on the third party concerned: while some interveners have an actual right to intervene, others may merely be "invited" to do so.

3.1 The Right to Intervene

3.1.1 High Contracting States Whose National Is an Applicant

The intervention of the applicant's State of nationality, set out in Article 36 § 1, is an updated version of former Article 48 (b) of the Convention of 4 November 1950. The latter gave these States standing before the Court to bring a case in their own right following a decision by the Commission on the admissibility of an application. The term "third-party intervention" was formally introduced by Protocol No. 11 when

---

[6]While this number may seem low, it should be stressed that the wording of the Explanatory Report to Protocol No. 14 emphasises that the Commissioner's role is to highlight "structural or systemic weaknesses in the respondent or other High Contracting Parties" (13 May 2004, § 87).

[7]Harvey (2015).

Article 36 was rewritten. Both Articles are rooted in the long-standing mechanism of diplomatic protection.[8]

While their interventions are limited to cases before the Chamber or the Grand Chamber, *de facto* excluding single-judge and Committee cases,[9] concerned States remain privileged third parties. Indeed, they are entitled to intervene on their own initiative without requesting the authorisation of the Court; in practice, they are systematically invited by the Court to intervene at the same time as the case is communicated to the respondent State.[10]

When the matter is brought against another Member State, States usually intervene in support of their nationals. Such was the case in *Perinçek v. Switzerland*, where the Turkish Government intervened in favour of the applicant's freedom of speech in respect of his criticism of the Swiss authorities' official recognition of the Armenian genocide.[11] Other States may use their intervention as an opportunity to stress additional legal issues which are less relevant for the applicant but are illustrative of their national position. In *Somogyi v. Italy* for example, the Hungarian Government intervened mainly to identify the international instrument on judicial assistance which was applicable to Italy and Hungary.[12] However, it cannot be ruled out that States will intervene against their own nationals. In *K.K.C. v. the Netherlands*, for example, the Russian Government informed the Court that they wished to avail themselves of their right to intervene in order to contest the applicant's allegation that her expulsion from the Netherlands to Russia would be in violation of Article 3 of the Convention.[13] Nonetheless, this represents a very rare practice.

3.1.2 Council of Europe Human Rights Commissioner

Since the entry into force of Protocol No. 14 on 1 June 2010, Article 36 § 3 has also enshrined the right of the Council of Europe Commissioner for Human Rights to intervene.[14] The Commissioner has made limited use of that right, although he/she has been more active in the past couple of years, particularly in sensitive cases.[15] According to Jean-Paul Costa, the reports produced within the Council of Europe

---

[8]Sicilianos (2005), p. 122.

[9]Explanatory Report to Protocol No. 14 to the European Convention on Human Rights amending the control system of the Convention, Strasbourg, 13.V.2004, Council of Europe Treaty Series No. 194, § 89.

[10]Rule 44 § 1 (a) of the Rules of Court.

[11]*Perinçek v. Switzerland* [GC], no. 27510/08, §§ 173-176, 15 October 2015.

[12]*Somogyi v. Italy*, no. 67972/01, §§ 59-60, 18 May 2004.

[13]*K.K.C. v. the Netherlands*, no. 58964/00, 21 December 2001.

[14]Rule 44 § 2 of the Rules of Court.

[15]As of January 2019, the last intervention was in December 2018 in the case of *Mehmet Osman Kavala v. Turkey*, which concerned the arrest and detention of the applicant, a civil-society activist and human-rights defender in Turkey, and the alleged use of this detention as a mean of silencing him.

and brought to the Court's attention through the Commissioner's observations compensate for the reduced number of on-the-ground investigations conducted by the Court.[16] The Court itself has acknowledged, at least indirectly, that the Commissioner's unique perspective and the valuable information provided by the Commissioner's Office, highlighting structural or systemic weaknesses in the respondent High Contracting Parties,[17] facilitate its task in reaching a decision.

3.2 The Conditional Ability to Intervene

In accordance with Article 36 § 2, third States Parties and third parties to the proceedings may, in the interest of the proper administration of justice, be invited by the President of the Court "to submit written comments and take part in hearings". These States and persons take part in the proceedings but are not parties to them[18]; it follows that they do not enjoy the same rights as the parties before the Court. Moreover, and since the decision pertains to the President of the Court, they do not have a fully-fledged right to intervene. However, while in practice the Court is very liberal in accepting the intervention of Member States and *amici curiae*, it is very cautious with regard to the "person(s) concerned".

3.2.1 Third States

Third States' interventions originate in arbitration and in the sovereign right to create and amend international law, and thereby to play a part in the law-making role of the Court.[19]

Unlike the States referred to in paragraph 1 of Article 36, third States generally intervene in favour of the respondent State, principally because they share a particular legal order or similar judicial practices. They exercise that right when the outcome of the case could affect their domestic legal system, mainly in high-profile cases or those involving public international law issues.[20] Thus, they intervene in their own interest, at least indirectly. As an example, in *Lautsi v. Italy*, ten Governments intervened in support of the Italian Government's position that the Cross was both a national and a religious symbol which inevitably had a place in State institutions.[21] This type of intervention is even more desirable given the *erga*

---

[16]Costa (2008).

[17]Explanatory Report to Protocol No. 14, § 87.

[18]Explanatory Report to Protocol No. 11, 11 May 1995, § 91.

[19]Bürli (2017), pp. 132–135.

[20]Harvey (2015), *op. cit.*

[21]*Lautsi and Others v. Italy*, no. 30814/06, § 47, 18 March 2011. The Governments of Armenia, Bulgaria, Cyprus, Greece, Lithuania, Malta, Monaco, Romania, the Russian Federation and the Republic of San Marino submitted written observations.

omnes de facto effect of some of the Court's judgments, and their impact on national legal systems other than that of the respondent State.[22]

3.2.2   Third Parties Concerned: *amici curiae* and Parties with a Stake in the Proceedings

Among third parties, there is first a category of *sui generis* parties, usually seen at the Court in the form of *amicus curiae*, and a second category, comprised of by parties who have an actual stake in the outcome of the proceedings. The first are, in my view, "interesting" parties for the Court, while the second are "parties with a stake, or direct interest, in the proceedings", as will be extensively discussed in the third section below.

The first category, the *amici curiae*, encompasses interest groups; companies; governmental and non-governmental organisations ("NGOs"), whether international or national (although the NGOs are mainly Anglo-Saxon)[23]; national human-rights institutions[24]; universities; academics; bar associations, etc. In theory, they are not directly affected by the outcome of the proceedings. Their role is rather to enlighten the Court with their expertise as to the legal and cultural issues, both national and international, of the case *sub iudice*.[25]

From my short experience as a Rapporteur to the Grand Chamber, admission of this group to the procedure appears to be subject to the assent of the experienced lawyers who prepare the case for the Grand Chamber and is based on the quality of their interventions in previous proceedings. It seems to me that the Judge Rapporteur in a case rarely has access to that information, particularly recently appointed judges. Hence, part of this preliminary task may fall outside judicial control. Moreover, one cannot exclude the possibility of some kind of manipulation of the Court, since certain of these *amici curiae* could primarily be using their intervention to obtain an implicit acknowledgment of their expertise by the Court. This risk could be avoided by various methods. First, seeking the parties' opinion about the competence of the *amici curiae* could lead to a better evaluation of their quality. Second, establishing a database containing past Rapporteurs' assessment of their interventions could facilitate the work of future Judge Rapporteurs, who could, on the basis of this information, form a more comprehensive opinion on their actual value and decide whether or not they should be granted leave to intervene. In other words, the whole point should be to guarantee that the Judge Rapporteur is in the best position to prepare the case file properly.

---

[22]In the case of "leading judgments", for example. On the issue of the reach of the Court's cases, see Pastor Vilanova (2018), pp. 120–121.

[23]Burgorgue-Larsen (2011), p. 73.

[24]Vincent Berger, Regional Consultation on Advancing a Pacific Regional Human Rights Mechanism, Suva, 28–30 November 2011.

[25]Burgorgue-Larsen (2011), p. 75.

4 Intervention by Original Parties to the Domestic Proceedings

4.1 Due Process As the Foundation

The second category of "persons concerned" under Article 36 § 2 refers to legal and natural persons who are directly involved in the facts of the case and who were usually parties to the domestic proceedings.[26] Their right to intervene is rooted in the principle of due process. One of the latter's main components is the common-law rule *audi alteram partem*, namely that the judicial function must hear both sides of every case, because not to do so would be unfair to the unheard party or because one might otherwise fall into error.[27] The principle of due process guarantees a set of procedural rights to any person who may be affected by a judicial decision, and therefore confers to the parties to the proceedings and to third parties indirectly concerned the right to be heard, through the submission of observations and participation in the debates. Their presence is therefore entirely compatible with, and even necessary for, the proper administration of justice before the Court.[28] In my view, it is precisely these persons who have a genuine *locus standi* and are principally "interested" by the outcome of the dispute. It is that interest, in particular, which distinguishes them from *amici curiae*.[29]

Their existence as a legal form is well known in comparative law. Examining this mechanism under various domestic legal systems (French, Spanish and Andorran) and under the law of the European Union is thus helpful in proposing solutions to increase the effectiveness of their intervention.

4.2 Third-Party Interventions Within Various Domestic Legal Systems and in the European Union

As a first example, the French legal system allows a third party voluntarily to join a lawsuit engaged between the originating parties[30] by becoming a party to the proceedings.[31] In its accessory form ("*intervention accessoire*"), the intervention seeks merely to substantiate or support one of the parties' claims, including by means of

---

[26]Bürli (2017), p. 9.

[27]On the origins of this rule, see J. M. Kelly, "Audi Alteram Partem. Note", *Natural Law Forum*, Paper 84, 1964, p. 103.

[28]Bürli (2017), p. 160.

[29]Bürli (2017), p. 161.

[30]French Code of Civil Procedure, Article 66 § 1.

[31]Chainais et al. (2018), § 435.

different arguments.[32] Its purpose is therefore to prevent any damage that this intervener could suffer, as well as to preserve their individual rights. Such intervention is admissible when the latter can demonstrate their interest in supporting a party in order to preserve their rights.[33] The Code of Civil Procedure stipulates that the third party is to be informed of any procedural steps adopted from the start of the proceedings, and is then able to submit observations on them.[34]

Spanish civil procedure provides for a form of intervention (*"intervención adhesiva simple"*) which allows a third party voluntarily to intervene and support the legal position of one of the parties to the proceedings.[35] The intervener is not a holder of the rights or bearer of the obligations at stake (as would be the case in the other form of *"intervención"*, known as *"litisconsorcial"*), but intervenes to prevent any adverse consequences that may follow from the judicial organ's decision. This is why, in order to be granted leave to intervene, these interveners must prove that the outcome of the case at hand could have indirect or secondary effects (*"efectos reflejos o indirectos"*) on their situation. Third parties are not a party to the proceedings; they take a subordinated procedural position, which depends on the position of the principal party, to which they adhere. Their powers are accordingly fairly extensive: they can plead, submit and provide evidence, appeal the decision, oppose termination of the proceedings by one of the principal parties, and challenge the establishment of the facts on account of the procedural behaviour of one of the parties...[36]

In Andorran administrative procedural law, any legal or natural person, whether public or private, who has a direct and legitimate interest in the object of the dispute can intervene as an adherent. However, these persons will never have the status of parties to the procedure, particularly since they cannot lodge an appeal or modify the claims of the parties.[37]

Finally, in the context of European Union law, any person, legal or natural, who has an interest in the outcome of a dispute pending before the Court of Justice of the European Union ("the Court of Justice") can support a party's claims.[38] The second paragraph of Article 40 of the Statute of the Court of Justice states that "any other person [than a Member State or an institution of the Union] which can establish an interest in the result of a case submitted to the Court" may intervene.[39] The interest must be direct and existing, as opposed to indirect, abstract and hypothetical.[40] In

---

[32]Fiche d'orientation: Intervention en Procédure civile, Éditions Dalloz, Septembre 2017.

[33]French Code of Civil Procedure, Article 330 § 2.

[34]French Code of Civil Procedure, Article 169 § 2.

[35]*Ley de Enjuiciamiento civil*, Article 13 § 1.

[36]Ortells Ramos (2005), p. 183.

[37]*Llei de la jurisdicció administrativa i fiscal*, Article 25.

[38]Bürli (2017), p. 159.

[39]They are, however, excluded from institutional disputes between Member States, institutions of the Union or between Member States and any of the said institutions.

[40]Bürli (2017), p. 159.

contrast, Member States and institutions are privileged interveners, who do not need to demonstrate any interest in the result of the proceedings. However, all interveners must support the form of order sought by one of the parties.[41] Ultimately, the interveners' interest is to be appreciated in the light of the objects of the dispute, i.e., its implications, so that judicial decisions result from thorough deliberations, taking into account all potentially affected interests.[42] Article 93 of the Rules of Procedure of the Court of Justice specifies that, once the application to intervene is granted, the intervener is to receive a copy of every procedural document notified to the parties, except for certain secret or confidential ones excluded by the President of the Court of Justice.[43]

4.3 Implementing an Actual Right to Intervene at the Court

Before the Court, the original parties to the proceedings do not have a priority right to intervene over *amici curiae*. This disconcerting equal status of both types of interveners arises from Article 36 § 2 as it is currently worded and the Court's practice in this regard. Consequently, the original parties' interests and opportunities to intervene are not effectively safeguarded, which may lead to practical inconsistencies when the time comes for domestic execution of the Court's judgment, particularly where domestic proceedings are reopened after the Court has found a violation of the Convention.[44] Another argument in favour of including the original parties and giving them priority over *amici curiae*, and one that is specific to the Court's internal functioning, is that these third-party interventions can be used to update the Court about recent legal changes in the respondent State or important case-law by the domestic tribunals. This is especially relevant when Court lawyers have already spent a long period at the Court, far from their national judicial system.[45] The risk of error may increase when the Court's Registry does not have any lawyers of the nationality of the dispute brought to the Court's attention (this is currently the case for Lichtenstein, Monaco and San Marino). The information brought to the Court's attention could therefore contain crucial aspects of the law that are likely to have a decisive impact on the outcome of the case at hand.

This section first examines, without claiming to be exhaustive, the potential "persons concerned" in relation to the actors in the domestic procedure. Some suggestions are then made as to how to secure these third parties' right to intervene in practice and which litigation rights should be conferred on them.

---

[41] Statute of the CJEU, Article 40(3).

[42] De Schutter (2005).

[43] Rules of Procedure of the Court of Justice, Article 93(3).

[44] Bürli (2017), p. 178.

[45] Rule 18 A of the Rules of Court.

4.3.1 Identifying "Any Persons Concerned"

It should be first noted that the "person(s) concerned" under Article 36 § 2 are the same persons covered by Article 34, namely natural and legal persons who are subject to the protection of the Convention. They are entitled to intervene so long as they can justify a legal interest in doing so. Their legal interest lies in the fact that, as Nicole Bürli explains very clearly, these persons would be affected in their rights by the measures taken by the respondent State in order to comply with the Court's judgment.[46]

We are referring mainly to the "original parties", that is, the claimant(s) or defendant(s) to the domestic dispute, but this group also includes the defendant in a civil action who brings a counterclaim in order to obtain an advantage other than the mere dismissal of the initial claim[47]: in other words, the "successful" party, who is not bringing a case before the Court against the respondent State. Additionally, this group could even include a third party who makes an intervention in the domestic proceedings.[48]

These "original parties" derive from a wide range of domestic disputes. In the context of criminal litigation, for example, victims who are *parties civiles* and join the proceedings initiated by the prosecutor may also wish to secure their interests in Strasbourg,[49] or even to ensure the correct establishment of basic facts. The Court's decisions are binding and authoritative; it would subsequently be extremely difficult (or simply impossible) for a third party to prove that the key facts as established in the Court judgment are false.[50] In the *Krombach v. France* cases, the father of the alleged victim, who was a civil party to the proceedings against the applicant, was granted leave to intervene twice, in 2001 and 2018.[51] The practice of the Court encompasses many other examples, in various specific civil[52] or administrative matters,[53]

---

[46]Bürli (2017), p. 161.

[47]For example, the French "*demande reconventionnelle*"; see French Code of Civil Procedure, Article 64.

[48]*Lambert v. France* [GC], no. 46043/14, 5 June 2015. One of the interveners, Vincent Lambert's half-sister, was also a third party to the domestic proceedings.

[49]Or any similar mechanism through which the victim intervenes as an accessory complainant, such as the "*Nebenklage*" in German criminal proceedings. This was the status of the interveners in *Gäfgen v. Germany* [GC], namely the parents of the child who had been killed by the applicant (no. 22978/05, 1 June 2010).

[50]Bürli (2017), p. 181.

[51]*Krombach v. France*, no. 29731/96, 13 February 2001 (judgment); no. 67521/14, 20 February 2018 (decision).

[52]See, concerning property law for example: *Brumărescu v. Romania* [GC], no. 28342/95, 28 October 1999 (Merits) and 23 January 2001 (Just Satisfaction); *Vrioni and Others v. Albania*, no. 2141/03, 24 March 2009; *Birzescu and Others v. Romania*, no. 9304/05, 25 September 2012; *Batkivska Turbota Foundation v. Ukraine*, no. 5876/15, 9 October 2018.

[53]*Lambert v. France* [GC], no. 46043/14, 5 June 2015.

employment law,[54] child-abduction disputes,[55] paternity disputes[56] or with regard to defamation and invasion of privacy issues.[57] The problem would be much worse if it turns out, *a posteriori*, that the Court has based itself on erroneous legislation or outdated national case-law.

However, is it actually necessary to have been "part" of the domestic proceedings? Can persons who are neither parties nor third parties intervene in Strasbourg? I am thinking, for example, of the victims of an offence who are not *"parties civiles"* to the criminal proceedings brought by the public prosecutor.[58] Have these interveners lost their right to legal action? I cannot accept that the answer should always be in the affirmative. First, we are aware that many legal systems do not recognise the mechanism of *"constitution de partie civile"*; instead, they separate criminal proceedings from any civil proceedings brought by the victims. Such is the case in English criminal procedure, where the victim has no particular status, and no formal *locus standi* to ask for compensation.[59] In the notorious case of *T. v. the United Kingdom*,[60] the parents of the child who had been killed by the applicant were granted leave to submit written comments, to attend the hearing and to make oral submissions, despite the fact that the parents had not been parties to the criminal proceedings which were being contested before the Court.

Moreover, interveners do not necessarily need to have taken part in domestic proceedings; the wording of Article 36 § 2 does not contain any such indication. Indeed, as noted above, it is the fact that the "persons concerned" have a stake, or legal interest, in the Court's decision which confers on them the *standing* to intervene. The "beneficiaries" of the outcome of civil proceedings, for example, although not parties to those proceedings, can also be granted leave to intervene. Family litigation, e.g., the adoption of a minor, does not necessarily involve the adoptive parents. The Norwegian adoption system, for example, provides for a mechanism whereby the county social welfare board (a public authority) orders the withdrawal of parental responsibility from the child's biological parents and gives its consent for him or her to be adopted by persons other than the biological

---

[54]For cases where the applicants were employed by religious institutions, see *Schüt v. Germany*, no. 1620/03, § 52, 23 September 2010; *Obst v. Germany*, no. 425/03, 23 September 2010; *Siebenhaar v. Germany*, no. 18136/02, 3 February 2011; *Fernandez Martinez v. Spain* [GC], 56030/07, 12 June 2014.

[55]*Neulinger and Shuruk v. Switzerland*, no. 41615/07, 6 July 2010.

[56]*Anayo v. Germany*, no. 20578/07, 21 December 2010; *Schneider v. Germany*, no. 17080/07, 15 September 2011; *Ahrens v. Germany*, no. 45701/09, 22 March 2012; *Mandet v. France*, no. 30955/12, 14 January 2016.

[57]*Feldek v. Slovakia*, no. 29032/95, 12 July 2001; *Hannover v. Germany*, no. 59320/00, 24 June 2004; *Aquilina and Others v. Malta*, no. 2141/03, 24 March 2009; *Bohlen v. Germany*, no. 53495/10, 19 February 2015; *Kahn v. Germany*, no. 16313/10, 17 March 2016.

[58]The process of *constitution de partie civile* can, for example, be found in Article 3 of the French Code of Criminal Procedure.

[59]Spencer (2002), p. 156.

[60]*T. v. the United Kingdom* [GC], no. 24724/94, 16 December 1999.

parents.[61] Thus, adoption proceedings oppose the biological parents to the public authority, although the beneficiaries of a decision in favour of adoption will ultimately be the adoptive parents. Accordingly, in the recent case of *Strand Lobben and Others v. Norway*, the second applicant's adoptive parents were invited to intervene in the written proceedings by the President of the Court *ex officio*.[62]

4.3.2   A Practical Problem: The Reopening of Domestic Proceedings

The main implication of a defective intervention system lies in the fact that most States Parties to the Convention have enshrined in their own legislation the possibility of reopening national proceedings subsequent to a finding of a violation in the applicant's favour.[63] In practice, the Court will specify, in its operative provisions and after indicating the relevant national provisions, that "the finding of a violation constitutes in itself just satisfaction". Indeed, the Court has repeatedly considered that, in principle, the reopening of domestic proceedings or trial *de novo* are, if requested, an appropriate, and often *the* most appropriate, way of putting an end to the violation and of affording redress for its effects.[64]

However, how can one preserve the equity of further domestic proceedings without hearing all the persons who had been initially involved? It is not impossible to imagine that, in criminal litigation as mentioned above, victims would have to return the damages awarded to them in the first round of proceedings because the applicant (who had previously been declared criminally and civilly liable) was ultimately acquitted after a retrial. Still in the context of criminal litigation, the reopening of cases may be detrimental to the victims in that evidence may have been lost and because of the time that has elapsed. Similar risks exist in civil litigation, such as that relating to succession, property disputes, paternity declarations, adoption, dismissals and defamation lawsuits. As mentioned above, however, our concern lies with the parties who have been (totally or partially) successful in the domestic proceedings, or who have at least benefited from their outcome.[65] This will not be the case for an unsuccessful party who did not deem it necessary to lodge any claim in Strasbourg, e.g. the applicant's co-accused or co-condemned in criminal proceedings who does not submit an application to the Court.

Some domestic courts have already openly criticized the ECHR's procedural deficiencies. As an example, the German Federal Constitutional Court (the

---

[61]Child Welfare Act of 17 July 1992 (*Barnevernloven*), section 4-20.

[62]*Strand Lobben and Others v. Norway* [GC], ECHR press release 347 (2018), 17 October 2018.

[63]In Germany, the possibility of reopening criminal proceedings is found in Article 359 § 6 of the Code of Criminal Procedure, and for civil proceedings in Article 580 § 8 of the Code of Civil Procedure.

[64]*Öcalan v. Turkey* [GC], no. 46221/99, § 210 *in fine*, 12 May 2005; *Moreira Ferreira v. Portugal (no. 2)* [GC], nos. 50541/08 and 3 others, § 52, 11 July 2017.

[65]Lambert-Abdelgawad (2008), p. 18.

"Karlsruhe Court"), in the context of execution of the well-known *Gorgülü v. Germany* case,[66] expressed the view that the procedure before the European Court of Human Rights does not necessarily provide a faithful picture of the positions and interests at stake, in particular when the national proceedings are private in nature. *In casu*, the Court had decided in favour of the applicant, the natural father of a child who was given up for adoption after his birth and had since lived with his foster parents. The latter had not intervened in the proceedings before the Chamber. The German court noted:

> In this respect, it is necessary for the national courts to evaluate the decision when taking it into account; in this process, account may also be taken of the fact that the individual application proceedings before the ECHR, in particular where the original proceedings were in civil law, possibly does not give a complete picture of the legal positions and interests involved. The only party to the proceedings before the ECHR apart from the complainant is the State party affected; the possibility for third parties to take part in the application proceedings (see Article 36.2 of the European Convention on Human Rights) is not an institutional equivalent to the rights and duties as a party to proceedings or another person involved in the original national proceedings.[67]

Similar criticism has been formulated within the Court, *inter alia* in the concurring opinion of Judge Wojtyczek in *Bochan v. Ukraine*.[68]

> 8. In examining applications alleging human rights violations in civil proceedings or arising from judicial decisions in civil cases, determining disputes between individuals or legal persons governed by private law, the rights of the party opposing the applicant party must never be overlooked. That is because the Court's finding of a violation of the Convention on account of a judicial decision in a civil case may have practical and legal consequences for the other parties to the civil proceedings and for the implementation of their rights. This problem is particularly acute in the case of applications against States whose legal systems (like that in Ukraine) allow the reopening of civil proceedings following a judgment of the Court. . . .

> 9. . . . The Convention does not guarantee the other parties to domestic proceedings who are concerned by the impugned judicial decision the right to be heard by the Court. . . . The approach adopted strikes me as inadequate, as the option, left to the discretion of the President of the Chamber, of hearing the views of a person who is concerned does not equate to a guarantee of the right to be heard. It is not always used where the rights of third parties are concerned.

> When sitting in cases dealing with violations of the Convention in civil proceedings or arising from a judicial decision in a civil case, I invariably wonder whether the other parties concerned should not be granted the right to submit observations to the Court. Is it right to give a decision without hearing the other parties concerned? Ensuring that they have the right to be heard would not only give greater effect to the principles of procedural justice, but in many cases would also afford greater insight into the issues under examination.

---

[66]*Gorgülü v. Germany*, no. 74969/01, 26 February 2004.

[67]Bundesverfassungsgericht, Beschluss, 14 October 2004 (2 BvR 1481/04) NJW 2004, 3407, § 65.

[68]*Bochan v. Ukraine (no. 2)* [GC], no. 22251/08, Concurring Opinion of Judge Wojtyczek, 5 February 2015.

4.3.3 The Solutions: An Effective Right to Intervene

The risks described above could in fact be neutralized were the Court to adopt a more voluntarist approach. This would consist in *systematically* inviting all the parties to the original proceedings to intervene, in as far as the outcome could have an impact on their own judicial sphere.

Some may argue, unconvincingly in my opinion, that third parties already have the possibility to intervene *proprio motu*. However, Article 36 § 2 of the Convention states that it is for the President of the Court to "invite" the persons "interested", on his own discretionary initiative.

In fact, I wonder how the parties to the original dispute would even become aware of the existence of a pending procedure before our Court in order to exercise their option to intervene. This drawback is even more acute in that, in theory, third parties have "only" 12 weeks after the respondent State has been notified of the application[69] or, before the Grand Chamber, once the Chamber judgment has been notified to the parties,[70] to submit their request to intervene. Although they may be informed by the opposing party in the domestic proceedings, such a formality is not compulsory, given that the obligation to protect national and international fair-trial guarantees lies only on States and not on private persons. Some may argue that these original parties should be proactive in seeking out information about cases that may be of concern to them, either on the Court's website or on Hudoc. However, using the internet to notify a *sub iudice* procedure seems both artificial and atypical, and it places an excessive burden on the interveners, especially as an extended period may elapse between the date of the final domestic decision concerning them and the point at which an application to the Court is made public. It is clear that notifying the existence of a case by means of an official journal (or web page) should be a solution of last resort, once all other avenues have been exhausted.

Others might argue that the initially successful party will necessarily be informed of any proceedings before the Court at the execution stage of the original domestic decision. Indeed, the unsuccessful party would, in theory, object to the execution of that decision by invoking the application lodged in Strasbourg. I imagine that most national tribunals would notify the other party of this challenge in order to comply with the right to an adversarial procedure. However, this hypothesis does not always correspond to reality. Depending on the legal system in question, some decisions, such as a judicial declaration on ownership or a declaration of paternity, are self-enforcing and require no formal procedure against the unsuccessful party. The same difficulty arises when the request for execution is considerably delayed, for many and various reasons.

---

[69]Unless another deadline is set by the President of the Chamber, see Rule 44 § 3 (b) of the Rules of Court.

[70]Unless another deadline is set by the President of the Court, see Rule 44 § 4 (a) of the Rules of Court.

Finally, some might argue that the obligation to inform the parties should lie with the State to which the case was communicated. However, unless there is a duty to do so under domestic law, such notification remains merely optional, since it is dependent upon the good will of the State. Indeed, without any legal obligation, the parties will probably not be able to seek pecuniary remedy if, due to an absence of notification, their rights are infringed as a result of the reopened national proceedings. However, the practice of some countries provides inspiration in resolving this practical issue. As an example, Germany systematically notifies the existence of proceedings to the original parties, an approach that the Council of Europe could recommend to all State Parties on a voluntary basis.

Thus, since one can count on neither the parties to the proceedings nor the State in which their dispute was adjudicated to inform all potentially concerned parties, it seems reasonable to request that the Court do so. In practical terms, this would require that our Registrar ask the respondent Government to provide the identity and contact details of these potential third parties. This was done without any difficulty in the recent Grand Chamber case of *Strand Lobben v. Norway*.[71]

4.3.4   The Extent of Third Parties' Litigation Rights

Another area of uncertainty concerns the actual extent of third parties' litigation rights. In the majority of cases, they are granted leave to intervene in the written proceedings by submitting their own observations within a certain time-limit. Only exceptionally, however, are they allowed to take part in hearings.[72]

In my view, third parties should have access to the written observations of both parties in order to support the pleadings of one of the parties, either the applicant's or the defendant State's, effectively and directly; but also, indirectly, to defend their own interests. This is not currently the case since, in practice, third parties are only supposed to answer very specific questions and have therefore no margin to develop their own position. This procedural limitation reveals a situation which threatens the protection of these persons' right to a fair trial and the legal certainty of the European human-rights system. It is even more worrying in situations where it is not necessary to reopen the proceedings and some of the Court's decisions can therefore constitute *res iudicata* for the third party, without any possibility of domestic appeal and without having been "heard" (or read) by the Court.[73]

---

[71] *Strand Lobben and Others v. Norway* [GC], ECHR press release 347 (2018), 17 October 2018.

[72] Rule 44 § 3 (a) of the Rules of Court. In *Lambert v. France* [GC], no. 46043/14, 5 June 2015, the three interveners were given leave both to submit written observations and to take part in the hearings.

[73] For example, *Neulinger and Shuruk v. Switzerland* [GC], no. 41615/07, 6 July 2010. In this case, the Court found a violation of Article 8 in favour of the applicant who had abducted her child, making it impossible for the Swiss authorities to enforce the domestic decision ordering the child's return to his father in Israel.

Moreover, third parties ought to be heard when this opportunity is afforded to the parties. Public hearings concern mainly Grand Chamber cases, and rarely Chamber cases. Additionally, I believe that third parties should also have a chance to participate in friendly-settlement procedures under Article 39 of the Convention and even to request that the case be referred to the Grand Chamber, in accordance with Article 43 § 1.

Taking that position further, these parties should also be entitled to apply for legal aid, in exactly the same conditions as the applicants. Currently, such aid is available only to applicants and not to interveners,[74] although it is essential in terms of access to justice. It is also difficult to ascertain whether State Parties have a duty to guarantee access to the Court by providing legal aid for that purpose. Indeed, the right to legal aid is covered only by Article 6 § 3(c) of the Convention, and is therefore limited to criminal proceedings. However, some countries have introduced legal aid for all parties intervening before the Court; one example is Germany,[75] where financial assistance can be granted from the federal budget once the case has been communicated to the Government.[76] While this type of domestic initiative is laudable and should be encouraged, it is my opinion that, in order to guarantee adequate access to justice to all potential third parties, an application for legal aid at the Court level should also be possible if this is justified by the individual's financial situation.

In my view, the examples from comparative law, such as those described above, should be encouraged and should not be excluded from international judicial instances. The Court should be able to integrate them, not only to set an example of due process, but also to facilitate the execution of its judgments.

References

Burgorgue-Larsen, L. (2011). Les interventions éclairées devant la Cour Européenne des droits de l'Homme ou le rôle stratégique des amici curiae. In *La conscience des droits. Mélanges en l'honneur de Jean-Paul Costa* (p. 73). Paris: Dalloz.

Bürli, N. (2017). *Third-party interventions before the European Court of Human Rights* (1st ed.). Cambridge: Intersentia.

Chainais, C., Ferrand, F., Guinchard, S., & Mayer, L. (2018). *Procédure civile. Droit interne et européen du procès civil* (34th ed.). Paris: Dalloz.

Costa, J.-P. (2008). Les enquêtes sur place de la Cour européenne des droits de l'Homme. In *L'État souverain dans le monde d'aujourd'hui. Mélanges en l'honneur de J.-P. Puissochet*. Paris: Pedone.

---

[74]Rules 100-105 of the Rules of Court.

[75]For an interesting description of this issue, see Gruodyte and Kirchner (2016), p. 41.

[76]Law to introduce Legal Aid for affected Third Persons in Proceedings before the ECHR or *Gesetz zur Einführung von Kostenhilfe für Drittbetroffene in Verfahren vor dem Europäischen Gerichtshof für Menschenrechte*, 20 April 2013, section 1 (1).

De Schutter, O. (2005). Les tiers à l'instance devant la Cour de justice de l'Union européenne. In H. R. Fabri & J.-M. Sorel (Eds.), *Les tiers à l'instance*. Paris: Pedone.

Gruodyte, E., & Kirchner, S. (2016). Legal aid for intervenors in proceedings before the European Court of Human Rights. *International Comparative Jurisprudence, 2*, 41.

Harvey, P. (2015). Third party interventions before the ECtHR: A rough guide, *Strasbourg Observer*. https://strasbourgobservers.com/2015/02/24/third-party-interventions-before-the-ecthr-a-rough-guide/

Lambert-Abdelgawad, E. (2008). The execution of judgments of the European Court of Human Rights. *Human rights files, no. 19*, 18.

Ortells Ramos, M. (2005). *Derecho Procesal Civil* (6th ed.). Navarra: Editorial Aranzadi.

Pastor Vilanova, P. (2018). La Contribution du droit de la Convention Européenne des droits de l'Homme à l'intégration européenne. In J. Andriantsimbazovina (Ed.), *Intégration et droits de l'Homme* (pp. 120–121). Paris: Mare et Martin.

Sicilianos, A. (2005). La Tierce intervention devant la Cour Européenne des droits de l'Homme. In H. R. Fabri & J.-M. Sorel (Eds.), *Les tiers à l'instance devant les juridictions internationales* (p. 122). Paris: Pedone.

Spencer, J. R. (2002). The English system. In M. Delmas-Marty & J. R. Spencer (Eds.), *European criminal procedures* (p. 156). Cambridge: Cambridge University Press.

The Judicial Path to European Constitutionalism: The Role of the National Judge in the Multi-Level Dialogue

Francesco Perrone

Contents

1   The "Judicial Path" to European Integration

The contemporary cultural debate on fundamental rights and European integration focuses mainly on the role played within the multi-level system by the international and supranational Charters on fundamental rights. The implementation process of these legal tools into the national legal systems is producing a broad array of consequences, both legal and political, which go beyond the macroscopic effect of increasing the uniformity of fundamental rights protection standards among the European states falling within the jurisdiction of the ECJ and the ECtHR. It also

---

Francesco Perrone is Labour Judge at Court of Padova. He holds a PhD in Constitutional Law.

F. Perrone (✉)
Court of Padova, Padova, Italy
e-mail: francesco.perrone@giustizia.com

© Springer Nature Switzerland AG 2019
P. Pinto de Albuquerque, K. Wojtyczek (eds.), *Judicial Power in a Globalized World*, https://doi.org/10.1007/978-3-030-20744-1_26

involves a significant side effect: an emerging progressive evolution of the institutional identity of the national judge, who is assuming an increasing role as a key player of a new judicial path to European integration.

Both doctrine and jurisprudence have broadly emphasised the central importance gained by the apical dialogue between the national Constitutional Courts and the European Courts in the European integration process.[1] In some cases, such dialogue takes the form also of permanent structures of cooperation, such as the Superior Court Network (SCN), which ties the ECtHR with the national Supreme Courts. Within this framework of institutional roles, mainly in the last decade, the traditional identity of the judge—thanks to the entry into force of the Lisbon Treaty, the increasing osmosis with the European levels of jurisdiction and the continuous contamination with a variety of different legal models—,[2] has begun to change its genetic code. This transformation does not come up as a unitary and homogeneous phenomenon. Given that the judicial function is a power divided by nature in a multiplicity of individual holders (single judges, panels of judges, Tribunals, Courts, etc.), this process of evolution can profoundly vary in intensity and characteristics, depending on the professional, cultural and even philosophical background of each individual-judge. However, judicial practice demonstrates that a crosswise direction exists.

The purpose of this essay is to reconstruct how the multi-level integration process is changing the essence of the identity of the judge as conceived by the traditional nation-state model. This evolution concurs to carve out a growing trend that sees the ordinary judge as a pivot player of a *judicial path* to the European integration process. This phenomenon appears to have an even more significant impact in light of the stagnant correspondent crisis, which is trapping the *political path* to European integration. Judicial implementation of the fundamental rights provided by both the CFREU and the ECHR into national legal orders is nowadays the most significant test-bench to verify the concrete features that such phenomenon is gradually taking on. This process particularly brings into question two aspects of the traditional view of the role played by the judicial function in the nation-state.

The first sensitive point regards the long-established way to conceive the illuminist idea of separation of powers, one of whose essential cores is the principle of submission of the judge to the primacy of statutory law, in which the states mostly tied to the civil law legal tradition are mainly rooted.[3] Integration into the EU legal order makes national judges more and more aware of the privileged relationship that the direct dialogue with the EU's supranational level permits to have with the political "substratum" which typically underlies the legislation of the Union. This osmosis allows the national judge to have access to an axiological dimension that, according to the traditional doctrine of the nation-state, should be strictly reserved to the competence of the legislative and executive branches of the state. On the other

---

[1]Cartabia (2007), p. 59.

[2]Garapon and Allard (2005), *passim*.

[3]de Charles Montesquieu (1748), Book XI, ch. 6.

hand, the para-legislative efficacy stemming from the precedents set by the ECJ and the ECtHR case law calls into question the rigorous illuminist way to conceive the principle of submission of the judge to the law,[4] which radically excludes judicial interpretation from assuming the nature of source of law able as such to bind the judge.

Second, the multi-level integration process calls into question the long-established conception of sovereignty in the modern state, arising from Westphalian order (*cuius regio eius et religio*), whose cornerstone is the legitimate claim of the nation-state to exert the sovereignty in an exclusive manner over its own territory (*ius excludendi omnes alios*). The current political crisis in the process of European integration makes urgent the need to find a fertile compromise between such a doctrine, never waned, and the principle of supremacy and direct effect of EU law. The classic conception of the judiciary as an authority by nature "national" or "domestic" is no longer able to describe the practical way in which the sovereignty-integrated European legal order is evolving. The multi-level dialogue puts in contact, and potentially in conflict, a different way of conceiving some critical aspects of the conception of the rule of law that the national constitutional order might consider an essential and uncompromising expression of its sovereignty. In the *Dansk Industri* case,[5] the Danish judge was called to balance the principle prohibiting discrimination on grounds of age, such as interpreted by the well-established case law of the ECJ, with the principles of legal certainty and protection of legitimate expectations, both recognised also by the domestic legal order, with an autonomous and potentially conflicting meaning, as fundamental constitutional values. In the *Taricco* case,[6] a nervous dialogue between the Italian Constitutional Court[7] and the ECJ[8] has brought out an irreconcilable different way (substantial, rather than procedural) to conceive the limitation periods for criminal offences and, consequently, the closely linked principle of interdiction of retroactivity of criminal provisions. It is interesting to note that a remarkably different way to understand the concept of criminal law retroactivity has marked a drastic distance also between the Italian Constitutional Court's view and the interpretation given in the *Del Rio Prada* case by the ECtHR to Article 7 of the Convention.[9]

This process of *sovereignty dilution* emerges with even more emphasis in states which are subject to the jurisdiction both of the ECtHR and the ECJ, thanks to the trilateral dialogue fuelled by Articles 6 § 3 TEU and 53 CFREU. The *judicial path* to European integration is a rocky path, not immune to provoke institutional tensions.

---

[4]See for example Article 101 § 2 of the Italian Constitution.

[5]GC, C-441/14, *Rasmussen v. Dansk Industri*, 19.4.2016.

[6]Gallo (2017), p. 249.

[7]C.C., no. 115 of 10.4.2018.

[8]ECJ, GC, C-42/17, *M.A.S., M.B.*, 5.12.2017, GC, C-105/14, *Taricco*, 8.9.2015.

[9]ECtHR, GC, 21.10.2013, *Del Rio Prada v. Spain*, no. 42750/2009.

1.1 *The Role of the* ratio decidendi *in the EU and ECHR Legal Orders*

The multi-level integration process requires national judges to be able to manage the logic inherent to judge-made law systems, and to put into play new professional skills that are not necessarily part of their genetic heritage.

Article 32 of the ECHR confers competence to the ECtHR on the interpretation and application of the Convention and the Protocols thereto. Article 46 ECHR binds each Member State as a whole—in its legislative, governmental and judicial branches—to abide by the final judgment of the Court and to ensure the implementation of the Convention, as interpreted by the ECtHR case law, into the domestic legal order. Therefore, the fulfilment of the obligation to ensure the interpretation of the national legislation in consistency with the ECHR principles implies an integration within the structure of judicial reasoning and also of the peculiar elements characterising the epistemological approach of the Court, as the *ratio decidendi*-oriented reasoning is.[10]

As to the interpretative competence of the ECJ, even before the entry into force of the Lisbon Treaty, the judicial system appeared to be the most federalised element of the European Communities.[11] Article 267 § 3 TFEU prescribes the obligation of the referral to the ECJ of any preliminary question on the interpretation of the Treaties raised before a court or tribunal of a Member State against whose decisions there is no judicial remedy under national law. The interpretation that the ECJ gives to a rule of EU law "clarifies and defines the meaning and the scope of that rule as it must be or ought to have been understood and applied from the time of its entry into force".[12] As affirmed by the Italian Constitutional Court,[13] ECJ judgements establishing an inconsistency of a domestic criminal law with EU law "have the same force as an abrogating supervening law", in such way recognising the substantially para-legislative nature of the interpretative competence of the ECJ.[14]

Civil law legal systems, particularly those mostly inspired by the Montesquieu state model, are traditionally grounded on the cornerstone of the primacy of the statutory law. In the logic governing this principle, the *ratio legis* is the direct and binding reference term that must lead the judge in the interpretation and application of the legal norm. The *ratio legis* (the essence of the logic/reason of the legal norm), is logically and chronologically placed *before* the case to decide, therefore it reflects,

---

[10]See, for example, the ECtHR judgment 20.11.1989, *Kostovski v. the Netherland*, no. 11454/85, which led the Dutch Supreme Court to amend its own well-established case law on the use of statements anonymously made by witnesses during the preliminary investigation in criminal trials (H.R., no. 2.7.1990). See Efthymiou and de Wit (2013), p. 75.

[11]Hartley (1986), p. 229.

[12]ECJ, C-292/04, *Wienand Meilicke and Others*, 6.3.2007.

[13]C.C., no. 311/2011, n. 241/2005, n. 125/2004.

[14]A. Rosas (2007), Separation of powers in The European Union. https://scholar.smu.edu/til/vol41/iss4/6.

by nature, the *abstract* structure of the provision of law that contains it. Coherent with this logic, in civil law systems, the reasoning of the judge traditionally presents syllogistic and deductive structure.

The *ratio legis* also plays an important role as a dividing line, which guarantees, as a coherent result of the principle of submission of the judge to the primacy of statutory law, the independence of the judicial ruling from any possible interference coming from the political will of the other branches of the state. The will of the legislator, as well as of any authority included within the policy-making sphere, has the force to bind the judge only as far as it assumes the role of an objective constitutive element of the formal structure of the legal norm (*voluntas legis*). Otherwise, the political purpose of the legislature, if left outside the objective structure of the norm, remains deprived of any possibility of interference on the judicial interpretation and application of the law (*voluntas legislatoris*).

On the contrary, the judge-made law systems are grounded on the *ratio decidendi* logic, which is the *concrete* reason of the judicial decision. The *ratio decidendi* orientation of the judicial reasoning is especially evident in the ECHR legal order, whose cornerstone is a very short Charter of rights (along with its Protocols), and above all the case law elaborated by the ECtHR. The *ratio decidendi* logically and chronologically comes *after* the case to adjudicate, so that the factual characteristics of the case have a decisive weight on the *ratio decidendi* shaped by the judicial ruling. Differently from the deductive and syllogistic structure characterising the *ratio legis*-oriented reasoning, in judge-made law systems, the *ratio decidendi* logic forges an inductive and concrete epistemological approach. Whereas the *ratio legis*-based interpretation is called to relate *abstract* entities to each other (*ubi eadem ratio, ibi eadem dispositio*), the *ratio decidendi*-oriented reasoning is grounded on the method of *distinguishing*, whose logic structure relates two entities both *concrete*: the case to be adjudicated and the *ratio decidendi* of a precedent relevant case.

1.2   The Result-Oriented Approach of the ECHR Legal Order

The case *Del Rio Prada v. Spain*,[15] ruled by the Grand Chamber of the ECtHR in 2013, is a particularly meaningful bench-test to verify in concert terms which kind of different implications a *ratio decidendi*-oriented reasoning implies. In 2006, the Spanish Supreme Court[16] changed its well-established case law concerning the interpretation of the legal criterion to calculate the reduction of sentences in a way less favourable to the accused. In force of this supervening change in the case law, the *Audiencia National* postponed the early release to which the convicted was entitled because of the work done during the imprisonment, formerly fixed in April 2008, to a new date in June 2017. The ECtHR held a violation of Article 7 of the

---

[15]ECtHR, GC, 21.10.2013, *Del Rio Prada v. Spain*, no. 42750/2009.
[16]S.C., no. 197 of 28.2.2006.

Convention considering that the Spanish statutory law applicable at the material time, if read in the light of the accompanying interpretative case law, did not satisfy the requirement of accessibility and foreseeability. The reasoning of the Court stems from the assumption that the new judge-made criterion to calculate the remission of the sentence had a significant impact on the concrete length of the detention. In the assessment of the Court, it is not the wording of the legal norm itself, but rather the concrete effect obtained by the judicial application of that norm that has to be considered to verify case by case the compliance with Article 7 of the Convention. The Court affirms that the *"law"*, read in the substantive sense in which the term is used in the wording of the Convention, comprises statutory law as well as case law.[17] Therefore, the domestic law has to be regarded as a whole, included how it is applied in the material time, and it is as such required to comply with the principle of foreseeability. The case makes evident the epistemological approach followed by the Court. First, the judicial assessment is oriented to focus not on the formal wording of the legal norm itself but on the *result* stemming from the application of that norm. Second, the Court considers such *result* as relating to all the concrete circumstances of the *fact*, of which the legal provision is one of the relevant elements to be considered.

It is interesting to consider the different approach followed by the Italian Constitutional Court in 2012, when the Court ruled on whether, and to what extent, the principles affirmed in the *Del Rio Prada* case are compatible with the fundamental principles of the domestic constitutional order.[18] The Italian case regarded the admissibility of the revocation of a final criminal judgment because of a supervening overruling of the well-established case law of the Supreme Court of Cassation favourable to the convicted person. The Constitutional Court was called upon to rule on the consistency with Article 25 of the Italian Constitution, the domestic *pendant* of Article 7 ECHR "no punishment without law", of a procedural norm establishing a list of exceptional cases permitting the revocation of a final criminal judgment.[19] The norm does not contemplate the favourable overruling excluding the existence of the crime as a case of revocation. The Court held the question of constitutionality ill-founded. The core of the reasoning followed by the Court was the assumption that, in civil law legal orders, the rule of law finds its cornerstone in the principle of primacy of the statutory law. According to the Court, this principle does not permit the interpreting case law, no matter how authoritative the judicial body providing the interpretation is, to be included within the concept of *law*, and consequently within the formal structure of the principle of legality. In the specific case, the convicted was sentenced based on a provision of *law* regularly in force at

---

[17]See also *Kokkinakis v. Greece*, 25.51993, no. 14307/88, §§ 40-41; *Cantoni v. France*, 15.11.1996, no. 17862/91, § 29; *Coëme and Others v. Belgium*, nos. 32492/96, 32547/96, 32548/96, 33209/96 and 33210/96, § 145; *E.K. v. Turkey*, 7.2.2002, no. 28496/95, § 51.

[18]C.C., no. 230 of 12.10.2012.

[19]Article 673 c.p.p.

the time of both the crime and the conviction, therefore the Court held that the principle of legality of crimes and punishments was not infringed.

1.3   The Para-Legislative Power of the ECJ

As demonstrated in the case *Del Rio Prada*, the meaning of the concept of *law* and the ensuing role reserved to the judicial interpretation directly interfere in the substantial meaning that the principle of the rule of law assumes in a particular constitutional system. In legal orders mostly tied to the illuminist model of separation of powers, the judge, as a constitutive structure of the rule of law, plays as an authority rigorously separated from the policymaking sphere. The judicial interpretation is a task with an essentially declarative nature, without any power for the judge to make or create law.[20] Any possibility of interference into the policymaking process is like a taboo. Therefore, the judicial practice reveals how deeply the mutual integration between this idea of jurisdiction and the para-legislative role played by the ECJ's interpretative competence can lead to a clash of cultures.

The nature of the legitimacy competence of the Supreme Courts mostly inspired by the French model makes clear the distance between these two different paradigms. The precedents of this type of Courts are not legally binding as such on any other national judge (*potestas*). They have rather compelling interpretative force inasmuch as grounded on a logical, exhaustive and well-founded reasoning (*auctoritas*).[21] The illuminist paradigm of separation of powers has deeply influenced the Italian constitutional model. The Italian doctrine often defines the judiciary as a "null power", to stress that the judicial function is by nature deprived of any power to make law. A still vital cultural link with the Montesquieu doctrine is evident.[22] The philosophe famously insisted that judges "must be no more than the mouth that pronounces the words of the law, mere passive beings, incapable of moderating either its force or vigour". Robespierre explained that, in a state with one constitution and one legislation, "the jurisprudence of the courts was nothing but the statutory law". Coherently with this view, the law 16th–24th August 1790 prohibited general rulings (*arrêts de règlement*) from the courts and invited judges to ask for authentic interpretation in case of doubt or gaps in the existing law through the *référé législatif* process, repealed in 1804 by the Napoleon Code.

The anti-historical Jacobin idea of the judge *bouche de la loi*, as well as all the extreme legal doctrines of the revolutionary period,[23] are today abandoned. Nevertheless, these philosophical roots are still seminal in the architecture of the Italian

---

[20]Pollard (2007), p. 15; Steyn (2006), pp. 243–246.

[21]On the difference between *potestas* and *auctoritas*, see *Res gestae divi Augusti*, Pars prima, cap. XXXIV.

[22]Halpérin (1989), p. 226; *Idem* (2014), p. 51; Palmer (1999), p. 277.

[23]A. Cochin, *L'esprit du jacobinisme*, Paris, 1779, *passim*.

Constitutional order. Article 104 of the Constitution explicitly constitutes the judiciary as an "autonomous *order*, independent from *any other power*". According to an influential part of the constitutional doctrine,[24] the wording of this constitutional provision formalises the idea that only the legislature and the government, as authorities provided with law-making competence, are *powers* of the state in the strict sense of the word. On the contrary, the judicial function, being devoid of any law-making prerogatives, has to lie by nature with a body (*l'ordre judiciaire* in the French Constitution of 1958) which is ontologically different from a *power* of the state. This theoretical approach evokes a remarkable parallelism with the preamble of the Declaration of the Rights of Man and of the Citizen of the 26th August 1789, which mentions only the legislative and the executive as *powers* of the State, with no reference to the "judicial" one.

In this respect, the different wording of Article 3 of the U.S. Constitution of 1787, which explicitly constitutes the judiciary as a "*power* of the United States", appears to be particularly meaningful. The U.S. constitutional tradition recognises in Article 3, in conjunction with Amendments I to X (the so-called "bill of rights"), the theoretical basis for a conception of the judiciary as a "guardian" of the civil and political rights established by the U.S. Constitution.[25] The judge is required to perform this task of guardianship employing the judicial review of State legislation,[26] even in opposition to the possible abuses perpetrated by the representative institutions and the will of the political majority. The U.S. constitutional order recognises for the judiciary an active role in the balance between the concurrent interests at stake, eventually in competition with the balance of interests struck by the policymaking authorities. This model of jurisdiction is far from the theory of a rigid separation between the judicial function and the policymaking competence reserved to the legislative-executive branches. Therefore, it is not surprising either how deeply the American Constitutionalism tradition is influenced by the doctrine of the "moral reading" of the Constitution.[27] According to the authoritative opinion of the U.S. Supreme Court judge W. J. Brennan, a morally and legally acceptable interpretation of the Constitution is necessarily the result of an aware application of a more or less clear and substantial political theory. Such a proximity of the jurisdiction with the political and ethical sphere of law[28] marks an evident distance from the state models mostly inspired by the continental legal tradition.

---

[24]Bartole (1964); Guarnieri and Pederzoli (2007), p. 76.

[25]Friedman (1994), p. 97; Casper (1980), p. 773; Garapon (1996), p. 31.

[26]U.S. Supreme Court, *Marbury v. Madison*, 1803; *United States v. Nixon*, 1974.

[27]Dworkin (1977), p. 184.

[28]Rawls (1983).

1.4 The Teleological-Orientation of the EU Legal Order: l'effet utile

The principle of primacy of EU law[29] requires the EU Member States to ensure the effective achievement of the aims of the Union. The fulfilment of such obligation refers not only to the results established by the Directives but embraces all the political aims pursued by the European institutions, such as results, for example, from the reasons on which EU legal acts are based (Article 296 TFEU). Furthermore, Article 4 § 3 TEU establishes that "the Member States shall take any appropriate measure, general or particular, to ensure fulfilment of the obligations arising out of the Treaties or resulting from the acts of the institutions of the Union". Therefore, the obligation to take any general or *particular measure* binds the state in all its institutional bodies—legislature, public administration, and judicial authorities—to adopt any effective measures, including judicial decisions, to ensure the compliance of the domestic legal order with the political aims of the Union (ECJ, C-14/83, *Von Colson*, 10.4.1984, § 26).

The consistent interpretation is a judicial tool permitting national judges to adopt *particular measures* of implementation of EU law. The integration of this tool into the commonly acquired expertise of the legal practitioners is one of the factors contributing the most to the evolution of the institutional identity of the judicial function. This interpretative competence, in light of the principles of the ECJ case law,[30] is characterised by the attribution of powers to the judge, hard to reconcile with the traditional idea of legal interpretation as an activity rigorously separated from the policymaking sphere.

The case *Pfeiffer*[31] provides a meaningful example. The ECJ decided on the conformity with Directive 93/104, whose purpose is to secure effective protection of the safety and health of workers by fixing the maximum period of weekly working-time at 48 h, of the implementing German law on minimum periods of rest. The domestic law has substantially transposed the 48-h maximum period of weekly working-time, but also permitting this upper limit in cases of duty time completed by emergency workers in the framework of emergency service to be exceeded by means of a collective agreement. The ECJ called the national judge upon to interpret national law, so far as possible, in such a way to apply it in conformity with the objectives of the Directive and to ensure that Directive is fully effective.[32]

---

[29]ECJ, C-26/62, *Van Gend en Loos*, 5.2.196; C-6/64, *Costa v. Enel*, 15.7.1964; C-106/77, *Simmenthal*, 9.3.1978.

[30]ECJ, GC, C-106/89, *Marleasing*, 13.11.1990. See also C-282/10, *Dominguez*, 11.11.2015; C-91/92, *Faccini Dori*, 14.7.1994; C-129/96, *Nier-Environnement Wallonie*, 18.12.1997; C-131/97 *Carbonari*, 25.2.1999.

[31]ECJ, GC, joined cases C-397/01 to C-403/01, *Pfeiffer*, 5.10.2004.

[32]ECJ, GC, C-106/89, *Marleasing*, 13.11.1990, § 26; C-63/97, *BMW*, 23.2.1999, § 22; joined cases C-240/98 to C-244/98, *Ocèano Grupo Editorial*, 5.10.2004; C-408/01, *Adidas-Salomon*, 23.10.2003, § 21.

Two observations are necessary.

First, Directive 93/104 imposes on the EU Member States the obligation to achieve a clear result, which is to prevent the maximum weekly working time laid down in the Directive from being exceeded. Therefore, an interpretation of the domestic law in such a way as to ensure an outcome consistent with the objective pursued by the Directive (*effet utile*), requires the judge to perform an activity implying, in practical terms, to set apart the national provision permitting collective agreements to exceed a 48-h weekly limit. In other words, it means recognising horizontal effects on the non-discrimination principle in disputes between individuals, notwithstanding that well-established ECJ case law itself has traditionally excluded a provision of a Directive seeking to confer rights or impose obligations on individuals from applying in proceedings between private parties.[33] Such activity, evidently, pertains properly to the law-making process, rather than being a pure declaration of the meaning of the existent law.

Second, this "strong" reading of the duty of consistent interpretation could result in a potential conflict with the national rules which prescribe the adoption of different remedies to ensure the implementation of EU law in the domestic order, for example, the mandatory referral of an incidental question of legitimacy to the Constitutional Court. Therefore, by employing the *effet utile*-oriented interpretation doctrine, the judge could end up seizing powers that the constitutional order reserves to different authorities of the state, such as the Constitutional Court.

This interference in the organisation of the powers of the state is the reason for the institutional turmoil that the multi-level integration process is potentially able to provoke on the domestic rules governing the demarcation of competences between Constitutional/Supreme Courts, policymakers and the judicial function.

Similar perturbing effects might derive from the fulfilment by the EU Member States of the obligation to "provide remedies sufficient to ensure effective legal protection in the fields covered by Union law" pursuant to Article 19 TUE, enshrined also in Article 47 CFREU. The effective judicial protection of individual rights is a general principle of European Union law, stemming from the constitutional traditions common to the Member States.[34] As previously focused, the state is bound as a whole—in its legislative, governmental and judicial branches—to ensure the implementation of EU law and the achievement of the aims of the Union. This implies that the obligation to adopt *particular measures* needed to make available effective judicial remedies binds the policymakers, as well as the judicial function when dealing with rights falling within the scope of Union law.[35]

The problematic point is that EU law might confer on the judicial function the duty to adopt certain types of implementing measures, which the domestic constitutional order reserve to the competence of a different branch of the state. Especially

---

[33]Bell (2003), p. 91.

[34]ECJ, C-64/16, *Associação Sindical dos Juízes Portugueses*, 27.2.2018.

[35]ECJ, C-32/12, *Soledad Durante Hueros*, 3.10.2013; joined cases C-568/14 to C-570/14, *Fernández Oliva and others*, 26.10.2016; C-101/01, *Bodil Lindqvist's*, 6.11.2003.

in civil law legal orders, the task to establish the catalogue of the judicial remedies for the protection of a particular right is often conceived as a duty falling within the competence of the legislative power.

The consumer protection law provides significant examples. Article 6 of Directive 93/13/EEC on unfair terms in consumer contracts, states that "unfair terms used in a contract concluded with a consumer by a seller or supplier shall [. . .] not be binding on the consumer". According to the well-established ECJ case law, the norm pursues the aim of replacing the formal balance between the rights and obligations of the parties set by the domestic law, with an effective balance that re-establishes equality between them. In the *Pannon* case, the ECJ established that the need to re-balance the weaker position of the consumer requires national courts to assess, of their own motion and without a specific application from the consumer to that effect, the unfairness of a contractual term on territorial jurisdiction laid down in a consumer contract. The judge must accomplish this duty notwithstanding that the national procedural rule applicable to the case precludes the possibility to raise that issue, *ex officio* or on application of a party, after the first filing of the defence to the substance of the dispute.[36]

In the *Sánchez Morcillo* case, the ECJ went even further. In mortgage enforcement proceedings, the Spanish legislation allows an appeal to be brought against a decision that, upholding the objection raised by a debtor, terminates the enforcement proceedings, while it does not allow the debtor whose objection has been dismissed for bringing an appeal against the judgment ordering the enforcement procedure to be carried out. In this case, the ECJ invoked for the first time Article 47 CFREU. The Court affirmed the obligation of national judges to ensure full implementation of the effectiveness of consumer protection, in the exercise of legal claims based on the rights derived from Directive 93/13, by interpreting the domestic law in such a way to make up for the lack of a domestic effective remedy.[37] This means, in practice, to open a *judicial path* to the creation of judge-made remedies required to pursue the concrete result envisaged by the political aims of the Union. It is evident that this interpretative competence goes far beyond the idea of interpretation as commonly accepted by the civil law legal background and leads the national judge to drift apart from its traditional identity as an authority rigorously separated from the policymaking sphere.

---

[36]ECJ, C-243/08, *Pannon GSM Ztr.*, 4.6.2009, § 25.

[37]ECJ, C-169/14, *Sánchez Morcillo*, 17.7.2014.

1.5   The Cultural Impact of the European Non-discrimination Principle on the Judicial Practice

The non-discrimination principle, recognised as a general principle of Community law also before the entry into force of the CFREU,[38] might play, thanks to the extensive and detailed case law developed by both the European Courts, a particularly important role as a gate to the "judicial path" to the integration process. The structure of the European framework of the sources of anti-discriminatory law develops on multiple levels. Within the ECHR legal order, the non-discrimination principle is provided by Article 14 ECHR, Article 1, Protocol no. 12 to the ECHR, such as interpreted by the case law of the ECtHR, and Article E of the European Social Charter. Within EU law,[39] primary sources of anti-discriminatory law are Article 21 CFREU and all the norms of the Treaties prescribing specific anti-discriminatory norms (Articles 2 TUE, 10 TFUE, 18 e 19 TFUE, 157 TFUE, etc.). In the range of secondary sources of law, a major role is played by the general anti-discrimination Directives: Employment Equality Directive (2000/78/EC), Racial Equality Directive (2000/43/EC), Gender Goods and Services Directive (2004/113/EC) and Gender Equality Directive (2006/54/EC). There are also particular anti-discriminatory provisions regulating specific matters such as, for example, Article 4 of Directive 1999/70/EC on fixed-term work. EU law also establishes some specific rules coordinating the EU and the ECHR legal orders, such as Articles 6 § 3 TUE, 52 § 3 CDFUE, and 151 TFUE.

Common to Articles 14 ECHR, Protocol no. 12 and 21 CFREU, is that all these norms establish a non-exhaustive list of protected grounds (sex, race, colour, language, religion, opinion, origin, association with a national minority, property, birth, as provided for example by Protocol no. 12). However, their scope considerably differs. An allegation of a violation of Article 14 ECHR is always to be done *in conjunction* with a substantive right established by the ECHR. Protocol no. 12, on the contrary, is greater in scope prohibiting discrimination to the "enjoyment of any right set forth by law" and "by any public authority". Finally, Article 21 CFREU, despite the fact that it does not provide any explicit limitation of scope, covers any matter falling within the competence of EU law, according to general principles of the Treaties.

The judicial implementation of the non-discrimination principle is a significant test-bench to focus on some particular aspects of the cultural challenges faced by national judiciaries, especially those mostly inspired to the civil law tradition, where legal education and practice usually forge the expertise of judges and lawyers to

---

[38]ECJ, C-43/75, *Defrenne v. Sabena*, 15.6.1978; C-11/70, *Internationale Handelsgesellschaft*, 17.12.1970; C-75/82, *Razzouk and Beydoun v. Commission*, 20.3.1984.

[39]M. Barbera (2018), Principi contesi e contese su principi. Gli effetti dei principi di eguaglianza e non discriminazione nella giurisprudenza della Corte di Giustizia. http://csdle.lex.unict.it/Archive/WP/WP%20CSDLE%20M%20DANTONA/WP%20CSDLE%20M%20DANTONA-IT/20181008-105240_Barbera_n372-2018itpdf.pdf.

handle the concept of *equality*, rather than the *non-discrimination* logic. The Italian legal tradition formally recognises the principle of "equality before the law" since the entry into force of the Constitution of the Kingdom of Sardinia in 1848 (*Statuto Albertino*), turned into the Constitution of the Kingdom of Italy in 1861. The non-discrimination principle started to seep gradually into the national legal order much later, from the moment when the judicial practice began addressing the question concerning the integration of the principles established by the ECtHR and ECJ case law into the national legal order.[40]

The concept of equality sinks its roots in a much older era than the period of the nineteenth-century Constitutions. It is often traced back to Aristotle's Nicomachean Ethics.[41] In modern continental Europe, the most influential political theory on equality is the illuminist doctrine on *égalité*. Contemporary European Constitutions generally provide, as a commonly recognised definition of equality, the principle "everyone is equal before the law" (Article 3 of the Italian Constitution, Article 1 of the French Constitution). The principle of equality, in its essence, is a procedural rule, establishing a formal criterion for the law-making process, which prescribes that "like cases must be treated alike". Irrespective of the centralised or decentralised structure assumed by the constitutionality review on the legislation in a particular legal order, the judgment of consistency with the principle of equality is by nature an abstract assessment, relating to the legitimacy/validity of a *legal norm*.

On the contrary, the non-discrimination principle (Article 14 ECHR, Article 21 CFREU) typically belongs to the Anglo-Saxon legal tradition. It is not an *abstract* criterion for verifying the legitimacy/validity of a *legal norm*, but rather a *concrete* criterion to assess all the *facts* of the specific case: whether a reasonable proportionality exists between the means employed and the aim sought.[42] The proportionality test requires to take into consideration not only the applicable legislation but also all the concrete circumstances of the case. The factual context where the discrimination is accomplished, corporate policies, codes of ethics, operational practices observed by individuals, groups and public authorities are elements to be taken all into account to assess whether a differential treatment is justified in the specific case. In judgments *Eweida*[43] (ECtHR), *Samira Achbita*[44] (ECJ) and *Asma Bougnaoui*[45] (ECJ), the European Courts were called upon to assess whether a blanket prohibition for employees to visibly wearing signs of religious beliefs is proportional and necessary

---

[40]ECJ, C-43/75, *Defrenne v. Sabena*, 15.6.1978; ECtHR, *Marckx v. Belgium*, no. 6833/74, 13.6.1979; *Abdulaziz v. The United Kingdom*, no. 9214/80, 28.5.1985.

[41]Aristotle, Nicomachean Ethics. Chicago: University Chicago Press, Book 5, Ch. 5.

[42]ECtHR, GC, *Burden v. the United Kingdom*, no. 13378/05, 29.4.2008; *Guberina v. Croatia*, no. 23682/13, 22.32016. ECJ, GC, *Egenberger*, C-414/16, 17.4.2018; GC, *IR v. JQ*, C-68/17, 11.9.2018; *Abercrombie & Fitch Italia Srl*, C-143/16, 19.7.2017.

[43]ECtHR, *Eweida v. United Kingdom*, no. 46852/13, 15.1.2013. See, in particular, the joint partly dissenting opinion of Judges N. Vučinić and V. De Gaetano.

[44]ECJ, *Samira Achbita*, C-157/2015, 14.3.2017.

[45]ECJ, *Asma Bougnaoui*, C-188/2015, 14.3.2017.

for the aim to pursue a policy of corporate neutrality.[46] Neither Courts hesitated to take into account, case by case, whether the employee was required to interact with the customers, whether the employer genuinely pursued the corporate policy in a consistent and systematic manner, whether the restriction to the rights of the employer was of crucial importance for the pursuit of the corporate policy.

It is emblematic that the CFREU recognises and embraces both these different cultural traditions, establishing both the non-discrimination principle (Article 21 CFREU) and the principle of equality (Article 20 CFREU) as fundamental rights of the Union.[47]

1.6 The Cultural Impact of the Balancing Test

The increasing familiarisation with the logic underlying the non-discrimination principle opens the way to a contamination between legal cultures. The integration of the *balancing test* into the judicial reasoning of jurisdictions belonging to the continental legal tradition is a meaningful example.

Under EU law, a specific set of grounds of justification exist allowing differential treatment to be justified in a limited set of circumstances. For example, all the anti-discrimination Directives (except the Gender Goods and Services Directive) provide the "genuine occupational requirement" exception, as well as the Employment Equality Directive provides the admissibility of age discrimination and the permissibility of discrimination based on religion or belief. By contrast, under the ECHR, lacking a detailed set of secondary sources of anti-discrimination law, the approach followed by the ECtHR is to operate a generally phrased justification.[48]

However, despite some peculiar differences, the approach to the justification test on objective grounds under both the ECHR and the exceptions from non-discrimination Directives has a substantially similar core. As demonstrated in the judgments *Eweida*, *Samira Achbita*, and *Asma Bougnaoui*, both tests involve an assessment on whether the measure leading to the differential treatment pursues a legitimate aim and is proportionate and necessary to achieve that aim. In doing this, both the ECtHR and ECJ seek to strike a fair balance between concurrent interests at stake. On the one hand, the legitimate interest of the employer to pursue a policy of neutrality towards its customers by imposing a blanket prohibition to visibly wearing signs of religious beliefs. On the other hand, the right of the employee not to be

---

[46]V. De Gaetano (2014), Riflessioni sulla libertà di religione e di coscienza: l'articolo 9 della convenzione europea dei diritti dell'uomo. *Online Working Paper*, 61. http://www.cde.unict.it/quadernieuropei/linguistico-letterarie/61_2014.pdf.

[47]Ghera (2003), p. 95; Kenner (2003), p. 19; Lenaerts and De Smijter (2001), p. 285.

[48]*Handbook on European non-discrimination law*, 2018 edition, European Union Agency for Fundamental Rights, European Court of Human Rights, 92. https://fra.europa.eu/en/publication/2018/handbook-european-law-non-discrimination.

discriminated against on the grounds of religious belief, because of its choice to wear an Islamic headscarf or a Christian cross at the workplace.

Therefore, national judges, insofar as obliged to fulfil the obligation to ensure the judicial implementation of the ECHR and EU legal principles, are called upon to apply also the logical structures governing the judicial reasoning followed by the European Courts in interpreting those principles. The *balancing test* is one of the structures that mostly characterises the argumentative approach of both Courts, not only in discrimination cases. The field of privacy protection,[49] for example, demonstrates how influential the *balancing test* is as a fundamental criterion of assessment of the interests at stake.[50]

However, it is far from obvious that, in many EU or ECHR Member States, the balancing test falls within the natural range of interpretative-applicative activities that are expected to belong to the judicial function. In civil law systems, the epistemic approach of the judge generally follows the logic of syllogistic reasoning. Coherently with this logic, the parity in treatment in a specific case, as much as a justified disparity, are considered the natural result of the consistency of the applicable legal provision with the principle of equality, as recognised by the clauses of national Constitutions. On the contrary, striking a balance between different concurrent interests is perceived as an activity in substance political, based on the deep-rooted idea that the selection of the values, which have to find legal recognition and protection, is a task reserved to the policymakers and eventually, within certain limits, to the Constitutional Court. The recent judgment of the Italian Constitutional Court no. 20 of 21 February 2019, pronounced in a case concerning transparency and publicity in the conferment of public offices, proves the cultural influence of this view. The Court, taking carefully into account in its reasoning both the Constitutional and European legal frameworks, has struck a complex balance of interests between the right to privacy of the holders of public offices and the right of citizens to have free access to data and information detained by the public institutions. The domestic constitutional order undoubtedly prohibits the ordinary judge from performing such an assessment.

The consideration made so far demonstrates how multi-level integration process is both a cultural and a professional challenge for the national judicial systems.

1.7   *The* Ordinary Judge of European Law

As described above, the European integration process within both the ECHR and the EU legal orders is having a considerable impact on the role traditionally played by the judicial function in the nation-state. This progressive transfiguration is not immune to generate institutional tensions. In recent judgments, the Italian

---

[49]ECtHR, GC, *Bărbulescu v. Romania*, no. 61496/08, 5.9.2017.
[50]Perrone (2018), p. 283.

Constitutional Court adopted some strong positions, which might be interpreted as a reaction to some of the most subversive effects apparently stemming from the multilevel integration process.

In 2015, the Italian Constitutional Court stated that only judgments that are an expression of a well-established interpretation of the ECtHR case law and pilot judgments could be considered as having binding effects.[51] Such a stance appears to have the purpose to orient the interpretative discretion of national judges in the judicial implementation of the ECHR, notwithstanding that neither Article 46 ECHR nor the ECtHR case law make any distinction between well-established case law, pilot judgment and any other type of decision in recognising the binding effects of final judgments of the Court.[52] Even if the stance of the Constitutional Court does not reveal any intention to bring into question the role of the ECtHR jurisdiction, the divergence between the view of the Constitutional Court and the ECHR perspective is undeniable.

A partially different way to conceive the role of the national judge as an *ordinary judge of EU law* also characterises the dialogue between the Italian Constitutional Court and the ECJ. On the one hand, the ECJ has traditionally supported the idea that the principle of primacy of the Community/EU law also implies that EU Member States and the Union are fully integrated into a unique legal order.[53] On the other hand, the Italian Constitutional Court has upheld the thesis of the existence of two different legal orders separated from each other, albeit coordinated by Article 11 of the Constitution and the provisions of the European Treaties.[54] However, after the entry into force of the Lisbon Treaty, a harsher line of conflict, concerning the controversial question of the direct effects of the CFREU and, generally, of the Community-EU general principles establishing fundamental rights (Articles 13 TEC, 119 TEC, 2 TUE, 10 TFUE, 18 e 19 TFUE, 157 TFUE, etc.), has emerged between the two Courts.[55] The ECJ's well-established case law[56] has repeatedly supported a "strong" interpretation of the principles of primacy of EU law and direct effect. A national court hearing a dispute between two individuals is obliged, where it is not possible to interpret the applicable law in conformity with EU law, to guarantee the full effectiveness of the CFREU by disapplying if need be any contrary provision of domestic law.[57]

---

[51]C.C., judgment no. 49 of 14.1.2015.

[52]*See, ex multis*, ECHR, GC, *Lekić v. Slovenia*, 11.12.2018, no. 36480/07, § 107-112.

[53]ECJ, C-106/77, *Simmenthal SpA*, 9.3.1978.

[54]C.C., no. 17 of 18.6.1984.

[55]Craig (2009), p. 349.

[56]In respect of Articles 21, 31 and 47 CFREU, see ECJ, GC, C-193/17, *Cresco*, 22.1.2019; GC, C-684/16, *Max-Planck*, 6.11.2018; *GC*, C-68/17, *IR c. JQ*, 11.9.2018; C-322/16, *Global Starnet Ltd*, 20.12.2017; GC, C-441/14, *Rasmussen v. Dansk Industri*, 19.4.2016.

[57]ECJ, GC, C-414/16, *Egenberger*, 17.4.2018.

By contrast, the Italian Constitutional Court, in a debated judgment pronounced in December 2017,[58] assumed a radically contrary stance. Where a provision of national law determines a concurrent infringement of a fundamental right provided by both the Constitution and the CFREU, the ordinary judge is obliged to observe the priority referral of a question of constitutional legitimacy to the Constitutional Court. The Court has affirmed the general interdiction in any case for the judge to disapply a domestic legal norm conflicting with whichever provision of the CFREU.

The Constitutional Court does not challenge the competence of the ECJ to establish the final interpretation of the CFREU Articles, but rather its role as an authority holder of the power to contradict the autonomy of a Member State to determine discretionally the internal procedure of implementation of the Charter within the domestic legal order. Therefore, the real question at stake is not the external division of competence between the ECJ and the Constitutional Court, but rather the internal allocation of functions between the Constitutional Court and ordinary judges. The constitutional judgment no. 20 of the 21th February 2019 reiterated such interpretative leanings, re-affirming the role of the Constitutional Court as the only competent authority to set aside any national legal provision because of its inconsistency with the CFREU, and excluding such a power from being decentralised among the ordinary judges.

The ECJ, with its judgment on *XC, YB, ZA* of the 24th October 2018 (C-234/17, § 44), gave a strong response to the Italian Constitutional Court. The ECJ reiterated once again the well-established principle that the national courts, where called upon to give full effect to EU law, are obliged to refuse if necessary *"of their own motion"* to apply any conflicting provision of national law. Furthermore, the Court expressly affirmed that it is not mandatory for these courts to request or to await the previous setting aside of that provision of national law by legislative or other constitutional means.[59]

In conclusion, the supranational jurisdictions encourage national judges to play a preeminent role within the multi-level dialogue as an *ordinary judge of European law.*[60] The challenge, both cultural and professional, is complex. First, it requires a deep sense of institutional balance. The ordinary judge is, willing or not, in a pivotal position in the dialogue between the national and supranational apical courts. There being not a hierarchical relationship between the ordinary judge, the Constitutional Court, the ECJ and the ECtHR, the last word on the concrete direction to give to the judicial path of the European integration process is up to its institutional sensibility. Second, such a crucial role imposes a great effort to increase the professionalization of the judge, which is an indispensable condition to be an authoritative and aware player within the European integration process.

---

[58]C.C., no. 269 of 14.12.2017.

[59]D. Gallo (2019), Efficacia diretta del diritto UE, procedimento pregiudiziale e Corte Costituzionale: una lettura congiunta delle sentenze n. 269/2017 e 115/2018. *Rivista AIC*, https://www.rivistaaic.it/images/rivista/pdf/1_2019_Gallo.pdf.

[60]R. Conti (2019), Giudice comune e diritti protetti sulla Carta UE. https://www.europeanrights.eu.

References

Bartole, S. (1964). *Autonomia e indipendenza dell'ordine giudiziario*. Padova: Cedam.
Bell, M. (2003). The right to equality and non-discrimination. In T. Hervey & J. Kenner (Eds.), *Economic and social rights under the EU Charter of fundamental rights. A legal perspective* (p. 91). Oxford/Portland: Hart Publishing.
Cartabia, M. (2007). *L'ora dei diritti fondamentali nell'Unione europea, in I diritti in azione. Universalità e pluralismo dei diritti fondamentali nelle Corti europee* (p. 59). Bologna: Il Mulino.
Casper, G. (1980). Guardians of the constitution. *Southern California Law Review, 53*, 773.
Craig, P. (2009). The legal effect of directives: Policy, rules and exceptions. *European Law Review, 34*, 349.
de Charles Montesquieu, H. (1748). *L'Esprit des Lois*. Geneva: Barrillot.
Dworkin, R. (1977). *Taking rights seriously* (p. 184). Cambridge: Harvard University Press.
Efthymiou, N. S., & de Wit, J. C. (2013). The role of Dutch Courts in the protection of fundamental rights. *Utrecht Law Review, 9*, 75.
Friedman, L. M. (1994). *Total justice* (p. 97). New York: Russell Sage.
Gallo, D. (2017). Controlimiti, identità nazionale e i rapporti di forza tra primato ed effetto diretto nella saga Taricco. *Diritto dell'Unione Europea, 2*, 249.
Garapon, A. (1996). *Le gardien des promesses. Justice et démocratie* (p. 31). Paris: Odile Jacob.
Garapon, A., & Allard, J. (2005). *Le juge dans la modialisation*. Paris: Seuil.
Ghera, F. (2003). *Il principio di eguaglianza nella Costituzione italiana e nel diritto comunitario* (p. 95). Padova: Cedam.
Guarnieri, C., & Pederzoli, P. (2007). *La magistratura nelle democrazie contemporanee* (p. 76). Roma-Bari: Laterza.
Halpérin, J. (1989). *Le Tribunal de Cassation et la naissance de la jurisprudence moderne. Une autre justice* (p. 226). Paris: Fayard.
Halpérin, J. (2014). *Five legal revolutions since the 17th century* (p. 51). London: Routledge.
Hartley, T. (1986). Federalism, courts and legal systems: The emerging constitution of the European community. *American Journal of Comparative Law, 34*(2), 229.
Kenner, J. (2003). Economic and social rights in the EU legal order: The mirage of indivisibility. In T. Hervey & J. Kenner (Eds.), *Economic and social rights under the EU charter of fundamental rights* (p. 19). Oxford: Hart Publishing.
Lenaerts, K., & De Smijter, E. (2001). A "Bill of rights" for the European Union. *Common Market Law Review*, 285.
Palmer, V. (1999). From embrace to Banishment: A study of judicial equity in France. *The American Journal of Comparative Law, 47*, 277.
Perrone, F. (2018). La tutela della privacy sul luogo di lavoro: il rinnovato dialogo tra Corte Europea dei Diritti dell'Uomo e giurisdizione nazionale dopo la sentenza Bărbulescu 2. *Labor, 3, 283*
Pollard, D. (2007). *Constitutional and administrative law: Text with material* (p. 15). Oxford: Oxford University Press.
Rawls, J. (1983). *Political liberalism*. New York: Columbia University Press.
Steyn, L. (2006). Democracy, the rule of law and the role of judges. *European Human Rights Law Review, 3*, 243–246.

Protecting the Independence of International Judges: Current Practice and Recommendations

Paulo Pinto de Albuquerque and Hyun-Soo Lim

Contents

All the rights secured to the citizens under the Constitution are worth nothing, and a mere bubble, except guaranteed to them by an independent and virtuous Judiciary.—Andrew Jackson

P. P. de Albuquerque (✉) · H.-S. Lim
European Court of Human Rights, Strasbourg, France
e-mail: Albuquerque@echr.coe.int

© Springer Nature Switzerland AG 2019
P. Pinto de Albuquerque, K. Wojtyczek (eds.), *Judicial Power in a Globalized World*, https://doi.org/10.1007/978-3-030-20744-1_27

1 Introduction

Much scholarship has been devoted to the independence of the judiciary as a concern for potential litigants. Given that "judges are charged with the ultimate decision over life, freedoms, rights, duties and property of citizen",[1] independence and impartiality of the court are indispensable to the rule of law. But an equally important area that has received less attention is how to secure the independence of international judges. Members of international courts share the problems confronting domestic judges like freedom from political influence and backlash, but they also face unique challenges deriving from the distinct nature of the international legal order.

Many factors are considered crucial from the perspective of protecting judicial independence in the international context. Selection, tenure and reappointment of judges are the most obvious elements. However, questions regarding the composition of the court, ability to write dissenting opinions, remuneration, judicial discretion over material and human resources, political mechanisms, exit options, and interstate competition are also important parts of the context in which international judges deliver justice.[2]

In hopes of contributing to the discussion on how best to secure the independence of international judges, this article reviews the rules for selection, status and immunities of judges in five international courts: International Court of Justice, International Criminal Court, European Court of Human Rights, European Court of Justice, and the Inter-American Court of Human Rights. After offering an analysis of the most common issues arising from current practice, this article will then offer suggestions on how to better support international judges to be independent and impartial actors, while protecting them from political retaliation during their tenure and beyond.

2 Overview of the Selection and Status of Judges at International Tribunals

2.1 International Court of Justice ("ICJ")

2.1.1 Selection

There are fifteen judges at the ICJ, all elected to nine-year terms by the United Nations General Assembly and the Security Council. Judges' terms may be renewed once. One-third of the Court is elected every three years to ensure continuity of the bench. Any candidate must receive an absolute majority of the votes in both organs,

---

[1] Basic Principles on the Independence of the Judiciary Adopted by the Seventh United Nations Congress on the Prevention of Crime and the Treatment of Offenders (1985).

[2] Pérez (2015), p. 182.

which vote simultaneously but separately. Some elections can be quite contentious, prompting multiple rounds of voting.[3]

All States Parties have the right to propose candidates. The proposals are made not by the government, but by a national group at the Permanent Court of Arbitration ("PCA") designated by that State (i.e. four jurists who can be called upon to serve as members of an arbitral tribunal).[4] If a country does not participate in the PCA, a group constituted in a parallel way makes the nominations. Each group can propose up to four candidates, no more than two of whom may be of its own nationality, while the others may be from any country around the world. In addition, a State Party to a case which does not have a judge of its nationality on the bench may choose a person to sit as an *ad hoc* judge in that case under specific conditions.[5] Judges *ad hoc* do not have to be, and often are not, nationals of the State that designates them. Judges *ad hoc* are on terms of complete equality with the rest of the bench vis-à-vis the particular case.

Members of the bench must be persons of high moral character, who possess the qualifications required in their respective countries for appointment to the highest judicial offices, or have recognized competence in international law. The Court may not include more than one national of the same State. Moreover, the Court as a whole must represent the main forms of civilization and legal systems of the world.

2.1.2 Safeguards for Independence (Immunity, etc.)

Once elected, an ICJ judge is not a delegate of any country. As such, all judges—including *ad hoc* judges—must exercise their powers impartially and conscientiously.[6] Independence of the judges is also ensured by the fact that they cannot be dismissed unless, in the unanimous opinion of the other members, the judge has ceased to fulfil the required conditions.[7] To date, this has never occurred.[8] Since the power of removal belongs only to the Court, judges are protected from potential retaliation through the form of impeachment or removal.

While engaged in the business of the Court, judges also enjoy diplomatic privileges and immunities.[9] These immunities continue beyond the judges' tenure for any liability concerning the words or actions during their term in office. The

---

[3]See, e.g., *No British judge on world court for first time in its 71-year history*, The Guardian (2017).

[4]For more details on the composition of the PCA national groups or equivalent groups for the purposes of nomination, see Mackenzie et al. (2010), pp. 69–73. See also Mackenzie (2014), pp. 737–756; Seibert-Fohr (2014), pp. 757–778.

[5]Under Article 31, paragraphs 2 and 3 of the Statute of the Court; Articles 35–37, Rules of the Court.

[6]International Court of Justice, Members of the Court.

[7]Statute of the International Court of Justice [hereinafter "ICJ Statute"], art. 18.

[8]International Court of Justice, Members of the Court.

[9]ICJ Statute, art. 19.

Registrar of the Court, with the President's approval, has the right and the duty to waive the immunity if the immunity would impede the course of justice, and can be waived without prejudice to the interests of the Court.[10]

2.2 International Criminal Court ("ICC")

2.2.1 Selection

The ICC has eighteen judges who are elected by the Assembly of States Parties for their "qualifications, impartiality and integrity".[11] No two judges from the same country may be elected.[12] The makeup of the bench must account for "the representation of the principal legal systems of the world, equitable geographical representation and a fair representation of female and male judges."[13] Judges serve nine-year terms that are not renewable.[14]

Any State Party to the Rome Statute can nominate candidates, either by the procedure for the nomination of candidates for appointment to the highest judicial offices in the State in question, or by the procedure for nomination of candidates to the International Court of Justice.[15] Each State Party may put forward one candidate for any given election who need not necessarily be its own national, as long as that candidate is a national of a State Party.[16]

The nomination rules are meant to "insulate nominations from political influence".[17] However, without more detailed guidance, States have essentially been left to establish their own practice. Judges are elected by a secret ballot at the Assembly of States Parties—namely those who obtain the highest number of votes and a two-thirds majority of the States Parties present and voting.

2.2.2 Safeguards for Independence (Immunity, etc.)

Articles 46 and 47 of the Rome Statute outline the removal and disciplinary procedures for judges. A judge is removed from office for committing "serious misconduct or a serious breach of his or her duties under [the] Statute" or being "unable

---

[10]Resolution 90 (I) of the General Assembly of the United Nations (1946), 4(B).

[11]International Criminal Court, Judicial Divisions.

[12]Rome Statute of the International Criminal Court (1998) [hereinafter "Rome Statute"], art. 36(7).

[13]Rome Statute, art. 36(8)(a)(i)-(iii).

[14]Rome Statute, art. 9(a).

[15]Rome Statute, art. 36 (4)(a).

[16]Rome Statute, art. 36 (4)(b).

[17]Mackenzie et al. (2010), p. 65.

to exercise the functions required by th[e] Statute."[18] For misconduct or breach of duty that does not amount to being "serious", disciplinary measures may be imposed.[19] A decision to remove a judge must be made by a two-thirds majority vote in the Assembly of States Parties by secret ballot.[20] Judges facing such proceedings are guaranteed a full opportunity to present and receive evidence and to make submissions.[21]

Similar to other international courts, judges enjoy diplomatic privileges and immunities when engaged in or with respect to the business of the Court. In addition, after the expiry of term in office, their immunity continues "from legal process of every kind in respect of words spoken or written and acts performed by them in their official capacity."[22] However, the privileges and immunities of a judge may be waived by an absolute majority of the judges.[23] In addition, the ICC has an Agreement on the Privileges and Immunities of the International Criminal Court, covering a range of areas from tax exemption to the status of family members of judges.[24]

2.3 European Court of Human Rights ("ECtHR")

2.3.1 Selection

Each Member State nominates three candidates, from the list of whom one judge is elected by the Parliamentary Assembly of the Council of Europe. Like the ICC, ECtHR judges serve a non-renewable term of nine years. The Court does not dictate the process through which national governments pick their list of candidates. However, concern about the quality of nominees has led to changes in the national selection procedure to make it more transparent and inclusive.[25] The result has been an increased judicialisation of the domestic selection processes, such as the inclusion of judges from the highest courts in the advisory selection committees.[26] Nonetheless, it is ultimately up to the national governments to decide the nominees.

---

[18]Rome Statute, art. 46(1).

[19]Rome Statute, art. 47.

[20]Rome Statute, art. 46(2)(a).

[21]Rome Statute, art. 46(4).

[22]Rome Statute, art. 48(2).

[23]Rome Statute, art. 48(5)(a).

[24]Agreement on the Privileges and Immunities of the International Criminal Court (2002).

[25]See Guidelines of the Committee of Ministers of the Council of Europe on the Selection of Candidates for the Post of Judge (2012).

[26]Council of Europe, Steering Committee for Human Rights (CDDH), Selection Of Candidates For Election as Judge to the European Court of Human Rights: Procedure And Selection Criteria In Member States (2017).

2.3.2   Safeguards for Independence (Immunity, etc.)

Judge are accorded the same privileges and immunities extended to those at the Council of Europe. In accordance with Article 51 of the European Convention on Human Rights, judges and ad hoc judges are entitled, during the exercise of their functions, to the privileges and immunities provided for in Article 40 of the Statute of the Council of Europe and in the agreements made thereunder.[27]

In addition, judges, their spouses and minor children have the privileges and immunities, exemptions and facilities accorded to diplomatic envoys under international law.[28] In order to secure freedom of speech and complete independence in the discharge of their duties, post-mandate judges are accorded immunity from legal process in respect of work done at the Court.[29] Spouses and minor children of the judge are also granted diplomatic immunity during the term of office. This jurisdictional immunity includes immunity from criminal proceedings as well as immunity from civil and administrative proceedings, with certain limitations.[30] However, the immunity may be waived by the Court sitting in plenary.[31]

As for removal, no judge can be dismissed from his or her office unless the other judges decide by a majority of two-thirds of the current judges that the person has ceased fulfilling the required conditions. Any judge may trigger the procedure for dismissal of another judge. Before such voting takes place, the judge must first be heard by the plenary Court.[32]

2.4   European Court of Justice ("ECJ" or "CJEU")

2.4.1   Selection

Starting in 2019, the General Court will comprise of two judges from each EU country; the bench of the Court of Justice will have 1 judge from each EU country, plus 11 advocates general.[33] Judges serve six-year terms, and may be reappointed.

---

[27]Sixth Protocol to the General Agreement on Privileges and Immunities of the Council of Europe, 5.III.1996, Preamble.

[28]Sixth Protocol to the General Agreement on Privileges and Immunities of the Council of Europe, 5.III.1996, art. 1.

[29]Sixth Protocol to the General Agreement on Privileges and Immunities of the Council of Europe, 5.III.1996, art. 3.

[30]Vienna Convention on Diplomatic Relations, art. 31.

[31]Sixth Protocol to the General Agreement on Privileges and Immunities of the Council of Europe, 5.III.1996, art. 4.

[32]European Court of Human Rights, Rules of Court (1 Aug. 2018), Rule 7.

[33]European Union, Court of Justice of the European Union: Overview.

National governments choose their own candidate, who is then confirmed by other Member States. Although the other Member States may oppose the candidacy, nominees presented are usually endorsed by the Council of Ministers "without any real discussion."[34] Thus, the candidacy almost entirely depends on the nominating government; there may be a "strong and direct accountability to the home state, but only very limited accountability to other states."[35]

However, there is some effort to introduce quality-check in the process. Article 255 of the Treaty on the Functioning of the European Union (TFEU) has established a panel that produces an opinion on the suitability of candidates. This panel was a response to calls for objective criteria to be applied for assessing nominees, and for an independent body to assist in this process.[36] But the influence of this panel is rather limited, since it is consulted only before the Member States proceed to the appointment phase.

2.4.2 Safeguards for Independence (Immunity, etc.)

Judges and advocates-general are immune from legal proceedings. After they have ceased to hold office, they continue to enjoy immunity in respect of acts performed by them in their official capacity. However, the immunity may be waived by the full Court; in such a case, criminal proceedings against the Judge may be commenced only by the court competent to judge the members of the highest national judiciary.[37] Judges may be removed from office only by a unanimous decision of the Court.[38] In addition, privileges and immunities of the European Union also apply.[39]

2.5 Inter-American Court of Human Rights ("IACtHR")

2.5.1 Selection

The Court consists of seven judges. Six months prior to expiration of the term to which the judges of the IACtHR were elected, the Secretary General of the Organization of American States (OAS) addresses a written request to each State

---

[34]Guillaume (2003), p. 163.

[35]Dunoff and Pollack (2017), pp. 225, 235.

[36]De Waele (2015), pp. 25–26.

[37]Protocol No 3 annexed to the Treaties on the Statute of the Court of Justice of the European Union, art. 3.

[38]Protocol No 3, art. 3.

[39]Protocol No 3, art. 3.

Party for nomination of candidates.[40] Each State Party may nominate up to three candidates, who can be the State's own nationals or of any other member state of the OAS; at least one of the candidates must be a national of a state other than the nominating one.[41] Judges are elected by the States Parties at the OAS General Assembly by secret ballot and by an absolute majority of the States Parties. Judges are elected to six-year terms, and may be reelected a second time.[42]

Thus, the entire process of appointment lies in the discretion of the States Parties. Civil society or other stakeholders have no means of participating in the national selection of the candidates or in the election. The OAS also has no independent institution to supervise the nomination of candidates by States Parties, and the States Parties do not control the process of each other; they have no mechanism to formally object to a candidature who does not meet the requirements.[43] While they nonetheless may raise concerns about the competence of a candidate with the General Assembly, there is no institutional process to make sure that these concerns are properly addressed before a candidate is confirmed.

2.5.2 Safeguards for Independence (Immunity, etc.)

From the moment of election and throughout their term of office, judges at the Inter-American Court enjoy diplomatic immunities and privileges under international law. During the exercise of their functions, they also enjoy the diplomatic privileges necessary for the performance of their duties.[44] The judges of the Court cannot be held liable for any decisions or opinions issued in the exercise of their functions after their tenure ends.[45]

However, judges may be dismissed for holding a concurrent position that is incompatible with the duties of the Court, such as high-ranking officials of the executive branch of government, or international organizations.[46] While there is no formal mechanism for dismissal laid out in the Statute of the Court, the General Assembly of the Organization of American States has disciplinary authority over the judges, which may be exercised only at the request of the Court itself, i.e. the remaining judges.[47]

---

[40]Statute of the Inter-American Court of Human Rights, art. 8(1).

[41]Statute of the Inter-American Court of Human Rights, arts. 7(2) and (3).

[42]Statute of the Inter-American Court of Human Rights, art. 5.

[43]Ruiz-Chiriboga (2012), pp. 111, 118.

[44]Statute of the Inter-American Court of Human Rights, art. 15(1).

[45]Statute of the Inter-American Court of Human Rights, art. 15(2).

[46]Statute of the Inter-American Court of Human Rights, art. 18.

[47]Statute of the Inter-American Court of Human Rights, art. 20.

3 Issues Surrounding the Independence of International Judges[48]

International courts and tribunals "serve a function where the legal and the political are intimately conjoined", such that "the work of international courts can never be entirely divorced from the world of international politics".[49] Such "fragmented"[50] nature of the international legal order gives rise to challenges that are distinct from those to a national system.

The selection and appointment mechanisms of international courts surveyed in Sect. 2—whether global or regional—uniformly emphasize the judge's nationality by imposing geographical or national representation requirements. For instance, the Assembly of States Parties resolutions dictate that the ICC bench must contain at least three judges each from Western European and Other Group, Africa, Latin America and the Caribbean and two from Eastern Europe and Asia.[51] Thus, there is a general, implicit "assum[ption] that the judges who sit on those courts are inherently and irreversibly partial to, and perhaps dependent on, their respective countries of origin."[52] Indeed, this reflects a decades-long scepticism that "international judges, like international arbitrators, would be inclined to determine cases according to the wishes of the government of which they were nationals, or according to what they perceived to be their country's political interests."[53]

Three common issues stand out in the survey of international courts. First, transparency regarding the nomination and election processes; second, the recognition of the judge as an actor with potential bias for one's own country; and third, the interference of or influence by the national government that threatens the judges' independence before, during, and after their tenure.

3.1 Lack of Transparency or Regulation in Nomination and Election Processes

The nomination and election of judges to international courts and tribunals are often "subject to little transparency, and to widely varying . . . nomination mechanisms at

---

[48]Here, we are discussing solely external independence, i.e. the independence of judges and the courts vis-à-vis extrajudicial influence. Judge Pinto has written about both internal and external independence in a separate article. See Albuquerque (2018), pp. 119–133. One of his main suggestions is that of a "cooling-off period" for holders of some state positions as regards applying for judicial posts at the European Court as well as for ECtHR judges as regards applying for certain state positions for a period of five years after their mandate. This period would put an end to any risk of a "revolving door" between the Court and Government-dependent posts.

[49]Terris et al. (2007), pp. xxi, 149.

[50]Mahoney (2008), pp. 313, 317.

[51]Mackenzie et al. (2010), p. 29.

[52]Dannenbaum (2013), p. 77.

[53]Gordon (1989), pp. 508–529. Internal quotations omitted.

the national level".[54] For instance, ICJ judges are nominated by national groups that are intended to be independent from national governments, but transparency is still limited. "Very little is known about the way they operate,"[55] and these groups' suggestions are not always binding on the States, either. This means that even where there is an independent body, States may be able to abuse the gaps in the system to nominate whoever they wish, but with a façade of accountability at the nomination stage.[56]

Poor transparency has a direct consequence on "enhancing the qualities of the judges selected."[57] Without an objective process in place, the chances of improper, external factors determining the 'desirability' of a judge are extremely high. For instance, the lack of scrutiny from the public eye has led to the practice of vote-trading between States.[58] At the ICJ and the ICC, most votes are based on 'reciprocals', or 'mutual support agreements',[59] a mechanism by which a State promises to vote for a candidate in exchange for a vote in the same or another election, or in exchange of other benefits. As the term suggests, these give-and-take agreements are "largely motivated by political considerations rather than merit."[60] Thus, States seek to serve their geopolitical interests across different candidates, or even elections at different international bodies.[61]

Lack of transparency is also an obstacle to achieving greater diversity and representation in the international judiciary. An opaque process hinders the "integration of diverse views and their open and deliberative processing",[62] which in turn decreases the chances of having a diverse judiciary. Diversity of the judiciary—in terms of social representativeness or gender balance—has increasingly been raised as a desirable, yet overlooked, goal.[63]

---

[54]Mackenzie and Sands (2003), p. 278.

[55]Keith (2017), pp. 137, 145 (2019).

[56]One scholar has pointed to an election of an ECtHR judge in 2004 as an example of government maneuvering to seat the candidate of their choice on the Court. The government in the case selected as the two other judges on the candidacy list those with significantly less experience at the top domestic courts so that the candidate of choice would have a huge comparative advantage at the Parliamentary Assembly. While such "rigged selection process at the national level" was eventually detected by the Council of Europe and another candidate was selected, this was a cautionary tale of governments attempting to override a checks-and-balances system. See Kosař (2015), p. 150.

[57]Mackenzie et al. (2010), p. 138.

[58]Mose (2014), p. 191.

[59]Mose (2014), p. 122.

[60]Mose (2014), p. 122.

[61]See The Institute of International Law, The Position of the International Judge (2011), art. 1 (6) Vol. 74 Annuaire (recommending that "elections of judges should not be subjected to prior bargaining which would make the voting in such elections dependent on votes in other elections").

[62]Bogdandy and Krenn (2015), p. 169.

[63]See, e.g., Lord Justice Etherton (2010) ("a judiciary with a diversity of experience . . . is more likely to achieve the most just decision and the best outcome for society").

3.2 Perceived—or Real—National Bias of International Judges

The perceived bias of international judges is different from *personal partiality* (based on the judge's personal interests as they pertain to the parties of the case or the subject of the dispute), or *jurisprudential partiality* (revealing the judge's inclinations that arise from a jurisprudential worldview). Instead, the traditional concern is that the judge, as a nationally-appointed actor, may be tempted or motivated to decide in a manner that favours one's own country or the country's allies.[64]

There is an additional issue of what Richard Falk calls "structural impartiality", or "the reality of a world of sovereign states in which the primacy of these states is critical to the effectiveness of law".[65] In other words, there is a worry that states with "power to implement their views as to what appropriate understanding of law is about can advance an interpretation of bias that is really a reflection of geopolitics and power."[66] At the level of individual judges, this translates to judges from countries with less political muscle power enjoying less authority than those from richer, stronger nations. A telling example of this imbalance is the low number of Eastern European judges elected as section presidents in the European Court of Human Rights and consequently as members of the highly critical "Bureau" of the Court[67] in spite of the fact that they represent more than half of the Council of Europe population.

The idea that different legal systems and the judges coming from them have unequal value also inspires misguided resistance to the international legal order. For instance, some politicians have argued that European Court of Human Rights judges lack political legitimacy to act as a subsidiary legislator, a problem aggravated by the fact that some judges come from "alleged second-class democracies".[68] According to these voices, the undemocratic pedigree of some Contracting Parties tainted in the past, and continues to taint, the judges' independence and the Court's authority.

Thus, this scepticism is related to the broader critique that international law is an "instrument of policy to encompass the policies also of interested ethnic, racial, or

---

[64]See Voeten (2008), pp. 417, 421 (highlighting that "international judges may favour important allies of their national governments").

[65]Falk (1989), pp. 508–529.

[66]Falk (1989), pp. 508–529.

[67]This body has no Convention basis, which has led some Judges to be rightfully vocal about its illegitimacy. See Loucaides (2010), pp. 61, 63–64.

[68]Albuquerque (2018), pp. 119–133. The same concern was expressed in Judge Pinto de Albuquerque's separate opinion in *Hutchinson v. the United Kingdom (GC)*, no. 57592/08, 17 January 2017, § 40, where reference is made to the "biased understanding of the logical obverse of the doctrine of the "diversity of human rights", namely the doctrine of the margin of appreciation".

religious groups, of ideological groupings, and of constituency interests."[69] Such perception of national bias can expand beyond the citizenship of the judge—it can pertain just as well to the so-called Western versus non-Western values, or different blocs of culture.[70] Critique of national bias can be especially salient vis-à-vis judges facing inter-state disputes. For instance, Israel challenged Judge Elaraby's impartiality in the ICJ's decision on the Israeli Wall,[71] which was echoed by Judge Buergenthal in his dissenting opinion.[72] Eric A. Posner and Miguel de Figueiredo have gone further, alleging "strong evidence that [ICJ] judges favour the states that appoint them, and . . . favour states whose wealth level is close to that of the judges' own state".[73]

Of course, this argument potentially conflates *implication* with *bias*. As with domestic judges, it is undeniable that the education and training, cultural background and values of individual international judges will impact their decision-making to varying degrees. Some have suggested that there is no evidence that this prevents international courts from adjudicating fairly.[74] Indeed, if such bias has been systematic and conspicuous, the international legal order would have lost the confidence of stakeholders long ago. This is a problem that is simply inherent in human judiciaries, and does not rise to the level of concern: "[i]f being implicated means bias, then everyone is biased, and perhaps then no one can judge."[75] There is thus a need to distinguish one's identity and perspectives from one's ability to judge impartially.

Nonetheless, there is some basis to suspect that the national bias of judges is not entirely disassociated from decision-making. For instance, Erik Voeten's quantitative study of the voting behaviour of the ECtHR bench revealed that a number of factors lead to judges not being "fully impartial when they evaluate their national governments."[76] A former judge of the European Court of Human Rights also lamented that:

---

[69]Burton (1989), pp. 508–529.

[70]Burton (1989), p. 514.

[71]*Legal Consequences of the Construction of a Wall in the Occupied Palestinian Territory,* Advisory Opinion ICJ Reports 2004, p. 3, at 4, para. 2. The exact complaint of Israel was that Judge Elaraby "had previously played an active, official and public role as an advocate for a cause that is in contention in [that] case".

[72]*Legal Consequences of the Construction of a Wall in the Occupied Palestinian Territory,* Advisory Opinion, p. 9, para 11.

[73]Posner and Figueiredo (2004). See also Kuijer (1997), pp. 49–67.

[74]See Hernández (2012), pp. 183, 185 ("Although factors such as national loyalty, the selection process, the manner in which judges align themselves into voting blocs on the bench and questions of procedural fairness could surely prove important considerations if empirically cognisable, there is no evidence that the Court's judges systematically "vote their preferences" or are instructed by their governments").

[75]Minow (1992), pp. 1201, 1207.

[76]Voeten (2008), p. 425.

[T]he majority of the judges were reluctant to find violations in cases that would present serious problems to a State's financial capabilities, to the general legal or governmental system or to the political objectives of the respondent State.[77]

[...]

During my term of office as a judge I also experienced a consistent general attitude of the Court toward not finding a violation of the right to a fair trial on the ground of unfair national court judgments. The Court was concentrating on the procedural safeguards of a trial and it has established a practice of not interfering with the result of a trial on the ground that such an interference would transform the Court into a court of "fourth instance".[78]

Even if these concerns do not amount to the same level at every international court,[79] such perception can constitute a basis for challenging the broader international legal order. Therefore, it is important to address it institutionally: after all, "justice should not only be done, but should manifestly and undoubtedly be seen to be done."[80] Nomination, selection, and immunity of judges can all have an impact on how those outside the judiciary evaluate the independence of the judge. In order to build confidence of the participants in international tribunals, it is necessary to build a framework that minimizes any risk of national bias among judges.

3.3 Interference or Influence by National Government

Judicial independence means that judges must be able to exercise their functions without direct or indirect interference by an unauthorized actor. In the context of international courts, the independence of judges must be guarded especially from the intervention of states, "since States are parties to disputes and it is usually States who nominate judges to international tribunals".[81] Given that international courts are more frequently involved in holding a government to its nation's laws than domestic courts, the stakes of independence in the former are even higher and more difficult to protect than in the latter.

---

[77]Loucaides (2010), pp. 61, 64.

[78]Loucaides (2010), pp. 61, 68.

[79]For instance, Permanent Court of Arbitration judge Dr. Bossuyt has suggested that the bigger problem is judicial activism against States exercising their political discretion in protecting human rights. See Bossuyt (2014). ("In M.S.S., the Court has also extended the applicability of Article 3 to the living conditions of asylum seekers. In doing so, the Court is transforming the civil right by excellence (the absolute prohibition of torture is an obligation not to do something, an obligation that has to be and can be respected regardless the available resources) into an obligation to provide social benefits to asylum seekers which requires considerable expenditures. At this very moment of a deep financial crisis, according to the Court, Greece should give priority to asylum seekers rather than to its own citizens.")

[80]R v Sussex Justices; Ex parte McCarthy [1924] 1 KB 256, 259.

[81]Shetreet (2003), p. 129.

It must be acknowledged that at the international level, the relationship between judges and their nominating States is more complex and nuanced than at the domestic level. Since actual separation of powers is difficult to achieve at the highly politicized process of international legal order, "appointments to international courts and tribunals cannot be entirely insulated from political processes."[82] Indeed, countries' voluntary participation in the international legal order may be premised on the "belief that having a national on the bench furthers the interests of the state in some way."[83] Some have even suggested that it should be openly accepted that international court judges are not wholly independent, arguing that acknowledging these vested interests would make decision-making in international courts more effective.[84]

As such, governments exert a great deal of influence over the choices of even formally independent international judges in all of the international courts surveyed.[85] A reasonable inference from the effort that goes into having their candidate of choice join the bench at international courts is that appointing States put forward only those candidates who generally share the values of the government. Indeed, looking back at his time at the ECtHR, Judge Loucaides lamented that "[t]here were countries in which the selection was made on the basis of criteria such as the friendly relations of the candidate with influential political personalities or the affiliation of the person proposed with the political party in power. It was therefore obvious that the States concerned did not aim to propose the most qualified candidate."[86]

Moreover, none of the international courts surveyed in Section II grants lifelong tenure to their judges. Therefore, there is an inevitable concern for 'what is next' in the life after the international court, especially for judges of younger age. In most cases, judges seek to return to their home countries—therefore, it is not in the judge's personal interest to be disfavoured by the national government. Of course, this consideration applies with less force to judges who reach the retirement age by the time they leave the international tribunal; however, it would be both unrealistic and undesirable to fill the bench with only judges of senior age.

There is thus a need to reform the current selection process and after-tenure conditions to counter the geopolitical forces that come into play. As seen in Section II, geopolitical influence needs to be combatted with particular vigour when judges are sensitive to the threats of noncompliance, legislative override, or withdrawal of institutional support. In other words, there must be safeguards in place that address the motivation of States to nominate those that they believe will tend to rule in their favour. Such mechanisms should also keep in mind the judge's personal concern for one's career after the expiry of his or her term in office at the international court, so that such external factors do not interfere with fair decision-making.

---

[82]Pocar (2010), p. 603.

[83]Mackenzie et al. (2010), p. 25.

[84]See, e.g., Posner and Yoo (2005), pp. 1–74.

[85]See, e.g., Carrubba et al. (2008), pp. 435–452; Stephan (2002), pp. 333–352.

[86]Loucaides (2010), pp. 61, 62.

4 Suggestions and Recommendations

Since international tribunals are a newer phenomenon than domestic courts, they do not have the luxury of "deeply rooted confidence in society and operating within one legal system with generally shared ethical principles."[87] Consequently, international courts have a *de facto* heavier burden to prove that they deserve the confidence of those under their jurisdiction. In other words, the independence of international judges tends to be more easily attacked than that of domestic judges.[88] To earn and maintain this confidence, it is essential to have "judges who are independent of political or other pressures" to "adjudicate the disputes brought to them with an eye to the guiding legal principles and without any undue influence by external sources."[89] Ensuring the reflection of this principle in reality requires structural safeguards to eliminate external leverage on judges—especially that coming from national governments—and to support their function as guardians of justice. This section makes a few proposals in this regard in hopes of inspiring further discussion on strengthening the independence of the international judiciary.

4.1 Checks and Balances in the Selection of Judges

How international judges are chosen and appointed is one of the most significant determinants of their independence.[90] Needless to say, selection and nomination of judges must be based on objective criteria, with paramount importance placed on the ability to exercise judicial functions. But in reality, as Sects. 2 and 3 have demonstrated, the process is often dominated by governments that attempt to seat candidates in their favour.

One alternative to a selection system controlled by national governments is to establish independent bodies at the national level to help oversee the nominations. Indeed, there is already a trend in favour of "advisory 'screening' procedure prior to the election or appointment of candidates, to review the qualifications and experience of nominees in order to ensure they meet the criteria established in the

---

[87]Mose (2014), p. 189.

[88]For instance, the Hungarian Government advanced an alarming position in *Baka v. Hungary*: "judicial service at an international court cannot be equated with national judicial service from the point of view of the independence, or the perceived independence, of the judiciary." See ECtHR, *Baka v. Hungary* [GC], App. No. 20261/12, 23 June 2016, Joint Concurring Opinion of Judges Pinto de Albuquerque and Dedov, § 21.

[89]Meron (2005), p. 359.

[90]See Malenovský (2011), p. 118 («En effet, [les accords internationaux] prévoient le plus souvent, soit les modalités de l'élection des juges internationaux (au cas où le nombre de candidats est supérieur au nombre de postes à pourvoir), soit celles de leur nomination (au cas où l'élection n'est pas prévue)»).

governing instrument of the court in question."[91] The ICJ and ICC[92] have sought to do this by having national groups or other selection-aiding bodies involved in the nomination process.

However, "[i]f the state has already decided to nominate a particular candidate, [such bodies] may be cut out of the picture and merely act as a rubber stamp for the formal nomination."[93] Similarly, while both the CJEU and the ECtHR have two dedicated advisory bodies to scrutinize the suitability of judicial candidates, the Member States still have wide discretion in assessing the independence and merits of their own candidates. Indeed, the "strong vested interest of governments in strictly controlling the nomination process in order to influence the composition of international courts" can often derail the insulation of elections from political lobbying.[94] After all, it is no secret that domestic and international political considerations heavily affect nominations.

Therefore, international courts should have a system in place to ensure that overriding of the choice of a selection or advisory committee is done only sporadically and with legitimate reason. If the national government wishes to go against the recommendations of the domestic independent panel, there should exist some reasonable basis for their disagreement, promptly communicated. In essence, such committee should really have the decisive say in the nomination of a national candidate.

Having a uniform model of selection across different countries also helps ensure that the level of different nominees will be on par. Presently, the considerable divergence across the different selection mechanisms at the national level accounts in large part for the discrepancy in the relative experience in or knowledge of international law among judges at the same court, as well as their skills and acumen; such disparity within the bench in turn affects the overall quality of the jurisprudence of the courts.[95] Moreover, it also affects judicial independence in that the less competent judges will be less inclined to vote with confidence or go against the wishes of their government.

One desirable alternative for selection of judges is that used by the Caribbean Court of Justice (CCJ). At the CCJ, the Regional Judicial and Legal Services Commission appoints all judges with the exception of the President, who is

---

[91]Mackenzie (2014), p. 752. The existence of such mechanisms is also implicit proof that governments "sometimes nominate candidates who do not fulfill the minimum requirements."

[92]ICC Article 36 (4) provides that the national nomination shall follow the procedure for the nomination of candidates for appointment to the highest judicial offices in the state in question, or the procedure prescribed by the ICJ Statute.

[93]Mackenzie et al. (2010), p. 74.

[94]Ibid. at 65.

[95]See Malenovský (2011), p. 135 («Ces divergences considérables entre les nombreuses procédures de sélection à l'échelle nationale sont regrettables. En effet, l'équivalence de ces différentes procédures n'étant pas assurée, celles-ci ne sont pas, en principe, de nature à produire des candidats équivalents. Les disparités de niveau des candidats sont susceptibles de se répercuter sur la qualité de la juridiction concernée et sur sa fiabilité...»).

appointed by the governments upon the Commission's recommendation.[96] The President also serves as the chairperson of the Commission, facilitating a systematic dialogue between the selection committee and the bench.[97] Other members of the Legal Services Commission "include bar representatives, academics, chairpersons of national judicial and public services commissions, and civil society representatives."[98] Furthermore, if any of the members of the Commission fail to make a nomination, the heads of judiciaries of the Member States can make the nomination jointly.[99] Thus, national judges also have a role in the selection process.

Similarly, judges of the Central American Court of Justice are elected by the supreme courts of justice of the Member States.[100] If the presumption of separation of powers holds and the judges are indeed more independent from political pressure in their home countries, this judiciary-led model could also be a suitable alternative. Another model is the domestic selection process for the ECtHR in Portugal, which involves the High Judicial Council, the Prosecutor General, the President of the Portuguese Bar Association, law professors and one senior ministerial official.[101] The makeup of this selection body, chaired by the President of the Supreme Court, reflects different and competing interests in the society while ensuring legal expertise in assessing the quality of a potential nominee.

4.2 Transparency in the Nomination and Election Processes

As a positive development, there is a "tendency in favour of increased transparency in election processes and insistence on the personal qualifications of judges."[102] However, the current system of selecting international judges remains largely obscure, taking place in "dark corners of political negotiation and deal-making".[103] Lack of transparency gives rise to concerns for independence that can prevent judges from freely exercising their decision-making power. Some judges may even feel indebted by a "sentiment of gratitude" to the governments that nominated them,

---

[96]Malleson (2009), pp. 671, 686. Jiri Malenovský also notes that States are increasingly open to the idea of conferring the competence to designate international judges to an international political authority. See Malenovský (2011), p. 143.

[97]The Agreement Establishing the Caribbean Court of Justice, art. V (1) (a).

[98]Tsereteli and Smekal (2018), pp. 2137, 2151.

[99]The Agreement Establishing the Caribbean Court of Justice, art. V(2).

[100]The Statute of the Central American Court of Justice, art. 10.

[101]See the Minister of Justice's Decree n. 11884/2018, of 28 November, published in the official gazette, II series, n.° 238, of 11 December 2018.

[102]Mose (2014), p. 197.

[103]Pérez (2015), p. 195.

affecting the independence of the judge in a strongly prejudicial way.[104] One way to ward off this danger is to reform the selection process to be more open, transparent and consultative of various stakeholders.

Transparency is particularly important where the rules governing selection of judges are vague and arbitrary, as is the case in many international courts. It counters the risk of governments choosing judges of their own liking, such as former or current government agents[105]; governments are likely aware that judges who served as diplomats or in other government functions tend to defer to stated national interests more than those who were human rights activists before joining the bench.[106] Indeed, a recent statistical study has noted that governments have gradually appointed more restrained judges at the ECtHR, and, as a result, the Court has "become more reluctant to rule against consolidated democracies".[107] These findings seem to be confirmed by another expert report which detected a more frequent use of expressions "margin of appreciation" and "wide(r) margin of appreciation" at the ECtHR after the Brighton conference, leading to these two striking conclusions: firstly, that "the supposedly new approach of weighting more procedural aspects of the national human rights protection creates a bias in favour of Western states that are assumed to provide more solid legal guarantees in this regard"; and secondly, that "an international institution like the ECtHR is receptive to external inputs of non-legal or semi-legal nature."[108]

As the Council of Europe has acknowledged, transparency of public authorities is particularly important in a pluralistic, democratic system.[109] Given that international courts and tribunals are part of this democratic, multilateral order, they should embrace transparency as an important value and a helpful tool for sustainability; more transparency in nomination and election of judges also enhances the legitimacy of the court in the eyes of all stakeholders.[110] A transparent process would pressure governments to convince the public and the voting body of objective grounds of qualification.

---

[104]Malenovský (2011), p. 115 («l'intéressé se considère, en conscience, comme le débiteur de ceux qui l'ont choisi de manière non impartiale et nourrisse ainsi à leur égard un sentiment de gratitude non désintéressée. Ce sentiment de gratitude suspecte s'avère fortement préjudiciableà l'indépendance d'un juge en fonction,...»).

[105]See Malenovský (2011), p. 132 («Il n'est donc pas étonnant que les Etats choisissent assez souvent et précisément, en tant que candidat à la fonction d'un tel juge, leur agent respectif.»).

[106]Voeten (2008), p. 422.

[107]Stiansen and Voeten (2019), pp. 30–31.

[108]Madsen (2017).

[109]Council of Europe, Convention on Access to Official Documents (18 June 2009), CETS 205, Preamble.

[110]See Res. 1726 (2010) on the effective implementation of the European Convention on Human Rights: the Interlaken process, 29 April 2010; CM/Res/(2010)26 on the establishment of an Advisory Panel of Experts on Candidates for Election as Judge to the European Court of Human Rights. The committee has seven members and is presided over by a previous president of the ECtHR.

Indeed, a transparent process of judicial selection would strengthen the independence of judges by bringing to the public eye any connections or conflicts of interest, thereby facilitating the scrutiny and vetting of candidates. As Justice Cullen of Scotland stated, quoting Jeremy Bentham, publicity is the best guarantee of probity.[111] In this way, transparency is interconnected to having healthy checks and balances in the nomination system—it allows more parties to check the quality and any grounds for impartiality of the nominees.

As discussed in Sect. III.A, having a more transparent process also leads to greater diversity, which in turn strengthens the democratic legitimacy of courts: a diverse bench is "essential to shore up public support for and confidence in the judiciary."[112] Of course, diversity as a concept is "plainly not restricted to, or synonymous, with gender, ethnicity or sexual orientation . . . [although] those factors are likely to be an indication of valuable experience which is different to the norm".[113] Different life experiences of judges also inevitably contribute to different perspectives and sensitivities,[114] which are particularly useful in an international court that must face a wide range of issues that crosses borders and cultures.

There is ample guidance at the domestic level for tools to enhance the transparency of judicial selection. Some examples are public recruitment of judges through open advertisements; consultation with civil society or academia; public hearings before parliamentary commissions or other advisory bodies that give an opportunity for public screening of the candidate.[115] In short, "[i]nformation regarding the nomination, election and appointment process and information about candidates for judicial office should be made public, in due time and in an effective manner".[116]

4.3 Removal and Discipline of Judges

It is uncontroversial that "[t]he security of tenure and conditions of service of judges are absolutely necessary elements for the maintenance of judicial independence, according to all international legal standards."[117] Indeed, in the domestic context,

---

[111]Cullen (1999), pp. 261–262.

[112]Rackley (2010), Oct, pp. 655, 656.

[113]Lord Justice Etherton (2010), pp. 745–746.

[114]See Caflisch (2003), p. 169 ("Members of international tribunals are, of course, conditioned, up to a point, by their upbringing, their former activities and their personal circumstances.")

[115]Committee on Legal Affairs and Human Rights, Nomination of Candidates and Election of Judges to the ECtHR. Part B of the Appendix to Assembly Doc. 11767: Overview of Member States' Replies to a Questionnaire, AS/Jur (2008) 52, 2 December 2008.

[116]'The Burgh House Principles on the Independence of the International Judiciary', the Study Group of the International Law Association on the Practice and Procedure of International Courts and Tribunals, in Association with the Project on International Courts and Tribunals, § 2.4 (University College, London).

[117]ECtHR, *Baka v. Hungary* [GC], App. No. 20261/12, Joint Concurring Opinion of Judges Paulo Pinto de Albuquerque and Dedov, 23 June 2016.

irremovability of judges from office by the executive is a "corollary of their independence."[118] As a general rule, international judges should also enjoy absolute protection from removal during their tenure—except for personal misconduct not associated with their role as judges or actual incapacity (because of a serious illness, for instance).[119]

As for disciplinary measures, it is important for each court to have rules of procedure to address misconduct or breaches of duty.[120] There should also be active participation of judges in the relevant disciplinary body. Disciplinary proceedings must also guarantee the possibility of recourse or appeal.[121] It appears that a few international courts have established clear procedures for disciplinary actions that are led by the courts themselves.

4.4 Re-election or Re-nomination of Judges

The practice of re-election in many international courts has implications for both the independence and diversity of the international judiciary. First, the independence of judges can be hindered by fear of putting the second term at risk, especially if the national government controls the process. The concern "that a judge on an international court who is apprehensive about the prospects of renomination by his government or reelection may decide cases so as not to antagonize powerful [] member states, and especially his own state"[122] is justified and reasonable: there is evidence that States sanction judges by precluding them from a second term if the decisions have not been favourable to the government.[123] Indeed, the length of tenure and possibility of re-election combined augments the possibility that judges "who need to secure re-election, particularly toward the end of their term, would allow political pressure to affect their decision-making."[124]

---

[118]Laffranque (2014), p. 132.

[119]See Opinions Nos 1(2001), 2(2001) and 3(2002) of the Consultative Council of European Judges for the attention of the Committee of Ministers of the Council of Europe on standards concerning the independence of the judiciary and the irremovability of judges, on the funding and management of courts with reference to the efficiency of the judiciary and to Article 6 of the European Convention on Human Rights (the ECHR), and on the principles and rules governing judges' professional conduct, in particular ethics, incompatible behaviour and impartiality ("the CCJE Opinions Nos 1, 2 and 3") Documents CCJE (2001) OP N°1, CCJE (2001) OP N°2 and CCJE OP N°3.

[120]See 'The Burgh House Principles on the Independence of the International Judiciary', § 17.1.

[121]See Consultative Council of European Judges (CCJE), Magna Carta on Judges (Fundamental Principles), 6, November 2010.

[122]Meron (2005), pp. 359, 363.

[123]Mackenzie (2014), p. 753.

[124]Pocar (2010), p. 603.

Diversity is another problem that is rarely discussed alongside re-election, but is certainly relevant. In theory, a diverse membership of the court would help ensure that the bench *as a whole* remains independent, because there are many competing forces of influence. But re-election has proven to entrench the status quo of membership as to impede the entry of judges from countries with less experience with the international judiciary. For instance, in the International Court of Justice, "[t]he 106 members of the Court elected since 1946 come from only 50 countries, and the nationals of just 11 of those countries – the P5, Brazil, Germany, Italy, Japan, Nigeria and Poland – have served on the Court for nearly half of the total judge years available."[125]

Therefore, a non-renewable term is recognized as an "efficient and less restrictive tool" for the independence of judges.[126] Indeed, the European Court of Human Rights eliminated a second term through Protocol no. 14, with the explicit intention "to reinforce their independence and impartiality".[127] All international courts should follow the lead of the ECtHR and the ICC, shifting towards "longer, non-renewable terms that will better protect judicial independence."[128]

4.5 Financial and Job Security for Judges During and Post-mandate

During their mandate, judges should not fear for their salaries and working conditions. The financing, management and personnel requirements of the courts should be set in stone, and not subject to changes deriving from political manipulation. For instance, unjustified salary reduction may be understood as punishment for 'unpleasant' jurisprudence. Only very exceptional, publicly demonstrated circumstances should lead to a decrease of the financial package accorded to serving international judges. And any such measure should be previously consulted with the affected judges.[129] This issue evidently deals with the broader problem of administrative and budgetary autonomy of international courts.[130]

The traumatic experience of the Southern African Development Community Tribunal, which was first paralysed and then scaled down by the Member States due to an unpopular judgment, is a haunting tale for international judges and judicial

---

[125]Keith (2017), p. 147.

[126]Malenovský (2010).

[127]Explanatory Report to Protocol no. 14 to the Convention for the Protection of Human Rights and Fundamental Freedoms, amending the control system of the Convention, para 50.

[128]Dunoff and Pollack (2017), pp. 225, 228.

[129]Laffranque (2014), p. 147.

[130]Opinion No. 10 of the CCJE on the Council for the Judiciary at the service of society underlines that judicial independence is increasingly perceived as also applying to the financing, management and personnel requirements of the courts.

staff.[131] There is a constant worry that the Contracting parties may financially asphyxiate or simply close down their respective courts. Indeed, they become "hostages"[132] of their own fear, being paralysed by the ever present critique of judicial activism.

Regarding post-mandate financial security, it is no secret that some former judges have experienced difficulties in finding appropriate functions at the end of their terms of office.[133] Naturally, the international judge who does not reach retirement age by the time of the end of mandate would be thinking about the career afterwards— usually, back home[134]; this may trigger national bias and other political consider- ations that affect one's decisions on the bench.[135] There is thus a need to ensure that the international judge would have financial autonomy after her mandate—either through a sustainable pension scheme or through a comparable post—so that she would not have to choose between casting the right vote and securing a livelihood for herself and the family.

In general, regardless of career prospects after tenure, international judges should be permitted a decent pension that allows them to carry out their functions in what Gilbert Guillaume called "en toute sérénité".[136] While the exact amount that allows such tranquillity would depend on the cost of living and financial circumstances back home, the general idea is that judges' pension post-mandate should not present an opportunity for political retaliation by States. For instance, courts should counter State efforts to impose excessive taxes on the pension of retired international judges. The pension scheme from the ICJ offers an ideal model: upon retirement from the Court, judges receive an annual pension which is equal to half the annual base salary.

The issue of pension does weigh on judges' minds; the provision of adequate pension cover for judges was a "constant demand" from the ECtHR[137] until Reso- lution 5 (2009) was passed, which included the Court's judges in the Council of Europe's new pension scheme.[138] If budgetary concerns restrict the court's ability to

---

[131]Mackenzie (2014), p. 741.

[132]Cohen (2017).

[133]Laffranque (2014), p. 145 [citing N. Vajic, 'Some Remarks Linked to the Independence of International Judges and the Observance of Ethical Rules in the European Court of Human Rights', in C. Hohmann-Dennhardt, P. Masuch & M. Villiger (Eds.) *Grundrechte und Solidaritat. Durchsetzung und Verfahren. Festschrift fur Renate Jaeger*, N.P. Engel Verlag, Kehl, 2011, pp. 179–193, at 186].

[134]See Pocar (2010), p. 605 ("As long as international judges are put in the situation of being forced to ensure that their positions are maintained in their home countries, the intimate connection between an individual and the country of origin could continue to pose a problem").

[135]See Voeten (2008), p. 417 ("There is some evidence that a career insecurities make judges more likely to favor their national government when it is a party to a dispute").

[136]Gilbert Guillaume, *La Situation de juge international*, Institut de droit international: 6 Res Fr Final (9 Sept. 2011, 6th Commission) (discussing remuneration of judges).

[137]Laffranque (2014), p. 146.

[138]Resolution CM/Res(2009)5 on the status and conditions of service of judges of the European Court of Human Rights and of the Commissioner for Human Rights (adopted by the Committee of Ministers on 23 September 2009 at the 1066th meeting of the Ministers' Deputies), as amended by

guarantee a proper pension system, international courts should at least require States to preserve one's domestic post upon election or appointment, so that the judges would have a secure job to which they may return. The period of service at the international court should also be included in the period of employment for pension rights and retirement purposes.

4.6 Extrajudicial Activity

Since a judge's impartiality must exist in fact and by appearance, judges should engage in extrajudicial activity with particular caution. Given their expertise in international law and high renown, many international judges are invited to teach, speak/write, or even serve on bodies of a similar nature where they are asked to share their knowledge and opinion. It is generally desirable for an international judge to contribute to legal and professional education and discussion outside of their judicial function.[139] The Bangalore Principles of Judicial Conduct, adopted by the United Nations, also recognize that "[s]uch professional activities by judges are in the public interest and are to be encouraged."[140]

International judges must, however, be mindful that indiscreet extrajudicial activity may hinder their independence—and thus, their legitimacy and authority. For instance, participation in fancy conferences where the judge is given particularly generous accommodation arrangements, honoraria, or other treats is vulnerable to challenges of favouritism, or even corruption. Where the occasion is organized by States or other potential parties appearing before the tribunal in which the judge serves, there should be additional caution to ensure that the interaction is strictly distinct from the interplay of any special interests. Generally, judges should proceed with care whenever they are in personal contact with potential parties, agents, advocates and advisers[141]—especially repeat players at the court.

In speaking or writing outside the court, judges must be particularly sensitive in the tone and language used so that they do not constitute a ground to suspect

---

Resolution CM/Res(2013)4 amending Resolution CM/Res(2009)5 on the status and conditions of service of judges of the European Court of Human Rights and of the Commissioner for Human Rights (adopted by the Committee of Ministers on 27 March 2013 at the 1166th meeting of the Ministers' Deputies).

[139] However, there must be concrete policy at the level of the court to guide such behaviour. The guidelines for judges' teaching activities, adopted by the ECtHR Bureau on 5 October 2011, are illustrative. According to these guidelines, teaching shall in principle take place during periods of 'light schedule' (when there are no hearings). Otherwise, it is only acceptable outside normal working hours, which means in the evening and weekends.

[140] Judicial Group on Strengthening Judicial Integrity, *The Bangalore Principles of Judicial Conduct*, ECOSOC, UN Doc E/CN.4/2003/65 (2002) [*Bangalore Principles*].

[141] 'The Burgh House Principles on the Independence of the International Judiciary', § 12.1.

apparent bias or prejudice.[142] Many international tribunals are not specialized—their work is not focused on a narrow area of law, such as labour matters or family law. Therefore, international judges could face dockets consisting of any number of issues, and the chances of a judge having written opinionated pieces on a topic that may be pending before the court are high.

Since many international judges have been diplomats, academics, and legal advisors who are accustomed to taking an active part in these occasions, such "adaptation and discipline" may not always be intuitive.[143] The best solution in this regard would be to empower the Court's President to evaluate and eventually reject certain judges' extrajudicial activities. This is indeed the common choice of national courts in Europe.[144] Having the President decide the judge's participation in extrajudicial activities serves to liberate judges from having to make difficult or sensitive decisions without institutional guidance, allowing them to benefit from the discretion of actors with experience. After all, a judge's primary responsibility should not be to "manag[e] public relations."[145] It also helps unify the practice of different judges at a particular court, diminishing room for controversy. On the other hand, too much power in the hands of the Court's President may raise an issue of internal independence. Respecting the principle that every judge may freely perform his or her extra-judicial activities, the list of grounds for refusal of such activities must be strictly established by the Rules of the Court and the President must explain his rejection on the basis of one or more of such grounds.

In deciding to reject judges' requests for outside activity, the following conditions highlighted by Lucius Caflisch, former judge of the ECtHR, are helpful: (1) they may not hamper the court's regular work; (2) they may not be detrimental to the judge's independence; and (3) they should not result in public disclosure of discreet information regarding the court's work.[146] To this, we would add that (4) even where the independence of the individual judge may not be at stake, the activity cannot cast into doubt the legitimacy of the court as a whole. For instance, an ad hoc judge should refrain from accepting touristic trips paid for by the government which he or she is called to represent.

4.7 Immunity

In 2017, Turkey convicted Judge Aydin Sefa Akay of the United Nations Mechanism for International Criminal Tribunals (MICT) to more than seven years in prison

---

[142]See, e.g., Moran (2015), p. 453 (arguing that judicial silence is desirable).

[143]Meron (2005), pp. 359, 360.

[144]See Blisa and Kosar (2018), p. 2031.

[145]Eltis and Mersel (2017), pp. 247, 277.

[146]Caflisch (2003), pp. 169, 172. See also 'The Burgh House Principles on the Independence of the International Judiciary', § 8.1.

over alleged ties to the Gülenist network, the group blamed for the failed coup d'etat attempt one year earlier. Judge Akay's conviction was a direct affront to extensive efforts by the MICT and the international legal community to secure Judge Akay's release; in January 2017, the MICT had ordered Turkey to "cease all legal proceedings against [the Judge] and to take all necessary measures to ensure his release" by a set deadline. When Turkey refused to comply, the MICT referred the matter to the Security Council.[147] Yet, despite these interventions, Judge Akay remains in detention.[148]

All international courts surveyed in Section II grant diplomatic privileges and immunities to their judges, as does the MICT. Indeed, granting of diplomatic immunity is an area where there is very little variation across international courts. Given that judges are involved in highly sensitive matters of international relevance, the immunities of the international judge should be much broader than those of national ones. This enhanced protection of international judges is "not only opportune but necessary."[149] However, as the detention of Judge Akay demonstrates, it is clear that such simple rules on the book are not enough to protect international judges from being implicated in domestic proceedings that are politically motivated.

Although immunity of judges from criminal proceedings on personal conduct unrelated to their function in international courts has not been the norm so far, it is worthwhile to think about mechanisms to ensure the independence of judges by strengthening their immunity. Indeed, there has already been some recognition that the current standard of 'lifelong functional immunity' is not enough—for instance, the Council of Europe's Parliamentary Assembly has called on State Parties to provide judges and their families with diplomatic immunity for life.[150]

While lifelong diplomatic immunity may sound like a radical proposition, it should trigger a serious consideration of all possible means to ensure that former judges are protected from the risk of reprisal or retaliation disguised in legitimate sanctions or proceedings. Judge Akay's case is explicit and easy to notice—but there are more nuanced ways of retaliation that are more difficult to pinpoint and condemn. For instance, a judge may face excessive tax inquiries once returning home, or other similar administrative procedure that can be incredibly stressful and burdensome. Others may be subjected to home searches, phone tapping, or interference with conversations or communications for matters that are on the surface unrelated to their actions on the bench but motivated by them. In sum, there are many ways to harass judges out of retaliation through seemingly lawful judicial proceedings; yet, current privileges and immunities provisions of international courts do little to

---

[147]Escritt and Jones (2017).

[148]See *Imprisoned UN Judge has no Diplomatic Immunity to be Released: Turkish Justice Minister*, DAILY NEWS (1 Feb. 2017), http://www.hurriyetdailynews.com/imprisoned-un-judge-has-no-diplomatic-immunity-to-be-released-turkish-justice-minister.aspx?pageID=238&nID=109239&NewsCatID=509.

[149]Pocar (2010), p. 605.

[150]Resolution 1914 (2013), adopted by the Parliamentary Assembly on 22 January 2013 (7.6.1).

address these nuanced and implicit methods of harassment, especially when they take place after the expiry of the mandate.

One proposal to address this issue would be to set up a procedural safeguard that falls short of lifelong diplomatic immunity, but gives equivalent protection on a case-by-case basis. Under such a scheme, the State would be required to prove to the plenary of the international court that the former judge's activities on the bench have not motivated and are not related to prosecuting or subjecting her to legal process. In other words, the court in which the judge served alone should "be competent to waive the immunity of judges; it should waive immunity in any case where, in its opinion, the immunity would impede the course of justice and can be waived without prejudice to the exercise of the judicial function."[151] The burden of proof on the State to convince the Court that the investigation is unrelated to the judge's time at the Court should be equivalent to the burden of proving the alleged wrong underlying the investigation—for instance, where it is a criminal proceeding, beyond reasonable doubt.

Courts have proven capable of exercising this discretion in a fair manner. For instance, the European Court of Human Rights originally backed a judge who claimed immunity for his wife investigated for corruption.[152] This was a principled response, since carrying out a search in the home of the judge inevitably implicated him as well. However, following a request from Romanian prosecutors, the plenary split the judge's immunity and waived only the part that applies to his wife "to the extent strictly necessary for the conduct of the investigation."[153] In this way, the Court did its best to both conserve the judge's immunity and facilitate the implementation of justice in the home country.

4.8   Other Issues

The freedom to choose with whom and to what extent staff members are involved in preparing cases is another crucial element of the judge's autonomy. It is an important responsibility of the judge to exercise the discretion not to work on cases with certain registry members, especially those seconded by governments. The number and legal competence of lawyers at international courts—who are often tasked with applying and developing case-law in "blurring boundaries" between professional staff and the judiciary—can "either reinforce or undermine judges' potential capture to the staff".[154] In other words, the responsibility lies with the judge to ensure that judicial discretion is not undermined by imprudent or irresponsible conduct of registry members.

This autonomy is particularly consequential in a system where the judge's workload makes it inevitable for registry lawyers to be heavily involved in

---

[151]'The Burgh House Principles on the Independence of the International Judiciary', § 5.2.

[152]Pop (2011a).

[153]Pop (2011b).

[154]Cohen (2017), p. 79.

decision-making. In an insightful reflection of his time at the ECtHR, Judge Loucaides noticed that "[t]he extent of intervention, supervision and work of the judge Rapporteur depended on the personality, diligence and industry of the particular judge. Not all the judges had such qualities. The result was that the view of the member of the Registry frequently prevailed".[155] Ultimately, with or without institutional safeguards in place, "it is up to the judges – and to each judge individually – to act independently in their daily activity."[156] At the end of the day, what matters most is the extent to which the judges themselves value the independence of the lawyers with whom they work on a daily basis.

5 Conclusion

The founding documents of international courts and tribunals consistently require that candidates for the bench be persons of integrity, independence, and impartiality. These "requirements are emphasized and supported by the rules and practices relating to the solemn declarations made by new judges as they take office, their tenure, including immunity from suit, and guarantee of salary, recusal, and removal from office."[157] In other words, having judges with the proper qualifications and decision-making ability is invariably interconnected with making sure that the various aspects of their function are protected from external pressure and political or personal considerations.

In today's increasingly intolerant world that is experiencing a renewed backlash against human rights and shared values, judges at international courts are indispensable guardians of the rule of law and democracy.[158] Protecting their independence by improving the nomination and selection procedures, removal and disciplinary procedures, as well as immunity and security after tenure are essential to promoting justice and upholding the international legal order.

References

Albuquerque, P. P. D. (2018). Plaidoyer for the European Court of Human Rights. *European Human Rights Law Review, 2*, 119–133.

Basic Principles on the Independence of the Judiciary Adopted by the Seventh United Nations Congress on the Prevention of Crime and the Treatment of Offenders, endorsed by General Assembly resolutions 40/32 of 29 November 1985 and 40/146 of 13 December 1985.

---

[155]Loucaides (2010), pp. 61, 62.

[156]Pocar (2010), p. 598.

[157]Keith (2017), p. 141.

[158]See generally Stiansen and Voeten (2019) (noting "increasing backlash from consolidated democracies" to international courts and how it affects the behavior of the courts).

Blisa, A., & Kosar, D. (2018). Judicial self-government in Europe. *German Law Journal, 19*, 2031.

Bogdandy, A. V., & Krenn, C. (2015). On the democratic legitimacy of Europe's judges. In M. Bobek (Ed.), *Selecting Europe's judges: A critical review of the appointment procedures to the European courts* (p. 169). Oxford: OUP.

Bossuyt, B. M. (2014). Judicial activism in Europe: The case of the European Court of Human Rights. *Open Europe website. September*, 7.

Bowcott, O. (2017, November 20). No British judge on world court for first time in its 71-year history. *The Guardian*. Retrieved April 10, 2019, from https://www.theguardian.com/law/2017/nov/20/no-british-judge-on-world-court-for-first-time-in-its-71-year-history

Burton, S. J. (1989, April 5–8). Remarks in the independence and impartiality of international judges. In *Proceedings of the Annual Meeting (American Society of International Law)* (Vol. 83, pp. 508–529).

Caflisch, L. (2003). Independence and impartiality of judges: The European Court of Human Rights. *Law and Practice of International Courts and Tribunals, 2*, 169, 172.

Carrubba, C. J., Gabel, M., & Hankla, C. (2008). Judicial behavior under political constraints: Evidence from the European Court of Justice. *American Political Science Review, 102*(4), 435–452.

Central American Court of Justice. The Statute of the Central American Court of Justice.

Cohen, M. (2017). Judges or hostages? Sitting at the Court of Justice of the European Union and the European Court of Human Rights. *The Academy of European Law*. Retrieved April 12, 2019, from https://iow.eui.eu/wp-content/uploads/sites/28/2017/04/EU-Vauchez-01-Cohen.pdf

Committee on Legal Affairs and Human Rights, Nomination of Candidates and Election of Judges to the ECtHR. Part B of the Appendix to Assembly Doc. 11767: Overview of Member States' Replies to a Questionnaire, AS/Jur (2008) 52, 2 December 2008.

Consultative Council of European Judges (CCJE). Magna Carta on Judges (Fundamental Principles), 6, November 2010.

Consultative Council of European Judges (CCJE). Opinions Nos 1(2001), 2(2001) and 3(2002) of the Consultative Council of European Judges for the attention of the Committee of Ministers of the Council of Europe.

Council of Europe, Convention on Access to Official Documents (18 June 2009), CETS 205.

Council of Europe. Guidelines of the Committee of Ministers of the Council of Europe on the Selection of Candidates for the Post of Judge, CM(2012)40-final, 29 March 2012.

Council of Europe. Steering Committee for Human Rights (CDDH), Selection Of Candidates For Election as Judge to the European Court of Human Rights: Procedure And Selection Criteria In Member States (2017).

Cullen, L. (1999). The judge and the public. *Scots L. Times (News)* (pp. 261–262).

Dannenbaum, T. (2013). Nationality and the international judge: The nationalist presumption governing the international judiciary and why it must be reversed. *Cornell International Law Journal, 45*, 77.

De Waele, H. (2015). Not quite the bed that procrustes built: Dissecting the system for selecting judges at the Court of Justice of the European Union. In M. Bobek (Ed.), *Selecting Europes judges: A critical review of the appointment procedures to the European Courts* (pp. 25–26). Oxford: OUP.

Dunoff, J. L., & Pollack, M. A. (2017). The judicial trilemma. *American Journal of International Law, 111*(2), 225, 228, 235.

ECtHR, *Baka v. Hungary* [GC], App. No. 20261/12, 23 June 2016, Joint Concurring Opinion of Judges Pinto de Albuquerque and Dedov, § 21.

ECtHR, *Hutchinson v. the United Kingdom* [GC], App. No. 57592/08, 17 January 2017, Separate Opinion of Judge Pinto de Albuquerque, § 40.

Election as Judge to the European Court of Human Rights: Procedure And Selection Criteria In Member States (2017). Retrieved April 11, 2019, from https://rm.coe.int/selection-of-candidates-for-election-as-judge-to-the-courtprocedure-a/168075ad58

Eltis, K., & Mersel, Y. (2017). Revisiting the limits on judicial expression in the digital age: Striving towards proportionally in the cyberintimidation context. *National Journal of Constitutional Law, 38*, 247, 277.

Escritt, T., & Jones, G. (2017, March 6). Turkey referred to U.N. Security Council over detained judge. *Reuters*. Retrieved April 12, 2019, from https://www.reuters.com/article/us-turkey-coup-un-judge-idUSKBN16D1MR

Etherton, T. (2010). Liberty, the archetype and diversity: A philosophy of judging. *Public Law, 727, 728*, 745–746.

European Court of Human Rights. Rules of Court (1 Aug. 2018).

European Union. Court of Justice of the European Union: Overview. Retrieved April 11, 2019, from https://europa.eu/european-union/about-eu/institutions-bodies/court-justice_en

European Union. Court of Justice of the European Union. Protocol No 3 annexed to the Treaties on the Statute of the Court of Justice of the European Union.

Explanatory Report to Protocol no. 14 to the Convention for the Protection of Human Rights and Fundamental Freedoms, amending the control system of the Convention, para 50.

Falk, R. (1989, April 5–8). Remarks in the independence and impartiality of international judges. In *Proceedings of the Annual Meeting (American Society of International Law)* (Vol. 83, pp. 508–529).

Gordon, E. (1989, April 5–8). Remarks in the independence and impartiality of international judges. In *Proceedings of the Annual Meeting (American Society of International Law)* (Vol. 83, pp. 508–529).

Guillaume, G. (2003). Some thoughts on the independence of international judges vis-à-vis states. *Law and Practice of International Courts and Tribunals, 2*, 163.

Guillaume, G. La Situation de juge international. Institut de droit international: 6 Res Fr Final (9 Sept. 2011, 6th Commission) (discussing remuneration of judges).

Hernández, G. I. (2012). Impartiality and bias at the International Court of Justice. *Cambridge Journal of International and Comparative Law, 1*(3), 183, 185.

Imprisoned UN Judge has no Diplomatic Immunity to be Released: Turkish Justice Minister. *Daily News* (2017 Feb. 1). Retrieved April 12, 2019, from http://www.hurriyetdailynews.com/imprisoned-un-judge-has-no-diplomatic-immunity-to-be-released-turkish-justice-minister.aspx?pageID=238&nID=109239&NewsCatID=509

Inter-American Court of Human Rights. Statute of the Inter-American Court of Human Rights.

International Court of Justice. Members of the Court. Retrieved April 11, 2019, from https://www.icj-cij.org/en/members

International Court of Justice. Rules of Court.

International Court of Justice. Statute of the International Court of Justice.

International Criminal Court. Agreement on the Privileges and Immunities of the International Criminal Court, adopted by the Assembly of States Parties, ICC-ASP/1/3 (2002).

International Criminal Court. Judicial Divisions. Retrieved April 11, 2019, from https://www.icc-cpi.int/about/judicial-divisions

International Criminal Court. Rome Statute of the International Criminal Court 1998.

Judicial Group on Strengthening Judicial Integrity, *The Bangalore Principles of Judicial Conduct*, ECOSOC, UN Doc E/CN.4/2003/65 (2002) [*Bangalore Principles*].

Keith, K. J. (2017). Challenges to the independence of the international judiciary: Reflections on the International Court of Justice. *Leiden Journal of International Law, 30*(1), 137, 141, 145, 147 (2019).

Kosař, D. (2015). Selecting Strasbourg judges: A critique. In M. Bobek (Ed.), *Selecting Europe's judges: A critical review of the appointment procedures to the European courts* (p. 150). Oxford: OUP.

Kuijer, M. (1997). Voting behaviour and national bias in the European Court of Human Rights and the International Court of Justice. *LJIL, 10*, 49–67.

Laffranque, J. (2014). Judicial independence in Europe: Principles and reality. In N. A. Engstad (Ed.), *The independence of judges* (pp. 132, 145, 146, 147).

Legal consequences of the construction of a wall in the Occupied Palestinian Territory, Advisory Opinion ICJ Reports 2004, Order of 30 April 2004 on the Composition of the Court ICJ Reports 2004, p. 3, at 4, para. 2.

Loucaides, L. G. (2010). Reflections of a former European Court of Human Rights judge on his experiences as a judge. *Roma Rights Quarterly*, (1), 61, 62, 63–64, 68.

Mackenzie, R. (2014). The selection of international judges. In C. Romano et al. (Eds.), *The Oxford handbook of international adjudication* (pp. 737–756). Oxford: OUP.

Mackenzie, R., Malleson, K., & Martin, P. (2010). *Selecting international judges: Principle, process, and politics* (pp. 25, 29, 65, 69–73, 74, 138). Oxford: OUP.

Mackenzie, R., & Sands, P. (2003). International courts and tribunals and the independence of the international judge. *Harvard International Law Journal, 44*, 278.

Madsen, M. R. (2017). Rebalancing European human rights: Has the Brighton Declaration engendered a new deal on human rights in Europe?. *iCourts Working Paper Series*, No. 100, 32 (2017).

Mahoney, P. (2008). The international judiciary-independence and accountability. *Law and Practice of International Courts and Tribunals, 7*, 313, 317.

Malenovský, J. (2010). Les opinions séparées et leurs répercussions sur l'indépendance du juge international. *ACDI-Anuario Colombiano de Derecho Internacional*, Bogotá, ISSN: 2027-1131 Vol. 3, 66.

Malenovský, J. (2011). L'indépendance des juges internationaux. In *Recueil Des Cours: Collected Courses of The Hague Academy of International Law, Tome 349 de la collection* (pp. 115, 118, 132, 135, 143). Leiden: Martinus Nijhoff.

Malleson, K. (2009). Promoting judicial independence in the international courts: Lessons from the Caribbean. *International & Comparative Law Quarterly, 58*(3), 671, 687.

Meron, T. (2005). Judicial independence and impartiality in international criminal tribunals. *American Journal of International Law, 99*(2), 359, 360, 363.

Minow, M. (1992). Stripped down like a runner or enriched by experience: Bias and impartiality of judges and jurors. *William & Mary Law Review, 33*, 1201, 1207.

Moran, J. (2015). Courting controversy: The problems caused by extrajudicial speech and writing. *Victoria University of Wellington Law Review, 46*, 453.

Mose, E. (2014). The independence of international judges. In N. A. Engstad, et al. (Eds.), *The independence of judges* (pp. 189, 191, 197).

Pérez, A. T. (2015). Can judicial selection secure judicial independence? Constraining state governments in selecting international judges. In M. Bobek (Ed.), *Selecting Europe's judges: A critical review of the appointment procedures to the European courts* (pp. 182, 195). Oxford: OUP.

Pocar, F. (2010). Reflections on the independence and impartiality of international judges. In C. Eboe-Osuji (Ed.), *Protecting humanity: Essays in international law and policy in honour of Navanethem Pillay* (pp. 598, 603, 605). Leiden: Brill Nijhoff.

Pop, V. (2011a, October 20). Strasbourg backs Romanian judge in jewellery-for-verdicts case. *EU Observer*. Retrieved April 12, 2019, from https://euobserver.com/justice/114006

Pop, V. (2011b, December 1). Strasbourg court waives immunity in Romanian corruption case. *EU Observer*. Retrieved April 12, 2019, from https://euobserver.com/justice/114451

Posner, E. A., & Figueiredo, M. F. (2004). Is the International Court of Justice biased?. *John M. Olin Program in Law and Economics Working Paper* No. 234: 1.

Posner, E. A., & Yoo, J. C. (2005). Judicial independence in international tribunals. *California Law Review, 93*(1), 1–74.

R v Sussex Justices; Ex parte McCarthy [1924] 1 KB 256, 259.

Rackley, E. (2010). In conversation with Lord Justice Etherton: Revisiting the case for a more diverse judiciary. *Public Law*, 655–656.

Resolution 1726 (2010) on the effective implementation of the European Convention on Human Rights: the Interlaken process, 29 April 2010.

Resolution 1914 (2013), adopted by the Parliamentary Assembly on 22 January 2013 (7.6.1).

Resolution 26 (2010) on the establishment of an Advisory Panel of Experts on Candidates for Election as Judge to the European Court of Human Rights.

Resolution 5 (2009) on the status and conditions of service of judges of the European Court of Human Rights and of the Commissioner for Human Rights (adopted by the Committee of Ministers on 23 September 2009 at the 1066th meeting of the Ministers' Deputies), as amended by Resolution CM/Res(2013)4 amending Resolution CM/Res(2009)5 on the status and conditions of service of judges of the European Court of Human Rights and of the Commissioner for Human Rights (adopted by the Committee of Ministers on 27 March 2013 at the 1166th meeting of the Ministers' Deputies).

Resolution 90 (I) of the General Assembly of the United Nations, 11 Dec. 1946 (Privileges and Immunities of Members of the International Court of Justice, the Registry, Assessors, and Agents and Counsel of the Parties and of Witnesses and Experts).

Ruiz-Chiriboga, O. (2012). The independence of the Inter-American judge. *The Law & Practice of International Courts and Tribunals, 11*(1), 111, 118.

Seibert-Fohr, A. (2014). International judicial ethics. In C. Romano et al. (Eds.), *The Oxford handbook of international adjudication* (pp. 737–778). Oxford: OUP.

Shetreet, S. (2003). Standards of conduct of international judges: Outside activities. *Law and Practice of International Courts and Tribunals, 2*, 129.

Sixth Protocol to the General Agreement on Privileges and Immunities of the Council of Europe, 5. III.1996.

Stephan, P. B. (2002). Courts, tribunals, and legal unification-The agency problem. *Chicago Journal of International Law, 3*, 333–352.

Stiansen, Ø., & Voeten, E. (2019). *Backlash and judicial restraint: Evidence from the European Court of Human Rights* (pp. 30–31).

Terris, D., Romano, C. P. R., & Swigart, L. (2007). *The international judge: An introduction to the men and women who decide the world's cases* (pp. xxi, 149). New Hampshire: Brandeis University Press.

The Burgh House Principles on the Independence of the International Judiciary, the Study Group of the International Law Association on the Practice and Procedure of International Courts and Tribunals, in Association with the Project on International Courts and Tribunals, § 2.4, § 5.2, § 8.1, § 12.1, § 17.1 (University College, London).

The Caribbean Court of Justice. Agreement Establishing the Caribbean Court of Justice.

The Institute of International Law, The Position of the International Judge (2011), art. 1(6) Vol. 74 Annuaire.

The Minister of Justice's Decree n. 11884/2018, of 28 November, published in the official gazette, II series, n.° 238, of 11 December 2018.

Tsereteli, N., & Smekal, H. (2018). The judicial self-government at the international level—A new research agenda. *German Law Journal, 19*(7), 2137–2151.

Vienna Convention on Diplomatic Relations.

Voeten, E. (2008). The impartiality of international judges: Evidence from the European Court of Human Rights. *American Political Science Review, 102*(4), 417, 421, 422, 425.

The General Court of the European Union: Characteristic, Competences and Reform

Nina Półtorak

Contents

1 Introduction

The General Court of the European Union celebrates its 30th anniversary in 2019. During 30 years, it gained a significant impact on the functioning of the European Union institutions as well as enterprises and EU citizens. The General Court is essentially an administrative court that settles disputes between private parties and EU institutions, but this function does not exhaust its role, as the General Court deals also with some disputes between Member States and EU institutions. The case-law of the General Court has contributed significantly to the development of such

Nina Półtorak is Professor of the EU Law at the Jagiellonian University in Krakow and Judge at the General Court of the EU. All the views and opinions expressed in this article are personal views of the author.

N. Półtorak (✉)
Jagiellonian University, Krakow, Poland
e-mail: nina.poltorak@uj.edu.pl

© Springer Nature Switzerland AG 2019
P. Pinto de Albuquerque, K. Wojtyczek (eds.), *Judicial Power in a Globalized World*, https://doi.org/10.1007/978-3-030-20744-1_28

domains of the EU law as competition and state aid law, EU intellectual property law, rules on EU liability for damages, rules governing the imposition of restrictive measures by the EU or issues regarding access to documents. The General Court has also played a special role in the development of the interpretation and application of the EU principle and right to good administration as well as the right to court being the problems which can appear in all areas in which the General Court has jurisdiction.

For years, the expanding jurisdictional competences of the General Court and the increasing number of cases resulted in delays in the proceedings before it. This gave rise to the need for changes in the organization and functioning of the General Court, which were already planned in 2011, but which were translated into legal changes only at the end of 2015.

This articles first presents the genesis of the General Court and describes its competences changing over the years; next it describes the current reform of the General Court and its outcomes up to date; and then it analyses the jurisdictional competences of the General Court in view of the requirements provided for in the Charter of Fundamental Rights of the European Union.

2   Genesis and History of the General Court

The General Court was created by the Council Decision of 1988, adopted at the request of the Court of Justice.[1] Its recitals mention that the establishment of the General Court (then called the Court of First Instance) will improve the judicial protection of individual interests in respect of actions requiring close examination of complex facts, while enabling the Court of Justice to concentrate its activities on its fundamental task of ensuring uniform interpretation of Community law (at present: EU law). The Court of First Instance, as it name indicated, was to act as a jurisdiction of first instance, which decisions could have been appealed to the Court of Justice. The Court of First Instance started its judicial activity in 1989.

Adopting of the decision on establishing of the Court of First Instance was possible on the basis of the changes introduced to the founding treaties by the Single European Act signed in 1986, which, inter alia, provided for a new Article 168a of the Treaty on the European Economic Community (EEC), stipulating that, at the request of the Court of Justice, after consulting the Commission and the European Parliament, the Council, acting unanimously, attach to the Court of Justice a court with a jurisdiction to hear and determine at first instance certain classes of actions or proceedings brought by natural or legal persons. According to the same provision, that court should not to be competent to decide on complaints lodged by Member

---

[1]Council Decision of 24 October 1988 establishing a Court of First Instance of the European Communities (88/591/ECSC, EEC, Euratom), OJ L 319, 25.11.1988, pp. 1–8.

States or Community institutions and national courts' questions for a preliminary ruling.

The 1988 decision on the establishment of the Court of First Instance confered on it the competences to hear disputes between the Communities and their servants; in the scope of the Treaty on the European Coal and Steel Community (ECSC)—actions brought by undertakings or by associations of undertakings which concerned individual acts relating to the application of given provisions of the ECSC Treaty (e.g. dealing with levies, production, prices, restrictive agreements); and—regarding the EEC Treaty—actions brought against an institution of the Communities by natural or legal persons relating to the implementation of the competition rules applicable to undertakings. In principle, therefore, the jurisdictional competences of the Court of First Instance included the complaints of natural and legal persons against the institutions of the Communities in certain classes of actions regarding an examination of complex facts.

Soon, by the Council decision of 1993, the jurisdiction of the Court of First Instance was extended to adjudicate in the first instance subsequent types of cases brought by natural or legal persons.[2] The extension of jurisdiction of the Court of First Instance led to an increase in its judicial workload, which was reflected in the decision of 1999 that allowed it to settle cases by a single judge.[3]

The role of the Court of First Instance was enforced by the Treaty of Nice, which entered into force in 2003. Since then, the Court of First Instance together with the Court of Justice was meant to ensure that in the interpretation and application of the Treaty the law is observed.[4] The Treaty of Nice also introduced further significant changes in the architecture of the EU judicature.[5] Firstly, it provided for the creation of additional judicial panels attached to the Court of First Instance, in order to exercise, in certain specific areas, the judicial competence set out in the EC Treaty. Decisions given by judicial panels were meant to be subject to a right of appeal before the Court of First Instance. These amendments gave rise to the creation, by a decision of 2004, of the Civil Service Tribunal, which was competent to deal with disputes between the EU and its servants.[6] The Civil Service Tribunal began its judicial activity in 2005.

---

[2]Council Decision 93/350/ECSC, EEC, Euratom of 8 June 1993 amending Council Decision 88/591/ECSC, EEC, Euratom establishing a Court of First Instance of the European Communities, OJ L 144, 16.6.1993, pp. 21–22.

[3]Council Decision 1999/291/EC, ECSC, Euratom of 26 April 1999 amending Decision 88/591/ECSC, EEC, Euratom establishing a Court of First Instance of the European Communities to enable it to give decisions in cases when constituted by a single judge, OJ L 114, 01.05.1999, pp. 52–53.

[4]Article 220 of the EC Treaty in the version from 2003 provided for in par. 1: "The Court of Justice and the Court of First Instance, each within its jurisdiction, shall ensure that in the interpretation and application of this Treaty the law is observed."

[5]See more Rodríguez Iglesias (2013), p. 39 et seq.; Granger and Guinchard (2017), p. 10 et seq.

[6]Council Decision of 2 November 2004 establishing the European Union Civil Service Tribunal (2004/752/EC, Euratom), OJ L 333, 9.11.2004, pp. 7–11.

Secondly, the Treaty of Nice gave the Court of First Instance the jurisdiction to adjudicate on the questions referred for a preliminary rulings in matters specified in the Statute.[7] The determination of the distribution of competences between the Court of Justice and the Court of First Instance was done in the Council decision of 2004 amending the Statute of the Court of Justice.[8] However, the changes of the Statute did not provide for the allocation to the Court of First Instance of competence in the scope of the preliminary rulings, and thus the competence conferred by the Treaty of Nice was not implemented in practice.

Thirdly, the new Article 224 of the EC Treaty stipulated that the Court of First Instance consisted of at least one judge from each Member State, and that the number of judges was determined in the Statute of the Court of Justice.

The next amending treaty—the Treaty of Lisbon, which entered into force in 2009, did not bring such significant changes in the organisation of the European judiciary, but it made it more structured. First of all, the name of the Court of First Instance changed to General Court (French: *le Tribunal*, German: *das Gericht*). Second, the Treaty of Lisbon introduced Article 19(1) to the EU Treaty which states that the Court of Justice of the European Union which shall ensure that in the interpretation and application of the Treaties the law is observed shall include the Court of Justice, the General Court and specialised courts. Third, the amended Article 256(1) of the Treaty on the Functioning of the European Union (TFEU) defines the scope of jurisdiction of the General Court, indicating that it shall have jurisdiction to hear and determine at first instance actions or proceedings referred to in Article 263 (review of the legality of acts of EU institutions), Article 265 (complaint about failure to act of EU institutions), Article 268 (action for damages), Article 270 (disputes between the EU and its servants) and Article 272 (arbitration clause), with the exception of those assigned to a specialised court set up under Article 257 and those reserved in the Statute for the Court of Justice. What is important, it maintains the rule that the Statute may provide for the General Court to have jurisdiction for other classes of action or proceeding. Article 256(3) TFEU also confirmed the jurisdiction of the General Court in the scope of the questions referred for a preliminary ruling in areas specified in the Statute.

However, the Statue, as amendment by the Lisbon Treaty, still does not provide for the concrete competences of the General Court in scope of the preliminary rulings procedure. In addition, Article 51 of the Statute provides for the derogations from Article 256(1) TFEU in a way that excludes the jurisdiction of the General Court in the scope of the actions for annulment and actions against failure to act instituted by the Member States against European Parliament or the Council or the Commission when it acts under Article 331 TFEU (enhanced cooperation

---

[7]Article 225(3) of the EC Treaty in the version from 2003.

[8]Council Decision of 26 April 2004 amending Articles 51 and 54 of the Protocol on the Statute of the Court of Justice (2004/407/EC, Euratom), OJ L 132, 29.4.2004, p. 5.

procedure).[9] The same provision of the Statute excludes also the jurisdiction of the General Court in the disputes between the institutions of the EU.[10]

Furthermore, the Treaty of Lisbon established a new and important institution, namely a panel whose task is to give opinions on candidates' suitability to perform the duties of judge and advocate general of the Court of Justice and the General Court before being appointed by the governments of the Member States (Article 255 TFEU). This panel began its work after entry into force of the Council's decision setting out the rules of functioning of the panel and appointing its members.[11] The panel consists of seven persons chosen from former members of the Court of Justice and the General Court, members of the national supreme courts and lawyers of recognized competence, one of which is proposed by the European Parliament. When adopting a decision laying down rules for the functioning of the panel and a decision appointing its members, the Council acts on the initiative of the President of the Court of Justice. The panel hears the candidates, except where a proposal is to renew the mandate of the judge or advocate general. The opinion on the candidates contains a statement of reasons indicating the principal grounds of the panel's opinion. This opinion is forwarded to representatives of the governments of the Member States.

3   The Reform of the General Court[12]

The above-mentioned amendments of the Treaties led to a significant extension of jurisdiction of the General Court, which after the Treaty of Lisbon included:[13]

- complaints lodged by natural or legal persons against the acts of the EU institutions,
- complaints lodged by natural or legal persons against a failure to act by the EU institutions,

---

[9]Protocol (No 3) (to the Treaties) on the Statute of the Court of Justice of the European Union, OJ C 115, 9.5.2008, pp. 210–229 with amendments. In accordance with Article 281 TFEU, the Statute may be amended by the European Parliament and the Council acting in accordance with the ordinary legislative procedure acting either at the request of the Court of Justice and after consultation of the Commission or on a proposal from the Commission and after consultation of the Court of Justice.

[10]In this respect, there are doubts concerning the acts of the European Council and Committee of the Region—see more Lenaerts et al. (2014), p. 42.

[11]Council Decision 2010/124 of 25 February 2010 relating to the operating rules of the panel provided for in Article 255 of the Treaty on the Functioning of the European Union, OJ L 50, 27.2.2010, pp. 18–19.

[12]The part of this article concerning the history and the reform of the General Court is based on the author's draft article titled "Reform des Gerichts der Europäischen Union" to be published in the book *Reformprozesse der Europäischen Gerichtsbarkeit*, B. Łukańko & A. Thiele (Ed.).

[13]See Article 256 TFEU and Article 51 of the Statute of the Court of Justice of the EU.

- complaints lodged by Member States against the EU institutions except for acts or failure to act of the European Parliament and/or the Council (with exceptions listed below) and acts or failure to act by the European Commission under Article 331(1) of the TFEU,[14]
- complaints lodged by Member States against the Council regarding state aid (Article 108 (2) TFEU), measures to protect trade (Article 207 TFEU) and acts by which the Council exercises implementing powers (Article 291(2) TFEU),
- complaints for compensation of damage caused by EU institutions, bodies or agencies or their employees,
- complaints about contracts concluded by the EU pursuant to any arbitration clause,
- claims against the decisions of European Union Intellectual Property Office concerning trademarks and designs,[15]
- claims against the decisions of Community Plant Variety Office,[16]
- claims against decisions of European Chemicals Agency,[17]
- claims against the decisions of European Union Aviation Safety Agency,[18]
- claims against the decisions European Supervisory Authority (European Banking Authority),[19]

---

[14]There are some doubts about such competence in relation to the acts of the European Council—see more Lenaerts et al. (2014), p. 42.

[15]Council Regulation (EC) No 6/2002 of 12 December 2001 on Community designs, OJ L 3, 5.1.2002, pp. 1–24; Regulation (EU) 2017/1001 of the European Parliament and of the Council of 14 June 2017 on the European Union trade mark, OJ L 154, 16.6.2017, pp. 1–99.

[16]Council Regulation (EC) No 2100/94 of 27 July 1994 on Community plant variety rights, OJ L 227, 01.09.94, p. 1.

[17]Regulation (EC) No 1907/2006 of the European Parliament and the Council of 18 December 2006 concerning the Registration, Evaluation, Authorisation and Restriction of Chemicals (REACH), establishing a European Chemicals Agency, amending Directive 1999/45/EC and repealing Council Regulation (EEC) No 793/93 and Commission Regulation (EC) No 1488/94 as well as Council Directive 76/769/EEC and Commission Directives 91/155/EEC, 93/67/EEC, 93/105/EC and 2000/21/EC, OJ L 396, 30.12.2006, p. 1.

[18]Regulation (EU) 2018/1139 of the European Parliament and of the Council of 4 July 2018 on common rules in the field of civil aviation and establishing a European Union Aviation Safety Agency, and amending Regulations (EC) No 2111/2005, (EC) No 1008/2008, (EU) No 996/2010, (EU) No 376/2014 and Directives 2014/30/EU and 2014/53/EU of the European Parliament and of the Council, and repealing Regulations (EC) No 552/2004 and (EC) No 216/2008 of the European Parliament and of the Council and Council Regulation (EEC) No 3922/91, OJ L 212, 22.8.2018, pp. 1–122.

[19]Regulation (EU) No 1093/2010 of the European Parliament and of the Council of 24 November 2010 establishing a European Supervisory Authority (European Banking Authority), amending Decision No 716/2009/EC and repealing Commission Decision 2009/78/EC, OJ L 331, 15.12.2010, pp. 12–47. The General Court will also have competences to decide certain claims against the decisions of European Public Prosecutor on the basis of Council Regulation (EU) No 2017/1939 of 12 October 2017 implementing enhanced cooperation on the establishment of the European Public Prosecutor's Office ('the EPPO'), OJ L 283, 31.10.2017, pp. 1–71.

- disputes between the EU and its servants (until 2016 the General Court adjudicated on the appeal from the decisions of the Civil Service Tribunal).

Simultaneously with the expansion of the General Court's competence, the European Union itself was constantly enlarged. At the time of the creation of the Court of First Instance, there were 12 Member States of the European Community, while with the entry into force of the Treaty of Lisbon, there were 27 Member States of the European Union. The degree of harmonization and unification in various areas of EU law was also increased; the EU and its institutions obtained competence to act in new domains, and in the consequence the EU courts gained the jurisdiction in these domains. The number of intellectual property cases, in particular complaints about decisions of the European Union Office for Intellectual Property (EUIPO), has also substantially increased.

All this resulted in a huge increase in the number of cases handled by the General Court. The average number of cases resolved annually was significantly lower than the number of pending cases. The average length of proceedings by the Court was prolonged, from 20.9 months in 2004 to 27.2 months in 2009. The procedure in the particularly complex cases of competition law or state aid lasted for several years.[20] There were also the first decisions regarding the possibility of claiming compensation for the excessive length of proceedings before the General Court.[21]

The EU institutions and the Member States therefore looked for a right solution to improve the efficacy of the work of the General Court.[22] In 2011, the first proposal for the reform of the EU judiciary system was put forward by the Court of Justice of the EU.[23] The proposal provided for increasing the number of judges of the General Court by 12 (from 27 at that time to 39). This proposal was motivated by the need to increase the efficiency of the General Court's work and to reduce the duration of the proceedings. In the light of this objective, the proposal also considered alternative scenarios. The proposal preferred by the General Court itself was the creation of a specialized court dealing with matters related to intellectual property. This solution, as stipulated in the motives of the proposal, was not considered optimal, because firstly it was doubtful if it could reduce the delays in finishing the complicated cases

---

[20]Draft amendments to the Statute of the Court of Justice of the European Union and to Annex I thereto z 7.04.2011, 2011/0901 (COD), http://data.consilium.europa.eu/doc/document/ST-8787-2011-INIT/en/pdf. Accessed 5 Apr 2019.

[21]In Case C-385/07 P, Der Grüne Punkt v. European Commission, ECLI:EU:C:2009:456, par. 188 and 195, the Court of Justice stated that the proceedings before the General Court were being carried out in breach of the requirements of a reasonable time of the proceedings and this could give rise to damages. Later, the compensations for excessive length of proceedings were granted in the judgments of the General Court in cases T-479/14, Kendrion v. European Union, ECLI:EU:T:2017:48; T-577/14, Gascogne Sack Deutschland v. European Union, ECLI:EU:T:2017:1 and T-673/15, Guardian Europe v. European Union, ECLI:EU:T:2017:377.

[22]See also Sarmiento (2017), p. 238 et seq.; Albors-Llorens (2017), p. 126 et seq.

[23]Council document of 7 April 2011, 2011/0901 (COD) containing the letter of the President of the Court of Justice concerning the amendments to the Statute of the Court of Justice of the EU, http://data.consilium.europa.eu/doc/document/ST-8787-2011-INIT/en/pdf. Accessed 5 Apr 2019.

in other areas. Secondly, when the specialised court began delivering judgments, the number of appeals to the General Court would increase and therefore, the reduction in the number of intellectual property cases decided by the General Court could not be significant. Thirdly, as the motives of the proposal state, this solution was more difficult in organizational aspect, while the appointment of additional judges to the General Court could have an almost immediate effect on the handling of cases and, therefore, on the backlog. Additionally, the creation of a new court would take a long time, which in the light of the urgency of the reform was not desirable. The justification for the proposal indicated as well that the solution consisting in increasing the number of judges is more flexible than creating a specialized court, because it allows responding to the increasing number of cases in various areas. The creation of a specialized court could also not be beneficial from the point of view of consistency of case-law, since intellectual property cases would be resolved by various courts (by specialized court and by the General Court as an appeal court, and by the Court of Justice as a court in the preliminary ruling procedure).[24]

The above mentioned proposal of the Court of Justice of the EU was approved by the European Parliament and received a positive opinion from the Commission, but was not accepted by the Council. In this circumstance and following the Court's call by the Italian Presidency to submit new proposals for reform of the General Court, the Court of Justice made a new proposal in 2014. This new proposal provided for doubling the number of judges at the General Court, meaning that each Member State could nominate two judges.[25] The proposal provided for three stages of reform; the first consisting of an increase in the number of judges by 12, the second—scheduled for 2016—increasing the number of judges by 7, dissolution of the Civil Service Tribunal and transferring of its competences to the General Court; and the third—planned for 2019—involving a further increase in the number of judges by 9. After completing the three stages of the reform, the General Court would consist of 56 judges, i.e. two judges being appointed upon a proposal by each of the Member States, and would take over the competence of the Civil Service Tribunal.

This proposal was accepted by the Council and in December 2015 the Regulation 2015/2422 of Parliament and of the Council amending the Statute of the EU Court of Justice was adopted.[26] In the motives of this Regulation, it was indicated that the main goal of the reform was to allow for a reduction within a short time of both the volume of pending cases and the excessive duration of proceedings before the

---

[24]Council document 2011/0901—see note 23 above, p. 8.

[25]Response to the invitation from the Italian Presidency of the Council to present new proposals in order to facilitate the task of securing agreement within the Council on the procedures for increasing the number of Judges at the General Court https://curia.europa.eu/jcms/upload/docs/application/pdf/2015-05/8-en-reponse-274.pdf, available also in the Council document of 17 October 2014, 2011/0901B (COD), http://data.consilium.europa.eu/doc/document/ST-14448-2014-INIT/en/pdf. Accessed 5 Apr 2019.

[26]Regulation (EU, Euratom) 2015/2422 of the European Parliament and of the Council of 16 December 2015 amending Protocol No 3 on the Statute of the Court of Justice of the European Union OJ L 341, 24.12.2015, pp. 14–17.

General Court being the result of expansion of its jurisdiction and the increase in the number and variety of legal acts of the institutions of the Union, as well as to the volume and complexity of the cases brought before it particularly in the areas of competition, State aid and intellectual property.[27]

4 Implementation of the General Court's Reform

The initial phase of the reform began in 2016 within which 12 posts were to be taken by judges from Czech Republic, Cyprus, Greece, Hungary, Latvia, Lithuania, Luxembourg, Malta, Poland, Slovakia, Sweden and Spain. In April 2016 seven judges took the office (from Cyprus, Greece, Hungary, Lithuania, Luxembourg, Poland, Spain), then three more in June 2016 (from Latvia, Malta, Sweden), and in September 2016 a judge from the Czech Republic. Due to the need to align the terms of office of both judges from a given Member State, the Regulation 2015/2422 provided that the term of office of six out of twelve additional judges who were to be appointed in the first stage of the reform expired on 31 August 2016 (so that the next full six-year term of their office, aligned with the term of the previous judges, could cover the period from September 1, 2016 to August 31, 2022).

The second phase of the reform was carried out in September 2016. On 1 September 2016, the jurisdiction in disputes between the EU and its servants was transferred to the General Court; the Civil Service Tribunal was dissolved, its competences taken by the General Court and the number of judges of the General Court increased by 7 (judges from Belgium, Bulgaria, Denmark, Ireland, Italy, the Netherlands and Portugal).[28]

As a result, after two stages of the reform, the General Court had 46 judges (one post of a judge from the first stage of the reform remained vacant). According to Article 254 and Article 255 TFEU, all judges were appointed by common accord of the governments of the Member States, after consulting abovementioned panel, whose task is to give opinions on the candidates taking into account in particular, their independence, impartiality, experience and professional and personal suitability.[29]

In parallel with the work on the reform, the General Court worked on its rules of procedure, aiming at simplifying procedures and speeding up the examination of cases. The work ended in 2015 with the adoption of a new Rules of Procedure, which entered into force on 1st July 2015.[30] The provisions of the Rules were structured in

---

[27]Recitals 1-3 and 5 of the Regulation 2015/2422.

[28]Regulation (EU, Euratom) 2016/1192 of the European Parliament and of the Council of 6 July 2016 on the transfer to the General Court of jurisdiction at first instance in disputes between the European Union and its servants, OJ L 200, 26.7.2016, pp. 137–139.

[29]See recital 7 of the Regulation 2015/2422.

[30]Rules of Procedure of the General Court, OJ L 105, 23.4.2015, pp. 1–66 amended e.g. in 2016.

such a way as to reflect the three main types of proceedings before the General Court, i.e. proceedings on direct actions (Title III of the Rules), proceedings relating to intellectual property rights (Title IV) and proceedings in cases of appeals against decisions of the Civil Service Tribunal (Title V). Some procedural rules were simplified. In particular, the Rules provided for only one exchange of pleadings (application and response) in cases concerning intellectual property rights; they extended the possibility of deciding the cases by one judge and the possibility of adjudicating the cases without an oral phase; the new Rules regulated also a few procedural issues that have not been addressed before. New provisions have been introduced regarding the treatment of information and materials pertaining to the security of the EU, the Member States or to the conducts of their international relations (Article 105 of the Rules of Procedure).[31]

On the basis of the new Rules of Procedure, the General Court adopted practice rules, which contain explanations and guidelines as to the application of the provisions of the Rules of Procedure.[32] In 2018, the General Court decided also about obligatory lodging and service of procedural documents by electronic means (e-Curia system).[33]

5　Organization of the General Court at Present and Prospects

Since September 2016, the General Court has been operating in a new enlarged composition, in a new judicial organization (new chambers), with new judicial powers (cases taken over from the Civil Service Tribunal), and on the basis of the changed Rules of Procedure.

In September 2016, the president and vice-president of the General Court were elected for three years, as well as the presidents of the chambers of five judges (Article 50 of the Statute). The judges were allocated to the newly created chambers. The present organizational model of the General Court provides for nine chambers consisting of five judges each, which can adjudicate both in a five-judge formation and in two three-judge formations headed by the president of the chamber. As indicated in the press release, the new organizational structure of the General Court was to allow to maintain three-judge formation as the ordinary formation, while facilitating the referral of cases to the chambers of five judges, and to enable

---

[31] See Decision (EU) 2016/2387 of the General Court of 14 September 2016 concerning the security rules applicable to information or material produced in accordance with Article 105(1) or (2) of the Rules of Procedure, OJ L 355, 24.12.2016, pp. 18–30.

[32] Practice Rules for the Implementation of the Rules of Procedure of the General Court adopted by the General Court on 20 May 2015, OJ L 152, 18.6.2015, pp. 1–30 with amendments.

[33] Decision of the General Court of 11 July 2018 on the lodging and service of procedural documents by means of e-Curia, OJ L 240, 25.9.2018, p. 72.

the replacement from within the same chamber of any judge who is prevented from acting. It was also to give the presidents of chamber an enhanced role in respect of the coordination and consistency of the case-law.[34] The General Court may sit in chambers of three or five judges, and in some cases be constituted by a single judge or may sit in a grand chamber (fifteen judges). According to Article 49 of the Statute, there are no permanent posts of advocates general in the General Court, but the judges may be called to perform the tasks of the advocate general.

At this stage, it would be premature to analyse and summarize the effects of the reform. However, it is worth citing several statistics showing the work in the General Court after the first two stages of the reform. In 2016, the number of new cases increased by 17% compared to 2015 (from 831 to 974), which resulted mainly from the transfer on 1 September 2016 of 163 pending cases from the Civil Service Tribunal to the General Court. In 2017, 917 cases were lodged to the General Court, which was a slight decrease compared to 2016, however, the upward trend persisted from 2010 until at least 2017. In 2018 the number of new cases also decreased—834 new cases were submitted.[35]

Within the cases lodged to the Court in 2017, 298 concerned intellectual property rights, 39 state aid, 38 competition laws, 86 civil servants disputes, and 346 related to other direct actions. In 2018, there were 301 new cases concerning intellectual property rights, 42 state aids, 28 competition laws and 94—civil servants disputes. The number of cases in specific areas of EU law is obviously variable in given years, so it is difficult to observe any major trends in this respect, however, there is an increase in the number of cases in the field of economic and monetary policy (98 cases brought in 2017 compared to 23 in 2016 or 3 in 2015).

The decisions of the General Court were issued in the vast majority by the three-judge chambers, but the number of decisions issued in the five judges chambers significantly increased (from 12 in 2016, 18 in 2017 to 87 in 2018), the number of cases submitted to the enlarged chambers of five judges also increased—from 29 cases submitted in 2016 to 84 cases submitted in 2017.

In 2017, the General Court closed 895 cases; that means 140 more than in the previous year (in 2016—755 cases). In 2017 still 1500 cases was pending.[36] In 2018, the General Court closed 1009 cases, which is the record number up to date. The number of cases pending in 2018 went down to 1333.

The most important objective of the reform, i.e. shortening the duration of proceedings, was already achieved in 2016 and 2017. In 2014, the average time of the proceedings before the General Court was 23.4 months, in 2015—20.6 months, in

---

[34]Press release of the Court of Justice of the EU, No 35/16, 4 April 2016, https://curia.europa.eu/jcms/upload/docs/application/pdf/2016-04/cp160035en.pdf. Accessed 5 Apr 2019.

[35]Press release of the Court of Justice of the EU, No 39/19, Judicial statistics 2018: the Court of Justice and the General Court establish record productivity with 1769 cases completed, Luxembourg, 25 March 2019, https://curia.europa.eu/jcms/upload/docs/application/pdf/2019-03/cp190039en.pdf. Accessed 5 Apr 2019.

[36]Press release of the Court of Justice of the EU, No 36/18, 23 March 2018, https://curia.europa.eu/jcms/upload/docs/application/pdf/2018-03/cp180036en.pdf. Accessed 5 Apr 2019.

2016—18.7 months, and in 2017 it was further reduced to 16.3 months. In 2018, the average duration of the procedure was 20 months what is balanced by the record number of cases finished in 2018 among which were time-consuming complex competition cases.[37]

The General Court's reform involved reflection on the division of jurisdictional competences between the Court of Justice and the General Court. The increase in the number of judges at the General Court, and hence the improvement of its effectiveness, have been seen as reasons for transfer to the General Court of certain jurisdictional competences of the Court of Justice.[38] According to Article 3(2) of Regulation 2015/2422, by 26th December 2017, the Court of Justice was required to draw up a report for the European Parliament, the Council and the Commission on possible changes to the distribution of competences between the Court of Justice and the General Court for preliminary rulings under Article 267 TFEU. Such report was submitted in December 2017.[39] The Court of Justice, having analysed the functioning and the significance of the preliminary ruling procedure, considered that at this stage it was not appropriate to transfer to the General Court a part of the jurisdiction in preliminary ruling cases. The Court of Justice has pointed out that "the introduction of adequate mechanisms to ensure that the reference for a preliminary ruling retains its role as the 'keystone' of the judicial system of the European Union is an extremely delicate undertaking."[40] In addition, as stated by the Court of Justice, the average length of time for dealing with references for preliminary rulings was established at 15 months in 2016 which was a period quite close to the irreducible minimum, and the dialogue engaged with the courts and tribunals of the Member States had never been as intense. At the same time, the number of cases brought before the General Court increased, and the General Court itself was subject to reorganization. Nevertheless, the Court of Justice emphasized that the conclusion regarding the referral of the preliminary rulings should not be regarded as the final position on the distribution of jurisdiction between the Court of Justice and the General Court. The transfer of competences in preliminary ruling cases in specific areas would be possible if the number and complexity of requests for a preliminary ruling submitted to the Court of Justice were to be such that the proper administration of justice required it.

The Court of Justice has also pointed out that, irrespective of the division of competences in the questions referred for a preliminary ruling, other competence changes might be introduced, in particular with regard to direct actions and the examination of appeals by the Court of Justice. It also announced the presentation in

---

[37]See Press release of the Court of Justice No 39/19, note 35 above.

[38]See also Sarmiento (2017), p. 247 et seq.

[39]Report submitted pursuant to Article 3 (2) of Regulation (EU, Euratom) 2015/2422 of the European Parliament and of the Council amending Protocol No 3 on the Statute of the Court of Justice of the European Union; https://curia.europa.eu/jcms/upload/docs/application/pdf/2018-01/en_2018-01-12_08-43-52_183.pdf. Accessed 5 Apr 2019.

[40]Report, see note 39 above, p. 7.

2018 of proposals in this area, which should translate into an amendment to the Statute. Such proposal was presented in March 2018.[41] The Court of Justice proposed to transfer to the General Court jurisdiction to adjudicate at first instance in actions for failure to fulfil obligations of the Member States under Articles 258 and 259 TFEU and in actions against Member States under Article 108(2) second subparagraph TFEU, subject to certain categories of these actions being still reserved to the Court of Justice.

The above proposition of the Court of Justice did not meet the favourable opinion of the European Commission. The Commission was not in favour of transferring to the General Court jurisdiction to adjudicate in actions for failure to fulfil obligations of the Member States because "the transfer proposed by the Court of Justice of some actions for failure to fulfil obligations would have a negligible impact on the workload of the Court but would significantly extend the judicial phase of actions for failure to fulfil obligations, which could undermine these actions as an instrument which ensures the uniform application of Union law in the interests of all Member States, economic operators and the general public".[42] The Commission considered that it would be appropriate to await the report on the operation of the General Court to be submitted by the Court of Justice by the end of 2020 before making structural changes to the division of powers between the Court and the General Court.

In response, the Court of Justice presented on 10 August 2018 a modified request and invited the European Union legislature to postpone to a later stage the examination of the component of the request concerning the transfer to the General Court of the jurisdiction to adjudicate, at first instance, on certain categories of infringement proceedings.[43] The modified proposal did not concern the transfer of the competences to the General Court but provided for other procedural changes. First regarding Article 51 of the Statute it reserved to the Court of Justice litigations concerning a lump sum or a penalty payment imposed on a Member State pursuant to Article 260 of the TFEU. As these litigations concern in practice the problem of enforcement by a Member State of the judgment delivered by the Court of Justice within the infringement procedure, the Court of Justice proposed that these cases should be decided directly by it. The second proposal concerned new Article 58a of the Statute introducing an initial admission procedure for certain appeals from the decisions of the General Court to the Court of Justice. That concerns the cases which have already been considered twice, initially by an independent board of appeal of an administrative authority (EUIPO; Community Plant Variety Office; European Chemicals Agency; European Union Aviation Safety Agency), then by the General Court, and in which many of appeals are dismissed by the Court of Justice because

---

[41] See the presentation of the proposal in the Commission Opinion of 11.7.2018 on the draft amendments to Protocol No 3 on the Statute of the Court of Justice of the European Union, presented by the Court of Justice on 26 March 2018, COM/2018/534 final.

[42] Commission Opinion of 11.7.2018, see note 41 above.

[43] See the description of the proposal in Document of the Council of 31 October 2018, Amendment of Protocol No 3 on the Statute of the Court of Justice of the European Union - General approach, 2018/0900(COD).

they are unfounded or manifestly inadmissible. The new article provides that the Court of Justice allows an appeal to proceed only where it raises an issue that is significant with respect to the unity, consistency or development of Union law. This modified proposal of the Court of Justice was approved in the opinion of the European Commission; adopted in the regulation of the Parliament and the Council and entered into force on 1st May 2019.[44]

It should also be mentioned that the Court of Justice is obliged to examine the effects of the reform of the General Court and draw any legislative proposals to amend the Statute accordingly. This will of course only be possible after the reform is completed, i.e. after its last stage has been carried out in 2019 and after sufficient time has elapsed allowing for analysis. This requirement comes from Article 3(1) of the Regulation 2015/2422, which states that by 26 December 2020, the Court of Justice shall draw up a report, using an external consultant, for the European Parliament, the Council and the Commission on the functioning of the General Court. This report shall focus on the efficiency of the General Court, the necessity and effectiveness of the increase of the number of judges, the use and effectiveness of resources and the further establishment of specialized chambers or other structural changes.

6 Characteristic of the Jurisdiction of the General Court

As it was mentioned before, despite the legal basis established in Article 256 TFEU, the General Court still does not have competences to decide the actions instituted by the Member States (with few exceptions provided for in Article 51 of the Statute) or by the EU institutions; neither to determine questions referred for the preliminary ruling by the national courts, nor to decide the infringement procedures against the Member States.

Even with this limited jurisdictional competences, the jurisdiction of the General Court is very diverse in respect to the subject matters as it includes e.g. intellectual property law cases, state aid and competition cases, civil servant cases, damages claims against the EU or other direct actions (claims against the decisions of the EU institutions on e.g. access to documents, EU funds, FEOGA, restrictive measures, etc.). All these various cases are decided mostly within three main procedures provided for by the TFEU—action for annulment (Article 263–264), action against the failure to act (Article 265) and action for damages (Article 268 and Article 340).

It can be said that the General Court has many different functions, including the function of the labour law court in matters of civil servants (in these cases the

---

[44]Document of the Council of 31 October 2018, Amendment of Protocol No 3 on the Statute of the Court of Justice of the European Union - General approach, 2018/0900(COD), Regulation (EU, Euratom) 2019/629 of the European Parliament and of the Council of 17 April 2019 amending Protocol No 3 on the Statute of the Court of Justice of the European Union, OJ L 111, 25.4.2019, pp. 1–3.

General Court has also a possibility to seek the amicable settlement of the dispute[45]) or civil court awarding compensation for the damage, but the essential function of the General Court is a function of the administrative court meaning a court adjudicating disputes between private entities and the public administration (EU institutions).[46] In some particular cases, the General Court likewise adjudicates the disputes between EU institutions and Member States.

Even if the private entities can lodge to the General Court only a claim against the EU institution, in some situations, such claim directly concerns the interests of other individuals—as in the case of trademarks, where the claim is lodged against the decision of EUIPO but the origin of this dispute is often a conflict between the private entities concerning the right to the trademark; or in competition cases, where the decision of the European Commission is contested but the origin of the claim might be the conflict between enterprises.

The jurisdiction and powers of the General Court have been shaped in a way that corresponds to its essential function of the administrative court dealing with disputes with EU institutions. This means, first of all, that the General Court controls the legality of the decision of the institution, i.e. assesses and verifies such decision, but does not substitute the institution's decision. In other words the General Court has the competence to annul the decision or to reject the complaint, but cannot change the decision or issue injunctions as part of the annulment. There are however exceptions to the above rule—cases of unlimited jurisdiction, where the General Court can replace the findings of the administrative authority with its own findings and replace the administrative decisions. This is the case provided for in Article 261 TFEU which states that the regulations adopted by the European Parliament and the Council may give the Court of Justice of the EU unlimited jurisdiction with regard to the penalties provided for in such regulations. In such cases, the General Court not only control the legality of the decision on the penalty, but is competent also to change (cancel, increase, decrease) the penalty on the basis of its own appraisal of facts and circumstances and legal aspects of the case.[47] The General Court also has an extended jurisdiction that gives it the competence to change the decisions of the EU institutions, if this is provided for in the relevant legal instrument governing the jurisdiction of the Court, for example in the case of decisions of EUIPO.[48]

The General Court also has plain jurisdiction in the damages cases—it determines and awards the amount of compensation (Articles 268 and 340 of the TFEU).

---

[45]Chapter 11a of the Rules of Procedure of the General Court.

[46]See also Schwarze (2011), p. 117.

[47]E.g. T-704/14, Marine Harvest ASA v. European Commission, ECLI:EU:T:2017:753, par. 581 and case law quoted there.

[48]See Article 72 (3) of Regulation 2017/1001, note 15 above.

Similarly, It also has extended jurisdiction in the dispute of financial character between the EU and its officials and servants.[49]

Specific jurisdiction of the General Court is also exercised on the basis of Article 272 TFEU where the Court can give a judgment pursuant to any arbitration clause contained in a contract concluded by the EU or on its behalf whether that contract is governed by public or private law. In such cases, the General Court applies its own rules of procedure however decides on the basis of the substantive law chosen by the parties or determined in accordance with the EU rules on the applicable law.

In the context of an action for failure to act, the General Court merely determines whether there has been a failure to act, but is not competent to issue directions to an institution in the context of such action nor, of course, it replaces that inaction with its own decision.[50]

7   Access to the General Court in View of Art. 47 of the Charter of Fundamental Rights

Access to the EU judicature is one of the essential elements of a union based on the rule of law; and for that aim, the Treaties established a complete system of legal remedies and procedures designed to permit the EU courts to review the legality of acts of the EU institutions.[51] The acts of the EU institutions must be subject to judicial review if they produce legal effects in relation to third parties.[52] However, access to the EU courts is guaranteed only to the extent provided for in the Treaties, which grant to the individuals limited locus standi to file a claim to the EU courts. According to Article 263 TFEU any natural and legal persons may institute proceedings against an act of the EU addressed to that persons or which is of direct and individual concern to them. It is a settled case-law of the Court of Justice that on the basis of Article 263 TFEU the natural and legal persons other than the addressee of a legal act can be individually concerned by a EU act, if it affects their legal position by reason of certain attributes peculiar to them, or by reason of a factual situation which differentiates them from all other persons and distinguishes them individually

---

[49] Article 91(1) of Regulation No 31 (EEC) laying down the Staff Regulations of Officials and the Conditions of Employment of Other Servants of the European Economic Community and the European Atomic Energy Community (OJ P 045 14.6.1962, p. 1385 with amendments) provides: "The Court of Justice of the European Union shall have jurisdiction in any dispute between the Union and any person to whom these Staff Regulations apply regarding the legality of an act affecting such person adversely within the meaning of Article 90(2). In disputes of a financial character the Court of Justice shall have unlimited jurisdiction."

[50] E.g. T-395/04, Air One SpA, v. European Commission, ECLI:EU:T:2006:123, par. 24 and the case law quoted there.

[51] T-461/08, Evropaiki Dynamiki v. European Investment Bank, ECLI:EU:T:2011:494, par. 118.

[52] 294/83, Parti écologiste "Les Verts" v. European Parliament., ECLI:EU:C:1986:166, par. 23–25; T-461/08, Evropaiki Dynamiki, par. 46.

in the same way as the addressee.[53] The second of the conditions laid down in Article 263 TFEU—direct concern—is fulfilled when the provision directly affects the legal situation of an individual and leaves no discretion to the Member State in its implementation.[54] Treaty of Lisbon modified Article 263 TFEU adding the possibility for the natural and legal persons to institute proceedings against a regulatory act which is of direct concern to them and does not entail implementing measures.[55] As explained by the General Court and confirmed by the Court of Justice, the regulatory acts mentioned in Article 263 TFEU mean all EU acts of general application apart from legislative acts.[56]

According to the case-law of the Court of Justice, the Treaties have established a complete system of legal remedies and procedures designed to ensure review of the legality of acts of the institutions, and has entrusted such review to the EU courts. Under that system, where natural or legal persons cannot, by reason of the conditions for admissibility laid down in Article 263 TFUE, directly challenge the EU measures, they should be able, either indirectly to plead the invalidity of such acts before the EU courts under Article 277 TFEU or to do so before the national courts asking them (since the national courts have no jurisdiction to declare those measures invalid) to make a reference to the Court of Justice for a preliminary ruling concerning the validity of EU legal acts.[57] That means that the legal systems of the Member States complete the EU system of judicial protection also in respect to the validity of legal acts of the EU institutions and therefore the Member States should establish in their national laws a system of legal remedies which ensure respect for the right to effective judicial protection. In consequences, it is also for the Member States and, in particular, their courts and tribunals, to interpret and apply national procedural rules governing the exercise of rights of action in a way that enables natural and legal persons to challenge before the courts the lawfulness of any decision or other national measure relating to the drawing up of an act of the EU or to its application to them and to seek compensation for any loss suffered.[58]

---

[53]25/62, Plaumann & Co v. Commission, ECLI:EU:C:1963:17, par. 107; C-452/98, Nederlandse Antillen *v.* Council of the European Union, ECLI:EU:C:2001:623, par. 60.

[54]C-386/96 P, Société Louis Dreyfus v. European Commission, ECLI:EU:C:1998:193, par. 43; T-198/95, T-171/96, T-230/97, T-174/98 and T-255/99, Comafrica SpA v. European Commission, ECLI:EU:T:2001:184, par. 96.

[55]For explanation of the concept of implementing measures see e.g. C-622/16 P to C-624/16 P, Scuola Elementare Maria Montessori v. European Commission, ECLI:EU:C:2018:873, par. 58.

[56]E.g. T-18/10, Inuit Tapiriit and others v. European Parliament and Council, ECLI:EU: T:2011:419, par. 45-46. The Court of Justice confirmed also that the concept of the regulatory acts extends to all non-legislative acts of general application and not only to certain subcategories of these acts, C-622/16 P to C-624/16 P, Scuola Elementare Maria Montessori, par. 28.

[57]C-50/00 P, Unión de Pequenos Agricultores v. Council, ECLI:EU:C:2002:462 par. 41; C-263/02 P, European Commission v. Jégo-Quéré & Cie SA., ECLI:EU:C:2004:210, par. 31.

[58]C-355/04 P, Segi, Araitz Zubimendi Izaga and Aritza Galarraga v. Council, ECLI:EU: C:2007:116, par. 56.

Entry into force of the Charter of Fundamental Rights, providing in Article 47 for a right to an effective remedy and to a fair trial, did not change this complementary system of legal protection. As explanations to the Charter confirmed, the inclusion of the case-law on the right to court in the Charter has not been intended to change the system of judicial review laid down by the Treaties, and particularly the rules relating to admissibility for direct actions before the EU court. This system is also not changed by the amendments to Article 263 TFUE made by the Treaty of Lisbon extending the scope of the locus standi of the individuals in the case of the regulatory acts. The complementarity of the EU and national systems of judicial protection is furthermore confirmed in new art. 19(1) of the Treaty on European Union introduced by the Treat of Lisbon, which states that the Member States shall provide remedies sufficient to ensure effective legal protection in the fields covered by the Union law.[59]

The compliance of the EU legal protection system with the standard required by the European Convention on Human Rights was confirmed by the European Court of Human Rights (ECtHR). In the judgment in *Bosphorus* case, the ECtHR stated that the access of individuals to the EU courts is limited, but it is essentially through the national courts that the EU system provides a remedy to individuals against a Member State or another individual for a breach EU law. Within the complementary EU and national legal protection system, the dialogue between the national courts and the EU court through the preliminary procedure plays a special role. Finally, the ECtHR stated that the legal protection of the fundamental rights offered by the EU law can be considered to be equivalent to that of the Convention system.[60]

8 Jurisdictional Competences of the General Court in View of Art. 47 of the Charter of Fundamental Rights

The judicial control exercised by the General Court, as a rule, is the control of the legality of the legal act, action or inaction of the EU institutions.[61] In addition, in some cases, the General Court has unlimited jurisdiction, conferred on it by a specific provisions of the EU law. As indicated above, assessment of the legality of the administrative decision means that the General Court does not replace the findings of the administrative body by its own findings, but examines the findings of

---

[59]See more e.g. in Półtorak (2015), p. 15 et seq.

[60]Judgment of ECtHR of 30.6.2005, 45036/98, Bosphorus v. Ireland, ECLI:CE: ECHR:2005:0630JUD004503698, par. 163 et seq.; see also judgments of 6.12.2012, 12323/11, Michaud v. France, ECLI:CE:ECHR:2012:1206JUD001232311 and of 23.05.2016, 17502/07, Avotiņš v. Latvia., ECLI:CE:ECHR:2016:0523JUD001750207.

[61]C-247/11 P and C-253/11 P, Areva SA v. European Commission, ECLI:EU:C:2014:257, par. 171. See more Lasok (2011), p. 169 et seq.

the given authority.[62] Subject to some exceptions, the General Court should adjudicate on evidence and circumstances known to the EU institution at the date of the decision and does not take into account the new facts and evidence unknown to the administrative body.[63] The prevailing principle of the EU law is the unfettered evaluation of evidence by the court.[64] It means that the General Court independently and freely assesses the evidence collected in the case, but also that it should evaluate all the evidence gathered therein.

The proceedings before the General Court are contradictory and even the exercise of the unlimited jurisdiction does not amount to a review of the case of Court's own motion.[65] With the exception of pleas involving matters of public policy which the General Court is required to raise of its own motion (such as admissibility of the action or the failure to state reasons for a contested decision), it is for the applicant to raise pleas in law against the given decision and to adduce evidence in support of the pleas. The General Court cannot decide beyond the pleas and demands of the application, unless it concerns lack of competence or infringement of essential procedural requirements in the administrative procedure.[66]

If the EU institution had a discretion when deciding the case, the General Court examines whether the limits of this discretion were not exceeded and the Court's review is limited to verify if the rules governing the procedure and statement of reasons have been complied with, that the facts are correct and that there has been no manifest error of assessment or misuse of powers.[67] However, that does not mean that the General Court must refrain from reviewing the institution's interpretation of information and facts.[68] The Court should inter alia, establish whether "the evidence relied on is factually accurate, reliable and consistent but also whether that evidence contains all the information which must be taken into account in order to assess a complex situation and whether it is capable of substantiating the conclusions drawn from it".[69] Moreover, where EU institution has a wide discretion, the review of observance of certain procedural guarantees is of fundamental importance. Those guarantees include the obligation for the competent institution to examine carefully

---

[62]E.g. C-246/11 P, Portugal v. European Commission, ECLI:EU:C:2013:118, p. 85 and the case law quoted there.

[63]E.g. T-279/04, Éditions Odile Jacob SAS v. European Commission, ECLI:EU:T:2010:384, par. 338.

[64]E.g. 261/78, Interquell Stärke-Chemie GmbH & Co. KG v. European Economic Community, ECLI:EU:C:1982:329, par. 11; T-110/07, Siemens AG v. European Commission, ECLI:EU:T:2011:68, par. 50.

[65]C-389/10 P, KME Germany and Others v. Commission, ECLI:EU:C:2011:816 par. 131.

[66]E.g. C-89/08 P, European Commission v. Ireland and others, ECLI:EU:C:2009:742, p. 34.

[67]E.g. T-377/07, Evropaïki Dynamiki v. European Commission, ECLI:EU:T:2011:731, par. 22 and the case law quoted there. See also Lasok (2011), p. 190 et seq.

[68]C-12/03 P, European Commission v. Tetra Laval, ECLI:EU:C:2005:87, par. 39; C-386/10 P, Chalkor AE v. Commission, ECLI:EU:C:2011:815 par. 54).

[69]E.g. C-12/03 P, European Commission v. Tetra Laval, ECLI:EU:C:2005:87, par. 39.

and impartially all the relevant elements of the individual case and to give an adequate statement of the reasons for its decision.[70]

Taking into account all these elements of the jurisdictional competences of the General Court, the case-law of the Court of Justice acknowledges that the intensity of the judicial review conferred to the General Court meets the requirements of the principle of effective judicial protection as provided for in Article 47 Charter of Fundamental Rights.[71]

Another component of the right to effective legal protection is the right to have the case decided within a reasonable time. The assessment whether the duration of the procedure was reasonable should be done on the basis of the circumstances of each case, and in particular the importance of the case for the persons concerned, its complexity and the conduct of the parties of the proceeding.[72] This is not an exhaustive catalogue, and there might be different circumstances justifying a long duration of the proceedings. The Court of Justice stated for example that five and a half year duration of the proceedings before the General Court couldn't be justified by the complexity of this particular case, in particular taking into account the importance of the ruling for the parties, the parties' lack of contribution to prolonging the proceedings and lack of special circumstances affecting its duration.[73]

Where there are no indications that the excessive length of the proceedings affected their outcome, failure to deliver judgment by the General Court within a reasonable time cannot lead to setting aside of the judgment as such setting aside would not remedy the infringement of the principle of effective legal protection.[74] Initially the Court of Justice considered that excessive duration of the proceedings before the General Court could result—as compensation for the delay—in a reduction in the fine imposed by the administrative authority and disputed before the Court.[75] Yet, in later case law the Court of Justice decided that an effective remedy for a breach by a General Court of its obligation to adjudicate on the cases within a reasonable time should be an action for damages against the EU.[76]

---

[70]E.g. C-525/04 P, Spain v. European Commission, ECLI:EU:C:2007:698, par. 58 and the case law quoted there.

[71]C-389/10 P, KME Germany, par. 133; C-199/11, Otis and others, ECLI:EU:C:2012:684, par. 63; C-386/10 P, Chalkor, par. 67.

[72]C-403/04 P and C-405/04 P, Sumitomo Metal Industries Ltd and Nippon Steel Corp. v. European Commission, ECLI:EU:C:2007:52, par. 116; C-194/99 P, Thyssen Stahl AG v. European Commission, ECLI:EU:C:2003:527, par. 155). This formulation is a reference to ECtHR case law, see for example 18996/91, Garyfallou AEBE v. Greece.

[73]C-185/95 P, Baustahlgewebe GmbH v. European Commission, ECLI:EU:C:1998:608 par. 29; see also C-385/07 P, Der Grüne Punkt.

[74]C-185/95 P, Baustahlgewebe, par. 49; C-385/07 P, Der Grüne Punk, par. 190 and 196.

[75]Case C-185/95 P Baustahlgewebe, par. 48.

[76]C-58/12 P, Groupe Gascogne SA v. European Commission, ECLI:EU:C:2013:770, par. 83. Such damages have been already granted in the judgments of the General Court, see note 21 above.

9 Conclusions

During almost 30 years of its activity, the General Court proved to be an institution of great importance for the functioning of the EU. Over these years it evolved from a court of first instance with very limited competences to an important jurisdiction deciding about the rights of individuals in their relations with the EU institutions. The case-law of the General Court in the scope of the competition and state aid law, intellectual property law, European funds or other economic issues had a significant influence on the functioning of the internal market. Its case-law concerning the restrictive measures, access to documents, right to good administration or any other rights of the EU citizens and entities confirmed in the Charter of the Fundamental Rights, contributed to the development of the right of good administration and right to the effective judicial protection on the EU level.

The creation of the General Court allowed to relieve the Court of Justice in its jurisdictional tasks and to make the EU jurisdiction more effective. The current reform of the General Court which is still being implemented should bring the reduction of the adjudication time and increase in the number of cases closed. The report to be prepared by the Court of Justice by 26th December 2020 will certainly provide more information for the assessment of the effects of the reform of the General Court and possible changes in the distribution of jurisdictional competences between the Court of Justice and the General Court.

References

Albors-Llorens, A. (2017). The Court of Justice in the aftermath of judicial reform. In E. Guinchard & M.-P. Granger (Eds.), *The new EU judiciary. An analysis of current judicial reforms* (pp. 123–141). Wolters Kluwer.

Granger, M.-P., & Guinchard, E. (2017). Introduction: The dos and don'ts of judicial reform in the European Union. In E. Guinchard & M.-P. Granger (Eds.), *The new EU judiciary. An analysis of current judicial reforms* (pp. 1–18). Wolters Kluwer.

Lasok, K. (2011). The nature of judicial control. In *De 20 ans à l'horizon 2020, bâtir le tribunal de demain sur de solides fondations. Actes du Colloque organisé le 25 septembre 2009 à Luxembourg - Célébration des 20 ans du Tribunal de 1e Instance de l'Union européennes* (pp. 163–214). Luxembourg: Publication de la Cour de Justice de l'Union européenne.

Lenaerts, K., Maselis, I., & Gutman, K. (2014). *EU procedural law.* Oxford University Press.

Półtorak, N. (2015). *European Union Rights in national courts.* Wolters Kluwer.

Rodríguez Iglesias, G. C. (2013). L'évolution de l'architecture juridictionnelle de l'Union européenne. In A. Rosas, E. Levits, & Y. Bot (Eds.), *The Court of Justice and the construction of Europe: Analyses and perspectives on sixty years of case-law - La Cour de Justice et la Construction de l'Europe: Analyses et Perspectives de Soixante Ans de Jurisprudence* (pp. 37–48). Asser Press, Springer.

Sarmiento, D. (2017). The reform of the General Court: An exercise in minimalist (but radical) institutional reform. *Cambridge Yearbook of European Legal Studies, 19,* 236–251.

Schwarze, J. (2011). Access to the Courts under the rule of law. In *De 20 ans à l'horizon 2020, bâtir le tribunal de demain sur de solides fondations. Actes du Colloque organisé le 25 septembre 2009 à Luxembourg - Célébration des 20 ans du Tribunal de 1e Instance de l'Union européennes* (pp. 115–127). Luxembourg: Publication de la Cour de Justice de l'Union européenne.

European Soft-Law and Organization of National Judiciaries

Elisabetta Rosi

Contents

1 Soft-Law Instruments in the System of the Legal Sources

It is known that there is no common definition for soft-law. In this article, by soft-law we mean a set of "rules of conduct which in principle, have no legally binding force but which nevertheless may have practical effect",[1] and we have to consider the "impossibility of developing categories capable of understanding all the soft law tools, the variety of the forms, .. [is] the main characteristic of the soft law .. ": recommendations, resolutions of the international organizations, non-binding agreements for the international law, recommendations and opinions for the communitarian law.

It is possible to assert that the soft-law instruments, which increasingly manage the relations between the actors of the international community to replace acts of

---

Elisabetta Rosi is Judge at Supreme Court of Cassation in Rome.

---

[1] Snyder (1994), p. 198. Identical definition is endorsed by Trubek et al. (2005).

E. Rosi (✉)
Supreme Court of Cassation, Rome, Italy

© Springer Nature Switzerland AG 2019
P. Pinto de Albuquerque, K. Wojtyczek (eds.), *Judicial Power in a Globalized World*, https://doi.org/10.1007/978-3-030-20744-1_29

"hard" international law, even though they are not subject to the fundamental principle of the right of the Treaties,[2] nonetheless they constitute an expression of the rules of international law in force. In international law the rules don't have an "uniform standard of intensity" which depends on their legal goal, but in any case are aimed at orienting the conduct of States, international organizations and the individuals themselves even if the rules don't provide international rights and obligations and are not sources of law in a strict sense.[3] In conclusion: soft-law is characterized by an attenuated legal force, but it has an international legitimacy.

2 European Soft-Law Related to the Organization of National Judiciaries

Regarding soft-law within national judiciary organization, the set of Recommendations provided by Council of Europe is fundamental as it represents the framework of the fundamental principles regarding the administration of justice. In particular, the Statute of the Council of Europe, signed in London on 5 May 1949, provides in art. 15, letter (b), that the conclusions of the Committee of Ministers—the Body that, according to the art. 13 of the Statute, acts in the name and on behalf of the Council—may take the form of Recommendations and the same Preamble to the text makes it clear that these are guidelines, aimed at "promoting relations between magistrates and between individual judges of the various member states in order to encourage the development of a common culture of jurisdiction".

The above example of soft-law is being used more and more often by the European Court of Human Rights,[4] among the others interpretative legal rules, in order to establish a common legal basis and to recognize it within the Member States of the Council of Europe in the scope of application of the Human Rights European Convention or its Protocols.

There have been difficulties in reconstructing a "minimum common denominator" on very sensitive subject, among different existing disciplines, in the 47 Member States (some with a federal structure, which often complicates further the operation), and to solve them the European Court of Human rights is increasingly using legal documents unrelated to the Convention and to the national legal systems, such as other International Conventions (also unrelated to the Council of Europe), the opinions of the Venice Commission, the recommendations of the Committee of Ministers (and sometimes documents approved by the Parliamentary Assembly), the

---

[2]That is: *pacta sunt servanda*; on the contrary, soft-law is subject to the principle *inadimplenti non est adimplendum.*

[3]Thurer (2000), p. 452. The attempt to construct a concept of it has been strongly led by the internationalist doctrine; Trubek et al. (2005). Senden (2004), p. 112.

[4]Cfr. *Moulin v. France*, no. 37104/06, November 23, 2010; *Colesnicov v. Romania*, no. 36479/03, December 21, 2010, *A., B. and C. v. Ireland, Grande Chambre*, no. 25579/05, December 16, 2010.

judgments of the Court of Justice of the European Union and of other international and national Courts, the opinions of the Consultative Councils of European Judges and Prosecutors, and even documents issued by NGOs with a recognized reputation for defending human rights. Doing so, the Judge of Rights shows a sort of "holistic approach" to collect legal sources of knowledge and carries forward a non-formalistic interpretation in its jurisprudence.

The principles of independence and impartiality of the judiciary represents one of the fundamental values of democracy and are included in the principle of "fair trial" set by the article 6 of the European Convention of Human rights.[5]

In the European Union, since the entry into force of the Lisbon Treaty, art. 47 Nice Chart refers to jurisdictional protection and provides for compliance with the rules of a fair trial and the right for every accused individual of being heard, in a reasonable time, by an independent and impartial judge, established by law.

The European Court of Justice has clearly underlined this fundamental principle in judicial activity, especially in relation to independence of judges. As part of a Commission infringement procedure, the Court[6] has ordered the Republic of Poland to suspend the application of the reform law of the Supreme Court. The Luxembourg Court reiterates that the institutional reforms within each Member State are not indifferent to the Union and to the other Member States, through the direct application of the Charter of Fundamental Rights.

2.1 In relation to the Judicial Systems and judiciaries organization, the opinions and reports adopted by the Venice Commission focus on the guarantees of independence and accountability of the judges.[7] The internal organization of the judiciary has to be independent from other branches of the Government and to ensure this it is necessary

---

[5]About the guarantee of independence, the European Court of Human Rights said that "in a democratic society, the right to a fair administration of justice plays a so important that a 'purely strict interpretation of' Article 6 para. 1 of the ECHR does not match the aims and 'object this provision" (Cfr. *Ryakib Biryukov v. Russia*, judgment of 17 January 2008, app. no. 14810/02, para. 33).

[6]Ordinance of 19 October 2018, C-619/18, Poland. The infringement appeal was introduced by the Commission to ascertain that, on the one hand, the lowering of the retirement age limit also for the judges of the Supreme Court and, on the other, the discretion granted to the President of the Republic of Poland to prolong the active judicial service of the judges of the Supreme Court, constitute a violation of the Treaties and of the art. 47 (right to an effective appeal and an impartial judge) of the Charter of Fundamental Rights of the European Union.

[7]CDL-AD (2010) 004, Report on the Independence of the Judicial System Part I, §22: "It is [...] indispensable to provide [...] a constitutional right to have access to independent tribunals, in accordance with Article 6 of the European Convention of Human Rights." See the basic principles of independence of the judicial system, adopted by the seventh United Nations Congress in 1985; Recommendation n. 12 (1994) of the Committee of Ministers of the Council of Europe 'to Member States on the independence, efficiency and role of judges; Opinion n. 1 (2001) of the Consultative Council of European Judges (CCJE) on standards concerning the 'independence of the judiciary and non-removability of judgments; Opinion n. 10 (2007) of the CCJE on the Council of the Judiciary at the service of society; European Charter concerning the Statute of Judges, adopted in 1998.

to have a definite discipline of the status of judges. Consequently, the basic principle is that the national organization of the judiciary should be set out in the Constitution or equivalent texts. In particular, it is recommended to regulate the procedure of appointment in [. . .] detail in the Constitution. [. . .]. "The grounds for suspension, dismissal or resignation should be laid down in the constitutional law. [. . .]".

The procedures for the appointment and promotion of judges should be regulated in order to avoid influence of the legislature by the executive: transparency makes it clear that the appointment is made only on the basis of the merit of the candidate and is based on his professionalism, ability, moral integrity, independence, impartiality and efficiency. [. . .] The Venice Commission is of the opinion that a judicial council should have a decisive influence on the appointment [. . .] of judges, and the mere existence of a high judicial council cannot automatically exclude political consider-ations in the appointment process, to guarantee the impartiality of the judicial activities.

The requirement of independence also requires that the disciplinary regime of those who have a judicial function present the necessary guarantees to avoid any risk of using such a regime as a system of political control of the content of judicial decisions.

In relation to the allocation of cases to individual judges, the Venice Commission strongly recommends that it should be based "to the maximum extent possible on objective and transparent criteria established in advance by the law or by special regulations on the basis of the law, e.g. in court regulations. Exceptions should be motivated."[8]

2.2 These principles are acquired also in the juridical-constitutional heritage of the European Union, considering the importance in democracy of the rule of law and the constitutional traditions common to all EU Member States. They are: the principles of legality, legal certainty, prohibition of arbitrariness of the executive power, independence and impartiality of the judge, effective jurisdictional control, also with regard to respect for fundamental rights, equality before the law.

It's essential to have not only a formal setting of legal systems, but also the rule of law in action, as it comes out of the judicial governance put into motion in the daily activity of the courts and the public prosecutors across the domestic borders of the EU. Judicial training has gained a central position in European rule of law promo-tion. Better trained judges and prosecutors are deemed to be more inclined to properly apply EU laws and enforce the fundamental rights of EU citizens.[9]

European Network of Judicial Training and the European Commission for the Evaluation of Efficiency of the Judiciary have developed a dialogue between policy makers and practitioners about the justice system, giving priority to making courts efficient and transparent, and more accessible for citizens.

---

[8]CDL-PI (2015)—Venice Commission—Compilation of opinions and reports concerning courts and judges.
[9]Piana (2016), p. 20.

Efficiency is of course in connection with the existence of sufficient financial basis: it is clear that, in order to guarantee judicial independence, the justice system has to receive sufficient public funds to ensure fair trials in accordance with international standards, and the High Judicial Council would represent the judiciary in this regard and influence on budgetary decisions regarding the needs of the judiciary.

3 The Recommendation n. (2010) 12 of the Committee of Ministers to Member States of the Council of Europe on Judges: Independence, Effectiveness and Responsibility. Challenges for Judicial Independence and Impartiality in the Member States of the Council of Europe

The Recommendation n. (2010) 12 of the Committee of Ministers to Member States of the Council of Europe on judges: Independence, effectiveness and responsibility (November 17, 2010) has overcome the prospect of independence, as emerged from the previous Recommendation on the subject, especially the n. (94) 12, in the light of the jurisprudence of the European Court of Human Rights on the art. 6 CEDU, which establishes that "each person has the right to have his case examined fairly, publicly and within a reasonable time by an independent and impartial tribunal established by law". This last Recommendation has developed also the other documents drawn up and approved in the matter of justice.[10]

The Recommendation on judges of 2010 contains, by general principles, a complete regulatory system on judiciary, from recruitment to the retirement of judges, affirming the close relationship between the independence of each judge and the independence of the entire judicial system (Article 4); but underlining that the independence is placed on a functional level to guarantee the efficiency of justice as an essential element of the rule of law. The recommendation provides that the effectiveness of judges and judicial systems is a requirement for the protection of the

---

[10]The joint opinion adopted on November 18, 2009 by the Consultative Council of European Judges (No. 12/2009) and by the Consultative Council of European Prosecutors (No. 4/2009), under the common title of Judges and prosecutors in a democratic society, also known as the Bordeaux Declaration. The Advisory Council of Judges CCJE approved, on November 17, 2010, during its 11th plenary meeting, a Magna Charta of judges (Fundamental Principles), aimed at summarizing and codifying the main conclusions contained in its previous twelve opinions, established that to guarantee the independence, and in order to avoid undue influence, judges shall receive appropriate remuneration and be provided with an adequate pension scheme, to be established by law. Judges shall be involved in all decisions which affect the practice of judicial functions (organization of courts, procedures, other legislation). In addition it has been underlined that material and financial resources necessary to the proper operation of the justice system.

rights provided by article 6 CEDU, to reach a high-quality decision "within a reasonable time and on the basis of a fair appreciation of the circumstances".

The authorities responsible for the organization and functioning of the judicial system are in charge to create the conditions that allow the judges to achieve efficacy, without prejudice to the independence and impartiality of the judges.

3.1 A recent report, jointly prepared by the Bureau of the CCJE and the Bureau of the CCPE: "Challenges for judicial independence and impartiality in the member states of the Council of Europe"(March 24, 2016) has addressed the issue of independence and impartiality, in the light of the functionality and efficiency of the justice-service, in particular dealing with:

- organizational independence of judges and prosecutors as exercised by Councils for the Judiciary and the Administration of Courts;
- shortcomings in the effective enforcement of judicial decisions;
- public criticism of judges and prosecutors and their decisions.

4   European Judicial Systems: Efficiency and Quality of Justice. The Evaluation Process of the European Commission for Efficiency of Justice

The European Commission for the Efficiency of Justice (CEPEJ) was set up by the Committee of Ministers of the Council of Europe in September 2002 (Resolution n. 12), to promote the effective implementation of existing instruments used for the organization of justice, and offering States effective solutions for reducing backlogs in the Courts.

This recent report, published on September, 18, 2018 (CEPEJ Studies n. 26), is really interesting even if it is limited to key issues, such as the budget of the judicial systems, judicial staff (including judges and prosecutors and others), organization of the courts, and state of Information Technology development in European judicial system. In particular a Group of Pilotage of the SATURN Center for judicial time management was instituted within the CEPEJ,[11] to develop its capacity to acquire better knowledge of the time required for judicial proceedings in the Member States. On 4 December 2018, European Ethical Charter on the Use of Artificial Intelligence in Judicial Systems and their environment has been drafted as first reference framework.

Getting an effective national justice system in place is also essential for the European Union, that wants not only to implement EU Law, but also to improve the mutual trust among the national judicial authorities.

---

[11]Resolution of Ministers of the Council of Europe, on a modern, transparent and efficient justice, during their meeting in Istanbul at the occasion of their 30th Conference (November 24-26, 2010).

The 2018 EU Justice Scoreboard has developed a series of indicators concerning the independence, efficiency and quality of the national justice systems. The independence of judge is not evaluated as a goal in itself, but must be appreciated instead of the guarantee of judicial impartiality[12] and the efficiency rating has to be considered a tool of transparency of the results of judicial activities and the compliance with the "fair trial" principle.

5 Conclusions

The short examples illustrated above show how the value of the efficiency of justice ad national level is moving to the front stage, as a tool to guarantee the independence and impartiality of judicial activities and as a path to obtain a fair trial, not only to ensure the just mentioned principles, but also as the correct approach to obtain a decision in a reasonable time.

Soft-law instruments and decisions provided by the Strasbourg Court and by European Court of Justice further prove this trend.

In Europe, without the action of the ECHR, the Council of Europe and the European Union, no common principles regarding judicial organization would have been established.

European citizens, in a broad sense, must continue to trust in the future development of common grounds with the purpose to improve jurisdictional activity, under the umbrella of the protection of human rights.

References

Contini, F., & Mohr, R. (2008). Reconciling independence and accountability in judicial systems. *Utrecht Law Review, 3*(2), 26–43. https://doi.org/10.18352/ulr.46

Piana, D. (2016). *Actors, Networking, and the Law Rule: A new puzzle*. Working paper 1/15, LUISS, Guido Carli, ICEDD-International Center on Democracy and Democratization, 20. https://www.luissuniversitypress.it/content/actors-networking-and-rule-law-new-puzzle

Senden, L. (2004). *Soft law in European Community law* (p. 112). Oxford: Hart Publishing.

Snyder, F. (1994). Soft law and institutional practice in the European Community. In S. Martin (Ed.), *The construction of Europe: Essays in honor of Emile Noël* (p. 198). Dordrecht: Kluwer.

Thurer, D. (2000). Soft law. *Encyclopaedia of Public International Law, IV*, 452.

Trubek, M., Cottrel, P., & Nance, M. (2005). "Soft law", "Hard law" and European integration: Toward a theory of hybridity. *Jean Monnet Working Paper* 2. https://jeanmonnetprogram.org/archive/papers/05/050201.html

---

[12]Contini and Mohr (2008), pp. 26–43.

Individual Religious Liberty Under Article 9 and Identity as Dignity

András Sajó

Contents

1 Introduction

This article is first and foremost a personal tribute to my dear friend and former colleague, Vincent de Gaetano, and at this point it is imperative to disclose the interaction of the personal/judicial and the scholarly perspectives. When *Ladele*[1] was decided, I congratulated Vincent and Judge Nebojša Vučinić on their dissenting opinion which reflected a principle that is crucial to liberalism as tolerance: "no one should be forced to act against one's conscience or be penalised for refusing to act against one's conscience." The state shall not force someone to choose between the

---

[1] Eweida and Others v. The United Kingdom, (App. nos. 48420/10, 59842/10, 51671/10 and 36516/10), Eur. Ct. Hum. Rts., Judgment of 15 January 2013.

A. Sajó (✉)
Central European University, Budapest, Hungary
e-mail: Sajoand@ceu.edu

© Springer Nature Switzerland AG 2019
P. Pinto de Albuquerque, K. Wojtyczek (eds.), *Judicial Power in a Globalized
World*, https://doi.org/10.1007/978-3-030-20744-1_30

imperatives of her (religious or other) conscience and livelihood. Certainly not, where there are less burdensome alternatives (accommodation).

On second thought I still believe that the frame the dissent applies is far more satisfactory than the majority view. The majority decided the case as a matter of two conflicting rights. On the one hand we have non-discrimination on religious grounds—Ms. Ladele's right, and, on the other the right of gay people not to be discriminated. Once the case was construed as a conflict of these two fundamental rights the majority just followed the usual cavalier approach of the European Court of Human Rights (the Court, ECtHR). Based on the margin of appreciation doctrine there is no need to decide on the merit: whenever there is a reasoned decision of the national courts, referring to both considerations, it will stay.[2]

Maintaining my admiration for the liberal support of tolerance provided by Vincent, in the broader context of the conscience wars I have some concerns. First, I am not so sure that Ms. Ladele had a genuine conscience claim, if one takes conscience seriously. Secondly, instead of the language of conscience dictated by Ms. Ladele's perspective, we should consider the whole problem of these competing interests from the perspective of tolerance.

In the last decade religious convictions about homosexuality and demands for protection against discrimination on grounds of sexual orientation clashed in politics and the judiciary got involved in this conscience (or identity) war. Beyond religious garb cases (burqa[3] and headscarf cases[4]) both in the UK and the USA cases concerning the denial of providing gay marriage wedding related cakes reached the respective Supreme Courts. In other contexts, manifestations of religion as identity and conscience dictated behavior regarding gay marriage and abortion were also brought to Supreme Courts and the ECtHR.[5] The argument of the plaintiffs who typically lost under anti-discrimination law was that these laws disregard the religious behavioral command and (in some cases) represent discrimination on grounds of religion. There is a common trend here to insist on the protection of religious sensitivities. I will refer to the mentioned cases as 'sensitivity' cases.

These litigations represent a strategic choice serving the political agenda of the respective communities. I will argue that courts should find ways not to be drawn

---

[2]The Court (including the dissenters) was bound by the strategic choice of Ms. Ladele's lawyers who insisted to frame the case as one of discrimination. As a consequence, the Court was not called upon to determine whether "the means used to pursue this aim were proportionate" (§ 106).

[3]S.A.S. v. France (App. no. 43835/11), Eur. Ct. Hum. Rts., Judgment of July 1, 2014.

[4]German Federal Constitutional Court (Bundesverfassungsgericht) 2 BvR 1436/02 (Judgment of the Second Senate of 24 September 2003); German Federal Constitutional Court (Bundesverfassungsgericht) 1 BvR 471/10 (Order of the First Senate of 27 January 2015); Dahlab v. Switzerland (Application no. 42393/98), Eur. Ct. Hum. Rts., Judgment of 15 February 2001.

[5]Eweida and Others v. The United Kingdom, (Applications nos. 48420/10, 59842/10, 51671/10 and 36516/10), Eur. Ct. Hum. Rts., Judgment of 15 January 2013; Burwell v. Hobby Lobby, 573 U.S. ___ (2014); Masterpiece Cakeshop v. Colorado Civil Rights Commission, 584 U.S. ___ (2018); Lee (Respondent) v Ashers Baking Company Ltd. and others (Appellants) (Northern Ireland) [2018] UKSC 49.

into this identity war which is often about symbolic differences. In this respect, courts apply different strategies based on the available judicial theories and concepts. I will argue that the choices of the ECtHR originating in its concept of religion and manifestation of religion are unfortunate, undertheorized and result in antagonistic conclusions and judicially intractable antinomies (most famously see the difference in two manifestation cases: *Eweida* and *S.A.S.*). In the last part of the chapter I will argue that in these 'sensitivity' conflicts considerations of tolerance shall prevail.

2   The Nature of the Freedom of Religion Argument: A Matter of Identity

Contrary to other rights dignity is seldom used in the freedom of religion context in the ECtHR, except that it is used to justify *restrictions* of the free exercise of religion. It is also of relevance that for the ECtHR conscience is not associated with dignity. In the seminal freedom of religion case of the ECtHR *Kokkinakis v. Greece*[6] the ECtHR premised the protection of religious liberty on the understanding that it is "one of the most vital elements that go to make up the *identity* of believers and their conception of life"[7] (emphasis added). For the Court not only that religion and its free exercise are not a value per se, but they are relegated to an important matter of identity. Certainly, this is not the way most religions consider their importance. Religion is most often related to transcendental salvation, divine command etc., and this is what makes it so important for those who insist on its importance.[8]

The ECtHR continued to move in the direction of religious manifestation as an identity exercise, culminating in *S.A.S v France.* Here the applicant admitted that she

---

[6]Kokkinakis v. Greece, (App. no. 14307/88), Eur. Ct. Hum. Rts., Judgment of May 25, 1993.

[7]Kokkinakis v. Greece, (App. no. 14307/88), Eur. Ct. Hum. Rts., Judgment of May 25, 1993. para. 31.

[8]The special protection of religion remains contested. It is of course protected because of its social power, and in law because the experience of religious wars and toleration as a way to avoid such wars has been frozen in the code of fundamental (human) rights. The religious war experience remains relevant to this day. However, religions refer to a higher moral (divine) source and the recognition of the special force of this claim is simply a social concession of the secular state, perhaps in exchange of the recognition by the believers and their communities of the sovereignty of the state. Centrality of the belief is another common ground for the justification of the right, but this fails as a matter of practice: freedom of religion exists even for those for whom religion is not the organizing principle of life; it continues to matter in fragmented forms, e.g. when it comes to burial (discussed by the ECtHR as a right to private life matter: when it comes to burial religion becomes decisive for many people for whom religion is not an extremely intensive life organizer nor a central belief.

Brian Leiter refers to three characteristics that justify or explain the special treatment of religion (as a right): religions make some categorical demands on their adherents; some of the beliefs in every religion are insulated from reasons and evidence as those are understood in the sciences and common sense); and religions provide existential consolation (death—afterlife). None of these is identity based. See Leiter (2013).

is not following a religious prescription about the burqa; indeed, she admitted that she wears it when she feels like it. For the Court "the clothing in question... is the expression of a cultural identity which contributes to the pluralism that is inherent in democracy." (*S.A.S.* para. 120) This is perhaps correct as an empirical observation, but the case was about freedom of manifestation of religion. This attitude (that reflects a narcissistic cultural development that turns personal and collective (organizational) identity into a life project) is not limited to the ECtHR. It can be traced in some US Supreme Court decisions. The consequences are twofold: sometimes religious manifestations and dictates of conscience receive lesser protection being a matter of identity "only", while on the other hand non-religious identity concerns are played out to the detriment of freedom to manifest.

The ECtHR is not alone in the identity based understanding of religious freedoms. The Court of Justice of the European Union (CJEU) did not hesitate to focus on the interference with asylum seeker's individual religious liberty, as protected under Article 10 of the EU Charter as a problem of identity.[9] In particular, the CJEU pointed out that "[t]he subjective circumstance that the observance of a certain religious practice in public, which is subject to the restrictions at issue, is of particular importance to the person concerned in order to preserve *his religious identity* is a relevant factor to be taken into account in determining the level of risk to which the applicant will be exposed in his country of origin on account of his religion, even if the observance of such a religious practice does not constitute a core element of faith for the religious community concerned."[10]

All this is far from the standard dignity based justification of freedom of religion exemplified by The Special Rapporteur on freedom of religion or belief, (Heiner Bielefeldt) who considered dignity for the justification of the non-discriminatory treatment in matters of granting specific status.[11] Likewise, the Canadian Supreme Court emphasizes that the protection granted to freedom of religion is related to the intrinsic value of religion related to dignity (a strong point of departure for freedom of religion) but manifestation is understood restrictively (worship, practice, teaching, dissemination).[12] The ECtHR in some instances (which will be relevant here) accepts that religious exercise (manifestation) is conduct based on the believer's personal conviction (as long as there is nexus).

The insecurity of the value (or troubling nature) of religion in the ECtHR is reflected in the way religious claims are presented. Applicant organizations may

---

[9]Joined Cases C-71/11 and C-99/11, *Bundesrepublik Deutschland v.* Y & Z, Court of Justice of the European Union, 5 September 2012.

[10]Joined Cases C-71/11 and C-99/11, *Bundesrepublik Deutschland v.* Y & Z, Court of Justice of the European Union, 5 September 2012 para. 70.

[11]Report of the United Nations Special Rapporteur of 22 December 2011 on freedom of religion or belief. (A/HRC/19/60), para 61.

[12]"The essence of the concept of freedom of religion is the right to entertain such religious beliefs as a person chooses, the right to declare religious beliefs openly and without fear of hindrance or reprisal, and the right to manifest religious belief by worship and practice or by teaching and dissemination." R v. Big M Drug Mart Ltd., [1985] 1 S.C.R. 295, 336–337.

mention that they respect dignity in order to be worthy of protection.[13] Respect of dignity seems to be a certificate of good citizenship. This preemptive defense is understandable as Governments tend to consider minority religions as an attack on the rule of law, public order and dignity. This was the argument of the Greek government in *Kokkinakis* (para 34) where the anti-proselytism law was intended "to protect the beliefs of others from activities which undermined their dignity and personality." In other words, the Greek position was that it is dignity that is underlying the right to hold beliefs undisturbed.

Judge Martens was critical of the position of the Court that construed the issue as one of respect of the identity of another believer. In his partly dissenting separate opinion he wrote: "it is not within the province of the State to interfere in [a] 'conflict' between proselytiser and proselytised. . . . [R]espect for human dignity and human freedom implies that the State is bound to accept that in principle everybody is capable of determining his fate in the way that he deems best."[14]

The fact that religious belief and its manifestation is a personal choice (emanating from dignity) that deserves respect by the state is generally missing in the majority views of the Court. Note that the approach advocated by Judge Martens is about dignity as *autonomous individual choice*, but that choice is not protected as part of personal (or group) identity: it simply sets a limit to state intervention.

The reluctance of an international court to develop a clear concept of religion and a justification for the protection of religious freedom across borders is understandable. However, the judicial choice to transform religious exercise claims into identity claims as the core foundation of individual protection is not only a doctrinal happenstance of the ECtHR.[15] It reflects an important cultural change in the West

---

[13]See, e.g. the argument of the minority Mennonite church in Magyar Keresztény Memmonita Egyhaz and Others v Hungary (App. nos. 70945/11, 23611/12, 26998/12, 41150/12, 41155/12, 41463/12, 41553/12, 54977/12 and 56581/12), Eur. Ct. Hum. Rts., Judgment of August 4, 2014.

In fact, it is rather common in contemporary European national laws to require respect of dignity of others as a condition of church authorization (See Church Act Hungary, Romania). "The belief must be consistent with basic standards of human dignity or integrity." by Scientology Kirche Deutschland e V v. Germany (App. no. 34614/97), Eur. Ct. Hum. Rts., Judgment of April 7, 1997.

However, as *S.A.S.* has clearly stated, protection of dignity (as least in the burqa prohibition context) is not an acceptable aim for the limitation of Article 9, at least to the extent that "respect for human dignity cannot legitimately justify a blanket ban on the wearing of the full-face veil in public places." (S.A.S. para. 120) This is contrary to the French approach which accepted that wearing the full veil, "clearly contravenes the principle of respect for the dignity of the person", including the dignity of others.

[14]Kokkinakis v. Greece, (App. no. 14307/88), Eur. Ct. Hum. Rts., Judgment of May 25, 1993. partly dissenting opinion of Judge Martens, para. 15.

[15]I advance the hypothesis that the ECtHR's reluctance to protect religious manifestations, especially minority (unusual) religious behavior, especially where the applicant demands exceptions from generally applicable laws (which reflect majority religion traditions turned into majority culture) is related to the fact that these early cases were decided at a time when the then existing member states of the Convention were very rapidly secularizing. This trend came to a halt, partly because of the increased presence of Islam, partly because in some of the new member states religion was more alive and religious organizations had growing political influence (see in particular

where identitarian concerns became crucial for politics. Religions (as political movements, or as movements in politics) lost their transcendence-based influence and are in search for new legitimacy. It is for this reason that they promise identity, and related confidence that is in great demand in an uncertain world. To a great extent religious identity replaces authoritative and authoritarian spirituality. To put it in simple terms, religion matters less for providing consolation, meaning of life, and afterlife. It is important as an identity component (with the intention to become again all-encompassing). It provides (at least promises) a stable and respect-deserving social and psychological position to the individual.

The couching of identity claim into religious garb is part of the religious Reconquista of the public sphere. Display of identity as religious appurtenance is construed as manifestation of religion and hence it can be presented as such, without reference to the supremacy or transcendental exceptionalism of religion. This trivialization for use in carving out religious exemptions in the public sphere runs the risk that under the guise of freedom of manifestation, a divisive identity war will emerge. What happens is different groups try to occupy and colonize the public space on the basis of their (allegedly superior) identity. This is destructive of democratic politics and it ends up in identity-based politics.

Of course, there is nothing a priori wrong or objectionable with the display of religion in the public space or in the competition for social and legal acceptance, unless the display claims rely on the inherently superior position of the religious. Identity politics is not a peculiarity of religion. The identity centered culture wars and the politics of identity originate in the interest representation and mobilization of other interests. Indeed, religion is a latecomer in this competition. Be that as it may, identity competitions are destructive of democracy as a process of rational deliberation.

As to the consequences of the identitarian concept of religion it is enough to consider the Eweida story (a member of the airline check-in staff who displayed a crucifix on herself, in violation of company policy.) In that case, the protection of the manifestation of religious conviction as identity resulted at the end in the protection of religious advertisement: the believer displays a religious symbol as if it were a command of religion, in practice she wanted (successfully) to act as a human billboard in the conscience war. It may well be that such confession of the faith is a profanation of religion as a matter of sacrality and spirituality; most likely the Christian religion (of Ms. Eweida) has a different understanding of bearing witness.[16] However, what is the meaning of bearing witness is not a concern for law. In

---

Russia and other orthodox countries, Poland, and to a lesser extent Hungary.) Most ECtHR cases concern unorthodox groups or practices, subject to government and social suspicion and bias; the Court, within its cult of subsidiarity, is not particularly willing to turn upfront against local understandings of "proper" religion (see the reluctance to recognize Jehovah's Witnesses as religious organization).

[16]"Be on your guard. For they will deliver you over to councils, and you will be beaten in synagogues, and you will stand before governors and kings for my sake, to bear witness before them. And the gospel must first be proclaimed to all nations." Mark 13:9–10.

consequence law's permissiveness to personal interpretations may contribute to religious fragmentation.

3 Freedom of Religion as Identity: Social and Legal Consequences (the Road to Identity Conflicts)

The protection granted to free exercise of religion is now judicially extended to the manifestations of identity as personal choice, simply because personal choice is to be respected. This attitude is clearly visible in the US Supreme Court approach to constitutional liberties which "extend to certain personal choices central to individual dignity and autonomy, including intimate choices that define personal identity and beliefs".[17]

The search for identity implies that the primary question for the human agent is to ask and answer who she is. Once such identity is identified (negotiated, or accepted (even if imposed)), the actor will take it more or less for granted that she has to live according to the dictates of such identity. In some circumstances this may entail the following demand: others shall respect such identity as it unfolds in her actions (including the prohibition of criticism). In a more extreme formulation others shall

---

Here is an interesting Christian view on the matter:

The crucifix is not a decoration; ... The crucifix is the mystery of the 'annihilation' of God out of love," Pope Francis told... So is it OK for Christians to wear a crucifix? I think what matters most is how we use the symbol. A cross or crucifix on a necklace should be regarded as more than just a piece of jewelry but as a tool to help us contemplate Christ's suffering and God's love for us.

During his homily on Tuesday, Pope Francis also said that to understand the "history of our redemption" we must look at the crucifix. I'd argue that this is why so many Christians have an attachment to the symbol in a tangible form... In addition to this, a crucifix doesn't just become a reminder to the wearer and the Christian community, it also reminds everyone the wearer comes into contact with. Our actions are the greatest way that we can define our identities but our appearance is a factor too, which helps to explain why so many Christians have fought for the right to wear their crosses. Wearing a crucifix can be an intentional act of visual witness.

As the pontiff said on Tuesday, salvation "was not accomplished with a magic wand" and so the wearing of a cross or crucifix shouldn't be viewed as a good luck charm but as a tool to guide us into deeper meditation on how Jesus gave his life for us and what that means. See Francis (2016).

Given the methodology and standards of courts it is not appropriate judicially to ask the commonsense question: if the wearing of the cross serves deeper meditation what is the religious reason for the display at the check in desk during work hours (certainly not the time for deeper meditation). These are only questions in the court of commonsense, but law cannot fully isolate itself from commonsense.

[17]Lawrence v. Texas, 539 U.S. 558, 574 (2003).

behave according to the needs of one's personal identity to the extent this is part of her good life. (No one shall live in conditions one finds sinful or unjust.)

While it sounds like an individualistic approach, it is often the case that identity demands originate from group identity and the individual's choice is to adhere or not to such a collective identity (or identities). But again, the main concern of a group is to find a set of attractive markers which enable cooperation within the group and with other groups (or rejection of co-operation with the outgroup). To what extent identity concerns are legitimate or necessary for a group and the individual in an uncertain multicultural and changing environment is not the concern of this paper: what this paper considers is what happens when concerns of identity prevail as central at the collective and individual level, in the context of freedom of religion. It seems that not much good happens as such an approach generates a high level of conflicts and domination where this could be avoided. This is not surprising as religious identity (like some other forms of single agenda identities) tends to "essentialize", i.e. a believer is perceived by the outside world and by herself as being an adherent to the religion in an all-encompassing way and nothing more: all aspects of her life are framed in the religious essence: she is not a mother or a woman or a trade unionist, but (at best) a Muslim or Christian mother, woman and trade unionist. Believers tend to essentialize their beliefs. This is certainly the position of only the minority among believers, but some people in that minority use law to reify and extend that essentialist position. Religious people claim the right to live in the world according to the precepts of the religion (as they see it) because this is *the authentic* life.

This is reciprocated by social prejudice in the growing essentialist treatment of religious people (the 'Muslim' in Europe, but also the 'Christian' in Europe (Christian as autochthonous being, with a *Leitkultur*; or the 'Djaur' in the land of Islam, etc.)).

One possible consequence of the replacement of the freedom to manifest with religious identity protection is that the scope of protection is extended (and perhaps diluted), although the Convention, like other international human rights instruments lists the specific form of protected manifestation ("to manifest ... his religion or belief, *in* worship, teaching, practice and observance"—9 § (1)). Such extension results in more and more conflicts with other rights. It is not the manifestation of the religion as described in four distinct activities in the Convention but religion driven *conduct* in public (and to some extent private life, controlled by public concerns, like the best interest of the child) that results from religious identity that will affect the undeniable rights of third parties. *Hobby Lobby* serves as illustration here: the corporation (in fact the owners) consider an act that they held to be against their religious beliefs is having a restrictive impact on the reproductive rights of their employees. The conduct in case (not to contribute to a government scheme) is a public conduct that applies to all under the general law and not a matter of manifestation of religion nor an act that is prohibited by religion, except that the Supreme Court is of the view that the contribution forces the owners of the corporation to engage in conduct that seriously violates their sincere religious belief that life begins at conception.[18] In this perspective this is a matter of freedom of conscience as it imposes a duty that is contrary to an allegedly imperative religious commands on what is right and wrong (once again: not a conduct demanded nor prohibited, as it only facilitates evil conduct of *others*). Even assuming that abortion is a sin, it is not clear that it is imperative not to enable it indirectly, given also that what is enabled is lawful and it is based on the constitutional reproductive right. The refusal to pay the contribution was a matter of the personal construction of the religious identity of the person. The refusal to contribute did not concern one's own act, it is not like the situation of a physician required to perform an abortion contrary to the dictates of his religion. In an alternative reading: if in *Hobby Lobby* the personal choice of the Greens (the owners) is accepted, the sphere of manifesting religion can be extended to all social activity in the public sphere.[19]

The consequence of the acceptance of extended religious demands in public life is that conflicts are generated that are hard to negotiate as the issues are formulated as rights issues which are intended to act as trumps.

It is noteworthy that in the Ladele/wedding cake scenarios the counterclaim is also identity based—hence the intractability. The refusal of Ms. Ladele to participate in the registration of civil partnership for same sex partners did not result in any denial of service as other civil servants provided the service; the prospective couples were not even aware of the arrangement. The objection came from gay colleagues who complained that they "felt victimized". In Ms. Ladele's case the authorities applied a "Dignity for All" policy, meaning a policy of non-discrimination that required that "staff and customers be treated with dignity." The Court of Appeal agreed: "Ms. Ladele's refusal was causing offence to at least two of her gay colleagues; Ms. Ladele's objection was based on her view of marriage, which was not a core part of her religion[20]; and Islington's requirement in no way prevented her from worshipping as she wished." (Ladele v London Borough of Islington [2009] EWCA Civ 1357 quoted after Eweida § 29). The Court of Appeal's concept limits freedom of manifestation to worship. Indeed, it was only the possibility to live according to one's own (religion motivated) idea of good life *within a government activity* that was affected. For a "separationist" (religion pertains to the inviolable private sphere) her claim makes no sense: once the religious is private it has no place

---

[18]Even assuming that free exercise is a special right it remains somewhat puzzling that conduct outside worship can be determined by religion. After all, there are so many obligations imposed on the citizen of a liberal democracy that are contrary to deeply held personal and collective beliefs. The message is that one can live in the state according to her religious assumptions about the good life, but that does not apply to other beliefs. Equal liberty means, however, that all people are entitled to live according to the personally chosen life plan as long as this is compatible with similar rights of others (and in realities of constitutional law: as long as it is compatible with communal goals and interests).

[19]United States v. Lee, 455 U. S. 252, which upheld the payment of Social Security taxes despite an employer's religious objection. (Of course, the majority is keen to show that this is not a tax case.).

[20]As shown below, I have some sympathy for a judicial review of the relevance of a belief for a religion but in this case the Court of Appeal states its view on the matter without evidence or a standard of what is a core part of a religion.

in the neutral world of the public, especially that part of the public that falls within state activities of authority. For the religious mind with an all-encompassing world view this separation makes no sense (except for those, who, like the Amish prefer total withdrawal). The Court of Appeal (and the borough of Islington) seems to stand for the separationist perspective and the impact on conscience on everyday behavior is left out. But it is relevant that in all the sensitivity cases the problem is construed as a matter of emotions (and it is here that the dignity as identity perspective becomes problematic): the homosexual colleagues sense of offense, a matter of pure identity was construed as a right to non-discrimination against the freedom of manifestation (and arguably against the often unmentioned conscience). For the parties the issue is: whose identity (as a set of feelings) is more important in the eyes of the authority of the law.

We got to a perfect identity conflict. Ms. Ladele perceived her right as a matter of identity: the case was not about worship but a secular conduct which she turned into a matter of expression of religious beliefs or conscience. Her colleagues took this as an offence to their identity.[21] But once again same sex couples partnership rights were not affected beyond their sense of pride.

Instead of searching for reasonable accommodation, the Court reached its conclusion relying on the standard methodological flaw that currently undermines its freedom of religion protection (and rights protection in general). The Court found that this is a case of wide margin of appreciation as it came "to striking a balance between competing Convention rights." But there were no competing Convention rights present, as the right of others was in reality the dignitarian offense to the sensitivity of her homosexual colleagues. (On dignitarian harm, see below). Nothing in the case indicated that the employment of anti-gay religious persons actually violates the right of same sex couples not to be discriminated (which may be construed as a convention right if non-discrimination is a right). The toleration of Ms. Ladele's employment, especially in a purely clerical position cannot be held as official endorsement by Islington of anti-gay discrimination nor was there a risk that discrimination might occur. The religious conduct may be an offence even to the imaginary identity of a collective as in S.A.S, where French identity (based allegedly on the Fraternity of living together) was competing with religious identity. Here again the domestic status quo survived by the sheer deferential logic of the margin of appreciation.[22]

But identity may also give religious claims the force to prevail against otherwise legitimate limitations, in situations where accommodation is possible, as it happened in *Eweida* where the applicant was offered a back office job with equal conditions which she refused in order to be able to demonstrate (manifest) her religion as her

---

[21]The complaint came from colleagues who felt victimized but the ECtHR discussed it as a discrimination of same sex couples.

[22]By the survival of the status quo I mean that "Decisions made on the grounds of margin of appreciation are decisions that favour majority narratives of church–state relations." See Adrian (2017).

identity (there was no impact on religious exercise) in disregard of alleged offense to the airplane customers.

The consequence of allowing identity concerns to prevail is legal inconsistency that is open to criticism in terms of identity preference. As some commentators observed, *Eweida* is in conflict with *S.A.S.*[23] More importantly, the identity driven understanding of manifestation of religion results in aggravating social conflicts. Reasonable accommodation becomes more difficult (as the state insists on a specific public identity and because the issues are formulated as winner takes all games) while a dignity enhanced religious identity right runs the risk of imposing antagonistic duties on third parties creating further tension.

4 Where All Conduct (Dictated by Identity) Can Be "Manifestation of Religion" the Potential for Conflict Further Increases. What Constitutes "Manifestation"?

In 2013 in *Eweida* the applicant's "insistence on wearing a cross visibly at work was motivated by her desire to bear witness to her Christian faith" was sufficient for the Court to classify it as protected manifestation, without testing whether it was a matter of worship, teaching, practice and observance.[24] It does not appear to be any of these, but it is certainly a manifestation of the person's identity. Likewise, wearing a headscarf is not required by a specific religious command: it expresses what the applicant claims to be, without engaging in religious activity. In 2014 in *S.A.S. v. France*, the Grand Chamber took the wearing of the burqa in public to be a personal choice for reasons related to beliefs to be protected under Article 8 and 9.[25] In 2015 in *Ebrahimian* the Court found that wearing a headscarf is the "undisputed expression of [applicant's] adherence to the Muslim faith."[26] It is in the identity context that public expression of adherence is crucial but display of adherence is ancillary for worship. In the identity perspective it is not the prohibition to faithfulness to religious tenets that matters (observance or practice, or teaching); instead the

---

[23]See Odusote (2018). The discrepancy with Ebrahimian v. France (App. no. 64846/11), Eur. Ct. Hum. Rts., Judgment of November 26, 2015, is even more pronounced: to wear a crucifix in a position of superiority (even if in private employment) is protected, while the headscarf on an assistant in a public hospital (a public employment) even if knowingly accepted from the day of employing her, is not protected. It is interesting that both in *Ebrahimian* and *Ladele* the ECtHR is accepting a presumption without the showing of actual harmful effect that toleration of religious manifestation in public office is the expression of official public policy.

[24]Eweida and Others v. The United Kingdom, (App. nos. 48420/10, 59842/10, 51671/10 and 36516/10), Eur. Ct. Hum. Rts., Judgment of 15 January 2013 para. 89.

[25]S.A.S. v. France (App. no. 43835/11), Eur. Ct. Hum. Rts., Judgment of July 1, 2014. para 106.

[26]Ebrahimian v. France (App. no. 64846/11), Eur. Ct. Hum. Rts., Judgment of November 26, 2015 para. 47. Likewise Dakir v. Belgium, (App. no. 4619/12), Eur. Ct. Hr. Rts., Judgment of July 11, 2017, para. 47 (joint application of Articles 8 and 9).

right to *unconditional display* of adherence or belonging, a matter of identity is at stake.

Identity in general and religious identity, in particular are notoriously difficult concepts to define, even for purposes of litigation.[27] Religious identity is as much about the sense of one's authentic self as about the terms of belonging to various communities, to one's own faith community and also to the larger political community. In sheer legal terms, the identity of believers may be expressed through various protected manifestations of religious liberty (as well as through other fundamental rights, such as freedom of expression[28] or private life[29]). Yet, as even this brief account suggests, it is not synonymous with these legal claims. Its elevation to a "core" freedom of religion right may go not only against the original intent behind the protection of freedom of religion, but—more importantly—it privileges religious identity vis-á-vis other forms of identity that is related to non-religious conscience. As such, it creates new hierarchies and generates new social conflicts. As a minimum, the Court should become conscious of this shift from religious liberty to religious identity claims and acknowledge that certain aspects of identity claims fall outside the originally envisioned forms of religious manifestation that Article 9 was meant to protect.

What made such shift towards an identity related subjective definition of conduct as religious manifestation possible? It is intimately related to the reluctance of judges to determine what is religion and in particular what is religious conduct or manifestation.

Even where it is admitted that a religious manifestation (in the US terminology: free exercise) claim follows from an applicant's *own* religious beliefs and is not required by an authoritative religious text or religious doctrine, the Court will accept it as a matter of religious belief, so long as it is held sincerely.[30]

The German Constitutional Court is somewhat more concerned about the subjective determination of religion dictated imperatives: "When assessing what qualifies as an act of practicing a religion or an ideological belief in a given case, one must not disregard what conception the religious or ideological communities concerned, and the individual holder of the fundamental right, have of themselves. However, this does not mean that all conduct by a person must be viewed as an expression of freedom of faith in the same way that the person views it subjectively."[31]

---

[27]For the key premises see Minow (1991); For an informed recent account focusing on religious identity see Lucas (2017) esp. 67–77 and Mancini and Rosenfeld (2018).

[28]Ahmet Arslan and others v. Turkey, (App. no. 41135/98), Eur. Ct. Hum. Rts., Judgment of February 23, 2010.

[29]S.A.S. v. France (App. no. 43835/11), Eur. Ct. Hum. Rts., Judgment of July 1, 2014. para 106.

[30]The recognition of subjective qualification of manifestations religious on the basis of sincerity and consistency of belief represents a major breakthrough for the protection of free exercise as it makes more likely that minority and non-traditional religions and non-religious beliefs will be protected.

[31]German Federal Constitutional Court (Bundesverfassungsgericht) 1 BvR 471/10 (Order of the First Senate of 27 January 2015); 10 para 86.

Of course, a less permissive understanding of manifestation, in line with the applicable text is always possible. Earlier case-law of the Court has indicated that freedom of religion does not protect each and every act or form of behaviour motivated or inspired by religion or belief. Behaviour which was motivated or inspired by religion or belief, but which was not an act of practice of a religion in a generally recognized form, fell outside the protection of Article 9 in a number of cases. Likewise, in Canada according to the seminal *Big M Mart* case: "the right to manifest religious belief [means] by worship and practice or by teaching and dissemination."[32]

The standard reasons for such deferentialism to personal beliefs are partly epistemological (courts are not in the position to know) but primarily related to state neutrality. As the Canadian Supreme Court has formulated it: the State is in no position to be, nor should it become, the arbiter of religious dogma.[33] In one formulation of the neutrality concern: "Secular judicial determinations of theological or religious disputes, or of contentious matters of religious doctrine, unjustifiably entangle the court in the affairs of religion."[34]

The courts of the neutral state are expected not to determine what religious truth is and abstain from reviewing what is and is not dictated by religion, fearing that they interfere in matters of religion. But such deferentialism comes at a price; see the excessive deference to church autonomy or pastoral privilege in *Hosanna-Tabor.*[35] Moreover, it is one thing to accept a deferential position on matters of what religious doctrines are and another one to accept the conclusions of some lay persons that a specific behavior (as the conclude) follows inevitably or even possibly from his understanding of the religion.

In *Eweida* (as in other cases) the ECtHR has refused to consider the centrality of the belief or practice for religion although the applicant herself admitted "that wearing the crucifix was a sign of her commitment to her faith" (§ 12) and the Employment Tribunal found that "the visible wearing of a cross was not a mandatory requirement of the Christian faith but Ms. Eweida's personal choice" (§ 14) Note once again the identity based understanding: signaling of commitment to religion is manifestation of religion. (For the ECtHR it did not matter that there was no evidence on record of this being an accepted practice in the religious community or by its authoritative leaders; sincerity, consistency and nexus were the only considerations). Likewise, in *S.A.S.* the applicant, by her own admission was not under a religious obligation to wear the burqa (and she had it upon herself depending on her mood). The judicial deference to the subjective understanding of the

---

[32]R. v. Big M Drug Mart Ltd., [1985] 1 S.C.R. 295, para.94.

[33]It does not require a decision on religious dogma (even less of its truth) that the claim of an individual is not within any recognized dogma.

[34]Syndicat Northcrest v. Amselem, [2004] 2 S.C.R. 551, para. 50, per Iacobucci J.

[35]Hosanna-Tabor Evangelical Lutheran Church and School v. Equal Employment Opportunity Commission, 565 U.S. 171 (2012).

commands of sincere (and central) beliefs may appear to be friendly to religious liberty, yet, it runs the risk of making "every citizen to become a law unto himself."[36]

For the Court, at least in some cases the "manifestation" of religion or belief within the meaning of Article 9 is not limited to acts of worship or devotion which form part of the practice of a religion or belief "in a generally recognised form".[37] Provided a sufficiently close and direct nexus between the act and the underlying belief exists, the Court will accept the act as religious manifestation. It is up to the person, to create the nexus, which as long as it is reasonably connected.

This should not be the end of the review. The Canadian Supreme Court will likewise inquire into the sincerity of belief that has a nexus with religion, and, if so, whether there is an interference with those beliefs that is more than trivial or insubstantial.[38]

5 Conscience Wars Facilitated by Identity Based Freedom of Religion

So far, I have discussed some of the problematic issues of legal doctrine reflected in conflicting judicial approaches to freedom of religious manifestation/free exercise of religion. Beyond legal doctrine, the hotly debated 'sensitivity' cases offer a glimpse into the cultural and legal state of liberal democracies through the analysis of the microcosm of refusal to celebrate same sex marriage and similar conflicts. These were (increasingly) discussed as fundamental problems of freedom of conscience and manifestation of religion by political movement activists and in religious organizations driven to politicking. In identity politics these issues are often construed as discriminatory acts, and all interested parties claim that they are victims of bigoted discrimination. From and external perspective, however, these are conflicts about minimal socially irrelevant per se issues; narcissism is pitted against

---

[36]Justice Scalia, in a different sense, Employment Division v. Smith, 494 U.S. 872, 879 (1990).

[37]In *Eweida* the UK Government argued unsuccessfully that manifestation is an "act of practice of a religion in a generally recognised form."

[38]See Syndicat Northcrest v. Amselem, [2004] 2 SCR 551, at paras 56–59.

As to impact, the Canadian Supreme Court held the not only direct coercion will raise serious constitutional concerns and "incidental effects" of a decision, can be "so great that they effectively deprive the adherent of a meaningful choice", rendering the impact of the limit "very serious". Alberta v. Hutterian Brethren of Wilson Colony, [2009] 2 SCR 567, para 94. Using this approach one can ask the following question in the spirit of tolerance (aiming at optimal accommodation): Would the compromise offered to Ms. Ladele to continue to work without participating in marriage celebrations or doing other, purely clerical work deprive her of a meaningful choice as to her religion or professional aspirations? Would Jack the baker be professionally or religiously deprived of a meaningful choice by not engaging in the business of marriage cake making; would the equality of the gay couple and their consumer rights be deprived of a meaningful choice in case they have to shop five blocks away even if they have to be aware that some religious people consider their lawful activity sinful?

narcissism. The microcosm of narcissism should serve as eye opener in understanding the nature of politics in and culture of liberal societies.

The culture of narcissistic identity enforcement resulted in a judicial approach to the 'sensitivity' cases[39] and in the dress code wars that seems to disregard tolerance, a guiding principle in the Canadian cases which are animated by the needs of a multicultural society, resulting in a strongly accommodationist position.

To some extent the absence of the tolerance perspective is surprising. After all, Europe is multicultural or at least many of its national societies are pluralistic.[40] Tolerant democracy is a judicially recognized and applied consideration and value in the case law of the ECtHR; Ms. Eweida's manifestation of religion was turned into a superior right, among others in the name of tolerance.[41] The protection of the manifestation is "a fundamental right: because a healthy democratic society needs to tolerate and sustain pluralism and diversity; but also because of the value to an individual who has made religion a central tenet of his or her life to be able to communicate that belief to others."[42] (§ 94).

If tolerance and social pluralism (as a fact that requires special consideration for maintaining social order on the basis of equal respect to all) is taken seriously, as it is promised, the religious and identity claims shall not be allowed to continue to blow out reasonable considerations.

5.1 Broadening Conscience

Is the characterization of Ladele's claim (or the claim of the Greens, or Jack the baker) as an issue of freedom of conscience correct? Are Ms. Ladele's or the Greens' (the Hobby Lobby controlling stockholders) complaints really about 'conscience' from a judicially tractable perspective? The courts are satisfied that this is a matter of sincerity and the US Supreme Court and the ECtHR are not willing to address the religious nature of the claim because of their 'fear of interference' into what is the domain of religion. The justification most often given is state neutrality, esp. *vis a vis* conscience.

The term conscience is used sometimes in an indiscriminate manner by the US Supreme Court and other courts, referring to certain instances of free exercise of

---

[39] *Eweida* is the exception.

[40] One could argue that the French position on living together, which is sometimes criticized as expression of anti-Muslim bias is not directed against pluralism in France, only against an extreme form of religious fundamentalism that is contrary to this very open concept of living together with a mutually open attitude towards the different.

[41] Tolerance was a consideration in favor of Ms. Eweida but it did not come up in the context of the admittedly more central conscience claim of Ms. Ladele, although Eweida and Ladele were decided jointly, applying the same general considerations by the same composition.

[42] Once again, see the identity-centered approach: religion is protected because it is a personal choice to communicate what you are.

religion. However, conscience is clearly distinguished in the Convention and other international instruments.

What conscience may entail in a philosophical, practical or legal sense is seldom discussed by judges, and most often it is confused with a kind of religious manifestation.[43] This judicial neglect disregards that conscience had historically opposite meanings, and those meanings continue to coexist.[44] Conscience as a superior consideration was successful in law where the claim had not direct impact on third party rights (see conscientious objectors in the army). Conscience is specific because it has more commanding power and it knows no grounds of restriction in the Convention. Conscience is recognized as a special category in the Universal Declaration and the European and Inter-American Conventions. It was singled out in Madison's draft to the Bill of Rights but it does not figure in the First Amendment. Early state constitutions were concerned about it and it is recognized by the Supreme Court. Conscience is given a very preferential treatment in law (as it is understood to compel exceptions to binding state law, and not only to accommodate wherever reasonable). Without a clear understanding of what makes it special, less meritorious claims will receive preferential treatment that would be appropriate only for genuine conscientious objection.

Moral philosophers argue that "conscience is typically a *morally neutral* concept. Appealing to conscience does not usually add anything to the moral justification of any particular conduct or principle. ... [A]ppeals to conscience ... might ground political reasons for respecting individuals' moral beliefs, such as for example tolerance or pluralism." (Giubilini 2016) The recognition of conscience as a supreme but politically and legally ambiguous and suspect claim follows in some context from religious arguments, or, in a secular world, from tolerance and public peace: the extreme intensity of some conscience claims calls for respect or caution: given the resoluteness of the person it could result in spectacular disobedience that is detrimental to social order, or its legitimacy.[45] Conscience claims are more powerful were they refer to otherwise legitimate (generally accepted) moral rules. Even socially minoritarian positions receive such recognition once they can be presented as religious, given the blanket respect granted to religion (especially if the religious group behind the religion is respected or politically influential). (What if Ms. Ladele, the Greens, Jack the baker, etc. refuse to perform their respective service? Compare their disobedience to Gandhi and you have the answer.)

Conscience implies the idea that one cannot be constrained by the state to act in *self-regarding matters* against the person's innermost convictions, in violation of the essence of a self-determined life plan. This prohibition of coercion originates from state attitudes to religion where the reference to conscience meant that one cannot be

---

[43]The Nebojša Vučinić—Vincent de Gaetano dissent are keen to remove this religious aspect.

[44]See Saada and Antaki (2018) and Schlink (2018).

[45]To withdraw the licence of conscientiously homophobic bakers would not cause much social harm but the mobilization that results from the construction of martyrdom among like-minded persons may cause social problems.

forced to change one's religion (*forced conversion*); beyond that, for example in the days of Christian persecution in Ancient Rome, individual conscience had no voice, and in all other matters the Christian shall be obedient to the law. The scope of the sphere where conscience dictates can be held relevant by the state (and the person) was extended in the modern liberal state: the liberal state is expected not to constrain action contrary to one's "conscience". The modern legal concern with conscience emerged in this specific context, namely in matters of forced conversion. Here and in some other instances (military service) there is a history and actual possibility of very serious negative consequences or punishment for a self-regarding ethical position (most often dictated by religious commitment as all-encompassing life plan) that results in disobedience. Conscientious objection to military service is the seminal example. A person who makes a convincing conscience claim expresses a readiness to accept the consequences of her moral choice (a choice between good and evil). A conscience claim in order to be of weight will make clear the readiness to endure serious sanctions. Jehovah's Witnesses know that they will go to jail. Or at least, in a belief friendly approach, the person claiming conscientious objection has to show that disregard of the dictate of conscience will have very serious consequences to here (e.g. damnation, endless moral remorse).

Conscience driven action is a potential challenge to social order because the person claims the right to be *law to himself*. It disregards general norms of the society in a solipsistic manner. This is what Bernhard Schlink calls the anarchism of conscience (conscience is anarchic in nature): an anarchism that is fundamentally antithetical to social order.

I hasten to add that while conscience is a 'scandal' to public order based on general laws, there is also social value and virtue in the conscience driven anarchism of Thoreau and many other dissenters and martyrs. But in a relatively decent liberal society conscience claims shall be exceptional and not trivial as in the 'sensitivity' cases. I find conscience claims more convincing where, even if they are religious in origin, reflect an ethical conflict that *any* person may confront. For example, killing is generally prohibited and morally generally condemned in an ordered society, therefore killing in a war remains contrary to this fundamental precept, and for that reason a matter of ethical conflict.

In evaluating the force of conscience as objection the nature of the coercion is of relevance: running the risk of serious punishment indicates the intensity (importance) of the moral conviction. Ms. Ladele was told originally that she could continue her employment as long as she registers civil partnerships (but not same sex marriage). This is not the same as serving jail time in Turkish or Greek military prisons. In *Masterpiece* to undergo a training for the 'refusnik' baker is not the same as losing the licence, or be subject to serious fine or prison). A minimal sacrifice even in matters claimed to be matters of conscience are not a proof that the person simply cannot live contrary to one's life plan: the burden that one suffers for living according to her conscience is not demanding. To accept the argument that refusal of producing a wedding cake for gay marriage is in the same category as refusal to serve in the army which runs the risk of taking the life of others is simply the trivialization of conscience and disregards what conscientious objection was historically: it was about forced conversion in a world where it was believed that religion is all encompassing for a human being.

The danger of trivialization and hence the possibility to use litigation to promote religious and other identity claims results from the unwillingness of judges to apply more objective and demanding standards as to what is a religious command or what is a legitimate claim under conscience.

5.2   Tolerance

While the ECtHR does not discuss toleration as a state duty in the manifestation cases, the state attitude is dealt under pluralism and neutrality. As mentioned, the State has "to ensure mutual tolerance between opposing groups (see, among other authorities, *Leyla Şahin*,[46] § 107). Accordingly, the role of the authorities in such circumstances is not to remove the cause of tension by eliminating pluralism, but to ensure that the competing groups tolerate each other (see *Serif v. Greece*, no. 38178/ 97, § 53, ECHR 1999-IX; see also *Leyla Şahin*, cited above, § 107) (*S.A.S. v. France*, § 127). Moreover, opinions "that offend, shock or disturb the State or any sector of the population" are protected, because "[s]uch are the demands of that pluralism, tolerance and broadmindedness without which there is no 'democratic society'." (Handyside v. The United Kingdom[47] § 49).

Many courts would like to forget that religion as a historical phenomenon contains many offensive positions and, if for no other reason they cannot expect a different treatment by outsiders. If 'those who choose to exercise the freedom to manifest their religion . . . cannot reasonably expect to be exempt from all criticism. They must tolerate and accept the denial by others of their religious beliefs and even the propagation by others of doctrines hostile to their faith' (*Otto Preminger*)[48] it would be simply unfair to claim that other identities (as "rights") even if minority identities or identities of persecuted or segregated groups (I deliberately avoid the term "vulnerable") are exempt of the same treatment (unless, like in the case of religion there is actual harm or danger of social violence).

In this respect religious views (too) have to tolerate offense. But are others expected to tolerate (alleged) offence coming from religious people? (In the cake cases the bakers were considered disrespectful and discriminatory). The idea of a leveled playing field indicates that the answer should be affirmative, but here the offensive opinion was expressed by conduct.

The religious conduct or view is construed in the 'sensitivity' cases as discrimination and the expressions of disrespect have a negative effect on self-respect

---

[46]Leyla Şahin v. Turkey (App. no. 44774/98) Eur. Ct. Hum. Rts., Judgment of November10, 2005.

[47]Handyside v. The United Kingdom (App. no. 5493/72) Eur. Ct. Hum. Rts., Judgment of December 7, 1976.

[48]Otto-Preminger Institut v. Austria, (App. no. 13470/87), Eur. Ct. Hum. Rts., September 20, 1994.

(again, an identity concern). Is there harm to third parties due to the intransigent religious behavior? This varies: in *Eweida* the customers of the airline may feel uncomfortable and this may influence negatively business interests of the airline. The harm is hypothetical, moreover, freedom of religion requires that others have to endure its manifestation. Physicians' refusal of abortion is to be accommodated according to French law, as long as a seamless enforcement of the right is provided but not in the case of pharmacists. (This was upheld as to the second category by the ECtHR.[49]) What is the difference between a doctor and a registrar, except that doctors are powerful?

On the other hand, it is rather obvious that there is direct harm to women's constitutionally recognized right in case their access to contraceptives is not covered by insurance paid by the employer. In the *Masterpiece Cakeshop* scenario there is minimal actual harm to a liberty or consumer interest: the gay customer has to go for shopping to another shop a few blocks away. But like in *Ladele*, there is (dignitarian) harm to the self-respect of those gay persons who were denied service or see service denial in a matter that disregards in their view their equality and there is harm to a community interest expressed in non-discrimination.

5.3 Conscience War and Intolerance

In the absence of a proper consideration of toleration as an individual right, the judge is forced to structure social problems in terms of friend-enemy relations. Such framing is contrary to liberalism as toleration. Be that as it may, this is the way how legal and social movements position themselves in the conflicts about the presence of religion in the public sphere at a moment where the most personal, i.e. conscience, together with claims of anti-religious discrimination are used as an argument, first for exceptions favoring religious people and secondly to reorganize public life according to those dictates.

What I find troubling is that a minor conflict around cakes, display of cross on uniform, and the like could become central in the political structure of contemporary Western societies. A sense of personal offense can generate social division and courts are sucked into this maelstrom, instead of throwing out many of the non-meritorious claims (at the first instance, or no significant harm in the Convention). Alternatively, the focus of the judicial interest should be toleration instead of declaring one or the other party a winner. The intolerant shall not be rewarded.

What matters for identity in the contemporary world is *recognition*,[50] which means equal treatment but on the terms of personal or group identity. In this logic the injury in fact is replaced by a *sense* of victimhood. These shifts reflect a cultural change dictated by narcissistic sensitivities that make living together in a tolerant

---

[49]Pichon et Sajous v. France, (App. no. 49853/99) Eur. Ct. Hum. Rts., October 2, 2001.

[50]Misrecognition is not *just* lack of due respect, but "a vital human need" See Taylor (1992), p. 26.

society more and more difficult. The result is culture wars or, in the religion context, a conscience war. It is telling that so far, some apex courts have tried to avoid deciding cases on their merit where both parties relied on very broad conscience claims.[51]

Let's consider once again the grievances and the way these were treated. Ms. Ladele was replaced informally by colleagues and seamless marriage service was provided to gay couples who were not even aware that one of the employees considers their marriage a sin. Two of Ms. Ladele's colleagues (not involved in civil partnership registration) denounced her. Their claim was that they were *"victimized"*. This is the sign of the times we live. The claim was accepted at face value. The state policy, at least in Islington was that equal dignity of all is to be protected, including gay people. After the "scandal" has erupted and action was taken against Ms. Ladele, she was offered the possibility of limiting her duties to register same sex partnerships where there was no ceremony. She refused and complained. Her complaint was that she felt *victimized* and picked on (discriminated) for her views.

Similar intransigence characterized Ms. Eweida. In her case the company's dress code had for some years caused no known problems to any employee including the applicant herself, who from 2004 until May 2006 appears to have worn a cross concealed under her clothing without objection. Suddenly she felt an urge to act in a way causing conflict. Perhaps she was right not to continue to hide her cross; all I am saying is that where tolerance would indicate some self-restraint, the spiral of unmitigated identity claims has pushed people towards demanding unconditional recognition of their choice. In both cases a personal desire referring to religion (on matters which are not central to religion and its exercise, at least according to more authoritative views) are elevated to religious manifestation and efforts of reasonable accommodation are rejected as discriminatory restriction of freedom of religion.

Or consider Ms. Ladele's sincerely held beliefs as a matter of conscience. This reference to conscience is not convincing as the conduct required by the state is simply not as evil as her claim pretends. Ms. Ladele was asked to sign a new job description requiring her to carry out straightforward signings of the civil partnership

---

[51]In *Masterpiece* the US Supreme Court avoided going to the merit of the dilemma and found that there was antireligious animus behind to fine imposed on the believe.

In Lee (Respondent) v Ashers Baking Company Ltd. and others (Appellants) (Northern Ireland) [2018] UKSC 49, the Supreme Court of the United Kingdom framed the issue as one of compelled speech and not a matter of religious manifestation (Evangelical bakers refuse to prepare an icing with the inscription "Support gay marriage".) In a most extraordinary way Lady Hale in her speech commented on *Masterpiece*.

In both cases the topping issue was accepted as artistic expression and expression of views where this could have been simply a matter of exercise of professional duties: in this perception there is no expressive element in the conduct or at least this is not decisive (see the conduct and speech situation of *O'Brien,* United States v. O'Brien, 391 U.S. 367 (1968)), just like a person who prepares a nail to the nuclear bomb does not support, in the eyes of the law the destruction of Hiroshima.

register and administrative work in connection with civil partnerships, but with no requirement to conduct ceremonies.

By the standards of religion and secular logic she was mistakenly led to a position that she will be instrumental to sin and later she was carried away by her assumption that she, as a religious person is victim of discriminatory persecution, just like her gay colleagues who felt being victims of sexual orientation based discrimination. The discrimination would have consisted in the alleged toleration of antigay personal position by a civil servant. The mildly sanctioned views of an employee were elevated to the official position of the municipality. Again, in a manner comparable to the intransigence of Ms. Ladele and Ms. Eweida, the gay colleagues are elevating the feelings of discomfort into humiliation (by whom? by a fellow worker's behavior not addressed to them) and they construe this into a matter of discrimination based on their sexual orientation.

The dissenters in *Ladele* refer to conscience as a matter of choice between evil and good and refusal to do evil. This is a common understanding of conscience, but one that is hardly compatible with an understanding of regulated human conduct in a free society: If this is accepted without qualification there will be little space for general laws as each individual will be law to herself.

The extension of identity protection resulted in sensitivity related claims. For strategic litigators this is a win-win game: if they win, the cause advances, if they lose the group can claim that they are *victims* of state persecution which increases group coherence and mobilizes further resources. The protection of feelings of alleged victims just for being the subject of dislike and contempt (to be told that what they do is sin) functions as heckler's veto. (It is a different matter, if such message of contempt amounts to harassment of identifiable people.).

With the broad understanding of conscience and manifestation of religion, and with an excessively sensitive understanding of identity (including religious, ethnic, racial and sexual identity[52]) identity driven actors are in constant search of evidence of denial of full recognition of their equal status. Everybody is in search of an intransigent position and total victory. But to bake or not to bake—this is certainly not the same dilemma as religious conversion under constraint.[53] Unfortunately, in the conscience war religious manifestation based claims remain antagonistic to other identity claims. In this war identities are in search of situations where they can feel

---

[52]In most of the cases these are unhappy identities: they come out of some kind of negative experience of discrimination and are often related to constructions of those who oppressed a certain group or its members. For example, race is a false concept, imposed upon a select group, and following that categorization is in a sense accepting the badge of inferiority, turned (in some unfortunate situations) into a source of supremacy. It is true, however, that such categorical discrimination continues to have negative effects and it is understandable why the affected continue to search for recognition.

[53]Ironically, in one important historical use of the term 'conscience' it meant to encourage forced conversion which was limited to external acts: after all *in foro interno* one could continue to maintain the original faith, so why not convert to save one's life. But, on the other hand this was an argument *against* forced conversion: constraint resulting in external acts did not produce genuine believers, therefore the whole exercise is futile.

victimized, because in the perverse social culture victimhood has mobilizing force, it becomes the source of superiority, it triggers state protection and even preferential treatment.

5.4   The Solution of Tolerance

The bottom line is that middle of the road solutions dictated by toleration were not considered in the 'sensitivity' cases of the conscience war, although many liberal legal systems aim at tolerance as a rule. For example, the German Constitutional Court has stated: "Resolving the normative tension among these constitutionally protected interests [freedom of faith, the state's educational mandate, duty of ideological and religious neutrality, parents' right to the upbringing of their children and the pupils' negative freedom of faith] in consideration of the principle of tolerance is a task for the democratic legislature, which, within the public process of policy formulation, must seek a compromise that all can reasonably be expected to comply with."[54] The principle of toleration would suggest reasonable accommodation as proposed by Justice Sachs in *Fourie,* regarding registrars in the same sex case.[55] Interestingly, earlier the *Eweida* chamber of the ECtHR was all in favor of tolerance and accommodation.

As Justice Bastarache (dissenting) stated "not merely a balancing of the respective rights of the parties, but a reconciliation of the rights that takes the general interest of the citizens of Quebec into account."[56]

A tolerance based solution should have been attempted in the 'sensitivity' cases. Judges should hold responsible the party who refused this optimal solution or was in the position to offer it but failed to do so. Such review can be smuggled into a proportionality analysis, but accommodation claims can be reasonably settled only where rigid, inflexible and extreme consciousness dictates are discouraged.

Ms. Ladele and company were not impaired in any way in their religious practice; it was an all encompassing life form, with spillover effects on third parties that they insisted upon that made the situation difficult, a difficulty aggravated by the rigidity of the right to non-discrimination and related policy. Ms. Ladele's claims, like the counterclaims of her gay colleagues were made in relation to a non-central matter, at least from the perspective of general community norms. Decisively, Ms. Ladele and Ms. Eweida were not ready to accept accommodation where it was offered to them. (Lack of acceptance of accommodation is an attractive criterion of adjudication for a

---

[54]German Federal Constitutional Court (Bundesverfassungsgericht) 1 BvR 471/10 (Order of the First Senate of 27 January 2015) para 96.

[55]Minister of Home Affairs and Another v Fourie and Another; Lesbian and Gay Equality Project and Others v Minister of Home Affairs and Others, [2005] ZACC 19.

[56]Syndicat Northcrest v Amselem [2004] 2 S.C.R. 551 (the Canadian 'succah on the balcony' case).

tolerance based approach in these conflicts because of the relative clarity of the standard of conduct to be considered).

But the intransigence of the religious manifestation remains only part of the equation and is countered by a similar intransigence by offended groups, arguing that disrespect of their vulnerable situation (*including special* treatment) amounts to discrimination. Note, once again, that both Ms. Ladele and her gay colleagues claimed to be victims of discrimination. Earlier there was a moment of collegial, informal accommodation, when colleagues were ready to replace Ms. Ladele who has accepted that solution. It was at this point the intransigence intervened. It was bad lack for Ms. Ladele that in the ECtHR case law discrimination on the basis of religion is not considered unequivocally as one where only the most stringent reasons serve as justification, while sexual orientation is.

But there is a further point: in *Ladele* the Chamber's majority considered her claim a matter of religious manifestation while the minority argued that it concerns conscience.[57] A more demanding concept of conscience claim would settle the case without bringing in tolerance considerations. To apply the heavy artillery of conscience in the 'sensitivity' cases is a sign of the banalization of rights that resulted in the current rights inflation. It is all about display of identity. Eweida's interest was to make others aware that she is a good Christian: she wanted to be recognized as Christian by displaying a cross even when she was primarily a stewardess in a private business. One can rightly ask the question: why is the display of a religious identity more protected than the display of any other identity? Would the case be different if she were to display an unconventional sexual identity?

Once again, a free ordered society cannot leave, as a matter of principle, the determination of evil to the individual where the resulting conduct seriously burdens third parties. The law of a free society grants exceptions to dictates of conscience, but these, as exceptions are narrowly construed. As exceptions there ought to be a serious scrutiny of the belief called conscience, and the resulting conduct must be compelling to the person regarding central issues of her life plan, and finally, the exceptional behavior's consequences cannot be fatal for social order in the case and where the behavior would become general.

Beyond the need for tolerance, especially in a pluralistic democracy, one of the reasons of this tolerant attitude of the state is epistemological. The state (its authorities) cannot take for granted, especially in view of the absolute commitment of the individual that its position, especially in matters of morals is right. The conscience exception is a tribute to the recognition of state fallibility. Of course for the toleration of anarchism we need and the self-confident power of the state that it can afford such exceptional anarchism.

---

[57]The case has further aspects which complicate the matter. Ms. Ladele was a civil servant with special obligations of loyalty but it is arguable that this did not encompass loyalty to whatever policies the state will follow in the future, as she was employed as registrar before gays were allowed to have their civil partnership registered.

6 Conclusion

Identity as dignity and the dignity of identity are constitutionally protected in many legal systems.[58] But it can be detrimental to ordered liberty if the right to live according to one's identity is replacing freedom of religious manifestation. Identity as essentialism can undermine both religious communities and social peace among religious and other (non-religion based) identity-centered communities.

From a mainstream liberal constitutional perspective there is nothing wrong with identity concerns; after all self-definition is a central matter of liberty and the protection of identity as self-development[59] may fit well into privacy protection. However, "It may also interfere with proper operation of the law, which should turn not on individualized conceptions of identity, but on the values and other principles by which we as a society choose to structure legal relationships between individuals and the state" (Lucas 2017).

The conceptual shortcomings in the understanding of the scope of religious freedoms have contributed to conscience wars and courts became instruments of such wars. Toleration can be the solution. Liberal toleration does not mean that religious and other idiosyncrasies should be allowed to destroy society as a community or a place of interaction on equal footing of different communities. We should not see compelled opinion *a la Barnette*[60] in every commercial activity. Flag salute expresses a dominant opinion of the state, and the children had no other way to understand it. Baking a cake, even if understood as celebratory by the customer, does not necessarily require celebration or agreement by the baker, and it is certainly not compelled agreement, unless we allow the baker to construe his secular world (professional activity) as fully religious, where every loaf is a matter of salvation and damnation and allow him to impose this worldview on the behavior of others. It is one of the perversions of the claim to recognition (and the effort of religious groups and religions to reconquest the public sphere by gaining full recognition) that purely professional activities are turned into politically, morally or religiously relevant acts. Here, exceptionally, the NRA slogan makes sense: it is not the gun that kills but the gunman. It is not the cake that celebrates. Nor the baker. Let others do their celebration. On the other hand, to denounce dislike as an act of anti-discrimination (and allow or require public authorities to take this seriously and impose serious sanctions) is also non-sensical.

Once again, taking all these complaints seriously is only breeding and reinforcing excessive sensitivities, and it legitimizes identity politics and narcissism. On both sides.

---

[58]"The Constitution promises liberty to all within its reach, a liberty that includes certain specific rights that allow persons, within a lawful realm, to define and express their identity." Obergefell v. Hodges, 135 S.Ct.2584, 2593(2015) at 2597.

[59]The problem is that fixed, imposed identities are an obstacle of self-development which presupposes self-criticism.

[60]West Virginia State Board of Education v. Barnette, 319 U.S. 624 (1943).

The conscience war is to be prevented, or diffused with techniques of tolerance including accommodation.

References

Adrian, M. (2017). The principled slope: Religious freedom and the European Court of Human Rights. *Religion, State and Society, 45*(3–4), 174–185.

Francis, A. (2016, March 22). Should Christians Wear a Crucifix? *Christian Today*.

Giubilini, A. (2016). Conscience. In E. N. Zalta (Ed.), *The Stanford Encyclopedia of Philosophy*. Retrieved April 4, 2019, from https://plato.stanford.edu/archives/win2016/entries/conscience

Leiter, B. (2013). *Why tolerate religion?* Princeton, NJ: Princeton University Press.

Lucas, L. S. (2017). The free exercise of religious identity. *UCLA Law Review, 64*, 54–115.

Mancini, S., & Rosenfeld, M. (Eds.). (2018). *The conscience wars. Rethinking the balance between religion, identity and equality*. Cambridge: Cambridge University Press.

Minow, M. (1991). Identities. *Yale Journal of Law and the Humanities, 3*, 1.

Odusote, A. (2018). The limits of law in resolving religions conflicts: Perspectives from Nigeria and beyond. In B. D. Lundy, A. G. Adebayo, & S. W. Hayes (Eds.), *Atone: Religion, conflict, and reconciliation* (pp. 57–78). Lanham, MD: Lexington Books.

Report of the United Nations Special Rapporteur of 22 December 2011 on Freedom of Religion or Belief, no. A/HRC/19/60.

Saada, J., & Antaki, M. (2018). Conscience and its claims. A philosophical history of conscientious objection. In S. Mancini & M. Rosenfeld (Eds.), *The conscience wars. Rethinking the balance between religion, identity and equality* (pp. 23–57). Cambridge: Cambridge University Press.

Schlink, B. (2018). Conscientious objections. In S. Mancini & M. Rosenfeld (Eds.), *The conscience wars. Rethinking the balance between religion, identity and equality* (pp. 102–108). Cambridge: Cambridge University Press.

Taylor, C. (1992). The politics of recognition. In A. Gutmann (Ed.), *Multiculturalism: Examining the politics of recognition* (pp. 25–73). Princeton, NJ: Princeton University Press.

The Popular Sovereignty and Its Constitutional Limits: The European Court of Human Rights as the Last Resto for Avoiding the Banality of the Evil

Emilio Santoro

Contents

The Diciotti case is a test of constitutionalism itself, that is the legal civilisation built after the tragedies of the first half of the twentieth century. Is the Italian Senate's assessment free from legal constraints or, in case the authorisation to prosecute is denied, there will be "a judge in Berlin"?

Over the last few months the Italian debate (particularly in the Italian left wing) looks focused on the problem of obeying unjust laws. Disobedience to unjust laws has been evoked in connection with the criminal prosecution of mayor Mimmo Lucano, which undermined the immigrant reception system in Riace, and then with the "Salvini law", when mayors have been called upon to ignore the law's provisions on the registration of asylum seekers. In sum, we seem to have come back to the age of Sophocles's *Antigone*, who opposed the moral law and disobedience to the law of Creon the tyrant. Sophocles has her say: "I did not think that your decrees were of such weight that they could countermand the laws unfailing and unwritten of the gods, and you a mortal only and a man. The laws divine are not for the now, nor yet for yesterday, but live forever and their origins are mysteries to men".

This approach to the problem seems to forget that we live no longer in ancient Thebes but in a constitutional state. Rigid constitutions were devised after World War II precisely to solve the problem that Hannah Arendt called of "the banality of evil": the idea that civil servants should obey the law as such, that they have a duty to apply the law regardless of its content. The cornerstone of constitutionalism, in particular of Italian constitutionalism, is the idea that the judge should not be simply the mouth of the law, of Creon, not even of a law expressing the will of the sovereign

Emilio Santoro is Professor at University of Florence.

E. Santoro (✉)
University of Florence, Florence, Italy
e-mail: Emilio.santoro@unifi.it

© Springer Nature Switzerland AG 2019
P. Pinto de Albuquerque, K. Wojtyczek (eds.), *Judicial Power in a Globalized World*, https://doi.org/10.1007/978-3-030-20744-1_31

people, as legal Enlightenment wanted. A judge should be, first and foremost, the judge of the law. Her first duty is to assess whether a law complies with the Constitution and, if she doubts that it is not, to refer the issue to the Constitutional court. The problem is not one of comparing the positive law, expression of the people's will, against the moral law, Antigone's "laws unfailing and unwritten of the gods". It is one of the law's constitutional legitimacy: to put it with Kelsen, an unconstitutional law is only a temporary, apparent law. As law school freshmen learn, a ruling of unconstitutionality removes a law since the time it was passed: it is effective *ex tunc*, in lawyers' Latin phrase.

Constitutionalism rests on a delicate balance expressed in the oxymoron of article one of the Italian constitution: "Italy is a democratic Republic established on labour. Sovereignty belongs to the people, that exerts it in the forms and the limits of the Constitution".

This article states an oxymoron for it reconciles sovereignty and its limits. If we read the creators of the notion of sovereignty, from Bodin to Hobbes and Austin, we see that for them the sovereign has no limits: to borrow lawyers' Latin again, *superiorem non recognoscens*. The sovereign should be he who has no higher rule defining the borders of his power. Instead, the Italian Constitution provides that sovereignty "belongs to the people", but at the same time requires that the latter must exert it within the limits established by the Constitution itself, without this undermining the democratic character of the Republic: article one begins with the proposition that the Italian Republic is democratic.

Article 9, § 3 of the constitutional act no. 1 of 1989, implementing article 96 of the Constitution, provides that the House of Parliament of which a people's representative is a member, or the Senate if a government member is not a member of Parliament, "may, by a vote of the majority of its members, deny the authorisation to prosecute if it deems, with an unchallengeable assessment, that the person being prosecuted acted to protect a constitutionally relevant interest of the state, or to pursue a prominent public interest in the exercise of the government's functions".

What makes the case of the sequestration of one hundred seventy seven people on board of the Diciotti ship an *experimentum crucis* on constitutionalism and its health is that not only the home secretary, Salvini, but the whole government did not deny that they detained one hundred seventy seven people, possibly (they were not allowed to apply) including asylum seekers, on the military ship with no legal justification. Thus, they did not deny that they had committed an offence of kidnapping, aggravated by their position as government officials. Rather, they chose to argue that the act was legitimated by the principle that the end justifies the means. The home secretary and the government chose to argue that they deliberately proceeded to the sequestration and that the latter, though with no legal justification, was necessary "to protect a constitutionally relevant interest of the state, or to pursue a prominent public interest".

This choice dramatically questions the meaning and limitations of constitutional government: may a government decide not to respect a basic right of some people, an expressed constitutional right, to pursue what they think is a prominent public interest or a constitutionally relevant interest of the state (I guess borders' defence)?

The problem arises first from the phrase, in the rule on the authorisation of prosecution, that I have emphasised, "unchallengeable assessment": may this phrase be read as negating article 1 of the Constitution? May a House of Parliament, representing the sovereign people, recognise as legitimate an act that breaks the constitutional limits on the exercise of people's sovereignty?

Probably the framers of the Constitution never thought that this problem might arise but, since it did, it needs a solution. According to press reports, the president of the Constitutional court limited himself to insist on the distinction between a "legal assessment" by the Tribunal of Ministers, called upon to establish if "a fact is an offence" and, if it is, to refer the case to the Parliament, and a "political assessment" by which "the House or the Senate assess [...] if the offence is justified to satisfy a constitutionally relevant public interest. If so the Parliament does not authorise prosecution".

If this distinction means that the Parliament's assessment is irrespective of the rights recognized by the Italian Constitution, I beg to differ.

In my view, the clause that defines the Parliament's assessment as "unchallengeable" cannot question the delicate balance underlying constitutionalism. It cannot empower the representatives of the sovereign people to establish the boundaries of the people's sovereignty. Once again, a Latin sentence reminds us: *nemo iudex in re sua*. After all, rigid constitutions and constitutional courts were born after World War II because the facts that happened before the war had disappointed the hope of Rousseau and the nineteenth century theorists of the rule of law that the sovereign people or the legislative could protect people's basic rights against the executive.

It surely falls within the powers of government and Parliament the power of limiting migrants' entrance in Italy (perhaps not the entrance of asylum seekers), but this power cannot be exercised by violating migrants' constitutional rights. It is not the policy of the government and the Parliament's majority that is in question, but the possibility of implementing it by violating people's basic rights.

In my view, the stakes of this case—constitutionalism, i.e. the legal civilisation that we have built after the tragedies of the first half of the last century—are very high. It is therefore very important to establish if, in the case—very likely after the decision of the Parliament's committee—that the Senate denies the authorisation to prosecute, "there will be a judge in Berlin"—to borrow the famous phrase—to protect people's basic rights. Even though the road of bringing the Senate's decision before the Constitutional court is inapproachable, I think that there will be a judge, not in Berlin but in Strasbourg: namely, the European Court of Human Rights (ECtHR).

This Court has consistently ruled that "while states are sovereign in establishing their migration policies, difficulties in the management of migration flows cannot justify practices incompatible with conventional obligations" (Grand Chamber decision in the case *Georgia vs. Russia*, communicated on 30 January 2019). On the basis of this principle Italy was already condemned in 2012, case *Hirsi Jamaa and others vs. Italy*, for rejecting migrants without allowing them to apply for asylum. Even more relevant is the condemnation in the case *Khlaifia and others vs. Italy*, where the Grand Chamber, while acknowledging the problems facing Italian authorities in the management of migration flows, ruled that they cannot exempt Italy from the obligation to guarantee detention conditions respectful of people's dignity and, most importantly, they do not allow forms of detention that are not provided for by the Italian law.

The obligations that the European Convention of Human Rights (ECHR) imposes upon member states include those descending from article 13. This article provides that "Everyone whose rights and freedoms as set forth in this Convention are violated shall have an effective remedy before a national authority notwithstanding that the violation has been committed by persons acting in an official capacity". Since in the case of the Diciotti ship a right has been certainly violated, namely the right to "liberty and security" of article 5 of the Convention, and the ECtHR considers this right of great importance because its violation is often conducive to the violation of the prohibition of torture and inhuman or degrading treatments of article 3, it appears obvious that the case can be brought before the Strasbourg court. The conviction that the case will be heard by the ECtHR is also supported by the fact that some people kidnapped on the Diciotti have already lodged an application and that, if the authorisation to prosecute minister Salvini is denied, it appears quite obvious that the applicants ask the Court to rule on this denial, too.

In a famous judgement against Italy the ECtHR has already declared its power to enforce the applicants' right to effective prosecution of the authors of a violation of articles 3 and 5 of the Convention.

Not only is it important to remind this case because it seems to shed light on the Court's attitude, but chiefly because it concerns an event that highlights the slippery slope that would open if it is admitted that a House of Parliament can prevent prosecution against some ministers for violating a basic right, in particular the right to personal freedom, by alleging that they did so for the sake of "a constitutionally relevant interest of the state, or to pursue a prominent public interest".

The decision I am referring to is particularly significant because the Court fulfilled its duty to protect the basic rights of the European Convention of Human Rights even when they are violated by a state's constitutional bodies, such as the government in the Diciotti case or the President of the Republic, both of which were surely convinced of acting "to pursue a prominent public interest" in their official capacities, even though for those facts the Tribunal of Ministers did not request the authorisation to prosecute.

The judgement is that made by the Court in 2016 in the case *Nasr and Ghali vs. Italy*. The fact was the extraordinary rendition of Abu Omar. The latter, already convicted for membership of a terrorist association at the time of the Court's judgement, was kidnapped, beaten, brought to the US military base of Aviano and then to the Cairo, where he was tortured to force him to cooperate with the Egyptian intelligence. The investigation found the liability of a CIA agent based in Milan and other US nationals, in total twenty six people, for whom the Minister of Justice did not request extradition.

During the investigation the prosecutors asked the Italian intelligence service for information about the US agents: "Upon this request the Prime Minister, in his capacity as the competent authority on state secrets, indicated that he had authorised the transmission of the requested information under the condition that its divulgation would not do damage to the constitutional order" (§ 55 of the ECtHR judgement). Subsequently the investigation led to the involvement of some agents of the Italian intelligence. It was closed with the indictment of 35 people, including 26 US nationals who were tried in absentia, for they failed to report themselves to the trial. Then the Prime Minister lodged two applications to the Constitutional court, against the Milan magistrates, alleging a conflict of attribution between state powers due to the use and divulgation of state classified documents and information.

When the Court accepted to hear the applications, the Milan prosecutors lodged themselves an application for a conflict of attribution, holding that the Prime Minister had acted ultra vires in classifying the documents and the information concerning the organization and commission of the kidnapping. According to the procurators a state secret could not apply to the kidnapping that amounted to a "fact subversive of the constitutional order", since the principles of constitutional government prevent some individuals from being kidnapped in the national territory and forcefully transferred to another country to be interrogated with the threat or use of physical or moral violence.

According to the Milan procurators, "*since the kidnapping was part of a systematic violation of human rights, mostly the prohibition of torture and of arbitrary deprivation of liberty, it was contrary to the basic principles of the Constitution and the international rules of human rights*" (§ 90, my emphasis).

With the judgement no. 106/2009 of 18 March 2009 the Italian Constitutional court "declared the prevalence of the interests protected by state secret over any other constitutionally guaranteed interest and reminded that the executive has the discretional power to assess the need of secret to protect these interests", a power "that can only be limited by the need for Parliament to make the essential reasons for a decision explicit and by the prohibition to classify facts subversive of the constitutional order". The Constitutional court specified that this power is not subjected to any judicial review, including its own, and stressed that in an application for conflict of attribution it was not called upon to express an assessment of the reasons for applying the state secret (§ 99).

The Court "acknowledged the unlawfulness of the practice of 'extraordinary renditions', but it found that 'an individual criminal act, however serious, [was] not in itself capable of constituting a fact subversive of the constitutional order, for it [was] not able to subvert, by disrupting, the overall arrangement of democratic institutions'. Therefore, the Court ruled that, even though the applicant's kidnapping was not itself eligible as a state secret, the use of state secret could not be ruled out in the investigation" (§ 102).

State secret notwithstanding, the Milan court found that there was sufficient evidence of the kidnapping and the liability of 22 US agents, convicted two Italian officials for aiding and abetting, but declared that the directors of the Italian intelligence could not be prosecuted for the state secret. They were convicted in the appeal trial after a long bouncing back between the Court of cassation and the Constitutional court about the limits of state secret. Not only was the conviction of the US agents upheld, but those who had been acknowledged diplomatic immunity in the trial were convicted, too. Moreover, the right of Abu Omar and his relatives to have them pay damages was recognised.

After the judgment became final no Italian government body requested the extradition of the convicted US nationals, and an international arrest warrant was issued only for the CIA agent of Milan. The latter and the two US nationals who were in Italy at the time of the conviction asked for and obtained the Italian presidential pardon.

In the judgement the ECtHR reiterated its orientation, that by now we can define settled, in matters concerning article 3, i.e. torture and inhuman or degrading treatments. I quote paragraph 262 of the judgment because it is so crystal clear that any restatement could only obfuscate it:

> When an individual makes a credible case that he suffered, by the police or other similar services of the state, or as a consequence of acts committed by foreign agents acting with the consent or connivance of the state, a treatment contrary to article 3, the latter provision, together with the general duty imposed by article 1 of the Convention on states to 'secure to everyone within their jurisdiction the rights and freedoms defined in [. . .] this Convention', requires by implication that there should be an effective official investigation. Such investigation must be able to lead to the identification and, if applicable, the punishment of those responsible and to the ascertainment of truth. If it were not so, in spite of its fundamental importance, the general prohibition of torture and inhuman or degrading punishments and treatments would be ineffective in practice and it would be possible in some cases for state agents to infringe, almost with impunity, upon the rights of people under their control (my emphasis).

In the judgement the Court reaffirms other settled principles of its case law on torture and mistreatments: criminal prosecution should not expire and, after the conviction, punishment cannot be subject to conditional suspension, pardon, amnesty and clemency (§ 263 points V and VI).

It is clear from these provisions that the will of Parliament, as representative of people's sovereignty, cannot be placed above the Convention of human rights as interpreted by the Court. For both pardon and amnesty, that would be in breach of the Convention, are passed by Parliament that, according to article 79 of the Italian constitution, must approve them with a two thirds majority. Thus, not even the certified will of two thirds of the sovereign people can suppress the right to have someone punished who is responsible for a treatment contrary to article 3 of the Convention.

However, the most relevant passage of this judgement, which determines its importance for the case of kidnapping on the Diciotti ship, is that where the Court stresses the central place of article 5 of the Convention. Again, for its clarity, I directly quote paragraph 296 of the judgement:

> First, the Court observes the fundamental importance of the guarantees of article 5 to secure to individuals in a democracy the right not to be subjected to arbitrary detention by the authorities. For this reason it never ceases to underline in its case law that any deprivation of liberty must comply with the substantial and procedural provisions of national legislation but also conform to the very end of article 5: protect individuals against the arbitrary use of power. The importance of the protection accorded to individuals against the arbitrary use of power is shown by article 5 § 1 enumerating the circumstances in which an individual may

be lawfully deprived of his or her freedom, being understood that such circumstances call for a strict construction for they are exceptions to a fundamental guarantee of individual freedom.

This emphasis should not surprise those who are used to be told that our legal civilisation arose with the consecration of habeas corpus by the Magna Charta and that modern constitutionalism was born with the reassertion of that institution by the 1689 Bill of Rights that sealed the success of the Glorious Revolution. However, the consequences that the Court draws from it are somehow shattering, at least for the case at hand.

Indeed the Court stresses (§ 297) that "the framers of the Convention reinforced individuals' protection against arbitrary deprivation of liberty by enacting a set of material rights designed to minimise the risk of an arbitrary use of power, by providing that acts of deprivation of liberty must be subjected to an independent judicial review, and that it must be possible to investigate the authorities' responsibility". For the Court, the rationale for the speedy operation of the habeas corpus procedures, required by paragraphs 3 and 4 of article 5 of the ECHR, is the need "to find out and prevent measures that can endanger the person's life or serious mistreatments violating the fundamental guarantees of articles 2 and 3 of the Convention". The protection of individual freedom, provided for by article 5, first paragraph, of the Convention, is crucial because the lack of the guarantees protecting individuals' physical freedom and people's security "might eradicate the prominence of law and make the most elementary forms of legal protection inaccessible to detainees".

Premised on this assumption, the Court declared the absolute equivalence of the guarantees—hence of the positive obligations—of article 3 and article 5. For, from the conviction of the Italian state in the Abu Omar case for violating articles 3 and 5 of the ECHR, the Court derived the "defensibility" of an application under article 13, i.e. for a breach of the duty to "carry out an effective official investigation". Thus, it condemned Italy because *the applicants should have had, for purposes of article 13, concrete effective remedies capable of finding and punishing those responsible, ascertaining the truth and according a satisfaction* (§ 334, my emphasis).

In order to clarify the content of the obligation to "carry out an effective official investigation", and considering the case of the Diciotti ship, it should be kept in mind that, according to the Court, "for an investigation to be effective and conducive to identifying and prosecuting those responsible, it must be initiated and carried out rapidly" (§ 263 I). Thus, a failure to initiate the investigation or to carry it out once it has been started is a violation of the Convention. The Court is very clear on the consequences of the failure to carry on prosecution once some evidence has been found:

When a preliminary inquiry has led to the start of an investigation before national judges, all of the proceedings, including the trial, must meet the requirements of the prohibition provided for by such rule. Thus, national judges should in no case appear willing to leave an aggression to people's physical and moral integrity unpunished. This is needed to maintain public trust and guarantee people's support to the rule of law, as well as to pre-empt any hint of tolerance of unlawful acts or of possible connivance with their perpetration (§ 263 II).

As to the circumstance that the state authority "acted to protect a constitutionally relevant interest of the state, or to pursue a prominent public interest in the exercise of the government's functions", one should remember that in that case Italy was condemned because:

(1) the President of the Republic had used his power of pardon, whose exercise is not bound by constitutional criteria;
(2) the government had applied state secret, and this had been deemed at least partly legitimate by the Constitutional court, as mentioned above;
(3) the government had opted not to request the extradition of the US nationals involved.

Lastly, with specific reference to the "constitutionally relevant interest", one should remember that in the case of the Diciotti ship the government appealed to the interest to defending borders against the illegal entrance of one hundred seventy seven migrants, whereas in the Abu Omar case the debate concerned the much more serious danger of an individual convicted for taking part in a terrorist organisation. Once again, the crystal clear words of the Court (§ 298) on the possibility that protecting the people against terror attacks allows an exception to article 5 of the ECHR, i.e. to the protection of the personal freedom of actual or alleged terrorists, are worth quoting:

> Undoubtedly the investigations on terrorist offences confront authorities with special prob-lems. However, this does not mean that they are free, with respect to article 5, to arrest and detain suspects without any effective review by domestic courts and, ultimately, the review bodies of the Convention, whenever they think there is a terrorist offence. In this connection the Court stresses that the incommunicado detention of an individual is a total denial of these guarantees and a very serious breach of article 5.

1 Postface

In the repeatedly quoted judgement the Court reminds (§ 263) of its duty to "keep its review function and intervene if there is a clear disproportion between the serious-ness of an act and the inflicted punishment. Otherwise states' duty to carry out an effective investigation would lose much of its meaning". Thus, it is worthwhile spending some words on the seriousness of the offence that might have been committed in the case of the Diciotti ship.

When, on 30 August 2018, the Agrigento Procurators' office referred the charges relating to the Diciotti case to the Palermo office for them to assess and possibly change them before transmitting the file to the Tribunal of Ministers in 15 days, they included the count of kidnapping for coercion purposes under article 289-*ter* of the Italian criminal code. In their view, the Home secretary had held one hundred seventy seven people hostages to "coerce" the European Union to redistribute migrants in breach of the Dublin Regulation.

For the reader's convenience I quote article 289-*ter* of the Italian criminal code, titled *Kidnapping for coercion purposes*:

> Anyone, except in the cases indicated in articles 289-*bis* and 630, kidnaps a person or keeps him in his power threatening to kill him, to hurt him or to keep him kidnapped in order to force a third party, be it a state, an international organisation of multiple governments, a natural or legal person or a group of natural persons, to perform any act or to refrain from it, making the release of the person kidnapped subject to such action or omission, is punished with imprisonment from twenty-five to thirty years.

Instead, the Tribunal of Ministers decided to prosecute only on count of aggravated kidnapping. Today a document is on file at the Catania procurators' office, signed by the Prime Minister Giuseppe Conte, in which the Prime Minister himself states that "in the case of the ship 'U. Diciotti' actions of the utmost severity were needed to pursue two goals, deemed of the highest priority". The first goal was to combat the trafficking of human beings. The second, more relevant one, is described in these terms by the Prime Minister himself:

> The Government performed all actions useful to promote a policy of combating illegal immigration shared as much as possible at the European level. In particular, there were talks with the Maltese authorities concerning the individuation of a port of landing, and a request was made to other member states of the European Union and to the European Commission for the redistribution of migrants.

The document concludes by stating that:

> Therefore, the case of the 'U. Diciotti' ship falls fully within the exercise of government functions to pursue goals of migration policy meant to combat the trafficking of human beings and to call upon other member states of the European Union to share the burden of managing the phenomenon, since the operations of search and rescue at sea.

I do not know if kidnapping one hundred seventy seven people is a lawful way of "calling upon" other European states and the European Union to share in the management of the migration phenomenon, or a way of "coercing" some states and "an international organisation of multiple governments [. . .] to perform any act". It should be kept in mind that in the offence of article 289-*ter* the problem is, once again, method, namely the kidnapping. The act that one wants the states or the international organisation to be coerced to perform may well be a legal duty, but one cannot use the kidnapping of people to obtain satisfaction of one's right or national interest, however legitimate.

In the light of these considerations, I think that the Prime Minister's statement may support a reassessment of the Italian government's behaviour, not a kidnapping aggravated by having been committed by a state official but the much more serious offence of article 289-*ter* of the Italian criminal code, an article introduced to combat allegedly terrorist actions.

Coming back to the Strasbourg court, one should keep in mind that article 33 of the ECHR allows *Inter-State cases*, providing that "Any High Contracting Party may refer to the Court any alleged breach of the provisions of the Convention and the Protocols thereto by another High Contracting Party". Interstate cases fell into desuetude after the introduction of individual applications by victims, but they have not been abolished and it is worthwhile noting their features. In an old case of 1961, *Austria vs. Italy*, the then-Commission observed that the interstate application is not a means for a state to report violations of the Convention against itself. It is a rather a remedy to bring "an issue affecting the public order of Europe" before the Court.

Thus, if Salvini and the other members of the government who took responsibility for the kidnapping of the one hundred seventy seven people on board of the Diciotti ship were not prosecuted, both the latter individually, and other contracting states of the Convention to pre-empt the temptation to settle international relations through political (or terrorist?) extortion, might apply to the Court alleging a violation of article 5. Malta, for one, could be tempted to do so, even though in the Diciotti case it has been accused of not allowing people's landing: it would be a legitimate way of reacting to the pressures that Italy is exerting for every boat moving from Libya towards the Italian coast.

I hope it is clear that I am not asking Italian prosecutors and judges, and the European Court of Human Rights, to make a political use of criminal law, i.e. to oppose the political choice of limiting the reception of asylum seekers. I am asking them to oppose, through the means that the legal system makes available, the way this choice is being implemented: namely, the fact that this way involves the violation of the basic rights set forth by the Italian constitution and the European Convention of Human Rights. I am asking them to keep that mechanism alive, constitutionalism, that modern states have created to avoid the tragedies originated from the belief that people's sovereignty has no limits. I am asking them to remember that, under a constitutional government, their first task is to avoid the "banality of evil".

Reflections on Contemporary Issues of Judicial Independence

Shimon Shetreet

Contents

1 Introduction

The national and international judiciary plays a significant role in the national democratic system of government as well as international legal order and the machinery of international tribunals. The domestic courts and international tribunals exercise their function and fulfill their duties to adjudicate disputes based on public confidence in the courts and in the independence and impartiality of the judiciary.

Shimon Shetreet is Professor of Law at the Hebrew University of Jerusalem, Israel, the Greenblatt Chair of Public and International law (Emeritus), President, International Association of judicial Independence, past president of the Sacher Institute of Legislative Research and Comparative Law.

S. Shetreet (✉)
Hebrew University of Jerusalem, Jerusalem, Israel
e-mail: shimon.shetreet@mail.huji.ac.il

© Springer Nature Switzerland AG 2019
P. Pinto de Albuquerque, K. Wojtyczek (eds.), *Judicial Power in a Globalized World*, https://doi.org/10.1007/978-3-030-20744-1_32

511

The confidence of the public is deeply affected by the way in which the Judiciary performs its responsibilities in the democratic system. Public confidence in the courts is due to their impartiality, integrity and transparency.[1]

This paper offers reflections on a number of issues relative to Judges and Judicial Independence on the national and international levels.

Judges are central figures in the legal system. They conduct the process of justice in courts and exercise the judicial process. The competence, personality and qualifications of the judges to the judicial process have a significant impact on the quality of the judicial system and on public confidence in the judicial process. Therefore, the method of appointment to a judicial office requires special attention in view of its substantial influence on the legal system.

One of the conceptual challenges in assessing domestic jurisdictions and their laws in comparative perspectives is in the maintenance of proper balance between the universally accepted position and the particular position that is practiced in a certain domestic jurisdiction. In certain matters, domestic circumstances and national constitutional practices supported by long democratic traditions can be considered legitimate even though they deviate from the universally accepted principles.

The examination of the issues of judicial independence will be reviewed in the context of the basic values underlying the justice system, and in the light of the fundamental principles of the democratic system of government.

The paper emphasizes the importance of creating culture of judicial independence by all relevant branches of government.

Security of tenure of judges requires that their term of office will be for fixed term, for life, or until retirement age. Procedure for extending the term of office of judges, or review of renewal of their term by executive or other officers, is a violation of the concept of judicial independence. These practices, of renewal of review of judicial term, which take place in a number of jurisdictions, is unacceptable.

The models of judicial appointment must preserve the basic principle of judicial independence, in all its aspects. This includes substantive and personal independence of the individual judge and the collective independence of the judiciary as a whole.

A central point in the culture of judicial independence is an adequate constitutional infrastructure for the protection of the judiciary. Recent years have witnessed crises of the rule of law in number of jurisdictions with adverse effect on judicial independence. Special attention will be given to developments in Eastern and Central Europe and elsewhere which attracted international criticism both from international political bodies and international judicial tribunes. We refer to Poland, Hungary and Romania in Europe, as well as Turkey.

We selected as case study of the judicial role in society the developments as they emerged in India In the past, India experienced major governance crises and had been under the declaration of emergency, during the term of Prime Minister Indira

---

[1]Shetreet (2003b), p. 360.

Ghandi. In addition, India experienced periods of tense relations between the judiciary and the other branches of government, of judicial independence in the various jurisdictions.

The analysis of the theories of judicial independence in the various jurisdictions should be done in the context of realities of challenging circumstances that have taken place in the past, as well as contemporary ones.

2 The Basic Values of the Judicial System

The main function of the judiciary is to serve as an institution for the resolution of disputes in society. In order to fulfill its role efficiently and successfully, there are basic values that must guide the actions taken by the judiciary. These values are judicial independence, quality of justice and procedural fairness, the efficient conduct of the judicial system, the accessibility to the courts, public confidence in the courts and democratic accountability.[2]

Regarding the issue of impartiality and fairness of process, Prof. Albuquerque suggests that the ECtHR should enforce its "rule of silence", i.e. that judges would not express their opinion in any other way except in their judgements.[3] Similar criticism of the involvement of judges in external activities was expressed by Prof. Zoll. He suggested that involvement of judges in preparing legislation and academic writings and debates may harm the public perception of judicial impartiality. This is particularly important when judges express their basic opinions on issues they or their colleagues may adjudicate in their judicial function.[4] Elsewhere I supported the view that carefully shaped restrictions should be put on the ability of judges to take part in external activities while in office. The appropriate ground for such restriction when such activity may damage the public image of impartiality in the particular case, or consume an unreasonable amount of time.[5] Articles 16–18 to the Mount Scopus standards regulate these matters:

16.1 Judges shall enjoy freedom of expression and association. These freedoms must be exercised in a manner that is compatible with the judicial function and that may not affect or reasonably appear to affect judicial independence or impartiality.

16.2 Judges shall maintain the confidentiality of deliberations, and shall not comment extra-judicially upon pending cases.

16.3 Judges shall exercise appropriate restrain in commenting extra-judicially upon judgements and procedures of their own and other courts and may upon any legislation, drafts, proposals or subject-matter likely to come before their court.

---

[2]Shetreet (2012a).

[3]Pinto de Albuquerque (2018), p. 128.

[4]Zoll (2014), pp. 220–222.

[5]Shtreet and Turenne (2012), pp. 243, 246.

17.1 Judges shall not engage in any extra-judicial activity that is incompatible with their judicial function or the efficient and timely functioning of the court of which they are members, or that may affect or may reasonably appear to affect their independence or impartiality.

17.2 Judges shall not exercise any political function.

17.3 Each court should establish an appropriate mechanism to give guidance to judges in relation to extra-judicial activities, and to ensure that appropriate means exist for parties to proceedings to raise any concerns.[6]

Prof. Albuquerque refers to the need to introduce post-retirement restrictions on judges in the ECtHR and national courts. This "revolving door" phenomenon, which occurs quite often these days, may create a conflict of interests for judges who start planning their next post during term.[7] It is important to consider a general post retirement restriction, limited in time. In general, it should be noted that judicial or executive post-retirements restrictions are much more common than in public or commercial occupations.[8]

In order to enable the courts to exercise their function successfully as an institution for resolving disputes and to make their decisions publicly acceptable, especially when one of the parties to the legal dispute is a governmental authority, it is necessary to ensure judicial independence.[9]

Therefore, one of the most fundamental values which enables the performance of duties of the judiciary is the value of judicial independence. Judicial independence is necessary for maintain proper relationship of the judiciary with the other branches of government.[10]

In order to create a culture of judicial independence there are a number of necessary conditions which ought to be fulfilled. The most basic condition is the separation of powers. After this condition is achieved, in order to prevent the fear of infringement of judicial independence by one of the authorities, it is necessary to safeguard the culture of judicial independence on several levels of government; on the institutional level, there is a need to establish institutions, and preserve their status, jurisdiction and powers. On the constitutional level, there is a need to ensure the judges' independence by denying the ability of another authority to violate the status of the judiciary or to change its powers. On the legal level, these is a need to prescribe the constitutional norms of judicial independence in legislation.[11]

The modern conception of judicial independence includes several essential elements of independence; the personal and substantive independence of the judges, the

---

[6]The Mount Scopus International Standards of Judicial Independence (approved 2018), Articles 16–17.

[7]Pinto de Albuquerque (2018), p. 128.

[8]Shtreet and Turenne (2012), p. 269.

[9]Shetreet (1985a), p. 591.

[10]Shetreet (2012a), p. 19.

[11]Shetreet (2012a), p. 19.

collective independence of the judiciary, and even the independence of individual judges vis-a-vis his colleagues or higher courts and superior judges.[12]

In order to preserve judicial independence, there are a number of accepted doctrines that guarantee the independence of judges and their independence in the jurisdiction: such as the principle of judicial immunity, the principle of *sub judice* that exists in some countries, and more.[13]

Another aspect of judicial independence, which also has not attracted sufficient attention, is the *internal* independence of the judiciary. Internal judicial independence requires that with regard to certain types of adjudicative functions, judges be independent from directives or pressures from his judicial superiors and colleagues. This also transcends both the substantive and personal independence of the judge vis-a-vis his colleagues and superiors. Adjudicative functions are those official functions for which judges are responsible in the discharge of their official duties. They are threefold: (a) administrative; (b) procedural; and (c) substantive. This include, for example, fixing stable and constant rules regarding the distribution of cases between judges, in order to limit the ability of the president of the court to apply discretion regarding distribution on cases between the judges.[14] Such power may change the results of the case, as to the wish of the Chief Justice, and grant him an unfair pressure on the other judges.

Prof. Albuquerque proposes to change the practice of the ECtHR, in order to strengthen the value of transparency. He suggests to introduce change in the activity of the judge rapporteur who writes the main opinion of the court. Although there is a clear tradition for choosing the judge rapporteur, the section's president has full discretion to break this tradition and choose a rapporteur as he wishes. In addition, the court does not disclose the identity of the judge rapporteur of the case.[15] This tradition has no basis in the ECHR constitution.[16]

Transparency is one of the most basic values of an independent and accountable judiciary. Therefore, I support prof. Albuquerque's suggestions for improving the ECtHR transparency and public accessibility. These including the publishing of the identity of the judge rapporteur.[17]

Public transparency as well as internal independence of the judges is strengthened by maintaining a practice of publication of separate and dissenting opinions. Prof. Albuquerque criticizes the practice of the ECtHR not to publish minority opinions or dissenting reasoning.[18] I share the view that the courts including international tribunals should allow separate and dissenting opinions. Legal systems

---

[12]Shetreet (1985a), p. 591.

[13]Shetreet (1985a), p. 591.

[14]Shetreet (2003a), p. 245; International Bar Association (1982), Article (11A).

[15]Pinto de Albuquerque (2018), p. 129.

[16]Pinto de Albuquerque (2018), p. 129.

[17]Pinto de Albuquerque (2018), p. 129.

[18]Pinto de Albuquerque (2018), p. 129.

that encourage the expression of separate or dissenting opinion contribute to creative thinking and reasoning and advance transparency.[19]

Alongside the principle of judicial independence, there are important theories on the role of the judiciary. These are two principles: accountability and reflection of society.[20]

2.1 Judicial Accountability

The model of judicial accountability in a given society determines, to a large extent, whether or not the judiciary is independent. Judicial independence cannot be maintained without judicial accountability for failure, errors or misconduct. Using the conceptual approach proposed by Professor Cappelletti, one can say that when the method of judicial accountability follows the repressive model, i.e., it is vested in the political branches of the government, particularly the executive, then judicial independence is not adequately safeguarded.

Prof. Cappelletti distinguishes between three models of judicial accountability. The models are the repressive or dependency model, which rests the power of controlling judges in the political branches of the government; the autonomous corporative model, which leaves the function of controlling judges in the exclusive hands of the judiciary itself; and the responsive consumer-oriented model, which is a mixed model, neither exclusively judicial nor solely in the hands of the political branches.

There are many forms of judicial accountability. They can be classified into a number of categories: legal accountability, public accountability, and informal and social controls. The first category includes the disciplinary supervision over judges, appellate review of their decisions, and their civil and criminal liability. The second category, public accountability, includes the controls over judges exercised by parliament or the legislative body existing in each society, the executive, the general press and pressure groups. The third category includes the social and professional controls exercised informally and often in private, away from the public gaze. Such informal controls and professional pressures are exerted on judges by their judicial bretheren and superiors, and by their professional colleagues.

The formal mechanisms of accountability of judges are subject to legal restraints such as judicial immunity from criminal and civil liability for acts or omissions in the discharge of the official function, by the *sub judice* rule and other doctrines of contempt of court, and by the doctrine of *res judicata*.[21]

Accountability—in most of the accepted models for the appointment of judges, the appointments are not made directly by the public, unlike other branches of

---

[19]Shetreet (2003a), p. 366.

[20]Shetreet (2012b), pp. 619–647; Shetreet (2009a).

[21]Shetreet (2012a), pp. 654–655.

government. However, the judges bear responsibility for the public, and their choice should reflect a commitment to the public's stance and to the balance of the existing power relations.

A government system in which the composition of the supervising body directly reflects the relative political forces in Parliament is a method that leaves the door open to a series of failures, from a constitutional point of view. Since it was already mentioned that at the heart of the concept of constitutionality is the view that there is justification to impose certain restrictions on the power of the representative legislature ... On the other hand, the fact that the institution of judicial review can (and should) be less representative than the legislature does not mean that these institutions should be free from any obligation of democratic accountability.[22]

Transparency is an important aspect of judicial accountability. In order to sustain public confidence, as far as possible, court deliberations should be open to public view.[23] Judicial decisions should be open to criticism by the public, the media and other branches of governance.[24] This is why it is also important that the court will provide a detailed reasoning for his decisions, which may also contribute to the continuing development of the jurisprudence.[25]

2.2   The Principle of Fair Reflection

Another fundamental principle, in this regard, is the principle of Reflection. Fair reflection can be socially-based, meaning that the judiciary's composition should reflect the variety of the society. This principle is often rooted in criticism directed at the social composition of the judiciary, traditionally drawn predominantly from the upper middle class. England, Canada, Greece, France and Germany are sensitive to this issue, as are African countries, where regional, tribal and cultural considerations are necessary to maintain at least appearances of impartiality and the confidence in the courts of diverse segments of society.[26]

There is ever-increasing awareness of the importance of the principle of a fair reflection of society. It is illustrated by legislation and conventions which demand that judges with certain characteristics be members of a bench of a particular court, by federal and multi-cultural countries where the constituent political units, cultures or geographical regions are expected to be reflected on the bench, and by

---

[22]Dotan (2007), pp. 495–496 (Hebrew).

[23]Shetreet (2003a), p. 243.

[24]Shetreet (2003a), pp. 443–449.

[25]Shetreet (2003a), pp. 257–258.

[26]Shetreet (2012c).

constitutional changes such as the *UK's Constitution Reform Act 2005*,[27] requiring diversity in the process of judicial appointments.[28]

Canada offers an instructive example of both legislated and non-legislated geographical reflectiveness. By statute, three of nine of the justices of its highest court, the Supreme Court of Canada, are drawn from Quebec, and by convention three are selected from Ontario, two from the western provinces, and one from the Atlantic Provinces.[29] Canadians believe that this formula helps ensure that the diversity of Canadian society is best reflected in the country's highest court.[30] The ad hoc judge procedure in the International Court of Justice[31] is another established practice of inclusionary model. Geographical and cultural reflection is maintained in Great Britain's Supreme Court formerly the House of Lords, which always has one judge from Scotland and one from Northern Ireland.[32]

The principle of fair reflection of society is an adequate conceptual remedy to the problem of an unbalanced judicial composition, whether upon ideological, social, cultural, geographical, or other grounds. Fair reflection builds the judiciary's credibility, and public confidence in its functions. This is because the judiciary is also a branch of government, not merely a dispute resolution institution, and therefore there is value in it sharing the diversity of the society from which it is drawn. Fair reflection is also important in order to ensure balanced panels in appellate courts, particularly in cases with public or political overtones.

A reflective judiciary is an imperative factor for maintaining the important value of public confidence in the courts. Although the over-emphasis on personal judicial biases pays insufficient credit to the balancing effect of social controls, system factors and institutional and traditions, it cannot be denied that all judges view the world to some degree through their own individually-tinted glasses.[33] Thus a reflective judiciary is required. The process and standards of judicial selection must ensure fair reflection of social classes, ethnic and religious groups, ideological inclinations and, where appropriate, geography. The reflection should be fair rather than strictly numerical or proportional.[34] Likewise, compliance with the principle of a fair reflection of society must be premised foremost on maintaining

---

[27]Constitutional Reform Act 2005, ch 4 (2005, UK); For a detailed analysis of the history of this act, see Windlesham (2005, 2006). For accounts of the main players, see Woolf (2008); Phillips (2007); Woolf (2004), p. 317; Bingham (2000), pp. 55–68. All three authors served as Lord Chief Justice in these formative years. Lord Woolf was active in the shaping of the legislation and Lord Phillips succeeded him.

[28]Shetreet (2012c).

[29]Supreme Court Act, R.S.C. 1985, c S-26, $30(2) (Can.).

[30]Cotler (2008), pp. 131–147.

[31]For a discussion of ad hoc judges in the International Court of Justice, see Pettiti I. E. (1985), Independence of International Judges.

[32]Shetreet (2012c).

[33]Shetreet (1979), pp. 399–402; Pinello (1999), (judges' party affiliations account for between 31% and 48% of ideological variance).

[34]Models of Constitutional Adjudication (2005), pp. 198–229.

impeccable judicial professional standards and moral values. Again turning to Canada, the selection of Supreme Court of Canada justices is based first and foremost on merit, and only after this criterion has been satisfied, are personal and reflective qualities weighed.[35]

The Mt. Scopus Standards (International Judges) Section 11.2 shares this sentiment:

> 11.2 While procedures for nomination, election and appointment should consider fair representation of different geographic regions and the principal legal systems, as appropriate, as well as of female and male judges, appropriate personal and professional qualifications must be the overriding consideration in the nomination, election and appointment of judges.

The concept of a reflective judiciary is applicable too to the panel compositions in specific cases. The doctrine of fair reflection demands balanced panels, hence promoting neutrality. Judges with convictions or experiences that strongly identify them with a particular side should refrain from sitting in cases that might lead the public to question their neutrality.[36]

Section 2.15 of the Mt. Scopus Standards provide for a fair reflection of society:

> 2.15 The process and standards of judicial selection shall give due consideration to the principle of fair reflection by the judiciary of the society in all its aspects.

> 2.15.1 Taking into consideration the principle of fair reflection by the judiciary of the society in all its aspects, in the selection of judges, there shall be no discrimination on the grounds of race, colour, gender, language, religion, national or social origin, property, birth or status, subject however to citizenship requirements.

Section 2.17 also speaks of a fair reflection:

> 2.17 The process and standards of judicial selection shall give due consideration to the principle of fair reflection by the judiciary of the society in all its aspects.

It is important to distinguish "reflection", which refers to members of the judiciary mirroring certain characteristics of the population, from "representation", which implies loyalty and continued contacts and links to segments of the population. We speak of judicial reflection rather than of representation for we expect judges after their appointment to be completely independent, without loyalties to the sector in society from which they were drawn. This contrasts with the representative nature of members of parliament, who are expected after their election to office to keep contacts with the people who elected them and to promote their constituents' often self-serving interests. In addition, whereas democratic representation should be numerically based, the judicial reflection of society is based on fairness rather than numbers.

The fundamental values of the judiciary as a branch of government, accountability and reflection, were recently adopted by the Supreme Court of Israel in the *Aviram v. Minister of Justice* case, where Justice Neal Hendel ruled on a matter that

---

[35]Cotler (2008).

[36]Shetreet (1979, 1985b).

has to do with the judicial appointments selection committee. as part of the judgement, Justice Hendel review the fundamental values of the judiciary as a branch of government, and ruled that reflection and accountability must be the basic values to be taken into account when discussing the judicial appointments system.[37]

2.3 Constitutional Protection of the Judiciary

Judicial independence calls for the provision for protection of the judiciary vis-a-vis the legislature. The constitutional position of the judiciary depends on the normative level of the legal norms, which provide for the courts and their jurisdiction, and for the terms of office and tenure of the judges. When these are provided for in constitutional provisions then one could speak of constitutional courts, or constitutional judges.

Normally any change in such provisions would require a constitutional amendment. Sometimes the existence of certain courts is provided for in the constitution, but the jurisdiction of such a court is defined by ordinary legislature. In such a case one can speak of a constitutional court and legislative jurisdiction. The same may occur with regard to judges. Some of them may be constitutional judges; others may be the creation of ordinary statutes ("legislative judges"). Constitutionally speaking, legislative freedom to abolish courts to change their jurisdiction or affect terms of judicial independence by ordinary legislation depends on the normative position of the provision in question, as explained.

The vast majority of national jurisdictions have to some degree, embodied guarantees of judicial independence into their constitutions. The main aspects that are found to be thus protected are: (a) life tenure of the judge or until a fixed retirement, (b) his non-transferability, (c) salaries and pensions, (d) provision for disciplinary proceedings, (e) for appointment and removal procedures, and (f) security of tenure. Other countries choose a less specific method of protection, and have rather attempted to guarantee the separation of powers, the ability to review government acts and naturally the right to establish courts.

The weakest form of constitutional guarantee of judicial independence is simply to affirm in the constitution that judicial independence will be respected. This type of guarantee must naturally be supplemented by further legislation to give it any meaning over and above the semantic one. There are countries without any guarantee, naturally those without a constitution included, but a suitable system of rules, conventions, statute and public opinion make for a fair substitute.

In the absence of constitutional provisions establishing them, the courts may be abolished by ordinary legislation. Legislative abolition of a court may result in a removal of a judge whose decisions are unfavourable to the ruling powers, or their philosophy. Such legislation may be passed to effect the removal of the bench of an

---

[37]HCJ 9029/16 *Aviram v. Minister of Justice*, (Jan. 2, 2016), pp. 22–26.

entire court which has shown itself hostile to executive acts or legislative enactments.[38]

One can enumerate a number of principles for the constitutional protection of the judiciary. Elsewhere, we have identified six principles.[39] The first principle of constitutional protection of judicial independence is a rule against ad hoc tribunals. The second is a prohibition against intentionally stripping courts of their jurisdiction and diverting cases to other tribunals, which do not enjoy the same conditions of independence as the original courts.

The third is the standard judge principle, or the ordinary-judge principle, which requires that judges be selected to hear cases by a predetermined internal plan or assignment schedule prior to the commencement of the case.

The fourth principle requires post-decisional independence of the judgment and its respect by the other branches of the government.

The fifth principle is that judges must not be part of the administrative arm of the executive branch; rather, they should be viewed as independent constitutional or statutory officers of the state, completely separate from the civil service.

The sixth principle is that changes in the terms of judicial office should not be applied to present judges unless such changes serve to improve the terms of judicial service.

In recognition of the importance of the basic values of the justice system, the JIWP resolved earlier in 2018 in London to specifically enumerate indicators of the justice system, And emphasized the importance of them be established, recorded and reported. These indicators include the independence of the judicial process and the independence and the impartiality of the judiciary, high quality of the adjudicative process, efficiency of the judicial process and judicial administration, accessibility of the courts and judicial services and ensuring public confidence in the courts, accountability of the judiciary and the transparency of the justice system.[40]

2.4   Judicial Independence and Judicial Appointments

The appointment of judges directly affects the public's trust in the legal system. The manner in which the judges are appointed determines the quality of the judges and their independence vis-à-vis the other authorities. The choice of a particular appointment process stems, inter alia, from the need to share the public's viewpoint in the selection process. Through the participation of representatives of the elected authorities, the public's position is expressed in the selection of judges, and grants authority and power to the higher courts based on public confidence.[41]

---

[38]Shetreet (1985a), pp. 610–611.

[39]Shetreet (2009b), pp. 316–317.

[40]The Mount Scopus International Standards of Judicial Independence (amended 2018), Article. 1.6.3.

[41]Shetreet (2009b).

There are different methods for appointing judges around the world. Among the possible models are the following: Appointment by the Executive Branch only, Appointment by the Judicial Branch only. A process that involves a number of authorities (Parliament + Executive Branch, Executive Branch + Judicial Branch), a procedure carried out in a collegial body composed of professional ranks and constitutional ranks, parliamentary elections, or elections by the citizens' general vote.

In various countries, and even in the same country, the various courts have appointment procedures based on one of these models or a combination of more than one of them. For example, the US Supreme Court judges are appointed by the president with the consent of the Senate. In contrast, judges in State Courts, such as in California, are appointed through public vote.

The security of judicial office is maintained by appointing judges for life. Life tenure can be given two possible interpretations. Either literally that a judge is appointed for life, or that he is appointed until he reaches a certain age until such time, he cannot be removed from office. A fixed-term contractual appointment does not accord security of tenure. It opens up the possibility of renewing an appointment of a 'desirable' judge, whilst letting that of an 'undesirable' to elapse, without renewal.

Only a small number of countries entrust the power of judicial appointments to the judiciary. Generally, a collegial judicial body (judicial council) performs the function. With few exceptions most countries give this function over to the executive which carries it out on either a uniform method for all the judges, or according to a split-system, whereby the system of appointments in the higher courts will differ from that in lower courts.

In the second model the judicial appointments and promotions are a proper function of the executive. Sometimes this function is performed exclusively by the executive and sometimes the executive only initiates the appointment subject to approval by other bodies. There is a distinction which should be made between the formal act of appointment normally by the Head of State, and the process of selection. There are countries in which the selection is the function of a committee or the Minister of Justice, but the formal act of appointment is vested in the Head of State.

The majority of countries do not allow for any extension, few states provide for any extension. The argument in favour of a practice of extension is that it is useful from the point of view of tapping the experience of a still healthy and sound judge, particularly where there is a shortage of judges or a backlog of cases. Where it exists, extension is used as a stop-gap measure which can last a few years at most. The possibility may indeed only exist where a fill-in post is needed for a very limited period, sometimes a matter of months.[42]

In many countries, there exists a probationary period for judges on their first judicial appointment, which is inconsistent with the independence necessary to judicial function. However, there might be a doctrinal justification for the probationary appointment in countries such as those of the civil law tradition, where the

---

[42]Shetreet (1985a), pp. 623–624.

ordinary judicial appointment comes immediately after completing the legal education.[43]

Another problem which arises is that of part-time appointments and ad hoc judges. The use of part-time judges is well known. In England they have existed for centuries and are styled Recorders. It is efficient, as it allows at short notice the temporary recruitment of lawyers to the bench to tackle with increasing caseloads. The system of part-time appointments has raised objections, while part-time judges still under the executive control are deprived of the protection of tenure, which in the view of the public could cast a doubt on judicial impartiality.[44]

The practice of the ad hoc appointment of judges of lower courts to appellate courts poses a problem to personal independence, and gives rise to appearances of impropriety. A judge holding temporary appointment to the court is susceptible to being influenced by external matters and pressures, and his independent judgment is liable to be affected. Temporary appointments to appellate courts should be used only in emergencies.[45]

Another undesirable feature is general temporary appointment to a judicial post made in some countries, to different levels of the court system. This can lead to a questioning of judicial impartiality by the public, since the motives for the appointment of such temporary judges may be influenced by political and other pressures and not from purely judicial interests.[46]

Prof. Albuquerque suggests a number of reforms regarding the practice of the ECtHR.

First, Prof. Albuquerque defends the current practice that judges of the ECtHR are appointed for a fixed, non-renewable term.[47] This approach is implemented in the US. Federal judges including Judges of the Supreme Court of the US are appointed for life.[48] Other countries, such as Israel, appoint judges until fixed retirement age, non-renewable term.[49]

In Scotland, the law granted the Lord Advocate the power to appoint judges for temporary terms. This arrangement was invalidated.[50] However, not every temporary appointment is for itself non-legitimate. In the *Clancy* case, the court ruled the in case that the judicial branch itself calls retired judges for fixed terms is a legitimate practice. In general, the question whether or not temporary appointments are legitimate depends on the context and the circumstances, such as the appointment

---

[43]Shetreet (1985a), pp. 624–625.

[44]Shetreet (1985a), pp. 625–626.

[45]Shetreet (1985a), p. 627.

[46]Shetreet (1985a), p. 628.

[47]Pinto de Albuquerque (2018), p. 128.

[48]Turley J. Essays on Article III: Good Behavior Clause.

[49]Most judges are appointed until retirement age (Article 7(1) of Basic Law: Adjudication (Israel)). Presidents of all courts are also limited to a term of seven years (Articles 8(B), 9(B) to the Courts Law (1984) (Israel)).

[50]*Starrs and Chalmers v. P.F. Linlithgow*, (2000).

method, terms of office, and other guarantees for independence in the exercise of office.[51] Accordingly, the Mount Scopus standards state that:

> 2.2. Each judge shall enjoy both personal independence and substantive independence
>   2.2.1. Personal independence means that the terms and conditions of judicial service are adequately secured by law.[52]

Prof. Albuquerque suggests to change the criteria for appointment of presidents of the sections or divisions of the ECtHR which are too vague and leave too wide discretion to the section's president. He suggests that some strictly objective standards of appointments should be adopted. I support the proposals of Prof Albuquerque. This is particularly true regarding the ECtHR, which consists of judges from many nationalities, which are sometime the rival parties.

3   Constitutional Culture and Judicial Appointments: Illustrative Case of Judicial Appointments India

The law of government in India from 1919 in article 101 of the Supreme Court constitution, states that all appointments to the Chief Justice of the Supreme Court position and all other Supreme Court judges are subjected solely to the discretion of the Thrown. The old law, amended in 1935, gave the authority of judicial appointment to all federal courts to the Thrown as well. It seems that under the old law, consultation with the judiciary was not significant, if it was required at all. When the Indian Constitution was drafted, there was a general agreement that judicial appointment to the Supreme Court should not remain solely in the hands of the government, and that was the reason for the enactment of the obligation for consultation with the Chief Justice, However, it was also agreed that this consultation is not binding, as the Chief Justice of India does not have supremacy in the matter of judicial appointments to the Supreme Court.[53] Despite this judgment, governments through the years tended gives supremacy in judicial appointments to the Chief Justice.[54]

At some point, the court changed his opinion and decided that he should be given the supremacy In the appointment process, as he is the authority that will complete the task better.[55] However, it was stressed that[56] the verdict should focus on the main goal—to enable a thorough and significant opinion of each participant of the judicial appointment process, understanding that the combination of all opinions will bring an appropriate solution.[57]

---

[51] *Clancy v. Caird*, (2000).

[52] The Mount Scopus International Standards of Judicial Independence (approved 2018), Articles 2.1–2.1.1.

[53] *Supreme Court Advocates-on-Record Assn. v. Union of India* (1993), para 21.

[54] *Supreme Court Advocates-on-Record Assn. v. Union of India* (1993), para 22.

[55] *Supreme Court Advocates-on-Record Assn. v. Union of India* (1993), para 27.

[56] *Supreme Court Advocates-on-Record Assn. v. Union of India* (1993), para 21.

[57] *Supreme Court Advocates-on-Record Assn. v. Union of India* (1993), para 28.

In 2014, in order to change that situation, the Houses of Parliament of India amended the 99th amendment, and enacted the NJAC Act in August 2014. The constitutional amendment added article 124A of the constitution that requires to assemble a committee, called "National Judicial Appointments Commission", which will consist of the Chief Justice of the Supreme Court, two other judges, the minister of Justice, and two member who will be appointed by the government together with Chief Justice and the Head of Opposition.

In October 2015 case of *Supreme Court Advocates-on-Record Ass'n v. Union of India*, the Supreme Court of India ruled on the matter of the 99th amendment and the NJAC act and invalidated it. According to the court, the suggested composition of the committee is no good, and the amendment caused that the "primacy of the judiciary, had been totally eroded through the impugned constitutional amendment".[58] The result of that ruling was to invalidate the amendment and the NJAC act,: *"Given our constitutional history, the established conventions, the views of various committees over the last seventy years and the views of scores of legal luminaries Act.."*

This judgment needs to be understood in its unique context. The contemporary debate on the model of judicial appointment, after the judgment in relates to the broader issue of judicial role of courts in society in India. Some argue, that the Supreme Court by its extremely activist role is challenging the nature of democracy in society. Thus, the Minister of Finances of India stated: "Indian democracy cannot be a tyranny of the unelected and if elected are undermined, democracy itself would be in danger".[59] To this argument, the proponents of the wide role of the Supreme Court in society in India argue, that there is no tyranny of the judiciary at all; it is all about the constitution's supremacy. The Supreme Court has merely ruled, as it should, to prevent parliamentary supremacy over the constitution, and by that preventing the tyranny of the elected. The Supreme Court was not exceeding its jurisdiction; it was carrying it out to protect the Indian constitution and the Indian democracy.[60]

The Indian Constitution does not include and restrictions on amending it. as to its constitutional roots in the British tradition, which opposes to the concept of unamendability.[61] This initial position has changed, though, due to historical circumstances. From the early days of the Indian republic, the Supreme Court have permitted, time after time, limitations on human right by constitutional changes.[62]

---

[58]*Supreme Court Advocates-on-Record Ass'n v. Union of India*, (2016), para 12.

[59]Constitutional, Judicial and Parliamentary Supremacy in India, *gktoday* (5 September, 2016).

[60]Constitutional, Judicial and Parliamentary Supremacy in India, *gktoday* (5 September, 2016).

[61]Roznai (2017), p. 42.

[62]In 1951, the government tried to lead a reform in a matter regarding to land owners, by changing their constitutional right to property *(Shankari Prasad v. India* (1951); Merillat (1960). Later, in the case of *Sajjan Singh v. State Of Rajasthan* (1965) the court declared that constitutional amendments may violate fundamental rights.

The turning point in the Supreme Court stance on the issue took place in *Golakanath v. State Of Punjab* case of 1967.[63] The court determined that constitutional cannot violate rights. Despite the fact that the amendment was not invalidated, the judgment was "the opening shot of a great war over parliamentary versus judicial supremacy".[64] Few years later, the court first presented the "Basic Structure" doctrine, without applying it. This thesis claims that there are significant restrictions on the power to amend the constitution. These restrictions subject the parliament to the "Basic Structure of the Constitution".[65]

As a reaction to the judgment, Indira Gandhi sought to reestablish the parliament's supremacy. The 24th and 25th amendments were put into motion in 1971. The 24th amendment enabled the parliament, while using its constitutional power, to invalid, amend or change any article of the constitution, including those who protect constitutional rights. The 25th amendment enabled property reform.[66] The Supreme Court ruled on these amendments. The court determined that the power to amend the constitution does not include the power to change its identity—i.e. applying the Basic Structure doctrine, in its primal form.[67]

This struggle between the legislature and the Supreme Court has repeated itself few more times during the years.[68,69]

The debate about the proper place of the judiciary in matters regarding to politics is not unique to India. In many democratic countries, the judiciary has adjudicated on matters that some might view as purely under the jurisdiction of the political branches of government. And yet, some degree of tension between the activist Supreme Court and the political branches of government is unavoidable, and "some would say that tension between the courts and the other branches is natural, even desirable".[70]

Some might question the necessity of a strong, activist constitutional court, but given the last six decades of the Indian republic's history of human rights violations and emergency state, it is very plausible to recognize and admire the fact, that the court "has not hesitated to innovate and improvise so that the poor and the disadvantaged people realize their basic and fundamental rights".[71]

The opponents of the position of the Supreme Court ruling argue, in support of their position that the ruling brought about a complete lack of democratic accountability of the Supreme Court judges, as put by Ashish Tripathi. Accountability means that the Judiciary, despite the need to be as independent as possible, has a

---

[63] *Golakanath v. State Of* Punjab (1967).

[64] Roznai (2017), p. 43.

[65] Roznai (2017), p. 43.

[66] Roznai (2017), p. 44.

[67] Roznai (2017), p. 44.

[68] *Indira Nehru Gandhi v. Raj Narain*, AIR 1975 SC 2299.

[69] Roznai (2017), p. 44.

[70] Roznai (2017), p. 365.

[71] Roznai (2017), p. 364.

responsibility towards the public, in order to maintain Public Confidence, among other things. By taking the constitutional authority to invalidate unconstitutional constitutional amendments and restoring the complete supremacy of the judiciary over the judicial appointments process, the Supreme Court has ignored, in the opinion of the opponents, the fundamental value of democratic accountability.

Other points of criticism of the 2015 judgement, as put by Akhilesh pillalamarri, are that the judgement created imbalance between the judiciary and the political branches of government in relation to judicial appointment. The judgment is viewed by many as a move of the judiciary that is now "hermetically sealed off from democratic checks and balances"—for it perpetuates the judiciary's supremacy in judicial appointment. The same author points to issues of transparency and accountability in the judicial appointment process by the Supreme Court of India.

Another critique, Rehan Abeyratne, passed criticism of the supremacy assumed by the court "while cloaking itself in the constitution". This has to do with a broader criticism of the globally unprecedented powers that the Indian Supreme Court has taken to itself in the last few decades, such as invalidating "unconstitutional constitution amendments" in other cases as well as here.

On the other side, while being well aware of the problematic issues arising from the judgment, Prashant Bhushan, the advocate who argued the case against the NJAC Act in court, emphasizes for the importance of judicial independence. He argues, that while full-time and independent institutions for selecting judges are much needed, as are other reforms in matters that have to do with the judiciary (in the hope that the decision would act as a catalyst to bring about these reforms), the judgement was very much in place:

> This judgment is welcome, particularly as it comes at a time when the government is seeking to control various independent accountability institutions. It is extremely important in the present climate, where there is a serious attack on diversity, dissent and freedom of speech at the hands of the ruling party and the government, that the independence of an important institution like the judiciary remains untouched.

Mr. Bhushan admits that judicial independence does not mean that the judges should appoint themselves. However, he argues that it is much preferable to vest the authority of the judicial appointments in the hands of the Judiciary, and not in the alternative option of executive control over the judicial appointments. He considers the judicial control option as the lesser of two evils.

4 Guiding Principles Regarding Permissible Executive and Legislative Role in Matters Relevant to Judiciary

We now turn to deal with a wider topic of discussion in democratic administrations, which is the permissible executive and legislative role in matters relevant to judiciary. Judicial appointments is just one of the issues in this topic—how to administrate the judiciary in a way that will maintain judicial independence, both on collective and individual levels.

Collective independence protects the Judiciary vis-à-vis the legislature. Collective responsibility also calls for protection of the Judiciary from Executive interference by way of administrative control by the Executive or by way of personal control over individual judges. Personal control on individual judges creates a collective dependence of the Judiciary. Due to the importance of the issue of Executive control over judges and Judicial administration, and because it is more common, the issue of the permissible boundaries of Executive roles in Judicial administration will be examined in detail.

Collective independence calls for a more significant Judicial participation in the administration of the courts. The greater role given to the Judiciary in the administrative responsibility of courts at the central level, in addition to its already important role at the court level, is supported by the different models of responsibility for Judicial administration. An essential element of Judicial independence, in my view, is that Executive control over Judicial administration is minimized only to areas in which such control is required under the concept of ministerial responsibility to Parliament.

When discussing the subject of independence of the Judiciary we should differentiate between the central responsibility for Judicial administration and finances, and the responsibility for Judicial administration at the court level. The Executive may legitimately have a greater role in the central responsibility for Judicial administration, as part of the application of the principle of responsible government in a parliamentary system. Notwithstanding that the principle of substantive, personal and collective independence of the judges requires that the Executive branch involvement and control be removed from Judicial administration at the court level.

A beginning of a proper solution to the challenge of maintaining Judicial independence and legitimacy is presented in the Mount Scopus Standards for Judicial Independence, which is a formulation of global standard criteria for Judicial independence which can serve us in judging whether a certain Judicial System is considered independent.

Mount Scopus International Standards of Judicial Independence stipulated primarily that the Judiciary must enjoy collective independence and autonomy vis-a-vis the Executive.[72] According to which, Judicial matters should be exclusively within the responsibility of the Judiciary, in central Judicial administration and in court level Judicial administration.[73] In addition, the document states that the exclusive responsibility for case assignment for judges should be vested in a responsible judge, preferably the President of the Court.[74]

While the document determines that the Judicial appointments and promotions by the Executive are not inconsistent with Judicial independence, it contest that these

---

[72]The Mount Scopus International Standards of Judicial Independence (approved 2018), Article 2.3.

[73]The Mount Scopus International Standards of Judicial Independence (approved 2018), Article 2.12.

[74]The Mount Scopus International Standards of Judicial Independence (approved 2018), Article 2.18.2.

should be done according to principles of the culture of Judicial laid down in the document.[75]

Regarding the issue of the power of the Executive to discipline the Judiciary, the document contest that the Executive may not by the adjudication of any disciplinary matters but only be able to refer complaints against judges or to initiate them,[76] and that it will not have the power to discipline or remove a judge.[77] As for the legislators, the document dictates that any rules of procedure and practice made by legislation or by the Judiciary should be done together with legal professionals and be subject to the approval of Parliament.[78]

The formulation of the boundaries of the Executive role in Judicial administration should be made in light of several propositions I wish to submit in this article concerning the role of the Executive in various administrative aspects of Judicial administration.

The first proposition is that Judicial appointments and promotions will be viewed as a proper function of the Executive branch. At times this function is performed solely by the Executive and sometimes the Executive only initiates the appointment subject to approval by other bodies.

The first model exists in countries such as Canada, England, Australia, Norway, and Uruguay, while the latter is practiced in many other nations. The other bodies which participate in the appointments along with the Executive vary depending on the state. It is important, when discussing the issue of appointments, to distinguish between the formal act of appointment, normally being made by the Head of State, and the process of selection. There are countries in which the selection process is being made by a committee or the Minister of Justice, but the formal act of appointment is vested in the Head of State. There are many examples for this type of process. To name a few: the United Kingdom or Canada, where the Head of State, the Queen or the Governor General appoints the judge upon the recommendation of the Lord Chancellor or the Minister of Justice, respectively.

Another example in this regard is Israel, whereby a Judicial Selection Committee selects the judge, and the President of the State appoints him upon the recommendation of the Committee submitted to him by the Minister of Justice. In the United States, judges are selected by the President that nominates them, and his nomination goes before the Senate for confirmation. When reviewing these appointments methods a line should be drawn between countries where the President is a ceremonial figurehead, as in Israel, and countries in which the President is vested with Executive power, such as the United States.

It is my view that we should favour the idea of a responsible committee for Judicial appointment, as the state practice of several countries with a selection

---

[75]The Mount Scopus International Standards of Judicial Independence (approved 2018), Articles 2.4, 4.

[76]The Mount Scopus International Standards of Judicial Independence (approved 2018), Article 2.6.

[77]The Mount Scopus International Standards of Judicial Independence (approved 2018), Article 2.7.

[78]The Mount Scopus International Standards of Judicial Independence (approved 2018), Article 2.10.

committee has been satisfactory. Committees are able to exclude irrelevant political inputs and other problematic considerations from the appointment process and generally speaking, their work has been successful.

The second proposition I wish to offer when formulating the boundaries of the legitimate Executive control in court administration is that the Executive may participate in the discipline of judges, but only by referring complaints against judges or in the initiation of disciplinary proceedings, not in the adjudication of such complaints. The ability to remove or discipline a judge must rest with an institution which is independent of the Executive, or in parliament. Evidently, the executive control over these disciplinary matters is prone to bring about interference with the personal independence of the judges. Prof. Cappelletti named this type of practice a "repressive model". It is safe to say that this proposition is supported and applied in most countries.

A number of countries have taken this principle further. Some countries prohibit any kind of Executive input with regard to the discipline of the Judiciary. On the other hand, I maintain that in order to insure the independence of the Judiciary, it is necessary to remove only the Executive control over the disciplinary tribunal. Beyond that, it appears that the removal of any Executive power in the discipline of judges is not imperative though, of course, very desirable.

My third proposition is that the Executive will not obtain control over matters concerning judges or on Judicial functions. In other words, the Executive cannot control the transfer of judges from one court to another, the division of labour among the judges, case assignments to judges, the setting of cases for hearing or the determination of sitting hours in the courts and judges' vacations; In addition, generally, the Executive branch must avoid controlling the case flow management and the courts' schedule. A control of this type is expected to interfere with the substantive and personal independence of judges and is inconsistent with the collective Judicial independence.

The fourth proposition I wish to make in this paper is that the courts will supervise the execution process of civil judgments and decide all matters of judicial nature relating to them, even though the physical execution of these civil judgments is a function which is suitably under the responsibility of the Executive. In the Netherlands, for example, the Executive has refused to execute the judgment in some civil cases. Many of these cases require the police help for execution, hereby leaving it to the Executive to decide whether or not the judgment of the court will be enforced. It is clear why this method was criticized as undermining the judgments of the courts and as a blatant violation of judicial independence.

The practice of Executive pardon of criminals was also, similarly, highly criticized. The practice has been debated in the United Kingdom and, at present, great Judicial, concerns stem from the Executive plans to reduce the prison population. These plans are perceived by many as an oblique attack on judicial power. The issue of Executive pardon was also debated in Austria and has been subject to criticism as well, in light of the proposal for a joint exercise of pardon by the Federal Minister of Justice and a central Judicial senate. Yet, at the moment, the Australian legislature is not inclined to follow such suggestions. In Italy, the use of "arnnistia" has often been criticized—but not because it is perceived as a threat to the independence of the Judiciary. An intense controversy was sparked in Israel in 1977 when a white collar criminal was granted pardon, shortly after his sentence was upheld on appeal. The Judiciary considered this pardon as an interference with the objectivity of the Judicial process.

Regarding the criticism on the Executive involvement in the Judiciary in Australia, a great source of complaint is the exercise by parole boards and their ability to permit the early release of prisoners, despite substantial "head sentences" imposed by the judges. This contradiction between the Judicially imposed criminal sentences and the administratively determined parole release of the Executive generated the need to make a substantial reform in parole in Australia.

Generally, the examination of the Executive control over judges implies that the Executive has excessive power over the Judiciary in many countries. There are abundant of laws which grant the Executive authority to initiate disciplinary proceedings against judges in countries like Italy, Australia, South Africa, and Israel. Even though this power is not considered as a violation of Judicial independence, it can still be harmful to the independence of the Judiciary. The Executive also controls the appointments and promotions of judges in many countries as well, and in some countries this includes the ability to transfer a judge from one court to the other, or to temporarily appoint a judge to a higher instance.

The concept of collective Judicial independence was recognized by the emerging transitional jurisprudence of the independence of the Judiciary, which emphasized the need to restrict the Executive role in Judicial administration and to increase the Judicial participation in the responsibility for court administration. The Montreal Declaration and the IBA Standards clearly recognize collective Judicial independence.[79] The Montreal Declaration provides that the main responsibility for court administration shall rest in the Judiciary; that the court budgets shall be prepared in collaboration with the Judiciary, and that the Judiciary alone shall be responsible for case assignment.[80] The IBA Standards call for exclusive Judicial responsibility over court administration at the central level, or at least joint responsibility with the Executive, and provide that Judicial matters shall be exclusively within the responsibility of the Judiciary, both at the central level and at the court level.[81] The IBA Standards and the Montreal Declaration both exclude the Executive from its current control over various Judicial functions.[82] Similarly, the International Standards specifically prohibit the exercise of an Executive power when it hinders the Judicial

---

[79]The International Association of Judicial Independence and World Peace (1983), *Universal Declaration on the Independence of Justice* Article 2.04; International Bar Association (1990), *IBA Standards for the Independence of the Legal Profession,* Article 2.

[80]The International Association of Judicial Independence and World Peace (1983), *Universal Declaration on the Independence of Justice* Articles 2.40–2.43.

[81]International Bar Association (1990), *IBA Standards for the Independence of the Legal Profession,* Articles 5, 8.

[82]International Bar Association (1990), *IBA Standards for the Independence of the Legal Profession,* Article 5; The International Association of Judicial Independence and World Peace (1983), Article 2.07.

process, as can be said in relation to the procedure of execution of judgments or the power of pardon.[83]

4.1 Reviewing and Renewing Judicial Tenure

Judicial independence requires security of tenure of judges. Certain practices raise serious issues concerning judicial independence and judicial term of office. These are renewal and review of judicial terms of office.

In Eastern European countries, which changed from a communist regime to a democratic system of government, they resorted to the procedure of lustration. Lustration of the Judiciary in a situation of a basic change in a regime raises central issues regarding the independence and accountability of the Judiciary.[84] This issue was raised particularly in the transition of governments from communist rule to democratic governments. But the theoretical issues have arisen in other contexts as well, such as in judicial appointment process. Thus, the issue was debated in cases involving introduction of reduction of retirement age or in situations of structural court reform, which require the closing of courts and the transfer of judges from one geographical area to another.

Lustration arose in Ukraine. Lustration legislation, when passed without careful respect for judicial independence, is a violation of the principle. Numerous cases of such violations, were adjudicated by international tribunals. Important example is the case of Baka v. Hungary.[85] What is important to note in this regard, is that whenever retirement age is introduced or changed, the new retirement should not apply to present judges. This was done in England in the Judicial Pensions Act of 1959.[86]

In numerous cases, the Court of Justice of the European Union and the European Court of Human Rights dealt with issues concerning Judicial independence and challenges to the rule of law. In their decisions, the Courts stressed the importance of the rule of law and emphasized the duty of the Member States to respect the rule of law in all its aspects, such as Judicial independence and human rights.[87]

---

[83]International Bar Association (1990), *IBA Standards for the Independence of the Legal Profession,* Article 18; The International Association of Judicial Independence and World Peace (1983), Article 2.07.

[84]Shetreet (2017), pp. 12–13.

[85]*Baka v Hungary,* App. No. 20261/12 (23 June 2016) (ECtHR).

[86]Judicial Pension Act, 1959 [UK].

[87]*Baka v Hungary,* App. No. 20261/12 (23 June 2016) (ECtHR); Case c-550/09 *E and F* [2010] ECR I-06213, at para. 44; Case c-456/13, *T & L Sugars and Sidul Açúcares v Commission* [2015] ECR 286, at para. 4; Case C-506/04 *Graham J. Wilson v Ordre des avocats du barreau de Luxembourg* [2006] ECR I-08613, at para. 49; Case C-583/11 *P, Inuit Tapiriit Kanatami and Others v Parliament and Council* [2013] ECR I-nyr; Case C-72/15 *OJSC Rosneft Oil Company v Her Majesty's Treasury and Others* [2016] ECR; Case C-411/10 *N. S. v Secretary of State for the Home Department* [2011] ECR I-13905; Cases C-404/15 and C-659/15 PPU *Pál Aranyosi and Robert Căldăraru v Generalstaatsanwaltschaft Bremen* [2016] ECR, at para. 94; Opinion C-2/13

The developments in Hungry,[88] Poland,[89] Romania[90] and turkey,[91] have been the subject of much discussion and criticism following Executive and legislative actions

---

Enquêtes Douanières v. Humeau Beaupréau SAS [2014] ECR; Case C-64/16 *Associação Sindical dos Juízes Portugueses v. Tribunal de Contas* [2017] ECR, opinion of Advocate General at Art. 19.

[88] In 2011, the Hungarian Parliament approved several Transitional Provisions and introduced a new criterion for the election of the new President of the Supreme Court, which eventually led to the early termination of office of the former President of the Hungarian Supreme Court, Mr. Baka. Baka lodged an application against Hungary with the ECtHR in 2012. The ECHR held that Hungary violated the right of access to a court of the former President of the Hungarian Supreme Court (see: The European Convention on Human Rights and Fundamental Freedoms (1953), articles 6,10; *Baka v Hungary*, App. No. 20261/12 (23 June 2016) (ECtHR). On September 2018, the European Union parliament voted to sanction Hungary for posing a "systemic threat" to European Union values and the rule of law, under Article 7 of the EU Treaty Staudenmaier (2018), EU Parliament Votes to Trigger Article 7 Sanctions Procedure against Hungary; France 24 (2018), 'Parliament Initiates Steps Under Article 7 Over Hungary's 'Systemic Threat' to EU Values'.

[89] In 2015 election of the right-wing PiS government (Law and Justice). Since coming into power, the party decided to restructure the Justice System in Poland. The most controversial new law the party initiated decreases the mandatory retirement age for the Supreme Court judges from 70 years to 65 years (and for the female judges to 60 years). This new legislation is effectively forcing 27 of 74 sitting judges to retire, including Malgorzta Gersdorf, the First President of the Supreme Court. Notably, all judges older than 65 wishing to continue to work after their "retirement" may file a request to the President of Poland.

On October 19th 2018, the European Court of Justice (ECJ) said in an interim ruling that "Poland must "immediately suspend" the application of its controversial law that lowers the retirement age of Supreme Court judges" (EU court stuns Poland's PiS with order to suspend ejection of judges (2018)).

See: Shetreet (2017).

[90] In Romania, a new cabinet led by the Social Democratic Party (PSD) fueled significant public disorder by attempting to pass emergency ordinances and limit Judicial independence, immediately after taking office in January 2017. Faced with this massive social upraise, the government eliminated two controversial amendments that were about to pass. At the end of 2017, only watered-down versions of the laws remained pending in the parliament. In August 2017, the new Minister of Justice (after the former resigned, published a large Judicial reform plan. Some of the amendments pose a threat to Judicial independence as a whole and to functional independence in particular The Superior Council of Magistrates gave a negative vote on the proposals in September and approximately 4000 magistrates (out of a total of about 7000) signed a letter of protest asking the government to withdraw the proposal. Other judicial actors and civil society groups also demanded that this initiative be dropped; several streets protests took place. A slightly amended draft was pending in parliament at year's end, with the ruling coalition key figures demanding a fast track procedure. The Superior Council of Magistrates equally vetoed the new version of the amendments, but its opinion was merely consultative. Freedom House (2017).

[91] In Turkey, in the context of Executive assaults on the rule of law and the institutions designed to protect it. Over 4500 judges and prosecutors have been discharged from their post after the botched coup. Moreover, about 3000 judges and prosecutors suffer in appalling prison conditions without an indictment yet to this day. These events took place in the post-coup attacks on government critics Ayasun (2018).

Since his re-election President Recep Tayyip Erdogan appointed a Council of Judges and Prosecutors which none of its members are elected by the judiciary itself. Furthermore, the Executive has retained significant influence over a number of key issues regarding the running of the judiciary, such as the process of selecting and recruiting judges, reassignments of judges against

that adversely effects the culture of the democracy and the independence of the justice system.

Certain legislations in Israel also attracted sharp criticism by opposition leaders in civil rights associations.[92] Criticism was also directed at statements and orders of the Trump administration in the US.[93]

In the matter of renewing term of office of judges, the issues of the recall and retention practices, as discussed above in relation to the popular elections based judicial appointments, are to be mentioned as well. Such practices are inherently different from the renewal and review of judicial tenure practices in Eastern Europe after the communist rule. In the recall and retention practices, the public, not the executive, decides in general popular elections whether the judgeship term will be renewed. While these practices of recall and retention might present other problems, the main issue of Separation of Powers is not offended by these procedures.

In a case from Scotland, the House of Lords determined that dismissal of a Scottish Sheriff 'for inability',[94] is not limited in meaning to either mental or physical infirmity, but can also include simple incompetence. The fact that the inquiry into the Sherriff's unfitness was conducted in private was not unfair.[95] This judgment is also an expression of reviewing of judicial term of office, and it is very concerning in regards to judicial independence.

4.2 Judicial Self-Governing in Court Administration

One of the many issues regarding the judicial and executive roles is court administration. On this issue, there are a number of models: Executive exclusive control of courts administration, judicial exclusive control and shared models of control. The models which gives the greatest powers for judges over court administration is the judicial self-governing model of court administration.

Self-Judicial governance means control of the Judiciary over the Judicial System. Self-Judicial governance includes budgeting, financial managing, managing human

---

their will and disciplinary procedures. The Council of Europe's 49-member Group of States against Corruption (GRECO) has also expresses its concern about fundamental structural changes that have taken place in Turkey recently, putting the independence of the judiciary from the executive and political powers at stake (Platform for Peace and Justice 2018).

Other legal amendments that were recently passed in Turkey provide the president the authority to appoint half of the country's most senior judges, while the Parliament was granted the authority to appoint the other half. Therefore, on paper, a single party could appoint all the judges to the highest courts United States Department of State (2017), pp. 14–15. Available at: https://www.state.gov/documents/organization/277471.pdf.

[92] Hovel (2017), Harkov (2018), Azulay and Hay (2018) and Leifer (2018).

[93] Orlofsky (2018) and Jude and Watters (2018).

[94] Article 12 of the Sheriff Courts Act of 1971 (Scotland).

[95] *Stewart v. Secretary of State for Scotland, Extra Division*, (1996).

resources and managing of a large system. In addition, it includes a few tasks which demand professional management, such as managing case assignment, engaging in rulemaking of the procedures of the courts and enforcing these procedural rules. For the Judiciary to engage in self-governance, it should possess a wide variety of administrative abilities, which are required for managing the system of justice. It should be stressed that self-governance also calls on the Judiciary to act in coordination with the other branches of government. In addition to these abilities, a Judiciary acting under self-Judicial governance must also obtain certain financial qualifications, in addition to his legal training and experience.

Furthermore, the development and the enforcement of a Judicial code of conduct is also included in self-governance. Part of the culture of Judicial independence in all countries is the maintaining of traditions and rules that ensure independence of the legal profession, and independence of the prosecutors.

The mount Scopus standards also accept the concept on judicial code of conduct,[96] judicial ombudsman,[97] disqualification rules, and limitations on political and social activities while in term.[98] These, alongside a general limitation on any activity which may harm the public appearance of his impartiality.[99]

The separation of powers doctrine is virtually a precondition for a self-governing Judicial System and has a lengthy history in political theory. It was celebrated as a fundamental principle of the foundation for a democratic government in arguments among colonial leaders drafting the United States Constitution, and it frequently is invoked in justifications for an independent Judiciary. However, achieving a Judiciary that can be characterized as institutionally independent (and, to that extent, self-governing) is not an easy task even where constitutional provisions outline a balanced authority model among the established powers of government. Reaching a situation where a country has a self-governing Judiciary is likely to entail an extended series of additional deliberative assessments and active lobbying by pro-independent Judicial coalitions. These efforts are likely to spark resistance from embedded interests which regard judges as civil servants no more deserving of collective self-governance than other government functionaries, and incremental legislative initiatives.[100]

As stated, the process of building a culture of Judicial independence is long and gradual. This process may significantly change the Judicial branch and even possibly demand changes and cooperation of the other branches of government. Nevertheless, it is important to stress that this process is achievable. The development of self-Judicial governance in the United States Federal Judiciary can be used as a good example for such a gradual process for building a culture of Judicial

---

[96]The Mount Scopus International Standards of Judicial Independence (approved 2018), Article 5.4.

[97]The Mount Scopus International Standards of Judicial Independence (approved 2018), Article 5.8.

[98]The Mount Scopus International Standards of Judicial Independence (approved 2018), Article 7.4.

[99]The Mount Scopus International Standards of Judicial Independence (approved 2018), Article 8.

[100]Zimmer (2011).

independence.[101] It took the United States Federal Judiciary 140 years to undergo a change from being under total control of the Executive to attaining the stage of self Judicial governance system.

4.3   Universality vs. Particularity

The determination of issues such as judicial appointments is very much dependent on an integration of two main approaches. The first, the Universal Theory, or universality, claims that an independent judiciary is a shared value of all legal systems, and is essential to the Rule of Law. This theory calls for defining a model of universal judicial independence, which is reflected in legal rules and other formal institutional arrangements—the judicial appointments process included.[102] But alongside the universality approach, particular circumstances in each jurisdiction must be taken into account, and recognition that in some countries it is justified to exempt certain practices from the universal standards is expected.

In England, for example, before the 2005 reform the Lord Chancellor had three different duties, in all three branches of government, as mentioned above. The problem of such a position is that it clearly violates the Separation of Powers principle, which is part of the universal standards of judicial independence. However, this particular practice of the Lord Chancellor in England, is a result of a historical practice and development, which prevailed for centuries. Thus, this unique historic tradition of the English practice must be taken into account. In the *New Delhi Code of Minimum Standards of Judicial Independence*, adopted in 1982 (prior to the 2005 reform in England), provided an exception to the general role of the separation between the justice system and the executive branch. Article 3(b) of the *New Delhi Code* provided that "Appointments and promotions by a non-judicial body will not be considered inconsistent with judicial independence in countries where, by long historic and democratic tradition, judicial appointments and promotion operate satisfactorily".[103] This exception was no longer needed after the Constitutional Reform Act of 2005,[104] which was passed as a result of a process of mutual impacts of national and international law and jurisprudence in the area of judicial independence.[105] This example shows clearly the cross conceptual fertilization and the

---

[101]For a detailed description of this process, see: Zimmer (2006), pp. 62–69.

[102]Neudorf (2017), p. 27.

[103]International Bar Association (1982), paragraph 3b.

[104]Constitutional Reform Act of 2005 (UK).

[105]The case of *Procola v Luxembourg*, (1995), and other similar cases, hold that a judicial function cannot be mixed an executive or legislative function. This means that the position of the Lord Chancellor in principle and in theory is a violation of the ruling of *Procola*. However, according to the exception provided in the New Delhi Code, the position of the Lord Chancellor was unique and supported by a "Long and democratic tradition" (International Bar Association (1982), Article 3b). see: Shetreet (2009b).

mutual impact and ideas that have enriched both international and domestic jurisprudence.[106] The exception is an illustration of recognition of particularity within the context of universal rules.

Another such illustration of recognition particularity within the context of universality in the *New Delhi Code* in other standards, is the proper conduct regarding political activities of judges. In the continent of Europe judges are involved in party politics, but in common law countries they are excluded. Seemingly, the universal theory of judicial political-impartiality would dictate the complete and utter prohibition of judges' political activity. Nevertheless, the particularity of the European countries' tradition in the matter, requires a compromise between the two legal cultures. This compromise is expressed in article 7.1 of the Mt. Scopus standards. It adopts the previous *New Delhi Code* standards, and provides that "Judges shall not hold positions in political parties".[107] This means that membership of judges in political parties will not be a violation of the universal principles, but holding an active position in a political party remains prohibited in the universal standards of judicial independence.

Another illustration of the need to reconcile between universality and particularity is the resolution of the issue of the nature and position of supreme constitutional institutions of several countries, including France, Italy and Belgium. The issue is that these institutions fail to stand the universal standards of independence and impartiality, as directed in article 6 of the European Convention on Human Rights (ECHR). In the background of the discussion of this issue we ought to mention the Procola vs. Luxemburg case of 1995 before the ECtHR.[108] In this case, Procola complained that some of the members of the Judicial Committee of Luxembourg who ruled on Procola's application for judicial review had previously given their opinion on the lawfulness of the impugned provisions in their other role as members of the Conseil d'Etat. Their interpretation was that Article 6 is applicable only when the proceedings are decisive for a civil right. The ECtHR determined that no administrative or legislative authority is allowed to be integrated with judicial authority.[109]

In France, the Conseil Constitutionnel (the Constitutional Council) raises a similar issue. The council consists of all former Presidents of the Republic, who wish to serve, and nine other members who serve a non-renewable term of 9 years, one third of whom are appointed every 3 years. The other nine members are appointed by the President of the Republic, the President of the National Assembly, and the President of the Senate—each of them appoints three members.[110] The President of the Republic selects the President of the Constitutional Council. The composition of this council is highly political. It consists of former politicians and

---

[106]Shetreet (2016a), p. 370.

[107]Id Shetreet (2016a), p. 376.

[108]*Procola v Luxembourg*, (1995).

[109]Shetreet (2009b), p. 304.

[110]French constitution, Article 56.

members of the Executive and Legislative branches. The council has the power of constitutional review. This composition, in addition to the fact that the high constitutional institute is a "council" and not a court, may be argued to be a violation of universal standards of judicial independence. In light of the unique particular circumstances in France, it should come within the exception of "long and democratic tradition",[111] and therefor this should be recognized within the universal rules, which exclude mixing judicial and executive functions.

In Italy, the Corte Costituzionale (Constitutional Court) is not viewed as part of the judiciary but as a constitutional organ by the mainstream approach in Italy.[112] Until recently, the court defined itself as a non-judicial body. It never functions as a Court of last instance, nor exercises appellant jurisdiction. The Court consists of 15 members: five are elected by the parliament, five by the top judicial bodies, and five by the President of the country (and approved by the Prime Minister).[113] This composition of the constitutional court in Italy raises issue of excessive input of political branches of government. In addition, it is not viewed as a judicial institution, but rather as a constitutional organ. These characteristics arguably contradict Article 6 of the ECHR providing for independent and impartial tribunal, which reflects universal standards of judicial independence. The particularity of the circumstances of Italy regarding the top court defined as constitutional organ exercising constitutional review, should be excepted as well on the basis of "long and democratic tradition".

In Belgium, the Constitutional Court consists of 12 members, six of whom are former politicians.[114] In 1987 the following question has arose: three of the judges of the Constitutional Court had, when they were members of the Flemish parliament, participated in voting for the decree which was subjected to the review by the Constitutional Court. The question arose whether they are qualified, to sit and pass judgment on the matter. The answer that the Constitutional Court gave was positive, due to the delicate balance between the two ethnic groups in Belgium, who are represented by an equal number of members on the Court. Disqualifying some of them would imbalance this delicate composition. The position regarding the situation in Belgium should be recognized as particular practice justified by "long and democratic tradition" as an exception to the universal rules.

The view of this author is that recognition of the particular practices which take place in these countries, should be accepted within the guidelines regarding permissible executive and legislative role in matters relevant to the judiciary. This means, that these exceptional cases should be recognized as particular and unique long-going traditions, and they should be exempted from universal standards. In the case of England, the unique practice regarding the Lord Chancellor combining judicial, legislative and executive functions, was resolved by the aforementioned

---

[111]International Bar Association (1982), Article 3b.

[112]Ferrari (2014), p. 154.

[113]Ferrari (2014), p. 155.

[114]Bossuyt (2014), p. 138.

constitutional reform act of 2005,[115] which separated between those functions and implemented the doctrine of Separation of Powers. The Lord Chief Justice was entrusted with all the judicial functions previously exercised by the Lord Chancellor. The Lord Chancellor ceased to be Speaker of the House of Lords, and he remained mainly Minister of Justice, exercising executive and administrative functions.

Concerning India, it may be argued that it falls within the exception of particularity. The universal judicial independence standards lay down standards for judicial appointments, which provide for permissible participation of the executive or the legislative branches in judicial appointments. The jurisprudence of India, beginning in the 1993 ruling,[116] and later in the 2015 ruling,[117] sets up a much higher and stricter standards regarding the executive and legislative branches involvement in judicial appointments. This represents a controversial approach regarding the balance of powers between the judiciary and the political branches of government. The Supreme Court of India, in its 1993 and 2005 judgements, adopted a higher standard of judicial independence, by establishing an preserving the supremacy of the judiciary over the executive and the legislature regarding judicial appointments. This jurisprudence arguably calls for recognition of particularity of the circumstances in India.

The fact that certain practices of legislative or executive role in judicial appointments are permissible conceptually or by legal practice in many jurisdictions and in international standards, does not prevent India from determining that such role of the executive and legislative branches in judicial appointment as practiced by other countries is not acceptable to them. India may justifiably decide to adopt higher standards and stricter standards, limiting the role of executive or legislative role in judicial appointment, because of the particular interests existing in India. Just as the international standards allowed exception for jurisdictions which do not comply fully with the universal standards, such as in political activity of judges in Europe, or the position of the Lord Chancellor before 2005, and the different concept in France, Italy and Belgium regarding the composition of the top constitutional courts—so India can expect the universality theory to accept its exception for a more restrictive role of the executive and legislative role in judicial appointments.

I do not accept the argument advanced by Professor Neudorf in his book "The Dynamics of Judicial Independence: a Comparative Study of Courts in Malaysia and Pakistan",[118] that the *Mt. Scopus International Standards of Judicial Independence 2008* adopted by the international associations of judicial independence,[119] were based only on universal theory. The fact is that the international standards, first shaped in the *New-Delhi Code* by the same scholars, recognize particularity as mentioned above—such as the case of the politically-involved judges in Europe,

---

[115]Constitutional Reform Act of 2005.

[116]*Supreme Court Advocates-on-Record Assn. v. Union of India*, (1993) (India).

[117]*Supreme Court Advocates-on-Record Ass'n v. Union of India*, (2016) (India).

[118]Neudorf (2017), p. 3.

[119]The Mount Scopus International Standards of Judicial Independence (approved 2018).

or the Lord Chancellor position before 2005. The *Mt. Scopus International Standards of Judicial Independence* were adopted by the International Association of Judicial Independence and World Peace, on the basis of universal theory accommodating special circumstances. Thus, the right approach is ordinarily to expect countries to respect the universal rules, but at the same time, in proper circumstances, an exception should be carved for particular jurisdictions. With regard to India, it is an open question whether the view of the Supreme Court of India denying the dominant role of the Executive in judicial appointments based on separation of powers is to be supported, but the theory of particularity vis-à-vis universality approach allows a conclusion, which accepts this position. Many national courts believe that International or Supranational courts should not interfere in issues that are already regulated by domestic law.[120]

An important issue regarding universality vs. is the relationship between international tribunals and top courts of domestic jurisdictions. This includes the ECtHR and the top courts of the domestic jurisdictions or the European Court of justice and the courts of the member States.

Prof. Albuquerque claims of the ECtHR writes that ECtHR should apply its universal standards and not not, be subject to domestic laws of each country, in order to fulfill its function as a multinational independent and valuable jurisdiction.[121] This is a typical case of the tension between particularity and universality. The European community stresses common values, such as human rights, using American and Canadian constitutional doctrines, often on the behalf of national laws and basic values. This idea is not always viewed favorably by national jurisdictions.[122]

One such issue arose with regard to European arrest warrants. The EU convention requires all member to respect an arrest warrant of other states of the union. However, some countries, like Germany, have basic limitations on extradition of their citizens in their constitution. In this clash between the national law and the and ruling of transnational legal order, the German Constitutional Supreme court, and so did the Polish Supreme Court, have decided to declare unconstitutional the national laws implementing the European Arrest Warrant.[123] Similarly, the British House of Lords ruled that he is not obliged to the ECtHR decision, declaring that deprivation of the right to vote from prisoners is unconstitutional.[124]

The ECtHR should consider the basic principles of the legal systems before making its decision. When examining domestic acts or legislations, the judges of the international tribunals and supra national courts must consider the basic

---

[120]Shetreet (2014), p. 476.

[121]Pinto de Albuquerque (2018), p. 128.

[122]Pinto de Albuquerque (2018), p. 128.

[123]Shetreet (2016b), p. 162.
The German Court Decision: BvR 2236/04, BVerfGE (2004); The Polish Court Decision: Wyrok [judgment] TK [Constitutional Tribunal] z [of] 27 April 2005 P. 1/05.

[124]*Secretary of the State for the Home Department v. AF and Or's* [2009].

principles of the national systems, and interpret the law regarding the basic constitutional values of this state.

I support the Constitutional Pluralism doctrine that while we are not sure which moral and jurisprudential set of values and principles is to be preferred, it is highly important to consider each formulation as equally legitimate.[125] This idea is expressed in the 2014 Vienna amendments to the Mount Scopus standards. The Article 1.3 states that:

> 1.3 It is vital that supranational and international Tribunals respect the fundamental principles of the legal systems of the Member States and to that end acknowledge the collegiality of the traditions of the courts of both the municipal and extra municipal courts.[126]

Therefore, I suggest that the relations between the courts should be based on a dialogue, respect and least conflicts as possible.[127]

References

Books

Bingham, T. (2000). *The business of judging: Selected essays and speeches*. Oxford: Oxford University Press.

Neudorf, L. (2017). *The dynamics of judicial independence: A comparative study of courts in Malaysia and Pakistan*. Berlin: Springer.

Roznai, Y. (2017). *Unconstitutional constitutional amendments: The limits of amendment powers*. Oxford: Oxford University Press.

Shetreet, S. (2003a). *On adjudication: Justice on trial*. Jerusalem: Yedioth Aharonot.

Shtreet, S., & Turenne, S. (2012). *Judges on trial: The independence and accountability of the English Judiciary* (2nd ed.). Cambridge: Cambridge University Press.

Woolf, L. (2004). The rule of law and a change in the constitution. *Cambridge Law Journal, 63*, 317–330.

Woolf, L. (2008). *The pursuit of justice*. Oxford: Oxford University Press.

Journal Articles

Cotler, I. (2008). The Supreme Court appointment process: Chronology, context, and reform. *University of New Brunswick Law Journal, 58*, 131–147.

Dotan, Y. (2007). Judicial review within a Constitution: The accountability issue - A comparative perspective. *Mishpat Vemimshal, 10*, 495–496. (Hebrew).

---

[125] Shetreet (2014), p. 477.

[126] The Mount Scopus International Standards of Judicial Independence (approved 2018), Article 1.3.

[127] Shetreet (2014), p. 476.

Merillat, H. C. L. (1960). The Indian Constitution: Property rights and social reform. *Ohio State Law Journal, 21*, 616.

Pinello, D. R. (1999). Linking party to judicial ideology in American Courts: A meta-analysis. *The Justice System Journal, 20*(3), 219.

Pinto de Albuquerque, P. (2018). Plaidoyer for the European Court of human rights. *European Human Rights Law Review, 2*, 119.

Shetreet, S. (1979). On assessing the role of courts in society. *Manitoba Law Journal, 10*, 357.

Shetreet, S. (2003b). Judicial appointments: Standards and process. *Hamishpat Law Review, 8*, 357.

Shetreet, S. (2009a). Culture of Judicial independence in Israel: Institutional and substantive aspects of the justice system in historical perspectives. *Law and Business, 10*, 525.

Shetreet, S. (2009b). The normative cycle of shaping judicial independence in domestic and international law: The mutual impact of national and international jurisprudence and contemporary practical and conceptual challenges. *Chicago Journal of International Law, 10*, 295.

The European Convention on Human Rights and Fundamental Freedoms. (1953). United Nations Treaty Series, 212 223.

Turley, J. (2005). Essays on Article III: Good behavior clause. In *Heritage Guide to the Constitution*. Washington, D.C.: The Heritage Foundation.

Windlesham, L. (2005). The Constitutional Reform Act 2005: Ministers, judges and constitutional change. *Public Law, 1*, 806.

Windlesham, L. (2006). The Constitutional Reform Act 2005: The politics of constitutional reform. *Public Law, 1*, 35.

Zimmer, M. B. (2006). Judicial independence in Central and East Europe: The institutional context. *Tulsa Journal of Comparative & International Law, 14*, 53.

Zimmer, M. B. (2011). Judicial system institutional frameworks: An overview of the interplay between self-governance and independence. *Utah Law Review, 1*, 124.

Chapters from Books

Bossuyt, M. (2014). The independence of the judiciary in Belgium. In S. Shetreet (Ed.), *Culture of judicial independence: Rule of law and World Peace*. Leiden: Brill Nijhoff Publishers.

Ferrari, G. F. (2014). The conceptual definition of the constitutional court in Italy. In S. Shetreet (Ed.), *Culture of judicial independence: Rule of law and World Peace*. Leiden: Brill Nijhoff Publishers.

Models of Constitutional Adjudication. (2005). *The legal cultures of China and Israel – The proceedings of Legal Conference of Zhengfa University, Beijing and Hebrew University* (p. 198). Beijing: Zengfa University.

Shetreet, S. (1985a). Judicial independence: New conceptual dimensions and contemporary challenges. In S. Shetreet & D. Jules (Eds.), *Judicial independence: The contemporary debate* (p. 591). Boston/Lancaster: Martinus Nijhoff/Dordrecht.

Shetreet, S. (1985b). The emerging transnational jurisprudence on judicial independence: IBA Standards and Montreal Declaration. In S. Shetreet & D. Jules (Eds.), *Judicial independence: The contemporary debate*. Boston/Lancaster: Martinus Nijhoff/Dordrecht.

Shetreet, S. (2012a). Creating a culture of judicial independence: The practical challenge and the conceptual and constitutional infrastructure. In C. F. Forsyth & S. Shetreet (Eds.), *The culture of judicial independence: Conceptual foundations and practical challenges* (p. 18). Leiden: Brill Nijhoff.

Shetreet, S. (2012b). Fundamental values of the Justice system in Israel. In A. Barak et al. (Eds.), *Or Book* (pp. 619–647). Herzeliya: Interdisciplinary Center.

Shetreet, S. (2012c). Formulation of a consensus in a legal culture of diversity. In C. F. Forsyth & S. Shetreet (Eds.), *The culture of judicial independence: Conceptual foundations and practical challenges* (p. 477). Leiden: Brill I Nijhoff.

Shetreet, S. (2014). Analysis of the amendments to the Mt. Scopus in international standards of judicial independence. In S. Shetreet (Ed.), *Culture of judicial independence: Rule of law and World Peace* (p. 495). Leiden: Brill Nijhoff Publishers.

Shetreet, S. (2016a). Amendments to the Mt. Scopus Standards (Moscow Conference, Osnabrueck Conference and Bologna and Milan Conference). In S. Shetreet & W. McCormack (Eds.), *The culture of judicial independence in a globalised world*. Leiden: Brill II Nijhoff Publishers.

Shetreet, S. (2016b). Relations between top courts and supra-national courts. In S. Shetreet & W. McCormack (Eds.), *The culture of judicial independence in a Globalised World*. Leiden: Brill II Nijhoff Publishers.

Shetreet, S. (2017). Comparative analysis of lustration in the judiciary: Theoretical and practical aspects. In O. Baller & B. Breig (Eds.), *Justiz in Mittel-und Osterupa*. Berlin: BMV Berliner Wissenschafts Verlage.

Zoll, F. (2014). On judges writing commentaries: Is it appropriate for a judge to engage in outside activities? In S. Shtreet (Ed.), *The culture of judicial independence: Rule of law and world peace* (p. 217). Leiden: Brill Nijhoff.

International Standards and Declarations

The International Association of Judicial Independence and World Peace. (1983). *The Universal Declaration on the independence of justice.*

The International Association of Judicial Independence and World Peace. (Approved 2018). *Mount Scopus international standards of judicial independence.*

International Bar Association. (1982). *The IBA minimum standards of judicial independence.*

Electronic Articles

Ayasun, A. (2018). Is Turkey's Judiciary Independent?, *The Global Post Turkey*, Available at: https://turkey.theglobepost.com/turkey-judiciary-independence-judges/

Azulay, M., & Hay, S. (2018). Herzog: Netanyahu's attacks on judiciary a clear and present danger to democracy, *Ynet*. Available at: https://www.ynetnews.com/articles/0,7340,L-5247664,00. html

Leifer, J. (2018). Attempts to 'Bypass' Israel's High Court will create a 'Tyranny of the Majority', *+972 Online Magazine*. Available at: https://972mag.com/attempts-to-bypass-high-court-could-end-protection-for-israels-minorities/134765/

Constitutional, Judicial and Parliamentary Supremacy in India. (2016). *gktoday*. http://www. gktoday.in/gk/constitutional-judicial-and-parliamentary-supremacy-in-india/

EU court stuns Poland's PiS with order to suspend ejection of judges. (2018). *bne IntelliNews*. http://www.intellinews.com/eu-court-stuns-poland-s-pis-with-order-to-suspend-ejection-of-judges-150554/

Freedom House, Nations in Transit. (2017). Romania Country Profile, *Freedom House*. Retrieved September 15, 2018, from https://freedomhouse.org/report/nations-transit/2017/romania

Harkov, L. (2018). Netanyahu, Levin Push for Dramatic Judiciary Restructuring, *The Jerusalem Post*. Available at: https://www.jpost.com/Israel-News/Top-Likud-minister-Well-even-go-to-election-to-limit-Supreme-Court-549850

Hovel, R. (2017). Israel's Chief Justice Warns Government in Landmark Speech: Judicial Branch 'Under Unprecedented Attack', *Haaretz*. Available at: https://www.haaretz.com/israel-news/israel-s-chief-justice-judicial-branch-under-attack 1.6062718

Jude, K., & Watters, K. (2018). Trump's attacks on courts undermine judicial independence, *ABA Journal*. Available at: http://www.abajournal.com/news/article/trumps_attacks_on_courts_undermines_judicial_independene

Orlofsky, S. M. (2018). *Judicial independence in the age of Trump, Blank Rome*. Available at: https://www.blankrome.com/publications/judicial-independence-age-trump

Parliament Initiates Steps Under Article 7 Over Hungary's 'Systemic Threat' to EU Values'. (2018). *France 24 News*. https://www.france24.com/en/20180912-european-parliament-calls-punitive-action-against-hungary-over-rule-law

Phillips. (2007). Constitutional reform: One Year On, the judicial studies board annual lecture (Mar 22, 2007). Available at: http://www.judiciary.gov.uk/media/speeches/2007/Judicial+Studies+Board+2007+Lecture (Visited Oct 3, 2010).

Platform for Peace and Justice. (2018). *Non-independence and Non-impartiality of the Turkish Judiciary, A comprehensive report on the abolition of the rule of law*. Available at: http://www.platformpj.org/wp-content/uploads/non-independence-1.pdf

Staudenmaier, R. (2018). EU Parliament votes to trigger Article 7 Sanctions Procedure against Hungary, *DW - Made for Minds*. https://www.dw.com/en/eu-parliament-votes-to-trigger-article-7-sanctions-procedure-against-hungary/a-45459720

United States Department of State. (2017). *Turkey 2017 Human Rights Report, Bureau of Democracy, Human Rights and Labor Country Reports on Human Rights Practices for 2017*. Available at: https://www.state.gov/documents/organization/277471.pdf

Court Decisions: ECtHR

Procola v Luxembourg, (1995) 326 Eur Ct HR (ser A) (ECtHR).

Case C-506/04 *Graham J. Wilson v Ordre des avocats du barreau de Luxembourg* [2006] ECR I-08613 (ECtHR).

Case c-550/09 *E and F* [2010] ECR I-06213 (ECtHR).

Case C-411/10 *N. S. v Secretary of State for the Home Department* [2011] ECR I-13905 (ECtHR).

Case C-583/11 *P, Inuit Tapiriit Kanatami and Others v Parliament and Council* [2013] ECR I-nyr (ECtHR).

Opinion C-2/13 *Enquêtes Douanières v. Humeau Beaupréau SAS* [2014] ECR (ECtHR).

Case c-456/13, *T & L Sugars and Sidul Açúcares v Commission* [2015] ECR 286 (ECtHR).

Baka v Hungary, App. No. 20261/12 (23 June 2016) (ECtHR).

Case C-72/15 *OJSC Rosneft Oil Company v Her Majesty's Treasury and Others* [2016] ECR (ECtHR).

Cases C-404/15, C-659/15 PPU *Pál Aranyosi and Robert Căldăraru v Generalstaatsanwaltschaft Bremen* [2016] ECR (ECtHR).

Case C-64/16 *Associação Sindical dos Juízes Portugueses v. Tribunal de Contas* [2017] ECR (ECtHR).

Court Decisions: Germany

BvR 2236/04, BVerfGE 113, 273 (Germany).

Court Decisions: India

Shankari Prasad v. India (1951) AIR SC 458.
Sajjan Singh v. State Of Rajasthan (1965) AIR SC 845. (India).
Golakanath v. State Of Punjab (1967) AIR SC 1643. (India).
Indira Nehru Gandhi v. Raj Narain (1975), AIR SC 2299. (India).
Supreme Court Advocates-on-Record Assn. v. Union of India, (1993) 4 SCC 441 (India).
Supreme Court Advocates-on-Record Ass'n v. Union of India, (2016) 4 SCC 1 (India).

Court Decisions: Israel

HCJ 9029/16 *Aviram v. Minister of Justice*, 22-26 (Jan. 2, 2016), Nevo Legal Database (by subscription, in Hebrew) (Isr.).

Court Decisions: Poland

Wyrok [judgment] TK [Constitutional Tribunal] z [of] 27 April 2005 P. 1/05 OTK ZU 4/A/2005 42 (Poland).

Court Decisions: Scotland

Starrs and Chalmers v. P.F. Linlithgow, 2000 S.L 2. (Scotland).
Clancy v. Caird, 2000 Scottish Law Times (Scotland).

Court Decisions: UK

Stewart v. Secretary of State for Scotland, Extra Division, (1996) SLT 1203 (UK).
Secretary of the State for the Home Department v. AF and Or's [2009] UKHL 28 (UK).

Legislation: Canada

Supreme Court Act, R.S.C. 1985, c S-26, $30(2) (Can.).

Legislation: Israel

Basic Law: Adjudication (Israel).
The Courts Law (1984) (Israel).

Legislation: Scotland

The Sheriff Courts Act (1971) (Scotland).

Legislation: UK

Judicial Pension Act, 1959 (UK).
Constitutional Reform Act, 2005 (UK).

The Subjective Right of Judges to Independence: Some Reflexions on the Interpretation of Article 6, Para. 1 of the ECHR

Linos-Alexander Sicilianos

Contents

1   Preliminary Remarks

I have had the privilege of working together with President Vincent De Gaetano since the beginning of my mandate at the European Court of Human Rights (ECtHR), either in the Committee on working methods, or in the Grand Chamber and in the Bureau. His sense of humour but also the clarity of his positions, defended with brio, has made this cooperation a real pleasure. The independence of the judiciary is always a recurrent theme in his thinking and legal discourse. This is the reason why I decided to focus the present contribution in his honour to the issue of the independence of judges and more precisely to the question whether one could

---

Linos-Alexander Sicilianos is President of the European Court of Human Rights.

L.-A. Sicilianos (✉)
European Court of Human Rights, Strasbourg, France
e-mail: linos-alexandre.sicilianos@echr.coe.int

© Springer Nature Switzerland AG 2019   547
P. Pinto de Albuquerque, K. Wojtyczek (eds.), *Judicial Power in a Globalized
World*, https://doi.org/10.1007/978-3-030-20744-1_33

interpret Article 6, paragraph 1 of the ECHR so as to cover the subjective right of judges to independence. This question has not been examined by the Court *expressis verbis*, but was closely related to the facts of the case *Baka v. Hungary* decided by the Grand Chamber in 2016.[1]

The applicant, a former judge of the European Court of Human Rights, was elected President of the Supreme Court of Hungary for a 6-year term ending in 2015. In his capacity as President of that court and of the National Council of Justice, he expressed his views on various legislative reforms affecting the judiciary. The transitional provisions of the new Constitution (Fundamental Law of Hungary of 2011) provided that the legal successor to the Supreme Court would be the Kúria and that the mandate of the President of the Supreme Court would end following the entry into force of the new Constitution. As a consequence, the applicant's mandate as President of the Supreme Court ended on 1 January 2012. According to the criteria for the election of the President of the new Kúria, candidates were required to have at least 5 years' experience as a judge in Hungary. Time served as a judge in an international court was not counted. This led to the applicant's ineligibility for the post of President of the new Kúria.

Examining the case under article 6 of the Convention, the Court found that as a result of legislation whose compatibility with the requirements of the rule of law was doubtful, the premature termination of the applicant's mandate was neither reviewed, nor open to review, by any bodies exercising judicial powers. Noting the growing importance which international and Council of Europe instruments, as well as the case-law of international courts and the practice of other international bodies, were attaching to procedural fairness in cases involving the removal or dismissal of judges, the Court considered that the respondent State had impaired the very essence of the applicant's right of access to a court.

Under article 10 of the Convention, the Court stressed that it was not only his right but also his duty to express his opinion on legislative reforms which were likely to have an impact on the judiciary and its independence. The applicant had expressed his views and criticisms on questions of public interest and his statements had not gone beyond mere criticism from a strictly professional perspective. Accordingly, his position and statements called for a high degree of protection for his freedom of expression and strict scrutiny of any interference, with a correspondingly narrow margin of appreciation being afforded to the domestic authorities. Furthermore, he was removed from his office more than 3 years before the end of the fixed term applicable under the legislation in force at the time of his election. This could hardly be reconciled with the particular consideration to be given to the nature of the judicial function as an independent branch of State power and to the principle of the irremovability of judges, which was a key element for the maintenance of judicial independence. The premature termination of the applicant's mandate undoubtedly had a chilling effect in that it must have discouraged not only him but also other judges and court presidents in future from participating in public debate on legislative reforms affecting the judiciary and more generally on issues concerning the independence of the judiciary.

---

[1] *Baka v. Hungary*, GC, no. 20261/12, 23 June 2016.

It thus appears that although the independence of the judiciary is omnipresent in the judgment of *Baka v. Hungary*, it is seen through the perspective of the right of access to a Court and the freedom of expression. In other words the issue of judicial independence is examined indirectly and not frontally, i.e. under article 6, paragraph 1 of the Convention which explicitly refers to an "independent tribunal". This approach is in conformity with the traditional case law of the Court (II). The question is raised, however, whether this provision can be interpreted in a way as to cover a fundamental aspect of the functioning of the judicial system, namely the subjective right of the judge to his or her own independence. In order to reply to this question it is important to refer briefly to other international instruments and relevant international practice (III–VII).

2 Judicial Independence in the Court's Case-Law Under Article 6 § 1 of the Convention: The Right of Persons Involved in Court Proceedings to an Independent Judge

It is well known that the ECtHR has repeatedly insisted, for more than 30 years, that a court must be independent both of the parties and of the executive. In the now classic wording of the *Campbell and Fell* judgment:

> [I]n determining whether a body can be considered to be 'independent' - notably of the executive and of the parties to the case (see, *inter alia*, the *Le Compte, Van Leuven and De Meyere* judgment of 23 June 1981, Series A no. 43, § 55) -, the Court has had regard to the manner of appointment of its members and the duration of their term of office (ibid., § 57), the existence of guarantees against outside pressures (see the *Piersack* judgment of 1 October 1982, Series A no. 53, § 27) and the question whether the body presents an appearance of independence (see the *Delcourt* judgment of 17 January 1970, Series A no. 11, § 31).[2]

The Court has added in this regard that what is at stake is "the confidence which such tribunals must inspire in the public".[3]

Similarly, the Court has also underlined the judiciary's necessary independence from the legislative. Thus, in the *Stran Greek Refineries and Stratis Andreadis v. Greece* judgment, it noted in general terms that "[t]he principle of the rule of law and the notion of fair trial enshrined in Article 6 . . . preclude any interference by the legislature with the administration of justice designed to influence the judicial determination of the dispute".[4] The formula in question, frequently repeated since,[5] conveys the idea of the separation of powers.

---

[2]See *Campbell and Fell v. the United Kingdom*, 28 June 1984, § 78, Series A no. 80.

[3]See *Clarke v. the United Kingdom* (dec.), no. 23695/02, ECHR 2005-X.

[4]See *Stran Greek Refineries and Stratis Andreadis v. Greece*, 9 December 1994, § 49, Series A no. 301-B.

[5]See, for example, *National & Provincial Building Society, Leeds Permanent Building Society and Yorkshire Building Society v. the United Kingdom*, 23 October 1997, § 112, *Reports of Judgments*

The principle of the independence of the judiciary is not simply a matter of its relations with the executive and the legislative branches. It also concerns judicial independence within the system of the administration of justice itself. Judges must be free, in their individual capacity, not only from any external influence, but also from any "inside" influence. This "internal judicial independence" implies that judges do not receive instructions and are not subjected to pressure from their colleagues or from persons exercising administrative responsibilities in a court, such as the president of a court or the president of a court's section.[6] The absence of sufficient guarantees ensuring judges' independence within the judicial branch, and especially *vis-à-vis* their superiors within the judicial hierarchy, could lead the Court to conclude that an applicant's doubts as to the independence and impartiality of a court may be said to have been objectively justified.[7]

Thus, the Court's case-law has addressed several aspects of the principle of judicial independence: independence *vis-à-vis* the parties, independence from the executive and legislative powers, and internal judicial independence (for a detailed overview of the Court on the subject see mainly Sicilianos 2017, pp. 265 et seq; Grabenwarter 2014, pp. 116 et seq; Harris et al. 2014, pp. 447 et seq; Renucci 2015, pp. 407 et seq; Schabas 2015, pp. 294 et seq). However, all these aspects of judicial independence have been assessed from the perspective of the right of "[e]veryone . . . to a fair and public hearing . . . by an independent and impartial tribunal previously established by law. . ." In other words, the letter of Article 6 § 1 of the Convention has led the Court to analyse the issue of judicial independence from the perspective of *the rights of persons involved in court proceedings* and not from that of *judges' subjective right* to have their own independence guaranteed and respected by the State.

The case *Baka v. Hungary* lent itself, *a priori*, to an examination of this latter aspect. However, under Article 6 the applicant relied solely on the more traditional aspect of the right to a fair hearing, namely the right of access to a court. In those circumstances, the Court, quite rightly, restricted its assessment to the right relied upon. Nonetheless, the principle of judicial independence is omnipresent in the judgment.[8] In the "Facts" part, the Court quotes numerous international, universal and regional texts, including case-law examples concerning judicial independence

---

and Decisions 1997-VII; *Zielinski and Pradal and Gonzalez and Others v. France* [GC], nos. 24846/94 and 34165/96 to 34173/96, § 57, ECHR 1999-VII; *Scordino v. Italy (no. 1)* [GC], no. 36813/97, § 126, ECHR 2006-V; and *Tarbuk v. Croatia*, no. 31360/10, § 49, 11 December 2012.

[6]See *Parlov-Tkalčić v. Croatia*, no. 24810/06, § 86, 22 December 2009, and *Agrokompleks v. Ukraine*, no. 23465/03, § 137, 6 October 2011; see also *Moiseyev v. Russia*, no. 62936/00, § 182, 9 October 2008.

[7]See *Parlov-Tkalčić*, cited above, § 86; *Agrokompleks*, cited above, § 137; *Moiseyev*, cited above, § 184; and *Daktaras v. Lithuania*, no. 42095/98, §§ 36 and 38, ECHR 2000-X.

[8]See in this regard, the observations of Judges Pinto de Albuquerque and Dedov in their common concurring opinion (annexed to the *Baka v. Hungary* judgment, cited above), mainly §§ 20–21.

and the related principle of the irremovability of judges.[9] In the "Law" part, these principles are examined *in extenso* from the perspective of the applicant's right to freedom of expression.

3 The Non-binding International Texts: Judicial Independence Includes the Judge's Subjective Right to Independence

Of the non-binding texts quoted in the judgment, several emphasise the judge's subjective right to his or her independence. Thus, after having asserted that "[j] udicial independence and impartiality are essential prerequisites for the operation of justice", the Magna Carta of Judges (Fundamental Principles), adopted by the CCJE in November 2010, adds that "[j]udicial independence shall be statutory, functional and financial. It shall be guaranteed with regard to the other powers of the State, to those seeking justice, *other judges* and society in general, by means of national rules at the highest level. . .".[10] Similarly, the Venice Commission has considered that "the interest of maintaining the independence of the judiciary and the good administration of justice requires that the judiciary be protected against arbitrary dismissal and interference in the exercise of the functions".[11]

4 The International Covenant on Civil and Political Rights and the American Convention on Human Rights: Essentially the Same Wording as the European Convention

Beyond these non-binding texts and opinions, the interpretation of conventions and agreements containing similar or even identical wording to that of Article 6 of the Convention with regard to the right to an "independent tribunal" is of even greater importance. It should be noted that Article 14 § 1 of the International Covenant on

---

[9]See *Baka v. Hungary*, cited above, §§ 72–87.

[10]CCJE (2010)3 Final, Magna Carta, 17 November 2010, par. 3.

[11]Venice Commission, Opinion on the draft law on introducing amendments and addenda to the judicial code of Armenia (term of Office of Court Presidents), adopted by the Venice Commission at its 99th Plenary Session (Venice, 13–14 June 2014, CDL-AD(2014)021 par. 47); see also paragraph 97 of the Joint Opinion of the Venice Commission and the Directorate of Human Rights (DHR) of the Directorate General of Human Rights and the Rule of Law (DGI) of the Council of Europe, on the draft law on amendments to the Organic Law on General Courts of Georgia, adopted by the Venice Commission a its 100th Plenary Session (Rome, 10–11 October 2014, CDL-AD (2014) 031).

Civil and Political Rights (hereafter the "ICCPR") states that "everyone shall be entitled to a fair and public hearing by a competent, independent and impartial tribunal established by law..." Article 8 § 1 of the American Convention on Human Rights also contains a similar provision: "Every person has the right to a hearing, with due guarantees ... by a competent, independent, and impartial tribunal, previously established by law..." In other words, the wording of these two binding instruments, like that of the ECHR, approaches the issue of judicial independence in terms of the rights of persons involved in court proceedings, and not from the perspective of the judge's subjective right to have his or her own independence guaranteed and respected by the State (including within the judiciary).

5 The Case-Law of the Human Rights Committee: Highlighting the Judge's Right to Independence

In spite of the above-cited wording of Article 14 § 1 of the ICCPR, the Human Rights Committee has nonetheless on several occasions approached the issue from the perspective of the rights of judges themselves, and of the State's obligations towards them in safeguarding their independence. Here, we would refer primarily to General Comment no. 32 on Article 14 of the Covenant (Right to equality before courts and tribunals and to a fair trial). This General Comment emphasises the various aspects of the guarantee of independence from the perspective of the judges themselves (appointment, qualifications, security of tenure, remuneration, promotion, transfers, suspensions, dismissal, disciplinary measures, etc.), and the measures that the States should take to guarantee judges' effective independence and their protection from "any form of political influence in their decision-making", and from conflicts of interest and intimidation (see also the commentary of Eudes 2011, pp. 342–344).[12]

This General Comment codifies, as it were, the Committee's practice, including with regard to "individual communications" concerning the right to a fair hearing. Thus, we note that the Committee has received various communications from judges themselves, alleging, in particular, that they were dismissed (or that their mandates were ended prematurely) in breach of the established procedures and safeguards. In these cases it has found that "those dismissals constitute[d] an attack on the independence of the judiciary protected by article 14 § 1 of the Covenant".[13] Admittedly, in this case, as in others, it dealt with this type of communication under a combination of Article 14 § 1 of the Covenant and Article 25 (c), which recognises the right

---

[12]United Nations Human Rights Committee, General Comment no. 32 on Article 14 of the International Covenant on Civil and Political Rights (Right to equality before courts and tribunals and to a fair trial), 23 August 2007, UN doc. CCPR/C/GC/32, par. 19.

[13]See *Munyo Busyo et al. v. Democratic Republic of Congo*, Communication No. 933/2000, 19 September 2003.

of every citizen to have access, "on general terms of equality, to public service in his country". It is also true that the right of access to public office is not, as such, expressly protected by the Convention.[14] However, as is clear from the above-cited wording in the *Mundyo Busyo* case, the Committee in that case examined the impugned dismissal not only under Article 14 § 1 of the Covenant in combination with Article 25 (c), but also from the perspective of judicial independence as protected on an autonomous basis by Article 14. This approach was confirmed by the *Bandaranayake v. Sri Lanka* case (Communication No. 1376/2005, 24 July 2008), where the Committee found, *inter alia*, that "the dismissal procedure [had] not respect[ed] the requirements of basic procedural fairness and failed to ensure that the author benefited from the necessary guarantees to which he was entitled in his capacity as a judge, thus constituting an attack on the independence of the judiciary".[15]

6   The Case-Law of the Inter-American Court of Human Rights: From the Right to an Independent Judge to the Judge's Right to Independence

Similar observations apply, *mutatis mutandis*, with regard to the recent case-law of the Inter-American Court of Human Rights on the same subject, quoted in paragraphs 84 and 85 of the *Baka* judgment. In this connection, it is significant that the Inter-American Court in its *Supreme Court of Justice (Quintana Coello et al.) v. Ecuador* judgment of 23 August 2013, on the removal by parliamentary resolution of 27 judges of the Supreme Court of Justice of Ecuador, built on its earlier case-law on the right to an independent judge, guaranteed by Article 8 § 1 of the American Convention in terms, as we have seen, that are practically identical to those used in Article 6 § 1 of the Convention. The following extract from the relevant judgment is particularly enlightening in this regard:

> The foregoing serves to clarify some aspects of the Court's jurisprudence. Indeed, in the case of *Reverón Trujillo v. Venezuela*, the Court concluded that the right to be heard by an independent tribunal, enshrined in Article 8(1) of the Convention, only implied that a citizen has a right to be judged by an independent judge. However, it is important to point out that judicial independence should not only be analyzed in relation to justiciable matters, given that the judge must have a series of guarantees that allow for judicial independence. The Court considers it pertinent to specify that the violation of the guarantee of judicial independence, as it relates to a judge's tenure and stability in his position, must be examined in light of the conventional rights of a judge who is affected by a State decision that arbitrarily affects the term of his appointment. In that sense, the institutional guarantee of

---

[14] It is well known that Article 3 of Protocol No. 1 to the Convention, although developed and supplemented through case-law, is more limited in scope than Article 25 of the ICCPR.

[15] Human Rights Committee, *Bandaranayake v. Sri Lanka*, Communication No. 1376/2005, 24 July 2008, par. 7.3.

judicial independence is directly related to a judge's right to remain in his post, as a consequence of the guarantee of tenure in office.[16]

This case-law was confirmed in the *Constitutional Tribunal (Camba Campos et al.) v. Ecuador* (28 August 2013)[17] and *López Lone et al. v. Honduras* (5 October 2015)[18] judgments. Thus, in the view of the Inter-American Court, it now appears established that Article 8 § 1 of the American Convention recognises not only the right of persons appearing before a court to an independent judge, but also the right of judges themselves to have their independence safeguarded and respected by the State.

7 Towards a Subjective Right to Judicial Independence, Protected by the Convention?

The above considerations give rise to the question of whether Article 6 § 1 of the Convention can be interpreted in such a way as to recognise, in parallel to the right of persons involved in court proceedings to have their cases heard by an impartial court, a subjective right for judges to have their individual independence safeguarded and respected by the State. A positive response to this question would indicate that the judges themselves could rely on Article 6, without necessarily having to prove that an interference with their independence had simultaneously amounted to an unjustified interference in the exercise of their right to freedom of expression or another right enshrined in the Convention. In other words, such an interpretation would strengthen the protection granted to judicial independence under the Convention.

It is well known that in the *Golder* judgment the Court interpreted the Convention teleologically, for the purpose of identifying the right of access to a court in Article 6 § 1. After noting that the provision in question "does not state a right of access to the courts or tribunals in express terms",[19] it referred to all of the principles of interpretation contained in Article 31 of the Vienna Convention on the Law of Treaties, including the importance of the preamble, which is "very useful for the determination of the 'object' and 'purpose' of the instrument to be construed".[20] In a similar vein, it drew attention to the "profound belief" of the signatory Governments in the rule of law, referred to in the preamble, and the key role of this concept in the

---

[16]Inter-American Court of Human Rights, 23 August 2013, *Supreme Court of Justice (Quintana Coello et al.) v. Ecuador*, par. 153.

[17]Inter-American Court of Human Rights, 28 August 2013, *Camba Campos et al. v. Ecuador*, par. 188–199.

[18]Inter-American Court of Human Rights, 5 October 2015, *López Lone et al. v. Honduras*, par. 190–202 and 239–240.

[19]See *Golder v. the United Kingdom*, 21 February 1975, § 28, Series A no. 18.

[20]Cited above, §34.

Convention system. It concluded in this regard that "in civil matters one can scarcely conceive of the rule of law without there being a possibility of having access to the courts".[21] It also reiterated the terms of Article 31 § 1 (c) of the Vienna Convention, which indicates that account is to be taken also of "any relevant rules of international law applicable in the relations between the parties", including the "general principles of law recognized by civilized nations" within the meaning of Article 38 § 1 (c) of the Statute of the International Court of Justice. It noted that one of those principles forbids the denial of justice. Taking all of these aspects into consideration, it reached the still renowned conclusion that "it would be inconceivable . . . that Article 6 § 1 should describe in detail the procedural guarantees afforded to parties in a pending lawsuit and should not first protect that which alone makes it in fact possible to benefit from such guarantees, that is, access to a court . . . the right of access constitutes an element which is inherent in the right stated by Article 6 § 1".[22]

The Court has since reiterated on numerous occasions the importance of the principle of the rule of law in the context of Article 6 of the Convention,[23] and also of the need to take account of the relevant rules of international law in interpreting and applying the Convention.[24] In my opinion, however, the rule of law is hardly imaginable without an obligation on the State to offer safeguards for the protection of judicial independence and, hence, without the corresponding right of judges themselves to independence. Moreover, as is clear from the entirety of the international-law materials cited in the judgment of *Baka v. Hungary*, judicial independence is today an integral part of the general principles of international law (this concerns both the national and the international judge, see Mose 2014, pp. 187–205) which must be taken into account in interpreting the Convention. Equally, an interpretation of Article 6 § 1 which finds that it protects the judge's subjective right to independence would be perfectly compatible with that provision's object and purpose. In this connection, I subscribe to the idea, set out in the Magna Carta of Judges, to the effect that "[j]udicial independence and impartiality are essential prerequisites for the operation of justice".[25]

Indeed, how can one hope that persons involved in court proceedings will enjoy the right to an independent judge if judges themselves are not afforded safeguards capable of ensuring that independence? In my opinion, a subjective right of this sort for judges is inherent in the safeguards of the first paragraph of Article 6, and in the concept of a fair trial. I believe that this approach is borne out by the above-mentioned case-law of the Human Rights Committee and the Inter-American

---

[21]Cited above.

[22]Cited above, §§ 35, 36.

[23]See, for example, *Siegle v. Romania*, no. 23456/04, § 32, 16 April 2013; *Varnienė v. Lithuania*, no. 42916/04, § 37, 12 November 2013; *Solomun v. Croatia*, no. 679/11, § 46, 2 April 2015; *Ustimenko v. Ukraine*, no. 32053/13, § 46, 29 October 2015; and *Amirkhanyan v. Armenia*, no. 22343/08, § 33, 3 December 2015.

[24]See, among many other authorities, *Hassan v. the United Kingdom* [GC], no. 29750/09, §§ 100 and 102, ECHR 2014.

[25]CCJE (2010)3 Final, Magna Carta, cited above.

Court of Human Rights. In view of the concerns about and challenges to judicial independence and impartiality in the member States of the Council of Europe,[26] it seems appropriate to interpret Article 6 so as to enhance the protection of judges.

References

Eudes, M. (2011). Article 14. In E. Décaux (Ed.), *Le Pacte international relatif aux droits civils et politiques. Commentaire article par article*. Paris: Economica.

Grabenwarter, C. (2014). *European convention on human rights—commentary*. Munich, Germany/ Oxford, England: C.H. Beck/Hart/Nomos/Helbing Lichtenhahn Verlag.

Harris, D. J., O'Boyle, M., Bates, E. P., & Buckley, C. M. (2014). *Law of the European convention on human rights* (3rd ed.). Oxford, England: Oxford University Press.

Mose, E. (2014). The independence of international judges. In N. A. Engstad, A. Laerdal Frøseth, & B. Tønder (Eds.), *The independence of judges*. The Hague, The Netherlands: Eleven International Publishing.

Renucci, J.-F. (2015). *Droit européen des droits de l'homme. Droits et libertés fondamentaux garantis par la CEDH* (6th ed.). Paris: LGDJ.

Schabas, W. A. (2015). *The European convention on human rights*. Oxford, England: Oxford University Press.

Sicilianos, L.-A. (2017). Article 6 par. 1. In L.-A. Sicilianos (Ed.), *European convention on human rights, commentary article by article* (2nd ed.). Athens, Greece: Nomiki Vivliothiki. (in Greek).

Legal Sources

CCJE (2010)3 Final, Magna Carta, 17 November 2010.

ECHR, *Agrokompleks v. Ukraine*, no. 23465/03, 6 October 2011.

ECHR, *Amirkhanyan v. Armenia*, no. 22343/08, 3 December 2015.

ECHR, *Campbell and Fell v. the United Kingdom*, 28 June 1984, § 78, Series A no. 80.

ECHR, *Clarke v. the United Kingdom* (dec.), no. 23695/02, ECHR 2005-X.

ECHR, *Daktaras v. Lithuania*, no. 42095/98, ECHR 2000-X.

ECHR, *Golder v. the United Kingdom*, 21 February 1975, § 28, Series A no. 18.

ECHR, *Moiseyev v. Russia*, no. 62936/00, § 182, 9 October 2008.

ECHR, *National & Provincial Building Society, Leeds Permanent Building Society and Yorkshire Building Society v. the United Kingdom*, 23 October 1997, *Reports of Judgments and Decisions* 1997-VII.

ECHR, *Parlov-Tkalčić v. Croatia*, no. 24810/06, 22 December 2009.

ECHR, *Scordino v. Italy (no. 1)* [GC], no. 36813/97, ECHR 2006-V.

ECHR, *Siegle v. Romania*, no. 23456/04, 16 April 2013.

ECHR, *Solomun v. Croatia*, no. 679/11, 2 April 2015.

ECHR, *Stran Greek Refineries and Stratis Andreadis v. Greece*, 9 December 1994, § 49, Series A no. 301-B.

ECHR, *Tarbuk v. Croatia*, no. 31360/10, 11 December 2012.

ECHR, *Ustimenko v. Ukraine*, no. 32053/13, 29 October 2015.

---

[26]CCJE, *Report on judicial independence and impartiality in the Council of Europe member States in 2017*, 7 February 2018, doc. CCJE-BU(2017)11.

ECHR, *Varnienė v. Lithuania*, no. 42916/04, 12 November 2013.

ECHR, *Zielinski and Pradal and Gonzalez and Others v. France* [GC], nos. 24846/94 and 34165/96 to 34173/96, ECHR 1999-VII.

Hassan v. the United Kingdom [GC], no. 29750/09, §§ 100 and 102, ECHR 2014.

Inter-American Court of Human Rights, 23 August 2013, *Supreme Court of Justice (Quintana Coello et al.) v. Ecuador*.

Inter-American Court of Human Rights, 28 August 2013, *Camba Campos et al. v. Ecuador*.

Inter-American Court of Human Rights, 5 October 2015, *López Lone et al. v. Honduras*.

Joint Opinion of the Venice Commission and the Directorate of Human Rights (DHR) of the Directorate General of Human Rights and the Rule of Law (DGI) of the Council of Europe, on the draft law on amendments to the Organic Law on General Courts of Georgia, adopted by the Venice Commission a its 100th Plenary Session (Rome, 10–11 October 2014, CDL-AD (2014) 031).

United Nations Human Rights Committee, *Bandaranayake v. Sri Lanka*, Communication No. 1376/2005, 24 July 2008.

United Nations Human Rights Committee, General Comment no. 32 on Article 14 of the International Covenant on Civil and Political Rights (Right to equality before courts and tribunals and to a fair trial), 23 August 2007, UN doc. CCPR/C/GC/32.

United Nations Human Rights Committee, *Munyo Busyo et al. v. Democratic Republic of Congo*, Communication No. 933/2000, 19 September 2003.

Venice Commission, Opinion on the draft law on introducing amendments and addenda to the judicial code of Armenia (term of Office of Court Presidents), adopted by the Venice Commission at its 99th Plenary Session (Venice, 13–14 June 2014, CDL-AD(2014)021).

The United Nations' Internal Justice System and Fair Trial Rights of International Staff Members in Disciplinary Proceedings

Teresa da Silva Bravo

Contents

1 Introduction

On 4 April 2007, the United Nations' General Assembly adopted a Resolution which provided the legal framework for the reform of its internal system of justice. The rationale of such Resolution was to transform the nature of the system and to pave the way to the creation of a more efficient, professionalized and independent one, whose features would be similar to those of sovereign States.

The scope of this text is to evaluate the UN staff member's normative status concerning defense rights in the context of the disciplinary proceedings. In fact, due

---

Teresa da Silva Bravo is Judge President of the United Nations Dispute Tribunal.

T. da Silva Bravo (✉)
United Nations, Geneva, Switzerland
e-mail: teresamaria.dasilvabravo@un.org

© Springer Nature Switzerland AG 2019
P. Pinto de Albuquerque, K. Wojtyczek (eds.), *Judicial Power in a Globalized World*, https://doi.org/10.1007/978-3-030-20744-1_34

to the jurisdictional immunity of the Organization, staff members cannot file an application in their national courts.[1]

Staff Members' normative status is of outmost importance due to the nature of the United Nations' mission, which employs thousands of people around the world in several field missions, developing humanitarian projects, participating in peace keeping missions and performing military interventions.

The normative status of the UN staff members is a combination of internal rules and regulations, as well of general international legal principles held in several instruments like the UN Charter, the Universal Declaration of Human Rights, the International Covenant of Civil and Political Rights, amongst others.

The text is structured in three parts: the first one addresses the origins of the internal justice system and the creation of its two tribunals: a first instance court—UNDT and an appeals court (UNAT). The second part, identifies the main legal principles that have emerged from the internal jurisprudence related to staff member's procedural rights and thirdly, the internal jurisprudence is tested under the hermeneutical framework of Article 6 of the European Convention of Human Rights.

The purpose of this evaluation was to assess whether there is a convergence between the jurisdictional practice of the United Nations and the parameters provided for by the jurisprudence of the European Court of Human Rights, concerning fair trials' rights.

In short, the main purpose of this work is to discuss whether the UN respects and aligns with international standards of fair trial in the context of disciplinary proceedings held against staff members, while performing their official functions.

2   Genesis of the (New) Internal Justice System of the United Nations

The United Nations, as a supranational organisation is granted jurisdictional immunity, in other words, the organization cannot be subject of a complaint in national jurisdictions, pursuant to article 105 of the UN Charter together with Article II, section 2 of the Convention on the Privileges and Immunities of the United Nations.

Similarly, UN staff members cannot have access to a national court to settle their employment disputes in relation to the terms and conditions of their appointments.

Pursuant to Articles 100 and 101 of the UN Charter, staff members are under the authority of the Secretary General of the United Nations who is at the top of the UN

---

[1]In this regard, recall the case law of the ECHR in Judgements of 18 February 1999—Waite and Kennedy (Case 28934/95) and Beer and Regan v. Germany (Case 26083/94) and the decision of 6 January 2015 held in Klausecker v. Germany (415/07-5th Section) available online at https://hudoc.echr.coe.int/eng#{%22fulltext%22:[%22Waite%20and%20Kennedy%20and%20Beer%20and%20Regan%20v.%20Germany%22],%22documentcollectionid2%22:[%22JUDGMENTS%22,%22DECGRANDCHAMBER%22]}, assessed on 3rd April 2019.

hierarchy. This is also applicable "mutatis mutandis" to the employees of the specialized agencies of the United Nations (for instance, UNICEF, the High Commissioner of the United Nations for the Refugees—UNHCR, or the United Nations Development Programme—UNDP—amongst other entities).[2]

This pyramidal structure was also clarified by the internal jurisprudence of the UNDT, (see, UNDT/GVA/2017/020/029/031/037 and 040), which held that:

(. . .)

57. It is recalled that staff members are barred from bringing any cause of action against the Organization before national courts, since the United Nations Charter and the Convention on the Privileges and Immunities of the United Nations grant the Organization immunity from jurisdiction. Consequently, the Convention demands that "the United Nations shall make provisions for appropriate modes of settlement of . . . [d]isputes arising out of contracts or other disputes of a private law character to which the United Nations is a party".

58. The Organization's immunity from jurisdiction may impair the staff members' right to access to court if the Organization does not provide them with a reasonable alternative dispute resolution mechanism. In this respect, the European Court of Human Rights ("ECtHR") held in *Waite and Kennedy v. Germany* (Application no. 26083/94, Judgment of 18 February 1999):

63. Like the Commission, the Court points out that the attribution of privileges and immunities to international organisations is an essential means of ensuring the proper functioning of such organisations free from unilateral interference by individual governments. The immunity from jurisdiction commonly accorded by States to international organisations under the organisations' constituent instruments or supplementary agreements is a long-standing practice established in the interest of the good working of these organisations. The importance of this practice is enhanced by a trend towards extending and strengthening international cooperation in all domains of modern society.

. . .

67. The Court is of the opinion that where States establish international organisations in order to pursue or strengthen their cooperation in certain fields of activities, and where they attribute to these organisations certain competences and accord them immunities, there may be implications as to the protection of fundamental rights. It would be incompatible with the purpose and object of the Convention, however, if the Contracting States were thereby absolved from their responsibility under the Convention in relation to the field of activity covered by such attribution. It should be recalled that the Convention is intended to guarantee not theoretical or illusory rights, but rights that are practical and effective. This is particularly true for the right of access to the courts in view of the prominent place held in a democratic society by the right to a fair trial (see, as a recent authority, the Aït-Mouhoub v. France judgment of 28 October 1998, *Reports* 1998-VIII, p. 3227, § 52, referring to the Airey v. Ireland judgment of 9 October 1979, Series A no. 32, pp. 12-13, § 24).

Before the reform of the internal justice system, it was commonly agreed that the original system was too slow and too cumbersome, it lacked fair trial guarantees and it was not independent since its members were under the SG's hierarchical power.

In fact, at that time, staff members could only address their complaint to the Joint Appeals Body (JAB) and/or the Joint Disciplinary Committee (JDC) which made recommendations to the SG without a binding effect. The members of these

---

[2]See recently, the UNDT Geneva's judgement (UNDT/GVA/2016/092) which clarifies the scope of the SG's powers, available online at https://www.un.org/en/internaljustice/undt/judgments_2016.shtml, assessed on 3rd April 2019.

committees were also staff members, chosen by their peers on a voluntary basis and who did not necessarily have any legal or judicial experience.

Those Committees sat in Nairobi, Geneva, New York and Vienna on an *ad hoc* basis to decide the cases. However, as highlighted by the Re-Design Panel Report, the results were globally unsatisfactory:

> 64. In recent years, there have been difficulties in recruiting volunteers and, with the increase in fixed-term contracts relative to permanent contracts, there is growing concern on the part of the staff about the Independence of both bodies. Moreover, problems with volunteers' availability generate delays.
>
> 65. Disciplinary proceedings are protracted, and frequently, more than one year will pass before the disciplinary measures can be implemented. Proceedings before a JDC usually take six to nine months, and its recommendations must then be considered at Headquarters in New York before any disciplinary measures can be taken.[3]

Moreover, the Administrative Tribunal of the United Nations (created by the General Assembly in January 1950) had a limited jurisdictional scope since it held meetings only twice a year to decide, on appeal, about the decisions taken by Committees.

It took almost three decades to implement a deep restructuring of the whole system. In fact, only in 1984, the General Assembly expressed its concern over the backlog and the high number of pending cases before those internal committees and decided to hire a group of experts to identify and evaluate the systemic needs of the UN administration of justice.[4]

Only in 2006, the Redesign Panel Report achieved a complete analysis of the internal justice system, identified its fragilities and suggested a global reform:

> (. . .) the administration of justice in the United Nations is neither professional nor independent. The system of administration of justice as it currently stands is extremely slow, under resourced, inefficient and thus, ultimately ineffective. It fails to meet many basic standards of due process established in international human rights instruments. For all these reasons, staff of the Organization have little or in the confidence in the system the it currently exists.

According to its Report, the Re-Design Panel suggested that the future internal justice system should include two tiers: a first instance court (UNDT) and an appeals tribunal (UNAT), which would be competent to decide on appeals. Moreover, the judges of those tribunals should be recruited, internationally, from a pool of

---

[3]*See*, Report of the Redesign Panel on the United Nations System of Administration of Justice, A/61/205, which was subject of discussion at the 61 session of the General Assembly of the United Nations, held on 28 de July 2006, available online at: https://www.un.org/ga/search/view_doc.asp?symbol=A/61/815, assessed on 3rd April 2019.

[4]*See*, Report of the Group of High Level Intergovernmental Experts to Review the Efficiency of the Administrative and Financial Functioning of the United Nations, UM Doc.A/41/49, August, 15, 1986, available online at https://undocs.org/pdf?symbol=en/A/43/16, assessed on 3rd April 2019.

pre-selected candidates, by a panel of independent experts (Internal Justice Council, or IJC[5]) and elected as UN officials by the General Assembly of the United Nations.

The first instance Tribunal (UNDT) was created by Resolution 61/261 of the General Assembly and began its functions on July 01, 2009. It was initially composed of a group of 7 judges elected to serve for a seven years' term. The UNDT's Statute was approved and adopted on December 24, 2009[6] whereas, the Statute of UNAT was adopted and approved under Resolutions 66/237 and 69/203.

UNDT has now its seats in three different geographical areas which also coincide with the scope of its jurisdiction: Geneva is competent to hear cases from Europe, Asia and Pacific, New York is competent to hear cases and pass judgements involving America and the Caribbean while Nairobi is competent to hear and pass judgements on cases from Africa and the Arabic Peninsula.

Pursuant to paragraph 64. of said Resolution 61/261 the main purpose was to:

64. (. . .) to establish a new, independent, transparent, professionalized, adequately resourced and decentralized system of administration of justice consistent with the relevant rules of international law and principles of the rule of law and due process to ensure respect for the rights and obligations of staff members and the accountability of managers and staff members alike.

3   Jurisdictional Scope of UNDT and UNAT

The competence of UNDT is held in the Statute and in the Rules of Procedure.[7]

Pursuant to Article. 2 of the Statute of UNDT, the Tribunal is competent to hear and pass judgement on the following cases:

(a) To appeal an administrative decision that is alleged to be in non-compliance with the terms of appointment or the contract of employment. The terms "contract" and "terms of appointment" include all pertinent regulations and rules and all relevant administrative issuances in force at the time of alleged non-compliance;

(b) To appeal an administrative decision imposing a disciplinary measure;

(c) To enforce the implementation of an agreement reached through mediation pursuant to article 8, paragraph 2, of the present statute.

2. The Dispute Tribunal shall be competent to hear and pass judgement on an application filed by an individual requesting the Dispute Tribunal to suspend, during the pendency of the management evaluation, the implementation of a contested administrative decision that is the subject of an ongoing management evaluation, where the decision appears prima facie to be unlawful, in cases of particular urgency, and where its implementation would cause irreparable damage. (. . .)

---

[5]The *Internal Justice Council* (IJC) consists of a panel of 5 member's which includes three outside experts, one representative of management and a representative of staff members.

[6]See, also GA Resolutions 69/203 and GA R. A/70/112, available at https://www.undocs.org/, assessed on 3rd April 2019.

[7]These Rules of Procedure were adopted by the UNDT Judges, gathered in New York during their Plenary Meeting and later approved by the GA Resolution 64/119, dated the 16 December 2009.

5. The Dispute Tribunal shall be competent to hear and pass judgement on an application filed against a specialized agency brought into relationship with the United Nations in accordance with the provisions of Articles 57 and 63 of the Charter of the United Nations or other international organization or entity established by a treaty and participating in the common system of conditions of service, where a special agreement has been concluded between the agency, organization or entity concerned and the Secretary-General of the United Nations to accept the terms of the jurisdiction of the Dispute Tribunal, consonant with the present statute. Such special agreement shall provide that the agency, organization or entity concerned shall be bound by the judgements of the Dispute Tribunal and be responsible for the payment of any compensation awarded by the Dispute Tribunal in respect of its own staff members and shall include, *inter alia*, provisions concerning its participation in the administrative arrangements for the functioning of the Dispute Tribunal and concerning its sharing of the expenses of the Dispute Tribunal. Such special agreement shall also contain other provisions required for the Dispute Tribunal to carry out its functions *vis-à-vis* the agency, organization or entity.

Access to the UNDT is limited to staff members, former staff members as well as their legal representatives pursuant to art. 3 of the Statute. This being said, consultants, interns and contracted experts do not have access to the internal judicial system.

Moreover, one of the issues that remains unsolved (contrary to was suggested in the Re-Design Panel Report, see paragraph 82) is the possibility of Staff Unions having access to the Tribunal on behalf of their affiliates. Collective action and access to the internal justice system by staff member's Union is not possible, contrary to what happens under the jurisdiction of ILOAT.

Nonetheless, despite said limitations, UNAT has enlarged the access to the internal system in a case decided in 2010 (which constitutes a precedent for future cases) *Gabaldon vs. SG*, UNAT-2010-115[8]:

28. (...) a contract concluded following the issuance of an offer of employment whose conditions have been fulfilled and which has been accepted unconditionally, while not constituting a valid employment contract before the issuance of a letter of appointment under the internal laws of the United Nations, does create obligations for the Organization and rights for the other party in good faith. (...) the Organization should be regarded as intending for this person to benefit from the protection of the laws of the United Nations and, thus, from its system of administration of justice and, for this purpose only, the person in question should be regarded as staff member.

Despite its shortcomings, one interesting feature of the UN formal system of justice is the flexibility of its rules of procedure, which is a combination of civil and common law. For instance, it is the judge's responsibility to evaluate each case file and to decide whether a hearing is necessary or not (exception made for disciplinary cases in which a hearing should take place).

The Rules of Procedure have also included other elements that can turn up the judicial proceeding more efficient:

[8]See, Judgement 2011-UNAT-120, available online at: https://www.un.org/en/internaljustice/unat/judgments_2011.shtml, assessed on 3rd April 2019.

- the referral of the case to the OMBUDSMAN person and the suspension of the proceeding up to 3 months (in cases in which the judge finds Mediation a possibility);
- the use of summary judgements in cases in which there is no controversy on the facts and the issue at stake is of a purely legal nature.

Pursuant to Article 5 (.1) of the Rules of Procedure, the case is heard before a single judge. However, in accordance to Article 5 (2) a panel of three judges can be conveyed. This usually happens in situations where the legal and factual issues of the case are of a complex nature and also when the internal jurisprudence does not have previously established a clear precedent.

On December 29, 2017, UNDT in Geneva, adjudicated on cases UNDT/GVA/ 020,029,031,037 and 040, following a hearing that took place between the 20 and 22 September 2017, before a panel of three judges.[9] These cases referred to the changes in the salary scales of staff members established in Geneva. One of the legal issues at stake was whether the applications should be declared irreceivable since the Respondent argued that the decision which was being contested was not of an administrative nature but a regulatory one. The panel of judges have decided to hear the case and dismissed the arguments raised by the Respondent (concerning receivability) based on the general legal principle of access to justice:

(...)

59. The International Court of Justice ("ICJ") explicitly recognised the role played by the former United Nations Administrative Tribunal in fulfilling the Organization's obligation to provide access to justice to its staff members in its *Advisory Opinion on Effects of Awards of Compensation made by the United Nations Administrative Tribunal* of 13 July 1954 (I.C.J. Reports 1954, p. 47, at p. 57), where it held:

When the Secretariat was organized, a situation arose in which the relations between the staff members and the Organization were governed by a complex code of law. This code consisted of the Staff Regulations established by the General Assembly, defining the fundamental rights and obligations of the staff, and the Staff Rules, made by the Secretary-General in order to implement the Staff Regulations. It was inevitable that there would be disputes between the Organization and staff members as to their rights and duties. The Charter contains no provision which authorizes any of the principal organs of the United Nations to adjudicate upon these disputes, and Article 105 secures for the United Nations jurisdictional immunities in national courts. It would, in the opinion of the Court, hardly be consistent with the expressed aim of the Charter to promote freedom and justice for individuals and with the constant preoccupation of the United Nations Organization to promote this aim that it should afford no judicial or arbitral remedy to its own staff for the settlement of any disputes which may arise between it and them.

In these circumstances, the Court finds that the power to establish a tribunal, to do justice as between the Organization and the staff members, was essential to ensure the efficient working of the Secretariat, and to give effect to the paramount consideration of securing the highest standards of efficiency, competence and integrity. Capacity to do this arises by necessary intendment out of the Charter.

---

[9]Available online at https://www.un.org/en/internaljustice/undt/judgments-orders.shtml, assessed on 3rd April 2019.

60. Similarly, the former United Nations Administrative Tribunal took into account on several occasions the staff members' right to access to justice in interpreting its jurisdiction (see, e.g., Judgment No. 378, *Bonh et al.* (1986); Judgment No. 461, *Zafari* (1990); Judgment No. 469, *Salaymeh* (1990).

61. Most significantly, when the former United Nations Administrative Tribunal set the definition of what constitutes an administrative decision in its seminal judgment *Andronov*, it was cautious to state the following:

The Tribunal believes that the legal and judicial system of the United Nations must be interpreted as a comprehensive system, without *lacunae* and failures, so that the final objective, which is the protection of staff members against alleged non-observance of their contracts of employment, is guaranteed. The Tribunal furthermore finds that the Administration has to act fairly vis-à-vis its employees, their procedural rights and legal protection, and to do everything in its power to make sure that every employee gets full legal and judicial protection.

62. Likewise, the Administrative Tribunal of the International Labour Organization ("ILOAT") relied upon "the principle that any employee is entitled in the event of a dispute with his employer to the safeguard of some appeals procedure" in its leading case *Chadsey* (Judgment No. 122 (1968)). In *Rubio* (Judgment No. 1644 (1997)), the ILOAT spoke more broadly of the principle that "an employee of an international organization is entitled to the safeguard of an impartial ruling by an international tribunal on any dispute with the employer". (. . .).

This was a landmark judgement because it reaffirmed the UNDT's jurisdictional powers to adjudicate in matters related to staff member's benefits and entitlements and reinforced their access to a judicial *forum*. This judgement reshaped and enlarged the concept of administrative decision and it applied general principles of labour law, such as, the protection of retribution and acquired rights.

This judgement was issued in a particularly difficult context, in which, important changes (namely, budgetary constraints and downsizing exercises) have been implemented throughout the UN system. The overall context highlights the extreme importance of an independent and fully resourced system of justice within the United Nations. On the other hand, it also clarifies the scope of the UNDT jurisdiction and the *sui generis* nature of its competences, as follows:

"In line with these principles, the Appeals Tribunal adopted a broad interpretation of the requirement that the administrative decision be of "individual application", distinguishing regulatory decisions from their execution where appropriate. Contrary to the Respondent's submissions, the Appeals Tribunal did not rule out the possibility that decisions of general application may constitute administrative decisions within the meaning of art. 2 of the Dispute Tribunal's Statute. In *Ovcharenko et al.* 2015-UNAT-530 and *Pedicelli* 2015-UNAT-555, the Appeals Tribunal found that decisions which negatively affect the terms of appointment or contract of employment of a staff member are reviewable administrative decisions, despite their general application. In this respect, it explicitly held in *Pedicelli* (see para. 29) that:

[I]t is an undisputed principle of international labour law and indeed our own jurisprudence that where a decision of general application negatively affects the terms of appointment or contract of employment of a staff member, such decision shall be treated as an "administrative decision" falling within the scope of article 2(1) of the Statute of the Dispute Tribunal and a staff member who is adversely affected is entitled to contest that decision.

UNDT has also clarified that:

> 138. In this connection, the Tribunal finds that the right to salary necessarily extends to its quantum. The salary is, by definition, the consideration paid for the staff member to perform his or her duties. It is part of any contract of employment and the agreement between the parties lays in the determination of its actual level. The balance between the rights and obligations of the parties would be broken if the Organization was allowed to unilaterally modify the level of salary, as suggested by the Respondent. In line with these general principles, the Organization indeed committed not to reduce the Applicants' salaries in specifying the initial amount in their letters of appointment and explicitly stating that this amount is "subject to increase", making this term of employment inviolable (see, e.g., *In re De Los Cobos and Wegner) (...)*.

However, as already pointed out, the decisions of the first instance court are subject to appeal before UNAT, pursuant to Article.2 of the Statute of the Appeal's Tribunal, in the following cases:

– when UNDT has exceeded or omitted the scope of its jurisdiction;
– when the tribunal of first instance has committed a factual, legal or procedural error.

Article 2.8 of the statute of UNAT grants the Appeal's tribunal the "*competenz-competenz*" *to* determine its own jurisdiction, in other words: the Appeal's tribunal can decide concerning its own competence to decide a dispute. Pursuant to Article 2 (4) of UNAT's Statute the appeals tribunal can decide:

– to upheld, vacate or modify the first instance's initial decision, based on the evidence produced before the UNDT;
– to remand the case back to the first instance court so that an issue of law or of fact can be fully clarified.

However, the appeal's tribunal doesn't work on a full time basis. Instead, it is composed of seven judges, who gather three to four times a year to decide on the cases. Those sessions usually take place in New York but can also be held in Geneva or in Nairobi.

The following chapter addresses the issue of fair trial rights in the context of disciplinary proceedings while establishing a comparison with the same international standards as defined by the jurisprudence of the European Court of Human Rights.

4 Fair Trial Rights in the Context of Disciplinary Proceedings: An Overview

As previously underlined, the main purposes of the establishment of an independent and professionalized internal justice system was twofold; to ensure staff members a jurisdictional forum and, at the same time, to have the internal mechanism in accordance with the international standards concerning fair trial.

Despite these intentions, the challenge lays in how to reconcile and to harmonize the internal norms with those international standards, while taking into account the particularities of a complex supranational organization.

The disciplinary status of the UN staff members is the combination of a complex set of legal principles, norms, rules and regulations from different sources: Norms of Conduct of the International Civil Service (soft law), Article .101 of the Charter United Nations, the Rules and Regulations of the Personnel of the United Nations (see, Chapter X, Article 10), ST/SGB/2014/1 and also the new ST/AI/2017/1, which contains a full description of what Misconduct is and establishes the framework of the disciplinary process and the subsequent sanctions.

Art. 101 (3) of the UN Charter establishes the general criteria that should be taken into consideration in the recruitment process of its staff members: the higher standards of efficiency, integrity and competence as well as geographical diversity.

Accordingly, Article I of ST/SGB/2014/1 states that:

- Staff members shall uphold and respect the principles set out in the Charter, including faith in fundamental rights, the dignity and worth of the human person and in equal rights of men and women. Consequently, staff members shall exhibit respect for all cultures; they shall not discriminate against any individual or group of individuals or otherwise abuse the power and authority vested in them;
- Staff members shall uphold the highest standards of efficiency, competence and integrity. The concept of integrity includes, but is not limited to, probity, impartiality, fairness, honesty and truthfulness in all matters affecting their work and status;
- Staff members shall follow the directions and instructions properly issued by the Secretary General and by their supervisors; (. . .)

Disciplinary proceedings may be instituted against a staff member who fails to comply with his or her obligations and the standards of conduct set out in the Charter of United Nations, the Staff Rules and Regulations, the Financial Regulations and Rules and administrative issuances.

On October 26, 2017 a new internal framework concerning disciplinary proceedings come into force and superseded[10] the former ST/AI/371 and ST/CPA/ Amend.1 (which is still applicable to the pending cases). Under Section 3 of ST/AI/ 2017/1 unsatisfactory conduct is an umbrella concept which includes misconduct. The difference between the two relates to the gravity of the offense and the possible outcome.

Article 3.1 of Section 3 defines unsatisfactory conduct as follows:

3.1 Unsatisfactory conduct is any conduct where a staff member fails to comply with the staff member's obligations under the Charter of the United Nations, the Staff Regulations and Rules of the United Nations or other relevant administrative issuances or to observe the standards of conduct expected of an international civil servant. Unsatisfactory conduct includes conduct of sufficient gravity that rises to the level of misconduct.

---

[10]See, ST/AI/2017/1, available online at https://undocs.org/ST/AI/2017/1, assessed on 3rd April 2019.

On the other hand, Articles 3.4 and 3.5 describe the situations and/or the behaviour that can fall under the definition of misconduct and, subsequently, lead to a disciplinary proceeding and a sanction:

> 3.4. Staff rule 10.1 (a) provides that "failure by a staff member to comply with [the staff member's] obligations under the Charter of the United Nations, the Staff Regulations and Rules or other relevant administrative issuances or to observe the standards of conduct expected of an international civil servant may amount to misconduct and may lead to the institution of a disciplinary process and the imposition of disciplinary measures for misconduct".
>
> 3.5 Misconduct for which disciplinary measures may be imposed includes, but is not limited to:
>
> (a) Acts or omissions in conflict with the general obligations of staff members set forth in article 1 of the Staff Regulations and the rules and instructions implementing it;
> (b) Unlawful acts (e.g. theft, fraud, the possession or sale of illegal substances, smuggling) on or off United Nations premises, and whether or not the staff member was officially on duty at the time;
> (c) Misrepresentation, forgery, false certification and/or failure to disclose a material fact in connection with any United Nations claim or benefit;
> (d) Discrimination, harassment, including sexual harassment, abuse of authority and retaliation;
> (e) Misuse of United Nations property, including equipment or files, and electronic files;
> (f) Misuse of office, including breach of confidentiality and abuse of United Nations privileges and immunities;
> (g) Sexual exploitation and sexual abuse;
> (h) Acts or behaviour that would discredit the United Nations.
>
> 3.6 Misconduct may also include assisting in, or contributing to, the commission of misconduct.

According to this framework, it is up to OIOS (Office of Internal Oversight Services) to decide which cases should be investigated. This means that OIOS has a discretionary power in relation to the outcome of the complaint or the information provided to it. Such decision is made after a "preliminary evaluation" or (preliminary assessment) during which the responsible entity can decide whom to enquire (the informer, the suspect or any other person who has relevant information) in order to assess if the case will proceed. At this stage, OIOS (or any responsible official to whom this decision was delegated) evaluates (under Article 5.5 of ST/AI/2017/1):

> (a) Whether the unsatisfactory conduct is a matter that could amount to misconduct;
> (b) Whether the provision of the information of unsatisfactory conduct is made in good faith and is sufficiently detailed that it may form the basis for an investigation;
> (c) Whether there is a likelihood that an investigation would reveal sufficient evidence to further pursue the matter as a disciplinary case;
> (d) Whether an informal resolution process would be more appropriate in the circumstances;
> (e) Any other factor(s) reasonable in the circumstances.
>
> 5.6 Upon conclusion of the preliminary assessment, the responsible official shall decide to either:
>
> (a) Initiate an investigation of all or part of the matters raised in the information about unsatisfactory conduct; or
> (b) Not initiate an investigation.

5.7 In cases where the responsible official decides not to initiate an investigation, the responsible Official should decide either to close the matter without further action or to:

(a) Take managerial action, without prior consultation with the staff member; and/or
(b) Issue a written or oral reprimand, provided the staff member has had the prior opportunity to comment in writing on the facts and circumstances, in accordance with staff rule 10.2 (c).

This norm evidentiates that the Administration enjoys a wide margin of manoeuver in deciding whether to proceed or not with a formal investigation. Even if an investigation starts it doesn't necessarily mean that a disciplinary proceeding will follow. Moreover, according the well-established case-law of the appeals tribunal (see, *Abu Hamda vs. Commissioner General* 2010-UNAT-022):

37. Disciplinary matters are within the discretion and authority of the Commissioner-General of UNRWA. It is however a general principle of administrative justice that administrative bodies and administrative officials shall act fairly and reasonably and comply with the requirements imposed on them by law. The roll-neck normal Courts/Tribunals of the not interferes in the exercise of the discretionary authority unless there is evidence of illegality, irrationality and procedural impropriety.

Also in *Abboud 2010-UNAT-100*, the Tribunal has decided that:

34. As a general principle, the investigation of disciplinary charges against a staff member is the privilege of the Organization itself, and it is not legally possible to compel the Administration to take disciplinary action against another part.

This was also the precedent followed in two other more recent cases; *Benfield-Laporte* 2015-UNAT-505 and *Oumih* 2015-UNAT-518:

37. As a general principle, the investigation of disciplinary charges against a staff member is the privilege of the Organization itself, and it is not legally possible to compel the Administration to take disciplinary action. (. . .)

31. (. . .) The Administration has a degree of discretion as to how to conduct a review and assessment of a complaint and may decide whether to undertake an investigation regarding all or some of the allegations. (. . .)

As a consequence, one must conclude that both the investigations and the disciplinary proceedings in the UN context are based in a principle of opportunity and administrative discretion rather than on a principle of legality.

From our point of view, this also means that investigations and disciplinary proceedings can be regarded as a "managerial tool" instead of an essential safeguard to ensure legality and the respect for the rule of law within the United Nations. ST/AI/2017/1 establishes the compulsory stages of the disciplinary procedure;

1. Preliminary assessment of the complaint or information obtained;
2. Investigation and drafting process of the investigation's report;
3. Decision of the Assistant-Secretary General (ASG) to open a disciplinary procedure;
4. Notification to the staff member of the summary content of the Investigation's report;

5. Thirty days' deadline is granted to the staff member to answer the allegations held against him or her;
6. Recommendation from the ASG to the Under-secretary for Management (USG) regarding the outcome of the disciplinary proceeding which can include and sanction to the applied.

In cases where a disciplinary proceeding is entertained and a sanction applied, the staff member can always contest this decision before the UNDT and subsequently, before UNAT.

UNAT's case law has constantly held that the role of UNDT in disciplinary cases is the following;

– To assess if the facts of the case were properly established,
– If the facts amount to misconduct and, finally,
– If the sanction is proportionate to the gravity of the offense.

See, for instance, *Haniya* 2010-UNAT-024:

31. When reviewing a sanction imposed by the Administration, the Tribunal will examine, whether the established facts qualify as misconduct, and whether the sanction is proportionate to the offence.[11]

And, in the case *Portillo Moya* (2015-UNAT-523):

19. It follows from the reasoning of the quoted jurisprudence that the matter of the degree of the sanction is usually reserved for the Administration, who has discretion to impose the measure that it considers adequate to the circumstances of the case and to the actions and behaviour of the staff member involved.

20. This appears as a natural consequence of the scope of administrative hierarchy and the power vested in the competent authority. It is the Administration which carries out the administrative activity and procedure and deals with the staff members. Therefore, the Administration is best suited to select an adequate sanction able to fulfil the general requirements of these kinds of measures: a sanction within the limits stated by the respective norms, sufficient to prevent repetitive wrongdoing, punish the wrongdoer, satisfy victims and restore the administrative balance, etc.

21. That is why only if the sanction imposed appears to be blatantly illegal, arbitrary, adopted beyond the limits stated by the respective norms, excessive, abusive, discriminatory or absurd in its severity, that the judicial review would conclude in its unlawfulness and change the consequence (i.e., by imposing a different one). This rationale is followed in the jurisprudence of this Tribunal. If that is not the case, judicial review should not interfere with administrative discretion.

The established case-law has limited the scope of judicial review in disciplinary cases and does not allow the first instance tribunal to replace the sanction (if it is illegal) since it is commonly understood that the Judge cannot act as "decision-

---

[11]This was also confirmed in Mahdi 2010-UNAT-018 para. 27; Masri 2010-UNAT-098; Applicant 2013-UNAT-302 para. 29; Kamara 2014-UNAT-398 para. 29; Nasrallah 2013-UNAT-310 para. 23; Walden 2014-UNAT-436 para.24; Koutang 2013-UNAT-374 para. 28; Portillo Moya 2015-UNAT-523 para. 17; Wishah 2015-UNAT-537 para. 20, available online at http://untreaty.un.org/UNAT/Judgements_English_By_Number.htm, assessed on 3rd April 2019.

maker "and replace the administration's role. As a consequence, the best the UNDT judge can do is to send the case back to the administration for the procedure to be redone.

5 ECHR *Fair Trial*'s Standards and the UN Disciplinary Framework

The UN framework, which establishes the steps of each disciplinary proceeding and the procedural safeguards granted to suspects (ST/AI/2017/1), evidentiates "a low level of guarantism" and is not in conformity to the international and other regional standards.

Indeed, ST/AI/2017/71 contains provisions which contradict the commonly recognized standards in disciplinary proceedings i.e. the presumption of innocence the right to be assisted by council and the right to have full access to the evidence and to be made aware of the overall set of facts held against the suspect.

In fact, Article 6.9 of said framework imposes on the suspect a duty to cooperate with the investigator, to answer questions and to allow them access to personal information held, for instance, in mobiles, laptops and/or any other means to gather evidence:

> 6.2 Pursuant to staff regulation 1.2 (r) and staff rule 1.2 (c), staff members are required to fully cooperate with all duly authorized investigations and to provide any records, documents, information and communications technology equipment or other information under the control of the Organization or under the staff member's control, as requested. Failure to cooperate may be considered unsatisfactory conduct that may amount to misconduct.

The justification for this can be found in section 2. 2.1 paragraph g) of ST/AI/2017/1 which specifically states that: Investigations are administrative in nature."

This rationale is also supported by the internal jurisprudence, based on the fact that disciplinary proceedings are not of a criminal nature and, consequently, staff members are not subject to the same level of guarantees as in a criminal proceeding. See, for instance, *Jahnsen Lecca*, 2014-UNAT-408, in which the tribunal has decided that:

> 24. Disciplinary cases are not criminal, so that criminal law procedure and the criminal definition of theft are not applicable to this case. There was no need to give notice of a specific charge of theft because from first to last, the charge against Ms. Jahnsen Lecca was "taking, without authorization, a staff member's property".

Also, in the case *Abu Ghali* 2013-UNAT-366, the tribunal held:

> 43. Misconduct based on underlying criminal acts do not depend upon the staff member being convicted of a crime in the national court. As the former United Nations Administrative Tribunal concluded, "different onuses and burdens of proof would arise in the . . . domestic criminal proceedings than would arise under an investigation for misconduct under the [Agency's] appropriate Regulations and Rules".

Once an international organisation comes into existence and starts actually functioning, it becomes a distinct – autonomous-organised community, with its own, internal legal order. The realm of such legal order is clearly different from the realm of international law, properly understood as the domain of interstate relations.(. . .) Within the autonomous internal legal system of an international organisation (which is essentially composed of statutory provisions, administrative rules, staff regulations and labour contracts), international rules and principles on the protection of human rights, including those established by treaties concluded under the framework of the organisation are not *per se* legal sources. They can be considered legal sources, having legal value, if and to the extent that legal sources of the internal order of the organisation make an explicit reference- a renvoi- to them; or also as general principles of law, which judges in international administrative tribunals can legitimately and usefully consider and apply to assess and decide cases brought before them.[12]

We agree that international organisations have a specific and self-contained internal administrative framework and benefit from immunity of jurisdiction. However, we submit that through general principles of law (particularly, human rights principles) the administrative judges can develop an internal case law that creates a favourable setting for staff members. As a consequence, the fact that the UN is not a contracting party to the ECHR does not prevent judges from using the principles enshrined therein and accommodate them within the scope of their jurisdiction.

The European Court of Human Rights (ECHR) has been consolidating its case-law regarding the rights of the accused not only in criminal proceedings but also in the context of disciplinary proceedings, under Article 6 of the European Convention of Human Rights.[13]

In the case *Funke vs. France*, (Case 10828/84, judgement dated February 25, 1993) the ECHR has decided that[14]:

The applicant was convicted is the failure to disclose documents asked goes by customs authorities. The applicant argued that customs was unwilling to procure the documents by some other means and thus attempted to compel him to provide evidence of offences he had allegedly committed (para. 44). The Court found a violation of Article 6(1) holding that there was an infringement of the right of anyone "charged with a criminal offence" to remain silent and not contribute to incriminating himself (para. 44).

However, in the UN system, the administration is entitled to draw adverse inferences, in the following circumstances, pursuant to section 6.8 of ST/AI/2017/1:

– if the suspect does not attend the interview (s) without providing a satisfactory explanation, if he or she supply false information or omit relevant data.

Two other essential dimensions of a fair process are the right to be assisted by a lawyer during the early stages of the investigation and the right to be fully informed

---

[12]See, Palmisano (2017), pp. 1 and 2.

[13]See, Engel and others, para. 81; (Applic.5100/71, 5101/71, 5102/71, 5354/72 and 5370/72), judgement held on 21 October 1976. https://hudoc.echr.coe.int/eng, assessed on 3rd April 2019.

[14]21, See also: *Salabiaku v. France*, (Case 1051/83) judgement dated the 7th October 1998, para. 28, *Västberga Taxi Aktiebolag e Vulic v. Sweden*, ECtHR, (case 36985/97) judgement 23 July 2002 at para. 113, alla available online at: https://hudoc.echr.coe.int/eng, assessed on 3rd April 2019.

about the content of the accusations held against the suspect and to have access to the evidence on file. Nonetheless, these two essential dimensions of due process have a limited application since the UN distinguishes between the investigation stage and the disciplinary proceeding *stricto sensu*. In fact, in the UN system due process rights only come into play when a disciplinary proceeding is initiated and even then, with some limitations.

As an example, pursuant to section 6.10 of the said administrative instruction, a staff member who has been identified as the subject of an investigation shall be:

a. Permitted to be accompanied by a staff member to act as an observer during an interview. An observer shall not participate in any way in the interview, including by speaking or gesturing in any manner. If the observer does not abide by this requirement, the observer will be removed from the interview. An observer may take notes of the interview in handwritten form and must provide a copy of such notes to the investigator(s). If the subject decides to bring an observer to the interview, the subject shall ensure that the observer is available at the time scheduled. Interviews shall not be rescheduled owing to the unavailability of the observer; However, the staff member cannot bring counsel to those early interviews.

This contradicts the perspective held by the jurisprudence of the ECHR in cases *Imbrioscia v. Switzerland*, (Case 13972/88, 24 November 1993) and *Salduz vs. Turkey*.—Grand Chamber Judgement (Case 36391/02, 28 November 2008).

Within the UN context, the Organisation has the power to decide which elements of the investigation will be made available to the envisaged staff member. It can also decide (based on a previous evaluation of the best interest of the organization or for security reasons) to provide only a summary of facts and conclusions of that Report. The jurisprudence has supported this view and only accepts the full disclosure of the Investigation Report to the staff member if "exceptional circumstances" are at stake.

In *Powell vs. SG* (2013-UNAT-295) UNAT has confirmed held that defense rights have a limited scope of application in the preliminary steps of the investigation:

24. During the preliminary investigation stage, only limited due process rights apply. In the present case, the UNDT was correct in finding that there was no breach of Mr. Powell's due process rights at the preliminary investigation stage in that, by 21 December 2004, Mr. Powell had been apprised of the allegations against him and had been given the opportunity to respond.

In *Akello* 2013-UNAT-336, the appeals tribunal has also declared that:

36. While the statutory instruments governing the investigation and disciplinary process in the present case are different instruments to those which governed the Applicant case, our jurisprudence remains that the due process entitlements, which every staff member has, come into play in their entirety once a disciplinary process is initiated. Furthermore, we have held in Powell that at the preliminary investigation stage, only limited due process rights apply.

37. In all the circumstances of this case, we are not persuaded that Ms. Akello has put forward any compelling argument to merit a departure from the established jurisprudence of this Tribunal.

47. [. . .] Furthermore, under former Staff Rule 110.4 (a) no disciplinary proceedings can be instituted against a staff member unless he has been notified of the allegations held against him. This is the stage when the staff member's due process rights come into operation. These rights have been enumerated in former Staff Rule 110.4.

We submit that this approach is not entirely satisfactory, due to the potential negative consequences that it may have, not only in the career but also at the personal level for the suspect. In fact, in cases of sexual harassment, rape, child abuse and exploitation, the internal investigations and the disciplinary proceedings are shared with national judicial authorities to pursue a criminal case against the accused.[15] It is our view that the organisation has a duty of care towards its staff and has to make sure that the evidence collected and the proceedings that lead to the sanction (and possible referral to national authorities) are in accordance with the well-established international jurisprudence concerning fair trial rights.

6   Conclusion

The main purpose of this chapter was to provide an overview of the (recent) internal justice system of the United Nations. Effectively, the UN is the biggest international organisation which is present worldwide and engages in different activities to promote and support human rights. The UN has thousands of employees in different countries and it is a cultural "melting pot".

In the actual political context, the organisation is facing huge budgetary constraints and is undergoing a complex reform. The internal justice system plays an important role in such a challenging environment since, through its case-law, provides guidance to both staff and decision-makers in regard to the correct interpretation and application of internal law.

However, the role of the internal judiciary goes even further since, through its jurisprudence it can also contribute to the improvement of the internal legal framework and administrative practises. Internal case law can also establish a convergence with other jurisdictions around the world in order to improve the rule of law in the United Nations system and keep it at pace with international and commonly accepted due process rights.

This text is a modest contribution to that effect.

---

[15]Concerning the issue of cooperation between the UN and law enforcement national authorities see UNDT/2017/091, held on 29.11.2017 available at http://www.un.org/en/oaj/files/undt/judgments/undt-2017-091.pdf.

References

Articles

Palmisano, G. (2017). *The European Social Charter as an instrument for the protection of fundamental rights within the international organisation.* In Common Focus and Autonomy of International Administrative Tribunals- International Colloquy, March 2017, Council of Europe. https://mycloud.coe.int/index.php/s/0cc69e006be76be09bc57556dc6e5a1c?path=%2

Electronic Resources

https://hudoc.echr.coe.int/
http://untreaty.un.org/UNAT/Judgements
https://www.un.org/ga/search/view_doc.asp?symbol=A/61/815
https://undocs.org/ST/AI/2017/1
https://www.un.org/en/internaljustice/undt/judgments_2016.shtml

United Nations Internal Justice System

UNDT/GVA/2017/020/029/031/037
UNDT/GVA/2016/092
UNAT/2015/530
UNAT/2015/555
UNAT/2015/505
UNAT/2015/518
UNAT/2015/523
UNAT/2014/408
UNAT/2013/366
UNAT/2013/295
UNAT/2010/115
UNAT/2010/022
UNAT/2010/024
UNAT/2010/100

European Court of Human Rights

Case 28934/95, Waite and Kennedy vs. Germany
Case 26083/94, Beer and Regan vs. Germany
Decision of the 5th Section 415/07, Klausecker. vs. Germany
Cases 5100/71, 5101/71, 5102/71, 5102/71, 5354/72 and 5370/72, Engel and Others
Case 10828/84, Funke vs. France
Case 1051/83, Salabiaku. v.. France
Case 13972/88, Imbrioscia .v. Switzerland

Case 36391/02, Salduz v. Turkey
Case 36985/97, Vasterberga Taxi Aktiebolag e Vulic. V. Sweden

International Labor Organisation Administrative Tribunal

Chadsey Judgement No. 122/1968
Rubio Judgement No. 1644/1997

The Role of the Proportionality Test in the Workplace Surveillance Field

Andrea Sitzia

Contents

1 Workplace Surveillance and Workers' Dignity

Surveillance of workers' activity is an unavoidable factor in labour organisation: It is an essential tool for coordinating and evaluating the work, as well as allowing the exercise of disciplinary power. The impossibility of separating the work from the person who performs it provokes an inevitable conflict between the employer's authority and workers' privacy, which can be deeply affected by surveillance. The structure of the employment relationship presupposes a contraposition between authority and freedom, so that legal systems have refined rigid frameworks for regulating employer's prerogatives, with the aim of ensuring a balance between the protection of the individual on the one hand and the economic freedom of the

Andrea Sitzia is Associate Professor at University of Padova.

A. Sitzia (✉)
University of Padova, Padua, Italy
e-mail: andrea.sitzia@unipd.it

© Springer Nature Switzerland AG 2019   579
P. Pinto de Albuquerque, K. Wojtyczek (eds.), *Judicial Power in a Globalized World*, https://doi.org/10.1007/978-3-030-20744-1_35

initiative on the other.[1] The general principles and constitutional provisions that address this topic reflect the degree of personality compression that legal systems consider acceptable in the context of legal subordination.

In fact, in the employment relationship, legal systems legitimise the exercise of private authority for the pursuit of a private interest, and thus, accept the attribution of legal importance to a form of domination of one person over another. The personalist principle justifies restrictions on the freedom of private economic initiative with the aim of respect for human dignity.

From the general perspective delineated above, we must consider the latest trends in the fragmentation of the figure of the employer, diffusion of the 'network' business model and improvement of networks and computer platforms. These processes have undermined the traditional criteria for identifying legal subordination. For labour lawyers, topics related to the application field in the discipline of subordinate employment classically evoke the attempt to subtract the employer's side from the operation of social legislation. Companies tend to resort to ingenious constructions to artificially exclude some of the 'collaborators', who ultimately work for them. The most advanced forms of operation on technological platforms do not limit the simple relationship between customers and service providers, but they define the terms of the exchange and organise the service.[2] These platforms pose a serious problem for labour law.[3]

The diffusion of the personal computer, individualisation of juridical statutes and progressive diversification and distribution of dependent work, where the boundaries with self-employment are always more difficult to identify, register an obfuscation of the boundaries between private and professional life.[4] The new forms of organisation of work, regardless of the types of contracts used, tend towards an ever stronger integration of the 'collaborator' with the company. Thus, in addition to the devaluation of the typical elements of the bond of legal subordination, we are witnessing a simultaneous tendency towards the development of a bond of control, which is growing narrower and more pervasive. Thus, the exercise of control characterises the relationship of authority, and in some recent doctrines,[5] it is considered the element qualifying the legal relationship of employment. At the same time, how the working tool is referred to has been profoundly modified, to the point that careful doctrine shows how the instruments of the biological human are increasingly inscribed and amplified in material objects.[6] The issue is the object of attention, mainly referring to the forms of so-called smart work[7] and relating to the problem of 'disconnection'.

---

[1]JILPT (2014), Perraki (2013), Sitzia and Barraco (2010), p. 705; Mathieu (2005).

[2]ECJ, 20 December 2017, C-434/15, Elite Taxi v. Uber System Spain.

[3]See Fabre and Escande-Varniol (2017), p. 166.

[4]See Ancel (2017), p. 219.

[5]Rosa (2019) and Lokiec (2018).

[6]Ziccardi (2015), Μίχος (2007), Supiot (2005), Leclerq et al. (2005) and Hazel (2002), p. 321.

[7]Ales et al. (2018).

As part of this overall scenario, we consider that the greatest risks to human dignity are manifested when the human being is reduced to an instrument—an object—to the detriment of the humanity it expresses. The constant connection of the person with the machine and the pervasive and hidden technological control relationship risk making the worker an unconscious object of observation of others.

To preserve human dignity, any interference in the personal sphere of the worker by the employer must be justified. The justification of the control is connected to the identification of the interest that, from the perspective of European Regulation 2016/679/EU (GDPR), can allow the processing of personal data, after demonstration of its 'legitimacy' beyond carrying out a balance sheet assessment between opposing interests. Under certain circumstances, this may impose the need for carrying out a 'data protection impact assessment' (Article 35 of the Regulation).

In a transitional age like the present one, faced with the intrusion of technologies in the control of expressive human activity and the awareness of the crisis of traditional labour law, understood as a protective apparatus, the judge has an essential role.[8] This is especially true when considering the EU Law perspective, in which the judiciary 'embodies an authority founded on independence, on its relationship with the law and on the resolution of disputes', and thus, it has 'a singular voice which [is] isolated from the political sphere and linked only to the will of the law'.[9]

2 The Balancing Test and Role of the European Court of Human Rights (ECtHR)

The European Court of Human Rights (ECtHR) has not yet fully addressed the complex problems outlined in the previous section, which urgently require an authoritative reconstruction capable of re-establishing a coherent relationship between the forms of explication of the entrepreneurial authority and the personalist principle. As highlighted in the dissenting opinion of Judge Pinto de Albuquerque in the *Bărbulescu* case,[10] 'the Court does not provide any guidance on the interests that the employer may invoke under Article 8 § 2 to justify interferences with the employee's privacy' (dissenting opinion, note 11). The persistent absence of a stable orientation criterion leaves a significant gap, especially where the difficulty of reconstructing the relationship between confidentiality and freedom of enterprise is

---

[8]Berramdane and Rossetto (2010) and Allard and Garapon (2005).

[9]Cf. the Opinion of Advocate General Ruiz-Jarabo Colomer delivered on 25 giugno 2009, Case C-205/08, who highlights the strategic role of the national courts in the enforcement of Community law, and considers the preliminary ruling dialogue an extraordinary instrument "to strengthening the institutional voice of an authority of the Member States: the judiciary" (see point 29 of the Opinion).

[10]ECtHR, Fourth Section, 12 January 2016, appl. n. 61496/08, Case of Bărbulescu v. Romania, riformata da ECtHR, Grand Chamber, 5 September 2017. For a comment cf. Pereiro and Rodriguez (2017).

considered from the perspective of the Charter of Fundamental Rights of the European Union (the Charter).

It is recognised that freedom of enterprise is the essence of the Treaty of Rome and the EU single market. The concept of business freedom, in the system of EU Law, is extremely broad and includes the exercise of all economic activity on both the individual and collective levels. However, Article 16 of the Charter states that the exercise of freedom of enterprise must take place in accordance with the Union's Law and national laws and practices, and thus, it is first in the EU Law that the guarantees and limits to the exercise of the business activity must be sought. It is also known that, pursuant to Article 52, para. 3, of the Charter, in the case of correspondence of the rights it establishes with those of the European Convention on Human Rights (ECHR) and related protocols, meaning and scope are defined by the latter.[11] This point is crucial because it allows the ECHR system to place the legal analysis of the relationship between freedom of enterprise and the workers' dignity (from the perspective of privacy) at the centre of its concerns.

The model referred to in Article 8, para. 2, and Article 10, para. 2, of the ECHR implies the prevalence of a 'reasonable expectation of privacy' in terms of the explication of the employers' surveillance power. In a democratic society, any interference by the employer in the employee's right to respect for his or her private life and freedom of expression, including the mere storing of personal data related to the employee's private life, must be justified by the protection of certain specific interests covered by the Convention.[12]

In terms of respect for the worker's privacy, Article 1 of the first Additional Protocol to the ECHR can only be read in combination with Article 8 of the Convention. In this sense, it can be assumed that, in relation to workers' privacy, an interpretive outcome, such as that achieved by the Court of Justice with the *Alemo-Herron* (see Prassl 2015) and *AGET Iraklis*[13] rulings,[14] should not be possible. The central role attributed by the Court of Justice to the freedom of enterprise, understood as freedom from intrusions and regulatory coercion, can only be rebalanced, at least in terms of the relationship with the confidentiality of the worker. This must be done in light of the parameter set out in Article 8 of the ECHR, which places the person at the centre of the system. In the model in Article 8, freedom of enterprise—and therefore, authority—is in a subordinate position in terms of human

---

[11]Milano (2016), Campeis and De Pauli (2014), Dorssemont et al. (2013), Senden (2011) and Braibant (2001).

[12]About these topics see the dissenting opinion of the judge Pinto de Albuquerque quoted above, who concludes by criticizing the solution offered by the fourth section in the *Bărbulescu* case because "the Court neglects the normative value of the "reasonability" criterion, leaving the impression that the employee's privacy at work is always deferential to pure management prerogative, as if the employer had the ultimate word on what kind of activity is not regarded as private in the workplace and the employee could not benefit from any expectation of privacy".

[13]ECJ, 18 July 2013, C-426/11, Alemo-Herron and others c. Parkwood Leisure Ltd.; ECJ 21 December 2016, C-201/15, AGET Iraklis c. Ypourgos Ergasias.

[14]See Giubboni (2017).

dignity. For all these reasons, it should be emphasised that the Strasbourg Court has a fundamental role in the elaboration of a general interpretative criterion of the balancing of interests in the matter, now assumed to be a benchmark for European law in relation to the processing of personal data in the GDPR. Concerning this point, it must be considered that, in specifying the object and purpose of the sector legislation, Article 1 of the GDPR explicitly delineates a balancing grid between the fundamental rights and freedoms involved in the processing of personal data.

The system configured by Article 1 of the GDPR evidently relates directly to the restrictive clause in Article 52, para. 1, of the Charter. This is shown by the fourth Recital of the European Regulation (directly related to Article 1), which states, 'The processing of personal data should be designed to serve mankind. The right to the protection of personal data is not an absolute right; it must be considered in relation to its function in society and be balanced against other fundamental rights, in accordance with the principle of proportionality'.

A stable interpretive model of the balancing criterion would also make it possible to harmonise the detailed regulatory interventions of the individual member states on the processing of employees' personal data in the context of employment relationships. In fact, Article 88 of the GDPR specifies that, in this matter,[15] the national rules are intended to 'ensure the protection of [. . .] rights and freedoms' (para. 1) and include 'suitable and specific measures to safeguard the data subject's human dignity, legitimate interests and fundamental rights, with particular regard to the transparency of processing, the transfer of personal data within a group of undertakings, or a group of enterprises engaged in a joint economic activity and monitoring systems at the work place' (para. 2).

Article 88 of the GDPR posits a criterion of mobile balancing that must respect the criteria of proportionality, necessity and purpose as reconstructed by the jurisprudence of the Court of Justice and ECtHR. All this was reiterated by point 10(c) of the 'European Social Pillar',[16] which was approved at the Göteborg social summit on 16 November 2017.[17] According to this point, 'Workers have the right to have their personal data protected in the employment context'.

It should be noted that the centrality of the person and protection of his or her privacy go well beyond the restricted scope of subordinate work. This is because the ECHR, GDPR and Charter do not attach importance to the legal qualification of the relationship binding the employer and worker, but rather, the simplest relationship between the 'controller' and the subject's data. Thus, the ECtHR has the important task of orienting national jurisprudence, which is recognised as a central role in the formation of European living law.

---

[15]"More specific rules", in the english version; "des règles plus spécifiques" in the french one.

[16]See Garben (2018).

[17]Cfr. European Commission, Recommendation on the European Pillar of Social Rights, C(2017) 2600 final, and Communication of 26 April 2017 establishing a European Pillar of Social Rights, COM(2017) 250 final.

National judges are part of the European rights protection system.[18] This is also demonstrated by the European Court of Justice's tendency to vest in the national judge the task of carrying out those balancing and proportionality operations that can only be performed in the most appropriate manner by examining the specific case. In this sense, it is sufficient to consider the sentence of the European Court of Justice of 15 March 2017, C-157/15, *Samira Achbita*,[19] where, after having outlined the principles regarding religious freedom, the Court recognised that they should be subject to limitations, as determined from the jurisprudence of the ECtHR. The Court then pointed out that the desire to show a policy of political, philosophical or religious neutrality in relation to both public and private clients must be considered legitimate, adding that the prohibition against workers wearing visible signs of political, philosophical or religious convictions is suitable for ensuring the correct application of the policy of neutrality, provided that this policy is really pursued in a coherent and systematic way.

The Court outlined the characteristics of direct and indirect discrimination corresponding to a company policy implemented in an undifferentiated way with reference to any religious belief. It asked the national judge to verify whether the prohibition on wearing visible signs or clothing that may be associated with a religious belief or political or philosophical conviction relates only to company employees who have customer relationships. Moreover, it asked if the same company would be in a position to move the employee to an activity that does not involve contact with the public. Thus, the Luxembourg Court requests the concrete verification activities necessary for determining the presence or absence of indirect discrimination to the national court, indicating the way forward for such an assessment to verify the proportionality of the limitations to the fundamental freedom. Similar protections are outlined in the Charter and ECHR. Thus, the national judge had the difficult task—exacerbated by the diversity of the social systems of the different member states—of addressing the conflict between freedom and fundamental rights via the balancing technique. The judge then had to subject the outcome of the conflict to the proportionality test.

---

[18]For a case of direct interpretative use of the ECHR see Tribunal Central Administrativo do Sul (Central Administrative Court of the South – Portugal), 2937/16.6BELSB (http://www.dgsi.pt/jtca. nsf/170589492546a7fb802575c3004c6d7d/f10b04d65e9975b28025812300515d9e? OpenDocument). In order to know what "personal data" means, the Court considers Article 8 of the Charter, in particular the doctrine that exists about it, in order to demarcate the correct meaning of that concept. At the same time, the Court uses the Opinion issued by the European Union Data Protection Working Group, in relation to Directive (EC) 95/46, in order to further clarify the meaning of personal data. It is possible to say that there is a direct relation between this decision and ECHR and that the meaning of "personal data" reached by the Court is consistent with that of the ECHR.

[19]Similarly, cf. ECtHR, 27 May 2013, application numbers 48420/10, 59842/10, 51671/10 and 36516/10, Case Eweida and Others v. the United Kingdom.

3   A 'Different Weight in the Future' for Employee's Protection

The advent of the so-called 'information society' immediately raises the problem of dangers to individuals' freedom and identity, emerging due to the electronic processing of information. Moreover, the European legal systems have always understood that the verifying of the accuracy of the employer's obligation to the workers is not detrimental to the workers' dignity per se. When the worker is working, what he or she does ceases to belong to the private sphere, and thus, it is not protected under the auspices of confidentiality. However, the problem relates to the surveillance that takes place without the worker's knowledge; this is where the legal appreciation of the violation of dignity comes into play.

In recent years, the ECtHR has begun to develop a balancing criterion between privacy and property related to the visual angle of worker surveillance. Especially, this has emerged from the *Köpke, Bărbulescu, López* and *Libert* judgments. The Court of Strasbourg is progressively developing a 'test' for balancing the right to the protection of 'private life' in the workplace (Article 8 of the Convention) and the employer's opposing interest in the protection of property (Article 1 of the first additional protocol).

In this historical phase of great technological changes, it is natural to have high conflict (and uncertainty) in the individual member states. Consequently, the interest of the Court, which has been significant for some time, is destined to grow progressively: 'The competing interests concerned might well be given a different weight in the future, having regard to the extent to which intrusions into private life are made possible by new, more and more sophisticated technologies'.[20] This type of warning, contained in the *Köpke* judgment, is especially relevant for our purposes, as it highlights how the Court is thinking about the potentially high level of intrusiveness of technological tools. The passage quoted above must be recalled when examining the Court's judgments, as it allows us to grasp the non-definitive nature of individual case-law lines, where the path is still under development.

Although it is also an especially important acknowledgment when considering the unfinished nature of the current juridical reflection, it can still address criticism on the Court's approach, above all because of the emergence of increasingly complex algorithmic forms of control. In the face of such developments, we need a jurisprudential position to be established quickly.

4   The "Reasonable Expectation Test" in the ECtHR Judgements

The *López* judgment represents the most advanced point in the jurisprudential elaboration of the ECtHR in the remote technological control field. The case is simple: Video surveillance was used for identifying the responsible parties in a series

---

[20]ECtHR, fifth section, 5th October 2010, Köpke v. Germany, application no. 420/07.

of losses that had occurred in a supermarket. The most relevant aspects of the story involve two details: First, the employer had noticed some irregularities and discrepancies between inventory counts and daily sales, recording increasing losses month after month. He proceeded to install a video surveillance system comprising some 'visible' cameras and some hidden cameras. The visible cameras, placed inside and outside of the supermarket, aimed to look for possible thefts committed by the clientele, while the hidden cameras were positioned to record the area behind the cash desks to capture any appropriative behaviours on the part of the employees. Information was only given to the employees about the 'visible' cameras; they were not told about the installation and use of the hidden ones. To describe this situation, we could posit a hypothesis of 'semi-hidden defensive control', where the adverb underlines the fact that some kind of warning regarding the presence of a system of ongoing video surveillance in the shop was provided.

The second detail pertains to the reasons for the employer behaviour: The suspicion that the staff were responsible for the losses was general and did not relate to any of the employees specifically. This is what distinguishes the *López* case from *Köpke*, where the hidden video surveillance system (still in a supermarket and still monitoring the checkout counter) was installed because of a series of suspicions involving two specific workers.

In the *Köpke* case, the employer installed the video surveillance system only after the discovery (made during the counting of the inventory) of losses and irregularities in the accounts of the beverage department in which a certain employee worked. Suspicion had also been raised about the possibility of appropriative conduct by that employee and a fellow worker. These two employees were the only ones subjected to video surveillance. The surveillance measures were put in place for a short amount of time (2 weeks); they were limited to the area of recovery, so that the monitoring would not relate to the whole work environment but only the cashiers' area. Access to the recorded information was limited to a small number of investigative agency operators and the personnel in charge of the company.

Before discussing the merits of the legal reasoning the Court followed, to complete the picture of the most recent judgments in the video surveillance field, it is also important to refer to the sentence rendered in the case of *Antović and Mirković against the Republic of Montenegro*,[21] which assessed the legitimacy of the installation of a video surveillance system in the auditorium of the Montenegrin University. In this case, the dean of the Faculty of Mathematics had informed the Faculty Council that a video surveillance system would be installed. A few days later, the headmaster decided to extend video surveillance to seven amphitheatres and the area in front of the bureau, all to protect the security of property and people, including students. Access to the recorded information was protected by a code held by the headmaster alone, and the data would be kept for 1 year. In this case, the domestic litigation was not work related, but instead, concerned a claim for damages brought

---

[21]ECtHR, second section, 28 November 2017, case of Antović and Mirković v. Montenegro, application no. 70838/13.

by some professors for alleged violation of the right to 'privacy'. While noting that the expectation for the protection of 'privacy' is not lost solely because the place of work is public or open to the public, the Montenegrin justice nevertheless concluded that the applicants had not shown that their rights had been violated.

The Strasbourg Court found that, although the aims pursued by the university were to be considered legitimate, it did not appear, in this case, that a fair balance between opposing interests had been guaranteed. The grounds for this decision were that it would have been impossible to resort to less invasive tools that would still be suitable for pursuing the objectives set, and furthermore, in this case, the information had been provided appropriately.

In *López*, the Court developed an argument based on the *Köpke* judgment. The *Köpke* ruling basically stated the following: (a) Article 8 of the Convention implies not only negative obligations for the contracting states but also a positive obligation to adopt suitable measures for guaranteeing the effective respect of family and private life; (b) effective compliance with Article 8 of the Convention requires the state to fulfil its positive protection obligations in favour of vulnerable persons, but the choice of specific measures to be adopted falls within the 'margin of appreciation'[22] reserved for contracting states; (c) under certain circumstances, the positive obligation imposed by Article 8 can be fulfilled through the introduction of a regulatory system suitable for reconciling the various conflicting interests in the specific context of reference; and (d) in relation to the overall installation of the relevant legislation (in the *Köpke* case, the German legal system), it can be assumed that a hidden video surveillance system in the workplace that follows grounded and demonstrable suspicions of theft, in the presence of an appropriate system of protections, can be said to be respectful of the protection of private life.

The specific circumstances that led the Court to consider that the balancing of the conflicting interests was carried out fairly in the *Köpke* case are represented by the following: (a) the area of recovery was restricted; (b) the surveillance was limited in time; (c) access to the recorded data was limited; (d) there was considerable interest in the protection of property rights; and (e) the domestic justice departments had verified that, in practice, other, less invasive tools were not available to protect the employer's property. The relevance of the principle of law is obvious; the *Köpke/López* strand makes clear when it is possible to deviate from the transparency rule (*sub specie* preventive information), thereby completing the picture compared with the 'test' of compatibility of the controls operated by the employer with the worker's interest in privacy, most recently elaborated by the Grand Chamber with the *Bărbulescu* ruling.[23] The profiles that the Grand Chamber found are as follows:

(a) The worker must have been informed of the possibility of monitoring and taking control measures;
(b) The information must be clear regarding the nature of the monitoring and provided in advance;

---

[22]See Harris et al. (2014), Jacobs et al. (2010) and Aliprantis (2005).

[23]ECtHR, Grand Chamber, 5 September 2017, case of Bărbulescu v. Romania.

(c) The extent of monitoring and degree of intrusion in the worker's privacy must be verified: From this perspective, there is a distinction between the monitoring of the flow of communications and that of their content, and it must be specified to the worker if all or only part of the exchanged communications are monitored, as well as the number of people who can access them;

(d) The employer must have legitimate reasons for justifying the monitoring;

(e) It must be ascertained whether there is a possibility of resorting to less intrusive monitoring measures;

(f) The consequences of monitoring and what use the employer intends to make of the information must be verified; and

(g) It must be verified that there are adequate safeguards, especially those guaranteeing that the employer cannot access the content of the communications without the worker being previously informed.

The *López* ruling reiterates the principles affirmed by *Köpke*. The reasoning is parallel, involving the following points: (a) hidden video surveillance of a worker in the workplace must be considered as a significant intrusion into the employee's private life; (b) the state must comply with the positive obligation imposed by Article 8 to guarantee effective respect for private life, including in the workplace; and (c) from this perspective, it is necessary to verify whether the state has achieved a fair balance between the opposing interests (privacy and property). However, in the case, the recorded information had been processed and examined by multiple subjects before the workers were informed of the existence of video recordings; the domestic legislation on the protection of personal data (section 5 of Spanish Law No. 15 of 1999) imposed (in compliance with EU Law) that prior, explicit, precise and unequivocal information concerning the existence of personal data files be provided. For the rights due to the interested party, the Spanish Personal Data Protection Authority had imposed the placement of a notice indicating the areas subjected to video surveillance, but nevertheless, domestic courts had considered the measure of hidden video surveillance as justified, appropriate, necessary and proportionate in relation to the legitimate interest pursued.

In the face of all these considerations, the Strasbourg Court established a different conclusion than that in *Köpke*. The Court found that Article 8 of the Convention was infringed, essentially because the installation of the hidden video surveillance system had not been the consequence of a preventive and probable suspicion against one or more specific workers. The judgement, in this regard, is condensed in a few lines in paragraph 68 of the sentence.[24]

The contribution that European jurisprudence makes to the debate on the reconstruction of the balancing criteria between opposing interests is twofold: First, it has

---

[24]In his dissenting opinion, judge Dedov criticizes the conclusion of the Court because, in the specific case, the decision to adopt surveillance measures had been based on a general suspicion against all staff members; for this reason, judge Dedov considers that the conclusion of the majority contradicts the general principle of law: "the applicant should not be legally allowed to profit from their own wrongdoing".

established the logical category of defensive checks, which may be considered legitimate if they are a necessary, proportionate measure, and above all, must be considered admissible, resulting from the emergence of a probable suspicion against one or more specific workers. Second, it emphasises the importance of compliance with the domestic legislation on the protection of individual rights, and especially, the legislation on personal data processing. The first aspect (which is also strongly related to the second) is certainly fundamental, and in some ways, confirms the conceptual elaboration that has been developed in several European countries, especially Italy, following the modification made in 2015 to Article 4 of the so-called Workers' Statute.

It must be emphasised that the common law doctrine has long been concerned with the possible elaboration of a 'proportionality test' valid for balancing between opposing interests in the matter of technological surveillance. In this regard, the most advanced perspectives are reconnecting to a 2009 study in which a list of 'objective indicators' was proposed to verify the intrusiveness of surveillance technologies.[25] These indicators are as follows: the nature of the observer (public, private, company or other); the level of personal identification; the place where the surveillance is carried out; the more or less 'sensitive' character of the extracted information; the level of accuracy (specified in the perspective of the 'granularity' of the surveillance, which depends on the level of precision of the recorded data); the purpose of surveillance; and the awareness of the observed subject. As an indicator of the impact of surveillance, another doctrine adds the evaluation of the original purpose for which the technology in use has been specifically designed.[26] This factor is certainly highly important with reference to more complex forms of surveillance in terms of the technology used, since there are strong differences related to risks for people's dignity and privacy. Different software programs or mathematical systems of reference can give rise to distinct results in relation to a use constituting an implementation of the functions for which the program was originally designed. The issue concerns the verification of the 'architectural' structure of the information system. Especially, it emphasises the need for careful consideration of the technological context of the design of the algorithm on which the program's operation is based.

These perspectives have been implemented by the European legislation with the GDPR, which is founded on the principles of 'privacy by design' and 'by default'. However, the issue of the infrastructural form has never been addressed by the ECtHR jurisprudence, evidently because the specific technology used in cases submitted to the Court do not present certain characteristics.

The most recent jurisprudence of the Court of Strasbourg insists on two profiles of the proportionality test, as follows: the purpose of surveillance and the awareness of the supervised subject. The Court admits that surveillance can be considered 'necessary in a democratic society in the interests of national security, public safety or the

---

[25]Thommesen and Andersen (2009).

[26]See Milaj (2016), p. 115.

economic wellbeing of the country, for the prevention of disorder or crime, for the protection of health or morals, or for the protection of the rights and freedoms of others' (Article 8, para. 2, Convention). An intrusion into the worker's private life consisting of a hidden video surveillance system can be justified by 'prior substantiated suspicion' towards the employee.

It should be noted that Article 8 of the Convention has a 'bipartite structure', in the sense that the norm consists of a first part that sets out the content of the protected right and a second that identifies the conditions under which the contracting state may subject the right to restriction. The limitations of bipartite property rights are permitted under the three following conditions: (a) the existence of a legal basis of the limitation; (b) the existence of a 'legitimate aim', the pursuit of which justifies the restriction of the right; and (c) the restriction's necessity in a democratic society. The protection of property rights, ensured by Article 1 of the first Additional Protocol, admits the power of the individual states to introduce normative provisions it 'deems necessary to control the use of property in accordance with the general interests'. However, the formulation of this rule leaves a wider margin of discretion in terms of Article 8 of the Convention.

5   Hidden 'Defensive' Surveillance

One of the fundamental passages of the *López* judgement concerns the recognition of a primary relevance to the domestic legislation regarding the protection of privacy, which is evidently *sub specie* regulation of the processing of personal data. The Court repeatedly clarifies that internal justice did not give sufficient prominence to the employer's breach of the prior and detailed disclosure requirement imposed by the legislation in force at the time related to the facts of the case in Spain. This aspect is also crucial concerning the transposition of the judgment related to the interpretive perspectives valid for all the legal systems of the EU member states.

The judgment of the Court of Strasbourg contributes to consolidating the importance of the regulatory link between labour discipline and general legislation regarding personal data, with reasoning that remains valid with the application of the GDPR. From this perspective, two factors must be underlined, as follows:

(a) Article 88 of the European Regulation does not require the harmonisation of the EU member states' legal systems for data processing in the context of employment relationships, given that member states are entitled to (may) provide more specific rules to ensure protection of rights and freedoms for processing employees' personal data in employment relationships. This means that the effect of the Regulation will relate exclusively to the portion of the discipline that interweaves the employment relationship in terms of the export of the general legislation; in contrast, it will not cover elements concerning the discipline that regulates the relationship and the labour market; and

(b) With a view to protecting personal privacy in the workplace, the problem of the relationship between labour law and privacy legislation is governed by a definitive and circular relationship between the two regulatory plans.

The question to be asked, considering all of the above, concerns the admissibility of hidden defensive checks. The problem arises because, as a condition of the legitimacy of data processing, the European discipline always seems to impose the necessary transparency to be guaranteed through information.

The jurisprudence of the ECtHR tends to rigorously favour the demands for freedom and dignity of workers. At the same time, it shows a certain interpretative effort aimed at achieving a point of harmonious balance between the opposing requirements of privacy protection concerning property, *sub specie* freedom of economic initiative: To be genuinely 'defensive', first, the controls must be aimed at ascertaining the worker's unlawful conduct to protect assets unrelated to the employment relationship.

Control does not have to take the form of a system designed to remotely monitor the performance of the work to be considered truly defensive; it can also involve a subsequent verification. Thus, the 'preterintentional' prohibition of remote control is intended to be valid for those control instruments with the purpose of monitoring the worker's activity. This is done by allowing the intrinsic possibility of monitoring the fulfilment of the work performance in real time, in a continuous way, and conferring this *ex ante* to the employer.

The employer's case is different, for example, if it involves cleaning up the information technology (IT) system following a virus attack and verifying—*ex post* and without any finalisation other than the restoration of the system—the illicit conduct of the worker (which can be traced via the authentication system). In this case, a punctual technical check is conducted, as opposed to a continuous one, avoiding the risk of excessive compression of freedom and the worker's dignity. These circumstances were taken into serious consideration, for example, by the Italian Court of Cassation, which provided a fundamental ruling in 2012[27]; to date, this continues to represent a rather balanced moment of synthesis. In this case, a bank had dismissed an employee for just cause. The individual was accused of having disclosed confidential news concerning a client of the organisation through confidential messages to strangers, and due to the news in question, having put in place financial transactions from which he had taken personal advantage. The bank had acquired the text of the emails exchanged by the employee with unrelated subjects, *ex post*, or after the occurrence of the behaviour attributed to the employee, when elements of fact had emerged that illustrated the need for a 'retrospective investigation'. The Supreme Court has specified that, in this case, the employer's right to protect its interest came into play, which constituted not only the whole of the company assets but also the bank's external reputation in relation to the public.

---

[27]Similarly, in the sense of illegitimacy of the installation of a geo-location system 'prepared ex ante and in general well before we could have suspicions about a possible violation by the worker' cf. Corte di Cassazione, 5 October 2016, n. 19922, in *Rivista Italiana di Diritto del Lavoro*, 2017, 1, II, page 26.

The results of defensive control can only be used in a proportionate and relevant manner considering the nature of the implemented control. For instance, the employer should be able to sanction a disciplinary measure or make a claim for compensation against an employee who damaged the company's computer system via use of the Internet for personal reasons. However, the employer cannot challenge the employee's absence from work for the time corresponding to the various connections. The latter represents a disproportionate use compared with the ratio of defensive control.

The problem of the relationship between hidden technology control, the provision of adequate information and compliance with the transparency rules imposed by the EU Law on privacy remains. To deny the legitimacy of any form of defensive control does not seem admissible. In fact, on this subject, part of the doctrine has proposed an interesting re-reading of the issue of defensive controls as a manifestation of legitimate defence in the civil sphere; this reconstruction is also based on the search for a balance between opposing interests, identifying the existence of a 'concrete, and not only imaginary, dangerous situation' (Maio 2015), as a hypothesis justifying the hidden control.

The theoretical perspective referred to as a final point intersects with the jurisprudence of the Court of Strasbourg, from which further argument must be drawn to confirm the persistent legitimacy of the defensive controls, where they pass the balancing test. In fact, we cannot neglect that an interpretation of the legal system that denies any space for effective protection of property rights (as well as the right to free exercise of private economic initiative, protected by Article 16 of the Charter in conjunction with Article 1 of the first Additional Protocol to the ECHR) would contradict a constitutionally and conventionally oriented reading of the system. This would result in a model that is unjustifiably unbalanced towards a disproportionate protection of privacy in the face of a compression of opposing interests, and this has no basis in the system of national and supranational sources. Furthermore, we would also have an imbalance effect in relation to the reconciliation of the worker's right to privacy with the employer's right to defence.

An Italian ruling from a few years ago emphasised that the privacy regulation is aimed at providing protection concerning the processing of personal data, and it is not intended to change the probation regime.[28] This must also be remembered from the perspective that the protection of the right to privacy should be excluded, under the prohibition of *venire contra factum proprium*, when it is asserted in correlation with an anti-dutiful behaviour previously held by those who request its application. In any case, it should not be forgotten that the law has long emphasised that 'in the case of processing of personal data, the need to protect other legally relevant subjective positions constitutes a limit to the protection of the right to privacy'.[29]

---

[28]Tribunale Torino, Italy, 8 January 2008, in *Argomenti di diritto del lavoro*, 2008, 4–5, page 1272.

[29]In this sense Corte di Cassazione, 30 June 2009, n. 15327, in *Nuova giur. civ. commentata*, 2010, 1, 71, perfectly consistent with ECtHR, 3 April 2007, application n. 62617/00, case of Copland v. the United Kingdom.

This principle implicitly confirms that the reference regulatory system must be interpreted in light of the interaction between labour law, general legislation on privacy and the civil order. The general model has long admitted, in full accordance with the ECHR, that the interest in confidentiality recedes when the latter is exercised for the defence of a legally relevant interest and only within the limits in which it is necessary for protection.

Ultimately, the need to identify a criterion of fair balancing between opposing interests emerges clearly from the GDPR system. Without going into too much detail, in the European Regulation, it is enough to draw attention to the centrality that assumes, among the conditions of lawfulness of the treatment, its necessity 'for the purposes of the legitimate interests pursued by the controller or by a third party, except where such interests are overridden by the interests or fundamental rights and freedoms of the data subject which require protection of personal data' (Article 6, para. 1, letter f); This should especially be read in correlation with Recitals 47, 48 and 49. The most recent doctrine attributes central importance to this rule, underlining how it plays a role of weakening the consensus as a parameter of lawfulness to feed a composite range of legal bases, among which, the balancing criterion assumes a certain importance in the GDPR's system.[30]

The balancing operation will be carried out by individual legislators and domestic jurisprudence in light of a rule of prevalence and loss of conflicting interests, primarily characterised by the reference to the good faith/correctness in Article 5 of the Regulation and strengthened by Article 40, which encourages the development of codes of conduct that also function to clarify the balancing model based on the criteria of fairness, correctness and transparency. Given all these considerations, in conclusion, how the balancing test elaborated by the jurisprudence of Strasbourg can fulfil the function of preventing abusive behaviours that see the right to privacy exploited via the legal protection of previous years' anti-dutiful behaviour can be highlighted in light of the criterion of good faith.[31] From this perspective, we must also consider the final rule set by Article 17 of the ECHR, which explicitly prohibits the abuse of the law, thereby revealing the exercise of the rights recognised by the Convention for the sole purpose of preventing that of others equally protected by it.[32]

The category of 'defensive controls' pertains to those controls aimed at ascertaining the presence of behaviours characterised by profiles of unlawfulness other than the mere breaches of the employment contract. The employer's control activity on the worker must always be compatible with the principles expressed by the jurisprudence of the ECtHR in matters of privacy protection; the restriction of the worker's right to privacy must be necessary in a democratic society to be considered

---

[30]In this sense Corte di Cassazione, 30 June 2009, n. 15327, in *Nuova giur. civ. commentata*, 2010, 1, 71, perfectly consistent with ECtHR, 3 April 2007, application n. 62617/00, case of Copland v. the United Kingdom.

[31]Astone (2006) and Zoli (1988).

[32]Piraino (2017).

an assessment of proportionality. The balancing judgment, which must incorporate the company policies and carry out the assessment in light of the criteria indicated in the *Bărbulescu* ruling, cannot fail to consider the purpose of the control.

The concrete application of the balancing test is referred to the responsible national court, as evidenced by the *Köpke* ruling, to address the eventual lack of accessibility and/or predictability of the formal legislative data. Thus, the proportionality test plays a fundamental role as a concrete instrument of European harmonisation through the intervention of the national judge.[33]

References

Ales, E., Curzi, Y., Fabbri, T., Rymkevich, O., Senatori, I., & Solinas, G. (2018). *Working in digital and smart organizations*. Basingstoke: Palgrave McMillan.

Aliprantis, N. (2005). Για μία διεύρυνση των κοινωνικών δικαιωμάτων. Ένα πρότυπο Ο Ευρωπαϊκός κοινωνικός χάρτης του συμβουλίου της Ευρώπης. Αθήνα: Παπαζήση.

Allard, J., & Garapon, A. (2005). *Les juges dans la mondialisation*. Paris: Seuil.

Ancel, B. (2017). Big Brother au bureau. Impératif sécuritaire ou crépuscule du droit à la vie privée? *Revue du droit du travail, 3*, 219–224.

Astone, F. (2006). *Venire contra factum proprium*. Napoli: Jovene.

Berramdane, A., & Rossetto, J. (2010). *Droit de l'Union européenne; Institutions et ordre juridique*. Paris: Montchrestien.

Braibant, G. (2001). *La Charte des droits fondamentaux de l'Union européenne*. Paris: Seuil.

Campeis, G., & De Pauli, A. (2014). *Carte e Corti europee. Diritti fondamentali e giustizia italiana*. Torino: Giappichelli.

Dorssemont, F., Lörcher, K., & Schömann, I. (Eds.). (2013). *The European Convention on human rights and the employment relation*. Oxford: Hart.

Fabre, A., & Escande-Varniol, M.-C. (2017). Le droit du travail peut-il répondre aux défis de l'ubérisation? *Revue du droit du travail, 3*, 166–174.

Garben, S. (2018). The European pillar of social rights: Effectively addressing displacement? *European Constitutional Law Review, 14*, 210–230.

Giubboni, S. (2017). *Diritto del lavoro europeo. Una introduzione critica*. Milano: Wolters Kluwer.

Harris, D., O'Boyle, M., Bates, E., & Buckley, C. (2014). *Law of the European Convention on human right*. Oxford: Oxford University Press.

Hazel, O. (2002). E-mail and internet monitoring in the workplace: Information privacy and contracting-out. *Industrial Law Journal, 12*, 321–352.

Jacobs, F. G., White, R., & Ovey, C. (2010). *The European Convention on human rights*. Oxford: Oxford University Press.

JILPT (Japan Institute for Labour Policy and Trading). (2014). *Protection of Employees' personal information and privacy*. Tokyo.

Leclerq, J.-F., De Roy, D., Neven, J.-F., Demez, G., Plasschaert, E., Wassenhove, S., et al. (2005). *Vie privée du travailleur et prérogatives patronales*. Bruxelles: Editions du jeune Barreau de Bruxelles.

---

[33]As an example of judicial decision based on an explicit reference to the normative and giurisprudencial system of the ECHR cf. Tribunale Padova, Italy, judgement of 24 dicembre 2018, n. 709, Judge Perrone, available at the web page http://www.europeanrights.eu/public/sentenze/ITALIA-Tribunale_di_Padova.pdf.

Lokiec, P. (2018). De la subordination au contrôle. *Semaine Sociale Lamy, 1841*, 17 décembre 2018.

Maio, V. (2015). La nuova disciplina dei controlli a distanza sull'attività dei lavoratori e la modernità post panottica. *Argomenti di diritto del lavoro, 6*(I), 1186–1215.

Mathieu, V. (2005). *Privacy e dignità dell'uomo. Una teoria della persona.* Torino: Giappichelli.

Milaj, J. (2016). Privacy, surveillance, and the proportionality principle: The need for a method of assessing privacy implications of technologies used for surveillance. *International Review of Law, Computers & Technology, 30*(3), 115–130.

Milano, I. (Ed.). (2016). *Convention européenne des droits de l'homme et droit de l'enterprise.* Paris: Arthemis.

Μίχος, Σ. (2007). *Η επιτήρηση των επικοινωνιών μέσω internet στο χώρο εργασίας.* Αθήν-α-Θεσσαλονίκη: Σάκκουλα.

Pereiro, J. C., & Rodriguez, E. (2017). Is the employer entitled to survey employee's internet communications in the workplace? Case of "Barbulescu v. Romania". In F. C. Freire et al. (Eds.), *Media and metamedia management, advances in intelligent systems and computing* (pp. 87–93). Basel: Springer.

Perraki, P. (2013). *La protection de la vie personnelle du salarié en droit comparé et européen: étude comparative des droits français, hellénique, britannique et européen.* Thèse. Université de Strasbourg.

Piraino, F. (2017). Il Regolamento generale sulla protezione dei dati personali e i diritti dell'interessato. *Nuove leggi civili commentate, 2*, 369–409.

Prassl, J. (2015). Business freedoms and employment rights in the European Union. *Cambridge Yearbook of European Legal Studies, 17*, 189–209.

Rosa, F. (2019). Nouvelles formes d'externalisation de la main d'œuvre: quelle réactions du droit du travail? In S. Laval (Ed.), *Contournement, optimization, evasion: les norms en danger?* Paris: Varenne éd.

Senden, H. (2011). *Interpretation of fundamental rights in a multilevel legal system. An analysis of the European Court of human rights and the court of justice of the European Union.* Cambridge: Intersentia.

Sitzia, A., & Barraco, E. (2010). Protection of privacy in labor relations: The Italian case within the European dimension. *Comparative Labor Law & Policy Journal, 31*(4), 705–744.

Supiot, A. (2005). *Homo juridicus.* Paris: Seuil.

Thommesen, J., & Andersen, H. B. (2009). *Privacy implications of surveillance systems.* Technical University of Denmark. Retrieved April 5, 2019, from http://orbit.dtu.dk/fedora/objects/orbit:56150/datastreams/file_4010841/content

Ziccardi, G. (2015). *Internet, controllo e libertà. Trasparenza, sorveglianza e segreto nell'era tecnologica.* Milano: Raffaello Cortina Editore.

Zoli, C. (1988). *La tutela delle posizioni "strumentali" del lavoratore.* Milano: Giuffré.

International Arbitration in the Adjudication System of a State Party to the European Convention on Human Rights

Inna Smirnova

Contents

1 Introduction: International Arbitration

Arbitration provides an alternative to classic litigation before governmental courts, generally speaking, when the latter are unavailable or inefficient. So, in the absence of a supra-national adjudicating authority, two sovereign States might choose to submit their dispute to arbitration. A company running into difficulties with a foreign country contractor might consider impractical to seek legal protection before the governmental courts of that counterparty for a number of reasons, but primarily due to significant differences of "procedural, choice-of-law and substantive legal rules" as well as "inconvenience, local bias and language".[1]

However, no adjudication mechanism, no matter how efficient, is flawless or the only available one. When a practising lawyer has to give a client an advice as to what judicial forum to submit a potential or an existing dispute, he or she needs to know

---

[1]Born (2016), p. 14.

I. Smirnova (✉)
Registry of the European Court of Human Rights, Strasbourg, France
e-mail: inna.smirnova@echr.coe.int

© Springer Nature Switzerland AG 2019
P. Pinto de Albuquerque, K. Wojtyczek (eds.), *Judicial Power in a Globalized World*, https://doi.org/10.1007/978-3-030-20744-1_36

which authority provides to whom and what kind of protection and what are the pros and cons of a particular litigation.

This article purports to assist in that task by giving a short general overview of three subjects, international commercial arbitration, investor-State arbitration and the ECtHR's approach to arbitration. Although each subject's description might not reveal something new to a specialist's view, bringing the three subjects together and having a look at their interplay and problems they currently face will hopefully ensure a better understanding of the complex and fascinating legal infrastructure of the contemporary global world.

2 International Commercial Arbitration

2.1 Definition and Legal Nature

Before discussing the advantages, critiques and potential future scenarios, some general definitions and notions, as developed by legal writers, could be reiterated.

Arbitration may be defined as "a process by which parties consensually submit a dispute to a non-governmental decision-maker, selected by or for the parties, to render a binding decision resolving a dispute in accordance with neutral, adjudicatory procedures affording each party an opportunity to present its case".[2]

International commercial arbitration is regulated by: "(a) international arbitration conventions, particularly the New York Convention, (b) national arbitration legislation, particularly local enactments of the UNCITRAL[3] Model Law, (c) institutional arbitration rules, incorporated by parties' arbitration agreements, and (d) arbitration agreements, given effect by international arbitration conventions and national arbitration legislation".[4]

There are currently four major theories explaining the nature of arbitration—contractual, jurisdictional, mixed (hybrid) and autonomous ones. The four theories attempt to answer the following questions, as put by some authors: "[as] a private, non-national system of dispute settlement, is [arbitration] subject to legal regulation? If so, to what legal order: a national law (which?), an international law or a mixture of the two? Alternatively, is arbitration, as a creation of the parties, subject only to their regulation (party autonomy)? In short, how does arbitration fit, if at all, into a clearly defined system of State justice?".[5]

The contractual theory is based on the idea that it is only the contract—the arbitration agreement, concluded between the parties, that determines the existence

---

[2]Born (2016), p. 2.
[3]United Nations Commission on International Trade Law ("UNCITRAL").
[4]Born (2016), pp. 16–17.
[5]Lew et al. (2003), p. 71.

of and regulates arbitration.[6] The proponents of this theory consider that as arbitrators derive their powers from the contract, they are not similar to judges and do not exercise public functions.[7] This theory, however, is often criticised for disregarding the role of national legal systems in the conduct of arbitration proceedings and enforcement of arbitral awards.

The jurisdictional theory, on the contrary, concentrates on the State's jurisdiction to control and regulate arbitration as it is national arbitration laws, especially the law of the arbitral seat, that provide the basis for parties to conclude an arbitration agreement.[8] An arbitration agreement is not considered to be a contract, but is only a means for parties to entrust dispute settlement to a private (instead of a public) judge.[9] Both arbitrators and public judges derive their authority from the national law, the only difference being in who nominates them.[10] Thus, an arbitrator exercises a quasi judicial function.[11]

The mixed (or hybrid) theory attempts to reconcile both of the above approaches in considering that arbitration has both elements of private and public law. The national arbitration laws determine the basis for arbitrations, while the agreement to arbitrate flows from the parties' will and consent.[12] Arbitrators, even if they perform the quasi judicial function, do not exercise State (judicial) powers.[13]

The fourth way to explain the nature of arbitration is the autonomous theory. To a certain extent, it is based on the mixed (hybrid) theory in that it also recognises private and public law elements in arbitration.[14] However, it shifts the focus to the autonomy of arbitration from those elements.[15] In particular, in business and law terrains arbitration develops its own reality. Arbitration users organise for themselves a flexible, non-national system of resolution of disputes, with procedures adapted to their needs.[16] To meet those needs, national arbitration laws are amended and international documents are elaborated.[17]

Whatever theory is preferred by legal writers, arbitration users consider that in practice it provides a number of important advantages by contrast to national judicial remedies[18]: neutrality and special expertise of arbiters, procedural flexibility, confidentiality and speed of arbitral proceedings, enforceability of arbitral awards.

---

[6]Born (2014), p. 214, with further references.
[7]Born (2014), p. 214.
[8]Born (2014), p. 215.
[9]Born (2014), p. 215.
[10]Lew et al. (2003), p. 75.
[11]Lew et al. (2003), p. 75.
[12]Lew et al. (2003), p. 75.
[13]Lew et al. (2003), pp. 79–80.
[14]Lew et al. (2003), pp. 81–82.
[15]Lew et al. (2003), pp. 81–82.
[16]Lew et al. (2003), pp. 81–82.
[17]Lew et al. (2003), pp. 81–82.
[18]Born (2016), p. 7.

2.2   Features of International Commercial Arbitration

2.2.1   Neutrality and Expertise of Arbiters

The major advantage of arbitration by contrast to national courts is considered to be the neutrality of arbiters.[19] A company having a transaction or some business with an "international element" might prefer to avoid litigation in the domestic courts of their counterparty. The same is equally true for the other party. The fears of "domestication" of disputes might arguably be even higher when States or State owned companies are a party to the contract. Even if there are no particular fears for partiality or corruption of domestic courts, a local forum, familiar legislation and legal counselling already in place immediately give an advantage to the party whose home-State courts are chosen as the adjudication forum. An arbitration, with (usually three) arbitrators chosen by or for the parties, is a logical compromise as either "domestic" courts are involved and, thus, either party has the advantage over the other. Arbitration, therefore, is often chosen not because it is "the most favourable forum, but because it is the least unfavourable forum"[20] that a party may realistically obtain during the negotiation of the contract and its dispute resolution mechanism.

The right to select arbitrators also allows the parties to choose people who are experts in a particular field relevant to the dispute. This is obviously an advantage for parties of disputes related to such technological fields of activities as space, aviation, medicine, information, construction, etc. Moreover, even simply commercial competence (by contrast to governmental judges who are mostly generalists) is perceived as an advantage by the parties.[21]

Finally, when choosing arbiters, the parties may take into account their availability,[22] which also helps to ensure a speedy examination of the dispute.

2.2.2   Procedural Flexibility

Parties may choose and modify the procedures to be followed during the arbitration. This allows them to drop certain formalities of governmental court proceedings and adjust the process to their needs.[23] So, the parties can set a particular timetable, define the scope of disclosure, determine the expert and witness participation.[24]

It should be noted that international arbitrations may be of two types: institutional ones and *ad hoc* arbitrations.[25] Institutional arbitrations are carried out with the help

---

[19]Born (2016), p. 8.

[20]Born (2016), p. 8.

[21]Born (2016), pp. 10–11.

[22]Born (2016), p. 11.

[23]Born (2016), pp. 11–12.

[24]Born (2016), pp. 11–12.

[25]Born (2016), p. 26.

of the registry of an arbitral institution[26] and, usually, in accordance with procedural rules elaborated by such an institution.[27] The parties may incorporate those procedural rules into their arbitration agreements[28] (with or without adjustments). Arbitral institutions do not examine the merits of cases, but usually provide only administrative assistance to the parties of an arbitration case, such as helping to choose or appoint arbiters (who are not employees of the arbitral institution), examine parties' allegations of arbiters' conflicts of interests, etc. *Ad hoc* arbitrations are carried out without the assistance of arbitral institutions, however, the parties may still choose to follow a set of procedural rules elaborated by an arbitral institution or even other authority (such as UNCITRAL arbitration rules[29] or IBA's various guidelines[30]).

2.2.3 Confidentiality

The confidentiality of the dispute resolution by means of arbitration constitutes another advantage for the parties. Companies might have sensitive business or other type of information they might prefer to avoid making public knowledge. "Trial by press release" might complicate the dispute[31] or give an unfair advantage to a party.

2.2.4 Speed of the Proceedings and Enforceability of the Arbitral Award

One of the main reasons which makes arbitration faster (and thus, more interesting for commercial actors), is that it is designed "to avoid the jurisdictional disputes, choice-of-law debates and multiplicitous litigation in different national courts".[32] A party willing to escape arbitration might, of course, contest the validity or scope of

---

[26]Examples of regional arbitral institutions: London Court of International Arbitration ("LCIA"), International Court of Arbitration of the International Chamber of Commerce ("ICC", located in Paris), Singapore International Arbitration Centre ("SIAC"), International Centre for Settlement of Investment Disputes ("ICSID"), the Permanent Court of Arbitration ("PCA", located in the Hague), Arbitration Institute of the Stockholm Chamber of Commerce ("SCC"), Vienna International Arbitration Centre ("VIAC"), Kuala Lumpur Regional Centre for Arbitration ("KLRCA"), etc. Industry-specific arbitral institutions: Court of Arbitration of Sports ("CAS"), London Maritime Arbitration Association, etc.

[27]Born (2016), p. 26.

[28]Born (2016), p. 26.

[29]UNCITRAL Arbitration Rules, adopted by the General Assembly of the United Nations in 1976 (original version), revised in 2010 and 2013 (either version may be chosen by the parties to an arbitration case).

[30]International Bar Association's ("IBA") Rules and Guidelines.

[31]Born (2016), p. 13.

[32]Born (2016), p. 8.

the arbitration agreement and, thus, protract the proceedings (see below). Still, a properly drafted arbitration agreement usually allows minimising this risk.

Furthermore, arbitral tribunal issues a final and binding award. The finality of the award is ensured by the lack of further reviews by appellate or other judicial instances. The award is not a recommendation or an advisory opinion, but a decision binding on the parties.

Finally, arbitral awards are recognised and enforced by States due to, among others, international treaties, such as the Convention on the Recognition and Enforcement of Foreign Arbitral Awards of 1958 ("the New York Convention"),[33] which set rules to ensure recognition and enforcement of arbitral awards.[34] So, the New York Convention provides that an arbitral award issued in one contracting State should be enforced in any other contracting State, subject to only a limited number of exceptions. International treaties are also supported favourable national arbitration legislation (often based on the UNCITRAL Model Law on International Commercial Arbitration of 1985[35]). As a result, both international treaties on recognition and enforcement of arbitral awards and national arbitration legislation "provide a "pro-enforcement" regime, with expedited recognition procedures and only limited grounds for denying recognition to an arbitral award".[36] This is a significant advantage when compared to the difficulty of recognition of foreign court awards. There is no a comparable international treaty ensuring the enforcement of foreign courts' awards similar to the arbitral ones.[37] Thus, from the practical point of view, which is always the primary interest for commercial actors, an arbitral award has more chances to be enforced than a governmental court's decision.[38]

Certainly, even arbitral awards are not immune to refusals of enforcement. If one party refuses to comply voluntarily with the arbitral award, the other party has to seek its recognition and enforcement in the national courts. Ideally, the national courts order or refuse an award's enforcement without revisiting the merits of the dispute. However, a party unwilling to comply may raise a number of defences to justify its refusal to enforce the arbitral award. Those defences may be related to the validity or scope of the arbitration agreement, notification about arbitration, subject matter of the arbitral award or "public policy" defence.

Such arguments as the validity of an arbitration agreement may easily be closely connected with the merits of a case. The "public policy" defence may lead to a similar result. An award which recognition or enforcement would be contrary to "public policy" refers to situations "when the core values of a legal system have been

---

[33]New York Convention currently has 159 parties.

[34]Other examples of international treaties on international arbitration are the Inter-American Convention on Commercial Arbitration ("the Panama Convention") of 1975; the European Convention on International Commercial Arbitration of 1961.

[35]UNCITRAL Model Law on International Arbitration Law 1985 (as amended in 2006).

[36]Born (2016), p. 9.

[37]Born (2016), p. 9.

[38]Born (2016), p. 10.

deviated from".[39] While this defence might have been reserved for exceptional circumstances, the concept is clearly open to various interpretations by national courts.

At this point the whole legal system of a particular State with its domestic law and practice, national courts and appellate instances and even the possibility of application to the European Court of Human Rights ("ECtHR") enters the dispute. In such a scenario the "winning" party is back to square one and the speed and costs of the dispute resolution change dramatically.

2.3 ECtHR and Arbitration

The ECtHR has already had a number of arbitration related cases submitted to it under the heading of Article 6 of the European Convention on Human Rights ("ECHR") providing fair trial safeguards. The recent case of *Mutu and Pechstein v. Switzerland*[40] is illustrative of the ECtHR's approach.

On the matter of admissibility the ECtHR considers that a State might be attributed responsibility for acts of private arbitrators even though they are not public judges in so far as the State formally or tacitly approves those acts.[41] Therefore, where the national courts "validate" the arbitral award, for instance, by allowing its recognition and enforcement, the State might be found responsible not only for those proceedings before the national courts, but also for the initial arbitral proceedings in so far as they have been encompassed by the national courts.

On the merits the ECtHR has held that the right to a fair trial by "a tribunal established by law" does not require the "tribunal" to be a classic governmental court. However, such an authority should provide the safeguards set by Article 6 of the ECTHR[42] unless the parties freely, lawfully and unequivocally waive certain of their rights.[43] Thus, in principle Article 6 of the ECHR does not prevent the creation of arbitral tribunals for examination of certain disputes on pecuniary interests between private parties, especially as such arbitral tribunals provide significant advantages for the concerned parties and for the administration of justice as a whole.[44] Arbitral tribunals must ensure the safeguards of the fair trial, even if the extent of those safeguards may be different and the parties may waive certain rights.

Regarding the extent of those fair trial guarantees, the ECtHR distinguishes between compulsory and voluntary arbitration. Where a person cannot opt out of an arbitration (due to, for instance, national legislation requirements or other types of

---

[39]New York Convention Guide.

[40]*Mutu and Pechstein* (2018).

[41]*Mutu and Pechstein* (2018), §§ 66–67.

[42]*Mutu and Pechstein* (2018), §§ 91–94 with further references.

[43]*Mutu and Pechstein* (2018), §§ 91–94.

[44]*Mutu and Pechstein* (2018), §§ 91–94.

regulations), the ECtHR expects that such arbitration should ensure to the person concerned the same guarantees under Article 6 of the ECTHR as governmental courts. However, if parties have a free choice and consent to arbitration voluntarily, they may thereby waive certain rights under Article 6 of the ECHR. So, in a recent case of *Mutu and Pechstein v. Switzerland*[45] the ECtHR found the situations of two applicants, professional sportsmen involved in arbitration proceedings, different due to a number of circumstances. One applicant, Ms Pechstein, had no other choice but to accept arbitration as a dispute settlement means as it was a pre-condition for her participation in sport competitions.[46] Thus, the arbitral proceedings in her case were compulsory and should have had all the safeguards of Article 6 of the ECHR.[47] The second applicant, Mr Mutu, by contrast, had an alternative to submit his dispute to national courts during the negotiation of his contract with the football club. The ECtHR rejected Mr Mutu's attempt to demonstrate that he had been in a weak negotiating position by contrast to the football club due to the absence of convincing support for such allegations.[48] The ECtHR, thus, considered that Mr Mutu's arbitration had been voluntary[49] and some fair trial rights could be waived.

The ECtHR then moved on to the applicants' particular complaints about lacking procedural safeguards. One safeguard invoked concerned the alleged lack of independence and impartiality of the CAS arbitral tribunal.[50]

The ECtHR reiterated that Ms Pechstein's arbitration proceedings had been compulsory for her and, thus, that they should have ensured the safeguards of Article 6 of the ECTHR. As for the second applicant, the ECtHR noted that even if Mr Mutu had voluntarily accepted the arbitration, that did not automatically imply that he had freely, lawfully and unequivocally waived his right to challenge the independence and impartiality of the CAS tribunal.

The ECtHR then examined the applicants' particular reasons to believe that the CAS tribunals in their cases had not been independent and impartial, but found no violations of Article 6 of the ECTHR. The ECtHR rejected, among others, Ms Pechstein's argument that the problem with independence and impartiality of CAS arbiters was structural due to the arbiters' nomination procedure. The parties could select arbiters only from the existing list, but the list contained at least 300 experts. According to the CAS regulations applicable at the relevant time, only one fifth part of arbiters placed on that list could be experts independent from various sports organisations potentially opposing athletes. The authority responsible for appointing even those "independent" experts was also composed of people issued from those sports organisations. The majority in the *Mutu and Pechstein*'s judgment admitted

---

[45] *Mutu and Pechstein* (2018), §§ 91–94.

[46] *Mutu and Pechstein* (2018), §§ 113–114.

[47] *Mutu and Pechstein* (2018), § 115.

[48] *Mutu and Pechstein* (2018), § 119.

[49] *Mutu and Pechstein* (2018), § 120.

[50] Court of Arbitration for Sport, established in 1984 and having its headquarters in Lausanne, Switzerland.

that sports organisations could have had a certain influence on the nomination mechanism, but held that it was indirect and was not a sufficient reason by itself to render all CAS arbitral tribunals as not being independent and impartial.

As some of commentators noted, the case of *Mutu and Pechstein* demonstrated that "the ECtHR will not shy away from interfering in certain types of what it called "compulsory" arbitration by invoking the responsibility of a State through allowing them in its territory".[51] No matter the assessment, the fact is that a party to arbitral proceedings may bring an application under the ECHR concerning issues of those arbitral proceedings or enforcement of an arbitral award.

3 Investor-State Arbitration

Investor-State arbitration is another type of international arbitration, having its specific history, subjects, objects and other features.

3.1 Particularities of Investor-State Arbitration

Originally, foreign investors enjoyed little protection in a host State if the latter decided to interfere with or expropriate their property or other "property" rights. In such situations foreign investors used to have only two options. First, apply to governmental courts. Second, seek the State of origin to provide them with protection via diplomatic means. Proceedings before the courts of the "host" State might appear less advantageous for foreign investors due to fears of partiality, corruption, protracted examination of the claims and else. Proceedings in the investor's domestic courts might run into State immunity, eventual award enforcement and other issues. The second option, diplomatic protection, is also not readily available as it depends on political relations between the two States involved, might be time-consuming. The idea of investor-State dispute settlement ("ISDS") was to provide an alternative to the above two options and, thereby, to promote international investment. The first bilateral investment treaties ("BITs") containing an ISDS provision were concluded in 1968–1969.[52] Since the 1990s multilateral treaties with investment provisions ("TIPs") (such as the North American Free Trade Agreement ("NAFTA")[53] or Energy Charter Treaty[54]) also began including an ISDS provision. In addition to numerous BITs and TIPs, another important for the

---

[51]Voser and Gottlieb (2018).

[52]International investment agreements' navigator of the United Nations Conference on Trade and Development ("UNCTAD").

[53]North American Free Trade Agreement.

[54]Energy Charter Treaty.

investor-State disputes international document is the Convention on the Settlement of Investment Disputes between States and Nationals of Other States ("ICSID Convention")[55] and the rules of procedure of arbitration and conciliation elaborated under its auspices.

Being a new way of dispute resolution, few investors actually used ISDS for almost 40 years. The first arbitration case based on the ISDS provision of a BIT was initiated only in 1987, and from that year until 2000 (included) only 57 arbitration claims were brought.[56] However, the next period saw a huge increase in the number of investors' claims against host States—from 2001 to 2018 (included) a total of 792 arbitration proceedings were initiated.[57] This trend has probably reached its climax as in 2018 the UNCTAD[58] noted the lowest number of new BITs concluded in 2017 (18) and the record number of BITs terminated (22).[59]

Initially ISDS was designed as a way for countries with developed economies to protect their investors from the alleged corruption and bias of State and especially judicial authorities of countries with developing economies. However, the globalisation of the commercial trade led to the reversal of the above trend. Nowadays, foreign direct investment ("FDI") is divided almost equally between both developed and developing economies. For instance, in 2018 FDI totalled $1,43 trillion, with $671 billion of FDI flows to developing economies, $47 billion to transition economies and $712 billion to developed economies.[60] Now ISDS began being used against countries with developed economies, even if their legal systems were well functioning. The mutual distrust, real or perceived, to local courts' even of those countries,[61] and the advantages provided by arbitration, lead to a serious increase in the number of arbitrations based on ISDS provisions of BITs and other international investment agreements ("IIAs").

Those arbitrations, in their stead, demonstrated a number of issues and provoked some serious critique. In particular, the older generation of ISDS were formulated in general terms the subsequent interpretation of which by arbitral tribunals was somewhat unpredictable. Arbiters, not unlike judges of other international fora, adopted a broad approach to such notions as "expropriation", "property", "investor", etc. Moreover, the terms of BITs or TIPs did not give the arbiters much room to take into account anything other than the commercial issues, such as protection of human rights or other public interests. The arbiters themselves had no professional expertise in other than commercial matters.[62] The sums claimed from States are always very

---

[55]ICSID Convention.

[56]Investment dispute settlement navigator of the UNCTAD.

[57]Investment dispute settlement navigator of the UNCTAD.

[58]United Nations Conference on Trade and Development.

[59]IIA Issues Note: Recent Developments in the International Investment Regime.

[60]World Investment Report, UNCTAD (2018).

[61]Explanatory report, PACE (2017).

[62]Laboratory for Advanced Research on the Global Economy, Investment & Human Rights Project.

considerable as they include future lost profits counted for decades of years, which could, obviously, have its effect on a government's readiness to settle the case. The practical result in some of such cases was the host State's inability to adopt and implement laws and measures aimed at sustainable development, protection of the environment and human rights without the threat of being sued by affected investors. The critics[63] claimed that private actors, thus, obtained a possibility to influence on public policy decisions taken by democratic governments.

To give an example, in 2015 President Obama denied permission to TransCanada company to construct a pipeline as a result of many environmental activists' protests. In reply, TransCanada sued the USA using the ISDS under the NAFTA for $15 billion. As critics pointed out, a case of public importance was to be decided in absence of any public, by three people who were not either American or Canadian judges, based on some widely formulated and, thus, unpredictable norms, without any regard to the environmental impact of the outcome.[64] TransCanada and the USA eventually settled their dispute. While the terms of the settlement are confidential, TransCanada did obtain the permission to proceed with the pipeline construction after the elections of the new President in the USA.[65]

Opponents of ISDS went to call the arbitral tribunals as "the shadow courts"[66] referring, among other ills, to the privacy and confidentiality of the arbitral proceedings despite their effect on public interests. There is also critique that the foreign investors have an unfair business advantage by contrast to domestic companies their ability to avoid the whole legal system of the host State even where that legal system does provide all requisite fair trial safeguards and is not considered to be corrupt.[67]

The backlash against the ISDS prompted various responses. Some States, like Argentina, unhappy about results of ISDS, refused to comply with the arbitral awards against them. Some, like Bolivia, Ecuador and Venezuela, withdrew from the ICSID convention. The United Nations[68] expressed their concern about investment arbitrations. In 2017 the UNCITRAL established a working group to elaborate possible reforms. The UNCTAD assists in the conduct of and records the reform of the current international investment regime.[69] According to its data, since 2012 about 150 States elaborated "new generation" (model) investment agreements designed to ensure sustainable development.[70] States also work on amending or replacing older BITs to bring them in line with the new approach.[71]

---

[63]Brekoulakis et al. (2016), p. 10, §1.23 with further references.
[64]Edwards (2016), p. 13.
[65]Romo (2018).
[66]Edwards (2016), p. 13.
[67]Edwards (2016), p. 13.
[68]OHCHR (2015).
[69]UNCTAD's Roadmap for IIA Reform.
[70]IIA Issues Note: Recent Developments in the International Investment Regime.
[71]IIA Issues Note: Recent Developments in the International Investment Regime.

The EU's attitude to investment arbitration is even more radical as evidenced by the *Achmea* ECJ case and proposal to create a new European Investment Court.

A Dutch insurance company Achmea obtained an arbitral award against the Slovak government based on the BIT between the Netherlands and Slovakia. As the seat of arbitration was in Germany, Slovakia sought the German national courts to set aside the arbitral award. The national court requested the ECJ's opinion and in 2018 the latter issued its pivotal decision in the *Achmea* case.[72] The ECJ held that as investments fell into common jurisdiction of the EU and EU member States (since the Lisbon Treaty), investor-State disputes between EU member States could involve issues of EU law interpretation or application. However, investment arbitral tribunals could not request the ECJ for preliminary rulings on EU law related issues and, thus, could not resolve a case "in a manner that ensures the full effectiveness of EU law".[73] Thus, the ECJ basically held that the BIT system between EU member States was incompatible with the EU law and should be replaced.[74] As a result, the Netherlands declared they would terminate all their BITs with other EU member States.[75]

Two weeks after the *Achmea* case the European Council initiated negotiations with the suggestion to establish a new multilateral and permanent investment court system ("ICS"[76]) to replace investor-State arbitration. However, this proposal faces serious critique and problems on many levels. The political crisis and economic challenges within the EU might make the agreement of member States on the matter of investment policies and creation of a whole new court system not feasible in the nearest future. Further, the ICS only concerns investors "foreign" to the EU and does not provide any help to "intra-EU" investors.[77] The business world might not appreciate the confusion and, while the debates continue, investors might want to avoid the risks of EU's approach and choose the seat of their arbitrations outside the EU, for instance, under the ICSID Convention[78] having its seat in Washington, the USA. Finally, the national courts, for instance, German magistrates, also opposed the ICS seeing no legal basis or necessity for it and suggesting to use the funds for improvement of the existing judicial remedies.[79]

The Council of Europe ("CE")[80] supported the EU's initiative to establish the ICS system instead of the ISDS clauses of IIAs. The CE expressed a shared concern that investor-State arbitrations might have negative impact on human rights and the rule

---

[72]*Achmea* (2018).

[73]As cited in Balthasar (2018), p. 228.

[74]Balthasar (2018), p. 227.

[75]Balthasar (2018), p. 229.

[76]Directorate-General for Parliamentary Research Services (European Parliament).

[77]Balthasar (2018), p. 230.

[78]Balthasar (2018), p. 229.

[79]PACE's Committee on Legal Affairs and Human Rights, Omtzigt, P., Explanatory report (2017).

[80]PACE's Resolution 2151 (2017).

of law. In particular, the CE also noted that investor-State arbitrations lack transparency and do not allow third parties to be heard; the arbiters are appointed from a small number of people from business circles or law firms, who might lack impartiality or have conflicts of interest; the threat of arbitrations might give the governments "regulatory chill" to amend their laws to ensure environmental protection, workers' and other human rights.[81] On the other hand, the CE considers that as the right to of property is a human right protected under Article 1 of Additional Protocol to the ECHR ("P1-1") without the difference between foreign or domestic legal persons, they cannot be said to be left without protection. Foreign investors enjoy the full "triple lock protection" in the EU—domestic law of an EU member State, EU law and ECHR.[82]

Some commentators see in the ECHR an additional[83] or even an alternative[84] protection available to investors.

3.2 ECtHR and Investor-State Arbitration

So far, the ECtHR case-law has not had a case whereby it would get directly involved in a classic investor-State dispute. However, it has examined a number of cases[85] which could be indicative of its potential approach to issues central to investor-State disputes.

An example of such a case can be the case of Stran Greek Refineries and Stratis Andreadis v. Greece.[86] The case differs from a classic investor-State dispute by the applicants' nationality (not foreign but domestic investor) and the applicable law (not an IIA, but national law). Still, like an investment dispute gone wrong, it had all the elements of arbitration and domestic court jurisdiction-merits-enforcement proceedings' saga, public policy interests of a democratic government, rule of law and a significant amount of money at stake.

In 1972 the applicants (a company and its sole shareholder) signed a contract for construction of an oil refinery with the Greek government, which at the relevant time was a military hunta. A year later the government refused to give them the land for the refinery. In 1973–1974 the applicants unsuccessfully sought to proceed with the work. After the democracy was restored, the new government issued a 1975 law on termination of preferential contracts concluded under the military regime. The applicants' contract was considered to be such a contract and was terminated in

---

[81]PACE's Committee on Legal Affairs and Human Rights, Omtzigt, P., Explanatory report (2017).

[82]PACE's Committee on Legal Affairs and Human Rights, Omtzigt, P., Explanatory report (2017).

[83]PACE's Committee on Legal Affairs and Human Rights, Omtzigt, P., Explanatory report (2017).

[84]Balthasar (2018), pp. 230–231.

[85]Dupuy et al. (2009), p. 219.

[86]Stran Greek Refineries (1994).

1977. In 1978 the applicants brought a civil law action for reimbursement of their expenditures incurred during the contract's period of validity. The State contested the jurisdiction of the domestic courts referring to the arbitration clause of the contract. The domestic court disagreed. The State then instituted arbitration proceedings to declare the applicants' claims unfounded. Despite the applicants' objections, the arbitration court found itself competent and proceeded to examine the dispute. On 27 February 1984 it partially granted the applicants' claims for about $16 mln. The State went back to the domestic courts and contested the arbitration courts' jurisdiction, claiming, among others, that the claims against them were statute-barred after termination of the contract. The domestic court disagreed relying on the autonomy of the arbitration clause surviving the termination of the contract. The appellate court agreed. When a cassation court's judge-rapporteur sent his opinion to the parties favourable to the applicants, the State sought to postpone the hearing. Eighteen days later Greece adopted a new law giving an interpretation to the 1975 law on termination of preferential contracts. The new law "clarified" that all terms of terminated preferential contracts were repealed including arbitration clauses; all arbitral awards in related cases were invalidated and could not be enforced. As a result of the new law the cassation court sent the applicants' case for retrial and their arbitral award was eventually declared void.

The applicants applied to the ECtHR. They complained, among others, under Article 6 about unfair trial and under P1-1 about loss of their possessions (arbitral award in their favour) as a result of the State's 1978 law declaring void arbitration clause and arbitral award.

The State attempted to contest the admissibility of the case on the grounds that the applicants had failed to exhaust statutory domestic remedies (by contrast to arbitration). The ECtHR found the State estopped from raising this objection as it was them who had instituted the arbitration.

The State then claimed that the applicants' complaint under Article 6 concerned the proceedings whereby the validity of the arbitration clause was contested, but no civil rights or obligations in substance were determined. The ECtHR rejected that argument as well finding that the validity of the arbitration clause determined the fate of the existing arbitral award and, thus, was directly decisive for the applicants' civil rights and obligations.

On the merits the government argued, *inter alia*, that it had been necessary to enact the 1978 law to resolve the contradictory judicial opinions. Furthermore, the public policy reasons required the democratic legislature to eliminate the consequences of the military regime. The ECtHR agreed that the government could well have pursued such an objective. However, the government should have still respected the rule of law principle. This principle and the notion of the fair trial "precluded any interference by the legislature with the administration of justice designed to influence the judicial determination of the dispute".[87] The ECtHR

---

[87] *Stran Greek Refineries* (1994), § 49.

concluded that the 1978 law adopted to directly influence the outcome of the applicants' case was, thus, a violation of their rights under Article 6.

Under P1-1 the applicants claimed that the adoption of the 1978 law had deprived them of the arbitral award in their favour. The government contested that the applicants had had "possessions" within the meaning of P1-1 because they had had no sufficiently established claims against the State. The ECtHR disagreed. It had found that the arbitration award had "clearly recognized the State's liability", it had been final and binding and had not "required any further enforcement measure and no ordinary or special appeal [had laid] against it" in accordance with the Greek arbitration laws. Moreover, until the 1978 law was passed, the domestic courts on two levels found no grounds to annul the award.[88] The ECtHR then held that the 1978 law had interfered with the applicants' right of property under P1-1 as it had rendered void and unenforceable the final arbitral award.

Furthermore, during the proportionality test, the ECtHR rejected the government's arguments that the applicants' preferential contract had been prejudicial to the national economy and had helped to sustain the military regime. In particular, the ECtHR considered that the State had had the right to terminate preferential contracts for all those reasons. However, the ECtHR believed that the termination of a contract could not have terminated the arbitration clause. To hold otherwise would have allowed for the State to evade jurisdiction in a dispute in respect of which an arbitration clause had been accepted. The Greek laws also recognized the principle of autonomy of arbitration clauses. The ECtHR concluded that by interfering at that stage of the proceedings by a law declaring void and unenforceable the arbitral award, the legislature "upset, to the detriment of the applicants, the balance that must be struck between the protection of the right of property and the requirements of public interest".[89]

Finally, it is worth noting that the ECtHR ordered the State to pay to the applicants just satisfaction in the amount of the arbitral award (about $16 mln) plus the simple interest of 6% for the 10 years' period between the date of the award and the date of the ECtHR judgment.

The judgment in the *Stran* case was adopted in 1994 before the backlash against ISDS. It would be interesting to see if the ECtHR reached the same conclusions nowadays, in a case involving a foreign investor and arbitration proceedings based on an ISDS of an IIA given the latest attitudes towards investor-State arbitration. As IIAs, the ECHR is formulated in rather general terms inevitably leading to varying and changing interpretations. Other important aspects are often disregarded by the proponents of the ECtHR as the protector of investors. For instance, while legal persons have the same standing as individuals, the ECHR does not protect them similarly. For instance, the ECtHR will not indicate any preliminary measures, even if a company risks getting liquidated because such consequences (by contrast, for

---

[88] *Stran Greek Refineries* (1994), §§ 61–62.

[89] *Stran Greek Refineries* (1994), § 74.

instance, to an individual's death) are not considered irretrievable. Further, as even the *Stran* case demonstrates, the ECtHR proceedings may unfortunately last years if not decades, rendering such proceedings incapable of providing a speedy response necessary in the business world. Finally, the ECtHR is not a commercial court not in terms of expertise nor in terms of damages it awards. It is thus doubtful that the ECtHR might provide a viable alternative to investor-State arbitrations.

4 Conclusion

Arbitration is a way to settle disputes where governmental courts are unavailable or inefficient. By choosing arbitration instead of governmental courts people waive certain rights, but, arguably, not the fundamental ones. The national legal systems and supra-national systems such as the EU law or the ECHR's practice, remain in place ensuring those fundamental rights and sometimes adding to the confusion at the same time.

International arbitration is praised for its neutrality and flexibility. Its proponents consider that arbitration is the most promising adjudicating tool at the current time. On the other side, arbitration is criticised for the lack of transparency, lack of impartiality of arbiters and disregard of environment protection, human rights and other important public interests. Its opponents consider it necessary to limit or even replace arbitration.

The opposing views on arbitration are also a matter of underlying ideology between individual and sovereign autonomy. It is, in essence the question of whether the decision makers believe in individual freedom to opt out of governmental legal and judicial systems or whether they believe that the State is the ultimate guarantor of the public interests and, thus, deviations from the governmental legal and judicial systems should be limited.

In any event, international arbitration is not a wild west territory anymore. The bulk of national and international laws, and expert rules or guidances is enormous and continues to grow and develop. As many times in history, international arbitration might prove having the capacity to improve and answer the new needs as it has already began doing. For instance, ICSID, UNCITRAL and ICC have elaborated new rules to increase transparency and third party participation in investment arbitral proceedings. The States began amending the IIAs in substance as well to clarify the terms and allow for protection of the States' possibility to ensure protection of human rights, environment and other public interests. Public lists of arbiters with full resumes might be provided by arbitral institutions for selection of candidates by the parties (maybe even based on a special qualification examination, including the knowledge of human rights' practice). These examples show that arbitration might be arguably quicker and easier to adapt than national or international adjudicating mechanisms. As one prominent legal writer put it, "…international arbitration is much like democracy"; it is nowhere close to ideal, but it is generally considered a good deal better than the alternatives".[90]

References

Journals and Articles

Balthasar, S. (2018). Investment protection in Europe: International Investment Treaties, the European Convention on human rights and the need for reform at EU level. *German Arbitration Journal, 16*(4), 227–233.

Books and Chapters

Born, G. (2014). *International commercial arbitration*. The Hague: Kluwer Law International.
Born, G. (2016). *International arbitration: Law and practice* (2nd ed.). The Hague: Kluwer Law International.
Brekoulakis, S., Lew, J., & Mistelis, L. (Eds.). (2016). *The evolution and future of international arbitration. International arbitration law library* (Vol. 37). The Hague: Kluwer Law International.
Dupuy, P.-M., Petersmann, E.-U., & Francioni, F. (Eds.). (2009). *Human rights in international investment law and arbitration*. Oxford: Oxford University Press.
Edwards, H. (2016). *Shadow courts: The tribunals that rule global trade*. New York: Columbia Global Reports.
Lew, J., & Mistelis, L. (2003). In S. Kröll (Ed.), *Comparative international commercial arbitration*. The Hague: Kluwer Law International.

Online Publications

Convention on the Recognition and Enforcement of Foreign Arbitral Awards of 1958 ("New York Convention"). Retrieved April 5, 2019, from http://www.uncitral.org/uncitral/en/uncitral_texts/arbitration/NYConvention.html
Convention on the Settlement of Investment Disputes between States and Nationals of Other States ("ICSID Convention"). Retrieved April 5, 2019, from https://icsid.worldbank.org/en/Pages/icsiddocs/ICSID-Convention.aspx
Court of Arbitration for Sport ("CAS"). Retrieved April 5, 2019, from https://www.tas-cas.org/en/general-information/history-of-the-cas.html
Directorate-General for Parliamentary Research Services (European Parliament). From arbitration to the investment court system (ICS), The evolution of CETA rules: in-depth analysis – Study. Retrieved April 5, 2019, from https://publications.europa.eu/en/publication-detail/-/publication/48636506-562d-11e7-a5ca-01aa75ed71a1/language-en/format-PDF

---

[90]Born (2016), p. 14.

Energy Charter Treaty. Retrieved April 5, 2019, from https://energycharter.org/process/energy-charter-treaty-1994/energy-charter-treaty/

European Convention on International Commercial Arbitration. Retrieved April 5, 2019, from https://treaties.un.org/pages/ViewDetails.aspx?src=TREATY&mtdsg_no=XXII-2&chapter=22&clang=_en

IIA Issues Note: Recent Developments in the International Investment Regime. Retrieved April 5, 2019, from https://investmentpolicyhub.unctad.org/Publications/Details/1186

Inter-American Convention on Commercial Arbitration of 1975. Retrieved April 5, 2019, from http://www.oas.org/en/sla/dil/inter_american_treaties_B-35_international_commercial_arbitration.asp

International Bar Association's Rules and Guidelines. Retrieved April 5, 2019, from https://www.ibanet.org/publications/publications_iba_guides_and_free_materials.aspx

International investment agreements' navigator of the United Nations Conference on Trade and Development. Retrieved April 5, 2019, from https://investmentpolicyhub.unctad.org/IIA

Investment dispute settlement navigator of the United Nations Conference on Trade and Development. Retrieved April 5, 2019, from https://investmentpolicyhub.unctad.org/ISDS/FilterByYear

Laboratory for Advanced Research on the Global Economy, Investment & Human Rights Project. Retrieved April 5, 2019, from https://blogs.lse.ac.uk/investment-and-human-rights/connections/resolving-investment-disputes/arbitration/

New York Convention Guide. Retrieved April 5, 2019, from http://newyorkconvention1958.org/index.php?lvl=notice_display&id=2321

North American Free Trade Agreement. Retrieved April 5, 2019, from http://www.naftanow.org/

OHCHR. UN experts voice concern over adverse impact of free trade and investment agreements on human rights (2 June 2015). Retrieved April 5, 2019, from https://www.ohchr.org/EN/NewsEvents/Pages/DisplayNews.aspx?NewsID=16031

PACE's Committee on Legal Affairs and Human Rights, Omtzigt, P., Explanatory report on 'Human rights compatibility of investor-State arbitration in international investment protection agreements'. Retrieved April 5, 2019, from http://assembly.coe.int/nw/xml/XRef/Xref-DocDetails-en.asp?FileID=23239&lang=en

PACE's Resolution 2151. (2017). *Human rights compatibility of investor-State arbitration in international investment protection agreements*. Retrieved April 5, 2019, from http://assembly.coe.int/nw/xml/XRef/Xref-XML2HTML-en.asp?fileid=23488&lang=en

Romo, V. (2018, September 10). *Native American tribes file lawsuit seeking to invalidate keystone XL pipeline permit*. Retrieved April 5, 2019, from https://www.npr.org/2018/09/10/646523140/native-american-tribes-file-lawsuit-seeking-to-invalidate-keystone-xl-pipeline-p?t=1551192813432

UNCITRAL Arbitration Rules. Retrieved April 5, 2019, from http://www.uncitral.org/uncitral/en/uncitral_texts/arbitration/2010Arbitration_rules.html

UNCITRAL Model Law on International Arbitration Law 1985 (as amended in 2006). Retrieved April 5, 2019, from http://www.uncitral.org/uncitral/en/uncitral_texts/arbitration/1985Model_arbitration.html

UNCTAD's Road Map for IIA Reform. Retrieved April 5, 2019, from https://investmentpolicyhub.unctad.org/IIA/KeyIssueDetails/552

United Nations Commission on International Trade Law. Retrieved April 5, 2019, from https://uncitral.un.org/

United Nations Conference on Trade and Development. Retrieved April 5, 2019, from https://unctad.org/en/Pages/Home.aspx

Voser, N., & Gottlieb, B. (2018, December 19). *How the European Court for Human Rights Interferes in (Sports) Arbitration*, Kluwer Arbitration Blog. Retrieved April 5, 2019, from http://arbitrationblog.kluwerarbitration.com/2018/12/19/how-the-european-court-for-human-rights-interferes-in-sports-arbitration/

World Investment Report (2018) (UNCTAD). Retrieved April 5, 2019, from https://investmentpolicyhub.unctad.org/Publications/Details/1187

Court Cases

Case C-284/16, *Achmea v. Slovak Republic*, ECLI:EU:C:2018:158 (Court of Justice).

Mutu and Pechstein v. Switzerland, nos. 40575/10 and 67474/10, 2 October 2018 (European Court of Human Rights).

Stran Greek Refineries and Stratis Andreadis v. Greece, 9 December 1994, Series A no. 301 B (European Court of Human Rights).

The Administrative Tribunal of the Council of Europe: Some Observations with Regard to Procedural and Substantive Guarantees

Zeynep Ucar Tagney and Mihail Stojanoski

Contents

1 Introduction

In order to ensure independent functioning of their powers, international organisations are furnished with privileges and immunities conferred upon them by their constituent statute or a general treaty.[1] That effectively means that they will be immune from the jurisdiction of national courts in matters including employment

---

Ms. Ucar Tagney is a lawyer at the European Court of Human Rights. M. Stojanoski is an assistant lawyer at the European Court of Human Rights and a PhD student at the University of Strasbourg, SAGE laboratory. The views expressed in this article are solely those of the authors and do not represent those of any institution.

---

[1]In the case of Council of Europe, see General Agreement on Privileges and Immunities of the Council of Europe, Paris, 2 September 1949 European Treaties Series No. 10.

Z. Ucar Tagney (✉) · M. Stojanoski
European Court of Human Rights, Strasbourg, France
e-mail: zeynep.ucartagney@echr.coe.int

© Springer Nature Switzerland AG 2019
P. Pinto de Albuquerque, K. Wojtyczek (eds.), *Judicial Power in a Globalized World*, https://doi.org/10.1007/978-3-030-20744-1_37

disputes of their staff. In order to enjoy this functional immunity and to provide their staff a means to resolve their disputes with the administration, international organisations have either set up their own internal administrative tribunals or have submitted to the jurisdiction of another existing international administrative tribunal.[2] Whether or not an international organisation's jurisdictional immunity will be recognised by domestic courts or the European Court of Human Rights ("ECtHR") depends on the existence and effectiveness of an internal dispute mechanism alternative to the jurisdiction of national courts.[3]

This article focuses on the International Administrative Tribunal of the Council of Europe ("ATCE", or simply "the Tribunal") as one tribunal among the international administrative tribunals and examines whether it offers ample procedural and substantive guarantees for staff disputes.[4] After a brief introduction on the structure and the functioning of the tribunal, it looks from a comparative perspective, some of the procedural guarantees and shortcomings of the Tribunal and then, on a substantive level, drawing on the case law of the Tribunal, it tries to establish whether the principle of subsidiarity, to the extent that an international court would not substitute its own assessment of facts for that of the administration of an organisation, plays out as a substantial bar to the examination of cases.

2   Structure and Functioning of the Tribunal

The Tribunal has its own statute and rules of procedure. It is not answerable to the Council of Europe Committee of Ministers or the general administration, nor does it receive instructions from the Secretary General.[5] Its independence is further

---

[2]The International Labour Organisation Administrative Tribunal (ILOAT) is the biggest international administrative tribunal competent to examine staff disputes of 57 other international organisations who have subscribed to its jurisdiction. However not all international organisations have followed the arduous path of setting their own tribunal or subscribing to the jurisdiction of another, the Commonwealth foundation, has for example chosen to lift its immunity for staff disputes and submitted to the jurisdiction of the national labour courts of the host State (England).

[3]The ECtHR has recognized that the attribution of privileges and immunities to international organisations is an essential means of ensuring the proper functioning of such organisations free from unilateral interference by individual governments, and that it pursues a legitimate aim. However, whether a claimant's right of access to court has been unduly restricted will be assessed by the yardstick of "availability of reasonable alternative means" see *Waite and Kennedy v. Germany* [GC], no. 26083/94, §§68-72, ECHR 1999-I, and *Chapman v. Belgium* (dec.), no. 39619/06, 5 March 2013.

[4]For a quantitative comparison of international organisations' internal justice systems, see the CoE-IJS legitimacy index, published every year at the International Administrative Law Centre of Excellence's website: http://www.ialcoe.org/legitimacy-index/. The index scores and ranks international organisations based on how compliant their internal justice systems are with the criteria set by customary international human rights law. In 2018 the Council of Europe's internal justice ranked third among the 35 organisations surveyed.

[5]See generally Sansotta (2013) and Arnim (2017).

guaranteed by the appointment of the chair and deputy chair, which are appointed by the ECtHR. Other two members and deputy members are appointed by the Committee of Ministers. Cases can only be lodged against the Secretary General, who represents the Council of Europe before the staff, and not against any other body or official of the Council.

The procedure before ATCE is called an appeal procedure. However, this appears as a misnomer for the Tribunal hears cases in the first-instance, but it is compulsory for complainants to lodge an administrative complaint against the Secretary General before they have recourse to the Tribunal. This mechanism reflects the general principle of administrative law where a complaint must first be brought to the related administrative authority in order to have an act annulled or obtain compensation. Therefore, claimants must exhaust the preliminary administrative complaint procedure respecting the applicable formalities and time-limits. Failure to do so will result in their case being rejected by the Tribunal on grounds of non-exhaustion.

Lodging a case before the Tribunal does not have suspensive effect. However, the Tribunal may issue an interim decision for the stay of execution at the request of the claimant where it considers that the execution of the impugned administrative act may result in irreversible prejudice to the claimant. Finally, the decisions rendered by the Tribunal are binding on the parties. The Secretary General is under an obligation to inform the Tribunal of the execution of its decisions within thirty days from the date on which they were delivered.

3 Procedural Guarantees and Shortcomings

The right of access to a court, or more generally the right of access to justice, is a basic principle of rule of law which has been set out explicitly in international human right treaties and instruments.[6] According to the well-established case law of the ECtHR right of access to court as such is not absolute and may be subject to limitations. Whilst rules and procedures regulating access to a court are required by the very nature of its right, they must not restrict or reduce the access left to the individual in such a way or to such an extent that the very essence of the right is impaired.[7] It follows that limitations which do not pursue a legitimate aim and do not have a reasonable relationship of proportionality between the means employed and the aim sought to be achieved will be deemed incompatible with the right of access

---

[6]See Article 10, Universal Declaration of Human Rights. 10 December 1948, General Assembly Resolution 217A (III). U.N. Doc A/810, p. 71; Articles 6 and Article 13 of the European Convention on Human Rights, 4 November 1950. 213 United Nations Treaty Series 221; Article 14 of the International Covenant on Civil and Political Rights, 16 December 1966. 999 United Nations Treaty Series 171; Articles 8 and 25 of the American Convention on Human Rights, 22 November 1969. 1144 United Nations Treaty Series 123; Article 7, African Charter on Human and Peoples' Rights. 27 June 1981. 1520 United Nations Treaty Series 217.

[7]See, for example, the *Waite and Kennedy* judgment, cited above.

to court. In that respect formal conditions of admissibility or standing may act as a bar to access from the get-go (such as standing, time-limitations, court fees) whereas certain procedural requirements or restrictions may prevent a claimant to have his or her case determined in an effective manner (complex legal proceedings, denial or unavailability of legal aid, non-execution of decisions). This sub-section looks at some of the procedural guarantees offered by the Tribunal, comparing it to the practice of other international tribunals where relevant.

3.1 Standing

3.1.1 Staff Members or Candidates

On the issue of right of access to a court and the *jus standi* to bring a case before the tribunal, the Tribunal follows the general practice in this field which is to allow cases to be brought by individuals who have direct and existing interest to bring a case concerning an administrative act that has adversely affected them. ATCE's jurisdiction *ratione personae* therefore covers employment disputes brought by current and former staff members with the organisation.[8] These disputes constitute the majority of the workload of the tribunal which range from issues concerning appointments, promotions, appraisals, dismissals, pensions and disciplinary measures. Candidates who have been allowed to participate in the recruitment procedure also have standing before the Tribunal in so far as they complain about an irregularity in the recruitment procedure. This last category also extends to seconded officials who have participated in a competitive selection process.[9]

---

[8]The fact that complaints procedure and therefore an appeal to the Tribunal is only open to staff members can be detected in the wording of Article 59 §§ 1–2 and 8 of the Staff Regulations.

[9]See *Sibel Sadir Yıldırım v. Secretary General* Appeal No. 580/2017 (ATCE, 24 January 2018) concerning a complaint brought by a Turkish national judge who had participated in a selection process for secondment to the Registry of the European Court of Human Rights as an assistant lawyer. The case is noteworthy because seconded officials are not considered as staff members in so far as they remain employed by the national state and receive no salary from the Council of Europe. Furthermore, secondment to the Council of Europe does not require the candidates passing a competitive recruitment procedure (see Resolution (2012)2 adopted by the Committee of Ministers on 15 February 2012 at the 1134th meeting of the Ministers' Deputies). Nevertheless the Tribunal held that the dispute fell within its competence *ratione personae* since, first and foremost, the applicant could not be expected to bring her grievances against Turkish authorities since they took no part in the part of the procedure the applicant complained of, and secondly, the tribunal found that the recruitment procedure effectuated by the Registry of the European Court of Human Rights was not a simplified procedure but had been in fact akin to the competitive recruitment procedure set out in Article 15 of the appendix II of the staff regulations. It would appear therefore that secondment through a simplified procedure, which is the case when the Secretary General appoints an official on the basis of the proposals received from the Permanent Representatives of the member States or, as the case may be, the Heads of international organisations without a separate competition procedure, would fall outside the jurisdiction of the Tribunal.

3.1.2 Staff Associations and Trade Unions

The Staff Committee, which is the official staff representative body of the Council of Europe can bring complaints on its own behalf so long as the administrative act complained of directly affects its rights or prerogatives. The explicit provision in the Staff Regulations which endows standing only to the Staff Committee in the category of staff association suggests that other staff unions or professional organisations do not have a right of action before the Tribunal.[10] It must nevertheless be noted that the approach adopted by the Council of Europe in granting *jus standi* to the Staff Committee in this respect is more progressive compared to other international organisations but more restrictive with respect to national administrative practices which generally permit anyone on the basis of general interest to challenge an administrative act (i.e., *actio popularis* or collective action).[11] It must be borne in mind that even among international organisations who have granted in their statute a right of action for their official staff association, no *actio popularis* as such are permitted. In practice this prevents the Staff Committee from bringing an action before the Tribunal to challenge a decision of regulatory nature which affect all staff or certain categories of staff. It seems therefore that there is a certain reluctance on the part of international organisations to recognise a right of collective action as this might undermine the decision making process at the administrative level, where every single regulatory decision might be challenged by a staff association for one reason or another. On the other hand, allowing a staff association to bring cases in the general interests of staff can contribute to the proper functioning of the administration as well as strengthen the confidence of staff members in the workings of rule of law, a key principle which most international organisations were set up to uphold. What is important in that respect that staff associations and trade unions in international organisations are not only the voice of opposition, but act as watchdogs of unfair administrative practices. For instance in *ad personam* decisions made by the administration, such as granting exceptional measures to a staff member's terms of employment by deviating from the regular practice, if staff associations are not granted leave to seek judicial review for the sole reason that the administrative act complained of did not directly affect them, there might be practically no one else

---

[10]It is interesting to contrast this with the statute of the administrative tribunal of the OECD, which does not limit standing to the official staff association but to other staff unions or other professional organisations.

[11]IMF administrative tribunal ("IMFAT"), the administrative tribunal of the Asian Development Bank, ILOAT or United Nations Dispute Tribunal ("UNDT") are notable examples which grant no standing to staff associations. However, unlike the situation in ATCE, a "regulatory decision"—that is any rule concerning the terms and conditions of staff employment, excluding the resolutions adopted by the Board of Governors of the Fund—may be challenged directly by a staff member before the IMFAT without there being an individual decision affecting that staff member.

who can, especially if the said administrative practice does not infringe upon the rights or legitimate expectation of another staff member.[12]

The issue of a staff association's ability to bring cases in their own name has not received much attention as a topic of debate and reflection in the doctrine, as most focus has hitherto been the right of staff members individual right of access to justice. Recently, whether and to what extent staff associations can rely on a right to freedom of association before national courts and contest the immunity of organisation which moreover has not granted such an association standing to bring cases in its own name has been brought before the Supreme Court of Netherlands. The case concerned interim relief proceedings brought by VEOB and SUEPO, staff unions of the European Patent Organisation, before Dutch national courts alleging that their right to freedom of association and their right to strike had been curtailed because of the introduction of new provisions on strike action after VEOB had begun calling upon their members to strike and that their right to communicate with staff members had been unduly restricted. The Hague Appeal Court dismissed the organisation's plea of jurisdiction immunity on the grounds that the staff unions in question had no access to the internal judicial processes of the organisation in their own name. Furthermore, it did not consider the possibility of staff members individually challenging the new restrictions on their right to strike an effective remedy to enforce the rights of collective action. It therefore held that their rights under Article 11 (freedom of association and assembly) and Article 13 (right to an effective remedy) of the European Convention on Human Rights would be curtailed if Dutch courts declined jurisdiction to hear their case. In its decision of 20 January 2017, the Supreme Court of the Netherlands quashed the appeal court's ruling by upholding the organisation's plea of jurisdictional immunity.[13] It noted in that respect that while the claimant staff unions did not have standing to bring complaints before the internal judicial process of the organisation, it considered that this was not a requirement *per se* under Article 11 of the Convention so long as the members of the association or staff representatives could bring contesting the measures affecting their right of collective bargaining, individually or in the name of collective interests of all staff contesting a general measure.[14] Having found that this option was available to the members of the staff union individually and the staff representatives for the protection of collective interests, the Supreme Court of Netherlands upheld the organisation's immunity and dismissed the case on the basis of the reasonable

---

[12]By way of example, in a case where the Staff Committee sought to set aside *ad personam* decision made by the Secretary General by means of a derogation from the rule that prohibited a staff member past the age of 65 being employed by the organisation, ATCE rejected the action on the grounds that the Staff Committee had no direct interest in the dispute in so far as it was not subject to the measure in question, see Staff Committee (VII) v. Secretary General, Appeal no. 305/2002 (16 May 2003).

[13]*European Patent Organisation & State of the Netherlands v Vakbondsunie Van Het Europees Octrooibureau (VEOB) & Staff Union of the European Patent Office (SUEPO)*, Case no. 15/02186.

[14]The Supreme Court of Netherlands relied on the case law of the ECtHR while noting that national law offered more protection in this respect.

alternative criteria. As one commentator notes it is open to doubt whether collective interests—such as the right to strike—can be effectively protected in practice only by allowing individual action since the threshold for an individual staff member to lodge a case on his or her own behalf is usually quite high.[15]

3.1.3   Third Parties

Third parties such as consultants hired through procurement and external contracts or persons injured by the organisation's tortuous acts do not have standing before the tribunal.[16] In the case of external contractors the General Agreement on the Privileges and Immunities of the Council of Europe require such disputes to be submitted to arbitration. There is no provision setting out how disputes arising out of tortuous acts would be settled. In any case tort claims fall outside of the jurisdiction of the tribunal which may only review administrative acts, the latter being confined to individual or general decision or measure taken by the Secretary General or any official acting by delegation from the Secretary General. In case of disputes arising out of tort, it is always of course open to the organisation to waive its immunity before national courts should the settlement negotiations fail and the tort victim takes the dispute before the nationals. In the case where the organisation does not waive its immunity before national courts, the latter may nevertheless examine the dispute since not doing so would infringe the tort victim's right of access to justice.

3.1.4   Political Organs or Representatives of the Organisation

The tribunal has no jurisdiction to hear disputes between the statutory organs of the Council of Europe, the Committee of Ministers (CM) and the Parliamentary Assembly (PACE) and neither does it have jurisdiction to accept claims coming from the members of those bodies even if such disputes may relate to disciplinary actions taken against them serving in their official (political) capacity.[17] In a recent case before the Tribunal the then President of PACE asked the tribunal to declare null and void of a draft resolution that sought to amend the internal rules of PACE by introducing a procedure which would allow PACE, among other things, to dismiss its president.[18] The applicant brought the case before the Tribunal before the draft resolution was adopted, and alleged in particular, that the resolution had in fact been an *ad hominem* decision that affected his honour. Moreover, relying on Articles 1, 6

---

[15]See Ryngaert (2017).

[16]See Kloth (2010).

[17]Similarly, it is doubtful whether the Secretary General himself may apply to the Tribunal, as a specially appointed official, see Sansotta (2013), p. 4.

[18]See *Pedro Agramunt Font de Mora v. Secretary General,* Appeal No. 584/2017 (24 January 2018).

and 13 of the Convention he argued the reason he brought the case to the Tribunal had been that he believed he had a right to an effective judicial remedy with respect to his grievances and that the Tribunal would be the only judicial body that could examine them. In the meantime, that is before the Tribunal examined the admissibility of the case, the resolution in question was adopted but the applicant had resigned before a motion to remove him from office had been put forward. The Tribunal rejected the case on *ratione personae* grounds noting firstly that the appellant did not belong any of the categories of persons who may lodge an "administrative" complaint. On that note, the tribunal pointed out that what the appellant challenged was not an administrative act, but concerned entirely of a political decision which the tribunal had no competence to review.

3.2   Costs and Legal Aid

There are no fees or security deposits that are required to lodge a complaint before the Tribunal.[19] On the other hand, no legal aid is available to staff. It must however be noted that legal aid before international administrative tribunals is uncommon and one such organisation who has institutional legal aid for its staff is the United Nations.[20] From the perspective of Article 6 § 1 of the Convention, legal aid in civil disputes is not a requirement unlike in criminal cases. That being said the ECtHR has found in some instances that denial of legal aid in civil cases can infringe an individual's right of access to a court. The question whether the provision of legal aid is necessary for a fair hearing must be determined on the basis of the particular facts and circumstances of each case and will depend, among others, upon the importance of what is at stake for the applicant in the proceedings, the complexity of the relevant law and procedure and the applicant's capacity to represent him or herself effectively.[21] Furthermore the Court has said that granting of legal aid in civil proceedings is not the only means to ensure effective access to a court, other measures such as a simplified procedure could also ensure the same principle. On the basis of these criteria, it cannot be said that the lack of legal aid before the Tribunal might hinder a claimant's right of effective access to justice. First, there is no requirement that a claimant be represented in the proceedings, they can choose to be self-represented or assisted by an adviser of their choice, and the latter category does not need to be a registered lawyer. Secondly, rules setting out lodging an

---

[19]Sansotta (2013), p. 6.

[20]Created during the reform of the United Nations internal justice system, Office of Staff Legal Assistance (OSLA) is unique in that it provides free and independent legal advice and representation for staff members falling within the jurisdiction of the UNDT and UNAT. While free legal advice is available to all staff, OSLA accepts formal representation only when it considers a case has a reasonable chance of success. When it declines representation, the staff members is accorded with a reasoned decision, see Leighton (2014).

[21]See *Steel and Morris v. the United Kingdom*, no. 68416/01, §§ 59–61, ECHR 2005-II.

application and the application form itself are straightforward and do not necessitate any specialised legal knowledge. The procedure itself is also claimant-friendly since it allows written round of pleadings which is always followed by an oral hearing where parties each have an opportunity to state their case before the tribunal. It must be mentioned in passing that the Staff Committee in practice helps staff members bringing a case before ATCE and can act as a third-party intervener in the dispute.

Looking at the flip side of the coin regarding costs, if they are not awarded at all to the successful party at the end of the dispute, or if the claimant as the losing party has to reimburse the defendant's costs, such practices may have a chilling effect on potential claimants from bringing a complaint to the tribunal, or they might, in certain situations, result in the unfairness of the proceedings.[22] The practice in international administrative tribunals is to let each party bear its own costs. The Tribunal's practice in this field has not drawn any particular criticism, unlike for example UNDT and UNAT, which do not have a mechanism for awarding litigation costs except in the case of manifest abuse.[23] The Tribunal's rules of procedure in fact give discretion to the tribunal to order the defendant to reimburse the costs of the claimant provided that they are properly vouched and reasonable as to quantum when it has allowed an appeal and even in exceptional circumstances to do the same when it has rejected an appeal.[24]

3.3 Procedural Guarantees

3.3.1 Disclosure of Documents: Equality of Arms and Adversarial Proceedings

According to the well-established case-law of the ECtHR, the concept of a fair hearing under Article 6 § 1 of the Convention implies the right to adversarial proceedings, according to which the parties must have the opportunity not only to make known any evidence needed for their claims to succeed, but also to have knowledge of, and comment on, all evidence adduced or observations filed, with a view to influencing the court's decision.[25] The principle of adversarial proceedings is reflected in Article 7 (6), of the Tribunal's Statute which provides that "every document included in the case-file shall be transmitted to the parties or made available to them for consultation in the offices of the Tribunal's registry". Despite this provision however, the Tribunal has established through its case-law an exception in that minutes of or views expressed at meetings of recruitment and promotion

---

[22]The ECHR has noted that the resolution of the issue of court costs may have implications for the fairness of the proceedings as a whole (see, for example, *Stankiewicz v. Poland*, no. 46917/99, § 60, ECHR 2006-VI).

[23]See, Leighton (2014), p. 142.

[24]See Arnim (2017), cited above, p. 354.

[25]See, for example, *Krčmář and Others v. the Czech Republic*, no. 35376/97, § 40, 3 March 2000.

panels are not disclosed to the claimants.[26] There are examples in the Tribunal's case-law where despite the express request of the claimants, certain documents, including for example sample of questions put to the candidates in recruitment tests, were not disclosed on the basis of the confidential nature of this information for the organisation.[27]

One might therefore wonder whether it is keeping up with the full guarantees of the adversarial proceedings and fair hearing where a party cannot have access to the full facts of the dispute. The disadvantage suffered by the claimant, is however to a great extent offset by the Tribunal which examines the contents of the non-disclosed documents carefully and in particular by determining whether they are damaging to the claimants. When it determines an irregularity in its contents, it will rule in favour of the claimant. If the tribunal finds no damaging elements in the contents of the confidential documents, it will set out the reasons for its consideration in detail in the judgment.

3.3.2 Anonymity

The statutory rules governing the Tribunal do not have a separate provision on anonymity.[28] In practice, claimants can request anonymity when filing their complaint and the Chair of the Tribunal gives a decision whether to grant or reject the request. It must be noted that anonymity is not granted generously by the tribunal most likely for reasons of transparency and this approach has been criticised by some commentators.[29] The claimants in certain disputes, such as those concerning appraisals and disciplinary actions, may have an interest to remain anonymous either for fear of retaliation or reprisals—whether such fears are founded or not—or they might simply not want their identity to be disclosed to the rest of the organisation which in any case does not have an interest to know who the claimant is but is more interested in knowing the particularities of the case and the conclusions of the Tribunal.

---

[26]See, Sansotta (2013), p. 7.

[27]See, *Bilge Kurt Torun v. Secretary General*, Appeal no. 543/2014 (30 January 2015) concerning the non-disclosure sample of questions put to the candidates during a recruitment procedure; See *Régis BRILLAT (III) and Riccardo PRIORE v. Secretary General*, Appeal Nos. 582/2017 and 583/2017 concerning non-disclosure of the findings of the harassment committee; see, *Levent Ercan v. Secretary General*, Appeal no. 460/2009 (28 April 2010) concerning the non-disclosure of the records of meeting of the Appointments Board.

[28]Contrast this with IMFAT, which has an explicit rule on anonymity where such requests are decided after receiving the defendant's comments.

[29]See the views expressed for and against more flexibility towards anonymity in international administrative tribunals, in International Colloquy: Common Focus and Autonomy of International Administrative Tribunals, held in Strasbourg on 19–20 March 2015 (Council of Europe, 2017) available at http://www.coe.int/T/AdministrativeTribunal/Source/ConferenceTACE2015_en.htm.

Since the Tribunal does not state the reasons for its decisions regarding anonymity, the criteria it uses in arriving at these decisions are difficult to ascertain. On the Tribunal's website it is indicated that it is inspired by the ECtHR's rules of the court when ruling on these requests. It can therefore be presumed that the burden rests with the claimant to demonstrate that disclosure of his or her identity would result in not just *some* but serious damage or prejudice to his or her privacy. In other administrative tribunals, too, anonymity remains to be the exception rather than the rule.

3.3.3 Oral and Public Hearings

Proceedings before the Tribunal are oral and public unless parties waive their rights to a hearing and the tribunal considers a hearing to be unnecessary. It must be noted that the Tribunal's practice in this respect is laudable since cases are rarely decided without a hearing, which is not always the case with other administrative tribunals.[30]

4 Substantive Guarantees

This chapter will attempt to present some issues of substantive law with regard to the Tribunal and problems which arise in that relation. It will then examine the power of the Tribunal to establish facts, the limitations thereto and the issue of burden of proof borne by the parties by examining its own, and the case-law of similar administrative tribunals. The examples provided below are not intended to be exhaustive.

4.1 Sources of Law

The primary source of material law relied on by the Tribunal are the Council Staff Regulations.[31] These are executed by means of rules issued by the Secretary General

---

[30]In that respect, in the case of most other international administrative tribunals, oral hearings are not mandatory ILOAT statute for example leaves it to the discretion of the tribunal to hold a hearing and it is observed that before this tribunal hearings are very rarely held. In the case of IMFAT, parties have a possibility to request it or the tribunal may decide on its own motion to hold a hearing. In the case of UNDT, statutory provisions require for a hearing in disciplinary measures. In others it is up to the discretion of the judge hearing the case.

[31]The Staff Regulations and the appendixes thereto are an extensive volume of law which govern employment issues with regard to Council staff members. They were adopted by Resolution Res (81)20 of the Council Committee of Ministers on 25 September 1981, with the exception of Appendix VIII, which was adopted by Resolution Res (83)12 of 15 September 1983. At the moment they are available in their integrity on the website of the Council at https://rm.coe.int/ 0900001680790b3f.

on the basis of Article 62 of the regulations themselves.[32] In addition, Resolutions of the Committee of Ministers of the Council are also considered a primary source of law, as they often regulate specific issues and fill lacunas with respect to the Staff Regulations. These sources form the core of positive law relied on by the Tribunal. Its Statute, being a source of procedural law, is also part of the staff regulations (Appendix XI). Lastly, the rules of procedure of the Tribunal, which are adopted by the Tribunal itself, should also be mentioned.[33]

In addition, the Tribunal applies general legal principles, concordant principles of systems of national law, international administrative practice and case-law emerging from its own practice, or that of other administrative tribunals operating in different international organisations. The Tribunal also has regard to the Statute of the Council of Europe and to Council of Europe practice in general.

The above sources will be examined briefly from the standpoint of their relevance in the decisions of the Tribunal.

For starters, the Tribunal often finds it sufficient to limit itself to the examination and interpretation of the staff regulations in order to reach a decision.[34]

For example, the application of the "salary step advancement" rule, which provides for an automatic promotion entailing a higher salary after a requisite period of employment by the Council was recently examined.[35] In this case the interpretation of Article 3 of Appendix IV to the Staff Regulations was called into question, which provided for advancement in step after having completed 24 months in the employment category of the plaintiff. The Tribunal held that a period of employment which was considered probationary should not count towards the overall 24 months required under that provision and subsequently dismissed the appeal as unfounded.

Another recent example comes from the interpretation of the right to an education allowance in respect of staff members' children, as provided for in Article 7 of Appendix IV of the Staff Regulations.[36] In the instant case the appellant was denied the allowance in question, but the Tribunal found in her favor, establishing that a study program similar to the one in question was not available in Strasbourg. Therefore, the request for allowance in respect of her daughter's studies in Paris had been justified.

---

[32] Article 62 stipulates: The Secretary General shall issue rules, instructions or office circulars laying down the provisions for implementation of these Regulations. Implementing provisions entailing a financial commitment shall be subject to approval by the Committee of Ministers.

[33] The rules of procedure entered into force on 1 September 1982. They were subsequently modified on 27 October 1994 and 30 January 2002.

[34] A brief search of its case-law, which is publicly available (https://www.coe.int/en/web/tribunal/case-law-of-the-administrative-tribunal) reveals that these cases do not lack in complexity, but rather the Tribunal had established case-law on the issue and was is possession of sufficient resources to reach its decision.

[35] *Yakimova v. Secretary General*, appeal No. 560/2014 (22 October 2015) (in some places the case number is reflected as 560/15).

[36] Case of *Dentinger v. Secretary General*, appeal No. 472/2011 (8 December 2011).

In these cases the Tribunal limits itself to the Staff Regulations and its own case-law, where necessary. Granted, it is difficult to rely on case-law of other administrative tribunals when interpreting rules so specific that they are virtually incomparable with other jurisdictions.

In some cases the Tribunal was forced to defer to national law instruments to rule on questions which lacked substantive definition in its own legal instruments. Such was the case of *Penninckx v. Secretary General*[37] where the definition of the term "residence" (or "*domicile*" in the French text) was called into question. The Tribunal held, on the basis of the personal circumstances of the appellant, that her place of residence before taking duties at the Council had been Belgium, and not Strasbourg. This entitled her to obtain an expatriation allowance. The case is interesting because the Tribunal deferred to the definition of the term used in French law to reach its decision:

> Having regard to the purpose of the expatriation allowance, the Tribunal considers that it can adopt these definitions for the purposes of its decision, even if these terms may have a different meaning in other member states of the Organisation.[38]

It is interesting to note that, being an organ of an international institution, the Tribunal chose to rely on French law in spite of the possibility to commission a comparative review and being aware that the said definition may vary across Member-States.

Further to the question of sources, it can be observed that although the Tribunal relies mostly on its own case-law, it frequently makes references to the case-law of the ECtHR, mostly in relation to its application of general legal principles. Although going into more detail on the former would require a very long analysis exceeding the aims of this chapter, a brief outline of the latter appears appropriate.

Among more recent examples, the appellants in the case of *Brillat (II) and Priore*[39] relied on case-law of the ECtHR to claim a violation of the principles of adversary proceedings and equality of arms with regard of access to certain materials. Further to the above, in the case of *Kling (IV)* the applicant invoked her freedom of expression citing Article 10 of the European Convention of Human Rights. In the latter case, the Tribunal even borrowed the proportionality test relied on under Article 10 of the Convention by the ECtHR to reach its conclusion.[40] The Tribunal has also relied on case-law from the ECtHR to reach a decision on

---

[37]More specifically, the Tribunal relied on a definition from the "*Vocabulaire juridique*", published by the Association Henri Capitant, ed. Gérard Cornu).

[38]Paragraph 66 of the decision.

[39]Appeals Nos. 582/2017 and 583/2017 (14 May 2018), paragraph 72 of the decision.

[40]Although, granted, it relied on its own case-law to support its findings. See paragraphs 62–66 of the decision. Similar issues are examined in the other three cases brought by the same appellant, appeals Nos. 316/2003 (22 December 2005), 345/2005 (22 December 2008) and 405/2008 (19 December 2008).

non-exhaustion[41] as well as various issues concerning Article 6,[42] Article 8,[43] Article 12[44] and Article 14[45] of the Convention. The operative part of its decisions is no exception.[46]

While still on the issue of general legal principles, it is worth mentioning that these usually go hand in hand with the reliance on the case-law of other administrative tribunals. Seen how the United Nations and the International Labour Organisation had operational administrative tribunals for several decades already at the point when the Council Tribunal was established, the above appears a logical recourse. For example, the Secretary General in case No. 563/2013[47] invoked ILOAT case-law to argue that loss of a staff members' pay in a period of work stoppage was an established legal principle. The Tribunal accepted this argument holding that the above had been "a general principle", but nonetheless found for the plaintiff.[48]

The Tribunal has also pronounced itself on the hierarchy of sources of material law relative to its decisions. For example, in the case of *Devaux (II)*[49] in addition to basing its decision, in part on general principles of law,[50] the Tribunal also held that:

> [...] l'arrêté n° 1232 constitue une source de droit de niveau inférieur aux principes généraux du droit et au Statut du Personnel qui dans son article 3 vise à garantir une égalité de traitement entre les agents [...]

The above reasoning rings familiar with constitutional lawyers, since it can be construed as a reiteration of the universally-held position of supremacy of international customary law vis-à-vis any individual decision or act by the State.

4.2   Power to Establish Facts

In view of the fact that the European Convention plays an ever increasing role in staff management and dispute settlement[51] it appears appropriate to examine the position

---

[41]*Marchenkov v. Secretary General*, appeal No. 294/2002 (28 February 2003), paragraph 21.

[42]*Inter alia*, *Vernau v. Secretary General*, appeal No. 413/2008 (31 March 2009), paragraph 37; and *Maria Grazia Loria Albanese v. Secretary General*, appeal No. 255/1999 (27 March 2000), paragraph 22.

[43]For example, in *Sorinas Balfego v. Secretary General*, appeal No. 114/1985 (25 October 1985).

[44]*Nyctelius v. Secretary General*, appeal No. 321/2003 (4 February 2005).

[45]For example, *Robert Diebold (II) v. Secretary General*, appeal No. 340/2004 (17 June 2006).

[46]*X v. Secretary General*, appeal No. 239/1997 (27 August 1998), operative part.

[47]Case of *Staff Committee v. Secretary General (XII)*, appeal No. 536/2013 (28 June 2013), paragraph 49.

[48]Paragraph 71 of the decision.

[49]Case of *Devaux (II) v. Secretary General*, appeal No. 587/2018 (25 September 2018), paragraph 111.

[50]Notably, equal treatment and equal pay for equal work.

[51]See, Sansotta (2013), cited above.

of the ECtHR when it comes to establishing of facts before we embark on the powers of the Tribunal in this domain.

In general, the ECtHR has broad powers to establish facts. It takes into consideration all the evidence submitted by the parties, including those submitted by way of *amicus curiae*. As a general rule, the ECtHR will rely on the evidence presented by the parties, but it also has the power to rely on other documents. It is worth mentioning that the Court has the power to conduct its own investigation pursuant to Article 38 of the Convention.[52] The Court, more notably in Chamber formation, has the power, at the request of a party or of its own motion, to adopt any investigative measure which it considers capable of clarifying the facts of the case.[53] This includes fact-finding missions on the site of the alleged violation in any member-State. Regardless of the Court's reluctance to frequently adhere to such measures, they remain an option available to it.

The Tribunal, similarly, has broad powers to establish facts. According to the Rules of the Tribunal, it has the power to hear witnesses and appoint experts at the proposal of a party, or *proprio motu*.[54] In addition, the Tribunal itself can interview the witnesses at an oral hearing, which is ordinarily held, unless waived by both parties.[55]

These powers are especially relevant when cases involve complex issues of fact which go beyond the legal sphere. For example, in the case of *Parienti v. Secretary General*, which dealt with alleged harassment, the Tribunal requested and obtained an expert report from a psychiatrist in order to determine the plaintiff's state of health at the time the alleged harassment took place.[56] The findings of that report were later relied on by the Tribunal to dismiss the appeal, in absence of any other means to reach a conclusion as to the appellant's state. In the instant case there was no lower instance to establish the facts in adversary proceedings to assist the Tribunal, and the administrative inquiry which preceded the Tribunal's examination does not appear to have the requisite procedural safeguards to meet the criteria of a fully-fledged dispute-solving organ.

Similarly, an expert report and several witnesses were essential for the Tribunal's decision in the case of *Rougie-Eichler v. Secretary General*, where the plaintiff contested the responsibility of the Council's medical service in a situation of medical emergency.[57]

---

[52]Only after an application has been declared admissible, and with the assistance of the States in question.

[53]Rule A1 of the Annex to the Rules of Court, added on 7 July 2003.

[54]"The Tribunal may, of its own initiative or at the request of a party, decide to hear any witness or expert as well as any person whose evidence or statements seem likely to assist the hearing", Rule 25 (1).

[55]Rule 23.

[56]*Parienti v. Secretary General*, appeal No. 285/2001 (16 May 2005) paragraph No. 7.

[57]Rougie-Eichler v. Secretary General, appeal No. 529/2012 (17 March 2015).

When facts are disputed before the Tribunal with regard to discretionary measures (such as the power of the Secretary General to grant a certain benefit or not, for example), it often makes reference to its subsidiary role. It will defer to findings of the administrative authorities of the Council and restrict itself to examining if the proper procedure was followed, or if any arbitrary conclusions were drawn from the submitted evidence. This long-held stance of the Tribunal on discretionary powers was recently reiterated in the case of *Andrea v. Secretary General*[58]:

> The Administrative Tribunal points out that [...] the Secretary General, [...] has wide ranging discretionary powers under which he is qualified to ascertain and assess the Organisation's operational needs and the staff's professional abilities. However those discretionary powers must always be lawfully exercised. Where a decision is challenged, an international court naturally cannot substitute its judgment for that of the administration. However, it must ascertain whether the decision challenged was taken in compliance with the Organisation's regulations and the general principles of law, to which the legal systems of international organisations are subject. It must consider not only whether the decision was taken by a competent authority and whether it is legal in form, but also whether the correct procedure was followed and whether, from the standpoint of the Organisation's own rules, the administrative authority's decision took account of all the relevant facts, any conclusions were wrongly drawn from the evidence in the file, and there was any misuse of power [...]

It follows that when there has been a lower instance which established the facts, the Tribunal will limit itself to ascertaining only whether the proper procedure has been followed and it will only intervene in cases of manifest arbitrariness. Cases in which the Tribunal found that such decisions had been manifestly arbitrary, are, understandably, rare.[59]

4.3 Burden of Proof

As seen above, where the case examines whether the Secretary General exceeded his discretionary power, the burden of proof is reasonably high on the part of the appellant. A standard of "manifestly unreasonable" must be proven to exist in the application of discretionary power, or a procedural defect.[60]

The general rule is that the onus falls on the claimant.[61]

---

[58]Andrea v. Secretary General, appeal No. 539/2013 (30 January 2014), paragraph 50.

[59]Such as, for example, *Pace Abu-Ghosh v. Secretary General*, appeal No.408/2008 (24 June 2009), paragraph 50: "En prenant la décision [...], le Secrétaire Général a méconnu la loi à laquelle il était lié et a tiré des conclusions manifestement erronées par rapport à l'avis de vacance de sorte à encourir la censure du Tribunal."

[60]*Ibid.*

[61]See, for example, *Tonelli v. Secretary General*, appeals Nos. 259, 260/2000 (9 March 2001), paragraph 46, and *Oristanio (I) v. Governer of the Council of Europe Development Bank*, appeal 559/2014 (29 January 2016), where the appellant claimed that she has been the victim of a disciplinary measure in disguise, paragraph 48: "The difficulties that she allegedly encountered

In cases of disciplinary misconduct, the onus would fall on the administration to prove the misconduct and that it meets the standard required for accountability under the applicable rules.[62] Once this standard has been met and a disciplinary decision has been made by the administration, the Tribunal will not replace its findings of fact with those of the administration.[63] However, it is not yet clear whether the burden shifts if the administration makes a *prima facie* case against the staff member.[64]

As to the burden of proof in cases of harassment, there seems to have been an evolving approach taken by the Tribunal.

The tribunal required a significant burden of proof to be met by the appellant in the case of *D.M. v. Governor of the Council of Europe Development Bank* who alleged harassment:

> [. . .] a staff member must unequivocally prove the existence of facts warranting a presumption of harassment, and the person accused of it must prove that his actions do not constitute harassment or are justified by reasons unrelated to any harassment.[65]

It would seem that the Tribunal refused any presumptions on the part of the appellant, but instead applied the standard of preponderance of evidence.[66]

However, the Tribunal opted for a somewhat different approach later on, when it decided on the case of *Seifert v. Governor of the Council of Europe Development Bank*.[67] Here it left the door open for the possibility of a shift in the burden of proof, had the appellant made a *prima facie* case:

[. . .] for which, moreover, she provides no proof either – does not exempt her from the burden of proof incumbent upon her before the Tribunal."

[62]See, for example, *Kling (IV)*, cited above. Also see ILOAT judgment *Pollicino*, No. 635 (1984), paragraph 7.

[63]See, for example, *R. V. (II) v. Governor of the Council of Europe Development Bank*, appeal No. 521/2011 (26 September 2012).

[64]See, *Pollicino* case, cited above. As far as possible to determine, this has not been accepted so far by the Tribunal. On several occasions it has been decided to the contrary, and supported by UN and ILOAT case law. See, for example *Fuchs (II) v. Secretary General*, appeal No. 130/1985 (10 November 1986), paragraphs 54–55: "The appellant submits that the [post] was deliberately transferred in order to make it possible to promote [. . .] to the post of Principal Administrative Officer in the Health Division. He considers that this procedure amounted to a breach of a principle of equality of opportunity for candidates in a competition. [. . .] Where such allegations are made in an appeal, it is for the appellant to present compelling evidence that the administrative decision relating to the selection of the person who was to occupy the post sought by him was based upon prejudice (UNAT, judgment No. 312, *Roberts v. Secretary General of the United Nations*)."

[65]*D.M. v. Governor of the Council of Europe Development Bank*, appeal No. 513/2011 (11 June 2006), paragraph 62. See also, *Lupas v. Secretary General*, Case No. 314/2003 (27 May 2004), paragraph 37.

[66]This standard seems to be widely applied in international administrative law. See, for example *Kogelmann (Nos. 1, 2, 3 and 4)*, ILOAT judgment No. 1373, paragraph 16. Also, see *Hasselback*, *World Bank Administrative Tribunal*, Decision No. 364 (2007), paragraph 50 and *Elobaid*, *United Nations Administrative Tribunal*, judgment No. 2018-UNAT-822, paragraph 35.

[67]*Seifert v. Governor of the Council of Europe Development Bank*, appeal No. 566/2015 (31 March 2016), paragraph 61.

[...] the fact remains that these facts cited by the applicant do not disclose any abusive
and/or systematic conduct. Consequently, even if the Tribunal were to accept, as the
appellant suggests, a shifting of the burden of proof in his favour, the Tribunal cannot find
that any psychological harassment occurred.

On the topic of harassment, it is worth noting that if harassment has been
established by the Commission against Harassment against a plaintiff, the Tribunal
will later easily find abuse on the part of the Secretary General when the appellant
was involuntarily seconded to another part of the organisation. In the case of
Zikmund v. Secretary General[68] the Tribunal held that the appellant had discharged
her obligation of establishing a *prima facie* case of the existence of an alternative
reason for her reassignment to another post by pointing to a declared need by the
administration to increase the staff at her former post. This was considered sufficient
for the Tribunal to shift the burden of proof to the Secretary General, who, on this
occasion, failed to explain why in spite of the above the appellant was reassigned
elsewhere.

From the cases presented it appears that the burden of proof does indeed lay with
the claimant. In cases of disciplinary sanctions the Tribunal will look into the
proportionality of the disciplinary measure applied while generally deferring to the
findings of the administration as to the facts, unless their findings have been
manifestly arbitrary. Notwithstanding the Tribunal's unlimited jurisdiction in issues
of pecuniary nature,[69] its power to establish facts is, at least in theory, unlimited, and
plaintiffs will frequently present evidence in order to support their claims.

A distinction, thus, must be made between cases where the facts have been
examined by an administrative authority prior to the case arriving before the
Tribunal, and those where they have not. In the case of the former, which involve
appointment (where the Council recruitment system has acted as an administrative
authority), appraisal (the appraiser him/herself), disciplinary proceedings (the disciplinary board), the Tribunal will generally not substitute its findings for those of the
administration, which are in a better position to establish the facts. This notion,
reminiscent of the ECtHR case-law, is comparable with the 'fourth-instance doctrine', being a reflection of the subsidiarity principle.[70] In the case of the latter type of
appeals, the Tribunal will exercise its power to establish facts to the fullest.[71] Its role
is therefore highly dependent on the nature of the case brought before it.

---

[68] *Zikmund (I and II) v. Secretary General*, appeal No. 459/2009 (30 October 2009).

[69] As provided for under Article 60, paragraph 2 of the Staff Regulations.

[70] While recognizing that both concepts mentioned are complex and merit further elaboration, the
paper, due to space limitations, will proceed under the assumption that there is no need to provide it.

[71] Such were, for example, the circumstances in the case of *Rougie-Eichler*, quoted above.

5 Conclusion

It appears that the Administrative Tribunal offers ample procedural and substantive guarantees for claimants. Although an act of general policy cannot be challenged before it, there is nothing preventing any staff member directly implicated by such a policy to bring a case before it. The tribunal, relying on the positive law of the Council of Europe, as well as national and international legal principles conducts a thorough review of the facts of each case, making use of oral hearings and free disposition of the parties with regard to evidence. It is not infrequent that the Tribunal itself will commission additional evidence with the aim of resolving the appeal. While in some categories of cases the burden of proof appears difficult to reach for a plaintiff, the Tribunal, in line with its often subsidiary role, will examine how the facts were established by the administration. If this is not possible, the Tribunal will make full use of its powers to establish facts, much like a first-instance national court should, in domestic labour disputes.

While some specificities remain present in its work (similarly to other administrative tribunals), one cannot state that the proceedings before the Tribunal suffer from any significant procedural defect, or that the plaintiffs are put before an unsurmountable obstacle to prove their case. While there is always room for improvement, it cannot be said that staff members' rights are not protected in a manner consistent with Article 6 of the Convention.

References

Arnim, D. V. (2017). In S. Schmahl & M. Breuer (Eds.), *The administrative tribunal* (pp. 345–368). Oxford: Council of Europe.

Kloth, M. (2010). *Immunites and the right of access to Court under Article 6 of the European Convention on Human Rights* (p. 137). Leiden: Martinus Nijhoff.

Leighton, R. (2014, September 15–16). Free advice and representation for staff members: The roles of the office of staff legal assistance in the United Nations internal justice system. In A. Talvik (Ed.), *Best Practices in Resolving Employment Disputes in International Organisations Conference Proceedings, ILO Geneva* (pp. 139–143).

Ryngaert, C. (2017). Jurisdictional immunity and infringement of fundamental labor rights. *International Labor Rights Case Law, 3*, 331.

Sansotta, S. (2013). *The Administrative Tribunal of the Council of Europe.* https://rm.coe.int/-the-administrative-tribunal-of-the-council-of-europe/16808b3d93

Advisory Opinions of the European Court of Human Rights: Do National Judges Really Need This New Forum of Dialogue?

Małgorzata Wąsek-Wiaderek

Contents

1   A Handful of Introductory and Terminological Comments

In the European legal space, the notion of a judicial dialogue has gained particular importance for reason of the institution of preliminary rulings passed by the Court of Justice of the European Union in response to the requests lodged by national courts. Indeed, this form of court-to-court dialogue has significantly contributed to the development of European Union law as a specific legal order.

Małgorzata Wąsek-Wiaderek is Professor of Criminal Procedure Law and Judge of the Polish Supreme Court.

M. Wąsek-Wiaderek (✉)
John Paul II Catholic University of Lublin, Department of Law, Canon Law and Administration, Lublin, Poland

© Springer Nature Switzerland AG 2019
P. Pinto de Albuquerque, K. Wojtyczek (eds.), *Judicial Power in a Globalized World*, https://doi.org/10.1007/978-3-030-20744-1_38

The subject of this elaboration is judicial dialogue conducted between the European Court of Human Rights (ECtHR) and national courts with regard to the application of the European Convention of Human Rights. First of all, the understanding of the notion of a "judicial dialogue" as used hereinafter needs to be clarified. The doctrine uses this concept to define different relations taking place among judicial organs. The rather common understanding of the notion is that in a process of adjudication, a court uses the verdicts of other courts (in the case of interest to us—the case-law of the European Court of Human Rights) in order to build or strengthen its own interpretative argumentation contained in the reasons for judgement. The process itself of a court referring to a decision passed by another court may have different forms. Among these, the doctrine specifies the so called affirmative and engaged dialogues. The latter contains the possibility of a dissenting dialogue or a concurring one. It is rightly noted that only engaged dialogue assumes the active inclusion of a national court in the critical analysis of a decision of international judicial organ. Even if the decision to which it refers is accepted, it must be preceded by a deeper analysis and a distancing from the argumentation on which this decision is based.[1] Such a form of dialogue has been seen as a dialogue in a broader sense of this notion. However, if the argumentation of the national court cannot have a reciprocate impact on the court whose judgment had been subject to a critical analysis, the process then actually constitutes a judicial monologue. As it has been indicated by A.M. Slaughter, a court monologue takes place in a situation when the court simply borrows the arguments or conclusions from another court, either at the domestic or the international level.[2]

The dialogue referred to henceforth will be understood in the narrow way as proposed by L. B. Tremblay,[3] i.e. as a deliberation. "In this sense, a dialogue [still] entails two or more persons, understood as equals, exchanging some words, ideas, opinions, feelings, and so forth, but the exchange is more formal and less spontaneous than in the dialogue as conversation. A dialogue as deliberation has specific mutual practical purposes: it aims at taking decisions in common; reaching agreement; solving problems or conflicts collectively; determining together which opinion or thesis is true, the most justified, or the best; or which particular practical view should govern actions or decisions."[4] The author also points to the conditions for carrying a dialogue which is understood as deliberation. These include: the perception of the interlocutor as an equal, the application of rational persuasion and not violence, and the will of each of the partners to subject their argumentation to critical analysis and to possibly change their opinions. Furthermore, the dialogue should aim to arrive at some "practical judgment, action or decision that can be the object to

---

[1]See, Górski (2017), p. 234 and literature referred therein.
[2]See, reference to the definition of A.M. Slaughter in: Amos (2012), pp. 558–559.
[3]Tremblay (2005), pp. 617–648.
[4]Tremblay (2005), p. 632.

reasoned agreement among the participants".[5] Although the definition here quoted has been constructed for the purpose of describing the interaction between courts and other national entities (the legislature), it is rightly noted in literature that it perfectly fits the description of a judicial dialogue between national courts and the ECtHR.[6]

In light of the definition of a judicial dialogue here adopted (dialogue *sensu sitricto*), for it to be present, there has to be an exchange of arguments and not just consideration and the possible adoption of the argumentation of another court in the process of its own decision making. Such a dialogue also requires simultaneity—one cannot talk about a genuine dialogue if the argumentation contained in the decision of another court participating in the dialogue evokes a reaction of another court in the form of a decision only some years later.

The notion of a judicial dialogue can also sometimes mean a non-formal dialogue carried on such fora as conferences or seminars dedicated to the exchange of the opinions of judges on the application of the Convention. Without prejudice to this very important form of dialogue and its role, it is a conversation rather than a deliberation.[7]

2   Judicial Dialogue Before the Entry into Force of Protocol No. 16

The procedure of an individual complaint lodged with the ECtHR does not really create an opportunity to conduct a judicial dialogue in the strict sense of the notion. The very supervisory nature of this procedure does not allow it. The indication of only two factors suffice to prove this view. First of all, despite the condition of the admissibility of an individual application in the form of the required exhaustion of domestic remedies, the national court of "the last instance" does not always present the interpretation of the provisions of the European Convention in the written reasons for judgement, which is later subject to the assessment of the ECtHR. The reasons for such a situation are varied. This may happen because the domestic supreme court does not always have the duty to formulate the reasoning of a final decision in the case in writing. The lack of such written reasons for judgment is not tantamount to the national court's forbearance on the consideration of charges of human rights' violation raised in the appeal remedy. Secondly, in line with the well established jurisprudence, for the condition of the exhaustion of domestic remedies

---

[5]Tremblay (2005), p. 632.

[6]Amos (2012), p. 559.

[7]About this form of dialogue, see: Tremblay (2005), p. 631. This form of dialogue is conducted very actively by the ECtHR and domestic judges, *inter alia*, in the framework of series of annual seminars titled "Dialogue between judges" organized by the European Court of Human Rights since 2005. Also activities of the Superior Courts Network established by President of the European Court of Human Rights may be considered as informal dialogue.

to be met, the applicant does not have to refer directly and clearly to the provisions of the ECHR in the course of domestic procedure. It is sufficient for the claim of his/her right guaranteed in the Convention to be raised at least in substance.[8] In such a situation, the court of the final instance, which usually considers the remedy within the limits of the claims raised, may refrain from referring to the arguments based on the Convention in its judgment and limit itself to only, for example, analysing the statutory and constitutional provisions. In such a case, the written reasons for judgment of the domestic supreme court will not contain that many arguments that could initiate a court dialogue with the ECtHR, including a broadly understood judicial dialogue.

The second factor which significantly limits judicial dialogue with the ECtHR is the temporal distance between the date of the final decision in a case issued by a domestic court and the ECtHR's judgment. Unfortunately, these two moments are a few years apart.[9] In addition, what should be taken into consideration are the frequent changes in domestic law—a situation particularly specific to new members of the Council of Europe. As a result, a domestic court's decision, which adopts a specific interpretation of the ECHR law, can be subject to an assessment by the European Court of Human Rights only some years later, i.e. when the same domestic court has already begun applying different, amended regulations of domestic law in a given field.[10]

What is most important, however, is the fact that the procedure followed to examine an individual complaint does not principally envisage any formal legal framework for a judicial dialogue between a domestic court and the ECtHR. Once a judgement is passed in a case which is later the subject of an individual application to the Court, the domestic court has no formal possibilities of "adding" new arguments for the defence of the position presented in the reasons of its judgment. The above is not an accusation of the procedure provided for adjudication of an individual complaint but a simple description of the factual state. As in any control procedure, it is also difficult to speak about a full equality of the courts which are interlocutors in the dialogue conducted.[11]

Therefore, it comes as no surprise that the practice in force thus far provides only scarce examples of a real judicial dialogue between the ECtHR and domestic courts. The first case which should be mentioned here is that of *Al-Khawaja and Tahery v. UK*.[12] The circumstances in which it occurred were very specific: upon the issue of judgement by the Chamber of the ECtHR in January 2009,[13] the Court of Appeal

---

[8]See, *inter alia*, Appl. No. 56581/00, *Selmouni v. France* (ECtHR 28 July 1999) para 74; Appl. No. 56581/00, *Sejdovic v. Italy* (ECtHR 1 March 2006) para 44.

[9]Amos (2012), p. 563.

[10]See, *for example*, pending Appl. No. 31454/10, *Ćwik v. Poland* concerning admissibility of private evidence. Since 2010 when the application was lodged to the ECtHR, the law concerning admissibility of private evidence has been changed twice by the Polish legislator.

[11]See, however, the contrary view: Amos (2012), p. 571.

[12]Appl. No. 26766/05; 22228/06, *Al-Khawaja and Tahery v. UK* (ECtHR 15 December 2011).

[13]Appl. No. 26766/05; 22228/06, *Al-Khawaja and Tahery v. UK* (ECtHR 20 January 2009).

and the Supreme Court of the United Kingdom considered another similar case (*R. v. Horncastle and others*), raising criticism against the judgment of the ECtHR, in particular against the Court's understanding of the right to a *fair trial* and the admissibility of hearsay evidence in a criminal case. The critical arguments presented by domestic courts were then raised in course of the proceedings before the Grand Chamber of the ECtHR and influenced the Court's decision to abandon the practice of considering hearsay evidence on the basis of the absolutely understood "sole or decisive rule" in lieu of a "counterbalancing" approach.

The judgment passed by the Grand Chamber presents an excellent example of a court-to-court dialogue. The ECtHR has several times expressed the fact that it took into consideration the arguments given by domestic courts.[14] One could risk a thesis that the change in the interpretation of Article 6 para 1 in connection with Article 6 para 3 d of the Convention introduced in this judgment was the result of a judicial dialogue between the ECtHR and the UK courts.[15] This is actually also the assessment of this case presented by the Court itself.[16] Scholars provide also other examples of a dialogue between the ECtHR and UK courts,[17] though situations in which the interpretation of the Convention's provisions has been changed as a result of arguments presented by domestic courts in the previously considered cases should be seen as manifestations of a judicial dialogue *sensu largo*. Examples of such dialogue are numerous and can be found, for instance, in the jurisprudence of the German Federal Constitutional Court (Bundesverfassungsgericht) and the ECtHR concerning preventive detention[18] or in the approach adopted by the ECtHR with reference to re-opening of judicial proceedings in cases examined by assessors (junior judges) in Poland.[19]

The recent jurisprudence of the Court proves that a strictly understood dialogue between the domestic supreme courts and the European Court of Human Rights can be conducted in course of considering the same case also after the passing of the final judgment by the Court in this particular case. In the judgment of *Morreira and Ferreira v. Portugal (no. 2)*,[20] the Grand Chamber of the Court found admissible the complaint concerning a violation of Article 6 of the ECHR with reference to the domestic proceedings conducted upon the application for review lodged by the applicant in consequence of a positive judgement of the ECtHR[21] founding a

---

[14]See, *inter alia*, para 49–62, 123, 131 and 160 of the judgment.

[15]See, Amos (2012), pp. 566–567; Elliott-Kelly (2012), pp. 81–87.

[16]See, European Court of Human Rights, *Preliminary opinion of the Court in preparation for the Brighton Conference*, 2012, para 27. See also concurring opinion of Judge Bratza attached to the judgment in the case of *Al-Khawaja and Tahery v. UK* (ECtHR 15 December 2011).

[17]Amos (2012), pp. 567–571.

[18]Peters (2012), pp. 757–772; Rinceanu (2017), pp. 1040–1041.

[19]Appl. No. 23614/08, *Henryk Urban and Ryszard Urban v. Poland* (ECtHR 30 November 2010) para 64–67.

[20]Appl. No. 19867/12, *Morreira and Ferreira v. Portugal (no. 2)* (ECtHR 11 July 2017).

[21]Appl. No. 19808/08, *Morreira and Ferreira v. Portugal* (ECtHR 5 July 2011).

violation of her right to a fair trial in criminal proceedings. The applicant complained that the Supreme Court of Portugal had dismissed her application for a review of the criminal judgment delivered against her. She submitted that the Supreme Court's judgment amounted to a "denial of justice", because that court had incorrectly interpreted and applied the relevant provisions of the Code of Criminal Procedure and the conclusions of the Court's 2011 judgment, thus depriving her of the right to have her conviction reviewed. She alleged a violation of Article 6 para 1 of the Convention. Declaring the application admissible in this scope, the Court continued a judicial dialogue initiated by the Supreme Court of Portugal which did not find any grounds for re-examination of the applicant's case at the national level. It should be underlined that the Supreme Court made its own assessment whether a violation of Article 6 of the Convention found by the ECtHR should result in re-opening of domestic proceedings. Arguments provided in the Supreme Court's decision were further assessed by the European Court in its judgment passed in 2017. Leaving aside the very decision of the Court on the admissibility of this complaint,[22] it should be noted that if the view expressed in this judgement is to be followed in other decision, it opens up an entirely new path of a *sensu stricto* judicial dialogue.

Furthermore, it cannot be excluded that the procedure envisaged in Article 46 para 4 and 5 of the Convention could, in the future, serve as a platform for such a formal dialogue. While examining the question of the Committee of Ministers whether a Party to the Convention has failed to fulfil its obligation to abide by a final judgment, the ECtHR may also indirectly assess the decisions of domestic judicial organs issued in order to execute the judgment of the Court. The experience in applying this procedure thus far is that it can only be launched in specifically exceptional cases.[23]

In conclusion, there is no doubt that a formal dialogue between domestic courts and the ECtHR in course of considering a specific case is significantly limited by the very nature of the individual complaint procedure.

3   Protocol No. 16 as a Platform of a *sensu stricto* Judicial Dialogue

The idea of advisory opinions of the ECtHR first emerged in 2006 in the report of the Group of Wise Persons, who had the task to indicate the means of ensuring the effectiveness of the ECHR in a long term, as well as to evaluate the effects of the

---

[22]I find convincing arguments against admissibility of this case with reference to the complaint submitted under Article 6 of the Convention, presented in joint dissenting opinion of Judges Raimondi, Nußberger, De Gaetano, Keller, Mahoney, Kjølbro and O'Leary.

[23]This procedure is rather aimed at supervising actions of executive power than judicial organs. See, Interim Resolution CM/ResDH(2017)429 adopted on 5 December 2017 concerning execution of the judgment of the ECtHR delivered on 22 May 2014 in the case *Mammadov v. Azerbaijan* (Appl. No. 15172/13).

adoption of Protocol No. 14 to the ECHR. The Group of Wise Persons considered and rejected the concept of equipping the ECtHR with the right to issue rulings on interpretation which would be binding upon domestic courts, thus recognising that the EU model of preliminary rulings would not fully play its role in the Strasburg system of human rights' protection.[24]

The concept of introducing the advisory opinions to the Strasbourg system of protection of human rights was discussed during the two following high level conferences of the Council of Europe in Izmir in 2011 and in Brighton in 2012. In the Izmir Declaration the Committee of Ministers was invited "to reflect on the advisability of introducing a procedure allowing the highest national courts to request advisory opinions from the Court concerning the interpretation and application of the Convention that would help clarify the provisions of the Convention and the Court's case-law, thus providing further guidance in order to assist States Parties in avoiding future violations".[25] The Brighton Declaration, on the other hand, included an "invitation" for the Committee of Ministers to draft the text of an optional protocol to the Convention introducing the institution of advisory opinions, by the end of 2013.[26]

The Protocol No. 16 was adopted by the Committee of Ministers on 10 July 2013 and entered into force on 1st August 2018 upon the 10 required ratifications.[27] By 1st of March 2019, 11 states have been parties to Protocol No. 16.

Together with Protocol No. 15, Protocol No. 16 constitutes a specific "package for subsidiarity" in the Strasburg system for the protection of human rights. Protocol No. 15[28] introduces to the Preamble of the Convention the definition of the subsidiary principle, which underlines the "primary responsibility" of the States-Parties to the Convention "to secure the rights and freedoms defined in this Convention and the Protocols thereto". At the same time, it has been indicated that the states should have in this respect "margin of appreciation" subject to the supervisory jurisdiction of the European Court of Human Rights". Furthermore, in the Preamble of the Protocol No. 16, it is specified that "the extension of the Court's competence to give advisory opinions will further enhance the interaction between the Court and national authorities and thereby reinforce implementation of the Convention, in accordance with the principle of subsidiarity". The key manifestation of this principle in its procedural aspect is the principle of exhaustion of domestic remedies before bringing the case to the Strasbourg Court, as well as the right to an effective remedy at the domestic level, as provided for in Article 13 of the Convention.[29]

---

[24]See, Report of the Group of Wise Persons to the Committee of Ministers, para 76–86.

[25]Izmir Declaration, Follow up Plan, para D.

[26]Brighton Declaration para 12 d.

[27]Council of Europe Treaty Series no. 214.

[28]Adopted on 24 June 2013 (not yet in force).

[29]See, *inter alia*, Appl. No. 30210/96, *Kudła v. Poland*, (ECtHR 26 October 2000) para 152; See also Lübbe-Wolf (2012), p. 12.

The concept of advisory opinions is based on an assumption that highest domestic courts which, by means of their judgments finally shape the legal situation of the applicant, should have the possibility of addressing the ECtHR with "questions of principle" relating to the interpretation or application of the Convention or the protocols thereto before resolving the case at the national level. The idea behind advisory opinion, which is not binding for the court who is requesting it, is to transfer the issue of compliance with the Convention to the domestic level at a stage before the passing of the final judgment in the case. It is assumed that this, in turn, should lower the number of cases lodged to the ECtHR.

Protocol No. 16 has been shaped as a normative concept of advisory opinions proposed by Dutch and Norwegian experts. It is based on four indicators: (1) the right to request advisory opinions is restricted only to "highest courts" of States-Parties to the Protocol; (2) lodging a request for an advisory opinion is optional; (3) the request for an advisory opinion is restricted in substance to "questions of principles"; (4) advisory opinions are not binding.

There should be no doubts that Protocol No. 16 provides an appropriate legal framework for conducting an actual dialogue between the domestic courts and the ECtHR, which is proven by the following features of the new procedure: its optional character; the non-binding nature of the advisory opinion and the admissibility of lodging an individual application in the case to which the advisory opinion had been issued; a procedural paths for a dialogue between the "requesting" court and the ECtHR in course of the issuing of an advisory opinion.

3.1   The Optional Nature of Requesting an Advisory Opinion

Article 1 of Protocol No. 16 stipulates that "highest courts and tribunals" indicated by the states will have the right but not the obligation to file a request for an advisory opinion. Already in the Report of the Group Wise Persons it was rightly recognised that a simple transfer of the preliminary ruling procedure to the Strasburg field could collide with the fundamental legal instrument of compliance with the Convention, i.e. the individual application. The optional character of the path of dialogue provided by Protocol No. 16 should guarantee its effectiveness. It should be assumed that a supreme court shall decide on seeking an advisory opinion upon its own interpretation of the ECHR or Protocols to the Convention. Since a decision to ask the Strasbourg Court for assistance is fully independent and free of any "force of legal obligation", one may assume that this domestic court intends to respect the opinion of the ECtHR in further proceedings.

The optional character of a request for an advisory opinion also releases the domestic courts from the obligation to explain to the parties to the proceedings the reason why their possible application for launching the procedure has not been taken into consideration. The court's decision in this respect requires no written justification. There are no good reasons for applying to this procedure the requirements which have to be filled by courts obliged to request preliminary rulings from the

Court of Justice of the European Union. Thus, the procedural requirements imposed by the case-law of the ECtHR with reference to a reasoning of a decision refusing to lodge a request for a preliminary ruling by a court bound by such an obligation[30] shall not apply to advisory opinions. Secondly, and most importantly, the optional character of this procedure does not limit the jurisdictional autonomy of a domestic court, which is an important element of the independence of courts and the impartiality of judges. Before a decision is made about submitting a request to the ECtHR, the court has the duty to autonomously consider the legal issue regarding the interpretation of the Convention law. Only once doubts are voiced as to the result of the process of interpretation, can it decide to address the ECtHR by means of the described procedure. Even if such doubts are voiced, the court may—but does not have to—come into a dialogue with the ECtHR. A request for an advisory opinion should be seen as seeking an important, authoritative source of non-binding interpretation of the Convention with reference to a set of factual circumstances specified in the request. From the point of view of the dialogue as a deliberation, the key value of this instrument is an exchange of arguments. A request for an advisory opinion drafted by a domestic court may be used as a platform for arguments aimed at influencing the Strasbourg Court's jurisprudence.

3.2 The Non-binding Nature of Advisory Opinions

In light of Article 5 of the Protocol No. 16, advisory opinions are not binding. It is of key importance for a *sensu stricto* dialogue and very precisely reflects the nature of this procedure as an interaction between courts based on persuasion.[31] It should be expected that an advisory opinion issued by the Grand Chamber will be taken into consideration in its entirety by the court who has asked for it voluntarily. At the same time, however, its non-binding nature allows for a continuation of the discourse with the Court. This circumstance should not be in any way seen as generating a risk of undermining the competence of the Court or the judicial dialogue as such.[32] To the contrary—it conditions the dialogue as an exchange of arguments. The complaint procedure has a vertical structure of relations, and a dialogue needs to be conducted horizontally, based on argument exchange. The possible reasons why a domestic court considering a particular case may decide to disregard an advisory opinion in full or in part, may be a change of factual and legal circumstances of the case after delivery of the opinion. Such a situation can take place only in exceptional

---

[30]See, *inter alia*, Appl. No. 3989/07, 38353/07, *Ullens de Schooten and Rezabek v. Belgium* (ECtHR 20 September 2011) and recently: Appl. No. 60934/13, *Somorjai v. Hungary* (ECtHR 28 August 2018) para 57; See, O'Leary and Eicke (2018), p. 224. Authors did not provide a conclusive view on this issue.

[31]See, Giannopoulos (2015), pp. 341–342.

[32]Criticism of the non-binding character of advisory opinions is based on such argument: Gragl (2013), p. 244.

circumstances as only "highest courts" adjudicating in the last stage of domestic proceedings, i.e. based on the already determined factual and legal state, are authorised to lodge a request for an advisory opinion.

A domestic court can also see the argumentation of the Court as not convincing thus opening up a path for a further *sensu stricto* judicial dialogue. It should be remembered that in case an opinion is rejected, it is highly probable that the party to the proceedings, upon their termination domestically, will lodge and individual application on grounds of a violation of the ECHR or the additional protocols to the Convention. It has been clearly stated in the Explanatory Report to the Protocol No. 16 that the advisory opinions will not have a direct effect on the complaints proceedings later on. Because they will formulate part of the Court's case-law, the interpretation there contained will have an effect similar to the "regular" judgements of the Court's Grand Chamber. Disregarding an advisory opinion the domestic court takes the serious risk that its final decision will be successfully challenged before the ECtHR. It is difficult to expect, for example, that a seven-judge bench adjudicating in a complaint procedure would reject an interpretation of the Convention expressed by the Court's Grand Chamber. Such a prospect should motivate the domestic court to double its interpretational efforts. If the court wants to effectively impact the change of the interpretation of the Convention, it will have to present important and significant arguments counteracting the views expressed in the advisory opinion.

In case an advisory opinion is taken into consideration by the domestic court and later an individual application is lodged on grounds of a violation of the Convention, it is expected that the Court would deem the application inadmissible or would strike it from the list of cases in the scope in which it is related to the decision of the domestic court which had correctly applied the advisory opinion (point 26 of the Explanatory Report). Rightly the "final word" in this dialogue is with the European Court of Human Rights.

3.3 Procedural Framework of Considering a Request and the Possibility of a Genuine Dialogue

A competent court can lodge a request for an advisory opinion only with reference to a case pending before it (Article 1 para 2 of Protocol No. 16). The request should include reasons and contain a description of the factual and legal circumstances of the case. It is stated in the Explanatory Report that it is not the aim of this procedure to move the dispute from before the domestic court to the ECtHR. The duty to give reasons for the request and for presenting the factual and legal circumstances of the case is to guarantee that before formulating the request, the domestic court carefully analyses both the necessity and the utility of requesting an advisory opinion in the case under consideration. Since the advisory opinion relates to the concrete case, the ECtHR should be provided with the following information: the subject matter of the domestic case, the facts that have been determined in the case or at least a summary of the relevant factual issues, the relevant domestic law applicable in the case, the relevant Convention issues, in particular the rights or freedoms at stake, if relevant, a summary of the arguments raised in the domestic procedure by the parties, and finally, should it be deemed justified and possible—the domestic court own view on the issue being subject to the advisory opinion with its own analysis of it (point 12 of the Explanatory Report; Rule 92 (2.1) of the Rules of the Court).

It is unacceptable to argue that, should a court express its view about the interpretation of the Convention in the request lodged with the ECtHR, there could be doubts about this court's impartiality and that this could serve as grounds for excluding this court from adjudicating the case further.[33] An identical problem has already been decided by the Court of Justice of the European Union in the context of the preliminary ruling procedure. The Luxemburg Court rightly excluded the possibility of deeming such a court as "biased".[34]

For the benefit of exchanging arguments by the courts in dialogue, it is important to have the possibility of presenting additional information by the domestic court in the process of considering the request for an advisory opinion. The Rules of the Court do not directly provide for such a possibility before the admissibility of the request is considered by a Panel of five Judges. However, the Guidelines[35] stipulate that also at the initial stage, the court or tribunal may be requested to supplement its request where it is considered to be deficient (para. 25). Once a decision on the acceptance of the request for consideration is issued by a Panel of five Judges, the written stage begins which, from the point of view of the domestic court, may be seen as quasi-contradictory. It is so due to the fact that pursuant to Rule 94 (2) of the Court's Rules, the court may be invited to submit "any further information which is considered necessary for clarifying the scope of the request or its own views on the question raised by the request". Importantly, Rule 94 (5) further stipulates that the domestic court is provided with and has the opportunity to comment on all the submissions filed by the parties to the procedure, i.e. third parties intervening in the proceedings, including a representative of the executive branch of its state, other High Contracting Parties, Commissioner for Human Rights of the Council of Europe, or parties to the domestic proceedings in the course of which an advisory opinion was requested, provided that these parties have been invited to participate by the President of the Grand Chamber (Rule 94 (3) of the Rules of the Court). Even if the advisory opinion is delivered without a hearing, the legal framework presented envisages contradictory procedure which gives the requesting court the possibility to speak and present arguments regarding every issue related to the subject matter of the proceedings. The judicial dialogue continues also upon the issuance of an advisory opinion due to the fact that the domestic court has been invited to inform

---

[33]Doubts were raised with regard to this issue by some NGOs. See, O'Leary and Eicke (2018), p. 229.

[34]Appl. No. C-614/14, *Ognyanov* (ECJ 5 July 2016), CLI:EU:C:2016:514.

[35]Guidelines on the implementation of the advisory-opinion procedure introduced by Protocol No. 16 to the Convention (as approved by the Plenary Court on 18 September 2017).

the Court of the follow-up given to the advisory opinion in the domestic proceedings and to provide it with a copy of the final judgment or any other decision adopted in the case (para 31 of the Guidelines).

As it has already been mentioned, one of the conditions for conducting a judicial dialogue as a deliberation is that the exchange of arguments between the court interlocutors should be restrained in time. The discussed procedure, at least in theory, seems to satisfy this condition by envisaging a priority for examining a request which, in addition, can be treated as "urgent". The practical enforcement of this rule is difficult to foresee. Only one request for an advisory opinion has been lodged with the Court thus far. It is a request of the French Court of Cassation. Only a month and a half passed from the date of submitting the request to the Court to the issuance of the decision on its admissibility.[36] However, the procedure of its examination as to the merit is still pending and has already lasted 3 months. Swift examination of admissibility of a request for advisory opinion by a Panel of five Judges is of crucial importance for the effectiveness of the new tool of judicial dialogue *sensu stricto*. It should be taken into account that the domestic court will usually have to suspend consideration of a case until the advisory opinion is issued. Long waiting times for the Court's decision on whether an advisory opinion can be issued at all would have a discouraging effect on the domestic courts.

A certain hindrance in conducting judicial dialogue in the framework of this procedure is the requirement to submit to the EtCHR a translation of the request into one of the official languages of the Council of Europe.[37] The Protocol No. 16 does not regulate this issue, however the Rules of the Court with amendments introduced on 19 September 2016 and with binding force as from 1 August 2018, allow for the submission of the original request in the language of the domestic proceedings. However, in line with the Rules of the Court, "where the language is not an official language of the Court, an English or French translation of the request shall be filed within a time-limit to be fixed by the President of the Court."

Another possible threat to the concept of advisory opinions is an excessively high number of courts authorised for filing requests to the ECtHR indicated by the States-Parties to Protocol No. 16.[38] Leaving this issue in the discretion of States-Parties to the Protocol and taking it out of the competence of the Court can lead to significant procedural perturbations. It should be stressed that by interpreting the notion of "highest courts and tribunals" the ECtHR could limit the scope of its own jurisdiction and the number of cases examined in this procedure. This matter should definitely be left to the Court. In my view appellate courts should not be authorised for the procedure if they can request domestic supreme courts for interpretation of the Convention law, for example, in the framework of incidental procedure of submitting legal questions. Therefore, there should be no doubts that a request for

---

[36]Appl. No. P16-2018-001, introduced on 16 October 2018, declared admissible on 3 December 2018.

[37]See, O'Leary and Eicke (2018), p. 235.

[38]For example, Romania listed 15 Court of Appeal as entitled to request advisory opinions.

an advisory opinion can be lodged not only by a supreme court which is considering, for example, a cassation case, but also when it is to resolve an important interpretational issue with reference to the circumstances of a specific case and in response to a legal question posed by a court of a lower instance. In such a situation, the request for an advisory opinion is also referred "in the context of a case pending before this court" within the meaning of Article 1(2) of Protocol No. 16.

4 The Impact of Advisory Opinions on the Courts of Countries Which Are Not Parties to Protocol No. 16

For an author coming from a country such as Poland, which has not decided to ratify Protocol No. 16, it is important to consider whether the non-binding advisory opinions can have a legal impact on the interpretation and application of the Convention by the courts of that country. It should be assumed that advisory opinions present the interpretation supported by the authority of the Grand Chamber of the ECtHR and thus build the normative content of the provisions of the Convention vis-à-vis all its States-Parties, including those who have not ratified Protocol No. 16. Thus, the advisory opinions shape the normative content of the provisions of the ECHR in similar way as judgments of the ECtHR issued in complaint procedure. Such effects of the advisory opinions have also been specified in the Explanatory Report to Article 5 of Protocol No. 16.[39] Looking at the question from the point of view of the case-law of the Polish Constitutional Court, it should be assumed that an observation contained in one of the judgements of the Constitutional Court also applies to advisory opinions[40]:

> . . .despite the fact that pursuant to Article 46 of the ECHR the judgements of the European Court of Human Rights are binding to the state-party to the proceedings in the given case, third countries, which are parties of the Convention, should aim at shaping their system of the protection of human rights in a manner which would take into consideration the standards developed in the Court's case-law on the basis of the Convention in the fullest possible scope. [. . .] In the Interlaken Declaration of 19 February 2010, [. . .] it is stated that member states of the Council of Europe have agreed that they should be "taking into account the Court's developing case-law, also with a view to considering the conclusions to be drawn from a judgment finding a violation of the Convention by another State, where the same problem of principle exists within their own legal system."

---

[39]Para 27 of the Report reads as follows: "Advisory opinions under this Protocol would have no direct effect on other later applications. They would, however, form part of the case-law of the Court, alongside its judgments and decisions. The interpretation of the Convention and the Protocols thereto contained in such advisory opinions would be analogous in its effect to the interpretative elements set out by the Court in judgments and decisions".

[40]Judgment of the Polish Constitutional Tribunal of 19 July 2011 r., K 11/10, OTK – A 2011, no. 6, item 60, para 3.3.3. of the reasons.

The view presented by the Polish Constitutional Court does not significantly differ from a concept adopted in the German doctrine of "Orientirungswirkung".[41] The German Constitutional Court (Bundesverfassungsgericht) has stated that German courts are bound by the Convention in the understanding which it has been given by the case-law of the ECtHR, and the German Bunderverwaltungsgericht has recognised that if it is possible, pursuant to the well-established jurisprudence of the Court in Strasburg, to establish a generally applicable and valid interpretation of the provision of the Convention, then the German courts should treat it as priority.[42]

Summing up, the advisory opinions will have an effect of a specific "*res interpretata*".[43] Although not binding, they will provide interpretation of the content of the Convention and in this way will specify the scope of obligations resulting from it for the contracting parties.[44] However, an opinion that should be seen as too far-fetched is that advisory opinions could be deemed to have an impact comparable to the ECtHR's pilot judgments, with *erga omnes* effects, rather than to an ordinary ECtHR judgments, with just *inter-partes* implications."[45]

5 Conclusions

Based on the above deliberations, my positive assessment of the usefulness of advisory opinions in the Convention-based system of the protection of human rights comes out very clearly. This assessment is no doubt determined by the domestic court perspective, and not that of the ECtHR. For the latter, this additional competence can mean additional workload and does not have to translate into a reduction in the number of individual applications. I also see other conditions, if not threats, such as the risk of losing the internal cohesion of the Court's jurisprudence determined by the circumstances of a specific case—also in the procedure of issuing advisory opinions. Apart from the undoubtful strengthening of the subsidiary principle, advisory opinions can indeed create a new legal framework for conducting a *sensu stricte* judicial dialogue between highest domestic courts and the ECtHR. In response to the question in the title of this elaboration: yes, it is the procedure which is needed for domestic courts. Possibility of engaging in a direct formal dialogue with the ECtHR strengthens their independence in the domestic system. This independence is, in itself, the essence of the right to court—the key value of the Convention-based system of the protection of human rights.

---

[41]Grabenwarter (2009), pp. 98–99; Garlicki (2011), p. 362.

[42]Meyer-Ladewig and Petzold (2005), p. 19.

[43]See, Paprocka and Ziółkowski (2015), pp. 290–291; Bodnar (2014), pp. 223–262.

[44]See, with reference to legal effects of the ECtHR' judgments beyond the boundaries of the case: Grzegorczyk (2008), p. 50.

[45]Dicosola et al. (2015), p. 1410.

References

Amos, M. (2012). The dialogue between United Kingdom Courts and the European Court of Human Rights. *International & Comparative Law Quarterly, 61*(3), 558–559.

Bodnar, A. (2014). Res interpretata: Legal effects of the European Court of Human Rights judgments for other states than those which were party to the proceedings. In Y. Haeck & E. Brems (Eds.), *Human rights and civil liberties in the 21st century* (pp. 223–262). Dordrecht: Springer.

Brighton Declaration adopted on 18–20 April 2012. Retrieved April 5, 2019, from http://www.echr. coe.int/Documents/2012_Brighton_FinalDeclaration_ENG.pdf

Dicosola, M., Fasone, C., & Spigno, I. (2015). The prospective role of Constitutional Courts in the advisory opinion mechanism before the European Court of Human Rights: A first comparative assessment with the European Union and Inter-American system. *German Law Journal, Special Issue – Preliminary References to the CJEU, 16*, 1387–1428.

Elliott-Kelly, J. (2012). Al-Khawaja and Tahery v United Kingdom. *European Human Rights Law Review, 1*, 1–87.

European Court of Human Rights, *Preliminary opinion of the Court in preparation for the Brighton Conference*, adopted on 20 February 2012, para 27. Retrieved April 5, 2019, from http://www. echr.coe.int/Documents/2012_Brighton_Opinion_ENG.pdf

Garlicki, L. (2011). Komentarz do art. 46. In L. Garlicki (Ed.), *Konwencja o Ochronie Praw Człowieka i Podstawowych Wolności. Tom II. Komentarz do artykułów 19-59 oraz Protokołów dodatkowych* (pp. 349–363). Warsaw: C. H. Beck.

Giannopoulos, C. (2015). Considerations on Protocol no. 16: Can the new advisory competence of the European Court of Human Rights breathe new life into the European Convention on Human Rights? *German Law Journal, 6*, 337–350.

Górski, M. (2017). The dialogue between selected CEE courts and the ECtHR. In A. Wyrozumska (Ed.), *Transnational Judicial dialogue on International Law in Central and Eastern Europe* (pp. 233–296). Łódź. https://doi.org/10.18778/8088-707-7.05

Grabenwarter, C. (2009). *Europäische Menschenrechtskonvention*. Wien: C. H. Beck.

Gragl, P. (2013). (Judicial) love is not a one-way street: The EU preliminary reference procedure as a model for ECtHR advisory opinions under draft Protocol no. 16. *European Law Review, 38*(2), 229–247.

Grzegorczyk, P. (2008). The effect of the judgments of the European Court of Human Rights in the domestic legal order. *Polish Yearbook of International Law, 28*, 39–82.

Izmir Declaration adopted on 27 April 2011. Retrieved April 6, 2019, from http://www.echr.coe.int/ Documents/2011_Izmir_FinalDeclaration_ENG.pdf

Lübbe-Wolf, G. (2012). How can the European Court of Human Rights reinforce the role of national courts in the convention system? *Human Rights Law Journal, 32*(1–6), 11–15.

Meyer-Ladewig, J., & Petzold, H. (2005). Die Bindung deutscher Gerichte an Urteile des EGMR – Neues aus Straßburg und Karlsruhe. *Neue Juristische Wochenschrift, 1–2*, 15–19.

O'Leary, S., & Eicke, T. (2018). Some reflections on Protocol No. 16. *European Human Rights Law Review, 3*, 220–237.

Paprocka, A., & Ziółkowski, M. (2015). Advisory opinions under Protocol No. 16 to the European Court on Human Rights. *European Constitutional Law Review, 11*(2), 274–292.

Peters, B. (2012). Germany's dialogue with Strasbourg: Extrapolating the Bundesverfassungsgericht's relationship with the European Court of Human Rights in the preventive detention decisions. *German Law Journal, 13*, 757–772.

Report of the Group of Wise Persons to the Committee of Ministers, adopted on 15 November 2006 r., CM(2006)203. Retrieved April 6, 2019, from https://search.coe.int/cm/Pages/result_details. aspx?ObjectId=09000016805d7893

Rinceanu, J. (2017). Judicial dialogue between the European Court of Human Rights and national supreme courts. In C. D. Spinellis, N. Teodorakis, E. Billis, & G. Papadimitrakopoulus (Eds.), *Europe in crisis: Crime, criminal justice and the way forward. Essays in Honour of Nestor Courakis* (pp. 1029–1041). Athens: Ant. N. Sakkoulas Publishers L.P. http://crime-in-crisis.com/en/wp-content/uploads/2017/06/54-RINCENAU-KOURAKIS-FS_Final_Draft_26.4.17.pdf

Tremblay, L. B. (2005). The legitimacy of judicial review: The limits of dialogue between courts and legislature. *International Journal of Constitutional Law, 3*(4), 617–648. https://doi.org/10.1093/icon/moi042

Judicial and Non-Judicial Elements in the Enforcement Mechanism of the European Convention on Human Rights

Krzysztof Wojtyczek

Contents

The European Convention on Human Rights is often presented as an example of a human rights system with a judicial enforcement mechanism. The Convention established an international judicial body for the purpose of ensuring the observance of this treaty. The question arises however, whether the assumption that the Convention enforcement mechanism has been judicialized, reflects the reality of the law and the practice. The aim of the present article is to determine to which extent the adjudication upon applications (both individual and inter-State) against the State parties of the Convention belongs to judicial bodies and to which extent non-judicial actors take decisions upon claims arising from human rights violations.

Krzysztof Wojtyczek is Professor at the Jagiellonian University in Krakow.

K. Wojtyczek (✉)
Department of Constitutional Law, Jagiellonian University, Kraków, Poland
e-mail: k.wojtyczek@uj.edu.pl

© Springer Nature Switzerland AG 2019
P. Pinto de Albuquerque, K. Wojtyczek (eds.), *Judicial Power in a Globalized World*, https://doi.org/10.1007/978-3-030-20744-1_39

1 National Legal Systems

Legal rules define the legal consequences of specific factual circumstances in general and of human acts in particular. They may define the legal consequences of acts undertaken in conformity with the law such as the conclusion of a contract, they also determine the legal consequences of acts undertaken in violation of the law such as driving in disrespect of the applicable legal rules or causing damage to another person's property. Sanctions for breaches of the law are a constitutive element of a legal system. As explained by H. Kelsen, *"[t]hat a person is legally responsible for a certain behavior or that he bears the legal responsibility therefor means that he is liable to a sanction in case of contrary behavior"*.[1]

The possible legal consequences of a breach of national law (legal sanctions) are defined in legislation. Usually, the law determines the catalogue of possible measures and general guidelines for their application leaving a certain scope for discretion in its application. In some cases, the scope of discretion may be extremely limited or even non-existent, while in other cases the possible measures may be defined in vague terms leaving broad discretionary powers to law-applying authorities.[2]

The question of legal consequences of specific factual circumstances in general and of a breach of the law in particular is an essential element of legal disputes and very often the most important element of a legal dispute. The claimant parties are usually interested in initiating legal proceedings because they enable them to obtain a favorable determination of the legal consequences of a breach of law, not just to obtain a statement that a breach of law occurred. In particular, the reparation of the damage is usually much more important than a mere finding of its existence.

Civil law guarantees the substantive right to adequate reparation for the damage caused by a civil delict. At the same time civil law is based upon the principle of dispositiveness: legal subjects may dispose freely of their claims and decide whether and to which extent they want to pursue them before the courts. It belongs to the claimant to elect the appropriate forms of reparation and to raise the respective claims. If the defendant refuses to satisfy these claims the plaintiff may initiate civil proceedings in order to obtain enforcement of his rights by the State. It belongs then to the adjudicating body to assess the adequacy of the reparation measures requested and make the final determination. In principle, the adjudicating body does not go beyond the requested measures. It may, however, decide to apply more limited measures, such as a pecuniary compensation lower than the amount claimed, or to order an apology as the sanction for personal rights violation, instead of awarding pecuniary compensation. The substantive right to adequate reparation for the

---

[1] Kelsen (2009), p. 65.
[2] Compare Wróblewski (1992), p. 34. and pp. 189–208.

damage is an enforceable right closely connected with the right to have the legal consequences of a civil delict determined by a court.

The purpose of the criminal proceedings is to decide whether a criminal offense has been committed and, if so, to impose adequate criminal sanctions, in accordance with the applicable criminal law. Criminal proceedings may be based upon the principle of legality or opportunity, but irrespective of this a criminal court cannot adjudicate without an act of indictment brought by the competent prosecuting authority. It is worth noting that—in some legal systems—establishing that a criminal offense has been committed and imposing sanction for theses offense belongs to two different bodies: the jury and the trial judge. In most legal systems, the same judicial body decides the question whether a criminal offense has been committed and if so, which punishment is adequate.

Even if the criminal court is not bound by the request of the prosecution and has the power to impose a harsher or a milder punishment, the parties play nonetheless an important role for the determination of the punishment and the gist of the dispute may be the punishment. If the accused pleads guilty, the dispute between the parties pertains usually only to the punishment and to the factors which are relevant for its severity.

In proceedings before administrative courts, the court has to assess the legality of a legal act contested by its addressee and, if necessary, to determine the legal consequences of the legal vices of this act. In particular the administrative court may declare an administrative act null and void *ex tunc* or annul it *ex nunc,* if the nature of breach of law justifies it.

In proceedings before a constitutional court, the court determines whether a legal rule is compatible with a provision of a higher rank. The consequences of a finding of incompatibility are determined by the national constitution and ordinary legislation and consist in the abrogation *ex nunc* or *ex tunc* of the legal rule under review. It may, however, be necessary to take other measures to restore the constitutionality, such as adopting a new statute filling the lacuna resulting from the abrogation of the unconstitutional provision, or pass specific legislation repairing the damages resulting from the application of the unconstitutional provision before its abrogation.[3] In this case, the specific measures to be taken are usually not indicated in the judgment itself but are left to the parliament or another competent norm-making body. Constitutional courts may nonetheless insert to the reasoning of their judgments certain recommendations to the parliament and other norm-making authorities concerning the way of executing these judgments.

Typically, in national law, the determination of legal consequences of a breach of the law is the power of the State organ which finds such a breach. If a breach is found by a court, the determination of the legal consequences of this breach belongs to the

---

[3]The question of legal consequences of constitutional courts' judgments has been studied particularly deeply in Polish legal scholarship—see in particular: Florczak-Wątor (2006), and Działocha and Jarosz-Żukowska (2013).

same court. In other words, the determination of a breach of the law and its legal consequences are part of the same judicial decision. This determination belongs to the core of the judicial power. As summarized by H. Kelsen, *[t]he judicial function consists, essentially, of two acts. In each concrete case (1) the court establishes the presence of a fact that is qualified as civil or criminal delict by a general norm to be applied to the given case; (2) the court orders a concrete civil or criminal sanction stipulated generally in the norm to be applied.*[4] The purpose of the judicial application of law is to formulate in the judgment a precise individual legal rule addressed at the person concerned. The process of application of law is often described with the model of legal syllogism.[5] In its most simple version, the major premise is the general legal rule to be applied, the minor premise consists in the factual circumstances of the case and the conclusion of the syllogism has the form of an individual rule expressed in the operative part of the judgment. The determination of this individual rule (obligation) is considered as a necessary precondition for the law enforcement: the law enforcing authorities need a precise determination of the individual legal obligation they have to enforce.

If the administration of justice is a power to be exercised by the courts, it is not compatible with this assumption to leave the determination of legal consequences of an act to a non-judicial body. This understanding of the judicial function at the national level is further confirmed by Article 6 par. 1 first sentence of the European Convention on Human Rights. This provision is worded as follows: *in the determination of his civil rights and obligations or of any criminal charge against him, everyone is entitled to a fair and public hearing within a reasonable time by an independent and impartial tribunal established by law.*

The determination of civil rights and obligations encompasses the determination of legal consequences of a civil delict or a breach of a civil contract. In other words, the determination of sanctions for breach of civil law is the exclusive power of a tribunal in the meaning of this provision. Similarly, the determination of criminal charge encompasses the determination of the punishment.[6] It means that the imposition of a specific sanction for a specific offense is also the exclusive power of a tribunal in the meaning of Article 6 of the Convention. A system in which a court limits itself to finding a breach of the law and leaves the determination of civil or criminal sanctions to a body which does not fulfill the criteria of Article 6 (independence, impartiality, establishment by law), contravenes the European Convention on Human Rights.

---

[4]Kelsen (2009), p. 273; see also, Wróblewski (1992), pp. 30–31.

[5]See Wróblewski (1992), pp. 189–209; see also: Pescatore (2009), p. 356 and Gianformaggio (2018), pp. 589–591.

[6]Compare the judgment of the European Court of Human Rights of 25 February 1997 in the case of Findlay v. the United Kingdom, application no. 22107/93, par. 77 in which the Court refers to *the well-established principle that the power to give a binding decision which may not be altered by a non-judicial authority is inherent in the very notion of "tribunal" and can also be seen as a component of the "independence" required by Article 6 para. 1 (art. 6-1).*

2   General International Law

In inter-State relations the rules of customary international law pertaining to legal consequences of internationally wrongful acts have been codified in the Articles on *Responsibility of States for Internationally Wrongful Acts*.[7] According to the Articles, the State responsible for an internationally wrongful act is under an obligation to cease that act, if it is continuing, to offer appropriate assurances and guarantees of non-repetition, if circumstances so require (article 30) and to make full reparation for the injury caused by the internationally wrongful act (article 31). Full reparation for the injury caused by the internationally wrongful act may take the form of restitution, compensation and satisfaction, either singly or in combination (article 34).

The Articles deal also with the procedural requirements for raising claim. Article 43 relevant in this respect is worded as follows:

Notice of Claim by an Injured State

1. *An injured State which invokes the responsibility of another State shall give notice of its claim to that State.*
2. *The injured State may specify in particular:*

   (a) *the conduct that the responsible State should take in order to cease the wrongful act, if it is continuing;*
   (b) *what form reparation should take in accordance with the provisions of part two.*

In interstate relations the claimant State is entitled to chose the appropriate method of reparation.[8]

State claims against other States resulting from internationally wrongful acts may be implemented by the way of self-help, countermeasures or the exception of non-performance of a treaty.[9] They may also be implemented through proceedings before international judicial bodies such as the International Court of Justice, the Permanent Court of Arbitration or an *ad hoc* tribunal.

Pursuance of claims through judicial proceedings triggered the development of case-law on reparation of damages resulting from internationally wrongful acts. Among the legal questions to be resolved, the international courts had to address the relationship between jurisdiction as to the breaches of international law and jurisdiction as to the forms of reparation. The Permanent Court of justice established the following principles in this respect:

---

[7]See the Annex to General Assembly resolution 56/83 of 12 December 2001, A/RES/56/83, with corrections inserted by the document A/56/49(Vol. I)/Corr.

[8]Crawford (2013), pp. 508–509.

[9]Crawford (2013), p. 675 ff.

(i) *An interpretation which would confine the Court simply to recording that the Convention had been incorrectly applied or that it had not been applied, without being able to lay down the conditions for there-establishment of the treaty rights affected, would be contrary to what would, prima facie, be the natural object of the clause; for a jurisdiction of this kind, instead of settling a dispute once and for all, would leave open the possibility of further disputes.*

This conclusion, which is deduced from the object of a clause like Article 23, and, in general, of any arbitration clause, could only be defeated, either by the employment of terms sufficiently clear to show a contrary intention on the part of the contracting Parties, or by the fact that the Convention had established a special jurisdiction for claims in respect of reparation due for the violation of the provisions in question, or had made some other arrangement regarding them.[10]

(ii) *In Judgment No. 8, when deciding on the jurisdiction derived by it from Article 23 of the Geneva Convention, the Court has already said that reparation is the indispensable complement of a failure to apply a convention, and there is no necessity for this to be stated in the convention itself.*[11]

This approach was farther confirmed by the International Court of Justice in particular in its judgment of 27 June 2001 in the La Grand Case (Germany v. United States Of America): "*Where jurisdiction exists over a dispute on a particular matter, no separate basis for jurisdiction is required by the Court to consider the remedies a party has requested for the breach of the obligation (Factory at Chorzów P. C. I. J., Series A, No. 9, p. 22)*".[12]

Similarly to the logic of domestic systems, the adjudicative international body assesses not only the existence of an internationally wrongful act, but also determines the forms of reparation within the limit of claims raised by the claimant.[13] The claimant party has to formulate specific claims which will be the object of assessment and decision of the judicial body. Moreover, the international body has the obligation to consider and respond to all the demands of the claimant (*non infra petita*).[14] In practice, the ICJ most frequently renders judgments finding that a wrongful act has been committed.[15] It rarely awards pecuniary compensation and very rarely orders restitution or guarantees of non-repetition.[16] It may also leave a choice of the specific measures to remedy the violations of an international

---

[10]Judgment of 26 July 1927 in the case concerning the Factory at Chorzow, Claim For Indemnity (Jurisdiction) *P. C. I. J., Series A, No. 9*, p. 25.

[11]Judgment of 13 September 1928 in the case concerning the Factory at Chorzow, Claim For Indemnity (Merits), Chorzów, *P. C. I. J., Series A, No. 17*, p. 29.

[12]*International Court of Justice. Reports of Judgments, Advisory Opinions and Orders, 2001*, p. 485.

[13]See Crawford (2013), pp. 615–621 and pp. 626–629.

[14]Santulli (2015), p. 349.

[15]Crawford (2013), p. 616.

[16]Crawford (2013), p. 619.

obligation.[17] On one hand, under the general State responsibility regime, forms of reparation are clearly an element of inter-state litigation, on the other hand, the case-law shows judicial self-restraint in respect of awarding reparation measures.

The Permanent Court of International Justice expressed the view that [t]*he decision whether there has been a breach of an engagement involves no doubt a more important jurisdiction than a decision as to the nature or extent of reparation due for a breach of an international engagement the existence of which is already established.*[18] The question of reparatory measures still appears to be less important than the question of compliance with international law. This may be explained by the fact that the States may try to resort to extra-judicial means of asserting their claims concerning the scope and forms of reparation.

3 The Text of the European Convention on Human Rights

The European Convention on Human Rights does not define with great precision the object of the proceedings before the European Court of Human Rights. The following provisions are of particular relevance in this respect. Article 32 defines the object of inter-state cases: *Any High Contracting Party may refer to the Court any alleged breach of the provisions of the Convention and the Protocols thereto by another High Contracting Party.* This suggests that the Court has to determine whether the responding State has breached the provisions of the Convention or the Protocols thereto. The accent seems *prima facie* placed here on objective legality rather than on subjective rights. Article 34 first sentence defines the object of individual applications as follows: *The Court may receive applications from any person, non-governmental organisation or group of individuals claiming to be the victim of a violation by one of the High Contracting Parties of the rights set forth in the Convention or the Protocols thereto.* The wording of this provision suggests that the Court has to determine whether the applicant's rights set forth in the Convention or the Protocols thereto have been violated. The letter of the treaty places the accent on the subjective rights.

Article 19 defines the mandate of the European Court of Human Rights in the following terms: *To ensure the observance of the engagements undertaken by the High Contracting Parties in the Convention and the Protocols thereto.* This definition is very broad and goes well beyond the determination whether a State has violated the Convention and encompasses the establishment of legal consequences

---

[17] [The International Court of Justice] *Finds that should nationals of the Federal Republic of Germany nonetheless be sentenced to severe penalties, without their rights under Article 36, paragraph 1 (b), of the Convention having been respected, the United States of America, by means of its own choosing, shall allow the review and reconsideration of the conviction and sentence by taking account of the violation of the rights set forth in that Convention* (La Grand Case, cited above, p. 516).

[18] Judgment of 26 July 1927 in the case concerning the Factory at Chorzow, cited above, p. 23.

of a breach of the Convention. The possibility of such an interpretation is further confirmed by Article 32 which defines the jurisdiction of the Court: *The jurisdiction of the Court shall extend to all matters concerning the interpretation and application of the Convention and the Protocols thereto which are referred to it as provided in Articles 33, 34, 46 and 47.* The term "all matters concerning the application of the Convention" in its ordinary meaning extends to matters concerning the reparation of the injury. One has to remind here that the Permanent Court of International Justice expressed the view that *[d]ifferences relating to reparations, which may be due by reason of failure to apply a convention, are consequently differences relating to its application.*[19]

The wording of Article 19 of the European Convention on Human Rights does not express the intention to remove from the jurisdiction of the ECHR questions of reparation for breaches of the Convention—questions which, as mentioned above, under the general rules of international law, do not require a separate jurisdictional basis.

Article 32 has to read in the context of Article 55 which is worded as follows:

Exclusion of Other Means of Dispute Settlement
The High Contracting Parties agree that, except by special agreement, they will not avail themselves of treaties, conventions or declarations in force between them for the purpose of submitting, by way of petition, a dispute arising out of the interpretation or application of this Convention to a means of settlement other than those provided for in this Convention.

One has to note that the same phrase *interpretation or application* [of the Convention] is used in both Article 32 and Article 55.[20] There is wide acceptance for the presumption that within the same legal act the same term is used in the same meaning.[21] It does not appear that the framers of the Convention wanted to limit the scope of the exclusion clause in Article 55 to disputes concerning the occurrence of a breach of the Convention. The purpose of the clause is rather to encompass by the exclusion clause *inter alia* the disputes concerning the reparation of the breaches of the Convention. Article 55 thus further confirms that the Court's jurisdiction defined in Article 32 extends to such questions.

Article 41 confers the following power to the Court: *If the Court finds that there has been a violation of the Convention or the Protocols thereto, and if the internal law of the High Contracting Party concerned allows only partial reparation to be made, the Court shall, if necessary, afford just satisfaction to the injured party.* The wording of this provision implies that one of the tasks of the Court is to decide whether there has been a violation of the Convention. It further confirms that the

---

[19]Judgment of 26 July 1927 in the case concerning the Factory at Chorzow, cited above, p. 21.

[20]The same phrase also appears in Article 28 par. 1 lit. b and Article 43 par. 2 but the wording of these two provisions does not appear to bring any guidance as to scope of the phrase in question.

[21]Lang et al. (1986), p. 443.

Court may decide at least certain questions concerning the reparation of the injury by affording just satisfaction.

Three questions arise however. Firstly, what "just satisfaction" exactly means? According to the Articles on *Responsibility of States for Internationally Wrongful Acts*, the State responsible for an internationally wrongful act is under an obligation to give satisfaction for the injury caused by that act insofar as it cannot be made good by restitution or compensation. Satisfaction may consist in an acknowledgement of the breach, an expression of regret, a formal apology or another appropriate modality. Satisfaction is therefore clearly distinguished from restitution and compensation. However, under the established case-law of the ECtHR "just satisfaction" means pecuniary compensation for moral or material damage.

Secondly, is "just satisfaction" in the meaning of the Article 41 of the Convention the only form of reparation or can a breach of the Convention require reparation in other forms? The Convention does not contain further provisions regulating the legal consequences of internationally wrongful acts consisting in the breach of its provisions. According to the case-law of the Court, the general rules on State responsibility apply, which means that the damage should be repaired if necessary by different means of reparation, not only through pecuniary compensation. The Court has expressed its view in the following terms: *The State Party in question will be under an obligation not just to pay those concerned the sums awarded by way of just satisfaction, but also to take individual and/or, if appropriate, general measures in its domestic legal order to put an end to the violation found by the Court and to redress the effects, the aim being to put the applicant, as far as possible, in the position he would have been in had the requirements of the Convention not been disregarded.*[22]

Thirdly, is "just satisfaction" the only form of reparation which may be awarded by the ECHR? In other words: is the jurisdiction of ECHR in respect of reparatory measures limited to awarding pecuniary compensation? Article 41 is an exemplification of reparatory measures which may be adequate in a specific case. An interpreter of the Convention may *prima facie* be tempted to use the *argumentum a contrario* which suggests that this provision would deny the Court the power to decide other reparation issues is not justified. One has to stress here, however, that any *argumentum a contrario* is valid only if a the purpose of a provision is to express an exception and not to specify a more general principle. Article 41 appears to be a specific provision implementing more general rules of State responsibility and not a provision that would establish an exception to the hypothetical principle that the Court is not otherwise competent to decide upon the legal consequences of the breaches of the Convention.

Under the Article 46 par. 1 of the Convention, *the High Contracting Parties undertake to abide by the final judgment of the Court in any case to which they are*

---

[22]Judgment of 30 June 2009 in the case of Verein gegen Tierfabriken Schweiz (VGT) v. Switzerland (no. 2), application no. 32772/02.

parties. If the parties "undertake to abide", this implies that there is a pre-existing legal obligation to be fulfilled. The formula used here suggests therefore that the judgments of the Court impose obligations upon the parties. This further implies that the obligation imposed is specified in the judgment itself, unless it is clearly specified in some general rules.

Under Article 46 par. 2 *the final judgment of the Court shall be transmitted to the Committee of Ministers, which shall supervise its execution.* If this provision speaks about the execution judgments, this further confirms means that judgments may establish obligations which have to be executed. Moreover, the wording of the provision makes it clear that the role of the Committee of Ministers is limited to the supervision of the execution. Article 46 par. 2, interpreted literally, does not give any mandate to determine or codetermine the obligations stemming from a judgment. The letter of Article 46 par. 2 presupposes that there are precise legal obligations which stem from a judgment and that the Committee of Ministers supervises whether the respondent State complies with these pre-existing obligations.

Finally, Article 46 par. 4 is worded as follows: *If the Committee of Ministers considers that a High Contracting Party refuses to abide by a final judgment in a case to which it is a party, it may, after serving formal notice on that Party and by decision adopted by a majority vote of two-thirds of the representatives entitled to sit on the committee, refer to the Court the question whether that Party has failed to fulfil its obligation under paragraph.*

This provision further suggests that the Committee of Ministers supervises whether the respondent State complies with these pre-existing obligations. The Committee has clearly the power to decide on questions whether those obligations have been met but it may also refer this question to the European Court of Human Rights. So far, the Committee has exercised this power only once.[23]

Given the qualification of the treaty body as a Court and the broad definition of its mandate in Article 19, the broad scope of the Court's jurisdiction defined in Article 32, the power of the Court—implied in Article 46 par. 1—to impose binding obligations upon the respondent Government and the very limited mandate of the Committee of Ministers defined in Article 46 par. 2, there is nothing in letter of the Convention which would prevent the Court from determining the legal conse-quences of the breaches of the Convention. On the contrary, it belongs to the core power of an international court to decide upon these issues. The interpretation of the Convention based upon its letter allows the conclusion that the Court has jurisdiction to decided on the forms of reparation for Convention breaches, whereas the role of the Committee is limited to the supervision of compliance with individual obliga-tions imposed on the respondent State found in breach of the Convention.

In these conditions, the letter of the Convention justifies the interpretation according to which the Court is competent to determine the legal consequences of

---

[23]In respect of the judgment of 22 May 2014 in the case of Mammadov v. Azerbeidjan, see the press release https://search.coe.int/directorate_of_communications/Pages/result_details.aspx?ObjectId=090000168076d57f.

a violation of the Convention. Under this approach, the object of the proceedings before the ECHR would be not only the occurrence of the breach of Convention rights but also the determination of the legal consequences such a breach entails.

One has to note here, however, the differences between the general regime of State responsibility vis-à-vis other States and the regime of State responsibility vis-à-vis the individual for violations of his human rights protected in international human rights instruments. Human rights litigation before the ECHR mixes elements of subjective and objective litigation (*contentieux subjectif* et *contentieux objectif*) with the former prevailing.[24]

The objective elements include *inter alia* the possibility of examining an individual application despite its withdrawal if respect for human rights so requires, as well as the question of identification of general measures susceptible to remedy a structural or systemic problem in a national legal system. The individual is necessarily much better placed than anyone to formulate and raise claims concerning the reparation of violations of his subjective rights, whereas he is not always as able to propose the optimal methods of restoring the objective rule of law, and especially to identify the general measures necessary to achieve this aim and ensure the compliance with the Convention in the future.

4 Practice Under the Convention

The case-law of the European Court of Human Rights and the practice of the Committee of Ministers of the Council of Europe have not followed the interpretation of the Convention based upon the letter of the treaty (the possible interpretation presented above). The Strasbourg Court made a deliberate choice of an approach guided by resolute judicial self-restraint. The whole system, as currently operating in practice, is based under the following assumptions:

(i) The Court stresses that its judgments are "essentially declaratory in nature",[25] which means that there are limited to deciding the question whether the Convention provisions have been observed and in principle refrain from addressing the questions of the forms of reparation of the damage caused.

(ii) If the Court finds a violation of the Convention it usually awards a pecuniary compensation for the moral damage suffered by the applicant and sometimes for material damage.

(iii) Other legal consequences of a judgment finding a violation of the Convention are in principle defined by the general rules of international law pertaining to

---

[24]See Wojtyczek (2018), pp. 674–676.

[25]Judgment of 12 May 2005 in the case of case of Öcalan v. Turkey, application no. 46221/99, par. 210.

State responsibility.[26] These rules were codified in the Articles on Responsibility of States for Internationally Wrongful Acts. They are further confirmed and developed in the rules of the Committee of Ministers which give the Committee of Ministers the mandate to examine:

- *if required, and taking into account the discretion of the High Contracting Party concerned to choose the means necessary to comply with the judgment, whether*
- *i. individual measures have been taken to ensure that the violation has ceased and that the injured party is put, as far as possible, in the same situation as that party enjoyed prior to the violation of the Convention;*
- *i. general measures have been adopted, preventing new violations similar to that or those found or putting an end to continuing violations* (Rule 6 par. 2).

The Court's case-law, recommendations issued by the Committee of Ministers and the practice of this organ developed further (more specific) general guidelines for certain types of cases concerning the most adequate forms of reparation. For instance according to the Court's case-*law where an individual [...] has been convicted by a court that did not meet the Convention requirements of independence and impartiality, a retrial or a reopening of the case, if requested, represents in principle an appropriate way of redressing the violation.*[27] General guidelines may also be derived from the individual decisions of the Court to recommend or impose certain measures in specific cases.

(iv) A Judgment of the ECHR finding a violation of the Convention entails the consequences specified in the above-mentioned rules. In particular, *a judgment in which the Court finds a breach imposes on the respondent State a legal obligation to put an end to the breach and make reparation for its consequences in such a way as to restore as far as possible the situation existing before the breach.*[28]

(v) The general obligations require specification in the circumstances of each and every individual case. The applicable general rules leave a broad discretion in the choice of specific measures for the reparation of the Convention violations in specific cases.

---

[26]See for instance the judgment of 30 June 2009 in the case of Verein gegen Tierfabriken Schweiz (Vgt) v. Switzerland (no. 2), application no. 32772/02, par. 86: *These obligations reflect the principles of international law whereby a State responsible for a wrongful act is under an obligation to make restitution, consisting in restoring the situation which existed before the wrongful act was committed, provided that restitution is not "materially impossible" and "does not involve a burden out of all proportion to the benefit deriving from restitution instead of compensation" (Article 35 of the Draft Articles of the International Law Commission on Responsibility of States for Internationally Wrongful Acts ...).*

[27]Judgment of 12 May 2005 in the case of case of Öcalan v. Turkey, cited above, par. 210.

[28]Judgment of 31 October 1995 in the case of Papamichalopoulos and others v. Greece, par. 34; see also *i.a.* the judgment of 13 July 2000 in the case of Scozzari and Giunta v. Italy, application nos. 39221/98 and 41963/98, par. 249.

(vi) The system is based upon the assumption of self-determination of the legal consequences of a Convention violation by the respondent State. The case-law of the ECHR expresses this principle in the following terms:

- *The Contracting States that are parties to a case are in principle free to choose the means whereby they will comply with a judgment in which the Court has found a breach. This discretion as to the manner of execution of a judgment reflects the freedom of choice attaching to the primary obligation of the Contracting States under the Convention to secure the rights and freedoms guaranteed (Article 1) (art. 1).*[29]

This approach is further confirmed by the rules of the Committee of Ministers in Rule 6 par. 1: *When, in a judgment transmitted to the Committee of Ministers in accordance with Article 46, paragraph 2, of the Convention, the Court has decided that there has been a violation of the Convention or its protocols and/or has awarded just satisfaction to the injured party under Article41 of the Convention, the Committee shall invite the High Contracting Party concerned to inform it of the measures which the High Contracting Party **has taken or intends to take** in consequence of the judgment, having regard to its obligation to abide by it under Article 46, paragraph 1, of the Convention* (emphasis added).

The Convention system adopts therefore a solution which is the opposite of the one admitted in general international law, where the choice of the means belongs in principle to the plaintiff.

(vii) The choice of the means to ensure compliance with a judgment is made under the supervision of the Committee of Ministers. It is therefore justified to formulate the principle of supervised self-determination: the self-determination of legal consequences by the State is subject to supervision by the Committee of Ministers. The Committee assesses whether the means applied or proposed are adequate and sufficient and may make recommendations in this respect to respondent State. If the Committee of Ministers finds that the means applied are sufficient, it closes the supervision procedure in respect of the judgment in question. The Committee has adopted rules on the supervision procedure as well as recommendations concerning the choice of means for the execution of judgments.

(viii) Exceptionally, the ECHR in the reasoning of its judgments recommends the adoption of certain individual measures (such as the reopening of the proceedings[30]) or general measures (such as *further improving domestic remedies in extradition and expulsion cases*).[31] More rarely, the ECHR imposes in the operative part of a judgment the adoption of certain individual (for instance to

---

[29]Judgment of 31 October 1995 in the case Papamichalopoulos and Others v. Greece cited above, par. 34; the same view was expressed *i.a.* in the judgment of 23 January 2001 in the case Brumărescu v. Romania, application no. 28342/95, par. 20.

[30]Judgment of 23 October 2003 in the case of Gençel v. Turkey, application no. 53431/99, par. 27.

[31]Judgment of 25 April 2013 in the case of Savriddin Dzhurayev v. Russia, par. 258; see also the judgment of 21 May 2015 in the case of Mukhitdinov v. Russia, application no. 20999/14, par.

return the land[32]) or general measures (such as the obligation to secure through appropriate legal measures and administrative practices, the implementation of the property right or provide them with equivalent redress).[33] It also happens that the reasoning expresses the view that the respondent State has an obligation to adopt certain measures, for instance:

- *In these conditions, having regard to the particular circumstances of the case and the urgent need to put an end to the violation of Article 5 § 1 and Article 6 § 1 of the Convention (. . .), the Court considers that the respondent State must secure the applicant's release at the earliest possible date.*[34]

The purpose of including recommendations or orders concerning the forms of reparation is to limit the scope of discretion left to the States by the general rules. In such a case the Committee of Ministers supervises the execution of these obligations.

One has to stress here that some of the measures ordered interfere deeply in national legal systems. For instance, in the operative part of one of its judgments, the Court has ordered *that Ukraine shall secure the applicant's reinstatement to the post of judge of the Supreme Court at the earliest possible date.*[35] At the same time, the Court has explicitly stated that ordering certain other types of less intrusive measures is out of the scope of its jurisdiction: *The Court reiterates that it does not have jurisdiction to order, in particular, the reopening of proceedings.*[36]

The Court, when it finds it appropriate, does not hesitate to encroach upon the sphere of the choice of reparatory measures which is otherwise presumed to belong to the jurisdiction of the respondent States and the Committee of Ministers.[37] As result, there is no clear line dividing the respective powers of these two sets of actors.

5 The Object of the Proceedings Before the European Court of Human Rights

The question of Court's jurisdiction in respect of reparation is closely connected with the rules of procedure before the Court and the practice of their application. Under the Rules of the Court (Rule 60),[38] and the practice directions issued by the

---

[32]Judgment of 31 October 1995 in the case of Papamichalopoulos v. Greece, cited above; of judgment of 23 January 2001 in the case Brumărescu v. Romania, cited above.

[33]Judgment of 22 June 2004 in the case of Broniowski v. Poland, application no. 31443/96.

[34]Judgment of 8 April 2004 in the case of Assanidze v. Georgia, application no. 71503/01, par. 203.

[35]Judgment of 9 January 2013 in the case of Volkov. v. Ukraine, Application no. 21722/11.

[36]Judgment of 11 July 2017 in the case of Moreira Ferreira v. Portugal (No. 2), application no. 19867/12, par. 48.

[37]Compare Lambert Abdelwagad (2009), pp. 474ff.

[38]https://www.echr.coe.int/Documents/Rules_Court_ENG.pdf (all documents quoted accessed 22.02.2019).

President of the Court the applicant has the obligation to formulate a precise claim for pecuniary compensation (rule 60) and show the material damage,[39] but on the other hand he is not required to provide any explanation justifying his claim in respect of moral damage.[40] The decision to award pecuniary compensation for moral damage is usually explained by an extremely short reasoning, often limited to a brief reference to equity.[41] In such judgments, there is no assessment of the nature of the moral damage suffered and no explanation how the amount of compensation for this damage was calculated. As result, the nature of the moral damage and the means of repairing it are usually not discussed more thoroughly by the parties.

The individual applicant may always present submissions requesting the Court to recommend or impose individual or general measures, but such requests are very rarely accepted in practice.[42] Much more frequently, the Court replies that is not empowered to make such orders.[43] Moreover, the Court does not have the obligation to examine and explicitly address such requests. In any event, the decision to reject such claims raised by the applicant is not explicitly mentioned in the operative part of the judgment, although it may be understood as covered by the usual formula used in the operative part "dismisses the remainder of the applicants' claim for just satisfaction".

All these factors have limited the actual object of the proceedings before the ECHR. The litigation before the ECHR focuses almost exclusively on the question of the occurrence of a violation of the Convention. Relatively little attention is devoted to the question of reparation. The main aim of the applicant is to obtain a finding of a violation of the Convention much more than to obtain the most favorable reparatory measures, whereas the main aim of the respondent State is to avoid such finding rather than to limit the scope of the reparation to be provided.

---

[39] Just satisfaction claims, Practice direction issued by the President of the Court in accordance with Rule 32 of the Rules of Court on 28 March 2007, https://www.echr.coe.int/Documents/PD_satisfaction_claims_ENG.pdf, par. 7–12.

[40] *Ibidem*, par. 13–15.

[41] See for instance the judgment of 14 March 2019 in the case of Kobiashvili V. Georgia, application no. 36416/06, par. 81: *As to the non-pecuniary damage, making its assessment on an equitable basis, the Court awards the applicant EUR 3500, plus any tax that may be chargeable on that amount.*

[42] The requests of the applicant were partly accepted in the judgment of 24 July 2014 in the case of case of Al Nashiri v. Poland, application no. 28761/11 - see par. 584–589.

[43] See for instance the Judgment of 14 September 1987 case of Gillow v. The United Kingdom (article 50), application no. 9063/80, par. 9; the judgment of 5 April 2007 in the case of Church of Scientology Moscow v. Russia, no. 18147/02, par. 106; the judgment of 1 October 2009 in the case of Kimlya and Others v. Russia, applications nos. 76836/01 and 32782/03, par. 109.

6 The Role of Committee of Ministers and of the Respondent State

Under the established case-law of the ECHR and the established practice of the Council of Europe organs, the determination of the legal consequences of a breach of the Convention belongs in principle to the respondent State, acting under the supervision of the Committee of Ministers.

The Committee of Ministers is a international body composed of representatives of 47 member States of the Council of Europe. Most frequently, the States are represented by their permanent representatives to the Council of Europe. This means that a decision, which is judicial in nature, is taken by a non-judicial body of a political nature. The European Court of Human Rights plays only a very limited role in the determination of legal consequences of violations of the European Convention.

As mentioned above, the Committee of Ministers has formulated a certain number of general recommendations concerning the execution of judgments by the States.[44]

The proceedings before the Committee of Ministers are regulated by Rules of the Committee of Ministers for the supervision of the execution of judgments and of the terms of friendly settlements.[45] These proceedings are of a non-judicial nature. The Committee of Ministers assesses the action plans and the actions reports presented by

---

[44]Recommendation CM/Rec(2010)3 of the Committee of Ministers to member states on effective remedies for excessive length of proceedings (adopted on 24 February 2010); Recommendation CM/Rec(2008)2 of the Committee of Ministers to member states on efficient domestic capacity for rapid execution of judgments of the European Court of Human Rights (adopted on 6 February 2008); Recommendation CM/Rec(2004)6 of the Committee of Ministers to member States on the improvement of domestic remedies (adopted on 12 May 2004); Recommendation CM/Rec(2004) 5of the Committee of Ministers to member States on the verification of the compatibility of draft laws, existing laws and administrative practice with standards laid down in the European Convention on Human Rights (adopted on 12 May 2004); Recommendation CM/Rec(2004)4 of the Committee of Ministers to member States on the European Convention on Human Rights concerning university education and professional training (adopted on 12 May 2004); Recommendation CM/Rec(2002)13 of the Committee of Ministers to member states on the publication and dissemination in the member states of the text of the European Convention on Human Rights and the case-law of the European Court of Human Rights (adopted on 18 December 2002); Recommendation CM/Rec(2000) 2of the Committee of Ministers on the re-examination or reopening of certain cases at domestic level following judgments of the European Court of Human Rights (adopted on 19 and 21 January 2000); Resolution CM/Res(2004)3 of the Committee of Ministers on judgments revealing an underlying systemic problem (adopted on 12 May 2004); Resolution CM/Res(2002)59 of the Committee of Ministers concerning the practice in respect of friendly settlements (Adopted by the Committee of Ministers on 18 December 2002 at the 822nd meeting of the Ministers' Deputies); Resolution CM/Res(2002)58 of the Committee of Ministers on the publication and dissemination of the case-law of the European Court of Human Rights (Adopted on 18 December 2002).

[45]Rules of the Committee of Ministers for the supervision of the execution of judgments and of the terms of friendly settlements (adopted by the Committee of Ministers on 10 May 2006 at the 964th meeting of the Ministers' Deputies and amended on 18 January 2017 at the 1275th meeting of the Ministers' Deputies), https://rm.coe.int/16806eebf0.

the respondent States. Exceptionally, the Committee of Ministers requests the respondent State to take a specific measure indicated by the Committee. The Committee decides in practice without issuing a formal decision stating these consequences. The determination of legal consequences is made in the form of the decision to close or not the supervision proceedings, accepting or not the measures presented by the respondent Government. The resolutions do not contain any legal reasoning which would justify the conclusion. In particular, the measures adopted by the States are not assessed in a more detailed way, which would encompass an evalutation of the individual circumstances of the case, and the final conclusion is not explained.

The respondent State plays a major role in the proceedings as it is, in principle, entitled to chose the appropriate means, whereas the applicant which obtained a judgment finding that his rights have been violated can only comment on the individual measures proposed. Unlike in the general State responsibility regime, in which it belongs to the claimant to specify the forms of redress he redress it wishes to obtain, in the Convention system, it belongs to the defendant to specify the forms of reparation it wishes to provide. Moreover, the representative of the State presents orally its views at the meetings of the Committee of Ministers the vote, whereas the individual applicant does not have such an opportunity. The right to be heard is not really guaranteed to the individual applicant. The representative of the State has also the right to vote, which means that the State takes part in the decision making process in the Committee of Ministers on an equal footing with all other Member States, even in respect of judgments against this State. It entails a privileged position of the State and a fundamental inequality between it and the individual applicant. The situation is different in the case of inter-state cases because both the applicant and the respondent State take part in the proceedings before the Committee of Ministers.

In practice, another actor plays an important role: the Department for the Execution of Judgments of the European Court of Human Rights, an organisational unit of the Council of Europe.[46] The Department assesses the action plans and action reports and prepares the drafts of the resolutions for the Committee of Ministers, which are later put on the agenda of this body by the President. Very often the draft resolution concerning the execution of judgments presented by the Department are adopted by the Committee of Ministers. This means that an international administrative body is actively involved in the process of determination of the legal consequences of the ECHR judgments and plays a key role in this process, assisting the international political body.

7 Conclusion

The Convention system, as shaped by the practice, is based upon a repartition of judicial tasks between the ECHR and the Committee of Ministers. The ECHR usually limits itself to deciding the question of violation of the Convention and, if

---

[46]See Dubois and Penninckx (2016), pp. 415–417.

necessary, awards a pecuniary compensation for the moral damage suffered by the applicant and sometimes for material damage. It usually refrains from imposing or even recommending means of reparation other than pecuniary compensation, leaving this question to the respondent State and the Committee of Ministers. The Committee of Ministers assesses the measures adopted or proposed by the State and makes the final determination in this respect by closing the supervision of a judgment's execution, and accepting those measures. It may also declare them—explicitly or implicitly—as insufficient. The legal consequences of violations of the Convention are therefore determined in a process in which the respondent State interacts with the Committee of Ministers and the Department for the Execution of Judgments of the European Court of Human Rights in non-judicial proceedings.

The above considerations allow the conclusion that the implementation of the Convention is only partly judicialized. The system is based upon the mixing of judicial determination of Convention breaches with non-judicial determination of legal consequences of these breaches. The question whether the substantives provisions of the Convention have been observed is decided by the European Court of Human Rights. The judicial decision triggers the non-judicial process of determination of legal consequences of the breach of the Convention. Fundamental questions belonging to the core of the judicial function, concerning the legal consequences of breaches of the Conventions (with the exception of pecuniary compensation for moral and material damage), are decided by non-judicial bodies in non-judicial proceedings. The system is based upon the principle of State self-determination of these consequences, under the supervision of a political body within the framework of very general rules of State international responsibility. The whole system may be seen as having certain parallels with the jury system: the Court, similarly to a jury, issues the "not guilty" or "guilty" verdict whereas the Committee of Ministers, similarly to the trial judge, takes decisions pertaining to the sanctions.

In such a system, abidance with judgments of the European Court of Human Rights becomes a metaphor. It does not mean abidance with precise legal obligations specified in the judgment itself but rather reasonableness in the choice of possible execution measures within very general and broad guidelines stemming from: the Articles on *Responsibility of States for Internationally Wrongful Acts*, the Court's case-law, the Committee of Ministers recommendations and its practice. The Committee of Ministers rather than supervising the execution of the judgment supervises the application of the relevant rules of State responsibility limiting the scope of discretion in respect of reparation of the breaches of the Convention. At the same time, the State performs two roles which are strictly separated in national legal system: on one hand, it is the legal subject against whom the enforcement proceedings are conducted, on the other hand, it determines the content of obligations to be enforced. To put it figuratively: it cumulates the roles of debtor and "co-bailiff".

Effective reparation of the damage caused by human rights violations may require far-reaching measures stepping deep into the domestic legal systems and sometimes important changes of the domestic legislation. The existing system aims at the protecting State sovereignty in the process of determination of legal consequences of Convention breaches. It considerably limits the impact of the ECHR judgments upon the legal systems of the States and enables a smoother adaptation of execution measures to the specificity of each of them. The mechanism of non-judicial determination is more acceptable to the States and therefore enhances the overall legitimacy and effectiveness of the whole Convention system. The existence of non-judicial elements in the system of Convention application seems the price to be paid for the acceptance of the judicial elements.

Given the specificity of the Convention mechanism, this instrument guarantees only certain elements of the right to an international tribunal: the right of access to international tribunal for the purpose of the determination of an occurrence of a rights violation but not for the purpose of a comprehensive determination of the legal consequences of such a violation.

Moreover, the right to claim the reparation of the damage resulting from a Convention breach is also guaranteed only partly. The applicant may claim a specific amount of money as reparation of the moral or material damage and may always request other specific measures to be ordered, but the Court has no obligation to grant any pecuniary compensation nor to address requests for any further (non-pecuniary) measures. Finding a Convention breach triggers subsequent proceedings, where the initiative and special weight are given to the respondent State and the individual does have only the right to present submissions, without the obligation of the competent bodies to examine and address them, let alone to issue any reasoned decision on their well-foundedness. Instead of a strong subjective right to claim adequate reparation there is at most a week subjective right to obtain a certain reparatory measures determined by the defendant State under the supervision of the Committee of Ministers. The question whether an alternative system based upon a strong and judicially enforceable right to reparation would ensure a more effective protection does not have an obvious answer and is a topic for a different study.

The above considerations clearly show that the syllogistic model of the application of law does not reflect the process of application of the European Convention on Human Rights. The European Court of Human Rights determines: (i) the content of a specific human right, (ii) the actions and omissions public authorities undertaken in the factual circumstances of a specific case and (iii) the question whether these action and omissions violate the right in question. The general rules establishing sanctions for Convention breaches are applied without the determination of the individual rule imposing a precise reparatory obligation upon the legal subject (in this case the State) liable for the breach of the law. In other words, the conclusion of the legal syllogism (the individual legal rule imposing—upon the person liable for the breach of the law—the individual obligation to provide reparation) is never formulated by any public authority. The Convention system appears to be a challenge to legal theory which develops its models looking almost exclusively at national legal systems.

References

Crawford, J. (2013). *State responsibility. The general part.* Cambridge: Cambridge University Press.

Dubois, C., & Penninckx, E. (2016). *La procédure devant la cour européenne des Droits de l'Homme et le Comité des Ministres.* Waterloo: Wolters Kluwer.

Działocha, K., & Jarosz-Żukowska, S. (Eds.) (2013). *Wykonywanie orzeczeń Trybunału Konstytucyjnego w praktyce konstytucyjnej organ ów państwa* [Execution of Constitutional Court's judgments in the Constitutional Practice of State Organs]. Warszawa: Wydawnictwo Sejmowe.

Florczak-Wątor, M. (2006). *Orzeczenia Trybunału Konstytucyjnego i ich skutki prawne* [Decisions of the Constitutional Court and their legal consequences]. Poznań: Ars boni et aequi.

Gianformaggio, L. (2018). Syllogisme juridique. In A.-J. Arnaud (Ed.), *Dictionnaire encyclopédique de théorie et de sociologie du droit* (pp. 589–591). Paris: LGDJ.

Kelsen, H. (reprinted 2009 from the 1945 edition). *General theory of law and state.* Clark: The Law Book Exchange.

Lambert Abdelwagad, E. (2009). The execution of the judgments of the European Court of Human Rights: Towards a non-coercive and participatory. *Zeitschrift für ausländisches öffentliches Recht und Völkerrecht, 69*(3), 471–506.

Lang, W., Wróblewski, J., & Zawadzki, S. (1986). *Teoria państwa i prawa* [Theory of state and law]. Warszawa: Państwowe Wydawnictwo Naukowe.

Pescatore, P. (2009). *Introduction à la science du droit.* Luxembourg: Université du Luxembourg-Bruylant.

Santulli, C. (2015). *Droit du contentieux international.* Issy-les-Moulineaux: LGDJ.

Wojtyczek, K. (2018). La procédure devant la Cour européenne des droits de l'homme - principaux dilemmes. In O. Dubos (Ed.), *Mélanges en l'honneur de Bernard Pacteau. Cinquante ans de contentieux publics* (pp. 673–688). s.l.: Mare et Martin.

Wróblewski, J. (1992). *The judicial application of law.* Dordrecht: Kluwer.

Transnational Law's Legitimacy Challenge for International Courts

Josephine van Zeben

Contents

1 Introduction

Transnationalism has long become a reality in most areas of life, including human rights. Relatively more recently, economic, political and cultural transnationalism has been accompanied with legal transnationalism and the acknowledgement of transnational law as a separate species of law. Governance that surpasses the geographical and jurisdictional boundaries of the nation-state raises important questions. This is particularly true when this governance is underwritten by enforceable legal rules that shape the rights and duties of states and private actors. This chapter reflects on the legitimacy of transnational law; how do we justify the creation and enforcement of legal rules that regulate and restrain individual and collective behaviours by actors beyond the nation-state? Specifically, it considers how the development of transnational law affects the legitimacy of international courts such as the European Court of Human Rights (ECrtHR).

The answers to this question are complicated not only by the geographical 'boundarylessness' of transnational law, but also by the involvement of non-state

Josephine van Zeben is Fellow Public and EU Law at Worcester College. I am indebted to Christiane Ahlborn and Joshua Pike for comments. Any errors or omissions are my own.

J. van Zeben (✉)
Worcester College, University of Oxford, Oxford, UK
e-mail: josephine.vanzeben@worc.ox.ac.uk

© Springer Nature Switzerland AG 2019
P. Pinto de Albuquerque, K. Wojtyczek (eds.), *Judicial Power in a Globalized World*, https://doi.org/10.1007/978-3-030-20744-1_40

actors, and the unilateral nature of transnational law compared to international law. The relationship between transnational law and legitimacy is one of reciprocity: on the one hand, law plays a formative role in providing and strengthening the legitimacy of transnational governance. This is particularly true in light of the increased formalization, and legalization, of transnational processes, which at first glance underlines their legitimacy. However, in the absence of a tailored approach, formalization risks reinforcing biases in favour of state-like actors and processes, which many consider to be the antithesis of transnational law. Transnational law is by definition developed by, and addressed to, a broader audience than those involved in traditional law-making. This has many potential advantages in terms of increased levels of expertise, participation, representativeness and democratic support. At the same time, these strengths could amount to weaknesses when expertise is used to pursue private rather than public interests, or successful lobbying results in unequal representation. To rely on the "law"—both substantive and procedural—as a source of legitimacy for transnational law is therefore not without its challenges.

Within this dynamic, courts play a crucial and complex role. This is true for national courts, which may decide to apply transnational laws that at times have been adopted unilaterally by foreign actors and/or originate from non-state actors, but also—and possibly even more—for international courts, such as the European Court of Human Rights. Transnational law subsumes both national and international law, provided that their application or subject matter is transboundary.[1] As key arbiters of the existence, interpretation, and application of international law, international courts are indirectly shaping the development and formalization of transnational law. At the same time, the mandate of international courts continues to be based on international law rather than transnational law. This juxtaposition both increases and challenges the legitimacy of international courts. Also here, a tension can be identified between the need to engage with these new sources of law in order to maintain the legitimacy of the courts themselves and the danger of undermining that same legitimacy by moving too far from the constitutive legal sources of their authority, and their original constituencies.

In light of these developments, this chapter will reflect on the relationship between transnational law and legitimacy in two steps: first, it outlines an understanding of legitimacy based on organizational sociology, which can be used to further analyse the legitimacy of transnational law and governance (Sect. 2); second, the role of international courts and tribunals in transnational law is discussed (Sect. 3).

2 Sociology of Legitimacy in Transnational Law

A comprehensive discussion on the relationship between law and legitimacy would require significantly more pages than available to the present author. Nonetheless, a few observations may be made to give an impression as to the ubiquity, and

---

[1] See in detail Sect. 2. See also Shaffer and Bodansky (2012).

continued fluidity, of the concept of legitimacy in legal scholarship. "Legitimate law" is a corner stone of the rule of law,[2] which in turn provides the foundation for most constitutional democracies.[3] Similarly, legitimacy is an important driver for the adherence to international law.[4] Legitimacy, or at least the perception of it, also helps to explain why people decide to obey the law.[5] Despite being a rich and well-researched field, conceptual debates on legitimacy remain; it is hard to provide a meaningful definition of legitimacy that is not linked to the specific context in which law is created—specifically referring to the actors creating the laws[6]—and the audience which it addresses.[7]

Transnational law creates several new challenges, and opportunities, in this regard. Transnational law has several features which are either unique in themselves, or unique in their combination with each other. As observed by Shaffer and Bodansky, transnational law can develop through the impact of unilateral legal developments in one jurisdiction,[8] as well as through the adoption of rules in transnational processes, which can involve the mediation by international law and institutions.[9] Moreover, these transnational processes tend to be shared between state and non-state actors, or even be entirely driven by non-state actors.[10] Examples of the latter type of transnational governance include environmentally focussed rules set by non-state actors in ways that reflect consumer preferences regarding the production and sale of products and services, such as wood, coffee, and tourism.[11]

In the grey area between national, international and transnational law, the legitimacy struggles of the European Union are perhaps the most well-documented.[12] A common way to categorize bases for legitimacy for the EU, and more broadly, is in

---

[2]The debate on what constitutes legitimate law, and the rule of law, is long standing. For an impression, see Bellamy (2015).

[3]O'Donnell (2014) and Rosenfeld (2001).

[4]See e.g. Weiler (2004) and Kumm (2004).

[5]There is a rich body of work on this issue within criminology, see for example Jackson et al. (2012) and Meares (2000).

[6]In the context of international law, consider Franck (2006).

[7]On the link between social organization theory and criminal law enforcement/compliance, see Meares (1998).

[8]In some contexts, this has also been referred to as "unilateral regulatory globalization", see e.g. Bradford (2012), p. 3.

[9]Shaffer and Bodansky (2012).

[10]For a detailed overview of types of transnational regimes within environmental law, see Heyvaert (2019) chapter 2.4.

[11]See in detail Cashore (2002).

[12]This is particularly interesting in the context of this chapter as the EU's legal system is not easily captured by existing models of national or international law but (arguably) also has not quite developed into a transnational legal system. See for a recent inquiry into the nature of EU governance, see van Zeben and Bobic (2019).

reference to input, output and throughput legitimacy.[13] Input legitimacy is achieved through participation by the people, output legitimacy through effective results for the people. Throughput legitimacy on the other hand is governance "with the people, analyzed in terms of their efficacy, accountability, transparency, inclusiveness and openness to interest consultation".[14] Unsurprisingly, these three types of legitimacy interact, with negative throughput processes having a strong negative effect on perceived input and output legitimacy.[15]

In an effort to accommodate the broadening of regulatory contexts, potential law-makers, and audiences, represented by transnational law, this chapter applies a legitimacy model based on organizational sociology instead of the more familiar "input/output/throughput" model traditionally applied by legal scholars. From an organizational sociology perspective, legitimacy can be defined as "a generalized perception or assumption that the actions of an entity are desirable, proper, or appropriate within some socially constructed system of norms, values, beliefs and definitions".[16] Specifically, Suchman identifies three types of legitimacy: interest-based pragmatic legitimacy, value-oriented moral legitimacy, and culturally focused cognitive legitimacy. These different types of legitimacy are based on different logics, as summarized in the table below.[17]

Type of legitimacy	Source
Interest-based pragmatic legitimacy	Narrow self-interest
Value-oriented moral legitimacy	Guiding values about the "right thing" to do
Culturally focused cognitive legitimacy	From a cognitive valuation that something is "understandable" or "to do otherwise is unthinkable"

Notably, legitimacy is seldom accidental. Rather it is an outcome that is actively pursued by organizations through the information, but also manipulation, of intended audience(s).[18] Moreover, different types of legitimacy have different durability.[19] For example, achieving interest-based pragmatic legitimacy is relatively easy to achieve—comparable to the output legitimacy enjoyed by the European Union—but also easiest to lose as it is very result-oriented and dependant on an organization's (perceived)[20]

---

[13] Schmidt (2013). A similar approach is applied by Cohen et al. in discussing the legitimacy of international courts. They refer to "source, process and result-oriented factors". See Cohen et al. (2018), pp. 4–5.

[14] Schmidt (2013), p. 2. See also Cohen et al. (2018), p. 2.

[15] Schmidt (2013). See also Cohen et al. (2018).

[16] Suchman (1995), p. 574.

[17] Table adapted from Cashore (2002), p. 515.

[18] Cashore (2002), p. 516.

[19] Cashore (2002), p. 516.

[20] Arguably, Suchman's definition of legitimacy depends more heavily on whether an organization is *perceived* to act in a certain way, rather than actually acting in a certain way. Space precludes a detailed discussion of the important questions this raises regarding events and information that form people's perceptions and how "sticky" these perceptions tend to be when people are faced with a change in facts. On this, see also Rowell (2019).

ability to continue to provide public, and/or private, goods to its audience.[21] In line with findings on the perceived legitimacy of substantive legal rules, moral and cognitive legitimacy are extremely durable—so much so that our perceptions of what the law *is* tends to be based primarily on what it *should be*, even when this is factually incorrect[22]—but also correspondingly harder to achieve. Once established, however, the value-oriented moral legitimacy of law (for example, a law prohibiting murder) can be such that it may extend to agencies that fail to obtain other types of legitimacy (such as an underfunded police force that fails to enforce laws against murder).

An important distinction between the model of legitimacy proposed here and the definitions often used within legal scholarship is the fact that legitimacy is something given to an organization by an *external* audience, which is either directly or indirectly affected by the organization's behaviour.[23] To a legal audience, the term "external" may be counter-intuitive as it may be thought to refer to an audience outside of the organization's jurisdiction. However, "external" in this context refers only to the relevant audience being outwith the organization, i.e. not part of the organization itself. Admittedly, the line between external and internal is not easily drawn when dealing with state actors—how to place oneself outside of the state whose rules affect your freedoms, apart from perhaps relinquishing citizenship and/or physically moving away? However, for questions relating to transnational law, this definition works remarkably well, given that there is no set jurisdiction or sphere of influence for the non-state actors that have become involved in law-making. Equally, unilateral acts of domestic state-based law that become influential in other jurisdictions tend to do so exactly due to their perceived legitimacy by "external" audiences. This is one of the reasons why viewing transnational law and governance from an organizational lens may have certain advantages.

Keeping this in mind, the application of an organization sociology model of legitimacy to transnational law requires us to consider the nature of transnational law in more detail. Several preliminary observations must be made: first, transnational law is by definition polycentric insofar that there is no one institution, subject matter or process through which we can define or earmark transnational law as transnational law. Second, and relatedly, transnational law has developed at different speeds in different areas of law. Transnational environmental law is now a relatively well-developed field of transnational law, in large part due to the intrinsic transboundary nature of many environmental issues and the corresponding need for transboundary solutions beyond the state.[24] Some regimes are further developed than others and

---

[21] On the EU, see Weiler (2012).

[22] See Rowell (2019).

[23] Rowell (2019), pp. 516–518, refers to these audiences as Tier I (directly affected) and Tier II (indirectly affected civil society) audiences.

[24] An illustration of this is the existence of the journal *Transnational Environmental Law*, available through https://www.cambridge.org/core/journals/transnational-environmental-law. Accessed 5 Apr 2019.

each subspecies of transnational law may be based on different logics and/or involve different actors. Third, as mentioned earlier, the relationship of transnational law with other species of law, such as international law and national law, is one of inclusion, rather than exclusion: transnational law subsumes other forms of law, provided that they apply to transboundary activities or have effect in more than one jurisdiction.[25]

To speak therefore of "*the* legitimacy of transnational law" would be a mischaracterization of transnational law as a field of law. More constructively, our organizational model may be used to recognize the types of legitimacy that more and less developed regimes within transnational governance—responsible for the creation of transnational law—pursue. Predictably, areas of transnational law linked to market processes currently rely most heavily, and often very successfully, on interest-based pragmatic legitimacy.

A prominent example of this is the regulation of chemicals. On the one hand, this area is an example of a unilateral act which has had transboundary consequences: namely, the adoption of the Registration, Evaluation, Authorisation and Restriction of Chemicals (REACH) Regulation by the EU.[26] The importance of the EU's market for chemicals for non-EU countries has meant that REACH has been effectively adopted far beyond the EU's borders.[27] In parallel, the Globally Harmonized System of Classification and Labelling of Chemicals (GHS) has developed.[28] This is a more 'traditional' transnational legal regime, involving a number of diverse actors such as the Organisation of Economic Cooperation and Development (OECD), the International Labour Organisation (ILO), the Inter-Organisational Program for the Sound Management of Chemicals (IOMC), delegates from national governments, trade representatives, industry representatives, public interest groups, and members from academia. Significantly, the "voluntary" standards developed by GHS has been incorporated into various national and regional laws.[29]

This is not to say that moral and cognitive legitimacy play no part in transnational law. Many transnational regimes, such as those related to corporate social responsibility,[30] are linked specifically to these legitimacy logics. Moreover, transnational legal regimes that start out as pragmatic systems may become internalized to such an extent that moral and/or cognitive legitimacy attaches to them.[31] One way in which

---

[25]On this, see also Shaffer and Bodansky (2012).

[26]Regulation (EC) No 1907/2006 concerning the Registration, Evaluation, Authorisation and Restriction of Chemicals (REACH) [2007] OJ L136/3.

[27]See Bradford (2012).

[28]See discussion in Heyvaert (2019), p. 15 onwards.

[29]This includes EU Regulation 1272/2008/EC on classification, labelling and packaging of substances and mixtures, amending and repealing Directives 67/548/EEC and 1999/45/EC, and amending Regulation (EC) No 1907/2006 [2008] OJ L353/1.

[30]See e.g. Sub-Commission on the Promotion and Protection of Human Rights (2003).

[31]While this may be a positive development with respect to the durability of that specific transnational legal regime, it also increases the risk of path dependency within the regime, making it less flexible and able to respond to changes in the needs of the affected audience. On path dependency

this process can be sped up is through the acknowledgement and reinforcement of transnational law through other institutions, such as courts, insofar that these institutions themselves are viewed as legitimate. The next and final section of this chapter will consider this interaction more closely.

3 International Courts and Transnational Legitimacy

Many consider the role of courts in applying and upholding the law central to constitutionalism and the rule of law.[32] Historically, this referred almost exclusively to the role of national courts upholding national law. This has changed significantly due to the growing importance of international law and international judicial dialogue. Even in countries with governments that do not always engage in multilateralism, courts have increasingly found it relevant, and appropriate, to cite judgments by foreign courts and/or international law that may or may not be binding on these courts.[33] The development of the European Union and the Court of Justice's creation of the doctrines of primacy and direct effect of EU law has—regionally—brought these developments to an even higher level with the enforcement of supra-national law becoming an integral part of national courts' mandates.[34] Increased multilateralism has also seen a proliferation of international courts and tribunals. Most of these courts, with the exception of the International Court of Justice, are specialized in particular fields of international law as set out in their constitutive instruments. Examples include the International Criminal Court,[35] the International Tribunal for the Law of the Sea,[36] but also the Appellate Body of the World Trade Organization.[37]

---

more generally, see Peters et al. (2005). On the need to responsive regulation, see Bennear and Wiener (2019).

[32] For foundational (and diverging) texts, see Dicey (1982) and Dworkin (1986).

[33] For examples from the United States, see *Lawrence v. Texas*, 539 U.S. 558, 575 (2003); *Grutter v. Bollinger*, 539 U.S. 306, 344 (2003) and *Roper v. Simmons*, 125 S. Ct. 1183 (2005). See also Kersch (2004) (discussing the use of foreign practices as a yardstick for American decisions) and Waters (2005). For a more general overview (covering 70 jurisdictions) see the Oxford Reports on International Law in Domestic Courts, available via http://opil.ouplaw.com/page/ILDC/oxford-reports-on-international-law-in-domestic-courts. Accessed 5 Apr 2019.

[34] See Case 26/62, *NV Algemene Transporten Expeditie Onderneming van Gend en Loos v. Nederlandse Administratie der Belastingen* [1963] ECR 1 ECLI:EU:C:1963:1, 41; Case 6/64, *Flaminio Costa v. ENEL* [1964] ECR 585 ECLI:EU:C:1964:66, 41.

[35] Created by the Rome Statute, document A/CONF.183/9 of 17 July 1998 and corrected by process-verbaux of 10 November 1998, 12 July 1999, 30 November 1999, 8 May 2000, 17 January 2001 and 16 January 2002. The Statute entered into force on 1 July 2002.

[36] Created by Convention on the Law of the Sea, Dec. 10, 1982, 1833 U.N.T.S. 397.

[37] Created through Article 17 of the Understanding on Rules and Procedures Governing the Settlement of Disputes (DSU).

The legitimacy of international courts depends on different factors as compared to national courts.[38] Whereas the decisions of national courts may be viewed as illegitimate when they overstep the separation of powers or amount to judicial activism,[39] or when corruption in decision-making and/or appointment becomes commonplace,[40] most national courts enjoy a presumption of legitimacy by virtue of being part of an otherwise legitimate system of governance within the nation-state.[41] By contrast, international courts seldom enjoy such "base legitimacy"; few international regimes have developed to a level of moral or cognitive legitimacy that can be transferred to related institutions, such as courts. As a result, similar to most other institutions, the legitimacy of international courts tends to develop over time.[42] A key challenge to international courts in this respect is the fact that most of them lack the police power that national courts can rely on for the enforcement of their judgements.[43] This makes their legitimacy even more important, as it is a key factor in the likelihood of compliance with their judgments, which in turn reinforces the likelihood of future compliance.[44]

As legitimacy is inherently linked to audience, regardless of whether one is applying an organizational sociology model or a more traditional legal model, it is equally important to consider the relevant audiences for specific international courts. For most international courts, states and individuals constitute its core constituencies. However, these constituencies are not equal in their influence and relationship vis-à-vis these courts. As captured by von Bogdandy and Venzke:

> [i]nternational courts then decide in the name of states as subjects of the international legal order. In view of democratic principles for the justification of international public authority, this seems to be increasingly unsatisfactory. [. . .] the starting point of democratic justifications are the individuals whose freedom shapes the judgments, however indirect and mediated this may be. In this vein, international adjudication in the post-national constellation should be guided by the idea of transnational and possibly cosmopolitan citizenship.[45]

This observation emphasizes that while the legitimacy of international courts is unmistakably connected to that of national institutions, specifically national parliamentary democracy,[46] this may not sustain it indefinitely. This emphasizes the

---

[38]Important work is being done on the legitimacy of international courts through the University of Oslo's PluriCourts project, see https://www.jus.uio.no/pluricourts/english/. Accessed 5 Apr 2019.

[39]See Kmiec (2004) and Abraham (1993).

[40]See Wallace (1998).

[41]Conversely, in countries where such base legitimacy of the state is missing, courts can either be seen as cures to this problem or expressions of this.

[42]See Shany (2014), pp. 145–147.

[43]The Court of Justice of the EU has a relatively special position in this respect. The effect on its perceived legitimacy is debated, see Pollack (2018), p. 143.

[44]It may be noted that some commentators have compared this lack of police power with the position of national constitutional courts, see Staton and Moore (2011).

[45]von Bogdandy and Venzke (2012), p. 41.

[46]The ECrtHR has also been instrumental in strengthening national democracies, see e.g. App. No. 24833/94, *Matthews v. Great Britain*, ECtHR (1999).

potential importance of transnational law for international courts, despite their different origins; transnational law, which is increasingly finding its way into traditional areas of international law, may provide opportunities for international courts to create bases for legitimacy in addition to, and separate from, nation-state-based processes.[47] Using the input/output/throughput terminology, one of the competitive advantages of transnational law is *inter alia* that it allows constituencies other than states to provide meaningful input into laws and law-making processes. The effect of this on the legitimacy of international courts is indirect however; its input legitimacy would only be affected if the resulting laws are also considered as input in judicial decision-making. This example purposefully blurs the line drawn in this chapter between the organizational sociology model and the legal model. It does so in order to emphasize that the input/output/throughput model is currently too state-centric to fully capture the developments in transnational law. By means of illustration, this section concludes by providing an example of the interaction of international and transnational law in the jurisprudence of the ECrtHR.

International environmental law is an especially rich field of international law. That said, transnational environmental law is at least as significant for the regulation of environmental impacts, and may even become more influential than international environmental law. This can be explained by, among other things, the centrality of private actors in environmental regulation; the importance of private information; and the difficulties posed to international negotiations by the collective action problems, long time horizons, and scientific uncertainty related to environmental regulation. In many areas, the absence of state actors, or at least their loss of monopoly over law-making processes, has allowed transnational environmental regulation to move quickly and flexibly in areas marred by political stalemate. There are potential pitfalls to these developments as well, especially linked to legitimacy as measured in the traditional sense (how to ensure equal input, transparency of process, and just outputs?). In terms of organizational sociology however, these transnational regimes enjoy a high level of pragmatic—if not (yet) moral and cognitive—legitimacy.

As a result of these developments, international and transnational environmental law increasingly interact. A key example of this can be found in the jurisprudence regarding the "greening" of human rights. The interpretation of human rights as incorporating environmental protection elements has been ongoing, and increasing, for some time. There are good reasons to advocate such a development, as well as some persuasive grounds for caution.[48] The ECrtHR has been at the forefront of this

---

[47]See by means of contrast the suggestions provided by von Bogdandy and Venzke as to how legitimacy of international courts may be increased, which prioritize the development and strengthening of national processes—such as expanding roles for the public in judicial elections and judicial proceedings and stressing the role of national organs in implementing international decisions. See von Bogdandy and Venzke (2012), p. 40.

[48]For an overview, see Boyle (2012).

development.[49] Specifically, the ECrtHR case law has shown the Court to interpret the right to private life and the right to life (Articles 8 and 2 ECHR respectively) to compel governments to regulate environmental risks or disclose environmental information.[50]

In shaping these environmental informational obligations, the Court has relied heavily on the Aarhus Convention on Access to Information, Public Participation in Decision-making and Access to Justice in Environmental Matters. While Aarhus' requirements are procedural, they are "gateway" rights to allowing individuals and NGOs to bringing substantive grievances before the Court. They also provide a particularly good example of the cross-over between international and transnational environmental law[51]: the Aarhus Convention is strictly binding only on states, but its principles have been adopted by numerous transnational environmental regimes.[52] The ECrtHR's increasingly broad reading of the Aarhus requirements therefore indirectly strengthens the transnational regimes modelled after the Aarhus requirements.[53]

4   Concluding Remarks

The ECrtHR's position that the ECHR is "a constitutional instrument of the European public order"[54] provides grounds for the integration of transnational law into its jurisprudence, on the basis that this allows for the inclusion of law originating from sources other than traditional state-made international law. In turn, this gives a voice to actors other than states—something which has arguably been integral to the Court's mandate since its foundation. However, in the short to medium term, these

---

[49]This has led to calls for an environmental protocol to be added to the European Convention on Human Rights (ECHR), which have been consistently rejected. The latest rejection was on 16 June 2010, when the Committee of Ministers again decided not to add a right to a healthy and viable environment to the ECHR. However, it also led to the adoption of a *Manual on Human Rights and the Environment*. See Council of Europe (2005) ('Council of Europe Report'). See e.g. Desgagné (1995), Francioni (2010), pp. 48–54; Verschuuren (2015).

[50]See generally *Guerra v. Italy*, 26 EHRR (1998) 357; *Taskin v. Turkey*, 42 EHRR (2006) 50, at paras 113–119; *Tatar v. Romania* [2009] ECtHR, at para. 88; *Budayeva v. Russia* [2008] ECtHR.

[51]See cases *López Ostra v Spain* [1994] App no 16798/90, ECHR 46, (1995) 20 EHRR 277; *Fadeyeva v Russian Federation*, App No 55723/00, ECHR 2005-IV, [2005] ECHR 376; *Öneryıldız v Turkey*, App no 48939/99, ECHR 2004-XII, (2005) 41 EHRR 20. For the Aarhus Convention, see Convention on Access to Information, Public Participation in Decision-making and Access to Justice in Environmental Matters, June 25, 1998, UN Doc. ECE/CEP/43, 38 I.L.M. 517.

[52]See also Heyvaert (2019), p. 224.

[53]See e.g. *Guerra v. Italy*, 26 EHRR (1998) 357 (where failure to provide information was found to affect right to life).

[54]See e.g. European Court of Human Rights., *Loizidou v. Turkey* (Preliminary objections), judgement of 23 March 1995, para.75.

developments, together with the growing importance of transnational law, will almost inevitably lead to the alienation of the Court's other constituency: states.

The ECHR's membership may be robust enough to wither such a storm—although the UK's Conservative Party's continuing insistence on withdrawal from the ECHR shows that even the cognitive legitimacy gained by the ECHR and the ECrtHR cannot prevent certain unilateral state acts.[55] Moreover, as a Court that derives some of its legitimacy from being seen to provide "justice", confronting and defying states is arguably central to its raison d'être.[56] Other international and regional courts, such as the International Criminal Court,[57] may face greater challenges in this respect as their foundations are less secure and presence too recent to have gained sufficient legitimacy in their right. As this process will continue to unfold over the coming decades, it is worth observing that in creating a short-term legitimacy challenge for international courts, transnational law may also provide the long-term answer to this challenge.

References

Abraham, H. (1993). *Judicial process*. Oxford: Oxford University Press.

Bellamy, R. (Ed.). (2015). *The rule of law and the separation of powers*. Routledge.

Bennear, L. S., & Wiener, J. B. (2019). Adaptive Regulation: Instrument Choice for Policy Learning over Time. *Draft Working Paper*. Retrieved March 18, 2019, from https://www.hks.harvard.edu/sites/default/files/centers/mrcbg/files/Regulation%20-%20adaptive%20reg%20-%20Bennear%20Wiener%20on%20Adaptive%20Reg%20Instrum%20Choice%202019%2002%2012%20clean.pdf

Boyle, A. (2012). Human rights and the environment: Where next? *European Journal of International Law, 23*(3), 613–642.

Bradford, A. (2012). The Brussels effect. *Northwestern University Law Review, 107*(1), 1–68.

Cashore, B. (2002). Legitimacy and the privatization of environmental governance: How non-state market-driven (NSMD) governance systems gain rule-making authority. *Governance: An International Journal of Policy, Administration, and Institutions, 15*(4), 503–529.

Cohen, H. G., Føllesdaland, A., Grossman, N., & Ulfstein, G. (2018). Legitimacy and international courts – A framework. In N. Grossman, H. G. Cohen, A. Føllesdaland, & G. Ulfstein (Eds.), *Legitimacy and international courts*. Cambridge, UK: Cambridge University Press.

Council of Europe. (2005). *Final Activity Report on Human Rights and the Environment*. DHDEV 006 rev, 10 Nov. 2005, App. II.

Desgagné, R. (1995). Integrating environmental values into the European Convention on Human Rights. *American Journal of International Law, 89*(2), 263–294.

Dicey, A. V. (1982). *Introduction to the study of the law of the constitution*. Indianapolis, IN: Liberty Fund Inc.

---

[55]See e.g. the Conservative Party's Manifesto for the 2010 General Election, available via https://www.conservatives.com/~/media/Files/Manifesto2010. Accessed 5 Apr 2019. At page 79: "To protect our freedoms from state encroachment and encourage greater social responsibility, we will replace the Human Rights Act with a UK Bill of Rights."

[56]On this, see also Land (2018), p. 83.

[57]See e.g. Ssenyonjo (2017).

Dworkin, R. (1986). *Law's empire*. Cambridge, MA: Harvard University Press.

Francioni, F. (2010). International human rights in an environmental horizon. *European Journal of International Law, 21*(1), 41–55.

Franck, T. (2006). The power of legitimacy and the legitimacy of power: International law in an age of power disequilibrium. *American Journal of International Law, 100*(1), 88–106.

Heyvaert, V. (2019). *Transnational environmental regulation and governance*. Cambridge, UK: Cambridge University Press.

Jackson, J., Bradford, B., Hough, M., Myhill, A., Quinton, P., & Tyler, T. R. (2012). Why do people comply with the law?: Legitimacy and the influence of legal institutions. *The British Journal of Criminology, 52*(6), 1051–1071.

Kersch, K. I. (2004). Multilateralism comes to the courts. *The Public Interest, 154*, 3–18.

Kmiec, K. D. (2004). The origin and current meanings of judicial activism. *California Law Review, 92*(5), 1441–1478.

Kumm, M. (2004). The legitimacy of international law: A constitutionalist framework of analysis. *The European Journal of International Law, 15*(5), 907–931.

Land, M. (2018). Justice as legitimacy in the European Court of Human Rights. In N. Grossman et al. (Eds.), *Legitimacy and international courts*. Cambridge, UK: Cambridge University Press.

Meares, T. L. (1998). Social organization and drug law enforcement. *American Criminal Law Review, 35*, 191–228.

Meares, T. L. (2000). Norms, legitimacy and law enforcement. *Oregon Law Review, 79*(2), 391–416.

O'Donnell, G. (2014). The quality of democracy: Why the rule of law matters. *Journal of Democracy, 15*(4), 32–46.

Peters, B. G., Pierre, J., & King, D. S. (2005). The politics of path dependency: Political conflict in historical institutionalism. *The Journal of Politics, 67*(4), 1275–1300.

Pollack, M. (2018). The legitimacy of the Court of Justice of the European Union: Normative debates and empirical evidence. In N. Grossman et al. (Eds.), *Legitimacy and international courts*. Cambridge, UK: Cambridge University Press.

Rosenfeld, M. (2001). The rule of law and the legitimacy of constitutional democracy. *Southern California Law Review, 74*(5), 1307–1352.

Rowell, A. (2019). Do people know the law? *Arizona State Law Journal, 51*(1), 50.

Schmidt, V. A. (2013). Democracy and legitimacy in the European Union revisited: Input, output and 'throughput'. *Political Studies, 61*, 2–22.

Shaffer, G., & Bodansky, D. (2012). Transnationalism, unilateralism and international law. *Transnational Environmental Law, 1*(1), 31–41.

Shany, Y. (2014). *Assessing the effectiveness of international courts*. Oxford: Oxford University Press.

Ssenyonjo, M. (2017). State withdrawal notifications from the Rome Statute of the International Criminal Court: South Africa, Burundi and the Gambia. In C. Jalloh & I. Bantekas (Eds.), *The International Criminal Court and Africa*. Oxford: Oxford University Press.

Staton, J. K., & Moore, W. H. (2011). Judicial power in domestic and international politics. *International Organization, 65*(3), 553–587.

Sub-Commission on the Promotion and Protection of Human Rights. (2003). *Norms on the Responsibilities of Transnational Corporations and Other Business Enterprises with Regard to Human Rights*. UN Document. E/CN.4/Sub.2/2003/12/Rev.2.

Suchman, M. (1995). Managing legitimacy: Strategic and institutional approaches. *Academy of Management Review, 20*, 571–610.

van Zeben, J., & Bobic, A. (Eds.). (2019). *Polycentricity in the European Union*. Cambridge, UK: Cambridge University Press.

Verschuuren, J. (2015). Contribution of the case law of the European Court of Human Rights to sustainable development in Europe. In W. Scholtz & J. Verschuuren (Eds.), *Regional integration and sustainable development in a globalised world* (pp. 363–385). Edward Elgar.

von Bogdandy, A., & Venzke, I. (2012). In whose name? An investigation of international courts' public authority and its democratic justification. *European Journal of International Law, 23*(1), 7–41.

Wallace, J. C. (1998). Resolving judicial corruption while preserving judicial independence: Comparative perspectives. *California Western International Law Journal, 28*(2), 341–352.

Waters, M. A. (2005). Mediating norms and identity: The role of transnational judicial dialogue in creating and enforcing international law. *Georgetown Law Journal, 93*(2), 487–574.

Weiler, J. H. H. (2004). The geology of international law – Governance, democracy and legitimacy. *ZaöRV, 64*, 547–562.

Weiler, J. H. H. (2012). Europe in crisis: On 'Political Messianism', 'Legitimacy' and the 'Rule of Law'. *Singapore Journal of Legal Studies*, 248–268.

Printed by Printforce, the Netherlands